STRANGE FASCINATION

'Buckley manages the ultimate achievement of any rock biog and sends you scuttling back to the records'

The *Guardian*

'*Strange Fascination* lives up to its title, presenting a compelling portrait of a complex man whose career has matched the shifting ideology of rock culture over the last 35 years'

Record Collector

'A mighty fine tome, as important as it is earnest'

Uncut

For my mum and dad,
Mabel and Harold Buckley

Also by David Buckley

The Complete Guide to the Music of David Bowie
(Omnibus Press, 1996)

The Stranglers: No Mercy –
The Authorised and Uncensored Biography
(Hodder and Stoughton, 1997)

R.E.M.: Fiction – An Alternative Biography
(Virgin Books, 2002)

The Thrill of it All: The Story of Bryan Ferry and Roxy Music
(André Deutsch, 2004)

David Bowie – The Complete Guide to His Music
(Omnibus Press, 2004)

STRANGE FASCINATION

David Bowie:
The Definitive Story

David Buckley

This edition first published in Great Britain in 2005 by
Virgin Books Ltd
Thames Wharf Studios
Rainville Road
London
W6 9HA

Copyright © David Buckley 2005

First published in 1999 by Virgin Publishing Ltd

A catalogue record for this book is available
from the British Library.

ISBN 0 7535 1002 2

Typeset by TW Typesetting, Plymouth, Devon
Printed and bound in Great Britain by Bookmarque Ltd, Croydon

CONTENTS

ACKNOWLEDGEMENTS

One of the main motivations behind the writing of *Strange Fascination* back in 1999, when Bowie's critical stock was only just recovering after his musical missing-time experience of the mid 1980s, was to share my enthusiasm about the man and his music with a wider audience. Today it's no longer passé to admit to loving David Bowie's music. From Ricky Gervais to Moby, from Jonathan Ross to Madonna, everybody's at it. Journalists no longer pen musical epitaphs on each new release. Bowie has regained his status as one of the biggest musical icons of our age.

I hope this revised and updated version will appeal to Bowie fans across the spectrum, from those who are new to David Bowie and want to find out more about him through to longstanding fans whose lives are marked out by Bowie songs: left junior school to the sound of *Station To Station*; watched Liverpool win the League (again) to the sound of 'Let's Dance'; had their first child to the sound of *Tin Machine* . . . Well, that's just a little bit of my story, but it's one that could be told by any of us who remember David Bowie in his pomp and who have stuck by him through the years.

Although as the author it is my name that is on the cover, all writers are only as good as the support they get. For the new version of *Strange Fascination* (published, appropriately, five years after the last paperback edition), I have been fortunate indeed to have had the help of Kevin Cann, a man who possibly knows more about David Bowie, or at least his early career, than anyone on the globe, including Bowie himself (Rock genius? Yes. Good on facts? Erm, not always). It was to Kevin that I turned for help with the first third of the book. Kevin helped weed out a number of factual inaccuracies (mercifully mostly of a relatively minor variety), suggested different interpretations of the events I described, and generally dotted the i's and crossed the t's. Another Bowie writer helped identify errors in the paperback. That man is actor, playwright and writer Nick Pegg, who at one stage during our email correspondence just happened to be playing the role of a Dalek at BBC Cardiff for the new *Dr Who* series.

In London, Carolyn Thorne, Eleanor Maxfield and Gareth Fletcher at Virgin Books have dealt with the author and the huge sprawl of edited and updated manuscript with both efficiency and understanding. I would also like to thank my literary agent Ros Edwards for being supportive of me and this project and for offering encouragement at all times. And thank you also to her colleagues at Edwards Fuglewicz Literary Agency – Helenka Fuglewicz, Julia Forrest and Lillian Jesner – for their friendly help.

I would like to signal my appreciation of Ian Gittins, my original editor at Virgin, who saw the potential in the idea of a celebration of Bowie's work and whose knowledgeable insights were invaluable, and to mention Kirstie Addis, Tim Wild and Melissa Harrison, all of whom worked on the original version. David Bowie's publicists, the Outside Organisation – particularly David's consultant, Alan Edwards, his former assistant, Vicky Hayford, and Julian Stockton – have given me much helpful advice and information and have kept David Bowie informed about the project over the years. David Bowie himself was kind enough to give me permission to interview some of his collaborators for the original version of the book.

Other helpers for this new edition include Paul Du Noyer, who contributed to his fourth David Buckley book with some great quotes, and the charming Erdal Kizilcay, Bowie's musical sidekick for twelve years. Jenny Bulley at *Mojo* magazine followed every twist and agonising turn of the writing process with astonishing patience, and sent me emails that made me laugh, (no mean feat on some days).

This version of *Strange Fascination* not only has a zappy new cover, but also a new chapter bringing the Bowie story up to 2005. The text in general has also been revised; some sections have stayed broadly the same, whilst others have been ripped up and reworked. Bowie fans will I hope get something new out of the book (such as the original title of the album *The Man Who Sold The World*, for example), whilst those coming to Bowie for the first time will be catered for too. If, however, you are the kind of fan who cannot sleep at night for not knowing the truth about Bowie's new teeth, or who is more interested in the sexcapades than the musical escapades, then this book is not for you.

The new material comes mainly from interviews conducted between 2002 and 2005. I want to thank Mark Blake, editor of

Mojo/Q's Special Collections, for permission to reproduce some of the material originally written for editions on David Bowie and Electronic Music respectively. I was fortunate enough to have been commissioned to write the official sleeve notes for three of David Bowie's reissues on EMI, and, during the course of that work I was able to speak to dozens of fresh faces. The freshest was Marc Riley, the artist formerly known as Lard, and proof that, to be a real David Bowie fan, you need to have an alter ego (like Blammo!). Other names featuring for the first time in this new edition of *Strange Fascination* include Ian McCulloch, Gary Kemp, Mick Rock, Geoff MacCormack, Alan Parker and Tony Newman. For the EMI releases I also spoke again to the perfect gentleman that is Ken Scott, the producer of Bowie's classic early work, as well as to Mike Garson, everyone's favourite out-there musician. My thanks go to Nigel Reeve at EMI for all his help and for permission to re-use this material. Full accreditation can be found in the Documents section on page 537.

This only leaves me to thank the original cast of people who were so kind as to offer their help, advice, expertise, insight and, in some cases, willingness to listen to the author drone on about David Bowie.

I would like to thank those people in Liverpool and elsewhere in the UK who helped during the writing of the original *Strange Fascination*. This list includes David Horn, for overseeing the successful completion of my postgraduate thesis on David Bowie, Geoff Ward, for invaluable feedback as the thesis turned into a book, and Ron Moy, a fellow postgraduate student at the time, for his encouragement and friendship. Due recognition should also be accorded to Richard Freeman, a schoolmate who braved the questionable delights of the Glass Spider tour concert at Wembley Stadium with me, and who patiently nodded in polite agreement whenever I spoke in awe (initially) of such master-works as *Tonight*. Thank you also to Keith Ansell Pearson, Martin Cloonan, Sara Cohen, John Corner, Simon Frith, Robin Hartwell, Mike Jones, Susan Mensah, Steve Murray, Robert Orledge, Steve Redhead, John Shepherd, Phillip Tagg, Michael Talbot, Liz Thomson and Jolande Van Bergen.

Two earlier projects which allowed me to test out theories about the former Mr Jones also gave me my first breaks as a professional writer. I would like to thank Liz Thomson and David Gutman for commissioning two articles for their anthology *The*

Bowie Companion, published by Macmillan in 1993, and Chris Charlesworth of Omnibus Press for asking me to write a short guide to Bowie's back catalogue. The result, a CD-sized Bowie primer entitled *The Complete Guide to the Music of David Bowie* and published in May 1996, was aimed at the general rock fan. David Bowie enjoyed the book and asked for a revised and redesigned limited edition to be produced as a media-only promotional gift to coincide with the release of his 1997 *Earthling* album. A second revised edition, again for key media only, was published with a review of *hours* . . . in the autumn of 1999. A completely revised and updated version was subsequently published by Omnibus Press in 2004.

Strange Fascination has benefited immensely from conversations I have had with many of the leading figures in Bowie's career over the years. My thanks go to all those people who have helped me in my research, corresponded with me, or have been interviewed for the book. Ken Scott gave me invaluable information about Bowie's brilliant work from *Hunky Dory* through to *Pin Ups*. Carlos Alomar spent many hours on the phone speaking candidly and with humour about his work with David. Tony Visconti, the co-producer of around half of Bowie's recorded work, provided me with dozens of emailed responses to the tonne of questions I asked him in 1998 and 1999. Further invaluable insights into David Bowie's life and work were provided by Adrian Belew, Patti Brett, Paul Buckmaster, Dai Davies, Bryan Ferry, Reeves Gabrels, Mike Garson, Hanif Kureishi, Gary Numan, Hugh Padgham, Tim Palmer, Mark Plati, Nile Rodgers, Earl Slick, David Stopps, Mike Vernon and Alan Winstanley. Sadly, one of the best (and certainly funniest) of the original cast of interviewees, Gus Dudgeon, died, along with his wife Sheila, in a car crash in 2002.

A huge thank you must go to those music-industry insiders, managers, publicists, journalists and writers who spoke or corresponded with me: Chris Charlesworth, Alan Franks, Paul Gambaccini, Dave Laing, Steve Malins, John Osborne at Slick Music, Jordyn at Nile Rodgers Productions, Mark Paytress, John Peel, Simon Reynolds, Chris Roberts, Paul Roberts, Jon Savage, Mat Snow and Rogan Taylor.

A debt of gratitude is owed by me to David Bowie's fans, many of whom answered questionnaires, corresponded with me, provided research material and generally offered encouragement during the writing of the original book. They include in particular David Priest, Paul Kinder and Dara O'Kearney. Dara also chipped in and helped with a couple of late queries for this new edition. I would particularly like to express my appreciation of the efforts of the following members (and in some cases ex-members) of the tribe of Bowie followers: Ian Aldous, Patti Brett, David Gough, Richard Guerin, Wolfgang Gurster, Neville Judd, Spenser Kansa, Steve Keay, Stefano Nardini, Steve Pafford, Bonnie Powell, Liz Racz, Evan Torrie, Stefan Westman, Michael Wiegers, Ruth Willis, Paul Woods and Tom Zuback. I'd also like to thank Colin Cunningham, Mark Russell and Stefan Westman for being so friendly and supportive during the writing of this new version.

In Munich I'd like to thank David Blackshaw, Graham Johnstone, Grant Coles and Klaus Federa. Chris Andrews, who was so supportive first time round, is sorely missed.

This book is dedicated to my parents, Mabel and Harold Buckley. My big brothers John and Harold also deserve a mention. They were Bowie fans before me, and it was John who arranged for Father Christmas to pop *Hunky Dory* into my pillowcase in 1973, so this book is possibly all their fault. My love, as always, goes to my two daughters, Louise and Elsa, and to my wife and very own in-house editor, Ann Henrickson.

David Buckley
Munich, 26 April 2005

UNCAGE THE COLOURS

Bowie was never meant to be. He's like a Lego kit. I'm convinced I wouldn't like him, because he's too vacuous and undisciplined. There is no definitive David Bowie.

(DAVID BOWIE ON DAVID BOWIE, 1976)

David Bowie has just entered his fifth decade of making pop music, and for four of those decades he has been one of the most photographed, adored, imitated, admired and talked-about rock stars of the post-Beatles period. He is a heroic heretic who in the 1970s redefined what it was to be a star, in the 1980s became a hugely successful, Hollywood-styled mainstream pop icon and in the 1990s ended up a self-reinvented cultural aesthete. In the Noughties, he is arguably the only rock star of his vintage still consistently making music that is not just listenable, but challenging and vital too. Perhaps, as for pop music itself, his years of true devilment and highest innovation are now gone. But his impact on pop music has been seismic. *Strange Fascination* tries to explain why.

After the eclipse of Marc Bolan, for two years – 1972 and 1973 – Bowie was the biggest pop star in the UK. Since then, his fortunes have waxed and waned, but he has always been able to count on a community of hardcore fanatics, a seemingly self-generating troop of doughty followers who make him still the biggest cult icon in pop. His work in the second half of the 1970s consolidated his reputation as a style guru, a man, so the story went, always one step ahead of his competitors. What Bowie did one year, the world did the next. He had both commercial clout and artistic kudos. By the 1980s, he was increasingly being regarded as played-out, and it became fashionable to denigrate his achievements, to trash each new album – good, bad, or indifferent – on release. Bowie has been on the receiving end of more petty literary vendettas than perhaps any other figure in pop. By the mid-1990s he had been partially rehabilitated and, at the time of writing, Bowie is once again one of the most revered artists in contemporary music.

Yet his influence and legacy have never been acknowledged in a major book. Unlike Dylan, Lennon, Zappa, Prince, Kraftwerk, Bolan, The Sex Pistols, Abba and Elvis Presley, all major players in post-rock'n'roll pop, Bowie's work (rather than his life) has never been the subject of a book-length study.

Bowie's career is littered with far more brilliant highs than infuriating lows. Just one person took glam rock to new rarefied heights and invented character-playing in pop, marrying theatre and popular music in one seamless, powerful whole. Two years later, that same person broke the then contemporary sounds of black America into the British white audience, the effect of which was to establish a tradition of blue-eyed soul in the UK pop charts. Two years further on and this same individual was producing, with collaborators Brian Eno and Tony Visconti, the most challenging pieces of modernist art housed in rock trappings that one could imagine. A little later again, the same person virtually defined the ways in which pop and video could be combined, with a series of stunningly inventive videos. No other pop star of Bowie's generation has survived the almost inevitable downswing in creativity that sooner or later occurs in order to go on to produce albums as experimental and flamboyant as *1. Outside* and *Earthling*. In the Noughties, Bowie received the best press of his long career for *Heathen* and *Reality*. If Bowie ever fails, it's almost always an interesting failure, which is the mark of a great artist.

This book is also about his great songs, his poor songs, his good movies, his not-so-good movies; those he's been influenced by and those he's influenced. It is about his brilliant performances and videos, his studio craft, his vocal style, his politics (sexual and otherwise) and his fans. Above all, it is perhaps about a tradition in British popular music: a tradition of irony and theatricality in popular music. It is for people who are quite comfortable when the aural stimulus is housed in visual information as powerful as the music it complements, not for those who look to pop to provide a package of pure sound and no vision.

For many teenagers (even pre-teenagers) and twenty-somethings in the 1970s and early 1980s, David Bowie was the only rock star who really mattered. He was, during this period, omnipotent without ever being omnipresent. In the UK at least, he was perhaps the most written-about pop star of his age. His music and personae were weighty enough to make legions of rock scribes wax lyrical, and his recreational pastimes and photogenic looks were resonant enough for the tabloid media to splash him on front covers for well over a decade. He was serious and trashy, manipulative and manipulated, and (for a time at least) both man and woman – figuratively speaking, of course. A very real sense of lack, despite this welter of comment, made him in a way unobtainable, at least to his fans. Even though huge quantities of albums (estimated today at around 140 million) and singles (around 10 million in the UK alone) were sold, fans' exposure to Bowie in the media was always rationed. In the 1970s he made just three appearances on the BBC's crucial *Top of the Pops*, the staple of every teenager's Thursday night, as much a part of the collective teenage consciousness as the Top 20 (by 1978 the Top 40) on a Sunday evening, or the first break of the new chart after *Newsbeat* on Radio 1.

Bowie was only marginally more visible in person. Two years after he broke big, in April 1974 he abandoned Britain, first for New York, and then for LA, before relocating to Switzerland and Berlin for the remainder of the decade. In terms of tours he was hardly a regular 'down your way'. True, his Ziggy Stardust creation was paraded with gusto in 1972 and the first half of 1973, but after that he made just nineteen appearances in concert in the UK over the next ten years. If you were an Australian or New Zealander, you would have had only eight opportunities to see a Bowie concert, and they were all in one year, 1978. One of Bowie's biggest markets, Japan, was graced with Bowie's presence only thirteen times in ten years. No wonder, when Bowie decided to relaunch his career in 1983, that the demand for tickets was colossal, making the UK leg of the Serious Moonlight tour the most oversubscribed in rock history up until the advent of Oasis in the 1990s.

Bowie appealed unashamedly to those precious teenagers who never felt happy with mainstream devotion. While it was faddish to like The Osmonds, The Bay City Rollers or even Gary Numan, Bowie fans thought of themselves as a race apart. They remained constant in their support for the man and regarded him as a serious artiste. While much has been written about Bowie's artifice, his followers at least regarded him as the real McCoy, separate from the pop mainstream despite his many commercially hummable pop tunes.

It's hard to believe, after the tarnishing of his legacy in the 80s, the celebrity chum-ups and the weightless, insipid mid-80s' albums, that Bowie once had that hold over his flock. But he undoubtedly did. Bowie had a greater hold on young people's lives in the UK arguably for longer than any other pop star living or dead, longer even than The Beatles. Between 1972 and 1983 Bowie wasn't simply liked or admired. In the UK at least, he was almost worshipped.

Just take a look at those rock and pop performers whose work borrowed – wittingly or unwittingly – from Bowie, or who were simply inspired to make music either wholly or in part by Bowie's example. It is inconceivable that punk would have turned out the way it did without the crucial input of a group of bored, arty, suburbanite Bowie fans (Siouxsie Sioux, Billy Idol et al). Johnny Rotten, who, 'Rebel Rebel' aside, hated Bowie, nevertheless borrowed his haircut, while Sid Vicious was a Bowie casualty first, rock casualty second. In the UK, those influenced by Bowie since the 70s are legion: Bunnyman Ian McCulloch, Holly Johnson, Boy George, Morrissey, Kate Bush (she even borrowed his mime tutor, Lindsay Kemp), Gary Numan (who borrowed Bowie's light show, sang-froid and sneer), virtually the whole of the new romantic scene, the slicked-back soulsters of the New Pop era (ABC, Associates, Spandau Ballet), and the synth-pop duos (Soft Cell, Pet Shop Boys, The Eurythmics). In America, the three biggest pop icons of the 1980s, Madonna, Prince and Michael Jackson, were hugely indebted to Bowie's sly shape-changing (Madonna dates her conversion to actually wanting to be a star to a Ziggy concert she attended at the age of fifteen). In the 90s, UK groups such as Suede (a neat rearticulation of Ziggy-era kitchen-sink gender-bending), and American bands such as Nine Inch Nails, Nirvana, The Smashing Pumpkins and, overwhelmingly, Marilyn Manson, all paid homage to Bowie's past. And, despite media attention to its impeccable Beatles and Kinks pedigree, Britpop, too, doffed a cap in Bowie's direction. In 1997, Oasis enjoyed a UK Top 3 hit ('Stand By Me') with a chorus which echoes Bowie's 'All The Young Dudes' riff, while Blur have given Bowie and Brian Eno a writing credit for their rather excellent Bowie parody/homage, 'M.O.R.'. 'Pumping On Your Stereo' by Supergrass is a chuckling slice of 'Rebel Rebel'-dosed riff-rock, while U2's reconstruction in the early 1990s from earnest power-chording stadium rockers to playfully ironic Enoesque stylists would have been unthinkable without Bowie. In the Noughties, it's now cool to say you love David Bowie, and everyone and his dog claims to be at least partly descended from the original Diamond Dog.

That Bowie had such an effect on fellow musicians is hardly surprising. His recordings amount to a stunning body of work: rich, exciting, fun, mysterious and deeply moving, encompassing pop, ambient, rock, soul, jazz, folk, techno, jungle (in 1997 he even performed a country-and-western version of 'Scary Monsters' in the States – one of the most surreal of many surreal moments in that most particular of rock careers). Bowie offered the paradigmatic proof that fleet-footed changes of image and music, packaged well and presented impeccably, were the perfect recipe for career longevity. In his wake came the pop star as businessman, hip to how pop could be packaged on video. Bowie's career was all about self-promotion, putting forward a whole philosophy along with the music. In all this, the message was clear: to succeed in the pop marketplace, it was necessary to take control of just about everything. Bowie wrote or co-wrote most of his own material, sang it, played it, often helped to design the album sleeves, chose all the personnel to work with him in the studio and on tour, helped design the tours, had a say in the videos, closely monitored the merchandising, jealously restricted media access to himself and, by the mid-70s, even managed himself with the help of lawyers and personal assistants. Smart, shrewd, sexy and immensely talented, Bowie proved that to stay ahead, to stay vital, it was necessary to change.

Where rock stars admired his music, sense of style and business acumen, for his fans what was important was that he directly mirrored their own lives and intellects. Bowie wasn't quite original enough to be a true academic or intellectual (like Eno), he wasn't somehow authentic enough to be an all-out rocker (like Jagger), and he was altogether too masculine to be an all-out drag queen (like Wayne County). Instead he was, and remains, the perfect liminal pop star, an utterly convincing media re-enactment of our times, deep and serious yet frivolous and lightweight. He was a one-man multimedia pop kit, years before technology brought 'interactivity' into the home. Bowie was living proof that our personalities are constantly in flux, constantly being made and remade, not fixed in stone by age, class or gender. His changes of character in the 70s, which began with Ziggy, were media-produced manifestations of how we all sift through ourselves, rummaging through the baggage to produce new, hopefully improved, versions for public consumption. There's no final version of Bowie. For every teenager who considered him or herself unfinished, who was not quite happy with his or her lot, who didn't like the way society worked but couldn't articulate that sense of disquiet, Bowie was the perfect foil. It's no wonder that so many punks were originally Bowie fans.

For those unsure about their sexuality or who were in agonies about 'coming out', Bowie at least let them know that someone (and someone talented and cool to boot) was listening: 'You got your mother in a whirl/She's not sure if you're a boy or a girl' – 'Rebel Rebel', 1974.

Through such simple (and simplistic) words, Bowie (and – at its best – pop in general) changed people's lives. For all those who felt lost, disenfranchised, alone or sad, Bowie acted out pop therapy: 'You're not alone? Gimme your hands, 'Cos you're wonderful' – 'Rock'n'Roll Suicide', 1972. Bowie was the 70s manifestation of pop as healing rite. He became the witch doctor of rock'n'roll, giving succour to his 'sick' brethren. In short, there was a lot riding on his success, a multitude urging him to even bigger and better creative endeavours for their own ends. Also, Bowie was unquestionably sexy and cool, shocking, outrageous and fun. Throughout the early 1970s he was particularly adored by teenage girls, that very community of record buyers crucial to any cult artist wishing to break into the mainstream.

Bowie has challenged and changed people. He's switched people on to whole new areas of popular culture, his fans following up on his literary or musical obsessions, making them their own. There are thousands of people out there who would never have read Burroughs or *Seven Years In Tibet*, or listened to the music of whatever band Bowie was championing at the time

(Kraftwerk or Eno or Human League, Placebo or, most recently, Arcade Fire), had it not been for Bowie. This is simultaneously liberating and manipulative. Bowie's detractors would simply call it sad. For some of his fans this obsession has driven them into a twilight zone of self-mystification. He's not only made people want to be him, be with him, touch him and sleep with him, he's made a minority think they are him, or a reincarnation of him. For a whole decade Bowie out-thought his competitors, and outpaced some of his fans, taking them too far, too quickly.

Bowie mattered then and, in different ways and for different reasons, matters now. This book suggests reasons why, or at least offers the reader as much of the available evidence as possible. This is the first book on Bowie to draw on exclusive, first-hand interviews with many of the major players in Bowie's career. Both Ken Scott and Tony Visconti, co-producers of more than half of Bowie's albums, have provided exclusive information. Carlos Alomar, who worked with Bowie almost continuously for thirteen years in the 1970s and 1980s and rejoined Bowie for the *1. Outside* project, and Reeves Gabrels, Bowie's writing partner for the last decade, have both had their say.

The book also deals with the media version of David Bowie – what one might term the 'fictive' David Bowie, the version he allows us to witness on record, in interview, on stage. Unlike almost all of the existing accounts, its focus is not so much on the private Bowie. The middle-aged dad, the everyday sleeping, eating, breathing, living David Robert Jones, is known by very, very few. 'David Bowie' himself is largely a media monster, the greatest rock persona ever created, and only tangentially part of the personality of David Jones himself. Some of the musicians who have spent months and months on the road with Bowie have little idea of what he's really like, so rehearsed is Bowie's bonhomie and so enshrouded is he by a network of aides, assistants and bodyguards, and by the trappings and accoutrements of superstardom. 'He's very insulated,' said one musician, guitarist Adrian Belew, talking of his time with Bowie on the 1978 tour. 'I don't know of anyone in rock who's more insulated. Sometimes I felt, Why are they protecting him from me? I'm part of this.' The layers of defence Bowie has erected, particularly post-1980 (in fact, specifically post-9 December 1980), tightly monitor the contact he has with both colleagues and public. Such a 'support' system is perhaps an inevitable consequence of huge international renown, but with Bowie one senses that these defensive layers are somehow part of the mystification central to his work. Bowie has made camouflage and misinformation part of his actual art. Even when in the late 1990s he set up a series of Internet chats, the answers were often jokey riddles (and Bowie does this very well, being a natural comedian), deliberate evasions and witty aphorisms. Bowie loves playing at being a rock star and, as he enters his sixth decade, he's brilliant at playing the role, and at playing at sending himself up.

This life of deliberate 'faction' is what makes many of the existing biographies rather extraneous: they try to create truths out of media fabrications. *Strange Fascination* deals with the same material (and much more besides), but rather than deferring to the biographer's brief of trying to reveal the truth, it accepts – indeed, celebrates – Bowie's deceits. However, in so doing, it also suggests that this fictive media monster, as shown through his existing commercially released work, is actually only part of an even more absorbing creative story. The version of Bowie as revealed in the neat chronology of the existing biographies or suggested by the assemblage of official CDs in the record stores is not the version of Bowie the artist himself would recognise. For every album release, stage performance, or celebrity guest slot, there's an unfinished song, an unrealised idea, a never-heard-before gem. It's a sad fact that Bowie's fans will probably have to wait until after his death for this material to be released. A wealth of brilliant archive footage from the major tours, as well as countless out-takes, unreleased songs, live audio tapes and video experimentation, remains locked in Bowie's vaults, to be exploited by the sharks and exhumed by the necromancers in the next century. This book can only hint at what one suspects is a huge archive yet to be fully activated.

Very few know the 'real' David Jones behind the fictive David Bowie. One suspects, crucially, that not even he knows what he is. But what we do know is that his whole career is a media enactment of a search for some sort of spiritual identity. Bowie has used the media as therapy. Just as he has 'healed' the emotionally 'sick', his records are media expressions of hurt, pain and doubt – private grief made public. Along the way, he's made some of the best pop music ever. *Strange Fascination* is the definitive story of amazing creativity, of huge, showboating theatricality, and of an unending spiritual quest enacted in music.

Part I

1947–1974

1. ELVIS IS ENGLISH, 1947–1967

Elvis is English and climbs the hills.

'THE BUDDHA OF SUBURBIA', DAVID BOWIE, 1993

David Bowie is a suburban English pop hero: he could be of no other time or place than post-war England. The tiresome ennui of lower-middle-class 1950s Britain, its staidness, deference and lack of splendour, was the stuff which Bowie, and thousands of others born in the baby boom, rebelled against in the 1960s. Bowie's rebellion was, like that of a minority of others lucky enough to have an outlet for their creative frustrations, encapsulated in his music and his performances.

Bowie was born David Robert Jones at 9.00 a.m. on Wednesday, 8 January 1947, by a quirk of fate twelve years to the day after one of his early heroes, Elvis Presley. The future rock god made his first public appearance at home, 40 Stansfield Road, Brixton, London SW9, in front of a midwife-cum-clairvoyant who allegedly remarked, 'This child has been on earth before,' as the babe snuggled into one of the coldest, snowiest winters of the century. Although home births were commonplace back in post-war Britain, the unmarried status of his parents was still sufficient to have the neighbours tut-tutting into their cuppas. His father, Haywood Stenton Jones (known as John Jones), the son of a shoe manufacturer, was born in 1912 in Doncaster, Yorkshire. He had one daughter, Annette, from a previous marriage to a nightclub singer and had served in the Second World War in the

Eighth Army in North Africa. He was by all accounts a likeable, reserved, mild-mannered, lower-middle-class professional. Bowie's mother, Margaret Mary Burns (known as Peggy), was then 32. She too already had a child, Terry, born in 1937, after an affair with a man called James Rosenburg. This liaison with a Jew was most odd, given the fact that, allegedly, Peggy was much enamoured by Oswald Mosley and his Nazistic Blackshirts. During 1946, John and Peggy had set up home in Brixton, a poor, working-class area of London then feeling the full force of deprivation in the immediate post-war, post-Blitz period. The two married in September 1947 in Brixton. David was to be their only child together. John Jones worked for Dr Barnardo's as a promotions officer. Peggy was an usherette at a local cinema.

Little David Jones soon developed a taste for exotica. At the age of three, Peggy found her son plastered in powder and eyeliner. Left alone for half an hour, the little lad had taken an 'unnatural' interest in the contents of his mum's cosmetics bag. 'When I found him, he looked for all the world like a clown,' Peggy told journalist Kerry Juby in 1985. 'I told him that he shouldn't use make-up, but he said, "You do, Mummy." I agreed, but pointed out that it wasn't for little boys.' How wrong she was.

David started Stockwell Junior School a few months before his fifth birthday. He shared a bedroom with his teenage half-brother, Terry, throughout his early school years, and the two became very close. If what is written in existing Bowie biographies is true, the austere, non-physical nature of his relationship with his parents (this certainly wasn't a kissy-cuddly household) may have left Bowie somewhat scarred. Terry was forever rowing with his mum; his dad was often in a state of quizzical, melancholic withdrawal. This is important in that much of the sang-froid of his music may be attributable to the sub-zero emotional climate in the Jones' house.

Until well into middle age, Bowie would admit that he was, underneath all the war paint and glitter, painfully shy, and that he found it very difficult to relate to people and enter into meaningful relationships with individuals. The cheeky, urbane chatterbox of today is, in fact, the direct antithesis of the young Bowie, who spent his first forty years on the planet acting like a man from the Andromeda galaxy. His sense of alienation was no artifice: both the public David Bowie and the private David Jones were struggling to make some sort of useful connection. This process wasn't helped, of course, when, for most of the 70s, it was virtually impossible for us, and for him, to disentangle the two facets of his personality in the first place.

Like most cultural icons, Bowie is supremely 'mythogenic'. Biographers who concentrate on 'revealing the real person behind the mask' are constantly missing the point: it's the myth which has far greater resonance and is far more intriguing than stolid attempts to identify some 'true' essence. Like all great names, whether from film (one thinks immediately of Orson Welles or Greta Garbo), sport (Muhammad Ali) or indeed politics (JFK), Bowie's appeal has lain in the generation of myths. By myths we don't mean simply falsehoods or 'inaccurate history'. What Bowie did as a cultural icon was to interrogate those accepted stereotypes that have symbolic meaning, such as heroism and villainy, comedy and tragedy; those archetypes which help form the narratives that underpin our culture. In becoming a hero, and a particular sort of hero – media-manipulative, cross-generic, pan-sexual – at that, he was playing around with the very fabric of how we make sense of what is around us.

That said, Bowie was also something of a past master at simply lying and getting away with it. In one interview he mythologised his early years, à la Andy Warhol, at times claiming to have been brought up in an "ouse full of blacks', and at other times to have lived for a while with relatives in far-off Yorkshire. In reality, he lived in Brixton until he was six, and then moved to suburban Bromley in Kent, some eight miles southeast of Brixton. After brief residences in Canon Road and then in Clarence Road, in 1955 the Joneses settled in at 4 Plaistow Grove, a small terraced house with a little garden front and back, which would be David's home for over a decade. His bedroom was at the rear of the house and overlooked the local pub.

The geography of the situation is crucial: living in the suburbs so close to London provided the perfect paradigm for escape. London represented exotica, freedom and change for youngsters driven to near-desperation by the blandness of the capital's environs. And it was close by – a mere half an hour away by train. The metropolis represented an escape from the leafy orderliness of Bromley. Thousands of teenagers could access the naughtiness and release represented by the clubs, pubs, shops and scandals of London and yet remain inside the dominant parent culture. This was a life of respectability and rebellion. Few actually went the whole hog and uprooted from the sticks. Those who did, like Bowie himself, were a brave minority.

Much of the impetus behind British popular music since the mid-1950s has come from these artistic, dreamy, bed-sit musicians. British pop has been dominated by white, middle-class autodidacts, from Pete Townshend, Jagger and Richards and Ray Davies in the 1960s through to Suede's Brett Anderson, Blur's Damon Albarn and Pulp's Jarvis Cocker in the 1990s. Just as the music business in Britain has been run by white, middle-class men, so much of British pop music has been produced by the bourgeoisie. Rather than being a source of embarrassment or restraint, this elite has produced some of the most wonderful moments in popular culture. David Bowie is, and remains, the finest product of this sensibility. All the shock, all the outrage, all the outreach which has dominated his music, comes from the predicament of this liminality; from not fitting in, from wanting to be different, from being brought up in a climate of suburban conformity, and wanting to belong to a community of urban hipness. To live in the suburbs conveyed a certain prestige, a certain eccentricity, an element of being the outsider looking in, and Bowie's whole career is a macrocosm of this search to be other, married to the desire to be part of a scene.

The cultural critic, Roger Silverstone, pointed out in an essay in the collection *Visions Of Suburbia*, that Bromley is perhaps the archetypal suburban habitat, the embodiment of the modernist programme which sought a miscegenation between town and country, thus setting up a bulwark between the hidden pleasures of the metropolis and the leafy greenery of the countryside. Conservative Bromley emerged as an unlikely crucible of talent. The writer HG Wells was born there in 1866 at the high-water mark of the gentrification of the town, when grandiose villas were erected for the petite bourgeoisie keen to ape aristocratic mores. In addition to Bowie, writer Hanif Kureishi and many of the leading punks came from the area, too. As writer Andy Medhurst aptly put it: 'Attacks on suburbia from pop culture originated in the rebellious, almost Oedipal wish to disavow one's parent culture, and the suburban audience for pop, all those teenagers skulking in the bedrooms of Hendon and Beckenham, latched on to this as a sign that escape was possible, that glamour was attainable once suburbia had been transcended.'

Another factor was crucial in shaping teenage suburban rebellion: America, an alien culture which, for a time, was the epitome of cool. America itself had pioneered the suburban conurbation (the term had been current there since the 1890s) and introduced the idea of purpose-built 'model communities' such as Beverly Hills in California and Forest Hills in New York. The tension between British and American popular culture was absolutely crucial. The advent of mass culture (first mass-circulation newspapers and magazines and cinema, and then, by the mid-1950s, jukeboxes, milk bars and rock'n'roll) was seen by certain wings of the intelligentsia (notably the old Left) as atomising society. Whereas in the past, communities and families had a communality of aims, both at work and at play, new mass culture forced young people into isolation. Radio, television and recorded music bred insularity and created a private space for enjoyment, separate from the previous participatory modes of entertainment which depended on a notion of 'togetherness', however rehearsed or stilted (the family singsong around the piano replaced in a decade by the self-absorption of sneaking upstairs to listen to Radio Luxembourg). Coupled with this perceived tyranny of mass culture was 'Americanisation'. Leftist writers such as Richard Hoggart in his *Uses of Literacy*, published in 1957, saw in America everything that was sterile, unthinking, artificial and heathen. In the milk bars, 'The young men waggle one shoulder and stare, as desperately as Humphrey Bogart ... Many of the customers – their clothes, their hair-styles, their facial expressions all indicate – are living to a large extent in a myth-world compounded of a few simple elements which they take to be those of American life.'

Bowie's generation was the first to feel the full force of this alleged cultural imperialism, and it was their response to it that gave them much of their identity. In his life and work Bowie has encapsulated not only the 'atomisation' of the individual, the alienation and the separateness of a consumer society which creates a 'false' notion of community through the media, but also this tension between 'Little England' and Americana. But, for the vast majority of teenagers, all things American had a wonderfully liberating effect.

Bowie had always loved listening to music. The fifty-something Bowie reminisces in his web journal about wintry family Sundays, with roast lamb, roast potatoes and peas, and a small fire blazing. *Two Way Family Favourites* would be on the wireless 'playing record requests for "our lads" serving abroad in the far-flung outposts of a rapidly crumbling empire, though it seemed to me that the entire armed forces were crammed on Malta. "Oh, I love this one," my mother would say as Ernest Luft [sic: his surname was, in fact, Lough] stroked the clouds with "Oh For The Wings Of A Dove". Her voice would soar in ambitious unison, effortlessly matching Ernest note for note as she delivered the gravy boat to the table. "All our family could sing," she'd inform my father and me. "We couldn't do much else but we all loved music." ' There would then be the usual berating of father from mother as Mr Jones was harangued for having dashed Peggy's dream of being a singer, of being a star. Peggy was a drama queen, John naturally nonconfrontational. In part it might be said that Bowie would inherit this complicated and unfortunate mix of character traits from his parents, often being frightened of confrontation (hence the need for all the various aides and 'protectors' to do his bidding?) yet supremely theatrical and show-stealing.

John Jones was nothing if not on the cutting edge of new technology. A television had been purchased in time for the coronation of Queen Elizabeth II in 1953, and the young David remembers half the street crowded round the flickering box in the corner for the event that spring. His dad also bought a gramophone, and David would delight in the latest Danny Kaye. However, in 1956, the Joneses' record collection was given a quite startling overhaul: one day, Dad came in with a stack of new-fangled 45s. 'Of course, we didn't realise that 45s don't play at the same speed as 78s,' says Bowie, 'and I would crouch over the heavy-armed turntable, twirling the plastic disc ever faster until it approached what I presumed would be its real speed. Although wonky and wobbly, these really great sounds came out of the horn. The Moonglows, Frankie Lymon And The Teenagers, The Platters, Fats Domino. Then I hit gold. "Tutti Frutti" by Little Richard. My heart nearly burst with excitement. I'd never heard anything even resembling this. It filled the room with energy and colour and outrageous defiance. I had heard God. Now I wanted to see him.'

Like many others of his generation, Bowie loved American music and American culture (he was a keen baseball follower as a youngster and in the school holidays of 1962, when the world was grooving to 'I Remember You' by Frank Ifield, Bowie was playing for a local team, the Dulwich Bluejays). But it was through the music that Bowie became inspired. When he first heard Little Richard, at the age of eight or nine, it was an almost epiphanic moment. Of course, for many young people the advent of American rock'n'roll into their lives had a cathartic effect, but for Bowie, and a tiny minority of others, it did more than that: it made him want to be a star.

According to Bowie's testimony in a variety of interviews, it was at that moment in the late 1950s that he knew there was nothing else he wanted to do in life other than make music. In his early teens Bowie was not just listening to R&B and rock'n'roll but the hep jazz of Charlie Mingus too. His half-brother, Terry, was a crucial influence here. He was the conduit through which Americana really influenced Bowie. Terry would talk to his kid brother about his love for the Beat poets, Kerouac and Ginsberg, and would frequent jazz cellars of an evening and tell tales of the thrill and excitement of modern jazz in the metropolis.

Good-looking and with an agile mind, Terry was also prone to bouts of gloomy depression and would later be diagnosed as a schizophrenic. The taint of 'madness' in the Jones family terrified the young Bowie: not only was Terry profoundly disturbed but many of his extended family on the Burns side had psychological or mental problems, too. Auntie Una, a schizophrenic, died in her late thirties after enduring electric shock treatment and internment in a mental institution. Auntie Vivienne also had schizophrenic episodes. Auntie Nora had been lobotomised in order to treat her nervous disposition. Peggy's mum was a self-confessed 'mad-woman'. Back in post-war Britain, when the diagnosis and treatment of mental-health problems was very different than it is today, it is estimated that in the UK alone there were around 150,000 inmates in various institutions for the mentally ill. The young Bowie saw disturbance all around him and felt the full force of society's stigma of the mentally ill, if only by proxy.

After returning from army service in 1958 unkempt and disturbed, Terry was turfed out of Plaistow Grove by his mum. For the next decade or so, Terry would intermittently reside at Plaistow Grove before being sectioned at local hospitals for the mentally ill. However, throughout his teenage years David and Terry remained very close. Bowie would accompany Terry on his excursions into the smoke to try out the latest breaking sounds. One episode during this time would haunt Bowie for years to come. In 1966 they walked to the Bromel Club at the Bromley

Court Hotel to see Cream in concert. On their way home after the gig, Terry became increasingly agitated until he fell to his knees and began pawing the road. He could see cracks in the tarmac and flames rising up, as if from the underworld. Bowie was scared witless. Aural and visual hallucinations, images of bright, searing lights (heavenly) and flames (hellish) would increasingly blight Terry's life. Like many schizophrenics – and some epileptics – he would often hear 'voices from God'. This example of someone so close being possessed was horrifying for Bowie. Frightened that his own mind would split down the middle, too, as the years of relative failure as a teenager and early-twenty-something turned into the glam-era days of heady excitement and adulation, Bowie became ever more fearful of and distant from his brother.

Bowie's first public appearance as a musician was back in the late 1950s when he went to the Isle of Wight with the Bromley Cubs. He and his lifelong mate George Underwood performed a few Lonnie Donegan skiffle songs using a makeshift double bass, made from a tea chest and a broom handle, and a ukulele. From that moment on, there was no turning back.

At school, Bowie would use 'wet breaks' to bash out a few riffs on a guitar. Whilst still at school he played in a band called the Konrads with his mate George Underwood. To finance his musical interests, he took a couple of part-time jobs, one, so legend has it (sadly the story may well be apocryphal), as a butcher's boy cycling round Bromley delivering meat (having had your sausages delivered by David Bowie must qualify as being one of the bizarrest claims to 'fame' for the citizens of Bromley), the other at the local record shop owned by a guy called Vic Furlong. Bowie was fired from the latter for daydreaming, but not before he had bought himself his first saxophone (with a little help from his dad). The white Bakelite acrylic alto saxophone (which Bowie still has) was made by Selmer and had gold keys. Bowie took sax lessons with Ronnie Ross, a top British saxophonist living in deepest Orpington, who remembered him as an enthusiastic though unexceptional pupil. At school, too, Bowie was far from conventionally gifted. Having failed his 11-plus, he attended Bromley Technical High School. He left school in 1963 after getting an O level in just one subject – Art.

Indeed, with hindsight, the most important thing that happened to him at school (in terms of his career development) was the sudden, and excruciating, acquisition of the weirdest eyes in showbiz the year before. During an argument with his then best mate (and still bosom-buddy) George Underwood over a girl, Carol Goldsmith, George's knuckle caught David's left eye. At Farnborough Hospital, it was found that the sphincter muscles in the eye were damaged, requiring David to have two operations. After a lengthy time off school, he was left with a paralysed and permanently dilated pupil (a condition known as an aniscora) and retarded vision. Just to kill off one particularly prevalent media 'myth', Bowie does not, in fact, have miscoloured eyes: the effect of the enlarged pupil on the iris only gives the appearance of different colours. He was born with blueish eyes but because of the paralysed pupil his left eye is unable to dilate or contract, appearing brown or green depending on the ambient light. The origins of his Technicolor eyes have been top, or at least near the top, of virtually every 'revelatory' tabloid article on Bowie for the past thirty years. Anecdote after anecdote has been piled up to mythologise the whole event, including news stories playing up the origins of Bowie's impeccable alien physiognomy. The whole affair is an index of the media fascination with a near sixty-something rock star who has retained close to physical perfection: perfect bone structure, a full head of hair, a tiny waist (at an age when most men's guts have well and truly flabbed over their belts) and an amazingly reconstructed set of gnashers. Bowie said in 2005, 'I've had nothing done really but to my teeth, and that helped prop up the visage.'

Bowie may not have covered himself in glory in terms of academic qualifications, but he did possess a vivid, unusual, imaginative flair for composition. Although his spelling and grammar were weak, he could write better stories than any of his classmates. Bowie is largely self-taught. His considerable eloquence and knowledge of a whole variety of topics from art (he claims to have visited every significant art collection in Europe) to politics are a testimony to his supreme mental acquisitiveness. Autodidacticism is stamped all over his work. He may not have been able to cut it as a professional saxophonist in technical terms, but the sound he did make (melismatic, croaky, almost asthmatic) when he blew into the instrument was idiosyncratic and distinctive. In fact, he had rather a punky attitude to the instrument before it became fashionable. Initially, his guitar, piano and saxophone playing were technically fairly limited, but his almost childish unconventionality rendered his playing and compositions quirky and effective. A muso Bowie certainly wasn't. The fact that ultimately his interests extended beyond music is crucial.

Whereas in the 1940s and 1950s it was America that originated and developed rhythm and blues, blues, country and rock'n'roll, it was Britain that stylised it, jumbled it up, mixed it with sources from outside of music and 'tarted' it up. The British changed forever the way pop was packaged and presented. Someone such as Bowie, or the Cure's Robert Smith, or Pulp's Jarvis Cocker, could only come from England. What it looked like, the casing (both conceptual and sartorial), was just as important, if not more so, than its original form. Bowie was at the centre of these developments. He wanted to be an English Little Richard, an English Elvis. And that's exactly what he became – the first British solo superstar of the art-school era.

Indeed, this was a defining moment within popular culture. The early part of the 1960s saw the appearance of the first 'bona fide' Brit-rockers (John Lennon, Mick Jagger), to contrast with the ersatz clones of Americana (Adam Faith, Cliff Richard). Billy Fury had set the tone for much to come by writing (under his Wilberforce pseudonym) and recording all his own material for his 1960 debut album, *The Sound Of Fury*, thus establishing a standard which The Beatles, The Who, The Kinks and The Rolling Stones would ultimately follow a few years later. Coupled with the novelty of acts who based their careers not on interpreting others' songs, which was standard up until the mid-1960s, but on originating their own, was the idea of the stylistic creation of a public identity which broke free from the stereotypical norm. Andrew Loog Oldham's selling of the Stones stressed authenticity and a maverick, oppositional stance ('Would you let your daughter go with a Rolling Stone?'), and contrasted with the rather more old-school packaging of The Beatles by Brian Epstein. The emphasis in these pioneering attempts at pop packaging was on the presentation of an identity that was separate and distinct from the American blueprint. Bowie, and the rock star who initially traded in the same currency of intellectualised artifice and outrage, Bryan Ferry, turned out the way they did because of a certain uncomfortableness: too young to be part of the first, distinctive and authentic packaging of the Britpop dream, there's a rehearsed, strangely distanced quality to the way in which they were presented, as if they were desperately trying to be authentic, but somehow falling short. Now the rules of the game in the earnestness stakes were no longer simply to be learned and rehearsed, they could be bent and exposed – hence Bowie and Ferry's fascination with pop as a construct, as an artificial state.

Despite claims in a press release for his 1966 single, 'The London Boys', that he had studied at Bromley Art School, Bowie never actually attended art school. His introduction to art came from Owen Frampton, father of famous guitarist Peter, initially of Humble Pie, and later in the 70s infamous for selling millions of copies of an album that briefly heralded in the delights of vocodarised voices and, rather more permanently, 'stadium rock', with *Frampton Comes Alive*. Owen Frampton taught at Bromley Technical High School, which Bowie attended from 1958 to 1963. Bowie, along with George Underwood, was in the arts stream, and he received a very solid grounding in art from a very well-respected teacher. Both Bowie and Underwood still have their portfolios, which were very thorough and had a bias towards commercial art. By all accounts, Frampton's liberal classroom regime indeed mimicked the nonconformity of the art-school ethic. Bowie undoubtedly socialised throughout the 60s with musicians and artists who had attended art schools themselves, and it was this art-school inheritance that set him off at a tangent. Art schools created a space for experimentation outside the codes of conformity which still operated in other institutions of higher education at the time: trial and error and freedom of expression were encouraged. Sociologists Simon Frith and Howard Horne in their seminal book *Art Into Pop* had this to say about the British art-school legacy: 'What distinguished 60s bohemians from previous angry young men and women was their collusion with (and direct intervention in) mass media . . .' They added that 'The artistic challenge was to seize control of the commercial process itself, to subvert pop from the inside. Art-pop (inspired more or less directly by pop art) meant not individual expression (like art-rock) but the manipulation of signs.' The list of pop musicians who went to art school in the late 50s and early 60s is like a roll call of the most important pop artists of their day: John Lennon, Eric Burdon, Keith Richards, Pete Townshend, Eric Clapton, Syd Barrett, Freddie Mercury, Charlie Watts, Bryan Ferry, Brian Eno, and many more.

Bowie had a painterly approach to his work and, in his middle age, raised this eclecticism to almost high cultural proportions.

But the impetus behind this layering of information, the serious-ness of intent, and the interest in eliding cultural art forms, whether it be painting, music, dance, mime or whatever, came primarily from the art-school tradition. Bowie is the collagist *par excellence*, and his best work in the 1970s was an extension of the work of many in the 1960s.

In 1992 he told *Life* magazine: 'From a very early age I was always fascinated by those who transgressed the norm, who defied convention, whether in painting or in music or anything. Those were my heroes – the artists Marcel Duchamp and Salvador Dali and, in rock, Little Richard . . . First it was John Lennon, some of the Stones and Kinks, and then it got hammered in with guys like [Roxy Music's] Bryan Ferry, King Crimson, Pink Floyd. It was usually Dada. Yeah, applying Dada, creating these absolutely frightening, extraordinary monsters of rock that nobody could possibly love . . . I would like to believe that I and a number of others in the early 70s changed the fabric of pop, made it a wider receiver; one that could incorporate ideas from other arts.' However, most of the mid-1960s art-school musicians made music which would later be classified as rock, or at least as rock-based. As Ken Pitt, the manager who guided Bowie's career from 1966 to 1970, is wont to point out, Bowie never expressed an interest in joining the league of macho journeymen rockers. In 1993 Pitt told Radio 1's Pete Frame: 'When he first came to me, I wasn't sure what he wanted to do. Certainly, he never implied that he wanted to be a rock'n'roll star. At that time I was looking for someone who could be called an all-round entertainer. There were very few people who you could hold out much hope for and I thought in David we had found someone who could be.'

This is certainly borne out by listening to Bowie's music from that time. Bowie's first ever band was the R&B group, The Konrads. After leaving his only permanent day job, as a 'junior visualiser' (basically the cut'n'paste boy) at Nevin D. Hirst Advertising in Bond Street, London (one of their products was the slimming biscuit, Ayds), Bowie's first recordings with The King Bees and The Manish Boys were intermittently listenable stabs at electric reworkings of the acoustic blues styles associated with John Lee Hooker.

The young Davie Jones was not without ample doses of barefaced cheek. So confident was he in his own talent that he sent a letter to John Bloom, a wealthy entrepreneur, asking him to cough up some dough for the new Beatles. Rather than consigning the letter to the wastepaper bin, Bloom passed on the request to Leslie Conn, a music person who ran Doris Day's music publishing company and was a talent scout for the Dick James Organisation. Conn booked the band for a wedding anniversary party at a club in Soho in order to check them out. They went down so badly with their brash, loud R&B that Conn had to stop the gig after just ten minutes. Davie Jones was in tears.

Nevertheless, Conn became The King Bees' manager and promoter for a few months in 1964. The band released their first single on 5 June 1964 – a cover of the old spiritual, 'Liza Jane' (although Conn is credited as the songwriter, then a common ploy to squeeze more money from the system). Bowie's career was finally up, if not exactly running. The single sold next to nothing.

Throughout the mid-60s, Davie Jones was just one of many teenage wannabes on the London pop scene, visible through performing gigs at the Marquee. The Manish Boys played a support slot on the Gene Pitney/Gerry And The Pacemakers tour and appeared on television shows such as *Juke Box Jury*, BBC 2's *Gadzooks* and *The Beat Room*.

Bowie then progressed through Who-sounding mod music with his next band, The Lower Third ('Can't Help Thinking About Me' is the best example, a catchy pop song on which the Americanised vocal accenting of his first recordings is replaced by a reedy, theatrical, south-London vocal), to the extraordinary eccentricity of his first Deram record in 1967, the acoustic folk/pop of Feathers in 1968, and that jumble of pop balladry and country rock found on *David Bowie* in 1969. But hardly ever did Bowie engage with rock as a style in the same way as The Kinks on their proto-punk 'You Really Got Me', or The Beatles on their classic countercultural put-down, 'Revolution'. Bowie disliked 'heavy music', calling it a 'fairly primitive form'. For Bowie, rock was blighted by false standards of musicianship and technique: 'I look for sensation rather than quality, and heavy music seems to be full of musicians who have quality rather than musicians who for some reason can chill your spine.'

And in this he has stayed remarkably constant. All his recordings, save those with Tin Machine, which elevated the playing of the music above the music itself, possess a maverick crankiness, and are about sensation above sense, vision before virtuosity. Bowie has seldom been interested in technique: in the studio he is often happy with performances which musicians themselves regard as flawed, discarding the complete and choosing the inharmonious, the right combination of wrong elements: 'It's like playing around with colours when you're doing a painting . . . You're trying to put this pastiche of things together, this juxtaposition. I was very heavily into the whole idea of Brion Gysin/William Burroughs "cut-ups" and knew that if you put the wrong things together you often got the right end result. It was trying to find out what the wrong things were. What could you put against each other that would make some none-sense.'

In fact, it might be just as well to stop referring to Bowie as a 'rock' musician at all. He has actually recorded very few lead-guitar-dominated albums, very few that would sit comfortably with those of pioneers of heavy rock such as Led Zeppelin, Black Sabbath and Deep Purple. Is *The Rise And Fall Of Ziggy Stardust And The Spiders From Mars*, with the whimsical pop of 'Starman' and the balladry of 'Five Years', really a rock album? Even those records that have an earthier bluesy feel only have it in parts. Of the ten songs on the 'Ziggy-goes-to-America' sequel, *Aladdin Sane*, only around half the tracks are rock songs.

In his time, Bowie has recorded in a whole variety of 'non-rock' styles (country, reggae, soul, disco, jazz, ambient, techno, jungle), interpreted songs by Jacques Brel and Kurt Weill (hardly stalwarts of stadium rock themselves) and has duetted with Bing Crosby. In fact, Bowie has produced only two bona fide rock albums, and for these he was almost universally panned, as the Tin Machine media saga amply showed. His least successful artistic collaborations have almost always been with stadium rockers (Queen, Mick Jagger, Tina Turner). His one constant attachment to the rock ethic has been his post-Ronson penchant for squealy lead guitarists on major tours, and gives a false impression of what his music is actually about.

Bowie's musical palette is in fact far broader, and this is what makes him especially interesting. A crucial influence on the young Bowie was that of his third manager, Ken Pitt. Pitt took over from Ralph Horton, who had managed The Lower Third. (Interestingly, although the band journeyed from gig to gig in a clapped-out ambulance, Bowie was driven in Horton's swish Mark 10 Jag – ever the star!) Indeed, Horton had pumped in considerable time, effort, and ideas into the promotion of the Lower Third. However, as the months rolled by, it was apparent to the rest of the group that Bowie stood out. Good-looking and with a stage presence, Bowie also always seemed to have the best girls, whilst the rest of the band toiled in a constant impecunious state. After seeing the band in action in September 1965 at the Marquee, Pitt agreed to manage David. According to Bowie engineer and producer Gus Dudgeon, Pitt was 'a very charming man, upper class, tall and impressive. He unquestionably had Bowie's interests at heart and he was influential on the sort of things he did or did not do.' An intensely private man, those who know him well speak of an absolutely charming and urbane character, now well into his eighties. Back in the 1960s, Pitt was a major-league player, having worked with Frankie Laine, Louis Armstrong, Duke Ellington, Frank Sinatra and Mel Tormé. These were all popular entertainers, but certainly not mascots of contemporary youth culture. Pitt also openly supported law reform with regard to homosexuality and joined the Conservative Campaign for Homosexual Equality. However, although biographers have speculated that he and Bowie were at times in a close relationship, neither Bowie nor Pitt have ever confirmed that this was so. 'My own impression, having observed Bowie and Pitt together at Manchester Street [where Pitt had his London flat]', says biographer George Tremlett, 'is that they probably did have a sexual relationship – but one that was never as important to Bowie as it was to Pitt.'

So Pitt's engagement with the music scene was more variety-based than streetwise, and this brought an interesting slant to the emergent Bowie style. His mark has been long-lasting. Taken in this light, the duets with Cher, Bing Crosby and Tina Turner become totally explicable. Pitt was also the very first to recognise that Bowie was a musician/actor with a wide range of interests both low- and high-cultural. Pitt encouraged and enlightened his young charge and was always willing to discuss and, in some cases, introduce Bowie to a wide variety of different cultural experiences, from the theatre and film through to literature (particularly the archly camp writing of Oscar Wilde) and art (Aubrey Beardsley). Of course, Pitt was just one of many people Bowie was influenced by in the 1960s as his musical and creative self was still forming. That said, Pitt helped to provide the high-cultural framework for Bowie to play around with in the 70s. If Bowie's half-brother Terry can be said to have given him a taste for hip Americana, then it would be Pitt who added to

Bowie's developing fascination with the 'legitimate' arts. Throughout his career, Bowie's interest in these two levels of artistic endeavour has constantly played itself out in his work. Bowie took from high art and brought it down to street level. In so doing, far from cheapening serious art, he made it into something entirely different. The collapse between high and low art is inextricably bound up with the advent of rock stars such as Bowie.

Bowie's eclecticism, inquisitiveness and acquisitiveness (he was already an avid collector of *objets d'art*) already existed, but Pitt gave him free rein to take on board and sift through the materials. In fact, Ken Pitt – urbane, charming, Conservative-voting (in truth, most managers save Brian Epstein voted Tory in those days) – was Bowie's link to a classical, rather than progressive, agenda. He provided all the room Bowie needed to test things out, bailed him out financially, and backed him to the hilt. His book, *The Pitt Report*, tells the tale far better than anyone else could and is an amazing insight into the amateurishness of the music business of the 1960s, in which ad hoc arrangements and general corporate torpor make for perversely amusing reading.

Pitt's first recommendation on meeting his young charge was that he should change his name. In fact, this was not to be the first name change for the fledgling singer. Back in 1963, in his first band, the Konrads, Davie Jones went under the stage name of Dave Jay. But now a change of name was more of a priority. The British singer Davy Jones had already secured more than his fifteen minutes as one-quarter of The Monkees, the first teen band to break almost exclusively through the media of television. 'Bowie', pronounced by the man himself and all his 'die-hard' fans to rhyme with 'slowie', as opposed to 'wowie!' as used by most 'casual fans' and chat-show presenters, was chosen for its connection with the Bowie knife. Jim Bowie (pronounced to rhyme with 'phooey') was a Texan adventurer who died at the Alamo in 1836, and carried a single-bladed hunting knife. Bowie's description of why he chose the name is typically highly ambiguous. In the 70s, Bowie proclaimed that the knife signalled a desire to cut through lies to reveal hidden truths (a highly ironic comment, give Bowie's capacity for deceit), while in a recent Radio 1 interview he said that he liked the connotations of a blade being sharpened on both sides, a signifier for all sorts of ambiguities. In fact, the Bowie knife has only one cutting edge, and is not double-bladed. This mistaken belief was held not just by Bowie, but by William Burroughs too. The choice of stage name nevertheless indicated a sense of being able to cut both ways, perfect for the pluralistic 60s. The name also derived, despite its association with Americana (a connection the English David was obviously happy about, his whole career musically being an English take on a largely American form), from a Scottish heritage, and Bowie quite liked that regional distinctiveness, too.

Like all successful 'artificial' names, it now feels, in the light of Bowie's success, completely natural. As writer Simon Frith rightly points out, we often forget how daft a name sounds on first hearing and forget the innate naffness or unsuitability of the name itself. Nostalgia turns even the most inappropriate name into one we all think of as totally fitting. 'The Beatles', for example, is one of the silliest names in rock history (a tiresome allusion to 'beat' music and an unfunny pun rolled into one), but, as Frith points out, 'successful groups' names always feel right; unsuccessful groups' names remain silly'.

So, on 16 September 1965, Davie Jones became David Bowie. However, no change was made by deed poll and David Bowie is merely the stage name of David Jones. All contractual, managerial and financial documentation is still presumably addressed to David Robert Jones to this day. 'David Bowie' was the singer's first alter ego.

The most remarkable thing about Bowie's 1960s' recorded output is that, with only one or two exceptions, it gives not the slightest hint of the greatness to come, save for one very important aspect: his innate sense of theatre.

Bowie emerged as a quite brilliant mimic: his mid-to-late-60s vocal is hugely indebted to Anthony Newley, the British singer who, significantly, performed mime in the hit musical, *Stop the World I Want to Get Off!* (1961), had huge American success, married actress Joan Collins and remained active in the theatre until his death in April 1999. Tim Hughes wrote in 1970: 'His [Bowie's] heroes are rather surprising – George Formby, Nat Jackley, Gracie Fields, Albert Modley – until one realises his admiration for the artiste as entertainer. Modern influences are Jacques Brel, Dylan, Tony Newley, John Lennon and Tiny Tim.'

In an interview from the late 1960s, Bowie told Gordon Coxhill, 'I'm determined to be an entertainer, clubs, cabaret, concerts, the lot . . . A lot is said and written about the musical snobbery with the fans, but I think the groups are just as bad. For some reason even the words entertainer and cabaret make them shudder.' At pains not to disassociate himself totally from the 'straight' world of cabaret, light entertainment and the theatre, while simultaneously signalling an interest in non-rock contemporary music, it now seems no surprise that Bowie went on to move his career away from rock music time and again.

Bowie's influences came from the music hall, light entertainment and the theatre as well as from Anglo-American popular music. Bowie was not alone in his appreciation of music hall: Tommy Steele, Marty Wilde and Joe Brown all covered music hall and The Kinks and The Beatles also pay homage to the genre. Like these earlier singers, and particularly like Lennon who sang in a rasping Scouse accent, Bowie also made sure he sounded like where he came from. In an era in which the distinctly parochial was making its first impact in the charts with the likes of Bernard Cribbins, Mike Sarne, Lionel Bart, Tommy Steele and, of course, Anthony Newley, Bowie's voice was that of south London, not south Alabama (as was the case with Mick Jagger).

However, Bowie was not aping music hall alone. His music was already influenced by all sorts of other elements – from theatre and from classical music – and this arguably made him unique among his contemporaries. His theatricality is in evidence throughout his first album, entitled *David Bowie*, released on the Deram label. The Herman's Hermits-sounding 'Love You Till Tuesday', with the little 'comic' aside ('Well I might be able to stretch it till Wednesday'), and the orchestral pop of 'Rubber Band' with its self-consciously quaint dénouement ('I hope you break your baton', 'Oh deary me') are as un-rock'n'roll as one could imagine, as is 'The Laughing Gnome'.

A flop single in 1967, but a UK Number 6 when re-released (without Bowie's permission) in 1973, 'The Laughing Gnome' is a supremely catchy children's song. Despite selling around a quarter of a million copies in the UK alone, it has never appeared on any officially sanctioned collection of greatest hits. Bowie appears embarrassed by it, yet he should be proud. It's a lovely little song and, despite Bowie's reputation for cool, arty, more serious songs, it's surely time now for it to be reappraised. According to some sources, it's Bowie's tenth-biggest-selling UK single. The fact that in a recent poll Channel Four viewers voted it the 78th worst pop song ever is likely to prolong its status as a banished Bowie song. The riff which forms the opening instrumental section of the song was later recycled on numerous occasions by Bowie, and can be heard, in slightly altered forms, on 'Speed Of Life' (1977), 'Scary Monsters (And Supercreeps)' (1980), 'Beat Of Your Drum' (1987) and 'The Last Thing You Should Do' (1997).

'The Laughing Gnome' is not a one-off either. 'When I'm Five', recorded in 1968 and included on the *Love You Till Tuesday* promo soundtrack, is another song which shows a quite well-honed affinity with the quiddities of childhood. Another is 'Rupert The Riley' (the long-lost cousin of Madness' 'Driving In My Car'), a song which dates from around early 1971. Although not quite the pop classic that is 'The Laughing Gnome', its nonappearance on any of the official Bowie reissues over the years is a shame. 'I had a Riley Gamecock', Bowie told Virgin Radio in 2003. 'It was an old racer . . . I think it probably goes back to the 30s or something. A mate of mine and me put it together – not very well as it happens – and it stalled outside Lewisham police station one day. I had really long hair in those days so I was standing round the front of the car, trying to pump it back to life again and all the cops were at the windows laughing at me and the bloody thing started up and I'd left it in first gear and it came at me. The crankshaft went through my leg and I was pumping blood like a fountain and I cracked both my knees as the bumper had kind of got me pinned to another car that was just behind it.'

The only competitor in terms of outright, although endearing, foolishness in the pop field (excluding 'comedy' records by the likes of Bernard Cribbins or the Avengers) was the art-school pop star, Syd Barrett. Barrett, the original lead singer with Pink Floyd, created aural collages of bangs, crashes and speeded-up demonic laughs on 'The Gnome', 'Scarecrow' and 'Bike' which actually outdid Bowie. When Tony Visconti, the brilliant young New Yorker a couple of years Bowie's senior who co-produced some of Bowie's most innovative work in the 1970s, turned down the opportunity of recording 'Space Oddity' in 1969, calling it a 'novelty record', he was, in a way, misreading his friend's act. Bowie might have a serious side, but a lot of his work, whether intentionally or not, is incredibly good fun, and 'Space Oddity', if it was a novelty record, was merely part of that particular body of work, certainly not an exception.

Bowie's eponymous first album, released on 1 June 1967 (the same date as *Sgt Pepper*) on the Deram label (the short-lived progressive ambit of the rather staid Decca), is undoubtedly the most bizarre record of his entire career. On the surface it is very different from the rest of his oeuvre, containing as it does short narrative songs framed by the squarest of pop backings (there's hardly a lead guitar anywhere in the mix), with brass, woodwind and strings thrown into the musical stew. Bowie already had a reputation for favouring odd musical combinations and, for his debut album, he and musical collaborator Dek Fernley rather astonishingly taught themselves the rudiments of music theory from the *Observer Book of Music*. They also provided the London Philharmonic with their own version of a score, which the orchestra dutifully transposed and amended. This captured Bowie's endearingly naive mindset perfectly. What other rock star would go on a two-week crash course in music theory to learn how to write musical parts for a bassoon?

The album was produced by one of Decca's in-house producers, Mike Vernon. Vernon, whose star was on the rise following his production of the first album by The Bluesbreakers featuring Eric Clapton, was immediately impressed by Bowie, whom he regarded as bright with an original lyricality. 'The one thing he did have,' Vernon remembered in 1998, 'was hooky little songs.' These included the 'incredibly trite' 'Love You Till Tuesday', which was recorded in two versions, one for single release. A German version, 'Liebe Dich Bis Dienstag', was also recorded, and remains one of Bowie's silliest moments to date, a comedic career high. Gus Dudgeon, producer of Bowie's 'Space Oddity' (1969) and later producer for many years of Elton John's platinum-selling albums, engineered the sessions for the first Bowie album and thought the track a potential hit: 'To be honest, I thought it was going to be his first hit single. I wasn't sure about the previous single, "Rubber Band", which I loved but thought might be too off-the-wall. He's still Anthony Newleying a bit there, but he's having a great time doing it!'

Dudgeon remembers the whole project with great fondness: 'It was so enjoyable because the music was very filmic, all very visual and all quite honest and unaffected and therefore unique.' What struck both Dudgeon and Vernon the most, though, was Bowie's acute sense of the bizarre. Mike Vernon: 'Occasionally he got into things where I thought, What the bloody hell's this? I don't understand this! "Gravedigger" was something I didn't understand at the time. I had no concept of what the hell it was!'

Completely unloved by the public and seemingly a source of some embarrassment to Bowie himself, the album is the vinyl equivalent of the madwoman in the attic. Bowie has never included it in any of the subsequent official reissue campaigns. 'It just so happens that he's in a position where he can avoid embarrassment if he wishes,' Gus Dudgeon said in 1998. 'If it doesn't suit him, he won't go with it. You know what he's like!' Its commercial failure at the time can partly be explained by Decca's completely anachronistic promotional policy. The company, as Ken Pitt noted in his *Pitt Report*, simply failed to promote an album they had paid good money to record. Decca was an antediluvian organisation, as Mike Vernon remembers: 'They didn't understand what rock music was. I did some sessions with The Yardbirds, which were rejected, same with The Spencer Davis Rhythm And Blues Quartet. It was getting played to the people who ran the company and they were stuck in a time warp with Vera Lynn, Mantovani, Frank Chacksfield and David Whitfield. My input was John Mayall and Graham Bond, but they didn't understand that at all.'

Despite flopping like a cowpat and being left destitute by its maker to fend for itself outside of the 'official' Bowie canon, the album does contain, in embryo, many of the themes Bowie was to develop, in a rather less insouciant way, throughout his subsequent career. Amazingly, it has, in a minor way, been an influence on the work of Britpop bands in the mid-1990s, particularly Blur. Lyricist Damon Albarn's nonconformist caricatures from the Britpop era (Ernold Same, Tracy Jacks) are strikingly similar to Bowie's Uncle Arthur and Little Bombardier. Bowie showed a predilection for writing three-minute narrative vignettes, depicting the worlds of a succession of 'little men' (and women), set in a bygone age, sung in a style which owed little to the traditions of rock'n'roll or the blues.

'Little Bombardier' is typical of this approach. The song tells the story of Frankie, a demobbed soldier who 'drank his money' and 'told his woes to no man'. The soldier befriends two children whom he spoils with treats, only to have to leave town a broken man after being warned off by the police, who suspect him of child molesting. The idea of the outsider, of the individual unable to connect with the rest of humanity, a theme of such power in Bowie's work throughout his career, was first explored in narrative songs such as these. Interestingly, 'Little Bombardier', like 'Maid Of Bond Street', another song on the album, is a waltz. In popular music the waltz form has tended to signify a bygone age, a yearning for a past emotional state, a sense of loss or regret. Kate Bush uses it on 'Army Dreamers' (1980), her condemnation of the 'Troubles' in Ireland and the senseless waste of life. The Stranglers' paean to heroin, 'Golden Brown' (1981), also uses the three-four time in part, as does Bowie's own 'After All' (1970).

In addition to 'Little Bombardier', two other tracks, 'She's Got Medals' and 'Rubber Band', were also set in a fictive wartime environment. The comedy cockney of 'She's Got Medals' is the tale of a woman who joins the army only to tire of 'picking up girls, cleaning her gun and shaving her curls'. It is Bowie's first song about cross-dressing and sexual ambivalence. Even the chord structure and lyric are a foretaste of his homage to The Velvet Underground on 'Queen Bitch' (1971). On his first album Bowie used a novel juxtaposition of instruments traditionally associated with pop – acoustic guitar, piano, bass guitar and drums – with those from music hall and classical music, such as tuba and trumpet. His incorporation of brass and woodwind instruments on a large scale on a track such as the single 'Rubber Band', released on 2 December 1966, predated their use on The Beatles' much-lauded *Sgt Pepper's Lonely Hearts Club Band* album.

Why all these references to wartime heroes and failed love affairs set in a bygone era of penny-chews, threepenny squibs, Scotch Emulsion and ringworm in the classroom? Other Bowie biographers have said that Bowie was haunted by tales of derring-do on the part of mentally unstable ancestors in the Jones family. What is more likely, however, is that Bowie was doing what he always does best – sniffing the intellectual wind and articulating it through song. Liverpudlian jazz hep cat and intellectual, George Melly, wrote in 1969: 'Following the success of The Beatles, States Worship has been largely replaced by a cool, if deep, chauvinism, but as it is impossible to think of England as having no past, this is dealt with by treating history as a vast boutique full of military uniforms, grannie shoes and spectacles, 30s suits and George Formby records. By wrenching these objects out of their historical context they are rendered harmless.' Bowie's first album articulated this 'chauvinism' perfectly.

Another theme running through his early work is a sort of naive critique of the counterculture and its attendant pill-popping hedonism. These are the first signs of Bowie's feelings of separateness from the 'flower power' era. 'The London Boys', a Bowie B-side in 1966, is a typical example. The city is viewed as a corrupting influence: it has lost its innocent charm in a show of conspicuous consumption and excess. In 'Join The Gang' he combines a further attack on drug use with a swipe at the counterculture, signalling his opposition to its fake camaraderie: 'This is what to do now that you're here/Sit down doing nothing altogether very fast' ('Join The Gang', 1967, author's transcription.)

This first Bowie album is already peopled by starlets. The idea of life-as-theatre and of the cinematic quality of everyday life, a theme that was later to become central to Bowie, was also beginning to manifest itself: 'This girl her world is made of flashlights and films/Her cares are scraps on the cutting-room floor.' ('Maid Of Bond Street', 1967, author's transcription).

The album's looniest moment is saved for the end. Just when you think you've survived an all-out attack of the barking mad, and just when you think Bowie couldn't actually get any sillier, the last two-and-a-half minutes or so reroute his weirdness on to a new plane of daftness. 'Please Mr Gravedigger' is Bowie's very own 'death disc'. The mid-60s charts were full of American tales of automobile pile-ups, decapitated girlfriends and smashed-to-pieces leather-clad teenage hunks (see the Shangri-Las' 'Leader Of The Pack' and Jimmy Cross' hysterical 'I Want My Baby Back'), often recorded with a surfeit of tacky sound effects from the throbbing torment of the motorbike to the creaking of coffin lids. However, Bowie gives the genre an added twist by mining British music hall, rather than James Dean-era bubblegum, for his story. Bowie narrates the story of a child-murderer, who watches the gravedigger at his work and who plans the latter's death so that he won't tell the police of the murders. The song itself reads like a macabre parody of the bonhomie of songs such as 'Oh Mr Porter'. Delivered without instrumental backing, the lyrics are supplemented by a number of stock-in-trade special effects such as thunderclaps, raindrops and a bell tolling, creating a bizarre sense of a 1940s or 1950s radio play. Bowie even fakes a sneeze or two. It was obvious, as far back as late 1966 when this track was recorded, that Bowie saw music and character as a whole. In fact, his sights were set as much on a career as a thespian as one of a singer: 'I want to act . . . I'd like to do character parts. I think it takes a lot to become somebody else. It takes some doing.'

The song is one of pop's genuinely crazy moments. Dudgeon enthuses:

I just love it. I just love 'Gravedigger'! The bottom end on the thunder is fantastic! Decca had the most fabulous sound-effects library. What I remember is Bowie standing there wearing a pair of cans with his collar turned up as if he was in the rain, hunched over, shuffling about in a box of gravel. And you thought Brian Wilson had lost it! I asked him, 'How long is this thing?' And he said, 'Well, five minutes should do it,' so I went off to the sound-effects library and found some thunder and some rain and I've managed to get it in extremely good stereo – the sound of the thunder is really hefty – plenty of low end! So I put together five minutes of rain and thunder and I threw in a few birds as well, and that became the backing track. Now is that weird or is that weird? The sneeze is a good piece of acting, isn't it? That's clever; that's when you see the actor in him. There's another weird thing about that track which has always freaked me out. It's about a bloody gravedigger and how [the narrator] is gonna chuck him in and dig his own grave for him, and he keeps on going on about 'Mr GD'. They're my initials and it bugs me! Every time I hear it I think, Oh no, don't do that, that's like sending me a chain letter, thanks very much. I had forgotten the horrible vibe I get every time I hear him singing, 'Oh, Mr GD'.

'Join The Gang' is almost as disturbed. Listening to the album for the first time in over a quarter of a century, Dudgeon remarked, 'It's the most peculiar thing. I love the sitar at the front, it's totally manic, bloody brilliant! The drums are also great on it and it's like the Bonzos at the end – the sound effects are great. There's a hoover, and there's farts, and there's munching. I think the farts sound pretty genuine to me. One of them's even got a delay on it, like a repeat; it goes from the right-hand side to the left on the stereo!'

These were Bowie's first faltering steps in the direction of theatrical pop. He knew that to project a sense of character it was necessary to embrace studio technology and utilise each new innovation as it came along. His recording history demonstrates a particular fascination with modifying his basic singing voice through the use of multi-track octave doubling (a second voice part, an octave above the first, recorded and often harmonised with the original vocal line) and a variety of studio tricks to distort the timbre of the vocal or to alter the speed of vocal delivery. The earliest attempts at this came, of course, on the 'The Laughing Gnome', and it is to this rock gem we must now turn. Daft as a brush, enormously catchy, and always a huge favourite of those members of the rock community who have only recently gained full control over their bodily functions, in the 1970s it was regularly introduced by Radio 1 DJ Tony Blackburn as being sung by Uncle David Bowie, an irony not missed by Bowie's fans, who were more used to him falling 'wanking to the floor' at the time.

They say time is a great healer, but the 'emotional scars' inflicted on the 25-year-old Dudgeon were still there, even after thirty years of trying to come to terms with a song he calls his 'own personal Troggs tape'. Bowie provided the voice of the Laughing Gnome himself, whilst Dudgeon was the voice of the second gnome ('his brother whose name was Fred') in the second verse and subsequent choruses: 'We did this bloody silly song and he finished the vocal and decided that he wanted to do a speeded-up voice. I got the tape operator to run it at half-speed, and as we took the tape down in speed, our voices went up. I mean, it's so corny, it's pathetic. And somehow we got this idea that we would try and incorporate as many jokes about the word "gnome" as we could think of. I mean, it was pathetic really. Well, in fact, it *is* pathetic. Somehow or other we got off on doing this. That's the really scary part. Technically it worked, but it's bloody embarrassing. We actually came up with those lines between us. I mean, what were we on?'

Here's a sample of the wit and wisdom of Dudgeon/Bowie:

Bowie: 'Ere, where do you come from?
Gnome: Gnome-man's land.
Bowie: Oh really?

Or try this:

Bowie: 'Ere, what's that clickin' noise?
Gnome: That's Fred – he's a metro-gnome!

The main problem for the fledgling singer was that he had no voice of his own, he merely had Anthony Newley's on loan, and his colleagues thought the impersonation was ultimately a handicap. 'He sounded like bloody Anthony Newley on all those first singles I made with him,' remembers Gus Dudgeon. 'It bothered Mike Vernon and me because we'd say, "Bowie's really good and his songs are fucking great, but he sounds like Anthony Newley." I was an engineer at the time and I didn't know if it was a plus or a minus but it felt like it was possibly a minus. But he did it so well that it was really rather good!'

Underneath this quaint and subdued surface of cheeky-chappy music hall and English whimsy, heavier themes lurked. The origins of Bowie's superman fixation of the early 70s is prefigured on one song, 'We Are Hungry Men', which, in an incredibly twee way, reflected the first stirrings of 'green' politics in the media and the moral panic engendered by reports that overpopulation would be an increasing global problem. Bowie casts himself as a Messiah figure who, through the blind allegiance of the populus, will right the wrongs of society: 'I prepared a document/Legalising mass abortion./ We will turn a blind eye to infanticide. ('We Are Hungry Men', 1967, author's transcription).

Again, it's hard to take seriously any track which starts with the session engineer impersonating a sort of BBC Home Service radio announcer, but there is a heavier lyric going down.

This song contains the seeds of so much to come. It is a vision of a future dystopia, peopled with desensitised dupes, searching for a Christ figure to save them. Bowie's obsession with strong men and his belief in the possibility of the rise of a new demagogy, which blighted many of his mid-70s interviews, are eerily prefigured by this extract from an interview he gave to Kate Simpson for *Music Now!* in 1969: 'This country is crying out for a leader. God knows what it is looking for, but if it's not careful it's going to end up with a Hitler . . . The only person coming through with any strength is Enoch Powell. He is the only one with a following. Whether it's good or bad is not the point. The fact is he has.'

Bowie's first album and singles, although now adored by some, were all commercial failures. Had he been starting out today, he would almost certainly never have become a rock superstar, and would quite possibly never even have had a career in music. He would probably have been dropped well before he'd had time to develop his act, find his voice, and set out his agenda. Today, the likes of David Bowie are simply not allowed to exist.

2. BECKENHAM ODDITY, 1967–1970

'You must think we out-of-towners are a strange and crazy bunch. Well,
I guess we are. He He Ha Ha Yes we dance a furious boredom.'

EXTRACT FROM A LETTER FROM BOWIE TO RADIO 1 DJ JOHN PEEL, 1969

By the middle of 1967, Bowie's career had reached something of an impasse. He had received some good reviews, but had had negligible sales. It was at this time that he met one of the most important figures in his career, Brooklyn-born would-be producer Tony Visconti, fresh over in London to learn his trade at Decca under producer Denny Cordell. Cordell was in partnership with the successful music publisher, David Platz, also Bowie's publisher, who handled such songwriters as Anthony Newley and Lionel Bart. Visconti was summoned to a meeting at Platz's office and played excerpts from David's debut album. 'I sat there amused by the eclectic styles of the singer. There was a quantum leap of styles between "The Laughing Gnome" and "When I Live My Dream". I think my comment was, "This guy's all over the place!" Platz found this amusing, but added that Bowie was looking for a producer to guide him in a more straightforward direction. He said something like, since I seemed to be an expert on working with hard-to-understand artists (he was alluding to Marc Bolan), the two of you should get along. Then he asked if I would like to meet him. I said yes and Platz replied, "He's in the next room." Inside was a twenty-year-old David Bowie, wearing shaggy, shoulder-length hair and nervously smoking a cigarette and pacing the floor. I recall that Bowie and I talked for a couple of hours. He had a vast knowledge of the American underground groups and particularly liked Frank Zappa, The Velvet Underground and especially The Fugs. I did, too. We spent the rest of the afternoon together and eventually ended up at a small art cinema in Chelsea, where we saw *A Knife in the Water* by Roman Polanski. Scratchy black-and-white foreign films were another passion we had in common.'

Bowie, at that stage, was a relatively unsuccessful pop singer, Visconti a virtually unknown producer. 'My track record, up to this point, was nil,' confirms Visconti. 'As an assistant to Denny Cordell I was on the second Procol Harum album, the first Joe Cocker album (I'd scored some parts for it and I mixed most of it) and the first [sic] Move album, *Shazam*. I had signed Tyrannosaurus Rex to Denny's Regal Zonophone label and that was my first real production – their first album, *My People Were Fair* . . . I was still unproven.'

However, in Visconti, Bowie had found a friend who shared similar interests and who was, very importantly, an American, and therefore by definition rather cool. But Visconti was a slightly complicating factor in the Bowie–Pitt axis. Visconti's relationship with Bowie's manager, Ken Pitt, was never close, and Visconti remembers Bowie making apologies for Pitt, saying he was an old-fashioned, theatrical-type manager who wasn't really into rock. 'When I saw the two of them together I got the impression of an awkwardness between them,' Visconti says. 'I remember Pitt telling me his plans for Bowie, but none of it registered with me. It all seemed like he didn't really have anything concrete, or things I could relate to. I remember talk of the bit part for Bowie in *Virgin Soldiers*. I felt that Pitt didn't care much for me. David felt like a nervous go-between and he would try to come up with some common ground that we could all discuss. I never became particularly close to Pitt and we kept a respectable distance. Ken Pitt dubbed me a "leftist draft-dodger". I knew nothing of politics then and I certainly didn't dodge the draft. I was, in fact, inducted, but rejected on medical grounds. Pitt was just frustrated and jealous that David and I were good friends.'

So Bowie was at the interface of the 'straight' and 'cool' worlds, both of which had their charms for a man as into Art Deco as he was The Fugs. However, the change of producer from Vernon to Visconti had no immediate impact on Bowie's fortunes. The first product of a recording session at Advison Studios, London, on 1 September, 'Let Me Sleep Beside You'/'Karma Man', was turned down by the antiquated Decca selection panel and never released.

In 1960s London, there were no better professions to be in than music, fashion or photography. These were young, happening areas, defining the pop culture of the day – new, flashy, vibrant and fun. Bowie colonised the first two of these professions, eventually weaving music and fashion into a seamless whole, and became objectified on Polaroid in the flashlight of the third. He was a natural convention-breaker. Personal style, and its articulation through dress, was central to this revolt. In 1997, he said: 'An outfit is an entire life experience. An outfit is much more than just something to wear. It's about who you are, it's a badge and it becomes a symbol.'

Even at school Bowie was a stylishly rebellious dresser, then, as now, something of a shoe fetishist: he was one of the first to wear what have now become known as winkle-pickers. Back in 1961 they were referred to as chisel-pointers, and were imported from Italy. One of his schoolteachers, Brian Lane, remembers that on one or two occasions Bowie came to school with dyed hair, a real taboo-breaking stand for the times. Bowie also backcombed his hair into a beautiful blond quiff. A school photograph from the very early 60s shows Bowie standing dutifully in line with his classmates, his head turned to reveal a quizzical, but photogenic, profile – giving the impression that he regarded the occasion as something of a photo opportunity.

In this, he was very much like his friend and rival Marc Bolan, born Mark Feld in 1948. Bolan, who as a teenager worked as a male model, was perhaps even more of a fashion fundamentalist than Bowie. Indeed, through producer Tony Visconti, Bowie and Bolan's rather uneasy friendship developed during the late 1960s into a mixture of mutual respect and bitchy rivalry. Visconti: 'According to both of them, they were always aware of each other. In their teens, both received a fair amount of exposure in the press, mainly for fashion statements. In one article, Marc was hailed as "King Of The Mods", for his chic Italian suits and his Vespa, which he merely posed on, but couldn't ride. My association with Marc began about six weeks earlier than with Bowie. They were often at my flat in Earls Court for many a musical soirée. Both lived with their parents when I first met them (and I had met David's father on an unexpected visit to my flat one weekend). Even when Marc married June, they often came back to my flat because their one-room flat in Notting Hill Gate lacked a proper bath. They bathed about three nights a week at my place. David often used my flat as a place to bring girlfriends back.'

Mod fashion was very important to both Bolan and Bowie – not the anorak-wearing, scooter-driving, soul-grooving mods of the Who generation, but their immediate antecedents. The first mods in the early 1960s were dangerous modernists: they wore expensive suits, lipstick, blusher, and eye shadow. They were yet another scion of gay subculture and sartorially part of glam's forbears.

Both Bowie and Bolan would hang around the chic joints of swinging London, raiding the dustbins of Carnaby Street for any discarded seconds which could be salvaged for night-time clobber. They took style very seriously. Bolan's biographer, Mark Paytress, says, 'Both were ex-mods on the make in mid-60s London, hustlers who'd congregate at the La Giaconda cafe in Denmark Street, hoping someone would notice them. Both were chameleons who could mould themselves to emergent trends. But whereas Bolan was probably the "natural" star, Bowie was more seriously engaged in intellectual pursuits.' An advocate of both Bolan and Bowie was DJ John Peel, the doyen of alternative music who was the longest-serving DJ on Radio 1. 'Bolan certainly gave the impression that he wanted to be a rock superstar and that was all he intended to do,' remembered Peel. 'I would describe him as cunning. That sounds a bit hard, but you were always aware that there was a side to him, a disagreeable side. He was certainly always an ambitious lad.'

In terms of personal style in the 1960s, Bowie for the most part followed, rather than set, fashion trends, although he was one of the first teenagers in Britain to have long hair. On 12 November 1964 he appeared as the president of the Society For The Prevention Of Cruelty To Long-Haired Men on the *Tonight* programme and told an amused Cliff Michelmore how members were being taunted for their sartorial excess. Bowie's whole demeanour revealed an innate campness – in fact his first television performance is probably the most limp-wristed of his whole career – but the young Bowie loved all this taboo-breaking and flaunting of moral codes. 'Well, I think we're all fairly tolerant,' he told Michelmore, 'but for the last two years we've had comments like "Darlin'" and "Can I carry your handbag?" thrown at us, and I think it just has to stop now.'

He wanted attention, he wanted to be known, and, back in 1964, to be a man and to have long hair was one way of achieving this aim. The rumpus he caused by having long hair in a world in which homosexuals were figures of ridicule was a lesson he would build upon in spades in the 1970s. In 1972, with the exception of the cropped skinhead look, short hair for young men would be equally novel, and would be the precursor to the post-Ziggy gay look. He may have appeared a mite gauche throughout the 1960s, but at least he was trying to look different. By the early 70s he looked as different from other rock stars past and present as one could imagine.

In 1965, Bowie was a mod, in 1966 and 1967 a hippy, but by 1968 he had begun developing his own post-hippy, slightly feminised cool. According to Ken Pitt, he divested himself of his beads just as the mainstream was about to embrace them and it was at about this point that Bowie started setting sartorial trends rather than aping them. At the same time, he began flouting the moral codes of the day in a more direct way. In performance, Bowie demonstrated a theatricality that was, for the time, certainly out of the ordinary for British pop. A typical gig by his mod group, The Lower Third, at the Marquee in London in the mid-60s would incorporate 'Mars' from Holst's *The Planets Suite* (used in 50s sci-fi classic serials *The Quatermass Experiment* and *Quatermass II*), and a cover of 'Chim Chim Cheree' from *Mary Poppins* – hardly standard rock/pop fare. Attending his first ever Bowie gig, future manager Ken Pitt witnessed the singer climax with 'You'll Never Walk Alone'.

Under the tutelage of dancer Lindsay Kemp (metaphorically, so he said, descended from William Kemp, Shakespeare's in-house clown at the Globe Theatre in London), Bowie's innate love of the bizarre flourished wildly. Kemp was born in Irby, near Liverpool, in 1938. At sixteen he attended evening classes at the Bradford College of Art and in 1964 he had set up the Lindsay Kemp Mime Company. When Bowie met him, Kemp lived in a flat in Bateman Buildings, Soho, above a strip joint. His one-time boyfriend, a brilliant near-blind dancer and mime called Jack Birkett, was a regular in Kemp's productions. Bowie and Kemp met during the summer of 1967. Kemp would play Bowie's first album in the classes he held at a dance centre in Floral Street. Bowie became a part-time enrollee and met designer Natasha Korniloff (later to provide Bowie's wardrobe for the 1978 world tour and the Pierrot costume for the 'Ashes To Ashes' video and promo shots).

Kemp's influence had less to do with the fact that Bowie attended some of his dance classes (Kemp is at pains to point out that these were not mime classes), and more with the fact that, by his very being, he increased Bowie's awareness of the bizarre. In 1997, Bowie said of Kemp: 'He lived on his emotions, he was a wonderful influence. His day-to-day life was the most theatrical thing I had ever seen, ever. It was everything I thought Bohemia probably was. I joined the circus.'

'I didn't really teach him to be a mime artiste but to be more of himself on the outside,' said Kemp in the mid-1980s. 'I enabled him to free the angel and demon that he is on the inside.'

Bowie's first performance with Kemp and his partner Jack Birkett, who went under the stage name of Orlando, came in *Pierrot in Turquoise* at the Oxford New Theatre on 28 December 1967. Bowie played Cloud to Kemp's Pierrot, and got to sing a few of his original songs. The show then moved via the Rose Hill Theatre, Cumberland, to the Mercury Theatre in Notting Hill for a run in the first half of March, 1968, and finished at the Intimate Theatre in Palmer's Green, north London, at the end of that month. Gus Dudgeon remembers that Bowie always kept a sense of humour about his excursions into mime. 'Bowie just talked to me about it one day when we were working. In fact, we were laughing about it. He said, "I've been studying mime with this fella and I'm going to do this mime show in Notting Hill Gate in this tiny little theatre, but the difference is, I'm going to sing some songs." Then he laughed: "But that's not really a mime show!" He was actually very good.'

Tony Visconti recalls that although Bowie threw himself wholeheartedly into mime, he never ever gave the impression that this would be his vocation:

I remember meeting Lindsay at a rehearsal for that show he put on at the Mercury Theatre in Notting Hill Gate. I used to study karate in those days and David seemed to think my moves were somewhat balletic. So, at the Kemp rehearsal, David introduced me to Lindsay with great panache, telling him that I was a karate expert (I wasn't). He immediately wanted me to show

Lindsay some moves and kicks and I complied. I can see the expression of repulsion on Lindsay's face, and afterwards received a warning not to try those kicks without warming up. I could see Lindsay's senses were more fine-tuned to more delicate body movement, so I just sheepishly sat and watched rehearsals. I later attended a dress rehearsal at the Mercury. I knew that David was spending a lot of time on this project, so I have to say that Lindsay was a big influence on David, if only for a short, intense period.

Lindsay Kemp behaved like the quintessential queen. His 'S's hissed like a steam radiator and he bent his wrists as often as he could. He was the epitome of a *femme*, gay man. His boyfriend, Orlando, was registered blind, very silent, but an expert at mime, too. David often said that Orlando had a slight edge over Lindsay. Both Lindsay and Orlando were shaved bald. Although I was wary of homosexuals in those days (I was told I was 'queer bait' because of my boyish, Mediterranean looks, and was hit on by gays constantly), I liked Lindsay a lot because of his wit and obvious expertise as a mime. At rehearsals he was intense and relentless when it came to perfecting a subtle nuance. I could see how closely David was watching him and learning invaluable techniques which he would apply in the future. But it was apparent to me then that being a mime was not David's final goal in life.

The tour was a bizarre affair indeed. Korniloff, the designer and driver, dressed Bowie in a 'huge pink shirt with maroon spots on, with a big maroon and pink ruff and little knee britches in grey with red velvet stripes on them'. At the time, and for a while unbeknown to Kemp and Korniloff, Bowie was conducting affairs with both of them. One night it was discovered that Bowie was cosying up with Kemp at the start of the evening, then rounding the nocturnal pleasures off with a stopover in the Korniloff boudoir. There were harsh recriminations over the breakfast table the following morning, and before that evening's show Kemp slashed his wrists, but not so badly as to hospitalise himself. Kemp performed with his arm covered in plasters after out-patient treatment at the local infirmary, bleeding through the show with aplomb, and the two mimes cried their way through the perform-ance. The audience thought it was all part of the act, and applauded wildly.

Bowie knew he had hit on something genuinely novel during his mime experiences. Kemp considered him rather wooden, and was hard on him during his dance classes, but while Bowie was no natural, he learned just enough from Kemp to take the essence or the attitude of mime and be able to apply it to rock. Bowie went on to mix rock and mime in the late 1960s, touring in early 1969 with Tyrannosaurus Rex as opening act and performing a mime called *Yet-San And The Eagle*, with 'Silly Boy Blue' as his backing track. To confront a rock audience in the late 60s with mime performances seems, with hindsight, an incredibly brave venture and one almost as incongruous as comedian Max Wall opening for rock band Mott The Hoople in 1972. It certainly didn't meet with everyone's approval. In 1996, John Peel, who supported Bowie's career in the interregnum between 'Space Oddity' and 'Starman' by regularly inviting him to play in concert for Radio 1, had this to say about the early Bowie:

I can't remember that he looked particularly androgynous. He certainly didn't look like a beer-sodden *Loaded* reader either. The people I used to hang out with at the time were Marc [Bolan], 'Beautiful Peter', a bloke who I was sharing a flat with who was a photographer and took the photo for the cover of the first Marc Bolan album (you actually couldn't tell if he was male or female), and a DJ called Jeff Dexter, who had long blond hair. Sheila [Peel's wife] thought he was a girl when she first saw him. By their standards Bowie was positively US marine!

The first time I remember him was on a Tyrannosaurus Rex tour. They had a support act, an Australian sitar player [Vytas Serelis] – one of the rarest of God's creatures – and David Bowie. I remember him sitting in the dressing room at the Philharmonic Hall in Liverpool and them shouting to him: 'It's eight o'clock, you're on, David.' He was a very edgy lad. But on the other hand he could have been edgy because perhaps he thought what he was doing was actually a load of piss. I'm sure mime is actually the oldest and the most important of the arts but to me it's a load of shite, I have to say. I always thought Marcel Marceau needed a good kicking. It's not my cup of tea unless there are howling guitars, and, by and large, in mime you don't get howling guitars.

The irony, of course, was that that was exactly what, in 1972, you did get: Ziggy, mime, and as many howling guitars as the heart could desire.

Bowie fan Geoff Ward, now a poet, writer and academic, remembers another gig on the tour – at the Manchester Free Trade Hall on 22 February 1969 – as one of the loudest he'd ever heard:

He was very, very loud – or rather, the tape to which he was miming was very loud. This was the golden era of the Marshall amp (made locally by Jim Marshall, of course) and I often left the Free Trade Hall with ears ringing. Even by the standards of the time he had the volume cranked up painfully high. This created an odd disparity (deliberate? perhaps not) between the necessarily silent and, in a pop-concert context, vulnerable nature of the physical performance, and what you heard. The mime itself was, looking back on it, conventional sub-Marcel Marceau type work ... Help! I'm trapped in an invisible telephone kiosk with existential overtones ... He was obviously a capable gymnast, but it wasn't an especially magnetic performance. He hadn't yet learned the kind of physical projection that I saw him show in London at the famous Ziggy shows, where he jumped on and off banks of speakers at the end of 'Suffragette City' and it made the hair on the back of your neck stand on end. On the Ziggy show you could tell what was obviously choreographed (kabuki costume being pulled off by young women rushing in from the wings etc.), but there was a dangerous grey area where the possibly choreographed and the possibly improvised were impossible to disintricate. I suspect everything in the 1969 mime act was rehearsed carefully. What was startling, above all, was not the act, but the benign and unquestioning acceptance verging on stoned indifference with which it was greeted. Today no rock act that wanted to get anywhere would abruptly switch medium for a particular tour and expect the audience just to go along with it. But then an audience that was willing to sit through John Peel reading fairy tales and listen to an antipodean sitar player is probably floating at the apogee of tolerance.

Visconti, however, remembers the whole tour as a rather cunning plan by Bolan to belittle the competition: 'David was open to friendship but Marc was quite cruel about David's as yet unproven musical career. I think it was with great sadistic delight that Marc hired David to open for Tyrannosaurus Rex, not as a musical act, but as a mime.'

In concert, Bowie may have sought to inject an epicene edge, but in private he was completely different. Almost all the interviewees for this book remember the young Bowie as likeable, hard-working and 'different'. But camp? 'Certainly not,' says Mike Vernon, 'although I don't know quite frankly if I would have known at that age if he was or not.' Ken Scott, who later went on to produce Bowie's classic glam-era records and who began his five-year working career with Bowie in mid-1969 as the engineer on Bowie's second album, recollects, 'I don't remember him being camp at any time.'

Of course, the whole idea of 'camp' is interpreted very differently over time. For some who would define camp less as playing the queen and more as an overstated, ironic playing around with gender roles, without any necessary link with homosexuality, the British comedian Eric Morecambe propped up in bed with his sidekick Ernie Wise in the 1970s was unquestionably camp, although he was not considered to be so at the time. For most, the idea of camp means overtly effeminate behaviour; the ostentatious demonstration of homosexuality. By this standard, Bowie was not camp at this stage.

Bowie's theatrical experimentation was to stand him in good stead over the next decade but it wasn't commercially or artistically successful. He undoubtedly had more false starts than any other superstar in pop, and his early work provides us with not even a glimpse of the greatness to come. However, in the 60s you were allowed to fail. Bowie would probably not have made it if he had started out today – record companies and managers would not stick with a consistently unsuccessful, if talented, artist (here we must give Ken Pitt the credit for sticking with 'his boy', despite year after year of commercial disappointments).

Given the extent of his later success, the sheer scale of Bowie's failure is quite remarkable, and it's a tribute to his tenacity that he seems never to have entirely lost faith in his calling. True, there had been some encouraging signs. He did have his supporters in the media, notably the journalist Penny Valentine, and two of his songs, 'Over The Wall We Go' and 'Silly Boy Blue', had been covered by Oscar Beuselinck (later singer and actor Paul 'Dancing With The Captain' Nicholas) and Billy Fury respectively. And then there was the customary high quotient of unrealised and unrealisable plans. Bowie interested himself in Buddhism, befriended the Buddhist priest, Chime Youngdong Rimpoche, and, according to some sources, came close to becoming a monk himself. However, Tony Visconti, himself curious about Buddhism at the time, doubts Bowie took his own interest too seriously:

If anything, I was a neo-Buddhist, with my introduction to the philosophy coming from Timothy Leary's psychedelic translation of *The Tibetan Book of the Dead*, especially written for acid trips (LSD). My politics were the politics of ecstasy. David and I had Tibetan Buddhism in common, and he talked a lot about meeting and studying with Chime Rimpoche. I was very envious, since it had been a two-year compulsion for me, to meet and study with a genuine Tibetan lama. When I finally met Chime Rimpoche, it was not through David, it was through a mutual friend, Mary Finnigan. I got the impression that David was very reluctant to bring us together, and I also got the impression that he exaggerated how much time he'd spent with Chime, although some biographies state that he studied with him for six months. Many years later, when we were mixing the *Scary Monsters* album in London, I called the British Museum, where Chime worked in the Asian section, and got him to pay David a surprise visit at my recording studio (Good Earth) in Soho. David was very happy to see him and I left them for a while. I knew that Chime had a fabulous idea to stage a rock concert at the Potala in Lhasa, Tibet, and he wanted David to be the star of the concert. I left him to pitch his idea to David, but nothing came of it.

By mid-1967, Bowie had finally flown the parental nest, to lodge with Ken Pitt, taking the spare room upstairs in Ken's flat and coming and going when he wanted. The two were close and would live together for around a year. Pitt says that their relationship was 'strong and affectionate'. It was time for Bowie to make the break from the confines of Plaistow Grove. Terry's mental illness and schizophrenic episodes were becoming more harrowing, the general domestic situation was confining, and Bowie needed space. Pitt's more expansive quarters, crammed full of books and records, was perfect.

During his residence *chez* Pitt, Bowie recorded a prototype rock musical, *Ernie Johnson*, about a character who throws a party to mark his intended suicide, planned for the next day. At the time of writing this has yet to be released, although a tape containing tracks from the project was put up for auction at Christie's in June 1996, but failed to reach its reserve price. The tape tells the tale of Ernie, nineteen, who spends the day leading up to the party thinking about his loves of the previous year and having a racist conversation with a tramp, before singing a song to himself in the mirror and then rushing off to Carnaby Street to buy himself a new tie. The tape dates from around February 1968, when Bowie often demoed work using a four-track tape recorder set up in his bedroom. The tracklisting is as follows: 'Tiny Tim', 'Where's The Loo', 'Season Folk', 'Just A Moment Sir', 'Various Times Of Day' (a song suite comprising three tracks – 'Early Morning', 'Noon-Lunchtime', 'Evening'), 'Ernie Boy', 'This My Day' and one untitled track. Additional tracks (from around February 1966) were appended to the Christie's tape: 'Going Down', 'Over The Wall We Go', and 'Love You Till Tuesday'.

Bowie continued to write and record after the sessions for his first album had been completed in 1967, and throughout 1968, but most of this material remains unreleased, officially at any rate. In December 1966, Pitt returned from a business trip to the States, during the course of which he met Lou Reed at the Factory (Warhol's workplace), with an acetate of the first Velvet Underground album, prompting Bowie, along with a band named The Riot Squad, to record 'I'm Waiting For The Man' with Gus Dudgeon. This stands as the first UK reaction to the avant-garde pop of the East-coast Factory scene and shows that Bowie was already into The Velvet Underground way before his much-publicised colonisation of the territory in the glam era.

Then as now, Bowie was a huge fan of new music. He was one of Britain's first Velvet Underground fans, to be sure, but he also admired a whole range of music, including some made by the most famous band of his or any other era. ' "I Am The Walrus's" "otherness" was transporting in a way that nothing before it had even approached,' Bowie would later say: 'A one-way ticket to ride out of Bromley.'

At this time, Bowie had a number of projects on the go simultaneously. He remembers that, 'Around '67, I was doing double duty with a couple of bands. It might even have been three.

One of them was The Buzz, my own band with whom I tried out all my new songs, good and bad. The other was indeed The Riot Squad. This was a far more democratic affair in which I shared vocals and played tenor sax. I also inflicted my taste for the theatrical upon them. This was the first band I was in where make-up and interesting trousers were as important as the music. I also made them cover Mothers Of Invention songs. Not happily, I seem to remember, especially as my big favourite was "It Can't Happen Here". Frank's [Zappa's] stuff was virtually unknown in Britain, and relistening to that song I can see why he wasn't on any playlists.'

There are numerous unrealised, unfinished, unreleased and unreleasable tracks from this era, including a remarkable song recorded with The Riot Squad in April 1967 called 'Little Toy Soldier' (also known as 'Sadie's Song'), which tells the story of Sadie, who has a clockwork toy soldier who comes to life and whips her when he is wound up. One day the girl winds it up too much and it beats her to death! The song itself is basically The Velvet Underground's 'Venus In Furs', with some changes.

By 1968, so dire were his financial circumstances that Bowie was forced, on an occasional basis, into operating a photocopier at Legastat. In the meantime, the Decca selection panel had rejected three self-penned songs intended for single release. Bowie was then turned down by Apple records, had a play, *The Champion Flower Grower*, rejected by the BBC drama department, failed auditions for *The Virgin Soldiers*, *Alain* and *Oh What A Lovely War* (although he was awarded a week's work as an extra in the first of these), and, to raise some cash, was forced into appearing in a television ad for Lyons Maid 'Luv' ice creams, incidentally made by future *Alien* and *Bladerunner* director Ridley Scott. He then acted in a short silent film, *The Image*, directed by Michael Armstrong, but with little impact. In addition, his new combo was regarded by manager Ken Pitt as a most undesirable extravagance.

In early 1968, Lindsay Kemp was asked by the BBC to choreograph *The Pistol Shot*, a play by Pushkin. For the production, Kemp chose Bowie and a beautiful red-haired dancer, Hermione Farthingale, to dance a poetic minuet. Very soon an item, the pair lived together.

Bowie's next project would be Feathers (originally called Turquoise after the Kemp production, *Pierrot in Turquoise*), a group consisting of Bowie, his then ever-faithful friend John Hutchinson (often simply known as 'Hutch') on bass, who had replaced the original band member, Tony Hill, and Hermione Farthingale on acoustic guitar. The band began live work in September 1968 and supported The Who at the Roundhouse in early 1969. Feathers, as Bowie later conceded, was merely a contrivance to be with Hermione for as long as possible, as often as possible.

By the summer of 1968, the 21-year-old Bowie had set up home in a flat in Clareville Grove, London, with Hermione. Hutch would be a regular visitor there. Hermione was determinedly middle class and it is rumoured that her parents disapproved very strongly of her dalliance with a would-be pop star. During his months of infatuation with Hermione, the smitten Bowie would devise projects simply to be around his amour, and Feathers was one of these.

They performed only a handful of gigs and their set, a mixture of Merseybeat, Roger McGough-inspired poetry, folksy whimsy and mime, was arty, but unsuccessful. One of their songs, 'The Ching-a-Ling Song', is a hidden classic in the oeuvre of daft pop songs, with extremely silly lyrics and a melody which all those familiar with Mike Leigh's 1976 BBC play *Nuts in May* will instantly recognise as the forerunner to the character Candice Marie's 'We're Going To The Zoo He Said'. Here's a snippet from the lyric:'I wish I'd play the doodah horn/The doodah horn is fine/I'd sell my house and ferny coach/To make this daydream mine.'

With Feathers destined to take their place in the ever-growing pantheon of Bowie pop flops, Ken Pitt set about raising finance for what he thought would be the project which would finally launch Bowie's career. But Ken Pitt's masterstroke, a Bowie film, also failed commercially.

Love You Till Tuesday, a collection of short promotional clips designed to kindle media interest in a flagging career, was in fact an extremely prescient work. Along with promos made by The Rolling Stones, The Kinks and The Beatles for their single releases in the mid-to-late 1960s, this collection is one of the very first attempts to sell pop in this way. Throughout the film, Bowie sports not so much a wig as a tailpiece. Having been cut short for the *Virgin Soldiers* audition, his hair had failed to grow back to the mandatory length by the time of filming, so a hair extension was used instead. Thus tonsorially transposed, Bowie paraded his least successful hairstyle to date – a sort of homage to John Noakes, the bluff Yorkshireman who was then a presenter on the BBC children's perennial, *Blue Peter*. Thirty-five years on, the film makes for rather embarrassing viewing in places, but it is Bowie's sense of theatre which comes through. 'When I'm Five', 'Rubber Band' and 'The Mask', a short mime sequence written and performed by Bowie, are quaintly engaging, and 'Let Me Sleep Beside You', much loved by Suede's Brett Anderson, is Bowie's first great pop song, with a killer riff and some slightly risqué lyrics: 'Wear the dress your mother wore/Let me sleep beside you.'

'Let Me Sleep Beside You' might have been strong enough for the charts. Nevertheless, as Bowie later commented, 'Had anything happened for me in the mid-60s, then I might have been cut off from an awful lot of influences.' Had he broken into the mainstream at that point, he would almost inevitably have had a career as either a standard pop balladeer or a light entertainer for the 70s – more Frank Spencer than Frank Black. On first inspection, this seems a bizarre comment to make about the boy David, but all the evidence is there: Bowie didn't play rock, was interested in acting, had a penchant for cheeky cockneyisms, could dance well, displayed a knack for (sometimes unintentional) comedy, and even went as far as creating and rehearsing (although never actually performing to a paying public) a cabaret routine which included Beatles covers and songs such as 'Trains And Boats And Planes'. At a time when many of the early Beatles-inspired beat combos (Gerry And The Pacemakers, Freddie And The Dreamers) were drifting into cabaret, the fact that Bowie didn't join their number and end up as Britain's answer to Dick Van Dyke is again due to the art-school inheritance. The Beatles included the art-school-trained John Lennon, a man imbued with a romantic ideology (his hero was Van Gogh), and therefore a willingness to embrace the new. This, together with Paul McCartney's interest in the avant-garde, ensured that The Beatles did not slide into self-parody or a career in light entertainment as the decade progressed, and it was a similar sensibility which in the end meant that Bowie would emerge as their natural successor.

Love You Till Tuesday was also a watershed in Bowie's love life for, during filming, he rowed bitterly with his lover and co-star, Hermione. His relationship with the classic 'English rose', with long strawberry-blonde hair, high cheekbones and 'Clodagh Rodgers' wispy folk vocal, and its abrupt termination in early

1969, appears to have had something of a devastating effect on Bowie. (Farthingale ran off with a dancer and later lived abroad after marrying an anthropologist.)

After the split, Bowie returned to live briefly at the parental home in Bromley, then went back to Ken Pitt's London flat before arriving on the doorstep of a certain Mary Finnigan who lived at 24 Foxgrove Road, Beckenham, Kent. (Bowie appeared to possess the knack of being simultaneously extremely sexually attractive to both men and women, and of presenting a waiflike helplessness.) Finnigan, a divorcee with two children of her own to look after, mothered Bowie, too, during their brief affair.

Bowie moved in with Finnigan in the first half of 1969 and, much to her horrified amusement, took over the entire flat – a bass amp here, a twelve-string guitar there. Soon the dining room of her small flat resembled something between backstage at the Roundhouse and a junk shop.

A freelance journalist, Mary Finnigan was at that time working regularly for the *Sunday Times* as well as for the underground newspaper *IT*. Bowie was in no position to help out financially: live work had petered out, his option with Deram had not been taken up and he was without record company backing. She therefore supported him financially for three months. Although nominally her lodger, Bowie paid no rent or household bills. The two were an item.

Together with friends Christina Ostrom and Barry Jackson, the couple started a Sunday-evening folk club at the Three Tuns pub in Beckenham. Finnigan claims that it was at her suggestion that the folk club became an Arts Lab later in 1969. Bowie appeared every week. The anchorman of the event, he performed much of the then unrecorded material from the *Space Oddity* album, backed by a pre-recorded tape or the stylophone, a new, cheap, downmarket synth played with what looked like a magic Biro. He wrote to DJ John Peel asking him to help fund the Arts Lab. Peel remembered being sent drawings for a lab Bowie had designed. Bowie took grass-roots mixed-media seriously. The Arts Lab soon had a suitably hippy-dippy name, Growth, and became moderately successful locally. The list of performers included Peter Frampton, Steve Harley, the Strawbs, Rick Wakeman, Keith Christmas, Tony Visconti, Mick Ronson and Lionel Bart. In a telephone interview with Chris Welch from the *Melody Maker* Bowie enthused:

There isn't one pseud involved. All the people are real – like labourers or bank clerks. It started out as a folk club, arts labs generally have such a bad reputation as pseud places . . . There's a lot of talent in the green belt and there is a load of tripe in Drury Lane. I think the arts lab movement is extremely important and should take over from the youth club concept as a social service . . . The people who come are completely pacifist and we get a lot of co-operation from the police in our area. They are more than helpful . . . Respect breeds respect. We've got a few greasers who come and a few skinheads who are just as enthusiastic . . . We started our lab a few months ago with poets and artists who just came along. It's got bigger and bigger and now we have our own light show and sculptures, et cetera. And I never knew there were so many sitar players in Beckenham.

'David was wonderful at those Arts Labs of his,' recalls Tony Visconti. 'He took me to someone else's, in Covent Garden, very early on. I think it was the first Arts Lab ever. I was impressed with the avant-garde atmosphere, the anything-goes spirit. He told me that night that he wanted to open one in Beckenham and, of course, he did, at The Three Tuns. I got along well with Hutch, and David really enjoyed "folking" around with him. In fact, I met David at this point in his life and that's what I thought he'd settled on. Little did I know that this was just one of many of his personas. What I liked about David's relationship with his Arts Lab was that it gave him a purpose. He had just been dropped from Deram but that didn't deter him from expressing himself. The Arts Lab and doing mime at rock shows was his way of buying time and sharpening a few skills when important people weren't looking. I admired this healthy attitude he had then.'

Although committed to this grass-roots populism, Bowie never really fitted into the hippy underground. While the rest of his peers were into dope and LSD, Bowie was more into drinking bottles of barley wine and falling over outside the pub. In fact, on occasion, Bowie would 'lecture' his audience at the Arts Lab about the dangers of hard drugs. Apart from cannabis tincture, which he seemed to be particularly fond of at the time, Bowie was into alcohol (much frowned upon by the counterculture). Perhaps fearful of the effect hallucinogenics might have on his personality, given his family's precarious mental state, acid was out of bounds.

But life in Beckenham was far from uneventful. Following a trip away, Mary Finnigan returned to her flat to find it, quite remarkably, spotlessly clean and well ordered. (According to Finnigan, the young Bowie was incredibly untidy, expecting his mess to be cleaned up pronto by the lady of the house.) She had been usurped by a certain Mary Angela Barnett.

Mary Barnett, or Angie as she was known, was born in 1950 in Xeros, Cyprus, of American parentage. As a teenager she had attended the same Swiss all-girls finishing school as Mary Finnigan and when Angie later moved into the Finnigan abode as Bowie's girlfriend, she and Mary would try and annoy David by speaking French together. She had met Bowie while both were dating the same lover, Calvin Mark Lee, who was working as an A&R man for Bowie's new record company, Mercury records. Angie had accompanied Lee on a scouting mission to see Bowie perform with Feathers in early 1969 as support to The Who and Scaffold. The two became 'an item' after an introduction by Calvin Lee at a press conference for King Crimson at London's Speakeasy. Lee himself was a very colourful character in a scene full of flamboyance. A San Francisco Chinese, he was also a doctor of philosophy. Angie was attractive, actively bisexual, extravagant, prone to huge self-dramatisation and scene-stealing faints, tantrums and collapses. She was also bright, cultured and likeable, if in a hugely demanding way. She also had aspirations of becoming an actress and a movie star. By attaching herself to a pop star on the make, she hoped to make her partner a star and, at the same time, become one herself in his wake.

For David Bowie, the first part of 1969 ran much as 1968 and 1967 had done: plenty of ideas, plenty of energy, but no commercial success. It was crisis time. His apprenticeship had to draw to a close soon, and it did so with the success of his first hit single, 'Space Oddity', written as a response to Stanley Kubrick's *2001: A Space Odyssey*, which he saw whilst out of his head on marijuana tincture. Commonly regarded as one of the best singles of his career, 'Space Oddity' came in at Number 14 in a 2005 Virgin Radio poll of the Top 500 singles of all time.

'Space Oddity' was just one of a whole batch of songs recorded in February 1969 in David's bedroom at Clareville Grove, Chelsea, where he had shared a flat with girlfriend Hermione, and friend and musician John Hutchinson. These recordings were the first songs completed post-Hermione. On them, Hutch and David performed as a duo in an attempt to become a sort of British Simon and Garfunkel. Apart from a version of 'Space Oddity', the duo also demoed 'An Occasional Dream', 'When I'm Five', 'I'm Not Quite' (which later became 'Letter To Hermione'), 'Conversation Piece', 'Life Is A Circus' (written by Roger Bunn, Roxy Music's first guitarist), 'Ching-A-Ling' and 'Lover To The Dawn' (an early version of 'Cygnet Committee'). These tracks can now be found on a bootleg called *A Beckenham Oddity*.

But 'Space Oddity' was the thoroughbred. It remains a beautifully haunting, if dated, masterpiece, a tale of alienation which thematically prefigured much of Bowie's work in the decade to come, telling the tale of astronaut Major Tom, destined to roam the universe for ever: 'Planet earth is blue/And there's nothing I can do.' Bowie liked to perform it in the 80s and 90s using quite a spartan arrangement, stripped down to its bare bones in the almost Lennonesque reading of 1980. But although its basic structure is folk-pop with acoustic guitar dominant, it only really works when this acoustic material is set against the stratospherics provided by lead guitar and synth. It is this tension – the homespun traditionalism of the acoustic instrumentation set against the technological sweep of the orchestration – which makes the song. Interestingly for a pop song from that era, 'Space Oddity' has no chorus. It's a seamless dialogue, a perfectly paced unravelling of events, and is the possessor of an instantly memorable melody, a superlative acoustic guitar riff and echoey hand clap for the middle-eight, and a lyric which burned its way in all its childlike beauty into the public consciousness.

Gus Dudgeon was brought in to produce the single after it had been turned down first by the 'fifth Beatle', George Martin (Pitt's choice as producer), and then Tony Visconti, who called it a 'cheap shot' to cash in on the Apollo 11 moon landing on 20 July that year. For Visconti, this unabashed pop song had absolutely nothing to do with Bowie's serious folk-rock sensibility and the anti-commercialism of his various mixed-media projects at the time:

Remember, my brief from David Platz was to keep him in one style. Yes, I believe he was trying to cash in on the first walk in space or moon landing, I can't remember which, but something like that was in the air at the time. I'm not sure it was motivated by *2001*. He never told me that, but the moonshot was being publicised for a year before it actually happened. My bias was for that reason and for the fact that it reminded me too much of David doing a John Lennon impression. Also, the 'here am I sitting in a tin can' sounded very much like a lift from a current album by Simon And Garfunkel called *Bookends*. I had to admit that it was a cleverly crafted song, but it was not in line with what he was writing at the time; it was more like a jingle. To me it was, anyway. I saw David as a more sensitive writer, writing about his own experiences rather than this third-person song about a Major Tom. As I predicted, I told him it would probably be a hit, but he wouldn't be able to follow it up. He never really did and it was very tough for him to finally get something going a couple of years later – and that was the Ziggy persona.

On reflection, it would've been a great feather in my cap to have produced it. What came out of it was a deeper friendship. I suggested that David record it with Gus Dudgeon. When I heard the results I thought that David would surely make the album with Gus. Instead he came back to me and said, 'That's over with. Now let's get on with making the album.' I was not expecting that. Gus always was a very clean, meticulous producer. I've worked for him as an arranger and I've seen his notes: Guitar overdub – 3:30, Tambourine overdub – 4:45, Break 5:00, backing vocals – 5:30, etc. This style of production is anathema to David, who likes to use the studio as an open canvas for his thoughts. To make it possible to record the rest of the album, David had to do a record with Gus. Once it was over he returned to his more favoured unstructured way of working with me. In Gus's defence I must say that other artists were not put off by his approach, especially Elton John.

Dudgeon, however, thought Visconti was passing up the opportunity of a lifetime. 'I was good pals with Visconti and his offices were next door. And he goes and turns it down! I thought to myself, Well, he's mad, he's completely mad. I could not believe that Visconti had passed on it, I just thought he was completely nuts.' Dudgeon was also well chuffed to be working with Bowie again. 'It was a pleasure to work with him again because he's a lovely bloke. I remember him sitting cross-legged in the lotus position in the office chair wearing a catsuit, actually pretty much like the one that he wore when he went through the Ziggy

Stardust thing, looking great as he always did, with the funny eye and everything – a very cool lad. I also remember him walking into my flat one day at Christmas time when I had my tree up in the sitting room and for a joke he went up and shook hands with it. Half the bloody balls fell off and I shouted at him!'

Whereas Visconti was more flexible in the studio, happy to create an overall environment conducive to recording, Dudgeon, at the time, was more fastidious and spent far more time in preproduction. The result, for 1969, was an incredibly detailed symphonic sound:

I planned it to the absolute nth degree before I went anywhere near the studio. I spent hours devising a wall map with the lyric written out based on his demo, which blew me away when I first heard it. So I planned it out like a military operation – brown lines were cellos, yellow were strings and all sorts of bollocks, so it was always going to have an orchestration on it. Then Paul Buckmaster got involved. Buckmaster had done some arranging that was very good on some unsuccessful records by William Kimber and had played with Marsha Hunt. I devised a system whereby I could think of an actual string line and remember it by looking at this thing that looked like a graph, basically, with lots of big gaps between the lyrics that I could write things in. So then Buckmaster scored it all out and it was all done fast; the whole thing was over in no time at all. In terms of my early productions it was closest to what I had intended it to be in my mind before it actually hit the studio floor. When I was talking about a possible bass player for the session, someone suggested Herbie Flowers and I just went, 'What a fucking brilliant name. We have to have him. With a name like that, how can he be bad?' And he was brilliant!! It was Terry Cox who was the weird choice. Why did I choose Terry Cox? I've no idea because I didn't particularly like him and he was in Pentangle, for fuck's sake! Of all bands! Why I was getting a folk drummer who went twiddlee twee most of the time with one finger in his ear, or, in his case, one drumstick in his ear, I have no idea. I must have been mad.

Rick Wakeman, then a jobbing session musician, turned up late for the session after being delayed on the tube. He made a mistake on his mellotron part on take one, but a second take was perfect.

The classically trained Buckmaster played flute and cello, and all this was backed up by a hired string section. For 1969, it was an ambitious production. It was also obvious to Dudgeon that this was a very special single. His only concern was that it might be too far out for the charts at the time. It was definitely not an instant hit. These were the days of the 'sleeper', when singles could take weeks, if not months, to detonate, totally unlike today when UK Number 1 singles can be in and out of the Top 75 within half a dozen weeks of release.

To start with, although in Visconti's assessment the single was a cash-in, its promotion was actually severely hampered by the moonshot itself (despite being used on the day of the moon landing during the BBC's live transmission), since the media, or rather BBC Radio, feared that it was in bad taste given the still uncertain status of the three astronauts on such a dangerous mission. Dudgeon again: 'The BBC banned it! I seem to remember it getting into the bottom half of the charts, around 75 or something. What happened was that the BBC didn't allow it to be played until the guys got back from the moon. As soon as they got back it started being played again, and subsequently charted and continued up. It was not a reissue as such, but it was reworked, and Calvin Lee, bless him, was one of the people who worked hard on it, very hard, as a promotions man. He was a pal of Bowie's who absolutely idolised him and was a doctor of philosophy or something, a Japanese guy, and he just ran around behaving like a tea boy. He promoted the fuck out of it. He was all over the place, pushing like crazy. He was unpaid as well, as far as I know. I got the impression he was pretty wealthy. He had long hair, was flamboyantly dressed, gay, a perfect companion in many ways for Bowie at the time because he helped to bring Bowie's flamboyance out.'

The single was given its first public airing on 5 July 1969, when it was relayed through the PA system to tens of thousands of steaming-hot fans just before the Rolling Stones set at the free concert given at Hyde Park. Released on the eleventh of the month (the same day as the Stones' 'Honky Tonk Women', incidentally), the single took three months to actually hit the Top 40.

Dudgeon also recalls that Calvin Lee lent Bowie his silver catsuit for Bowie's first ever *Top of the Pops* performance, in which our intrepid astronaut was filmed 'spinning in stars and floating in air'. For the performance, recorded on 9 October 1969, Bowie accompanied himself on the Dubreq Stylophone. Described on the box as a 'pocket electric organ', this quaintly dated monophonic instrument, famously endorsed by Rolf Harris in the late 1960s, made a noise like the sound of a hornet being sawn in two. It had no speaker, only two settings ('normal' and 'vibrato'), and was played with a metal pick-up.

Dudgeon went on to bigger, if not necessarily better, things as producer of a string of massive-selling Elton John, Elkie Brooks and Chris Rea albums in the 70s and 80s. He still regards 'Space Oddity' as a classic single. 'Every time I hear it on the radio, I have to turn the fucker up! "Let's Dance" and "Ashes To Ashes" come close, but for me, this is his most classic single.' Clearly, he counts it among his best work: 'I'm not sure whether I've ever done as well actually, to tell the truth!'

Tragically, Gus and his wife Sheila were killed in a car crash on 21 July 2002. Dudgeon was 59. Before the fatal accident, Dudgeon's lawyers had initiated a legal action against David Bowie for unpaid royalties. Dudgeon claimed that he had never been paid any royalties for the single, despite it reaching the Top 20 in the States and charting twice in the UK Top 5. Speaking in 1999, he said:

I was never paid for 'Space Oddity'. The advance was about £100. David Platz, who was co-director of my company, signed a contract which I co-signed, and which basically was crap. He was a very wealthy man, and bright, and also had The Who, The Rolling Stones and Anthony Newley. I fell out with Platz. There was a court case, which I lost. Platz died three or four years ago and I now deal with his son. Can you believe that my partner, my supposed mentor, signed a contract which said that, if David Bowie left the label, the record company was not required to pay the producer any royalties? I'd inadvertently relinquished my claim to royalties from that moment, even though my name has been printed on reissues over and over.

In March 2003 news reports claimed that Dudgeon's estate was about to file a £6 million lawsuit claiming unpaid royalties after failing to settle the matter amicably out of court. According to one report, 'Lawyers for the estate allege Dudgeon was only paid a £250 advance for producing the record, but claim he was promised 2 per cent of future royalties. With interest and damages, they now estimate he would be entitled to some £6 million.' On behalf of Bowie, Henry Wrenn-Meleck of RZO, Bowie's business managers, countered: 'We see no basis on which David Bowie is liable to Gus Dudgeon or any other party for producer royalties.' As of April 2005, media reports suggest that the case is on-going. Dotmusic.com quoted Dudgeon's royalties' investigator David Morgan as saying, 'We had rather a lot of evidence of the money that we claim was owed him. Apart from the huge sale of the Bowie albums, the single has been on almost every compilation of top hits. I was with Gus the day before he died, and he seemed disappointed. He wanted Bowie to sort it out, and instead we got a letter of rejection from his representatives. I gave him my word that I would not give up . . . Bowie sent flowers to [Dudgeon's] funeral, with the message: "Farewell to the Laughing Gnome" '.

Far from being simply a cash-in single, 'Space Oddity' was the first indication of Bowie's interest in outer space as a metaphor for inner space. Paul Buckmaster, who remembers Bowie as 'a warm-hearted kind of guy, very nice, very friendly, easy-going', recalls him being very taken indeed with the whole sci-fi vibe which had invaded popular culture, if not popular music, at the time. 'We had some wonderful intellectual discussions. The first ones we had had a lot more to do with a sort of pop science-fiction mysticism mixed with a bit of metaphysics and spiritualism. We were talking about aliens and UFOs a lot when we first met. It seemed to be the primary topic of debate. Many baby-boomers were besotted with it – comic strips, sci-fi literature. I remember one publication in the mid-1960s called *The Magazine of Speculative Fiction*, which was a euphemism for sci-fi.'

Visconti also remembers Bowie being very bookish, 'David always impressed me as being well read. Back in the late 60s we often talked about the sci-fi books we had both read; the usual pantheon of writers like Bradbury, Asimov and Sturgeon, as well as some obscure writers. For nonfiction he turned me on to *The Origin of Consciousness In The Breakdown of the Bicameral Mind* by Julian Jaynes, a theory about the evolution of the human brain and mind.'

Visconti also remembers Bowie as a UFO-spotter, though Bowie has given the impression that it was a passing phase:

It's no surprise that David was interested in UFOs, but we never spoke much about that subject. He introduced me to his friend, songwriter/singer Lesley Duncan. We both visited Lesley at her top-floor flat in West Hampstead one day. Leslie and her boyfriend talked about UFOs for hours. It was their speciality and the purpose of our visit was for David to introduce me to them. After dark I went out on their balcony with the boyfriend who eventually said, 'They are up there all the time.' Then he suddenly pointed up and we could see a faint moving object, about the size of a medium-bright star, moving rapidly across the night sky. 'There's one,' he said. I said it couldn't be; it was only a satellite. He said it wasn't and we should just keep watching it. Quickly, very unlike a satellite, the object did a ninety-degree turn and moved more rapidly, then it disappeared. David was inside the flat when this happened but we ran in to tell him and Lesley about it.

Given the comic-book nature of Bowie's interests at the time, as a piece of sci-fi writing 'Space Oddity' is remarkably, perhaps deliberately, naive. Rather than dealing with the correct terminology, Bowie's lyrics are childlike and quaint. So we get 'ground control' for 'mission control', 'space ship' for 'rocket', 'Major Tom' instead of, perhaps, 'Commander Tom' (indeed, the use of the Christian name further distances the narrative from reality), and 'countdown' instead of 'ignition sequence'. The result is that Major Tom is a puppet, a Mr Punch launched into space in a toilet-roll rocket covered in tin foil, flying around the nursery ceiling rather than the cosmos. In this respect, 'Space Oddity' is merely just another 'Laughing Gnome'.

Intentionally or not, the 'Space Oddity' single acted as a requiem for the flower power age, as Camilla Paglia wrote in 2004: 'As his psychedelic astronaut, Major Tom, floats helplessly into outer space, we sense that the '60s counterculture has transmuted into a hopelessness about political reform ("Planet Earth is blue/And there's nothing I can do").'

'Space Oddity' was Bowie's first 'classic' single, and has also entered the ranks of the rock mondegreens, or famously misheard lyrics, with the line 'Ground control to Mao Tse-tung' being almost, although not quite, in the same class as 'The girl with colitis goes by' from The Beatles' 'Lucy In The Sky With Diamonds'. It has been followed up not only by Bowie's own

'Ashes To Ashes' in 1980 but also by Pete Schilling's Euro hit of 1984, 'Major Tom (Coming Home)'. And, of course, three years after 'Space Oddity' was recorded, producer Gus Dudgeon went on to cut the thematically very similar 'Rocket Man' with Elton John.

However, on its first release that summer of 1969, it was touch and go for a while. Initially, it made no impression on the charts, despite Ken Pitt's attempt to buy it into the Top 50 by offering a chart-rigger £140. By September it had entered the UK Top 50 at Number 48. An anxious week followed when it promptly dropped out again, but the Bowie camp needn't have worried. It re-entered the next week and then climbed the chart steadily, finally reaching Number 5 in the chart published for the week ending 1 November. 'Sugar Sugar' by the Archies was by then enjoying its second of an eventual total of eight weeks at Number 1. If not yet a household name, Bowie had at least finally cracked the charts.

In line with his penchant for recording in foreign languages, the boy David was moved to sing the lyric, or at least what he thought was the lyric, in Italian. Gus Dudgeon remembers the farce of recording 'Ragazzo Solo, Ragazza Sola' (roughly translated as 'Lonely Boy, Lonely Girl'), at Trident Studios:

David Platz told me that there was an Italian version of 'Space Oddity' by two Italian boys, and that they'd done it really well and that it would obviously threaten the chances of the original version in that country. So I booked a studio and an Italian translator to work with Bowie on his pronunciation. We went into the studio and put the track up, and the guy had it written out phonetically on paper. It was all pretty funny most of the time because Bowie was crackin' up and I was crackin' up and this bloke was saying, 'No no no! You've got to say it a-like thees: "Reg-az-za So-lo". Make it a-fall at the end.' We finally get there, and he's happy with it and so Bowie's saying to him casually as he's putting his jacket on, 'You must have had a bit of a problem translating the lyric – the astronaut up in space and that sort of thing,' and the Italian bloke is frowning and saying, 'No, is no problem. What you just sing is a love story. It's about a boy, he meets a girl in a mist at the top of a mountain and they fall in love and they have a long kiss and they go home.' But Bowie said, 'Well, my story is about fuckin' astronauts!' But the man said, 'No, no, that's a-no good for Italy,' and Bowie just laughed it off. He said, 'Well, that's hilarious. I've just put in all that time singing some bloody love song about some tart in a blouse on a mountain in a mist falling in love!' Bowie's got a great sense of humour. But it did the job. Our version was the hit.

Sadly for Bowie, the single became a hit just a matter of weeks after the sudden death of his father from lobar pneumonia in August 1969. At the suggestion of Pitt, Bowie had been in Malta and Italy where he had entered, and won, two song contests with 'When I Live My Dream'. Ostensibly this had been an expenses-paid holiday for Bowie and Pitt. Healthy and tanned, he returned in early August and played his usual spot at The Three Tuns. Mary Finnigan had been prewarned of John Jones' deteriorating health but chose not to tell the buoyant, prize-winning singer until after that night's performance. Bowie was beside himself with rage when he finally found out that his dad was seriously ill.

Allegedly, Bowie rushed to his dad's bedside and showed him the statuette he had won on the Continent. It would be the last time he would see his father alive. Two days later, on 5 August, news reached Bowie during sessions for *Space Oddity* at Trident Studios in Soho that his father was dead. Bowie was in tears but completed the session.

After the funeral, Bowie and Angie were left to pick up the pieces. There was an air of recrimination at Plaistow Grove. According to Angie Bowie's memoirs, Bowie's distress at losing his father was compounded by the fact that Peggy had taken it upon herself to nurse her ailing husband and had waited until it was too late to call for a doctor. 'In the end John Jones had asphyxiated alone in an upstairs room,' reports Angie, 'trying to get to an oxygen tank just out of his reach.'

'On reflection, I think David is a young version of his father,' says Tony Visconti. 'He was certainly affable and very articulate. Reserved, but warm and respectful. He gave the impression of being well educated. His accent was that of an educated south-erner (but, as a Yank in a strange land, I was no expert on British accents yet. I'm recalling this from a memory of some thirty years ago). I think he was almost as tall as me – five foot eleven. He was thin. David's mom and Terry were there, too. I encountered his mom several times. She was a quiet, sombre, sad woman in those days. Well, her husband had just died. But she never quite got out of that. So every time I was with her she spoke very little.'

Without the support of his dad, Bowie increasingly turned to others for professional and emotional succour. Angie was the most important of these but other workmates such as Tony Visconti were by now very close to Bowie, too. After the death of his father, Bowie had only sporadic contact with his mum throughout the 1970s, and she complained bitterly that her son had abandoned her, and Terry, during the period of his greatest fame. She did, however, attend her son's performance as the elephant man on Broadway in 1980, and his marriage to Iman in 1992, and, according to reports, the two became close again during the 1990s. Peggy later moved into a private residential old people's home near Watford, where she lived until her death in April 2001.

Just five days after his father's funeral, Bowie performed at the Beckenham Free Festival at Croydon Road, which he also helped organise. Held on 16 August, the event, which attracted a crowd of around 3,000, was staged to raise money for permanent premises for the Arts Lab. While Angie cooked hamburgers in a wheelbarrow, the crowd were entertained by Bridget St John, Keith Christmas, Tony Visconti and The Strawbs. Bowie himself played a solo set which included 'Janine', 'An Occasional Dream' and several other songs which would feature on his upcoming second album. According to Tony Visconti, 'Space Oddity' was performed as a reggae number! David Bebbington, who co-hosted some of the Arts Lab shows and on the day of the festival itself was a puppeteer in the Brian Cole Puppet Theatre, took a series of photographs. 'At the time I was a professional photographer,' said Bebbington. 'At Bowie's request, I took shots of him, both at the festival and elsewhere. Bowie was flat broke at the time and was unable to pay me.' According to Bebbington, one of the pictures, showing Bowie with permed and tousled hair, hippy shirt and white trousers, seated playing an acoustic guitar, became one of Peggy Jones' favourites. Today, it stands as a study of a man on the very cusp of stardom, a matter of weeks before he would be transformed from a local hero, a Beckenham Oddity, into a UK pop star.

Bowie's second album came out in the autumn of 1969. It was certainly more coherent and less scatty than his first Deram effort, but 'Space Oddity' aside, there was little to suggest the greatness to come. Bowie was still reflecting the governing ideologies of the day and the dominant musical modes (acoustic balladry, folk, country and prog rock) rather than developing a distinct music of his own. However, it was the first Bowie album proper, has been deemed worthy of inclusion in subsequent reissue programmes, and has gone on to become a very respectable seller, so far clocking up an impressive 38 weeks in the UK album chart.

'Unwashed And Somewhat Slightly Dazed' is a country-meets-prog-rock collision of ideas. Lyrically it's a song about perception, about how Bowie thought others saw him: 'raving mad', 'a phallus in pig-tails'. The writing is heavier, more ornate, loftier and more serious. Writer Rogan Taylor has argued that if pop in the 50s was all about 'Dream Lover', then 60s pop was all about the dream. His book, *The Death and Resurrection Show: From Shaman to Superstar*, is a brilliant exposé of the shamanist origins of modern entertainment: 'In the 1960s, pop music goes from being a puberty rite into being a magical rite. It's not about growing up and making sexual contact as it was in the 1950s, it's about the big questions. The egg had been cracked open and we saw at the heart of show business what has always been there: an ecstatic core.'

Bowie, like pop itself, was maturing fast. 'Cygnet Committee' is wildly ambitious, ending in a rant, an emotional tirade against the counterculture which is underpinned by an almost militaristic musical backdrop. 'The Wild Eyed Boy From Freecloud' is more succinct, poetic and observational.

Lyrically, however, the most important song is also the most direct – 'Janine'. When he sings 'But if you took an axe to me/You'd kill another man not me at all', the concept of Bowie at a distance from his real self, the idea which would dominate the whole of his work in the first half of the 70s, comes across loud and clear. On 'An Occasional Dream' and 'Letter To Hermione', which concerns his first real love, Bowie is as vulnerable and quavering, almost as feminised, as the love he sings about. There's an earnestness about the vocal on tracks such as these which seems at total odds with the contrivance of Bowie's later, more representative work.

Looking back on his production work, Visconti is far from satisfied with his contribution to the album: 'I loved the arrangements and the performances, but sonically it was a terrible record for me. I knew nothing then. The songs were brilliant, not a bad one. I'm glad I was able to redeem myself as a producer by re-recording 'Memory Of A Free Festival' in between *Space Oddity* and *The Man Who Sold The World*, with Mick Ronson on the team. I knew a little more by then.'

'Space Oddity' itself was an exceptional song, and a deserved hit single in the UK, staying in the UK charts for fourteen weeks. With hindsight, Paul Buckmaster thinks that Bowie's career was assured after this success, but Ken Scott, who engineered the album, remembers having his doubts: 'I thought the material on that album was very good, but nothing earth-shattering. Musically, at that time I didn't see it, it didn't strike me as different. I'd kind of heard it all before. He hadn't quite got the right recipe for taking all his influences and putting them together.' Would Scott have predicted a 30-year-plus career for the 22-year-old back then? 'No way! But then again I wouldn't have predicted a thirty-year career for any artist back then.'

Gus Dudgeon was also unsure of the likely scale of Bowie's success. 'I thought we were dealing with a unique, enigmatic, imaginative person. But there's a very difficult line to cross sometimes between artistic integrity and commercial successes. It's a balance that artists such as Randy Newman, or Tom Waits, despite being wonderful songwriters, have only seldom achieved. And Bowie could have fitted into that category. There was no question that he was going to be known, that he was going to make it on one level or another. But quite on what level was difficult to say.'

On the back of the success of the single, Bowie played a number of UK dates. 'An Evening With David Bowie' at the Purcell Room at the Royal Festival Hall on 20 November was by all accounts a tremendous performance from Bowie in front of friends and music executives from Mercury. However, someone had forgotten to send out invitations to the press, and the event went completely unnoticed. Ten days later, Bowie played Save Rave, a charity event held at the London Palladium. Also, that autumn 1969, Bowie was added to the Humble Pie UK tour. However, such exposure, along with the big single, did not secure his career. In fact, it was rather the opposite, as the young singer met with indifference and, on occasion, outright hostility. 'With "Space Oddity" it was very hard,' said Bowie many years later. 'It was 1969, and I went out in front of these gum-chewing skinheads. As soon as I appeared, looking a bit like Bob Dylan with this curly hair and denims, I was whistled at and booed. At one point I had cigarettes thrown at me . . . It turned me off the business. I was totally paranoid and I cut out.' In fact, Bowie would later say that one 'terrifying' gig in Sunderland was the worst show he had ever done.

'I had the natural sympathies for the underdog,' says music journalist Paul Du Noyer, who as a teenage music fan saw Bowie's Liverpool Empire leg of the tour. 'He was at the bottom of the bill. There was a pretty rampant Liverpool rock audience, and here was this fey, curly-haired folk singer coming on and trying to hold people's attention. It was just him and his acoustic guitar. To either side of him were the mountains of Marshall amps that were going to be used by the big heavy groups such as Humble Pie later on. He did seem nervous; he fumbled a few songs and his introductions were hesitant, and you felt some sympathy for him. Nevertheless the songs he was playing got under my skin. I remember being haunted by them for a long time afterwards.'

Folky, impressionistic, whimsical, the second David Bowie album was still the product of an 'out-of-towner'. An extract from a letter written that summer to DJ John Peel (one of the very few media supporters at the time) shows that the young David (or simply 'Bowie', as he signed himself) was still very much a suburbanite at heart:

> I find myself in the arms of just about the biggest garden in the world, deep in the heart of (God forbid) Beckenham. I got an itchy bum after the tour so with a guitar and memories of Hermione on my back I thumbed through my mind and got involved with writing. I have walked through no less than fifteen songs in two weeks and some of them were very bad. So I came to this lawn which has a large flat attached to it . . . We had a great feast in the garden at about ten with a big fire. The foxes sat in a circle just outside of the flamelight and waited for scraps of stuff. I hope they weren't too mad at us but we were pretty hungry.

This David Bowie, the suburbanite, was to be the first media version of him to be killed off, along with the folky acoustic guitar sound which he had developed in tandem with it. Despite the hit single, the new album flopped badly, as did the follow-up to 'Space Oddity', 'The Prettiest Star'. Pitt was convinced that the song 'London By Ta Ta', a racy though lightweight piece of MOR not dissimilar to the pop of Herman's Hermits, was the obvious single. But the rather plodding billet-doux to new lover Angela Barnett was insisted upon by Bowie and the single stiffed.

'The Prettiest Star' was, of course, revamped and much improved during the *Aladdin Sane* sessions three years later, but the original single showcased the talents of Marc Bolan on guitar. Visconti, who was already working with T.Rex, thought it a useful bridge-building exercise to bring the two pretenders to the crown together and, for a while, the session went well. Visconti reminisces: 'I finally brought the two of them together on "The Prettiest Star", only because I loved both of them and thought that Marc was playing the electric guitar better than most I had met. David loved the idea and so did Marc. Only June Bolan stopped it from being the magical union I had longed it to be, by running up to David at the end of the session and hissing, "Marc is too good for you, to be playing on this record!" A very self-satisfied Marc was suddenly stunned by June's outburst and ensuing bad vibes, then silently followed June out into the night, leaving David and me baffled by June's remark. I suppose it was because, for the first time, Marc wasn't feeling any rivalry; he was simply grateful to be acknowledged as a good guitar player. He was actually feeling genuine camaraderie towards David for the first time – but June felt it necessary to remind him of his pop-Messianic mission!'

By 1970, Bowie had become skilful at communicating with music journalists: charming, good-looking and intelligent, he had already learned the art of keeping the caption-writers in the weekly music press fully employed. Penny Valentine, the leading writer for *Disc*, was particularly enamoured of the young David, spotting his rising star well before the breakthrough with 'Space Oddity'. 'He would always listen to me on the phone when I was taking about PR and giving advice to people. Also, he was very nosy . . . inquisitive, always looking at papers on my desk,' Ken Pitt told Chris Charlesworth. 'He's got to take the credit because he had a lot of natural charm, [but] I certainly gave him advice from the very beginning,' says Pitt. 'He was anxious about what to say. I would tell him exactly what the interviewer's interests were, and I told him, whatever you do, don't argue, don't get into a heated conversation. I told him to try to anticipate the interviewer, tell them what they want to hear, and adopt a different style according to the different types of media.'

But Bowie sensed that he needed a more hard-headed, hard-hitting management style to make him a star, and in May 1970 Ken Pitt was dropped. Bowie then signed to Gem, a production company owned by Lawrence Myers. By 1971 his career was being marshalled by one of Gem's employees, lawyer Tony Defries, who saw in Bowie a massive star quality. His MainMan organisation ran Bowie's affairs until early 1975. Pitt maintains that, had Bowie stayed with him, his career would have developed even quicker than it actually did, arguing that many of the strategies later adopted had their origins with him. There is some truth in this. It was at Pitt's instigation that Bowie talked to the gay magazine, *Jeremy*, at the end of 1969, and Pitt had already planned a promotional tour of the States for Bowie in 1970. But Pitt was deemed too old-school by Bowie's entourage of friends and associates, and the verdict is still open as to whether he could have matched MainMan's spectacular promotional success. That said, Pitt was a crucial influence on the emerging talent, and he took Bowie to the very brink of stardom.

What Bowie needed, however, was both a strategy and competition. His some-time friend, Marc Bolan, who broke big in the UK with T.Rex's 'Ride A White Swan' single, provided the latter. And in the first years of the 70s, Bowie launched a devastating critique of the rock establishment, wrapped up in make-up, glitter and flame-coloured hair.

3. LOOK OUT ALL YOU ROCK'N'ROLLERS, 1970–1972

We never got off on all that revolution stuff
Such a drag – too many snags.

MOTT THE HOOPLE, 'ALL THE YOUNG DUDES', 1972, WORDS AND MUSIC BY DAVID BOWIE

In 1970, pop had become laboured and dull. The scene lacked a sense of danger, excitement and generational angst. Hippy-dom had now gone mainstream. By 1971, your average concert-going sixteen-year-old male had long hair, sideboards and a trenchcoat: stylish, elegant and groundbreaking it was not. For some the route out was through the northern soul music being played in the new wave of clubs and dance halls in the provinces, the precursor of acid house and rave culture in the late 1980s. For others the escape route led them straight into the incipient heavy metal scene, and to the grass-roots populism of Black Sabbath, the beginnings of Goth and the apotheosis of biker culture. But those teenagers and twenty-somethings who were crying out for something different, something more than a decorous neo-classical keyboard run or yet another well-crafted pop song, turned to Bowie, Bolan and Roxy Music.

Bowie started the decade not only with his first hit single under his belt but also with a string of commercial and artistic failures to his name, too. In 1970, he made a number of important commercial and personal decisions which would dictate the course of his career for the first half of the decade. First, he sacked his manager, Ken Pitt; second, he 'invented' glam rock; third, he hooked up with a totally inexperienced rock manager but very smart businessman-lawyer named Tony Defries; and, last, he decided to get engaged to his girlfriend, Angela Barnett, who for a while basked in his limelight and joined his sequin-spangled journey to stardom.

There's a minor dispute between Bolan and Bowie aficionados as to who actually started the whole glam thing off. Marc Bolan does have a pretty strong claim to being the godfather of glam in that, on *Top of the Pops* in early 1971, he wore glitter under his eyes while performing 'Hot Love' with his band T.Rex, thus sparking off tabloid interest in 'Glitter Rock'. Up until mid-1972 Bolan was also undoubtedly the bigger teen idol and made the poppier material. He had a string of British Top 10 hit singles (eleven in all, from 'Ride A White Swan' in late 1970 to 'The Groover' in June 1973) with an infectious, if formulaic, brand of pop which mixed surprisingly punky 50s-influenced rock'n'roll with some deft orchestral arrangements, all topped off with Bolan's instantly recognisable cheeky bleat of a voice. Singles such as 'Metal Guru', and especially '20th Century Boy', still cut the mustard. The hop-a-long 'Hot Love', a song whose only mission, like 'Hey Jude', appears to be to get to near the end then stay there, is intensely annoying, although in a charming sort of way.

What mattered most to Bolan, though, was stardom at any cost, even if the music, by 1973, resembled a shell – a formula of a tired formula. His producer, Tony Visconti, says, 'Marc and David both had enormous strength as songwriters and as dynamic performers. Marc's weakness was his sense that he had "arrived", and he never developed himself as a musician beyond the stage he was at during his hit-single years. He also got caught lying too many times – he felt he could say anything to manipulate journalists. His tall tales were legend! David never shared any of Marc's weaknesses.'

'Both drew heavily on the talents of their associates,' says Bolan's biographer, journalist Mark Paytress, 'though Marc was less of a diplomat than Bowie, and tended to piss people off more easily. And, it has to be said, while Marc knocked off some tremendous records, Bowie was the more gifted craftsman.'

In many respects, Bolan paved the way for Bowie. This is even acknowledged by Bowie himself, who wrote in 1998, 'The little imp opened the door. What was so great, however, was that we knew he hadn't got it quite right. Sort of Glam 1.0. We were straining in the wings with versions 1.01 and 1.02 while Marc was still struggling with satin.' Both had ploughed similar furrows in the late 1960s. Both were from a folk-pop base (Bolan more so), but Bolan made the transition from minority acoustic elfin cult artist to mainstream-rogering pop god first. Bowie followed, doing it better, and taking it further, but Bolan had opened the door.

In fact, calling glam a 'movement' is a bit of a misnomer as it implies a sort of united front. There were far too few American bands to actually even form a glam-rock scene over there. What scene did exist centred around the Warhol crowd in New York in 1970/71, an absurdist movement concerned not so much with music, but with theatre and film and focused on Rodney Bingenheimer's English Disco in LA (founded in response to Bowie's visit to the States in 1971). Furthermore, WASP middle-America always had major problems with any form of masculinity in pop which didn't come housed in a white T-shirt and blue jeans. In the UK, any notion of a common ideology should be abandoned completely. David Bowie had absolutely nothing in common with Alvin Stardust, save, perhaps, for an interest in the Number 1 spot.

Very broadly speaking, there were always two wings of glam, or 'glitter rock' as it was more commonly referred to at the time. There was the arty, serious, more subversive end (Bowie, Roxy Music, The New York Dolls, Alice Cooper and, for a time, Lou Reed) and then there were the lads in silly trousers (Gary Glitter, Sweet, Alvin Stardust). With the exception of Suzi Quatro, glam was almost overwhelmingly male as well as overwhelmingly heterosexual. Despite all the limp-wristedness, few of the glam-rock acts were actually gay. Elton John (who wore the joke spectacles but remained more AOR than glam) 'came out' in 1976, well after the high-water mark of the glam-rock movement. For the first half of the 70s, Elton was at pains to hide his homosexuality from the media and his fans, although, as Scott remembers, in the recording studio he dropped his guard and revealed the real Elton. Lou Reed, whose own bisexuality was an obvious factor, stayed on the glam bandwagon for one album only. No, UK glam rock was unremittingly male and laddish, despite the make-up and posing. Gary Glitter was 'the leader of the gang' and indeed was 'doing all right with the boys again' in a display of sing-along homosociality which perhaps, with hind-sight, camouflaged a less playful psychology. The Sweet, too, were all lads together, 'hell raising' on a 'teenage rampage', while Slade, the boozing Midlands skinheads-turned-glitter-freaks, and probably the best of the glam pop bands of the time, also demonstrated their impeccably laddish credentials by misspelling their first half a dozen hits. They were naughty boys who wailed 'Mama Weer All Crazee Now' and in so doing invented Sham 69's terrace-stomp and quite a bit of Oasis, too. But you had to have real nerve to be, or indeed even to look like, David Bowie. He soon had a community of fans who dared to be different and who, as we shall see, were a race apart from the rest of the glam-rock fans.

In general, Bowie was dismissive of most of the competition, although Alice Cooper (with 'School's Out' and 'Elected'), Elton (with half a dozen or so great singles) and Rod Stewart and the Faces were releasing very strong material in 1972 and 1973. Bowie's competition with Bolan was a feature of the 'glam wars' during the period. One of the few contemporary acts Bowie had any time for would appear to have been Roxy Music.

Roxy Music were regarded as glam's in-house avant-gardists, although they could also be relied upon to make the coolest of singles. Along with David Bowie they straddled the pop/rock divide and defined early-70s cutting-edge pop music in the UK. However, Bryan Ferry says that he had no affinity whatsoever with the sort of music Bowie was making in 1972, and regarded it as being too poppy to be bracketed along with Roxy. Some critics consider Roxy Music, and possibly Steve Harley and Cockney Rebel, as the only true glam-rock bands in that they actually started their professional careers as glam or art-rock acts rather than as twiddly folkies. Cockney Rebel were by far the least critically lauded of the glam bands, despite two classic pop singles in 'Judy Teen' and 'Make Me Smile (Come Up And See Me)'. Steve Harley was initially very taken with Bowie, and even performed at his Beckenham Arts Lab. Indeed, it is impossible to imagine some of the orchestral songs in Suede's catalogue in the 90s, such as 'Still Life', without the hugely haughty though strangely moving 'Sebastian' twenty years before.

The glam era was possibly the last big male-band era in UK pop: Gary Glitter (three Number 1s, four Number 2s) versus Sweet (only one Number 1, but four Number 2s) versus Slade (six Number 1s and three Number 2s) versus T.Rex (four Number 1s and four Number 2s) versus Wizzard (two Number 1s). This was an intensely competitive period. That's why the Oasis versus Blur face-off in 1995, when the two Britpop acts scheduled their single releases for the same day, was important. It was a reminder of an age when pop-chart dogfights were commonplace rather than exotic.

So, what was glam rock all about? Was it simply, as John Lennon once put it, 'just rock'n'roll with lipstick on'? Or was it a bit more radical than mere frock-pop? If glam was simply about make-up and tinsel, then surely, Liberace would have an equal claim to glam-rock fame, as would a host of other performers from the 50s and 60s. Roy Wood, for example, could be seen singing with The Move in 1968 in a tastefully sparkling purple waistcoat, and he was later to form the pantomime Phil Spector-inspired outfit, Wizzard, in the early 70s. Glam rock definitely had a more show-business side, in the form of the often fun Gary Glitter (real name Paul Gadd) and the hardly ever fun Alvin Stardust (real name Bernard Jewry and a minor star in the 60s as Shane Fenton). However, these singers were more in the tradition of old-fashioned 'variety' entertainment than anything else. This was Butlin's glitz for the mass teen-market, and it was very successful, too.

The Bowie version of glam was as much to do with the flouting of gender codes and injecting a certain artiness and detachment into popular music as with attempts to shock the masses in the era of hippy, joss-stick-tinged stupefaction. Its origins are to be found in figures such as Little Richard, whose stage persona was flamboyantly garish and androgynous, with his make-up and that devastating bouffant. Richard, the first 'gender-bender' of the rock'n'roll era, was never going to be in a position to doubly disadvantage himself as a black person by admitting he was gay.

Then there was Pink Floyd's Syd Barrett, the first of the 60s psychedelic performers to wear make-up and an acknowledged influence on Bowie in particular. Before his collapse into mental illness, Barrett briefly promised an alarming future for pop, a future full of spaced-out tripping and flaunted convention. His music, particularly live, destroyed song structures completely. Huge washes of discordant sounds cascaded down from the speakers while the audience were befuddled by an eerie collage of death-green and bloodshot-red swirls and splodges of tie-died psychedelic colourings, the hues of Pink Floyd's light show and back-slide projections. Barrett prefigured Bowie's space-age fascination with songs such as 'Interstellar Overdrive' and the twee but brilliant 'Astromine Domine'. 'Arnold Layne', a song about a man stealing women's clothes from washing-lines, was deemed too daring and was banned from the national airwaves. Had Barrett continued, there might have been less room for Bowie to manoeuvre in the 1970s. But he didn't. By the early 1970's, he was, very sadly, a comatose wreck, pop's most famous acid casualty; an innovator destroyed before his prime.

In the hands of Bowie, glam challenged pop's masculine ethos. Bowie's version of glam was about gender violence. Lou Reed and Iggy Pop only started to wear obtrusive make-up on stage once Bowie and Bolan had begun to do so. By 1973 a degree of laddish femininity had become an absolute prerequisite for even the most mainstream of pop acts, as bands such as Mud and The Sweet had their lead guitarists camp it up seemingly ad nauseam for camera 1 on *Top of the Pops*. Soon every self-respecting British teen-band was to have at least one of its members kitted out in a fake leopard-skin jumpsuit with assorted glittery attachments. Bowie, though, had very little to do with these glitter rockers. Slapping on the slap was a surefire way for hetero rockers to snap up the girls, but Bowie took it well beyond this, tapping into a centuries-old tradition of shamanistic sexual play. There was an intensity to Bowie that no other glam-rock act possessed. So when did it all start for him?

The origins of glam, Bowie-style, can be traced back to the very first months of the 70s, an era in which the lumpen-rock of the post-Woodstock generation and the overdone earnestness of the new singer-songwriters fought against the tide of bubblegum spilling into the charts from the likes of The Archies and Edison Lighthouse. At the Roundhouse in London in February 1970, Bowie and his band, Hype, a hard-rocking line-up in stark contrast to the one-man acoustic folk-pop of Bowie's ill-starred tour as support to Humble Pie the previous autumn, played one of the most significant and most indifferently received concerts in rock history.

Hype were intended as a cartoonesque caper, a sort of rock'n'roll pantomime for the new decade, and the name was intended to run counter to hippy-era notions of an anti-commercialistic rock community. Here was a group which announced itself as a fraud from the outset, and which embodied Bowie's first faltering attempts to draw attention to the strategies put into place to sell pop, which the current rock orthodoxy of the time either disingenuously rejected or tried to cover up. In this sense, Hype was a dry run for Ziggy Stardust two years down the line. Bowie was Rainbow Man, wearing a cape of many colours and lots of diaphanous scarves. Drummer John Cambridge was Cowboy Man, Mick Ronson on lead guitar was Gangster Man, wearing a borrowed gold lamé suit from Bowie and matching fedora, and bassist Tony Visconti was Hype Man, a kind of comic-book superhero, in a white leotard, a cape and a pair of crocheted knickers. The whole event was filmed professionally (Hype were in fact just one of the acts on the bill that night) and some of the footage was later used by the Biography Channel for a programme on Bowie.

Bowie himself remembers that some people in the audience were so hostile to this pioneering rock spectacle they didn't even bother to boo, and instead simply turned their backs to the stage! But he is in no doubt that this was the first British glam-rock gig. Marc Bolan – in an attempt to get into the theatricality of the project – stood at the foot of the stage wearing a child's plastic Roman breastplate. Tony Visconti: 'We had absolutely nothing to do with glam rock. It was all David and Angela's idea to dress us up for that Roundhouse gig. Nevertheless, we saw the theatrical sense in it. We had to do something to get noticed. By then, we knew enough to listen to David. I think that is the night that the germ of glam rock was born.'

Hype impressed on Bowie the importance, for musical, theatrical and personal reasons, of finding a stable band structure. He was already a close friend of Tony Visconti. And in the 24-year-old Mick Ronson, a quiet, instantly likeable and supremely talented guitarist from Hull in the North of England, he had found a musical confrère and good-looking sidekick. Ronson was no intellectual, and might at times have given the impression of being not quite as switched on as some of the other people around Bowie. But get him in the studio, and he was a giant. The elements of his future success were beginning to fall into place.

Ronson was a very important musical component in the Bowie sound at the time. Loved by his fans and all those who worked with him, Ronson was a gifted but naive and slightly guileless man. Bowie was always the star, always the creative genius, and those who suggest he would never have made it without Ronno are simply wrong. However, without Ronno, the early Bowie records and stage shows would have been considerably the poorer. Visconti remembers him as charming, but adds, 'He always looked a bit lost; he hardly had an ambitious bone in his body.' Gus Dudgeon also remembers Ronno with great affection:

Bowie and Ronson met as a result of me working with Ronson. [Although Visconti claims that Bowie's introduction to Ronson was effected through John Cambridge, who played with Ronson in The Rats.] Ronson came down to play guitar on the Michael Chapman album on 'Harvest' and played really well. I seem to remember Bowie heard the album and liked it. They sort of hooked up, and became pals, and it went on from there. But Ronson, as you may know, was also an utterly charming fellow, I mean, just a total sweetheart and desperately embarrassed at having to pull all those stunts every night during the Ziggy period. He hated doing it. But when I first met him he worried me a bit because he wasn't very bright, but I don't want to use that word. I think maybe he was very shy. However, the minute he started to play the guitar he just went bazoooom! And he was happening, he was roaring. I really admired some of the arrangements he came up with. He had a very definite guitar-hero image, with the long hair. It might have been a tad corny in a way. He had a very striking face – he had a face like a Red Indian, I always thought. Very aquiline.

Eventually, Ronson's strengths – his virtuosity, his melodic gift, his arranging skills, his admiration for the late-60s power-pop of Cream and Jeff Beck – would root Bowie's music in a too traditionalist stance and become a constraining factor. However, for the moment, Ronson was the perfect foil for the developing Bowie.

Bowie was also by now a married man. On 20 March 1970, he and Angie were wed at Beckenham Registry Office. Although no family was invited, Bowie's mum Peggy turned up in any case, having notified the press. The marriage party was late, having overslept. Bowie asked John Cambridge to be a witness. Just as he was about to sign the register, Bowie's mum jumped up and signed it instead. Bowie allegedly looked over at John and shrugged his shoulders in a 'sorry mate, what can I do?' sort of way. Angie was dressed in a second-hand, purple-and-pink, floral silk dress bought the day before at Kensington antique market. David, with his permed, shaggy hair, tight leather trousers, black satin shirt and Afghan coat, cut something of an unconventional dash for the wedding day. Instead of rings, they exchanged Peruvian bangles during the brief ceremony. The night before their wedding was spent in bed with a mutual friend. The night after was spent down the pub getting blasted.

Angie's influence on her new husband is almost impossible to gauge after the self-mythologisation of her two autobiographies (the cover blurb for her 1993 autobiography, *Backstage Passes*, claims this to be her first book: it is in fact her second, after her early 1980s autobiography, *Free Spirit*). However, she did undeniably 'press the flesh' on Bowie's behalf, acting as a behind-the-scenes promoter of her husband's talents, persuading and pressurising record companies and pluggers, helping with the costumes, making phone calls, suggesting ideas, entertaining friends, listening to Bowie's work-in-progress. It is also certain that she was, at least for a time, as 'out there' as Bowie himself, if not more so. She was into outrage and bisexuality in a big way; her hair was often shorter, spikier and punkier than her husband's.

Many contemporaries are at pains to point out that Bowie only really weirdified his image after living with Angie. It is probably true to say that, before the Angie years, Bowie was actually fairly quiet as an individual and had not yet discovered the flair for sartorial flamboyance we now associate with him. Angie would constantly encourage Bowie to try on new, and ever weirder, designs. The checkboard jacket he wore on the *Hunky Dory* cover, for example, was Angie's. And, in the interregnum between Ken Pitt and Tony Defries (a period of almost eighteen months, in which Bowie was more or less kept solvent by royalties from his first hit single), Angie was important in getting Bowie's career moving. Although occasionally out of her depth, at least initially, she learned how to deal with the people that mattered in the music business, making calls and even writing up an agenda for the Haddon Hall habitués.

Bowie and Angie always had a love/hate relationship. It was only much later in the relationship that what love there was dissolved into what seemed like mutual detestation. Meanwhile, Angie certainly polarised opinion in the Bowie camp at the time. Manager Ken Pitt apparently strongly disliked her. Gus Dudgeon didn't 'get' Angie either: 'I didn't like her. I thought she was just a typical groupie. I just thought she was really loud and full of crap, and I still do. Sorry, Angie! I don't particularly want to upset her. There's no point. She's upset enough. She's not married to a superstar any more.'

'She was very flamboyant,' remembers Ken Scott. 'When she walked into a room, you knew it. I think David probably saw the effect she had on people and started to emulate it. I think it was part of him taking from everything around him and making it part of him. Because, in the early stages, he was much more quiet and subdued. And he became more flamboyant as time went on. Musically she had no influence whatsoever. She would stop by the studio once in a while with a "Hello, dahlings! Oh, that's lovely, yes!" and then go out and do some more shopping or something. But she was fine. I had no problems with her.'

According to Angie's second biography, Bowie was quite upfront about his feelings. He told her back in 1969 that he didn't really love her, and if they married it would be something of a marriage of convenience: both would aid and abet each other in the quest for stardom. Neither partner made any pretence of being faithful. 'Their relationship, though, was weird; supposedly an "open relationship",' says Scott. 'But every time I've heard of that, it always ends up with someone jealous, and that's what eventually happened.'

Many Bowie fans remember Angie as fun, approachable and thoroughly charming. One fan contacted for this biography was at pains to tell me how considerate she was, and how upset she has been by the media demonisation of her as a loud-mouthed gold-digger. Indeed, Tony Visconti saw her as an essential cog in the Bowie machine, at least at first:

Angie was a great team member up to a point. After Ken Pitt and before Tony Defries, it was Angie wheeling and dealing with Mercury records, getting more money out of them and even getting a small deal for Hype, so that we could buy stage equipment to support David on the road. She also gave great support to David at a time when he was beginning to grow in confidence as a performer. She was there for him in a difficult transitional period. But I could see when this wasn't enough for her.

At one concert David was surrounded by fans and Angie was next to him dressed even more outrageously than he was (her breasts were visible). Since all the attention was on him, she feigned fainting (something she did often) and suddenly she created an emergency drama around herself, taking the limelight away from David. This one time, my girlfriend Liz bent down to help Angela, putting a hand under her head. Angie opened her eyes briefly, saw it was Liz and gave her a knowing wink, then pretended to be unconscious again. I could see that Angie, who was invaluable at the start, would be a big hindrance in the future.

For a while though, everyone was one big happy family. And they were under one roof, too. In the days before the 'wonders' of Margaret Thatcher's home-owning 'democracy', even relatively wealthy rock stars rented, rather than bought, their homes. Bowie had set up home in a huge, rambling, redbrick Victorian house at 42 Southend Road, Beckenham, Kent, named Haddon Hall.

Bowie and Angie had soon turned their home into something of a sex-and-style laboratory, picking up blokes and girls from venues such as gay disco The Sombrero, a night-spot frequented by Bowie not primarily as a pick-up joint but rather as a way to get a hit of the flamboyance of gay style and hear some decent music. After a night of entertaining various friends picked up after a bout of hard partying, Bowie would rush to the bathroom to try out the new hairstyles or looks he'd seen the previous day. Like the teddy-boy style of the 50s and the mod style of the 60s, Bowie's glam-rock style of the 70s was in part appropriated from the gay subculture, to become part of the 'straight' world of high-street fashion.

Mick Ronson, John Cambridge and the roadie, Roger Fry from Hype, slept on second-hand mattresses on the landing. The cellar was turned into a practice room for Bowie and the band. It was here that *The Man Who Sold The World*, *Hunky Dory* and *Ziggy Stardust* were plotted. The garden was also big enough for a kick around, and Tony Visconti has photos of the young David relaxing playing footie. For a while, Visconti and his then partner Liz Hartley, an art student, also stayed at Haddon Hall, and Visconti remembers the place with a good deal of affection:

Hah! It was a crazy place. But one would expect that with all of us young artistic types living there. Liz and I moved in with David and Angela in December 1969. We moved out the following summer, around July. The main reason we moved out was that David and Angela had really made the place their own. There was great inequity between us because David was the only one among us (including the musicians and roadie) who had any money, and it was all going into his bedroom furniture and artworks, etc. He and Angela would disappear for days at a time and arrive home with valuable pieces of Art Deco and Art Nouveau. He was eager to share his new-found knowledge, and I learned a lot from him about these periods. The rest of us could barely scratch up the £8 a week for housekeeping. If David and Angela did the week's shopping, there would sometimes be arguments about whether they were thrifty enough and had bought a practical week's worth of staple items. Not that they were thieves or gourmets, but David and Angela ate what they wanted, not what they needed, compared to the rest of us. The Spartan life was not for them. As for wild sex – it only happened occasionally, when David and Angela would go out to clubs and bring dates back. I have no idea what went on in their bedroom, except we used to be wide awake in ours hearing all the laughter and screams emanating from theirs. When their guests tried to enter our bedroom in the early hours of the morning, we knew we had to move. David and Angela never tried to involve us in their 'sexcapades'.

The Haddon Hall house was also an abode possessed of genuine mystery – the lack of artificial light meant that the house was in permanent semi-gloom. With its massive polished oak doors, dark wooden staircase which led up to a stained glass window, Gothic chairs (upholstered in crushed velvet by Angie), and vast fireplace, the whole house looked like a discarded set from a Hammer Horror production. In fact Haddon Hall was apparently haunted, and Bowie spent some of the most creative years of his life there, tapping into the eerie vibe of this rambling Victorian mansion. Visconti again:

All of us, at one time or another, saw a mysterious young lady dressed in white, possibly a burial shroud, walking in the garden, slowly, along the hedged border around dawn. She looked Victorian. She was probably a darkish blonde and had very elegant, delicate features and she looked down remorsefully as she walked along the right wall of hedges towards the back hedge and just faded out around there.

Funny things used to happen in the apartment, too (my scalp is tingling as I remember this). Liz was cleaning the bathtub and a big explosion happened in midair over her head, making a very audible bang heard through the entire apartment. We (members of Hype and David himself) all ran into the bathroom to find her semiconscious on the floor. There was a strong smell of ozone in the air. There was no evidence whatsoever of an electrical short, in fact, electrical outlets were banned in bathrooms in those days – even shaver sockets. It was the middle of the afternoon, so even the overhead light was switched off. Liz described hearing the bang and seeing the entire room turn bright white and the repercussion sent her to the floor. Very strange. No one ever stayed in the apartment alone. Other tenants in the building also saw the lady in white.

It was in this spooky Victorian mansion that Bowie and Angie set about starting a family of their own. By the end of the summer of 1970, Angie was pregnant.

In the 1970/71 period, Bowie searched around for a new approach to pop. He rejected the communality of the counterculture ('We never got off on that revolution stuff') and imbued the 'stardust' of the 'Woodstock generation' with a new gender violence. He led the massed ranks of the confused, disconnected post-flower-power children. His stance was part remoulded progressive rock (he was still a serious pop artist), part revolutionary collagist. In 1973, he told William Burroughs: 'The idea of getting minds together smacks of the flower-power period to me. The coming together of people I find obscene as a principle. It is not human. It is not a natural thing as some people would have us believe.'

If his career in the 1960s was characterised by a rather manic rummage throughout the costume department of contemporary culture in an attempt to find the right combination of tastelessly mismatching attire, then Hype's Roundhouse gig saw the beginning of a phase in which his mismatching began to take on some sort of significance.

The failure of the gig was accompanied by the commercial failure of all the follow-up singles to 'Space Oddity'. 'The Prettiest Star' corpsed, and there were plenty more DOA singles to follow, 'Memory Of A Free Festival' and 'Holy Holy' being the next two to fail to trouble the scorers. The latter was rerecorded during the sessions for *Ziggy Stardust* and later found its way back on to general release as a B-side to the 'Diamond Dogs' single in 1974. The influence of 'Memory Of A Free Festival' would prove to be a little more enduring. It's the sort of record *Screamadelica*-era Primal Scream would have made had they been around in 1970 – a sort of trippy retake of the Stones' 'Sympathy For The Devil' but with a smiley lyric. It's a storming single with its joyous 'Sun Machine is coming down/And we're gonna have a party' hoedown finale. Although another flop when released, it has been reused twice in the dance-dominated 90s, once by E-Zee Possee ('The Sun Machine') in 1990, and then more successfully in the form of 'Sun Machine' by Dario G in 1998.

According to most authoritative sources, the rerecording of 'Memory Of A Free Festival' is the first recording to feature Mick Ronson. However, according to Tony Visconti, Ronson was around during the mixing stage of the album version of 'Wide Eyed Boy From Freecloud', adding a lead guitar lick and some hand claps during the middle eight. Visconti claims that Ronno was introduced to him by drummer John Cambridge. What is certain is that the rerecorded 'Memory . . .' single would be the last Bowie song to feature Cambridge on drums. Apparently, he had had problems nailing the drum part, and a dissatisfied Ronson, together with Angie, put pressure on Bowie to have his friend replaced.

Bowie's musical influences continued to be bizarrely eclectic, as Tony Visconti remembers:

It's no secret that he was always into The Velvet Underground. While he had some respect for his rock contemporaries, his own record collection was extremely eclectic. He also liked Van Morrison, resulting in us doing 'Madame George' in our live set. He also liked that writer of 'Buzz The Fuzz' [Biff Rose], which we did live. Oh yes, and Jacques Brel, but not in the original French, but the Mort Shuman English versions in *Jacques Brel is Alive and Well* on Broadway (hence the eventual recording of 'Port Of Amsterdam'). He was also impressed by a spoken-word record by a man called Ken Nordine. I think the record was called *Word Jazz*. He appreciated what Marc Bolan was doing as Tyrannosaurus Rex, and [was] very impressed by Marc's transition into T.Rex.

However, the sound Bowie was developing both live and in the studio was becoming heavier, more focused and theatrical. The material to be found on his next album, *The Man Who Sold The World* (released in November 1970 in the US and April 1971 in the UK), was decidedly more bleak and forbidding than the progressive chic of the *Space Oddity* era. His most autobiographical work to date, it was also of real quality, a haunted piece of Gothic rock'n'roll, all sinister shadings and bleak presents.

In an interview with Radio 1 in 1993, Bowie spoke openly for the first time about the fear of insanity which hung over him in the 1970s and influenced a large proportion of his work: 'One puts oneself through such psychological damage in trying to avoid the threat of insanity. You start to approach the very thing that you're scared of. It had tragically afflicted particularly my mother's side of the family. There seemed to be any number of people who had various mental problems and varying states of sanity. There were far too many suicides for my liking – and that was something I was terribly fearful of. I think it really made itself some kind of weight I felt I was carrying. And I felt that I was the lucky one because I was an artist and it would never happen to me. As long as I could put those psychological excesses into my music and into my work I could always be throwing it off.'

Against this background, the album's signature song has to be 'All The Madmen', which directly references his stepbrother Terry's plight (Terry spent much of this period in Cane Hill, the local asylum, where he lived until his suicide in 1985). It empathises with him and contrasts the derangement of the internees with the corrupt values of a society which institutionalises madness. Lyrically, this is one of Bowie's most disturbing songs, particularly the surreal coda of 'Zane Zane Zane, *Ouvre Le Chien*'. Musically, the descant recorder gives the song a childlike dementia, like a seven-year-old's first music lesson turned evil.

'All The Madmen', like 'The Supermen', shows that the young Bowie was hip to Nietzsche. Although there are no direct allusions to it in the lyric, the power of Bowie's depiction of madness must surely draw a little on Nietzsche's 1882 book, *The Joyful Wisdom*, and the section entitled 'The Madman'. Nietzsche makes his madman rant and drool in the market square in a parody of the ravings of a demented preacher: 'Are we still deaf to the noise of the gravediggers digging God's grave? Has the smell of divine putrefaction not reached our nostrils? Gods putrefy too. God is dead! God is still dead!' At a time of taboo-breaking secularism (the 1970s), such words sounded like prophecy for Bowie and his generation.

'After All' is the hidden gem on the album, a gorgeous melody with a stomach-churning merry-go-round synthesised section in the middle eight in waltz time. The 'Oh by jingo' refrain running through the track echoes the sort of song performed in the music halls a hundred years earlier. Bowie later said that songs from his childhood, such as Danny Kaye's 'Inchworm', with its slightly sinister, measured melancholy, also informed the nursery-rhyme waltz of 'After All', and, much later, the sublime 'Ashes To Ashes'. 'After All' is the first of Bowie's mini-manifestos for his chosen children, depicting himself and his flock 'painting our faces and dressing in thoughts from the skies'. With the line in the final verse, 'Live til your rebirth and do what you will,' Bowie is echoing the occultist teachings of the eighteenth and nineteenth-century diabolist Aleister Crowley, whose maxim was 'Do what thou wilt.' Bowie seems to be envisaging a fan base of star-child occultists.

The much-lauded title track is lyrically Bowie's boldest statement yet of his sense of psychic unease. Here Bowie (already dead?) runs up against his doppelgänger. 'The Man Who Sold The World' has a lilting melody, an almost bossa-nova-style rhythm section, step-by-step ascending guitar riff from Mick Ronson and perfect pop delivery by Bowie, who intones each line as if reciting The Lord's Prayer or some other holy text. It was later covered by Lulu, whose Bowie-produced sax-driven version arguably matches the original. With a chill and dreadful appropriateness, it was also covered in 1993 by Nirvana for their *Unplugged* session for MTV. 'I thought you'd died alone, a long, long time ago,' sang Kurt Cobain in a tortured, cracked voice, just a year before his suicide.

'The Width Of A Circle' shows Bowie at his most daring. The song, in a shorter form, had been in Bowie's live repertoire for several months prior to recording but, in the studio, it grew into a frightening art-pop behemoth. It contains one of Mick Ronson's most explosive moments on a Bowie album, as his lead guitar soars through the mix, the perfect riposte to Bowie's tale of Kafkaesque transmogrification: 'Then I ran across a monster who was sleeping by a tree/And I looked and frowned and the monster was me.'

In the second half of this nine-minute thriller, Bowie describes a homoerotic encounter with God in the devil's lair: 'He swallowed his pride and puckered his lips/And showed me the leather belt round his hips.'

The closing track, 'The Supermen', is just as sinister. Powered by a riff 'given' to Bowie in the 1960s by Jimmy Page (and later reused for 'Dead Man Walking' in the 90s), the song is all towering spirals of sound. The timpani is well to the fore, referencing the German romanticism of Richard Strauss, and the whole song is deliberately monumental, primal and triumphalist.

The Man Who Sold The World depicts a world of almost satanic, neo-occultist perversion ('The Width Of A Circle'), a future hell in which the interface between man and machine has corrupted the species ('Saviour Machine'), where lust and desire replace the sort of cosy, clichéd, heterosexualised monogamy peddled by the pure pop tunesmiths of the 60s ('She Shook Me Cold'). Bowie is haunted by the real possibility of his own personality shattering into so many constituent parts ('Width Of A Circle', 'All The Madmen', 'The Man Who Sold The World').

The album cover, which portrays Bowie with flowing golden locks and wearing a full-length dress (his Symbolist Gabriel Rossetti Pre-Raphaelite look, claimed Bowie), is now a classic collector's item. Contrary to popular belief, the dress cover was never withdrawn from the US market because it was never actually used there in the first place.

Another interesting fact about the album is that the title was changed very late on in the day. It has been confirmed by more than one source that, when delivered, the tapes were clearly marked *Metrobolist*, a pun on the title of Fritz Lang's silent science-fantasy epic *Metropolis*, then nowhere near as well known as it is today. Semiotically, Bowie's title also seems to hint at the words 'diabolist' or 'miserablist'.

The 1960s were collapsing into emotional, economic and political uncertainty, creating the perfect terrain for an agent provocateur like Bowie to clean up in. The twenty-first century was starting right now. As he told the *New York Times* in 1998: 'I think in the 70s that there was a general feeling of chaos, a feeling that the idea of the 60s as "ideal" was a misnomer. Nothing seemed ideal any more. Everything seemed in-between. We thought, Are we entering a great flux from which we'll never come out again?' Bowie and his generation represented nothing short of a new way of looking at the world: a mix-and-match existence, a 'take-away' culture – a bit of Buddhism here, a helping of liberalism there, and a few old-fashioned Victorian values to top things off.

The Man Who Sold The World also sounds so oddly formed and dark. The seeds of cyborg space-pop, later developed by the likes of the Futurists John Foxx, Gary Numan, Bill Nelson and Thomas Dolby, are to be found on songs such as 'Saviour Machine'. The sort of childlike paranoia found on 'After All' and 'All The Madmen' was a new form of Gothic melodrama, and a direct influence on Siouxsie And The Banshees and The Cure in the 70s and 80s, and America's Nine Inch Nails in the 90s. Also, at a time when Led Zeppelin and Black Sabbath were turning their hands to what would later become 'hard rock' and 'heavy metal' respectively, Ronson's solo guitar work, particularly on 'She Shook Me Cold', is as hard-hitting as any to be found in 1970. The band was deliberately recorded to sound as 'fat' as possible, according to Visconti, 'with no overdubs, so that we could play that song live and not disappoint'.

Key to this bleak soundscape was Visconti and Bowie's desire to harness the newly arrived musical possibilities of the synthesizer. 'The synth was a passion of mine at the time,' Visconti remembers:

I saw immense possibilities, not so much in sci-fi sounds but as a kind of larger-than-life Wagner or Beethoven-type device. I scored the first parts and asked Ralph Mace, a middle-aged executive at Phonogram, to play the parts because they were beyond our abilities and he was a classically trained performer. David and I had an agreement to try and create the most startling, evocative electronic effects when we wanted to follow that route. It was a kind of sonic one-upmanship that was going on in those days. The biggest compliment anyone could give you was, 'How did you make that sound?' We came up with outrageous sonic landscapes like 'The Supermen', which was kind of prescient for the sound that Queen eventually came up with – not only the vocal style, but the high-pitched backing vocals and the guitar solo, too. *The Man Who Sold The World* was a primer for many generations to come.

However, the actual recording of the record was a nightmare for the young Visconti. According to Visconti, Bowie appeared distracted and undisciplined during the sessions, spending more time with Angie in the lobby of the recording studio kissing, cuddling and cooing ('naughty Uncle Tony says I have to do a vocal now, Bye bye Angie-wangie'), or collecting objets d'art in order to turn Haddon Hall into a decadent, arty abode fit for a rock star, than worrying about the demands of finishing the album before the money ran out. Visconti in particular regarded Bowie's 'malingering' in the recording studio with his new wife Angie as particularly unprofessional. Much of the music was 'arranged' by Visconti and the band:

All the songs on *The Man Who Sold The World* were 'head arrangements', worked out communally or made up on the spot. It's an arrangement spontaneously contributed to by all the players in the group, then perfected and memorised. 'Head' in this context means not written out on paper – it comes out of your head. David did not write my bass parts or Mick's guitar parts, but he often interacted and suggested variations on what we came up with. He also came up with riffs of his own, but it was my experience that *The Man Who Sold The World* was a team effort. It was an early-70s thing to call what our band did 'arranging', not 'writing'. There is no question that David was the author of every song on *The Man Who Sold The World*. Those instrumental passages contained many of David's ideas (the instrumental of 'Saviour Machine' was based on his own 'Ching-a-ling Song' recorded with Feathers earlier).

As the sessions for the album ran their course, Visconti was living on his nerves. As the producer, he was ultimately responsible for delivering the product on time and within budget. Not only was the band trying to pull off some quite innovative stuff in an era when studio gadgetry was still quite basic, but the album's protagonist was time and again arriving in the studio in a lyricless state, further driving the stomach-churned producer into a state of mild apoplexy. He recalls the panic of the sessions vividly:

Bowie was writing at the last minute because (one), he wanted to, and (two), he was preoccupied in the lobby of the studio with his new-found love, Angie – they were kind of honeymooning. At the very end of the album we had finished backing tracks, but no melody or lyrics. I remember the title song's vocal being recorded on the final day of the mixing and we were already overdue and over budget. Mick Ronson, Woody Woodmansey and I were working out most of the arrangements by ourselves, in David's absence. Of course, it was all subject to his approval, but his long absences from the studio created a kind of 'him and us' situation. I have to give lots of credit to an unsung hero in all of this, our engineer Gerald Chevin. He was an engineer whizz-kid and was able to go wherever our imaginations took us.

This tactic of writing in the studio and coming up with lyrics for songs at the eleventh hour may have fazed his friends, but Bowie was learning a new technique, which involved the almost spontaneous last-minute assembly of a song's lyrical content in the studio. Bowie has never really been a conventional craftsman and, as his career progressed, he turned expediency into a tactic, developing a spontaneous creative environment.

The Man Who Sold The World worked well in artistic terms. Visconti now considers the album, along with *Scary Monsters*, to be the finest he made with Bowie. As a commercial product, however, it was another near-fiasco, selling moderately for a while in the States, but disastrously in the UK. Ronson went back to Hull to live with his parents and to work as a gardener. Moreover, shortly after the recording of the album, Visconti departed the Bowie scene to concentrate on his production work with Bolan. There were a number of reasons for Visconti quitting, but the main one was Bowie's business relationship with Defries:

I was pleased, at first, that David had such a sharp businessman working for him. He could certainly talk that talk. He told us, confidentially, that he was interested in Bowie as an artist and me as a producer, but that we should drop the band. This was immediately after *The Man Who Sold The World* was finished, after the band slept on the gallery floor at Haddon Hall for months and played the album and gigs for very little money. I thought at the time that this was pretty ruthless and I guess that was what happened because the band did disperse after I went my separate way. As for my personal dealings with Tony Defries, I caught him bullshitting me and overcharging his fees from the beginning. Our agreement was for ten per cent, but when a long-sought-after cheque came in (this was independent of any business with Bowie), he informed me by letter that this fee was now fifteen per cent. I smelled the beginnings of a very unsavoury relationship here and decided not to go with him as a manager. I warned David about him and he protested that Tony was not devious, and that we were all going to make lots of money. This was the deal breaker between us. With the exhausting experience of *The Man Who Sold The World* behind us, with virtually no approval of the album from the record company and Tony Defries in front of us, I decided to concentrate on Marc's blossoming career instead. It seemed more stable and more positive. We parted company on the corner of Regent Street and Great Castle Street, outside the offices of Defries and Lawrence Myers. I can't remember what we said to each other, but David had a very hurt expression on his face and I just turned and left quickly. I didn't feel all that great, but I couldn't stand Defries and I couldn't get it across to David that Defries was not all that he seemed.

Tony Defries may have put Visconti off, but without him it's arguable whether Bowie would have ever attained superstar status. Perhaps Bowie would have been comfortable remaining a prolific artist on the margins; perhaps, had Ken Pitt remained in charge, he would have detonated and become a fireball of glam-era gender violence. But what is certain is that, once Defries realised what he had, he channelled all his energies into making Bowie big. Born in Rickmansworth on 3 September 1943, Defries was an extremely able lawyer, blessed, so some have said, with an almost photographic memory. 'Everybody I have spoken to who has worked with him directly has been astonished by his knowledge,' says Bowie writer Kevin Cann. 'Somebody told me that they were once in the library of his house in Connecticut. He had an entire wall of law books, mainly American law, and Defries said to this person, "Pick one of those books, open it, and ask me a question." And Defries reeled off the answer almost word for word. The guy just could not believe it.' Enthused, at least initially, by his new manager, a new phase in Bowie's career was about to begin.

By way of contrast to the shilly-shallying of the recording of *The Man Who Sold The World*, the previous year, 1971 was an enormously disciplined and prolific year, productive in more ways than one. On 30 May 1971, Bowie's son, named Duncan Zowie Haywood Jones, was born in Bromley Hospital. He was a whopping 8 lb 8 oz. It was a painful birth for Angie, who cracked her pelvis during the thirty-hour labour. Bowie himself was at home when the news of the arrival of his son was relayed to him, listening to a Neil Young record. Trading on the vibe of wistful folksiness, Bowie wrote 'Kooks', a pastiche of early-70s Neil Young and a present for his new son.

For their part, the arrival of little Zowie (so called as to be a male version of Zoë – the Greek word for 'life') appears to have had little discernible impact either on David and Angie as a couple, or on Bowie's muse. Bowie has always liked children. His friends and work associates often comment that he's good with their sons and daughters and finds time to play with them. Suzie Frost, who lived in the basement of Haddon Hall, was asked to take care of the baby. For Angie's part, the trauma of the birth and subsequent depression had exhausted her, and so post-birth she went on holiday to Italy with her friend, the singer Dana Gillespie. Thereafter, she and David were part-time mum and dad. It was only in the late 1970s that Bowie realised he was missing out, and that his son needed his dad around.

Professionally, things really kicked into gear during 1971. On 1 August, Bowie signed a contract with the music production company, Gem, co-owned by his manager Tony Defries and music lawyer Lawrence Myers. Throughout 1971, Bowie began building up a stockpile of songs which would be recorded as two albums, almost back to back, at Trident Studios in London between early April 1971 and late January 1972.

In the absence of a big hit single after 'Space Oddity' Bowie managed to maintain a media profile of sorts through live sessions for the BBC. Between December 1967 and May 1972 he recorded twelve BBC sessions. However, a goodly part of this cache of songs were either never finished, given away, or remained locked in the vaults waiting for their chance in the big time.

Bowie began this period more as a songwriter than performer. He fancied himself as a songwriter craftsman, despite his earlier dalliance with theatrical pop with Hype. Bowie and Defries were more than keen to have self-penned songs picked up by major acts and so were delighted when 'Oh You Pretty Things' was covered by ex-Herman's Hermit Peter Noone. Produced by one of the hottest producers of the era, Mickie Most, it became a hit, reaching Number 12 in the summer of 1971. But prior to this songwriting breakthrough (a breakthrough which was to help secure the major label backing of RCA), Bowie gave away songs willy-nilly to anyone with a voice. Or even half a voice; like Sparky King. In an Internet chat in 1998, Bowie explained:

Sparky King was in fact Mickey King, part of our little gang in the early 70s. We were a ragbag of sorts and numbered among our throng Freddie Barratt (Burretti, clothes designer of the earliest 'clockwork-orange' and 'space-shoulders' costumes for Ziggy) and Daniella, a fantastic-looking Anglo-Indian girl who was a friend and try-out for all Freddie's new designs. She was also the first woman of colour who I had seen with short peroxided white hair. Plus, she had cut various shapes into the back like ice-cream cones and flags and then dyed them red or pistachio or whatever. She just looked oh-so stunningly tomorrow. This was 1969, remember. I will try really hard to find some good pics of her as I believe her whole thing was probably quite important in the putting together of the glam scene. We seemed to attract everyone from tran-somethings like Amanda Lear to gangsters. Johnny Binden, friend of the Krays, was a regular for a while before he went off to break legs for Zeppelin. So Mickey was a 'club boy' who I encouraged to sing. I would try and get anyone who would open their mouths to do my songs. He recorded a homage to my car called 'Rupert The Riley'. Mickey, tragically, was stabbed to death around 1974 by one of his many affairs. Daniella was, in fact, Freddie's platonic girlfriend, and would also, on occasion, stay over at Haddon Hall and babysit for Zowie.

As an aside, the said Riley car was, just before the birth of Zowie, responsible for Bowie himself having to spend a week in hospital after he got the starting handle of the car impaled in his thigh, narrowly missing a main artery.

Another side project, and something of a dry-run for Ziggy, was Arnold Corns, the early-70s answer to Milli Vanilli. For a band in the early 1970s not to be a proper band at all was indeed playing on the stickiest of wickets. For Arnold Corns was merely a front for Bowie himself to get some product out and to gauge the potential market for theatrical pop, just as he had done with Hype. Arnold Corns were a band from Dulwich College (featuring Mark Carr-Pritchard) and David had agreed to write for them. At the time he had also agreed to write for nineteen-year-old Freddie

Burretti (aka Rudi Valentino) whom he met at The Sombrero, the trendy gay discotheque whose clientele, so it is rumoured, would often find themselves sandwiched between Bowie and Angie in the Haddon Hall master bedroom. Freddie became a regular visitor to Haddon Hall. Bowie and Angie studied his art of dressing up, and quickly began copying his style. Bowie came up with the idea of combining Freddie and Arnold Corns and with the help of Ronson, Woodmansey and Trevor Bolder, a friend of theirs, a revised version of Arnold Corns was created during the spring of 1971. Bowie was writing material that would later become *Hunky Dory*, as well as songs earmarked for Freddie, but Freddie was, like Sparky King, several octaves short of a soprano. In the studio, David's vocals were mixed on top of Freddie's guide vocal.

Freddie was one of Bowie's Warholian starlets, vicariously testing the waters for a Ziggy-type figure. Indeed, the band's first waxing, 'Moonage Daydream'/'Hang On To Yourself', released on B&C Records on 7 May 1971 and a stunning flop, would showcase not one but two future Ziggy classics, totally scuppering any notion that Bowie wrote the album as a coherent concept album (the view which has hitherto predominated in the press). Despite this zero-unit-shifter of a flop, a second single, 'Looking For A Friend'/'Man In The Middle', was planned but never given a UK release. Burretti, however, was the Andrew Ridgeley to Bowie's George Michael. Bowie could write the songs and look supremely stylish and beautiful, but Burretti was all style. Style, style and more style. He had cheekbones and a cherubic countenance even Bowie could only sit back and admire. He designed and made many of the costumes used on the 1972 Ziggy tour, a not inconsiderable feat, thus playing a small – though not unremarkable – role in the glam-era Bowie saga. Sadly, Freddie died of cancer in Paris in 1999.

For his next recording project proper, Bowie retained Ronson for these sessions and Woody Woodmandsey. Trevor Bolder replaced the cheesed-off Visconti on bass. Although they weren't known as such at the time, The Spiders had formed. Bowie now had a stable backing band, and in addition recalled Yes pianist Rick Wakeman to play keyboards on the *Hunky Dory* session. He also brought in Ken Scott as producer.

Scott, a couple of months younger than Bowie, had engineered *Magical Mystery Tour* and *The Beatles* at Abbey Road Studio as well as the two previous Bowie albums. He'd also just worked on

George Harrison's *All Things Must Pass* and some of that aggressive acoustic sound would be imported into the *Hunky Dory* sessions. Now connected with Trident Studios (incidentally the first studio in Europe to acquire sixteen-track recording equipment in 1971), Scott was one of that first wave of rock engineers to move into production work. This move was an indication of the shifting division of labour within the rock business at the time, as he recalls:

We had reached a point in time in music history where engineers were doing more than just sitting there and turning knobs. We were starting to come up with musical ideas of our own, although we weren't getting credited for these by the producers, who often passed off my ideas as their own. Engineers such as Roy Thomas Baker and myself wanted to move into production. I was the first to break out of simply being an engineer because, luckily, at that time I was engineering with Bowie and he rather nervously said, 'I was going to do the next album on my own, but I'm not sure if I can. Will you co-produce with me?' So I formed a company, Nereus Productions, with the owners of Trident Studios, and *Hunky Dory* was my first album as a producer rather than an engineer.

Bowie played Scott a number of demos, and from these the two began selecting tracks for what is many people's favourite David Bowie album. Scott was immediately impressed with Bowie's studio craft. His vocals were almost always first takes, exceptionally unusual in the rock field, and Bowie's judgement of which takes would work was almost alchemic. Often Scott remembers both himself and Ronno thinking that a particular guitar part, or a certain vocal section, would have to be redone, but Bowie would say, 'No, wait, listen,' and when all the parts were played together, much to Scott's astonishment, it was apparent that Bowie had been right all along.

Although Bowie had an excellent ear, and could work extremely quickly (the *Hunky Dory* album was started in late May 1971 and completed in the August), he was, as Scott points out, not an especially good musician in standard technical terms. His saxophone playing, Scott remembers with a chuckle, 'left a lot to be desired', and as a guitarist he was only adequate. Indeed, Woodmansey and Bolder were themselves only 'OK' musicians, although Ronno was in a different class altogether. An excellent guitarist, Ronson was also a quirky and effective arranger for strings. 'But I wouldn't agree with those who have said that without Ronno, Bowie was nothing,' says Scott. 'Ronno was an incredible guitarist. He was also a unique arranger strings-wise, orchestrally. As far as taking a rock band and doing the arrangements was concerned, he was very typical, very average. But, as a guitarist and as an orchestral arranger – brilliant.'

According to Scott, for *Hunky Dory* the new, mature Bowie had the basis of a stable team: 'On *The Man Who Sold The World* he was still more of a trend-follower than a trend-setter and it wasn't until *Hunky Dory*, when it was "To hell with everyone. I'm gonna do what I want to do," that he began to hit his stride.'

Hunky Dory was recorded when Bowie was out of contract, but on hearing the tapes the huge American-based company RCA snapped him up for their roster, which included the biggest recording act of the rock era, Elvis Presley. Indeed, Dennis Katz at RCA signed Bowie and later Lou Reed in part to 'de-countrify' RCA's safe, heterosexual image. The record deal signed on 9 September in New York was to pay $37,500 for the next three LPs. Bowie had also signed a separate management deal with Tony Defries on 1 August that year. It appeared that finally Bowie was guaranteed a regular income.

Released in December 1971, *Hunky Dory*, despite its overall excellence, is musically quite a conservative record, and now sounds like something of a retrenchment after *The Man Who Sold The World*. It's almost as if Bowie deemed it necessary to appease a potential new record label with something a little more conventional, in the same way in which *Let's Dance*, again recorded out of contract, would be so much more commercial than *Scary Monsters* in 1983. Along with its successor, *Ziggy Stardust*, and *Let's Dance* from the 1980s, *Hunky Dory* is the album most likely (along with any of the greatest-hits compilations) to be found in the non-Bowie-fan record collection. It's a beautiful, poetic record which is musically seamless.

In a pop world in which 'originality' was awarded the highest of commendations, side two has three tribute songs: to Warhol ('Andy Warhol'), Dylan ('Song For Bob Dylan') and The Velvet Underground, or perhaps more specifically the soon-to-be-sponsored Lou Reed ('Queen Bitch'). With these, Bowie redefined the notion of pop star as fan, and elided the boundaries between the two. Prior to this, homages tended to be the exclusive preserve of blues acolytes, whose guitar playing was judged in terms of its fidelity to the original. Bowie, however, began the process of quoting directly from sources other than the blues, and promulgated the idea of a self-reflexive pop in which influences were not hidden from public consumption but laid bare for all to see. By 1973, this process had developed to such an extent that artists such as Bryan Ferry could record a whole collection of covers in the form of a homage. This was something separate from the age-old practice of singers covering other well-known standards or singing specially written songs. At a time when, in pop, more and more artists were writing their own material, a singer-songwriter's willingness to do cover versions indicated a deeper shift towards a post-modern sensibility in which pop stars became fans and drew attention to pop's own history. It was this sense of rock star as fan/star that gave Bowie the ammunition to create Ziggy Stardust later in the year.

Of the three homages, 'Queen Bitch' works the best. It's probably Bowie's poppiest song from the early 1970s never to be released as the A-side of a single, and is made all the more interesting by Bowie's curious, and quite wonderful, vocal accenting. His attempt at hip New York jive at the song's dénouement ('Uh ha?, 'You betcha', 'Umm') sounds so fey as to render the whole song an exercise in high-camp melodrama.

For 'The Bewlay Brothers', Bowie looked inward. Thematically, the song updates and improves *The Man Who Sold The World*'s central concern of familial dysfunction. The song itself is a (fictionalised?) account of a relationship between two brothers. Bowie delivers the lyric (his vocal, as it is throughout the album, high in the mix) in short bursts of activity, which then give way to long pauses filled in by Ronson's acoustic guitar work, imbuing the song with an overall impression of nostalgia, of a steady flow of remembrance. A series of weird-angle snapshots concentrate firmly on the concept of identity, its mutability, and its eventual disintegration: 'I was Stone and he was Wax/So he could scream, and still relax, unbelievable.'('The Bewlay Brothers', 1971.)

Later in the song Bowie directly references the tag which would become the much-overused (to the point of cliché) sobriquet for the rest of his career – the 'chameleon'. A homosexual relationship is also suggested: 'In the Crutch-hungry Dark/Was where we flayed our mark.'

'The Bewlay Brothers' remains one of Bowie's most disquieting moments on tape, an encapsulation of some distant, indefinable quality of expressionistic terror. However, Ken Scott remembers that, far from being self-consciously deep or meaningful, the song was a deliberate wind-up for the critics. 'That was almost a last-minute song. Just down the street from Trident Studios, there was a tobacconist which apparently gave him the inspiration for the lyrics. Let's say it gave him the inspiration for the name. He'll probably deny this to his death! As I remember it, he came in and said, "We've got to do this song and it's specifically for the American market." I said, "OK, how do you mean?", and he replied, "Well the lyrics make absolutely no sense, but the Americans always like to read things into things, so let them read into it what they will." ' The song's importance seemed to be confirmed when Bowie used its title for the name of his publishing company. Its mythic quality was reinforced by its absence, until 2002, from any Bowie set list, an absence due, at least so the fans thought, to the extremely personal nature of its subject matter.

'Oh You Pretty Things', a sort of 70s update of McCartney's 'Martha My Dear', also hides blacker themes behind the pop *lite*. Seeing 'cracks in the sky' certainly qualifies the young Bowie for a course of psychoanalysis, and 'the homo superior' and 'the golden ones' are direct references to the teachings of occultist Aleister Crowley. Bowie's children appear artificial, like John Wyndham's 'Midwich Cuckoos', alien clones of humanity. And all this wrapped in the sweetest of Bowie melodies.

Another perennial favourite is the twee 'Kooks', written for the newly born Zowie. Producer Ken Scott thought it was great: 'I loved it. Maybe it just touched me personally. I had one daughter at the time. I seem to remember him saying that one day he'd like to do a kids' album. He could have done it so well with that kind of material. Whether he's capable now, with all that he's gone through, I have no idea.'

'Quicksand' is almost Buddhist in its spiritualism ('Knowledge comes with death's release'). If 'Oh You Pretty Things' was Bowie's take on McCartneyesque 'Martha My Dear', 'Quicksand', was his 'My Sweet Lord'. Scott had just engineered George Harrison's sprawling *All Things Must Pass*, and he attempted to recreate that album's gutsy wall of aggressive acoustic guitars on 'Quicksand', with up to seven tracks of acoustic guitar being deployed in the more aggressive sections.

On the rest of the album, Bowie is at pains to stake a place for himself in the pantheon of rock gods. 'Song For Bob Dylan' is probably the weakest song on the album, but its lyric analyses the lack of a hero figure in rock. Bowie had been much enamoured with Dylan. The whole *Space Oddity* album had Dylanesque shadings with its mix of harmonica, folk-rock and acoustic deliberation. But by 1971, it appeared to wannabes like Bowie that Dylan was a has-been. Bowie was to tell *Melody Maker* in 1976 that the song 'laid out what I wanted to do in rock. It was at that period that I said, "OK, if you don't want to do it, I will. I saw the leadership void." '

One song, the opening track, 'Changes', was Bowie's edict for the 1970s. Bowie sings: 'So I turned myself to face me/But I've never caught a glimpse/Of how the others must see the faker/I'm much too fast to take that test.' ('Changes', 1971)

These four lines illuminate three of the most important active ingredients in Bowie's quest for stardom. The lyric emphasises the themes of identity, the mutability of character, and a sense of play with first and third person, providing us with an important anticipatory signal for the creation of Ziggy Stardust. Bowie plays up the self-made myth of his butterfly nature, his innate ambivalence, and his endless musical, sexual and political vacillation. In the 1970s he had an almost pathological fear of repeating himself, not just musically but visually too. Most important, Bowie gave himself the epithet 'faker'. He announced himself as pop's fraud; the arch-dissembler.

In the middle-eight section Bowie sings: 'Strange fascination, fascinating me/Changes are taking the pace I'm going thru.'

'Strange fascination' is a phrase that not only embodies a continued quest for the new and the bizarre, but also carries with it the force of compulsion, the notion of having to change to stay afloat artistically.

'Life On Mars?', a soaring, cinematic ballad, was an intentional parody of the quintessential standard, 'My Way'. In fact, in 'Life On Mars?' Bowie settled a little-known musical score (no pun intended). Way back in February 1968, Bowie was asked to submit a set of English lyrics for a French song, 'Comme D'Habitude'. Bowie's version, 'Even A Fool Learns To Love', was rejected (although it was scheduled to be in the set of Bowie's aborted cabaret act), and lyrics by Paul Anka were used instead – the result being Frank Sinatra's calling card, 'My Way', a staple of endless karaoke evenings down the pub. In 1993 Bowie commented: 'There was a sense of revenge in that because I was so angry that Paul Anka had done "My Way" I thought I'd do my own version. There are clutches of melody in that that were definite parodies.'

Bowie's four-bar theme cheekily rewrote the song's main musical motif, and his hammy, hysterical plea, 'Is there life on Mars?' (with the word 'Mars' drawn out to an almost preposterous effect), was a deliberate swipe at Sinatra's vocal-chord-snapping dénouement ('I did it mmmmmmeyeyeyeyeye-waaaaaayyyy – thank you, London!').

'Changes' was 'My Way' inverted, not a valedictory farewell but a prophetic hello ('turn and face the strange'). Mick Ronson's perfectly crafted piano line is both an echo of The Beatles and a musical appropriation of the Americana of the bar-room piano accompaniment, something Bowie and the band would play up live. With a nice touch of irony, Bowie stutters (and thus repeats) the 'ch' at the beginning of the word 'changes' and gave Canadian combo Bachman-Turner Overdrive a hint for their rather more blatantly speech-defective 'you ain't seen n-n-n-n-nothin' yet' in 1974.

The line in the last verse, 'Look out you rock'n'rollers', is crucial. Bowie is not only throwing down the gauntlet to existing rockers, but putting a distance between himself and the rock fraternity. When he spoke about rock, he stressed that he was using the medium and had no strong ties with it. In 1971 he said: 'I think [music] should be tarted up, made into a prostitute, a parody of itself. It should be the clown, the Pierrot medium. The music is the mask the message wears – music is the Pierrot and I, the performer, am the message.' Over twenty years later he reiterated the stance: 'I think I remember at the time saying that rock must prostitute itself. And I'll stand by that. If you're going to work in a whorehouse, you'd better be the best whore in it.'

With hindsight, 1971 was the year in which Bowie became something of a pop-art agent provocateur. What really fired him was the desire to be different, radically different, to challenge and overturn both the dominant musical conventions and the moral and sexual codes of his day. He developed the idea of becoming a pop poseur at a time when rock musicians looked to the classics for high cultural stimuli, or to the blues tradition – and all that implied about fidelity to tradition and 'paying one's dues' on the live scene. This, of course, is not to say that Bowie was a poseur per se. He was, rather, posing at being a poseur, which is quite a different thing. What many people mistake for shallowness and a lack of substance is in fact an outward manifestation of a very astute customer, of a man adept at dissembling the rock charade. When Bowie told one journalist in 1972 'I lie an awful lot', he was, after all, being brutally honest.

Bowie did indeed tart up his art in a radical and shocking manner. Lindsay Kemp and his 1960s absurdist mime-and-dance troupe was an influence, and Bowie took a special interest in the Warhol scene, too. For a promotional visit to the States in January 1971, Bowie took to wearing a man's dress, as designed by London's Mr Fish, and was threatened by a gun-toting redneck less than chuffed with the cut of Bowie's jib. However, the Bowie at the time was long-haired, willowy, and wont to wearing a huge floppy hat and singing acoustic pop. In February that year he met a PR man from Mercury records, the flamboyant Rodney Bingenheimer, who guided Bowie round Hollywood. During August, Bowie went to see Andy Warhol's *Pork* at the Roundhouse, and befriended the cast of starlets, including several people who would become apparatchik in MainMan, Tony Defries' management company: Tony Zanetta (who played Warhol in the production and would become Bowie's personal assistant), Wayne County, Cherry Vanilla (Bowie's future press agent), Leee Black Childers (his tour photographer), and the future president of MainMan, Jaime Andrews.

Bowie initially disappointed the *Pork* crowd. Jayne (formerly Wayne) County said this of seeing Bowie on his club tour in early 1971: 'We'd heard that David Bowie was supposed to be androgynous and everything, but then he came out with long hair, folky clothes, and sat on a stool and played folk songs. We were so disappointed with him. We looked over to him and said, "Just look at that folky old hippy!" ' 'David was disappointing,' said Leee Childers, 'but we loved his wife, Angela Bowie. Angie was loud, she was pregnant, she was crazy, she was grabbing our crotches, laughing it up, and having a good time.'

However, back in the UK, Bowie's stage performances were certainly causing more of a stir. As 1971 progressed, Bowie's sound became harder and harder. On 20 January he had worn a dress on Granada TV for 'Holy Holy', and throughout 1971, dresses would be part of the Bowie wardrobe. David Stopps, manager of the Friars Aylesbury venue and later manager of pop star Howard Jones, played a part in helping to break Bowie in the UK during 1971 and 1972. Friars Aylesbury was a small though important landmark on the gig circuit and Stopps was approached during the summer of 1971 by Bowie's agent, eager to get a gig for Bowie. Stopps had been aware of Bowie, not simply because of the 'Space Oddity' single, but also because Bowie had written for a band called Chameleon who came from Princes Risborough. The lead singer of Chameleon was Les Payne, who prides himself on, and makes media capital (including Radio Four appearances) out of, being the self-styled most unsuccessful pop singer in the history of pop music! 'Although very talented, he ended up making a career of being unsuccessful,' Stopps remembers.

Payne recalls that in the late 1960s and early 1970s, Bowie was thought of primarily as a songwriter, rather than a performer. Bowie met Chameleon in a rehearsal studio near Victoria Station and played them 'Oh You Pretty Things' and 'Star' and although Payne preferred the former, Bowie told them that it had already been earmarked for Peter Noone to record. Payne wanted Bowie to produce 'Star' for them but the band's label, Chrysalis, said that they had to use a 'proper' producer instead, John Schroder. The song was never released by Chameleon, although it did, of course, make Bowie's own Ziggy album two years down the line.

Stopps was also incredibly impressed with Bowie, and recalls that it was at this gig that the band became formalised as one unit (a unit later to be dubbed The Spiders From Mars). He was also rather shocked by the Bowie persona at the time: 'Bowie was fantastic. I think it was one of the first gigs he did with the band and he decided to form the band that night. He did the gig on 25 September 1971. They all liked it, so they said "Let's do it." In September 1971 he was dressed as a woman, as he was on the original cover of *The Man Who Sold The World*, which I wasn't quite expecting. I remember he came up to me in the afternoon and said, "Oh, it's ever so cold in the dressing room, can you get us a heater?" And he came on stage in what I think was a dress. I remember my wife, Budget Stopps (who had previously been married to Les Payne, the singer with Chameleon), mentioning "Star" to him. He'd forgotten about the song for some reason and he said, "Ooh, I must dig that one out." He was a very nice bloke, charming, pleased he had the gig, very excited after the gig.'

Stopps also paints a revealing picture of manager Tony Defries:

We had a regular clientele, so I thought we would get a half-decent audience. I remember we paid him £150, which was probably more than we should have. Defries was a bit of a hustler, shall we say. He was fine to me, but I remember that night when we paid David, for some reason we were short on cash and it was a cash deal, and I had to pay the last bit of it in 50p coins. Defries went back to the dressing room and counted it all, and came back and said it was 50p short. I then coughed up another 50p and that was that!

With the inclusion of 'tributes' to Lou Reed and Bob Dylan, a record written for the US market ('The Bewlay Brothers') and a cover of a Biff Rose song, 'Fill Your Heart', which had been part of Bowie's live repertoire for over a year by the time of recording, the *Hunky Dory* album was meant to make Americans part with their dollars in rather more significant volume than hitherto. America was still a mythic land for those teenagers and twenty-somethings brought up on rock'n'roll, and the memory of The Beatles' huge American success was still fresh. Rock acts like Bowie were as interested in breaking into the American market as they were in the UK (which generated only around a quarter of the potential earnings of the US).

Bowie, however, was naturally drawn to the fringes of American culture and the likes of Iggy Pop, Lou Reed and Andy Warhol. In the autumn of 1971, he made a trip to the Factory in New York. Bowie remembers Warhol as possessing a rather unearthly hue, his skin a preternatural waxy yellow. On a personal level, the meeting itself was far from a howling success. Warhol apparently hated Bowie's tribute to him on the *Hunky Dory* album, presented to him in the form of an acetate during the meet-and-greet, and was more interested in Bowie's shoes.

Despite this lead balloon of a détente between would-be pop star and seen-it-all-recently-shot New Yorkian pop-art doyen, Bowie nevertheless developed an approach in pop which was very similar to Warhol's in film and art. In the Factory, Warhol constructed fame and made 'talentless' people into movie stars. In doing so he challenged the notion of how stardom was attained by showing how easily it could be manufactured. The mythical, magical aura that enshrouded some Hollywood superstars was shown up for what it was – constructed and artificial. Anyone could be a star (if only for fifteen minutes).

Bowie found the idea that stardom could be fabricated immensely alluring. In fact, Warhol and Bowie may be said to have shared many psychological states. Both had a morbid fear of premature death. With Bowie this manifested itself in a fear of being shot on stage, and the final Ziggy Stardust shows were redolent with references to his own mortality ('Time', 'My Death' and 'Rock And Roll Suicide'). Warhol only narrowly escaped with his life after being shot by Valerie Solanas, a radical feminist, in 1968. Both had an abiding fear of flying. Both had a consuming passion for notoriety and fame. Even their careers followed certain similarities in trajectory.

Warhol assembled an entourage of people around him for work and recreational purposes who might live out his psychosexual fantasies vicariously for him on film and in real life. Bowie himself had his own, admittedly smaller-scale version, in Haddon Hall, at the Sombrero nightclub, and later his MainMan entourage, created for him by Defries out of the actual remnants of the cast of the production of Warhol's *Pork*. Warhol also 'reinvented himself', donning a wig to cover his baldness, changing the manner in which he spoke, the way he carried himself and his entourage in an effort to keep himself and others interested in the art and the hype. Perhaps most importantly, both Warhol and Bowie were unashamedly 'commercial' in their art. Despite both men's link with the avant-garde, they flaunted the consumerism of popular art and eventually became businessmen themselves.

Another major influence on Bowie (and on Warhol) at the time came from the camp aesthetic. The camp figure – witty, dry, ironic, sardonic, standing aloof and commenting with a bitchy, wry disdain – to be found throughout much nineteenth- and twentieth-century art, literature, theatre, film and television, has also made his mark in popular music (Morrissey and Neil Tennant being good examples). It is remarkable how many of the sensibilities described in Susan Sontag's article, 'Notes On Camp', are possessed by Bowie: 'Camp is a vision of the world in terms of style – but a particular kind of style. It is the love of the exaggerated, the "off", of things-being-what-they-are-not.' Sontag goes on to argue: 'Camp sees everything in quotation marks. It is not a lamp but a "lamp".' Most importantly, Bowie's penchant for fabricating a personality, for seeing life in terms of theatre ('It was cold and it rained, so I felt like an actor', he would sing on 'Five Years' in 1972), is prefigured in Sontag's comment that, 'To perceive camp in objects and persons is to understand being-as-playing-a-role. It is the farthest extension, in sensibility, of the metaphor of life as theatre.'

This sense of playfulness, married with a Warholian sense of pop as art, was a relatively new stance in the early 1970s and the very antithesis of the commanding rock ideology of the times. This rock ideology had a hegemonic position: almost everyone agreed unconsciously with its central tenets while never quite recognising that it was an ideology in the first place. So singers and performers, sometimes unwittingly, followed standards of excellence and decorum which, until Bowie, had never been fundamentally challenged before.

For some writers in the 1970s, who totally missed the point, Bowie was all glitz and show, with no substance. Journalist Dave Laing wrote in 1973, 'One thing all great music has in common is that it stands outside the dominant ethos of traditional pop: the ethos of showbiz ... OK, Bowie isn't Humperdinck. At times he has the poetic power of Dylan, the demonic presence of Jagger. But he has compromised with showbiz, with the whole manipulative process of image and stardom.'

What Bowie was actually doing was not simply being a commercial entity himself but showing that all rock was commercially based. It is absolutely no surprise that Bowie became such a shrewd businessman in later years, exploiting his position as rock star to the full through a succession of lucrative recording contracts in the 80s and 90s (RCA to EMI-America to BMG), culminating, of course, in 1997's 'Bowie Bond' scheme. In the 70s, jeans-clad, joint-smoking hippies might have spouted off about connecting with the kids, singing songs from the heart and feeling a sense of togetherness, but they were as implicated in the machinations of capital as any other pop star, as willing to be compensated by cash as The Partridge Family or The Wombles. For the young David Bowie, pop was pop art, a new form to be toyed with, to be combined with other related art forms – not a simple code to be truthfully revealed.

Up until January 1972, Bowie's career still showed all the signs of the stasis it had been in since the success of 'Space Oddity' more than two years previously. *Hunky Dory*, released just before Christmas, had failed to dent even the lower reaches of the charts, and the single, 'Changes', despite the highly dubious honour of being Tony Blackburn's single of the week on Radio 1 (surely proof, if proof were needed, of *Hunky Dory*'s melodic mainstream sensibility), also failed to chart. By this time, however, Bowie had another trick up his sleeve. Another album was already in the can, and he knew it was his best yet. However, his biggest act of prestidigitation was a casually slipped in but totally premeditated admission which would set the rock world alight.

On 22 January 1972, *Melody Maker* had Bowie on the front cover wearing an early-Ziggy catsuit, his hair cut spiky and short. During the course of the interview with Michael Watts, Bowie proudly announced, 'I'm gay and I always have been, even when I was David Jones.' Ken Pitt was apparently horrified: 'I wasn't at all happy when the "I'm gay" interview appeared,' he says. 'It wasn't the kind of thing I would have advised him to do.'

What Bowie *intended* is unclear. As a married man with a child, it was obviously closer to his lived experience to admit that he was bisexual. What strikes us now is how low-key the admission was. Given its legendary status in terms of helping to queer British pop, the really striking thing about the whole interview is how unsensationalist it is. There's no 'Pop star in "I'm gay" revelation' headline on the cover. Instead, there's a shot of Bowie having a fag next to the lead story, 'Crimson Break Up'. Yet it's probably true to say that this one interview made David Bowie, or, at least, was a significant addition to the mythic Bowie public persona of the day. In a recent interview for *Mojo*, Michael Watts told Chris Charlesworth:

I think he said it very deliberately. I brought the subject up. I think he planned at some point to say it to someone. He definitely felt it would be good copy. He was certainly aware of the impact it would make ... I think he'd had a relationship with a man at some time in his life, so it wasn't a lie. I don't think he was lying ... I think it was something Defries encouraged. He (Defries) understood the news value of something like that. I was aware of a changed mood towards gay people, not just in rock, but in culture as a whole.

Bowie was a very alluring, charismatic figure. You couldn't help but feel he had a hell of a lot of magnetism. He looked like a star. It was a mixture of film star and rock star appeal – he was so much better-looking than other rock stars.

In a real sense Michael Watts, a white, middle-class, heterosexual journalist, did more to unleash the Bowie phenomenon to the world than anyone or anything else. Of course, the brilliance of the music mattered, too, but up to that point it had gone largely unnoticed. Watts saw in Bowie a new Dylan-like figure, a figure who might build up a body of work to confront the latter's legacy. Watts remained impressed with the intellectual content of Bowie's work throughout the 1970s and recognised that he was not only a heavyweight, but also the best bet for a new rock icon there was. He was right.

Anyone following Bowie's career at this time (and there weren't that many) might have remembered an interview Bowie had given, at the suggestion of Ken Pitt, to the gay magazine, *Jeremy*, in January 1970. The contents of that interview had nothing whatsoever to do with Bowie's sexual orientation, and Bowie did not use the occasion to out himself, but the very fact that he spoke to a gay magazine surely indicated that he was at least sympathetic to the gay cause. In fact, Bowie used the *Melody Maker* interview to distance himself from gay politicking, and this action has damned him in the eyes of many gays ever since. As ever, Bowie would not commit himself to 'the cause'. This has led some gay critics, most notably John Gill in his provocative book *Queer Noises*, to brand Bowie as a closet homophobe who cynically manipulated his own sexuality in order to impress a straight rock critic like Michael Watts. But the 'myth' of 'Queer David' was, according to Gill, strong enough to allow 'real queers' (like himself) to come out of the closet. 'For gay musicians, Bowie was seismic,' said singer and now broadcaster Tom Robinson. 'To hell with whether he disowned us later.'

Bowie's ambivalent stance, as a gay man with a wife and child, and his subsequent claim that, in the 1970s, his bisexuality was more a form of sexual tourism, a compulsion to flout moral codes than a real biological and psychological state of being, were, perhaps, something of a smoke screen. It is not easy to simply accept that all this was mere play-acting and that Bowie was, in fact, just a straight man into experimentation. Although at the time, with gay liberation chic, with even straights coming out as gay, the fact of the matter is that Bowie was, to a small degree, bisexual.

As he got older, his attraction to the same sex receded in the same way that it might develop in another individual over time.

Ken Scott for one remembers that Bowie had male as well as female lovers: 'I'm sure he had escapades (although I myself had no first-hand knowledge), but I'm also sure they were far fewer than intimated.' Tony Visconti maintains that Bowie never gave the slightest hint of feminisation: 'He was never camp. I was not close to him during the Ziggy period, but I think he was being more flamboyant and theatrical rather than making a sexual statement. He was never a cross-dresser. I think he suddenly realised that he could do something outrageous to get noticed – he was ignored for years until he appeared on the front pages of the tabloids, pushing a pram and wearing a dress. It was a clever move – the first of many.'

In the 1990s the record company entrepreneur David Geffen apocryphally quipped, 'Say what you will about bisexuality, you have a fifty per cent better chance of finding a date on a Saturday night.' Bowie, borrowing a line from The New York Dolls' David Johansen, was a 'try-sexual' (he would have a go at anything). Perhaps he can best be described as being into what has been called 'experimental bisexuality'. The writer Marjorie Garber has identified the 'erotic appeal of transgression' and 'the role of cross-dressing' as being 'part of bisexual play'. For Garber, bisexuality is about many things, but it is perhaps crucially about disorientation. This sums up Bowie, and his art, perfectly.

As a publicity stunt, the 'Bowie is gay' line was perfect. Like Michael Watts, Ken Scott suspects that it has all the hallmarks of a Defriesian coup: 'Defries knew it would be a great selling point. The bisexuality thing was perfect. It was done early enough in his career to help boost his career, unlike Elton, who, when he came out, was so far into his career that he lost some of his audience because of it.' This view is not universally held, however. Apparently Angie and Bowie were concerned about how Defries would react to Bowie's admission. It was not until some months later, when Bowie had become a UK chart success, that the tabloids would turn their attention to his sexuality. The revelation was just one component in a sequence of events which helped make him a star.

Bowie's 'celebrity bisexuality' didn't link his rising star to the pop world so much as allude to the Hollywood tradition of gender-bending iconography, of which there was ample evidence. Garbo, Dietrich (known as 'the best-dressed man in Hollywood'), Brando, Olivier, James Dean, Montgomery Clift and Danny Kaye were all bisexual or gay, some publicly so. But the bisexual pop stars such as Edith Piaf, Janis Joplin and Little Richard, gay record producers such as Joe Meek, and gay managers such as Brian Epstein, were often forced to keep their sexuality away from the media. With a certain public acceptability in the post-Stonewall, post-legalisation of the homosexual act era, a pop star such as Bowie was a little less restricted in coming out. Bowie was the first to do so, and scores of other media people felt able to follow in his wake.

So Bowie's admission was more than a mere publicity stunt. Despite the relative sang-froid with which Watts reported the first ever outing of a gay British pop star, and despite Bowie's rather flippant, bitchy persona in the interview, the effect, in cultural terms, was absolutely revolutionary. After a decade of sexual experimentation for heterosexuals, Bowie's openly bisexual stance united all those psychically and sexually dispossessed people looking for a symbol for their own feelings of insecurity and lack of rootedness. As a bisexual mainstream pop star, Bowie represented taboo-smashing, rule-breaking and experimentation. Despite the traditionalism of some of his music at the time (there was very little to separate the pretty pop of 'Starman' from Elton John's 'Rocket Man'), Bowie was now the personification of something other. And, even more importantly, his name became synonymous with one character: the ultimate fabricated rocker, Ziggy Stardust. It is Ziggy's tale that must now be told.

4. COSMIC SURGERY, 1971–1972

I'm going out to bloody entertain, not just get up on a stage and knock off a few songs. I couldn't do that. I'm the last person to pretend that I'm a radio. I'd rather go out and be a colour television set.

BOWIE IN 1972

You couldn't fuck a lot of hip girls unless you were wearing some mascara.

BOWIE PHOTOGRAPHER AND PROMO MAKER MICK ROCK IN 1998

He had his own album. He had his own, very particular, hairdo, which was copied by both men and women. He brought cross-dressing, glitter and make-up to the high street. He's the most famous fictional rock star ever. He has a website devoted to him. He's had whole books written about him. Numerous tribute bands have sprung up in his wake. He's had a film, *Velvet Goldmine*, based, in part, on him. His last ever performance was turned into a film, a documentary about a complete fiction. There was even a Ziggy Stardust hotel in Thailand, although rumour has it that it is now closed. His creator, David Bowie, né Jones, has been inundated with offers to resurrect him in a musical. Quite simply, Ziggy made David Bowie a star.

Ziggy Stardust will go down in history as Bowie's finest creation. It's a truism that in pop one is almost always re-membered for what one did first and, in Bowie's case, this means that his name will forever be linked with his most famous doppelgänger. Some critics have argued that Bowie's truly ground-breaking work is not found until later in the 70s, and it could be argued that the Ziggy stage show was bettered by subsequent tours. But, it's a fact that, along with *Let's Dance* a decade later, the albums made with Ken Scott as producer are Bowie's biggest-sellers in the UK and, in general, it is this era that many fans hold most dear.

There were, of course, a number of dry runs for Ziggy. We've already seen how, aided by the supremely beautiful clothes designer, Freddie Burretti, a man severely more feminised than Bowie himself could ever be, the would-be star tried out a number of swishy camp looks for the Arnold Corns project. This piece of artifice was, of course, perfect for the sort of rock-as-pose stance Bowie took at the time. Another involved Bowie's mid-60s interest in mime, captured by manager Ken Pitt in a succession of eerie studies in black-and-white. In mid-1971 Bowie was shot by photographer Brian Ward as a strikingly androgynous sphinx in lipstick. According to Jungian readings, the sphinx is an icon which fuses the animus and anima, male and female.

Bowie first mentioned his character Ziggy on tour in Amercia in 1971. Ziggy was a composite rocker, and was based on two cult pop artists in particular. One was The Legendary Stardust Cowboy (real name Norman Carl Odom), a sort of thrash country-and-western star, four months Bowie's junior. That Bowie knew about him at all bespoke a certain engaging idiosyncrasy, since Mr Cowboy, or 'The Ledge' as his friends call him, was hardly a regular in the UK charts, or any charts for that matter. He did, however, reach the Billboard Top 200 with his remarkable single, 'Paralyzed', one of those almost surreal pieces of rock history. Essentially a bloody racket with whoops, hollers, incomprehensible screamed lyrics and various massively assaulted percussion instruments, 'Paralyzed' was included in Kenny Everett's hysterical 1978 compilation, *The Worst Records Of All Time*. The single has a certain perverse charm – so bad it's good – and is to pop what Ed Wood's *Plan Nine From Outer Space* is to film: intoxicatingly awful. As a totally madcap, fringe figure, The Legendary Stardust Cowboy was perfect Bowie fodder: an outsider, a pioneer, and extremely funny.

Bowie actually owned a copy of 'Paralyzed'. He may have also seen 'My Life', a press release in the form of a short biography to accompany the Cowboy's second single, 'I Took A Trip (In A Gemini Spacecraft)', later to be covered on Bowie's 2002 *Heathen* CD, which more than hints at some of the themes which would become Ziggy trademarks:

At this age [six] I used to look at the moon and told myself that some day man will go to the moon. I would like to go to Mars instead of the moon. When I was seven years old I was walking down the street after school and told myself that some day I was going to be famous ... I was sitting in my backyard thinking about cowboys and stardust in outer space. I put them together and came up with Stardust Cowboy. After that I added 'legendary', which means that I am a legend in my own time ... I figured that by singing I was able to attract all the girls but I attracted all the boys instead ... I kept up with the space programme and studied it while writing songs about space and rockets ... I got tired of working in a warehouse so I wrote Tiny Tim a letter with a picture of myself and musical instruments. I wanted him to help me record a record. By the way, my dad died when I was seventeen and he never heard me sing. Then my mother remarried. I wanted to be on the Johnny Carson show like Tiny Tim.

So The Ledge was given to delusions of a cosmic nature, was something of a hit with the boys, and was obsessed with the idea of becoming a star (all of which he arguably had in common with young Mr Bowie). Both men admired the Australian music-hall pop of Tiny Tim (whom David encountered when he shared the bill with him at Save Rave in 1969), with Bowie even going as far as recording one of Tim's B-sides, 'Fill Your Heart', by the equally dotty fringe figure, Biff Rose.

Bowie the rock'n'roll historian was also drawn to the story of Vince Taylor (real name Brian Holden, born in west London in 1939), the leather-clad 'French Presley', so called because he took that country by storm in the 1960s with his hit, 'Brand New Cadillac', later covered by The Clash. Taylor was thus a piece of exotica and a cult artist, again perfect Bowie material. He was given to week-long drink-and-drugs binges that reputedly make Keith Richards' broken-toothed 70s excesses look almost genteel. Bowie actually met Taylor while the latter was in London, his career in a tailspin. 'I met him a few times in the mid-60s and I went to a few parties with him. He was out of his gourd. Totally flipped. The guy was not playing with a full deck at all.' Bowie remembers him stopping outside Charing Cross tube station, unfolding a map of the metropolis on the pavement, crouching on his hands and knees, peering through a magnifying glass and pointing out sites where UFOs were going to land.

Bowie himself has claimed that Taylor's career effectively ended when, during an encore for one of his concerts, he came on stage dressed in a white sheet and sandals and proclaimed to the audience that he was the new Messiah. In fact, following mental health problems and a few wilderness years, Vince Taylor did indeed perform again (he even had a new album out around the same time that *Ziggy Stardust* was released). Taylor spent the last eight years of his life in Lausanne, Switzerland, working in a factory, before dying in 1991 at the age of just 52. Taylor was a cult figure possessed with a mad genius, his story a rock'n'roll tragedy and a perfect example of rock martyrdom.

Another immediate influence on the Ziggy creation was Stanley Kubrick's film version of the Anthony Burgess novel, *A Clockwork Orange*. A surreally cruel film, Bowie 'deviolenced' the *Clockwork Orange* look for The Spiders' earliest costumes. The inside photographs of the band on the album sleeve, portraits of four grotesquely artificial street urchins, was intended as a direct homage to the look of the film. Bowie had, in fact, toyed with the idea of taking to the stage wearing a bowler hat like the film's leading character, played by Malcolm McDowell. Bowie referenced the 'droogies' (the name given to the film's gang members) in his own 'Suffragette City', written months after the release of the film in 1971. Most importantly, Bowie borrowed the film's soundtrack, a haunting, synthesised interpretation of Beethoven by Walter (later sex-changed into Wendy) Carlos (specifically track five, 'March From A Clockwork Orange'). This music heralded Ziggy's arrival on the stage in 1973, and later, on the *Sound + Vision* tour in 1990, was used to announce the arrival of the sombre-suited walking jukebox of that year.

But perhaps the biggest influence of all came not from rock music at all, but from Japanese culture. First, Bowie has said that Japanese designer Kansai Yamamoto was 'one hundred per cent responsible for the Ziggy haircut and colour'. Second, Japan's influence on Ziggy came from its peculiarly stylised theatre. Bowie was fascinated by Japanese kabuki and No theatre and appropriated their essence for the Aladdin Sane shows, giving his performances the air of a secularised ritual debasement of one of the most formal of theatrical presentations. It is perhaps understandable that Bowie's 1972 and 1973 tours are now regarded as his Ziggy Stardust phase. This is encouraged not only by the fact that Bowie's famous gig at Hammersmith in July 1973 was known as Ziggy's last stand, but also in part by Bowie himself, whose own *Moonage Daydream* book, subtitled 'The Life and Times Of Ziggy Stardust', takes the story well into 1973. But, in fact, there appear to be two quite distinct eras. The 1972 shows in support of Ziggy were rocky, punky and brash; not without theatricality, but still very much part of the accepted way of framing a rock gig. However, once Bowie started promoting *Aladdin Sane* in 1973, the costuming becomes far more elaborate and garish. And Bowie's fascination with all things Japanese was crucial in defining the Aladdin Sane era.

In the West, Japan was traditionally viewed as an 'alien' culture, at least in the way that it was represented in the tabloids. It was often crudely caricatured as an incomprehensible, rule-bound society in which ritual humiliation was the order of the day for its citizens. Bowie's Ziggy dignified Japanese culture and showed him open to ideas outside Anglo-American rock. Bowie helped internationalise pop, starting a long-running fascination with the East. He later became one of Japan's biggest idols, and has retained an interest in the Far East, travelling extensively, particularly in Indonesia. The result, sartorially, of this kabuki appropriation, was a violent clash between the logic of the rock gig (connection and camaraderie) and that of kabuki theatre (stately though garish formality).

The use of kabuki styles in rock performance was an innovation. Some of the costumes for the Ziggy Stardust and Aladdin Sane shows were actually first used in kabuki theatre, others were designed for Bowie by Kansai Yamamoto, again based on traditional designs. The first item Bowie bought was the bright-red Kansai-designed jumpsuit emblazoned with woodland animals, which he wore at the Rainbow in 1972. Apparently he got it cheap in a sale because no one wanted it. Bowie then sought out the costume's designer, Kansai Yamamoto. In early 1973, returning to the States on a promotional tour for *Aladdin Sane*, he met Kansai in New York. Kansai had produced several new original costumes for Bowie, including the brilliantly outrageous design with the flap at the back, which he would flip sexily to reveal his undies to the audience. By the time the *Aladdin Sane* tour reached Japan in April 1973, Bowie had a full stock of new Kansai designs for the upcoming UK tour. In Japan, Bowie even wore a pair of Sumo wrestler's pants on stage, to brilliant effect.

The overall visual effect of these shows was that of a blurring of 'found' symbols from science fiction – space-age high heels, glitter suits and the like – with kabuki-style garments whose effect was to signify the codes of another culture, one alien to Western society. In the context of the times, Bowie's appropriation of kabuki theatre was, for a Western pop audience, in equal measure unsettling and fascinating. And kabuki was innovative and cool: for instance the Mawari-butai – a revolving stage now a staple in some glitzy entertainment and rock shows – was invented in Japan almost 300 years ago.

Kabuki was perfect for the Aladdin Sane shows in that, by its very nature, it is a 'gender-bending' theatrical form. In kabuki theatre, all parts, both men and women, are played by men. Its androgynous nature was elevated by Bowie to a position of fundamental importance. It was the kabuki aesthetic of visual excess, its garish though formal juxtaposition of colours, which attracted Bowie while he was drawing the Ziggy character ('some cat from Japan ... well hung and snow-white tan'). The Ziggy haircut hinted at the 'Siamese' style of hair and the heavily made-up red or gold lips, black eye-liner and blusher, set against the whitened pallor of the rest of the face, echoed the make-up used in kabuki theatre. The constant changing of costume, so evident in both the Ziggy and Aladdin Sane stage shows, also had its origins in kabuki. A change of kimono meant a change of personality. Bowie explained these costume changes as a way of expressing new facets of the personality, particularly necessary in his portrayal of the schizoid Aladdin Sane.

Like all the best pop creations, Ziggy/Aladdin was brilliantly photogenic. His angular and vulpine face with its high cheekbones is one of the most distinctive in the business. Of course, central to the look was the new hairstyle, which Bowie says originated in early 1972. He had seen a photo by Sukita of a model with red spiky hair wearing one of Kansai Yamamoto's designs for his first London show, probably in an issue of *Honey* magazine. Suzy Fussey, who worked in the Evelyn Paget salon in Beckenham, just opposite the Three Tuns Pub, attempted a copy of the cover hairdo. Like Phil Oakey's famous asymmetrical haircut six years later, Bowie's was a male version of a female model's barnet. Later, with the application of a product made by Schwarzkopf called Red Hot Red, it turned into the haircut that defined glam rock. 'I had her cut my hair short in early January 1972. No dye. Laid flattish,' said Bowie. 'I believe that it went red and stood up between the 20th and 25th of January 1972, therefore that's when the Kansai show must have been given maximum press.'

Suzy Fussey remained with Bowie throughout the Ziggy and Aladdin Sane shows, attending to his hair and costuming. She later became Mick Ronson's personal assistant and, in 1973, his wife. Another essential element in the sartorial redefinition of David Bowie was added with the arrival of make-up artist Pierre Laroche in 1973. La Roche applied the famous thunderbolt across the face of Aladdin Sane in 1973 (a look which, although often copied by Bowie imitators, was never actually used on stage). He also created the mystical astral sphere on Bowie's forehead, perhaps the most striking piece of make-up in the entire history of Bowie's stage career. David borrowed the 'astral sphere' idea from Calvin Lee. Lee wore a similar silver disc on his forehead which intrigued Bowie, and it was this that inspired the Aladdin sphere. Mick Rock: 'Pierre La Roche, or "Pierre Le Poof" as he was affectionately known, began doing the make-up, and that stepped up David's appreciation for a more elaborate look. Pierre was a brilliant make-up artist. David learned a lot, because at the time he mostly still did his own make-up, as there wasn't that much money around.'

Back in early 1972, Bowie, although striking, was not quite the shock of the new he would become in 1973. That said, the cover of his fifth, and, so many would say, greatest album, is one of rock's most iconic images. The cover which houses the *To Be Played At Maximum Volume* vinyl album is now the stuff of rock legend. With his blond feather-cut, Bowie stares rather coyly, his platform boots resting on a dustbin, the detritus of the inner city piled up before him, the lad on the verge of the big time. Suffused with the eerie reflected glow of a wet London night, the picture has a blurry, slightly distorted realism, as if this were not London but a mock-up of it in Moscow or some parallel universe. Even more striking, the back shows Bowie camply entombed in a red telephone box, his left hand bent at the wrist, lamely raised to eye level (as if about to limply tap at the window?), the right clasping his hip. Bowie's eyes, half-open, avoid our gaze. The figure in the phone booth looks like a mannequin, an almost lifeless simulacrum of camp. The effect is one of deliberate mystification. The telephone box has been rendered a kind of style laboratory, a sort of one-man-or-woman 'vogueing booth'.

It is quite ironic, given the unnatural, nonrealistic essence of London that the cover artwork suggests, that 23 Heddon Street, the venue for the picture shot by Bowie photographer Brian Ward (who later, with supreme irony, went on to work with Gary Numan), has become something of a shrine for Bowiephiles. Bowie has had hundreds of Polaroids sent to him by young Ziggys, foot on dustbin outside number 23, mimicking the album cover. The 'K. West' sign is now long gone – indeed, the building which looms large over Ziggy has been refurbished, but every year hundreds, maybe thousands, of Bowie fans make a pilgrimage to this locale just off Regent Street. A red telephone box was returned to the street in 1996 as part of the council's policy of reconstructing the inner city's historical look, and thereby returned some seventies authenticity to the locale. The council dutifully paints over the Ziggy graffiti about once a month. 'It's such a shame that sign went. People read so much into it,' said Bowie in 1993. 'They thought K. West must be some sort of code for a quest. It took on all these sorts of mystical overtones. We did the photographs outside on a rainy night, and then upstairs in the studio we did the *Clockwork Orange* lookalikes that became the inner sleeve.'

It is rather strange, then, that historically, Ziggy has been taken as a true rocker, or at least as a rocker with an authentic intelligence and as an inhabitant of a real city, on the basis of an album cover that appears to do everything to announce itself as a tampering with reality. This was the essence of Bowie's attraction. Like all the best pop, Bowie's work transformed the mundane, denatured it and blurred the distinctions between lived experience and fictionalised versions of it. It was this crisis, this extremely clever experiment in what could be taken as real and fake, which drove Bowie into even bolder artistic endeavours.

Work on the *Ziggy Stardust* album in 1971/72 also took place at Trident Studios. Bowie told Ken Scott, who had again been brought in to co-produce, that he wanted a very different sound. 'I remember David coming to me, prior to doing the album, and saying, "You're not going to like this album. It's gonna be much harder." I don't know who he compared it to; maybe it was Iggy. He thought I would hate it, but I loved it!'

According to Ken Scott, however, although Bowie was keen to harden the sound, the influence of the then contemporary proto-punk sound of Iggy Pop and Lou Reed was minimal at best.

David said he wanted a more rock'n'roll album. He wanted it to sound more like Iggy Pop. Now, at the time, I had no idea who Iggy Pop was. The Iggy and Lou influence has definitely been overplayed. The influence it had on David getting into that album was crucial. It was important in forming the way he wanted the album. But for anyone else connected with the album, and this goes for the listening public as well, I don't think it came out sounding anything like Iggy Pop.

The first thing to be changed was the drum sound. Woody had hated the one on *Hunky Dory*, it was much too dead for him. 'As far as I'm concerned, the drum sound on *Hunky Dory* was just like cardboard boxes,' Scott remembers Woody telling him. ' "Don't worry, it's not going to be like that," I told him. But on the first day of recording I sent the tea boy out to buy various-sized boxes of Kellogg's cornflakes and me and the roadie set up a whole drumkit made entirely of these boxes. I wish I had a picture of it – it looked amazing! Woody walked in and just fell on the floor laughing. He couldn't believe it!'

During recording there was little or no interference from either RCA or MainMan. Scott remembers: 'It was a remarkable set-up because no one from the record company ever came down and that was unusual back then, and impossible now. They would leave us alone, we would hand in our product, and then they would make their comments after that. And it was much the same with Defries. He would come down whatever the temperature was, in his fur coat and his cigar, which was his standard uniform once the money started to roll in. We were left to our own devices, which was great. I never heard him comment on the music at all. I always knew him as Deep Freeze! He handled success better than Bowie did! It was all for him, always.'

Keeping regular hours from two in the afternoon to around midnight, the sessions went along smoothly. Many of the songs were demoed before Bowie committed them to tape, a process he would abandon in favour of a more experimental approach in the studio as the decade wore on. These demos were not actually played to either The Spiders or producer Ken Scott. Bowie would introduce each new song on acoustic guitar and the structure was worked up in the studio from this blueprint.

Ken Scott produced a detailed, instantly recognisable sound, with acoustic and lead guitar interweaving perfectly. The Trident Studios piano, used earlier by The Beatles on classics such as 'Hey Jude', and later by Elton John, Genesis and Supertramp amongst others, was played by Ronson to superb effect on both *Hunky Dory* and *Ziggy*. In fact, on both albums, the meld between piano and rock guitar is what brings many of the songs to life. Some of the production tricks employed by Scott, such as the phasing on the strings at the end of 'Moonage Daydream', are simply perfect. The album has a wonderful unity, from the heartbeat-like drum intro on 'Five Years' to the calamitously overwrought ending of 'Rock'n'Roll Suicide'. And Bowie sings brilliantly. Ken Scott was astonished by the singer's vocal technique and his ability to nail a melody line perfectly and almost instantly. Beautifully melodic throughout, *Hunky Dory* and *Ziggy Stardust* are probably the two albums which the listening public in general would vote as the best Bowie albums of all time. *Ziggy* the album is as near to pop perfection as Bowie has ever got. 'The arrangements were by Mick and I, or Mick alone', Bowie said in 2002:

Mick wrote stunning string arrangements. A perfect foil and collaborator, Mick's raw, passionate Beck-style guitar was perfect for Ziggy and the Spiders . . . Another of Mick's singular abilities, which I have encountered in only a few players since, was the facility to take a hooky line that I might whistle to him or play badly on my guitar, and he would make it sing, often reinforcing it with a second line overdub . . . I would also literally draw out on paper with a crayon or felt-tip pen the shape of a solo. The one in 'Moonage Daydream', for instance, started as a flat line that became a fat megaphone type shape and ended in sprays of disassociated and broken lines . . . Mick could take something like that and actually bloody play it, bring it to life. Very impressive.

The final track listing for the record wasn't decided upon until quite late in the day. One dated 15 December 1971 shows that

'Velvet Goldmine', 'Holy Holy', 'Port Of Amsterdam' and a cover of Chuck Berry's 'Round And Round' were slated for inclusion. 'Suffragette City', 'Rock'n'Roll Suicide' and 'Starman' had yet to be recorded. Missing from the track listing, but already recorded, was 'It Ain't Easy'. By 2 February the list had been finalised in the form we now hold dear, with the exception of the rather perfunctory cover of Chuck Berry's 'Round And Round', where 'Starman' would later be. Indeed the first single, 'Starman', was very much a last-minute offering after pressure from RCA/ MainMan for a lead-off single.

During 1971, Bowie also cut a number of songs at Trident which have yet to be officially released. These tracks include 'How Lucky You Are' (also known as 'Miss Peculiar'), recorded at Haddon Hall in May 1970 with Sparky King as vocalist. Bowie's version was recorded at Trident in April 1971 but not included on either *Hunky Dory* or *Ziggy Stardust*. It's a piano-led theatrical showtune with a swaying, continental melodicism to the music. It's also very filmic and certainly worthy of release in some guise in the future. There's also the fun-time 'Rupert The Riley', recorded on 23 April 1971 under the name of The Nick King All Stars. Two versions are known to exist, one with Bowie on lead.

'The Man' (also known as 'Shadowman') is an acoustic ballad in the *Hunky Dory* style, with a melody slightly reminiscent of The Bee Gees' 1967 hit, 'To Love Somebody'. This song was first recorded at Haddon Hall in May 1970, the second version at Trident on 23 April, and the final version on 14 September 1971. Its lyric, with the line 'but the shadowman is really you', again rehearses Bowie's attraction/repulsion vis-a-vis the idea of the pookah, the doppelgänger, haunting and threatening his individuality. It was as if Bowie was forever starring in his own kiddies' pantomime in which the audience's shout of 'he's behind you!' echoed round his brain. And what was behind him was a clone of himself. His writing at this stage was full of the child's fear of the unknown, of nervously turning round to locate an unwanted imaginary guest. In Bowie's case he was terrified of seeing another version of himself peering over his shoulder.

'Don't Be Afraid', 'He's A Goldmine' (later 'Velvet Goldmine' of course) and 'Something Happens' are rumoured to be from pre-*Ziggy* sessions conducted in 1971 and have a harder rock edge than the *Hunky Dory* material. 'Only One Paper Left' and 'It's Gonna Rain Again' are also rumoured to have been started in

1971 but both remain unfinished. Ken Scott does remember the first of these, although, interestingly, he has no recollection of recording 'Sweet Head', the mildly risqué track put out in 1990 as part of the Ryko reissue. There is also said to be another song, 'Blackhole Kids', from this period; it, too, remains in Bowie's vaults.

Later, in 1972 and 1973, Bowie also worked on a stage presentation of Ziggy. Two songs, 'Rebel Rebel' and 'Rock'n'Roll With Me', eventually found on 1974's *Diamond Dogs*, were originally part of this separate project, and the likelihood is that Bowie still has unrecorded material from this writing spree.

What is clear, though, is that Bowie did not set out to write a concept album. Bowie spent a huge amount of time writing, demoing and recording in 1971 and after finishing *Hunky Dory* in the spring of 1971 soon stockpiled dozens of new songs with no home for them. Many of these songs were intended for release on the *Hunky Dory* follow-up, then jettisoned at the last minute once the contingent Ziggy idea provided a better framework on which to hang together already existing ideas and songs. Once the concept was in place, Bowie fine-tuned it, wrote a few additional songs very much at the last minute and a rock legend was born – in a rather more haphazard fashion than rock history would have it.

Released in June 1972, *The Rise And Fall Of Ziggy Stardust And The Spiders From Mars*, together with Roxy Music's eponymously titled debut, which came out a few weeks later that summer, did, for different reasons, bring 1960s rock culture to a close.

If Bowie was still essentially an excellent pop craftsman, then it was Roxy Music who were the avatars of change. The Roxy Music project might have had more virtuoso playing and have relied more, in part, on the 'difficult' time signatures of progressive rock music (particularly the work of Robert Fripp's King Crimson) than Bowie's *Ziggy*, but it also conveyed a more powerful sense of rupture with the past. The production by Pete Sinfield (King Crimson's original lyricist) is imaginative, though time-pressured, and the playing often decidedly unsure, but the result was, for 1972, something not of this world. Guided by singer Bryan Ferry and sound collagist Brian Eno, the group eschewed traditional rock structures almost completely, and yet largely abandoned the otiose trappings of prog-rock too. Their songs were synthesised edifices: Ferry's mannered vibrato warbled over a wash of electronically produced noise, while Andy MacKay's oboe usurped the role of soloist more often associated with the electric guitar.

Thematically, if not musically, there were similarities between Bowie and Roxy. Roxy Music's early songs such as 'For Your Pleasure' (1973), 'The Bogus Man' (1973) and 'In Every Dream Home A Heartache' (1973) dealt with the pliability of the psyche and the alienated spirit. The latter is perhaps one of the most frightening songs in pop history, as Ferry sings stranded in 'penthouse perfection' with a blow-up doll as his saviour, against a creepy synth line. The penthouse is transmogrified, giving the impression of being the site of some kinky sect. As a song, it is a perfect comment on the 1970s fascination with the surface, rootlessness and the emptiness that consumer society brings. The same year, Bowie's lovers in 'Drive-In Saturday' would have to relearn sex through watching videos, so detached have they become from 'real' emotion. This blast of icy nonemotion would have its disciples later in the decade (such as Gary Numan) and Marilyn Manson and Nine Inch Nail's graphic, cruel psycho-porn has its origins in the Ferry/Bowie artifice.

Roxy Music had a more obvious connection with the art-school tradition. Ferry had studied under pop-art guru Richard Hamilton in the 1960s at Newcastle University, while Brian Eno had attended Ipswich and Winchester art schools. 'I met for the first time other creative people who were, if you like, bohemian and unusual. They would be kind of the freak from each school! Richard Hamilton was still teaching there, so there was this amazing connection between him and figures like Duchamp, who was a friend of his,' says Ferry. Songs such as 'Virginia Plain', their first hit and one of the signature singles of the first half of the 1970s, spoke about a world in which the sights and sounds of art and advertising, experimental music and The Beach Boys collided in one glamorously sterile package. ' "Virginia Plain" was a collage of images,' says Ferry. 'I don't think I would have written that had I not been in the same place as Richard Hamilton. And later the title 'In Every Dream Home A Heartache' was inspired by Hamilton, too.'

Bowie and Roxy were both serious and contrived, pop and rock, jokey yet serious. Both Bowie and Ferry saw stage performance as drama and milked theatricality for all it was worth. Ferry made it an absolute prerequisite that his band looked good. 'Going back to my jazz days I'd go and see the Modern Jazz Quartet, and they'd all be in black tie, immaculately dressed, and that tradition I liked. When I went to see Otis Redding and the Stax Roadshow the presentation was very strong. And I said that Roxy would have to be like that as well. There was quite a bit of direction involved: "You wear this, you wear that." Not with Brian or Andy but the others, you had to help them out a bit.'

Like Bowie, Ferry and Roxy Music delighted in the artificial. There was nothing natural about Roxy Music, from Phil Manzanera's joke glitter glasses through to Eno's make-up and fake leopard-skin jumpsuit. Ferry's voice was also amazingly contrived, with a vibrato so unnatural and so mannered that it redefined the boundaries of the absurd. 'But we started to tone things down almost straight away after the first year,' recalls Ferry, 'after we saw The Sweet and Slade on the scene. I guess we were a bit snooty, because we thought our music was a lot deeper. Our music was not so much designed for the charts as for a thinking audience. We didn't see ourselves as part of a glam-rock movement at all,' adds Ferry. 'It's always very irritating when you see people lumped together when you don't really feel part of a scene. When we started playing I'm not sure how conscious we were of other people. We were conscious of Marc Bolan and Bowie but we thought we were very much doing our own thing. We felt we were providing a different musical theme than any of the other people. We didn't feel that our music was as commercial as what other people were doing. I was astounded when we had a hit record with "Virginia Plain", and a hit album.'

In seeing the beauty in the mundane, sterile objects of Americana and mass production, and elevating them to objects of art, Roxy Music were the first pop group to articulate what was in fact quite an old idea, first promulgated as far back as the early 1950s by the Independent group, a small coterie of arty British intellectuals who set up shop at the ICA in Dover Street, London. George Melly wrote that they possessed 'an exclusive fascination with the American dream. As you might expect, the working-class adolescents who "went ape" for Presley were naive and uncritical, whereas the intellectuals' enthusiasm for the subculture of billboards, Pin Ups and auto-styling implied a certain irony, and the wholehearted rejection of "good taste" in their assessment of pop imagery was in itself the attitude of the dandy in the Baudelairean sense.'

Roxy Music and Eno were actually the other side of the same coin. Bowie took from high art (such as a steal from Baudelaire, or a namecheck for Jean Genet) and used it in pop; Ferry and Eno took from 'un-artistic' popular culture and turned it into art – pop into art: art into pop. Whatever the spin, it made for a thrilling musical experience.

According to John Peel, Roxy Music seemed to come from nowhere. 'They were terrific because they were a proper band,' is how he put it in 1996. 'I went to see them at a place called, unbelievably, the Hobbit's Garden in Wimbledon, with Genesis. They were about the only band that came along at that time that didn't contain at least one member of a previously successful band, which was how the record industry would work then. Band A would break up and the constituent parts would go on to form bands B, C, D and E with varying degrees of success. That was the only way you would get signed to a record label. Roxy Music was about the only completely new band to appear in the first half of the 1970s.'

Many critics were initially highly sceptical of them and they criticised them for almost exactly the same reasons that they did Bowie. They were not proper rockers; their music and their attitudes were too arty and therefore fake. Roxy hadn't paid their dues in the form of years of hard slog on the club circuit. They had hatched out as fully formed butterflies without having to go through the grub stage. Tank-topped 'Whispering' Bob Harris, the *numero uno honcho* on BBC 2's prog-rock-era television show, *The Old Grey Whistle Test*, reportedly found Roxy Music's instant glitzy appeal and lack of good honest gigging pedigree so reprehensible that he prefaced their live performance by announcing his disapproval on air. Roxy Music were a manufactured marketing scam, and their high-cultural fashionableness further irritated the counterculturally-minded.

However, Roxy Music had the last laugh, of course, and eventually found themselves at Number 1 in the UK album charts late in 1973 with their third album, *Stranded*.

Roxy were the only serious rivals to Bowie in the period 1972 to 1975. Although the media hype was centred on Bowie's rivalry with Bolan, in actuality it was Roxy Music who were Bowie's direct competitors. A huge number of Roxy fans were Bowie fans, too. It's no surprise that in 1975 and 1976, when punk was breaking, many of the leading lights would declare for Bowie and Ferry, while trashing Rod and Elton.

In the heavily made-up, balding but long-haired feather-boa-wearing Brian Eno, Roxy Music had a man whose startling androgyny made even Bowie jealous, and Ferry, too. It was rumoured that one of the reasons Eno left the band was because Ferry was envious of his astonishing success with the ladies. Roxy Music possessed the ultimate in heterosexual gender-bending in Eno, while Ferry came on like a decadent 30s movie star, draping his videos with women whose legs were the longest in pop history. Each new album was housed in a cover even more brazen than the one before, an endless parade of female glamour, model after model. At the same time, the Roxy models looked so artificial that they may as well have been androids. They became the female equivalent of Kraftwerk's robots. Roxy, one of the cleverest bands in the business, perhaps recognised this, and the cover of their 1979 album, *Manifesto*, was populated by shop dummies.

Bowie and Roxy kept a deliberate, watchful distance in the glam-rock era. Roxy Music played with Bowie at the Croydon Greyhound in June 1972. 'He was on a roll at the time and we were just emerging. I think he asked for us to join him on tour. It was a very good audience for both turns,' says Ferry.

If with Roxy's first record we can see the beginnings of a definite rupture with the past, then conceptually, *Ziggy Stardust* is more important. The writer Jon Savage called Ziggy Stardust the 'first post-modern pop record', and it's easy to see what he's getting at. Bowie littered the songs with allusions to the real world of pop. The reference in 'Ziggy Stardust' to Jimi Hendrix is unmissable – 'He played it left hand, but made it too far' (Bowie himself, although a leftie, plays the guitar right-handed), the one to Bolan in 'Lady Stardust' a little more opaque but, according to Bowie, certainly intended ('People stared at the make-up on his face/Laughed at his long black hair, his animal grace'). This was an album by a (would-be) pop star, about a fictional pop star who may or may not have been merely a distillation of David Bowie himself. 'Star' – like 'Changes' before it – is another brazen declaration of intent: 'So inviting – so enticing to play the part/I could play the wild mutation as a rock and roll star/I could do with the money.' ('Star', 1972)

Bowie drew our attention to the fact that a person could play the part of a rock star before actually becoming one. This idea was taken up by many artists – from Kajagoogoo ('Ooh To Be Ah'), and Bros (whose first single was 'When Will I Be Famous') in the 1980s to Oasis in the 1990s – who wished themselves into the limelight with the opening salvo on their debut album ('Tonight, I'm a rock'n'roll star'). It was a strategy that worked, and Bowie started it. He also acted it out in real life.

Between the summer of 1972, when he finally broke into the UK Top 10 good and proper with 'Starman', and February 1974, when he brought the glam-rock phase to a close with 'Rebel Rebel', David Bowie was, in commercial terms, the biggest act in the UK, with eight Top 10 singles in eighteen months and four UK Top 5 albums (with three Number 1s). He was selling both albums and singles at a rate unknown since the heyday of The Beatles. In 1973, Bowie spent a total of a record 182 weeks on the album charts. In fact, Bowie, together with Elvis Presley, virtually kept RCA afloat in the UK in the first half of the decade. In terms of the singles market, Bowie, together with The Sweet, was again crucial to RCA. Between 1 September 1972 and 31 August 1973, RCA released 153 singles. Only fourteen made the Top 20, and half of these were from the 'big two'.

For some pundits, the huge UK success which Bowie had been preparing for was an inevitability. Bowie had been visible all through 1972, both on tour and recording no less than five sessions for BBC radio and one for *The Old Grey Whistle Test* in February, on which he sang the as-yet unreleased 'Five Years', as well as 'Queen Bitch' and 'Oh You Pretty Things' from *Hunky Dory* (although only the first two were broadcast at the time). The *Whistle Test* appearance in particular significantly raised Bowie's UK profile, and, by now a big live draw, the momentum became unstoppable. Producer Ken Scott, however, thinks very differently: 'I don't remember too much of a groundswell of support for Bowie before the sudden success of *Ziggy*. I remember sitting in the reception area of Trident Studios and Gus Dudgeon coming in and saying, "Congratulations!" I said, "What on?" And he said, "Well, *Ziggy Stardust* entered the charts this week at Number 7."

'Starman', the second RCA single, was released on 28 April 1972, although it took until the chart for the week ending 8 July for it to hit the Top 40. The band played it on ITV's *Lift Off* in front of a backdrop of huge gold stars, and on *Top of the Pops* on 5 July 1972. It was these two televison appearances in the early summer of 1972 that were crucial in making David Bowie a star.

Many fans date their conversion to all things Bowie to this *Top of The Pops* appearance. Lavishly plastered in make-up, his hair dyed a brilliant carrot-orange, and a lovingly limp arm draped round guitarist Mick Ronson's broad shoulders, a little piece of pop history was made. An event changed people's lives. Nobody had seen anything quite like it before, as two Bowie fans remember:

The most memorable part of that Thursday night was when David Bowie sang the line, 'I had to phone someone so I picked on you ooh ooh,' while at the same time pointing his index finger and rotating it in what I now describe as a 'camp manner'. It was as if Bowie actually singled me out . . . a chosen one . . . it was almost a religious experience!

I grew up in Huddersfield, which is a fairly nondescript place and, in common with most of my mates from school, we had all been big Bowie fans since the famous *Top of the Pops* 'Starman' appearance in 1972. Incidentally, this ought to be the subject for a book in itself.

And many a future rock star would be looking too. Ian McCulloch from Echo and the Bunnymen recalls:

As soon as I heard 'Starman' and saw him on Top of the Pops I was hooked. I seem to remember me being the first to say it, and then there was a host of other people saying how the *Top of The Pops* performance changed their lives. In 1972, I'd get girls on the bus saying to me, 'Eh la, have you got lippy on?' or 'Are you a boy or a girl?' Until he turned up it was a nightmare. All my mates at school would say, 'Did you see that bloke on *Top of the Pops*? He's a right faggot, him!' And I remember thinking, 'You pillocks', as they'd all be buying their Elton John albums, and *Yessongs* and all that crap. It made me feel cooler.

With people like me, it helped forge an identity and a perspective on things – helped us to walk in a different way, metaphorically, and to see things differently. And that's the major influence it had – as an inspiration in itself – to find yourself, not to clone yourself.

Gary Kemp, later to find international fame with Spandau Ballet, remembers:

I watched it at a friend's council flat. My reality was so far removed from this guy's place, that my journey from that moment on was to get there, and I think the same applies to most of my generation.

Marc Riley, formerly of the Fall, and now a radio broadcaster, also remembers the colossal shock of the very new:

I first saw Bowie performing 'Starman' on a kids' TV programme called *Lift Off*, presented by Ayshea Brough and an owl puppet called Ollie Beak. 15 June 1972, I believe. I'll never forget the moment my friendly little mate Ollie left the screen and on came this ... *thing* with his weird mates. I was absolutely gob-smacked. My gran was shouting insults at the TV (which she usually saved for Labour Party political broadcasts), and I just sat there agog. I was experiencing a life-changing moment. I know it sounds ridiculous, but it really did knock me for six. It was three weeks later when he popped up again on *Top of the Pops* . . . and for the second time in my life I was transfixed by a bloke in a quilted jump suit and red leather boxing boots! There's no doubt that Bowie's appearance on *Top of the Pops* was a pivotal moment in British musical history. Like the Sex Pistols at the Lesser Free Trade Hall in Manchester in '76, his performance lit the touchpaper for thousands of kids who up till then had struggled to find a catalyst for their lives.

It's hard to envisage today a scenario whereby one television appearance could have such a devastating impact. And, for some, the threat posed by Bowie was real. Bowie's gender-bending was a direct affront to straight society, a society which was still, in general, unwelcoming and intolerant of homosexuality. Hitherto, direct challenges to the heterosexual mainstream had been restricted to the world of theatre, to literature and the fine arts. But this was pop music! For all those parents none too keen on their sons and daughters hero-worshipping a man in make-up, Bowie was a truly subversive figure, as music journalist Chris Roberts recollects: 'Bowie and Bolan were the two for me who gave me a sense of otherness, a sense that there was some weird fantasy world outside the school classroom. They gave me a sense of magic and mystery. I had to persuade my dad to let me buy *Ziggy Stardust* and he insisted on coming to the shop with me. He was a bit dubious about the sexual imagery and he didn't want me absconding with some Moonie cult!' And this is no exaggeration. You had to be brave to be a Bowie fan: Ziggy Stardust scared the parent culture witless. Being a (male) Bowie fan meant that your schoolmates branded you a 'poof', too.

'Starman' itself was an excellent pop song. Just as 'Life On Mars?' cribbed 'My Way', so 'Starman', with its grand octave sweep from C to C, sounded rather similar to another great show tune – this time 'Over The Rainbow'. Bowie was adept at filling his songs with quite intentional nifty lifts from other songs. The baritone sax and flute instrumental line in the middle section of 'Moonage Daydream', which sounded almost Elizabethan, was in fact a deliberate attempt by Bowie to mimic the melody of an old Coasters song from the 1950s. Bowie, however, said he borrowed it from Hollywood Argyle's song 'Sure Know A Lot About Love' (1960).

As a character, Ziggy struck such a chord with people. Ziggy as star-child, as an alien visitation, was a sure-fire winner. He tapped into the public fascination with science fiction and fantasy. Films such as 2001: A Space Odyssey (1968), A Clockwork Orange (1971) and even Barbarella (1968), and television programmes such as Outer Limits, The Twilight Zone, Star Trek and Doctor Who, had positioned the two genres at the centre of popular culture. Ziggy therefore had the air of a cartoon, comic-strip figure. The Tomorrow People was actually directly inspired by Ziggy, after the show's creator, Roger Price, met Bowie on the set of the television show Lift Off With Ayshea. Bowie fan Mike Jones, lyricist with the band Latin Quarter and now an academic, was fascinated by the Ziggy character and Bowie's role-playing: 'What Bowie invented was a new cartoon figure, a semi-serious, almost human commentator on contemporary conditions, from an imagined universe (combining 'real' and 'imaginary' events, people, places), just like Superman, Batman or the Marvel comics.' In fact, Bowie's persona-switching finds its most obvious counterpart in the central role of the Doctor in Doctor Who, an alien Time Lord who is permitted thirteen regenerations throughout the entirety of his lifespan. As the swish Jon Pertwee was morphing into bog-eyed Scouser Tom Baker, Bowie himself was morphing from glam-rock androgene into dandified soulster, a new version of the same character. It's of little surprise that many Bowie fans are also fascinated by all things Gallifreyan. By one of those little twists of fate that are totally inconsequential yet somehow so appropriate, David Bowie shares his birthday with the actor who played the first Doctor Who, William Hartnell, born in 1908.

The *Ziggy* songs also constituted something of a modern-day secular morality story, the rise of a media-age Christ figure and his destruction by his acolytes (with 'Rock'n'Roll Suicide' as the crucifixion scene). The infectious and cocky 'Starman' was a deliberate attempt to compare pop hero-worship with religious fervour. A literal reading of 'Starman' ('There's a Starman waiting in the sky/He'd like to come and meet us but he thinks he'll blow our minds') merely suggests that Bowie is commenting on the Second Coming of Christ. In conflating orthodox Christianity with popular culture, however, Bowie's lyric takes on a second, more subversive, meaning. In 1966, John Lennon had famously (and accurately) told the media that The Beatles were bigger than Jesus. In *Tommy*, Pete Townshend had written about Tommy's 'disciples'. Now Bowie was completing the picture, highlighting the fact that the new gods were media fictions rather than the 'fables' of the gospels.

Although *Ziggy Stardust* has been regarded as a concept album, there is, in fact, no consistent plot development beyond an opener, which temporally places the events five years from the apocalypse, and an ending which wraps things up with a suicide. Indeed, Ken Scott reports that no narrative was ever discussed in the recording studio and that the songs themselves just fell together into a coherent whole over time. It now seems that the whole idea of the *Ziggy* album comprising a coherent storyline based round a fictional character was something Bowie developed in interviews well after the fact. Fans have, of course, also analysed every line for hidden meaning, and have tried to fit each song into a coherent whole. But in actuality, *Ziggy Stardust* was no concept album.

Read, however, as a critique or exposé of pop stardom, the album makes perfect sense. 'Star', for example, then becomes a shameless exercise in destroying the myth of art for art's sake, and reveals the grasping self-promotion that is at the centre of most popular music. 'Starman' loses its comic-book sci-fi trappings and becomes a statement about the Messianic nature of our rock idols. Bowie used *Ziggy Stardust* very cleverly to carry on the anti-rock ideology attack he'd begun on *Hunky Dory*. The main point of

Ziggy was to explode the myth of stardom in pop and show up the essential phoniness of the rock pose through posing as a rocker himself.

Ziggy Stardust formed something of a bridge between the 'rock' and 'pop' worlds of the early 1970s. The post-*Sgt Pepper* era had witnessed a widening gap between 'rock' (album-based, weighty and conceptual, performable live with 'great' virtuosity) and 'pop' (singles-based, frivolous and banal, contrived in the studio with production techniques overriding musical ability). What *Ziggy Stardust* presented was a thematically organised collection of pop songs that did not rely for its overall effect on high literary allusion (save, perhaps, Bowie's borrowing from Spanish poet Manuel Machado's *Chants Andalous*: 'Life is a cigarette/Cinder, ash, and fire/Some smoke it in a hurry/Others savour it').

Here was an album which was astute and weighty but which inhabited the pop world, too. Sure, Bowie appealed to the more intellectual types and the ex-hippies, but his records, like other glam-rock records, were also bought by a larger consumer base, those who had hitherto been into Tamla Motown or the pop of The Beatles and the Stones.

Perhaps the most curious thing about the album was that, although Bowie's own approach was a very English one, lyrically he created a pop world totally dominated by hip American jiving. As journalist Chris Brazier pointed out in 1976, Bowie appropriated the argot of rock'n'roll: 'The language on Ziggy was different because it was rock colloquialism with words like "cat", "jive", "blow our minds", "hey man", "wiped out" and "chick".' Perhaps the pivotal song in this respect is 'Five Years'. Lyrically, Bowie strikes a deliberately unstable register, depicting a world five years from Armageddon in terms of universals or stereotypes – the priest, the soldier, the policeman, etc. Bowie uses 'Cadillac' instead of 'car', 'cop' instead of 'policeman', 'bobby' or 'copper', 'news guy' instead of 'newsreader' and thus gives the lyric a slangy, American feel. Crucially, Bowie's society in crisis deals with minorities: a black (cast as the good guy), a gay (who is repulsed by the priest and not the object of society's repulsion for once), a woman (out of control, downtrodden) and a physically handicapped person ('I kiss you/You're beautiful/I want you to walk'). 'Five Years' has a radical edge which helps position Bowie as a speaker for the dispossessed.

* * *

In 1972, Bowie worked tirelessly to build up an impressive body of work, and was also in demand as a producer. Early in the year he had come to the aid of Mott The Hoople, Ian Hunter's good-time rock outfit, who were on the verge of splitting up after a run of unsuccessful albums and singles.

First off, Bowie gave them a tape of 'Suffragette City', but this was rejected by the band. Bowie was a songwriter with no real track record of producing hits, and Hunter and Co. had doubts about the song's chart potential. Undeterred, Bowie wrote 'All The Young Dudes' cross-legged on the floor of a room in Regent Street, London, with Hunter watching. An arrangement and backing track, with a Bowie guide vocal (phrased and pitched intentionally for Hunter's voice), was hastily recorded, at which point it was obvious to Hunter and the lads that they had a sure-fire hit. For his part, Bowie couldn't believe it when it dawned on him what he had done. Hitless himself for nigh on three years at the time (an eternity in the pop world) he'd just given away a song which constituted probably his best shot at becoming a star himself.

'All The Young Dudes' became to the glam era what 'All You Need Is Love' was to hippydom. As a summation of the preening narcissism of the times it was ideal, and never since has Bowie dressed a song in such obvious, deliberately anthemic garb. Lyrically it has everything – twenty-something suicide, inner-city alienation ('Is that concrete all around or is it in my head'), and a wearied swipe at the previous generation ('We never got off on that revolution stuff/What a drag, too many snags'). This was a hit single on a plate, and a gesture of astonishing largesse. The song reached Number 3 in the UK. Bowie performed it live with the band twice that year, too, in Guildford in the UK and at the Tower Theater, Philadelphia, in the States. Bowie also brought Mott into the MainMan stable, and produced their comeback album, *All The Young Dudes*.

However, as 1972 turned into 1973, Bowie and Defries began to lose interest in the group. Central to this was Bowie's offer of 'Drive-In Saturday', which he later recorded himself for the *Aladdin Sane* album. Hunter changed the arrangement and Bowie didn't like it. The single was, in the end, never put out under the Mott banner and, soon after, the band felt that they had been dropped from Bowie's circle. Hunter remains grateful for Bowie's help, but he always suspected that, having put something into a project with other artists, Bowie would always want something back from them in return at a later date. Whatever, Hunter was forced to come up with quality pop singles of his own, and this he duly did, most notably with the classy 'Roll Away The Stone', a big UK hit at the end of 1973, at the high point of the glam era when Roxy Music, Gary Glitter, Bowie, Wizzard, Slade, Elton John, Suzi Quatro and T.Rex were all in the Top 40.

Bowie also found time to help out two of his musical heroes: Lou Reed and Iggy Pop. Both were hugely fascinating to Bowie, and for almost identical reasons. They were more 'real' than Bowie ever could be. On stage, Lou Reed was horrendously forbidding, while Iggy Pop's bloodletting and physical and musical violence revealed the ecstatic core at the heart of pop. Bowie could not be either Reed or Pop: he was too distanced, detached and studied to be a 'real' rocker.

Perhaps surprisingly, Bowie befriended both Iggy and Reed. Lou Reed was Bowie's 'special guest' when The Spiders played the Royal Festival Hall in July 1972 in aid of Friends Of The Earth (all the proceeds went to the 'Save The Whale' fund). This was the first ever UK appearance of Lou Reed. That night, Reed and Bowie played together, belting out some old Velvet Underground standards. Reed was flattered by Bowie's obvious enthusiasm for his work at a time when Reed's profile in the UK was low. He also genuinely admired Bowie's songcraft, his ability with a melody and his intelligent theatricality.

A closer bond was formed between Bowie and Iggy. At first glance, this might seem one of the most bizarre team-ups in rock history, but far too much has been made of the contact Iggy and Bowie had in the early 1970s. They did not actually record or perform together during this period (in fact, Iggy And The Stooges played the UK just once, in 1972 in London that July). Iggy, more of a fringe figure than Lou Reed, and in an almost perpetual state of mental instability, needed MainMan's attention and money badly. However, to see Iggy as the Wild Man Of Borneo and Bowie as the cultured English dandy is a gross oversimplification. Along with Iggy's wrist-slashing and other self-abuse went a supremely intelligent mind.

Bowie and Iggy became close in the 1970s. In 1975, when Iggy voluntarily checked himself into a psychiatric hospital, Bowie was his only visitor, although he did, it has to be said, take in a load of drugs to help cheer Iggy up, when perhaps the traditional bunch of grapes would have done fine. In 1976 the two escaped to Berlin in an effort to try and kick their drug problems (unsuccessfully, by all accounts – Bowie would comment in *Q* magazine in 1993 that the drug intake on Iggy's 1977 tour was astronomic), and in the 1980s, when Bowie became a global rock superstar, he made a habit of covering Iggy songs to keep his friend solvent. The mid-80s' budding Franz Klammer version of Bowie even taught the Ig how to ski.

Iggy was a source of constant fascination to the aesthetic, cerebral Bowie. Here was a figure who appeared on stage like a demented tiger, stripped to the waist, mutilating himself with shards of glass, falling headlong into the audience, and showing off his penis when the mood took him (which was often enough). On stage as Ziggy, Bowie often exuded a haughty artiness. Iggy was animalistic, his movements showing a demonic spasticity, as if he was trying to get out of his body. His blood-letting is also part of the shamanistic tradition (self-mutilation was occasionally part of the witch-doctor's act), and parallels one of the characteristics of schizophrenics, who may slash their wrists, feeling themselves in some way 'unclean'.

So Bowie was also earning a reputation as something of a pop sister of mercy, bankrolling both Pop and Reed through MainMan and helping out on their comeback albums, although an (uncredited) mix of Iggy And The Stooges' *Raw Power* has been roundly criticised for its sterility (Iggy was to remix it in the 1990s). Bowie also produced arguably the finest album of Lou Reed's long and illustrious career, *Transformer*, and even wrote one of the album's lesser tracks, 'Wagon Wheel', although he went uncredited. Ken Scott, who worked on the album with Bowie, remembers that the sessions with Lou were very different from those with Bowie. Whereas, according to Scott, Bowie was totally clean during his time in the recording studio throughout their collaborations, Reed was 'out of his skull, permanently. He would come in and you'd know he was completely wrecked, and that was the way it would remain for the entire session. Once he understood what you were talking about he could actually deal with it. It was just that getting through in the first place was a little tough! He was in such a world of his own that it was difficult to tell what was going on in his brain. He wasn't a happy user, that's for sure.'

Not only was Scott having problems with Reed, but Reed was in a huge interpretative quandary over Ronson. Reed could hardly understand a word Ronno said; so alien to Lou was Ronno's Hull accent that Bowie had to act as interpreter.

Despite the lingo problems, musically the dialogue was just great. Almost every track on the album was a bull's-eye. 'Walk On The Wild Side', Reed's UK Top 10 hit in 1973, is a sleazy snapshot of the Warhol crowd, and, with its sassy rhythm and the unexpected and beautifully incongruous sax solo at the end, justifiably one of the most famous songs in pop. During rehearsals the drum part was played using sticks, but the end product was much too rocky for the song, so Scott suggested the use of brushes instead to give that smoky, sleazy, Manhattan nightclub vibe. The bass part, played on bass guitar and double bass, was Herbie Flowers' idea, and the sax part Bowie's. He thought a jazz saxophonist would be the perfect choice, called in his old sax tutor Ronnie Ross, and simply told him to solo over the final minute of the song on his baritone. But it's the bass line that marks out the song as a pop classic. Lou Reed:

> Session guitarist Herbie Flowers saw a way of making the bass line sound more interesting (which also meant he got paid more!) by double-tracking an electric bass-line a tenth higher. Arranged by Mick Ronson the bass-line is quite unique in that it provides its own melody as well as rhythm. This bass-line melody is played in a portmanteau style which also runs as a counter-melody to the vocal melody.

The lyric itself depicted the lives of the transsexuals and transvestites in the Warhol scene – Holly Woodlawn, Candy Darling and Jackie Curtis – whilst 'Joe' is Joe Dallesandro, a notorious hustler.

Given the graphic lyrical content (including, as it did, a line about oral sex) it was astonishing that the song was given needle time at all, although it is always possible that the suits at the BBC simply didn't know what 'giving head' actually meant. Initially bravely championed by BBC Radio 1's Johnny Walker, it eventually became a sizeable UK hit. In the more censorious USA of the early 1970s, the song was reduced to a series of bleeped-out naughty words, much to Reed's amusement.

Along with *Ziggy Stardust* and Bowie's next masterpiece, *Aladdin Sane*, *Transformer* defined the glam-rock era. The songs, the cover image by Mick Rock and the title itself brilliantly captured the changeling nature of the era. The album's opener,

'Vicious', is a stunning rock song, with its jokey put-down of the flower-power children. The brilliant 'Satellite Of Love', the second UK single off the album, ends in a fantastic vocal crescendo (Bowie's own 'Drive-In Saturday' would end in a very similar way – orgiastic, orgasmic). Remixed and reinvented as 'Satellite Of Love 04', it became a hit over thirty years after its original release. Duran Duran later covered 'Perfect Day' in 1995 on their covers album, *Thank You,* produced by Ken Scott himself, and the song ultimately became a UK Number 1 in 1997. The BBC originally chose 'Perfect Day' to showcase the myriad musical styles available on the Beeb; the song was eventually released as a charity single for *Children In Need,* on which Bowie appeared alongside Bono and various illuminati from the blues, pop, rock, classical and jazz worlds. Admired by some, it alarmed others who cringed at some of the interpretations and indeed at the very legitimatisation of Reed's song in the hands of 'proper' musicians.

After Mott, Iggy and Reed, fledgling pomp-rockers Queen approached Bowie to produce their second album, but his diary was already full to bursting. He was on the road for almost eighteen months in 1972 and 1973, and the reason was his truly revolutionary Ziggy Stardust stage show.

Ziggy made his first appearance at a pre-tour warm-up gig in Friars Aylesbury on 28 January 1972. The official tour opener was on 10 February at the Toby Jug in Tolworth. David Stopps, the owner of Friars, who had put on Bowie's last pre-Ziggy gig the previous September, saw the new, short-cropped Bowie premier one of his most powerful ever songs: 'I remember him doing "Rock'n'Roll Suicide", maybe for the first time. He shouted at the audience, "Gimme your hands, 'cos you're wonderful" and nobody got up. In those days they used to sit on the floor, and the stage was reasonably high, a good four feet high and somebody got up to give him their hands, but only half-heartedly. He sort of looked at the audience and the body language was, "Oh, you're useless." I remember thinking, Oh, that's a strong song, but nobody had heard it.' Unsurprisingly, the band suffered from first-night nerves. 'Woody Woodmansey was saying, "I'm not bloody wearing that!" ' remembers Bowie. 'There were certainly comments, a lot of nerves. Not about the music – I think the guys knew that we rocked. But they were worried about the look.

That's what I remember: how uncomfortable they felt with their stage clothes. But when they realised what it did for the birds ... The girls were going crazy for them, because they looked like nobody else. So within a couple of days it was, "I'm going to wear the red ones tonight." '

Six short months later, by the summer of 1972, Bowie had become one of the biggest acts of the decade. Although almost constantly on the road, he nevertheless found time for an astonishing trans-Atlantic dash to see one of his musical heroes. Presumably before his flying phobia had taken hold, on Friday, 9 June 1972 Bowie flew to see Elvis perform at Madison Square Garden. 'I had a gig on the Thursday night at the Polytechnic in Middlesbrough so I dashed down to London that night after the gig, got the plane early in the morning, just made the concert – I got in late to the concert and he was already doing "Proud Mary". I walked in in full Ziggy garb into Madison Square Garden to see Elvis. They nearly crucified me! I felt such a fool and I was way down at the front. I got incredible seats and I sat down there and he looked at me. And if looks could kill!! I just felt – Elvis is roasting me! I just hobbled down in my high-heeled shoes as fast as I could and got to my seat ... but, we nearly stopped the show.' Bowie goes on: 'Then I got up early the next morning and got the flight back to London and played the gig the next night. So I literally saw him between gigs. I absolutely had to see him before anything happened to him. He was pretty good at the time. He was still in great shape and it wasn't that long after the black-leather show that was on television.'

Whilst not at Elvis's level of fame, Bowie was nevertheless growing into something of a phenomenon, in the UK at least. A selection of the American press was flown in to Aylesbury at a cost of $25,000 to witness the Ziggy-era Bowie. Stopps again:

The gig on 15 July was used as a showcase for record company executives from all over the world. I remember doing a little history of the town and giving this out to these high-flying executives. That was an amazing gig, there was real hysteria. We had a hard time with security, too. It really was that intense. It was also quite clear at that point that it was breaking huge. I had put on a gig in Dunstable the previous month and Bowie was extremely good. I remember the fellatio with Ronson at that gig and I remember everyone being pretty shocked. It was breaking literally by the day and by the time 15 July came around there was great excitement in the air. Needless to say, the gig had sold out instantly.

Summer 1972 was a classic period. We sold the Bowie tickets at the previous week's Caravan gig and the queues went all the way down through the venue. All the tickets were sold at that one gig. It was very odd; Caravan came on to play to the back of the queue to some extent! The week after was David, the Saturday after that was Lou Reed, and the Saturday after that was Roxy Music. All three gigs were absolutely extraordinary. Lou came on with all this make-up and he was pretty out of his head. I spoke to him in the 80s about those gigs and he said 'Look, I'm really sorry, I don't remember anything about the 70s man, it's all just a complete haze. I'm sure I played the gigs you're talking about, but I have no memory at all.'

Playing generally to small or medium-sized halls, the Ziggy show was intimate. These relatively small venues were almost always packed out, and the audience reaction more often than not bordered on a hysteria not known since the mid-60s and Beatlemania. The days of embarrassing gaps in rock gigs when the bassist lights a fag, the lead singer gulps down a Jack Daniels and the roadie fixes the drum pedal were over, or at least rendered anachronistic by the likes of Bowie. This was rock as theatre, each move executed with precision, choreographed and perfectly lit.

From the end of January 1972 to the beginning of July 1973, Bowie and The Spiders were almost constantly on the road, playing medium-sized venues in Britain, America and Japan before an increasingly fanatical audience. There were several historic shows during this period. Among the most theatrical were undoubtedly Bowie's two sold-out performances at the Rainbow Theatre in London on 19 and 20 August 1972. Ever industrious, by night Bowie rehearsed these shows with the Lindsay Kemp mime troupe, and by day produced Lou Reed. Although Bowie's Ziggy performance was pretty remarkable, perhaps even more remarkable was the work of Jack Birkett, a dancer Bowie had worked with back in the 1960s. Although almost completely blind, Birkett was able to navigate his way round the stage by learning the lighting in rehearsal, a particularly risky business since rock lighting often went wrong during the actual show. Mercifully, Birkett carried it all off with aplomb and managed to stay on his feet, and on stage, despite several of his routines taking him to the very edge of the stage. Bowie and The Spiders performed a blazing set, while the Lindsay Kemp mime troupe added a further level of the bizarre, appearing as they did atop scaffolding erected on stage far above the singer, as well as on stage, at ground level.

Bowie really rubbed the critics' noses in it during one of the gigs when he wailed 'Somewhere, over the rainbow' during the mid-point of 'Starman', not only a little name-drop for the venue but also signalling gross inauthenticity and plagiarism. He was loving every minute of it.

In the audience at one of these concerts were Elton John and Bernie Taupin. Ken Scott vividly remembers the two leaving disgruntled halfway through Bowie's act. 'He's blown it now. He'll never mean anything any more!' raged Elton as he stormed off into the night. Too much mime and too little actual music of quality was, as far as Elton was concerned, a recipe for artistic disaster.

In 1972, Bowie replaced Dylan, in the UK at least, as the serious-minded rock critics' ideal of cool, and would retain the mantle of 'most important rock artist' until deposed by Prince in the mid-1980s. A crucial notice, which helped set this agenda, was printed during the summer of 1972, as Bowie's hold on the media began to tighten. Ray Coleman, writing in that bastion of serious-minded rock criticism, *Melody Maker*, pronounced, 'A Star Is Born':

> When a shooting star is heading for the peak, there is usually one concert at which it's possible to declare, 'That's it – he's made it.' For David Bowie, opportunity knocked loud and clear last Saturday at London's Royal Festival Hall – and he left the stage a true 1972-style pop giant, clutching flowers from a girl who ran up and hugged and kissed him while a throng of fans milled around the stage. It was an exhilarating sight.

Ziggy was, in part, a defence mechanism. It was less scary to play him on stage than be David Bowie.

Ziggy started out as an artistic conceit for himself as a writer and performer. Bowie intended to play Ziggy, not become him. 'I play my part right the way down the line,' Bowie told BBC's *Nationwide* in 1973. 'That's what "Bowie" is supposed to be all about.' Revealingly, by 1973, Bowie was referring to 'Bowie' as if it was a media creation like a fan enthusing about a pop star, not a real person talking about himself. 'Bowie' was an abstract, an idea, not a real person at all. Bowie, like Ziggy, was just another character for David Jones to play. The boundaries between all three were dissolving fast.

Bowie played around with audience expectations of identification and the correspondence between what was sung and what was felt. On stage, he attempted to present a composite rocker, a Frankenstein's monster, whom he directed. However, what started out as an artistic exercise for Bowie, the creation of a 'plastic' rocker who would live out his thrills vicariously on stage for him, soon collapsed into confusion for both the singer and his fans. Bowie's audience began to blend the real Bowie with his alter ego and began reading Bowie as Ziggy in reality. This tendency was encouraged by Bowie himself, who called his backing band The Spiders after their fictitious counterparts on vinyl. Bowie began extending the scope of the impersonation, as he later commented: 'I was a character when I performed all those albums ... and I carried the character into interviews, newspapers, on stage, off stage – whenever there was media around I had to keep those characters concrete. The fabric of my work is using my body, my personality as well as my songs and stage performance ... rather like a canvas.'

Embattled by the gruelling touring schedule MainMan had devised for him, and genuinely unsettled by his alarmingly quick rise to superstardom after almost a decade in the wilderness, Bowie, too, began confusing the character of Ziggy with his own. By the beginning of 1973, they had become one overwhelmingly powerful suprahybrid. David Jones now had not one, but two alter egos and, by the spring of 1973, had added a third – Aladdin Sane. Bowie was attaining rock-mythological status by becoming one huge aggregation of real and imagined personalities. As if releasing an alien virus, Bowie had set in train the idea of David Bowie – a one-man collective of media personae – changing form and content rapidly, shedding personalities like unwanted shards of skin and inhabiting different terrains of pop music and culture in the process.

For the next ten years, Bowie had an insatiable desire to change and be changed. In 1974, he commented: 'I don't know if I'm writing the characters or the characters are writing me.' By the mid-1970s, he was consumed by his fictional creations, his own personality having become fragmented and lost. Ziggy was indeed a monster: 'I fell for Ziggy, too. It was quite easy to become obsessed day and night with the character. I became Ziggy Stardust. David Bowie went totally out of the window.'

Bowie told Pete Frame in 1993: 'Now we started hitting real problems, because I enjoyed the character so much, and it was so much easier for me to live within the character, along with the help of some chemical substances at the time. It became easier and easier for me to blur the lines between reality and the blessed creature that I'd created – my doppelgänger. I wasn't getting rid of him at all; in fact, I was joining forces with him. The doppelgänger and myself were starting to become one and the same person. Then you start on this trail of psychological destruction and you become what's called a drug casualty at the end of it.'

By 1972/3, Angie was encouraging him to wear the same flamboyant clothes whether 'on' or 'off' duty. The Bowie/Ziggy/Aladdin Sane personalities had soon destroyed any vestiges of the 'real' David Jones. Despite this, however, these were not years of psychic terror for Bowie. His coke addiction had not yet started, nor was Bowie as terrifyingly thin as he would be in the States in 1974/5. The constant pressure of tour/album/tour/album was certainly crushing, but Bowie had not yet entered his own 'mindwarp pavilion'.

In 1987, Bowie commented, 'It's very hard to convince people that you can be quite different off stage in rock'n'roll than you are on stage. One of the principles in rock is that it's the person himself expressing what he really and truly feels – and that applies to a lot of artists. But to me it doesn't. It never did. I always saw it as a theatrical experience.'

When Ziggy sang 'Give me your hands, 'cos you're wonderful' in 'Rock'n'Roll Suicide', the words embodied not only the desperation and isolation felt by the rock star at the nadir of his career, but were also a critique of all those show-business platitudes uttered in concerts ('You were a really wonderful audience tonight').

If Ziggy confused both his creator and his audience, a big part of that confusion centred on the topic of sexuality. Bowie was first and foremost a taboo-breaker and a dabbler. He mined sexual intrigue for its ability to shock, and the Ziggy shows were as close to theatre as they were to rock. As one *NME* journalist wrote in 1973: 'Study still photos of his performance and unless there happens to be a guitar or a microphone in the picture, then it's not really obvious that the shot was taken at a rock show.'

Bowie moved with a languid grace on stage. Certain segments of the show were choreographed as mime sequences. 'Width Of A Circle' saw Bowie on tiptoes staring intently into the audience as if possessed, arching his arms like a bird in flight (a pose later appropriated by fellow Lindsay Kemp student, Kate Bush, for her 'Wuthering Heights' video). During Ronson's lengthy solo, Bowie performed a piece associated in the popular imagination with the French mime, Marcel Marceau, which involved running into an imaginary brick wall and feeling its contours and dimensions before finding a crack to squeeze through. The moment when Ziggy squeezed through, his fingers looking for release, was perfectly choreographed to the music.

Bowie's Ziggy Stardust character queered pop, challenged the machismo of cock rockers such as the Stones and Led Zeppelin, and helped to deconstruct the whole rock edifice. Cock rockers' musical skills were equated with their sexual prowess. Hendrix's hard-on is captured for all time in the form of a plaster cast. We've already seen how Iggy Pop was wont to direct his donger at the audience. The 'Miami dick flash' executed by The Doors' Jim Morrison managed to get him arrested, even though the member was, according to Ray Manzarek, only brought out for the briefest of appearances, and then only for the band's edification. Even when rock stars weren't actually flashing their willies, their music was doing it for them. The cock rocker pushes himself to extremes and indulges his animalistic appetites. Women are objects of both desire and abuse, to be dominated, manipulated and debased. Bowie positioned himself at a tangent to these constructs of masculinity. His public persona was not dominating or aggressive in any traditional 'masculine' sense. He was, as producer Ken Scott remembers, an absolutely pristine specimen: 'There was one time when I saw him being made up for a Russell Harty show in January 1973 and I remember looking at his reflection in the mirror and thinking, this is the most beautiful man I've ever seen. I don't remember him being camp at any time but he was beautiful. It comes from the bone structure, I think. It was beauty as opposed to handsomeness.'

Ziggy may have been suitably 'well hung' in the tradition of male rock machismo, but this was set against a whole range of non-macho attributes which rendered him less of a stud and more a sort of Eastern drag queen masquerading as a high priest/ priestess. This reflected Bowie's awareness of the fact that many of the ancient Eastern religions had transvestite elements in them. He defined himself in performance not as animalistic and raw but as an aesthete; a cerebral outsider debarred from strong feeling. His body – skimpy and angular – was the antithesis of cock-rock machismo. Bowie flaunted his physicality but replaced clichéd displays of masculinity with his own brand of homosexual leitmotifs. He used the guitar, such a powerful icon of male supremacy, as a phallic symbol, but a homosexual one. One of the most startling photographs in rock history, taken in 1972, shows Bowie grasping Mick Ronson's bum and fellating his lead guitar.

The interplay on stage between singer and guitarist, one of the key elements in a rock gig, was taken to new heights in the Ziggy shows. The two strutted back and forth across the stage, Ronson in make-up and glitter suit, preening and pushing, Bowie cocking his leg and flashing his arse (one Aladdin Sane garment actually had a little tail-piece at the back which acted like a flap). The interplay was, at times, even quite punky, as rock publicist and later (in the 90s) Bowie consultant Alan Edwards recollects: 'I remember him playing a gig at Worthing Town Hall in 1972. He got off stage and came into the admittedly small crowd on Mick Ronson's shoulders while continuing to sing. Ronson kept churning out the riffs despite being a long way from the stage. Very punky, in fact!'

While the media have concentrated on Bowie's friendship/ rivalry with Lou Reed and Iggy Pop, in terms of theatricality it was a progressive rocker who had more in common with Bowie: Peter Gabriel. Like Bowie, in the early 1970s Gabriel devised surreal stage costumes for his performances with the art-rock band, Genesis. If Bryan Ferry was Bowie's equal as art-rock agent provocateur, then Gabriel was, to many, Bowie's equal as a showman.

Gabriel infused the early Genesis shows with a theatricality as manifest as either Roxy Music's or Bowie's. He sought to give a literal visual interpretation of the song's narrative. During 'Willow Farm' (1972) Gabriel appeared as a daffodil; for 'Watcher Of The Skies' (1972) he wore a dark cloak and bat's wings; for

'Dancing With The Moonlit Knight' (1973) he was Britannia with trident and shield; and, most tellingly, for 'The Musical Box' (1971) he played the song's crumbling old man, fumbling at the microphone stand.

However, the closest equivalent to the spirit of Bowie's Ziggy-era performances came not from British pop but from American funk, most noticeably George Clinton's Funkadelic and Parliament. In his book *Extended Play*, John Corbett draws attention to the fact that three performers, Lee 'Scratch' Perry, Sun Ra and Clinton, have been fixated with space as a metaphor in their music and performances. Corbett writes, 'Within the distinctive worlds of reggae, jazz and funk, Lee Perry, Sun Ra and George Clinton have constructed worlds of their own, futuristic environs that subtly signify on the margins of black culture. These new discursive galaxies utilise a set of tropes and metaphors of space and alienation, linking their common diasporic African history to a notion of extraterrestriality. Ra worked with his free jazz big band, the Intergalactic Jet-Set Arkestra, and asked, "Have you heard the news from Neptune?" Perry helped invent "dub" reggae in his own Black Ark Studios and reminds us that "not all aliens come from outer space". In his spectacular mid-70s live concerts, funk-godfather Clinton staged an elaborate "mothership connection" and says, "Starchild here! Citizens of the universe: it ain't nothing but a party y'all!" '

So Bowie was certainly not alone in looking to the stars for inspiration. Right up to his death in 1993, Sun Ra claimed to have been born on Saturn. All three, like Bowie, used aliases and played around with stage personae. Perry was the Upsetter, Inspector Gadget, Pipecock Jackxon; Sun Ra the Ambassador to the Ambassador of the Omniverse or plain Herman Blount; George Clinton and various band members were Dr Funkenstein, Mr Wiggles, Starchild and Bumpnoxious Rumpofsteelskin.

But it was Clinton who was more obviously linked to, and perhaps indebted to, Bowie and glam rock. His mid-70s stage shows were outrageously tacky gatherings. His band was dressed in elaborately kitsch spacesuits, platforms and multicoloured hairdos, as spaceships landed and the sound of rocket-boosters thundered through the auditorium.

The main difference between Clinton and Bowie, however, is that Clinton sought to actively engage the audience. His music was about an extreme and elaborate form of consciousness, and a reciprocity with the audience. Bowie, on the other hand, for the most part acted like the audience was there to be played with, to be shocked. He exuded an otherness which connected with his audience in a manner completely unlike the communion of the rock spectacle. For Bowie, the rock gig was no house party.

By the summer of 1972, Bowie had finally achieved UK success. The *Ziggy Stardust* album rocketed into the charts and was to stay there for two years.

At that time, Bowie was fortunate enough to be able to count on the services of his own in-house photographer and promo maker, Mick Rock. Rock had studied modern languages at Cambridge then learned his trade at the London Film School. The first promo he made with Bowie was for 'Moonage Daydream', a collage of live footage shot on a 16mm camera in April 1972. Rock also cut the promo for Bowie's new single, the storming 'John, I'm Only Dancing', a song whose gender-bending proclivities are there for all to hear as the protagonist reassures his male lover that he's only flirting with a girl on the dance floor.

The promo was a study in cool: shots of a luring and pouting Ziggy were intercut with images of the Lindsay Kemp mime troupe from the Rainbow concerts. It wasn't ever played on *Top of the Pops*, though. Rumour has it is that the suits at the Beeb thought it substandard, with Bowie's poorly synched miming the main issue. Since the whole promo was produced for £200, his performance shot in two and a half hours, and David had to mime to a record player that was running very erratically, this maybe wasn't surprising. A film of butch, leather-clad motorcycle riders was substituted in its place, which, as Bowie writer Nicholas Pegg says, 'inadvertently ended up looking ten times more camp. The biker clip was later featured in a 1992 BBC compilation called the *Gay Rock'n'Roll Years*, to demonstrate how broadcasting attitudes have changed over the decades'. The single – a sort of glam rock meets rockabilly workout with the freakiest Ronson-dominated Gibson ending you could wish for – eventually reached Number 12 in October 1972.

By the end of 1972, Bowie had already built up a repertoire of lyrically provocative material, referencing a variety of 'taboo' and non-heterosexual preferences. 'Width Of A Circle' was almost sacrilegious in its depiction of God and the Devil in the throes of sexual desire. On *Hunky Dory*, 'The Bewlay Brothers' had alluded to the intimate nature of the relationship between the song's singer and the notional brother. *Ziggy Stardust* as an album was full of references to bisexuality ('I'm a mama papa comin' for you/I'm a space invader'), while songs such as 'Queen Bitch' and 'Suffragette City' had overtly bisexual narratives. 'John, I'm Only Dancing' was Bowie at his most blatant yet.

America and its lucrative market became increasingly the most overriding consideration in the promotion of David Bowie, at least in Tony Defries' mind. Bowie was not exactly unknown in the States, but then again he was hardly a household name, with the *Ziggy* album adrift in the lower reaches of the Billboard Top 100. Bowie himself must have been puzzled. After they had completed it, both Scott and Bowie thought the album, with its more up-front rock edge, would stiff in the UK but triumph in the States. But they were wrong. As a result, from the end of 1972 to the end of 1974, MainMan carried out an all-out assault on the US market. Ziggy was going to America.

5. KILLING THE KABUKI MONSTER, 1972–1974

I looked at the way Bowie presented himself in that whole 72–73 period and I just thought, and still do to this day, that it was the greatest rock'n'roll star image that there has ever been.

GARY NUMAN, 1998

The Elvis of the 70s

LILLIAN ROXON, NEW YORK NEWS, 1972, ON BOWIE LIVE

In the autumn of 1972, Bowie set sail for the States. Already the biggest pop star to have emerged in the UK during 1972, it was vital that the holy grail of American success came Bowie's way, to justify the hype, the promotional budgets, the intense media interest and the backing of American-based RCA records. Despite the fact that virtually all of Bowie's management and promotions entourage were American, and that many of them were deliberately drawn from the Warhol crowd of freaky avant-gardists, never before had a figure as confrontational as Bowie made it big in the States. That said, the Bowie contingent were on a high, full of hope, and sure that American success was just around the corner.

One aspect of British pop that had completely failed to grab the Americans' attention was its androgyny. In certain areas of America, you would be very likely to have a shotgun pointed at you if it was obvious that you were a 'faggot'. This is not to say that being gay in the UK is entirely stress-free. However, whereas Britain has had an arty wing of lipstick-glossed rockers since the

1970s, America has, despite the early intervention of Little Richard, been very late in developing the tradition, with The Smashing Pumpkins, Nine Inch Nails and, of course, Nirvana's Kurt Cobain pictured in a frock comparatively recent examples. The bottom-smacking foppishness of Brett Anderson and his band Suede in the 1990s earned them three Number 1 albums in Britain and a legion of admirers, but they were largely unbought by the mainstream American public.

It's usually only a certain type of act that can clean up the dollars. In the 1970s, Elton John's high musical values in the studio and showmanship on stage made him the biggest-selling British artist there, with Rod Stewart not far behind. The largely anonymous Mick Jones (of Foreigner, not The Clash, fame) sang his way to multi-dollar success, as did Fleetwood Mac, who were at least half-British. But the likes of art rockers Roxy Music went largely unloved. Bolan had had some limited success, but he was hardly a big star. Intensely competitive and driven, Bowie was determined to go one better.

Although only the fourth biggest market in terms of global sales (around a third as big as the States, and behind Japan and Germany), the UK was still big enough to make a rock star very rich indeed. In fact, as a territory, it was easily winnable, as long as the promotional strategy was right. This comprised Radio 1 or 2 airplay, several appearances on *Top of the Pops*, and widespread coverage in the press. Nevertheless, for real 'five homes and 25 limos' superstardom (and that's just for the manager), i.e. greedy superstardom, it was vital to conquer America.

In the States this three-pronged attack on radio, television and the press had to be deployed not once but in every single state. When Bowie played concerts in 1972 and 1973, the results were uneven. Like a presidential hopeful awaiting the outcome of the primaries, Bowie discovered that, while he was hot stuff in Philadelphia and New York, he was almost unheard of in most other areas. Shows were cancelled at the last moment because of poor ticket sales and on occasion, the Spiders took the stage to barely quarter-full arenas. But whilst Bowie found it tough going in the Midwest, the gigs in the areas that mattered – New York and LA amongst them – were a sell-out. And coverage in the media built and built as the tour progressed.

Nobody could say that the Bowie management team failed to pull out all the stops to get their man noticed. The campaign devised by Defries was massively costly, and carried off with barefaced cheek. Defries' strategy, although hackneyed now, was somewhat revolutionary back then. Its central tenet was simple. Bowie would be sold to the Americans as a de facto superstar. He would stay, as would the band, the MainMan support team, and the various hangers-on, in the most expensive hotels and with the most lavish of budgets. Like Ziggy, Bowie would act the star, even if his record sales suggested little actual public support.

Bowie, his band, and the whole MainMan entourage were placed by Defries in a wonderfully incongruous position. They may have dined on the most sumptuous food, drank champagne until it poured out of their ears, been flattered with flowers, and partaken of only the best drugs, but in reality all this was on credit. In every hotel they stayed in, they put everything down on their expense account to be settled by MainMan or RCA, while they were paid next to nothing in actual wages, at least initially. They had to eat in the hotel because they didn't have enough money for the taxi ride to the local McDonald's, let alone a few dollars to buy a hamburger. It was all part and parcel of Defries' big plan. MainMan's Tony Zanetta had this to say:

> RCA had agreed to certain kinds of support that got out of hand. They were willing to charge the hotels against royalties. The room service kind of crept in and since we didn't have any cash, we charged meals. We charged everything. We sat in the Beverly Hills Hotel for two weeks and ran up about $20,000 worth of room service. People didn't have money for taxis so we took limousines. It was total insanity.

Angie, however, was an unwanted distraction on tour. After causing a 'disturbance' in a hotel pool with one of her affairs late at night during a tour of the Southern states, she was packed off home. From that moment on, Angie was never an integral part of Bowie's touring regimen. She would, on occasion, drop in at Bowie's bidding, or when she was bored, but she was not welcome as a full-time member of the touring party. The cracks in the Bowie marriage were already beginning to show. Both were massively promiscuous, and when both started to parade their affairs in front of each other's noses (and then to make love to each other's friends), jealousy started to rot their 'open' relationship. Angie, convinced that Bowie and MainMan would make her a star, became increasingly disillusioned when the focus resolutely remained on her husband.

Despite generating a fortune for his record company and manager, the artist himself lived on advances, handouts and credit in rented accommodation in the UK, and hotels and apartments abroad. He lived the myth of being David Bowie, driven, almost maniacally, from album to tour to album by a cold, indomitable will.

Bowie's friends and workmates noticed him becoming more distant, and perhaps less friendly. Reminiscing in 2004, Bowie said that he felt 'displaced . . . out-of-sync, not in touch . . . There was a time when what I was doing . . . didn't seem to resemble anything anybody else was doing. I didn't understand what I was doing, but it just seemed out of touch with what everyone else was doing.' Trevor Bolder recalls that, whilst, at the beginning, the Spiders and Bowie travelled together, as Bowie got bigger, all this changed: 'We only saw him as we walked on stage. He separated himself from us towards the end, he was like a solo artist that didn't need us, while in the beginning, he definitely needed us.' He added, 'The bigger he got, the bigger his head got, and the less important you were to him. When he didn't need you, he'd discard you, but while he needed you, he was very friendly towards you.'

As Bowie himself became less connected, his success became more apparent. Many of his performances in America during late 1972 and early 1973 saw him really beginning to hit his stride as a singer and showman. The much-bootlegged and now officially released live set from the Santa Monica Civic Auditorium (broadcast on FM radio in October 1972) gives an indication of his increasing confidence as a performer. Newer songs such as 'The Jean Genie', which had been written on the tour bus, and 'Drive-In Saturday', premiered by Bowie at the Celebrity Theater, Phoenix, Arizona, on 4 November 1972, merely confirmed his pop sensibility. Bowie also played a number of covers from his American heroes, including Lou Reed's 'I'm Waiting For The Man' and 'White Light White Heat', and Chuck Berry's 'Round And Round', as well as a bold and daring reading of Jacques Brel's 'My Death'.

On some American shows, pianist Mike Garson fulfilled the dual role of performer and fan, unbeknown to the rest of the band. 'I didn't play every song in the set. They did about eighteen numbers, and I only played on around ten of them. So, when I wasn't playing, I went out into the audience and watched this guy! I'd be out in the audience having an absolute ball. That's the only way you'd see what the guy was really like.'

The architect of the US campaign, Tony Defries, has kept a low media profile since the 1970s. Few, if any, interviews and photographs survive from the days when he steered the Bowie juggernaut. If Angie was Bowie's 'authentically' bisexual other half, pressing him on to more and more sartorial outrage, Mick Ronson Bowie's musical foil, the translator of his ideas, and Ken Scott his George Martin, then Defries was his Colonel Tom Parker, a charismatic, behind-the-scenes fixer with no doubts that the artist he had on his books was the biggest since The Beatles.

Many people in the Bowie camp now remember Defries as a terrifying, Afro-permed, cigar-smoking behemoth of a character, utterly unbeatable when it came to business, but this fear is also mixed with backhanded admiration for his strategies and acumen. What was Defries really like? 'I think most people are too scared to say,' was Ken Scott's view in 1998. 'My personal opinion is that Defries was brilliant. He would be the perfect manager if he could work for someone other than himself; if he was not out all the time for himself. He knows exactly how far to bend the law. You will find lots of people he has pushed to one side and left. I was one of them.'

Dai Davies, a young, enthusiastic Welshman who went on to manage the new-wave group, The Stranglers, and was a leading promoter and manager on the new-wave scene, was brought in to do the advance pretour promotion for Bowie in the States:

He was a really good negotiator. He came into the music business without any preconceptions as to how it should work, and he had a different set of rules to traditional music people. The only thing that was wrong was that his mode of operation was so extravagant that it probably left Bowie bankrupt. There's only one way to get money and that's to take it off the record company in advances. The more expensive your campaigns, the longer you have to wait for any real royalties to come in.

His way of doing things was so flash that it ate up all the money. For instance, when we went to LA in 1972, we all stayed in the Beverly Hills Hotel, and that included the road crew. It was all done to create this aura of instant superstardom around Bowie, but it was funded by RCA and they exacted a price when the whole thing ran out of money. But it was a brilliant campaign. I really admired it, but I always had the nagging doubt that it was a far too expensive way of doing things. If you run up those kind of costs it puts the artist in a very vulnerable position.

Although he was obviously working on something for himself in the long term, it should be remembered that the 50 per cent of the overall money that was Defries' share was being ploughed straight back into Bowie's career. On tour in the States, they would often be paid by the promoter in cash, and Defries would have to take a few dollars out of the overall earnings for his petty cash, as he himself was broke.

Defries was still finding his way in the music business. However, nobody could say that he wasn't a quick learner. In the USA he could be found quizzing promoters on how to structure deals; once he got a handle on what was possible, there was no stopping him. The contracts he drew up for the Bowie live concerts were tough, exacting, and got the most for the artist. It is true to say that Defries tied Bowie to a very tight contract, one that was possibly very unfair, but it was with the long-term objective of making a ton of money for them both.

Looking back, Bowie is reluctant to give Defries any credit whatsoever for making him a star. 'I think it probably impeded the success of what I was trying to do,' he said in 2000. 'I think Ziggy Stardust would have been a monumental success without him. I think he was a very lucky man being there at the time.'

Bowie signed an employment agreement with MainMan management and production company in September 1972 that assigned to Defries a 'timeless' term of office as Bowie's manager. Under the terms of the agreement, Bowie was given a guaranteed allowance of £300. In return, he'd signed his life away. Mainman had exclusive rights to Bowie's person and image and could also 'fictionalise' the singer's biography for press purposes. In effect, MainMan could tell a pack of lies about Bowie and he would have no comeback.

In the light of this, Bowie's *Mirabelle* diaries from May 1973 to April 1975, which purportedly came hot from Bowie but were actually written by MainMan employee Cherry Vanilla, are just one manifestation of the willingness to play around with the truth.

Vanilla was the sexy, flamboyant actress and performer who was Bowie's PR at MainMan. That said, the overall picture provided by the diaries was a more or less accurate picture of Bowie's life at the time. They include stories of Bowie seeing a live Monty Python show, celebrating Christmas 1973 with Mick and Bianca Jagger, reporting the visitation of a ghost in his New York apartment, detailing Angie's attempt to get fit by joining a gym, and enthusing about plans for a Ziggy Stardust stage play. These monthly diaries can now be found in full on Paul Kinder's *Bowiewonderworld* website. Appearing to be a (slightly) fictional report of what the real David Bowie was doing, they make for intriguing reading and are a forerunner to the Bowie weblogs of the BowieNet era.

By late 1973, as Ken Scott recollects, Defries' influence over Bowie was all-encompassing. 'It was difficult to tell how much was David and how much was Defries. For example, I'd been recommended a book by Gus Dudgeon called *Stranger In A Strange Land*, by Robert Heinlein. One afternoon, David and Angie came round to my house. The book was lying around and David happened to see it. He started reading it and said, "You're reading this?" and I said, "Yeah." He said, "That's fuckin' amazin', I'm going to be starring in the movie of this!" I said, "No, get away," and he said, "Yeah." I told him it would suit him perfectly and we started talking about it. Cut to a month, maybe six weeks later, I happened to say to David, "What's happening about the film?" Bowie said, "Ah, well I'm not really doing it." I said, "Pardon?" and he replied, "Tony and I just devised that as a ploy. Tony didn't want to go to the trouble of asking for movie roles for me, so we just announced to the press that I was going to be starring in the movie, and the scripts have suddenly started pouring in." '

This little footnote is quite revealing, as it demonstrates the extent of Defries' control over Bowie. Scott is adamant that Bowie genuinely believed he was starring in the film, and covered this up by pretending he knew of Defries' wiles all along, so as not to appear duped. So, all the stories put out about Bowie starring in this film, recording with that singer, playing a gig in whatever country, which turned out to be false were very likely part of MainMan's misinformation campaign intended to keep Bowie in the papers during fallow periods or to drum up interest among potential financiers for actual projects.

It should be pointed out that the only crime Bowie was guilty of was believing Defries' hype. And believe it he did; at least initially. This was an era in which managers were supposed to wear big fuck-off coats, chew cigars, and basically frighten the shite out of absolutely everyone. Such people performed the function of making the star even more the star, of rendering even the simplest of requests from potential courtiers and suitors (the press, fellow collaborators) into a personal trauma. These were the days before most rock musicians took an interest in legal matters, or knew or even cared about their contractual duties and rights.

The MainMan days were possibly the most controversial of Bowie's career, involving as they did a hugely extravagant 'shagathon', with Bowie largely broke, and his wife Angie running up colossal debts in shoe shops and boutiques while desperately trying to cut it as an actress (she was later notably turned down for the lead in *Wonder Woman*). What is of particular interest is not so much the interpersonal politics, much discussed in Tony Zanetta and Harry Edwards' 1986 book *Stardust*, but the way in which Bowie was, in his own words, 'oversold'; how he was made into a huge Frankenstein's monster of a rock star in the USA, without a hit album to his name there.

Friend and photographer Mick Rock puts it like this:

The whole game was theatre. It was, like, David going to America with three bodyguards. When he got to America, yes, there was interest in certain areas, but if you went to the Midwest, you couldn't drag people off the streets to see him. It was part of the theatre to treat him like a star. And there I was; I came very cheap – in fact, I came for nothing! Not that Defries paid anyone very much for anything, including David. Defries could then start talking about David having 'an exclusive photographer'. People were saying, 'David Bowie's got an exclusive photographer. Who the fuck is David Bowie?' The people reasoned: 'If he's got an exclusive photographer and bodyguards, there must be something going on.' That was a piece of living theatre, if you like, part of the whole thing that Tony and David cooked up between them.

The whole MainMan operation had a wonderfully incongruous air to it. The US side were zany, druggy, promiscuous and into arty shock tactics, while the band and sections of the UK touring party were far more likely to go out for a beer than discuss make-up. Dai Davies:

> Zee [Tony Zanetta] was a terrific guy and very efficient. Leee (Black Childers) was a real character, and I really liked him, but he wasn't thorough or efficient, which you need to be as well as everything else. It was odd really because there were two contingents working on the tour. There were the gay, American, Warhol-type people such as Leee, Zee and Cherry Vanilla, and there was the British contingent, who were sort of down-to-earth, provincial types such as myself, Mick Ronson and the bodyguard, Stu. We were about as far removed from the Warhol contingent as you could imagine. After a gig we'd be looking to find a pool table and to drink loads of beer, while the Warhol/gay crowd would be looking for completely different types of pleasure! Bowie got on well with both sections. He had this kind of chameleon thing as you know; not exactly Zelig-like, he's too dominant for that, but he's a charming bloke who could get on with and adapt to those different types of people. In fact, he was great to work with.

'Defries made a fortune for himself. I've cursed him till the cows come home because it affected me personally, but that didn't stop his brilliance,' is Ken Scott's opinion. He continues:

> Bowie was completely stiffed by Defries and when something like that happens, you just pass it on, it's a fact of life. It's like any rock'n'roll band. They don't get sound checks when they're on the way up. The headliner never lets the opening act have a sound check. So what happens when what was the opening act becomes the headliner? They say, 'We never got sound checks, why should we do it for them?' And that's the way it goes. Bowie got completely stiffed by Defries and he passed it on to others. Bowie had to become tight to survive and he just kept it going because he certainly wasn't tight to start with. Bowie was broke! He was putting on these incredibly extravagant tours and he was paying for them completely out of his 50 per cent. It was completely unheard of! That's why the whole situation came about with The Spiders being paid so little money. Just a couple of weeks before they went on tour to Japan, I think it was, they said, 'OK, unless we get some more

money, we're not doing this tour.' That threatened David and more especially Defries. Then it started that they considered getting rid of the band. The only one they couldn't get rid of was Ronno, and Defries promised to make him a star like he had made David a star. So Ronno hung around. With disastrous results.

The result was indeed a miserable situation all round. Bowie was beside himself when he discovered that he was financing the tours, the promotional budget and almost everything else out of his cut. Ken Scott was unhappy because MainMan were habitually late on royalty payments – that is, if they paid them at all – and the band were pissed off at being paid the minimum Musicians' Union flat rate, even when Bowie was doing so well, in commercial terms, in the UK.

The personality of Bowie's band was changing rapidly. Bowie's new pianist, the avant-garde jazz maestro, Mike Garson, was a scientologist, and his proselytising efforts had converted Woody Woodmansey. The result was that, as Ken Scott puts it, 'No one wanted to sit next to Garson on the tour bus, not even other scientologists. It was all he would talk about.' Woody and Trevor became completely different people to deal with in the studio, and the whole Bowie entourage, according to one insider, was becoming considerably more weird than Bowie himself. A contrite Mike Garson says, 'I haven't been a scientologist since the early 80s. I think there's a lot of good knowledge in the subject, but I was into it pretty heavy and I was probably too fanatical. I probably owe some people apologies from that viewpoint because I was a little pushy. But it was coming from a good intention. I wanted to share what I knew and help people. But I'm not proud of that.'

This general unrest among the ranks came at a time when Bowie was called upon to deliver new product, the first album to be written from a position of fame. In many cases such albums (and in some cases the rest of the artist's career) are either a frightened excursion in water-treading, with the artist cowed into giving the punters more of what they know (the boring option and one preferred by artists too numerous to mention), or a confused melody of paranoia and unhappiness in an interesting gee-it's-hell-at-the-top-having-all-this-money sort of way. For his new album, Bowie chose the second option, but fashioned the paranoia of the superstar into a fantastically innovative record.

* * *

Aladdin Sane has always been regarded as Ziggy's slightly inferior companion piece. Written in the main on tour in the States during the latter part of 1972, and released in the April of the following year, it was very much 'Ziggy goes to America', an English stylisation of American sounds, ideas and images.

In an interview in the mid-1990s, Iggy Pop said that although the Ziggy-era Bowie had a great pop sensibility, his music lacked a 'groove':

> The real difference between us is that he doesn't have the groove that a band like The Stooges had. The hired-hand situation that he has always used doesn't give rise to that real groove thing. What he did have that was very strong was a sense of structure. Compare *Raw Power* and *Ziggy Stardust* and the structure of Bowie's album is wonderful. The groove on those records is Mickey Mouse but the structure is there. The Stooges had a lot of groove but no la-la-la choruses that will get 'em singing along on the radio. We had our own unique groove structure, an internal logic, if you will, but it wasn't commercial.

Aladdin Sane represented a definite step towards a harder, punchier sound. 'It was almost like a treading-water album,' Bowie would later say, 'But funnily enough, in retrospect, for me, it's the more successful album, because it's more informed about rock'n'roll than Ziggy was.'

While this is undoubtedly true, it is the album's sense of sonic daring which sets it apart from *Ziggy Stardust*.

He was extending himself,' Ken Scott remembers, 'and in doing so, trying to do the same thing with the audience, trying to extend them. It's like the journey from "Please Please Me" to "I Am The Walrus". The people who stay with an artist are those that grow and grow with the music and the artist has to make sure that he or she develops the music slowly enough so that the audience can grow with it. Bowie was very good at that. Eventually he did veer off in a direction that the public couldn't grasp with his Berlin work and it took some time for them to catch up. So you can extend too far for the general public. Even with *Aladdin Sane* he'd gone too far for some of his audience.'

The Aladdin Sane character itself was a schizoid amalgamation, and the music reflected this fracturing down. Ken Scott remembers that, at the time, Bowie's own personality was undergoing a series of quick-fire changes: 'Bowie was such that, when he changed, it was good for him to have everyone around him change, too. He was becoming a different person, and if he had the same people around him they always thought of him and acted with him the same way as he used to be. But he wasn't that person any more, so he couldn't have anything to remind him. The only constant at the time, apart from myself, was Ronno. They started off friendly, but not bosom pals, but they got much closer as time went on.'

Most of the *Aladdin Sane* album was written on the road during the autumn of 1972. Bowie himself was unsure of what direction to go in. 'I kind of knew that I had said all that I could say about Ziggy, and what I'd end up doing would be "Ziggy Part 2". I thought, well, you know, I'm very tempted to go further with this Ziggy thing only because it's so popular, but actually it's not really what I want to do ... as an interim measure I did this "Ziggy Goes To America".'

Speaking in 1993, Bowie told the BBC about the mythic quality America had at the time:

I think for any Englishman that goes to America for the first time they probably write some of their best stuff. I don't know how much of a culture shock it is now ... But I think for us back then, going to America was it. It used to blow us away. It was our language, but it was this other world, and for me, of course, wanting this other world, I just fell into it completely. Here was this alternative world that I'd been talking about, and it had all the violence, and all the strangeness and bizarreness, and it was really happening. It was real life and it wasn't just in my songs. Suddenly my songs didn't seem so out of place. All the situations that we were going through were duly noted down and all the remarks I had heard, real Americanisms that caught my ear. Just the look of certain places like Detroit really caught my imagination because it was such a rough city and it almost looked like the kind of place that I was writing about. I thought, 'Christ, these places really exist and people live in them!' I thought, 'I wonder if Kubrick has seen this town?' It makes his kind of world in *Clockwork Orange* look kind of pansy!

Aladdin Sane was recorded in New York and London in January 1973. 'The Jean Genie' had been recorded for single release the previous November and was remixed by Ken Scott for the album. 'It was done to be a big hit,' says Ken Scott. 'Yeah, it's cute, but it's not one of my favourites.'

The song was, of course, a homage of sorts, as Bowie reveals:

> 'The Jean Genie' was an ode to Iggy, I guess, or the 'Iggy-type' person – white trash, trailer-park kid thing – the closet intellectual who wouldn't want the world to know that he reads. I think it's a really good song and I actually enjoy playing it and singing it. It's one of the few that I can keep going back to. I guess it's because it is essentially rooted in straight old-fashioned blues. I mean, it's basically Muddy Waters' 'I'm A Man', isn't it?

The single became Bowie's biggest seller to date, peaking at Number 2 just after Christmas. And, to clear up one area of mild controversy amongst Bowie fans over the years, according to Bowie expert Kevin Cann, Bowie *definitely* performed the song on *Top of the Pops* in December 1972, although no footage of the performance is known to exist, and the BBC tape itself was wiped. 'Blockbuster', a song with an almost identical riff from fellow label-mates The Sweet, kept Bowie off the top spot. And in 2003, the electro-duo Goldfrapp updated the riff for their excellent 'Train' single, proving that old riffs never die.

For the single release, MainMan funded Bowie's first ever pop promo, which was filmed over two days in San Francisco. Jerry Slick, Grace Slick's first husband, was the cameraman for the shots of Bowie and the Spiders in the studio, and striking blonde Cyrinda Foxe, almost certainly the addressee of the song, was added to provide, as Rock says, 'some local colour':

> We shot Bowie and Cyrinda on the streets outside the Mars Hotel fairly early in the day. He played the Winterland that night – I remember Sylvester and his band were one of the support acts. I viewed the footage we had the next morning, and thought we didn't have enough stuff, but, of course, there was no more budget. Somehow I got some more dollars off Defries to rent an Arriflex camera, a silent one, and I went and shot all the live stuff myself the next night, because David did two nights at the Winterland. So, I filmed him singing 'The Jean Genie' that night, processed it overnight and, because there was

no time, edited it in one ten-hour rush. If you look at it now, there are no effects whatsoever, they're all cuts. But lots of the cuts were a matter of necessity because I had to chop it up a lot to keep everything in synch with his live performance, which was fairly close to the recorded version, as he'd only just recorded it. Necessity, as ever, is often the mother of interesting art, and it certainly was in this case.

Foxe was a famous scenester and star of Warhol's film *Bad*. 'When Bowie first stepped off the *QE2* arriving in New York City, the first thing he wanted to see was The New York Dolls and he came to the Mercer Arts Center,' wrote Sylvain Sylvain. 'Like an alien abduction, Billy (Doll) Murcia and Cyrinda Foxe vanished into Angie and David Bowie's suite at The Plaza Hotel, only to re-emerge several long nights and short days later. David Bowie was now in love with Cyrinda and Angie had a new lover, Billy Doll!' Foxe went on to marry first the New York Dolls' singer David Johansen, then Aerosmith's Steven Tyler. She died in 2002 of a brain tumour, aged just 51.

'Drive-In Saturday', the second single off the album, was vastly superior, and it and 'Rebel Rebel' are his finest glam-era singles. It's a 'futuristic nostalgia' song, the narrator in an imaginary future, looking back on events which have yet to happen. Bowie's future is one in which sex has to be relearned through watching old films. The music builds, through a sequence of step-by-step ascending and descending major chords (a Bowie trademark), to a cacophonous, orgiastic saxophonic ending.

'Time' is one of his most successful songs from any period – five minutes of wired perfection. In the middle section Bowie's heavy breathing, brought to the fore in the mix by Ken Scott, sets up a wonderfully overwrought tension to the melodrama. Snatches of Beethoven's Ninth (a piece then recently reworked by Walter Carlos for the *Clockwork Orange* soundtrack) played by Ronno are seamlessly incorporated as the music builds and builds with one of Bowie's trademark 'la la' endings (or 'lie lie' as in 'Starman' and the earlier, unreleased 'Miss Peculiar'), like a glam-rock Phil Spector symphony. In the 90s, Suede would source this sort of Bowiesque moment on tracks such as 'The Power' and 'The Beautiful Ones'. This was always one of Ken Scott's favourite Bowie tracks. Although as an album he preferred *Ziggy Stardust* because 'I love the road that one travels on *Ziggy* from beginning to end,' Scott concedes that there are 'better tracks on other albums'. The heavy-breathing section in the middle of the song was deliberately brought up in the mix by Scott after recording. 'He never came to the mixing sessions,' remembers Scott. 'It was always just me. So it would have been on there and I would have chosen to have pushed it up that bit louder.'

The beautiful ballad, 'Lady Grinning Soul', is, for Bowie, unusually sensual. Its direct, intimate appeal and lush mix, with twelve-string guitar and almost Latino piano part, provide an unusually emotional and sexual ambience. It was recorded back at Trident Studios in London and, again unusually, was one of the very few occasions when Bowie got involved with mixing during his time with Ken Scott. The song obviously meant a lot to Bowie at the time, but it's a largely forgotten gem, and certainly one of his least discussed songs.

The pivotal song on the album, though, is the title track, the clearest indicator of how Bowie was trying to free himself from the confines of rock. Much of its nerve-shattering power comes from a two-minute solo by pianist Mick Garson. Garson had come to Bowie's attention through his work on an album by avant-garde singer Annette Peacock, and she recommended Garson to Bowie's people. 'Tony Defries called and said, "Would you audition for a rock musician called David Bowie," ' recalls Garson, 'and I said, "Who's he?" I was giving piano lessons at the time, and I had one of my pupils baby-sit for me while I went for the audition. I went to RCA and there was Mick and David. I auditioned on "Changes". I played on about ten bars, and Mick said, "That's it." I said, "What do you mean? I haven't even started!" And he said, "You're the guy." I think the audition was twenty-five seconds!'

Garson was on board and he would remain with Bowie for the next three years. Bowie was becoming jaded with pop/rock and, in Garson, he saw a talented, eccentric musician who he could learn from. It is no surprise that Bowie's experimental phase started with *Aladdin Sane*. Born in 1945, Garson had been both on the fringes of the New York avant-garde jazz scene and the rock scene. In terms of the overall development of pop circa 1972/73, having an out-there jazz keyboard player on a pop album was nothing short of revolutionary.

Garson's allure for Bowie was profound. He represented a world way away from most rock music, a world of abstraction, improvisation and extreme peculiarity. Some of the best moments on any David Bowie album have come from Garson. 'I view myself as a window in this man's career; a small one, but a powerful one,' said Garson in 1999. 'Every time I'm not with Bowie I'm back in the jazz and classical world or a combination of both. I know that a great artist such as David – and you're probably really talking genius and I don't use that word loosely – they have the ability when you're in their space to absorb telepathically what you're about. When he got in my space, he absorbed a part of me. It's almost like spiritual vampirism, but in a good way! He's been able to run with it for twenty-five years. Bowie saw my abilities and my talents and knew how to filter them through into his music.'

According to Ken Scott, the addition of Garson was a crucial final piece in the *Aladdin Sane* jigsaw:

All our ears and minds had changed, and we were looking for different things. The drum sound was much more live than it had been before. With David's arrangements – he threw a lot more in than he did in *Ziggy*. And then there was the addition of Mike Garson. There had been acoustic piano before, which Ronno or Bowie had done, but they're not the greatest keyboard players in the world, and Mike made a big difference. On *Ziggy* it was all very sparse – there had been two bits of synth, that was it. Now on *Aladdin Sane* there were a lot more keyboards, mellotrons, a Moog synthesizer, as well as acoustic piano.

According to Garson, Ken Scott was the producer who got the best piano sound out of any of his performances for Bowie. And it's undisputable that Garson is truly inspired on *Aladdin Sane*. His improvised solo on the title track is a landmark recording. Speaking in 1999, Garson said:

I came into the studio and Mick Ronson was there and Ken Scott was there. When that track came up, I tried a blues thing and David said no, and then I tried a Latin thing and he said no. He complimented me on both of them and he said, 'I'm looking for something else. Remember when we were driving in the limo in the States a few months ago?' I had given him a whole synopsis of the avant-garde jazz scene in the 60s which I was somewhat part of. I was definitely playing in a lot of wild styles that were ahead of their time, and David was fascinated. When I was playing this stuff, there might be three people in the audience in a club or a concert hall where I was playing this music. But he was able to see how it could be made commercial. So he said, 'Play that sort of music that you were describing that you used to do on the jazz scene.' So I played that solo on the phenomenal Beckstein piano that they had at Trident, one shot, and that was it – never changed a note, never edited.

I've had more communication in the last twenty-six years about that one solo than the eleven solo albums I've done on my own, the six that I've done with another group that I'm a co-leader of, hundreds of pieces I've done with other people and the three thousand pieces of music I've written to date. I don't think there's been a week in those twenty-six years that has gone by without someone, somewhere, asking me about it!

Garson was also the star of three other tracks on *Aladdin Sane*. 'For "Time" I used the old stride piano style from the 20s and I mixed it up with avant-garde jazz styles, plus it had the element of show music, plus it was very European,' says Garson. 'For "Lady Grinning Soul", my playing is about as romantic as it gets and as beautiful as I could play the piano in that style. It's French with a little Franz Liszt thrown in there. And for "Let's Spend The Night Together", I was pretty much on the fringe there, just banging away!'

Another track, the opener 'Watch That Man', has baffled fans for close on three decades. The question on most people's lips has been a simple one: 'where the hell is David Bowie?' Buried beneath a wall of glam-rock freak-out, the lyric is almost inaudible. However, the truth can now come out. Ken Scott:

'Watch That Man' was very much a Stones-sounding thing, with the vocal used as an instrument rather than as a lead. When it came to mixing the track, to get the sort of power of it, I just put everything up front, which meant losing the vocal. So I did the mix the way I felt. When we delivered the tapes of the album, I heard from MainMan, 'Great, but can we get another mix on "Watch That Man" with the vocal more upfront so we can hear a bit more of David?' So I said, 'Fine,' and did the mix with David more upfront. The problem though is that with the vocal more up front, the other instruments have to drop back. Then, a couple of weeks later, I get a phone call from RCA, and they said, 'You were right in the first place. We'll go with the original.'

As with *Ziggy Stardust*, the cover shot for the album was as stylish as its contents. The album cover, a head-and-shoulder shot of Bowie with hair dyed reddish-orange and a painted thunderbolt splitting his face in two, is one of the most eye-catching and alarming ever made. The divine thunderbolt hinted at Bowie's continued fascination with the deification of pop idols. It split the face, and by implication the psyche, in two. Bowie didn't look like anything resembling a human being at all. The shot turned his physiognomy into a sort of tribal death mask, a shaman for the 1970s. When the album hit the shops in the spring of 1973, the cover was as startling as rock covers ever got.

Aladdin Sane well and truly established Bowie as a major-league pop star, in the UK at least. On its release in April 1973, it debuted at the top of the UK charts. RCA claimed advance orders of over 100,000 – the highest figure since the heyday of The Beatles over five years previously. The album was Number 1 for five weeks. Bowie also had a string of UK hit singles under his belt, with 'Starman', 'John, I'm Only Dancing', 'The Jean Genie', 'Drive-In Saturday' and the two-year-old 'Life On Mars?' released as a single to coincide with the summer UK tour (with typical perversity, just as the single hit the UK Top 3, Bowie dropped it from the set). For the promo made at a West London studio that June, Bowie again used Mick Rock. 'I wanted to do something that looked a little like a painting,' said Rock in 1998. He succeeded. It was eerie, garish and strangely beautiful, showing a kabuki monster encased incongruously in a suit and framed against a totally white backdrop.

Looking back at the Bowie of that era – a war-painted, sex-change harlequin with a fast-growing repertoire of songs about galactic apocalypses, suicides and 'try-sexuality' – one might reasonably wonder how on earth he became the biggest mainstream commercial success of 1973. In fact, it is not so difficult to work out why. Musically, Bowie had a lockerful of soaring, catchy melodies conventional enough for your mum or dad to whistle along to. Perhaps more importantly, his work was also at the very core of English pop sensibility. It was a reincarnation for the pop world of the British love of theatricality and make-up.

As the *Ziggy* tour morphed into the *Aladdin Sane* tour in early 1973, the shows became even more ambitious. An extract from a review by *Rolling Stone* journalist Stephen Davies of Bowie's 1973 Valentine's Day concert at the Radio City Music Hall gives an idea of their structure:

> The giant auditorium was filled with Walter Carlos' recorded cybernetic music from *A Clockwork Orange* as several layers of curtains parted to reveal a giant screen, on which was projected an animated film of the cosmos rushing at light-year speed at the viewer. A single spotlight opened up on a set of large concentric spheres welded on to a cage and suspended 50 feet above the floor of the stage, in the middle of which was standing a sternly staring Bowie, clad in a black silver garment, the first of what would be five different costume changes that night. It was a truly amazing sight . . .
>
> At times Bowie acted out his role as a straight pop singer, a sort of hyperthyroid Anthony Newley; at others he would change into a progressively more skimpy costume and whip his arse around, a campy gamine leg-throw here, a cute barefoot pirouette there. Those songs dealing with Bowie's starkly paranoid themes of rock-star death, impending planetary doom and up-and-coming suicide were treated as little theater pieces, playlets recited and acted rather than sung and played.

By the middle of 1973, Bowie had been on the road, almost nonstop, for eighteen months, in a punishing schedule that included six British tours, two American tours and a tour of Japan – more than 170 gigs in all. The Japanese tour was also a huge success. At the start of the tour, Bowie was a virtual unknown with negligible record sales; by the end, it was mass hysteria at the concerts. Japan was also one of the last times the Bowie family would be together on the road. There was a brief, though ultimately short-lived, rapprochement between Mr and Mrs Bowie, and Zowie came along, too. Zowie was now nearly two, with long, golden locks and his mum's features. He would play backstage with the toddler daughter of Bowie's costume designer, Kansai Yamamoto.

After the Japanese gigs, there was a large gap before the next gig, at London's Earls Court. His fear of flying meant that Bowie decided to return to Europe on the Trans-Siberian express. Bowie and his mate and singer on the tour, Geoff MacCormack, travelled 'soft class', which meant that they were lucky enough to have a bed. Bowie would sit for days in his kimono, drink cheap Riesling and play songs on his acoustic guitar for the waitresses who would serve him tea. Wolves chased the train as it ambled through Siberia. Bowie did decide to get dressed for the May Day celebrations in Red Square, Moscow and filmed proceedings with his video camera.

As the summer drew closer Bowie was nearing exhaustion, despite the onset of what the tabloid media had dubbed 'Bowiemania', a level of hysteria not witnessed since the Fab Four in the mid-1960s. Bowie had gone mainstream with a vengeance with profiles on BBC's *Nationwide*, massive exposure on Radio 1, and avid interest from the tabloids and the rock press. However, on 12 May, The Spiders played a thoroughly dispirited gig at Earls Court. The ambience was zero, the acoustics appalling because the PA was too small for the venue, and it was all but impossible to see the stage itself. It was one of the first times that Earls Court had been used for a rock concert, and the stage was also too low and fans couldn't even see it properly. There were punch-ups and major disgruntlement amongst the fans, and ensuing bad press in the rock inkies. It was one of the few real failures of the Ziggy/Aladdin Sane era. But no one could have expected Bowie's next move.

'Not only is it the last show of the tour, but it's the last show that we'll ever do . . . Bye bye. We love you.'

Bowie's retirement announcement from the stage of the Hammersmith Odeon, immortalised in that rather grainy DA Pennebaker film, left his fans in a state of complete disbelief. Bowie, just eighteen months into his fame, was bowing out for good. Little did we know that this was not the end of the story but simply the conclusion of one chapter in Bowie's career: Ziggy and glam rock were over.

The show itself defined post-hippy bacchanalian excess. One 'disgusted' fan wrote to the *Sun* to complain that people were copulating at the back of the stalls. Pennebaker's film depicts row after row of delirious teenagers, mostly female, writhing to the music, hands outstretched, enchanted. As a historical event, the Hammersmith gig has attained a mythic dimension. In the same way that almost every right-on journalist and would-be rock star claimed to have seen The Sex Pistols on their 'Anarchy In The UK' tour, so there must have been a Wembley-Stadium-sized multitude packed into the 2,500-seater venue that night. It wasn't the best gig The Spiders ever played, but it was their last, and it marked the end of an era. Although concealed from The Spiders until the night of the show, Bowie's announcement was in fact carefully leaked to the press beforehand. Charles Shaar Murray, wunderkind at the *NME*, was tipped off days before the event, and *NME* had the 'Bowie Quits' cover story ready to roll within hours of the abdication from the throne of glam.

'I heard all those stories of what was going on in the audience and I tend to believe them,' says pianist Mike Garson, 'because I remember seeing crazy stuff at Carnegie Hall earlier on the tour. I looked out in the audience and I saw rows of David Bowies, girls and boys. I don't know which was the real David Bowie, it was like a freak show. The Hammersmith gig itself was phenomenal. I was pissed off though because Tony Defries had come over and made me sign something before the show. I think I made $52 from that performance, the soundtrack album and the rights of the movie and that didn't seem fair! What people don't know about that gig is that I opened the show on solo piano. David asked me to be his opening act. So, for just fifteen minutes I took some of his hits, "Changes", "Life On Mars?" and "Ziggy", and made a medley for the gig. I came out to do the spot and I was scared to death. So was Bowie. He told me backstage that he was more frightened for me that night than for him!'

The show was famous also for the appearance of guitar hero Jeff Beck on an encore and, of course, for Bowie's final song, 'Rock'n'Roll Suicide', prefigured with the on-stage declaration that this would be 'the last show we'll ever do'. After the gig, Bowie threw a huge 'retirement' do, with Mick Jagger, Lou Reed, Ringo Starr, Barbra Streisand and Lulu all in attendance. The concert was a definite turning point for Bowie. He was shedding another skin that night at Hammersmith, throwing off glam rock and paving the way for a new, bolder era of experimentation. It was a rite of passage.

But why retire at the height of your fame? The answer lies in a combination of Bowie's low boredom threshold and, more importantly, his tour weariness. Bowie was genuinely exhausted after eighteen months' gigging. Just as Ziggy bit the dust at the end of the album, so Bowie used the Hammersmith Odeon show to fuel the myth and 'retire' in actuality. Since neither he nor his audience was sure whether it was David Bowie or Ziggy Stardust up there on stage, Bowie's fans assumed Bowie's retirement was the end of his, Bowie's, career, not simply that of his alter ego.

As we have already seen, there's also a good deal of revisionism going on with regard to the Ziggy myth, and quite a bit of it originated from Bowie himself in interviews. Bowie talked a lot about Ziggy, and his role playing, after the retirement, not so much about role playing during the glam-rock period itself. All the talk of masks, personae and alter egos came later, particularly around late 1974 and early 1975 when Bowie was in the USA and looking back on what he'd done, and how he'd done it. When Bowie 'retired' that night, his audience thought it was the end of Bowie as a performer. Angie Bowie, for her part, didn't believe a word of it and never thought her husband's musical career was at an end.

There were also strictly commercial reasons behind the decision to bow out. It was better to follow that age-old (and generally sound) showbiz maxim to 'leave 'em wanting more'. Frank Sinatra was forever playing goodbye concerts, and the hype surrounding these valedictory performances ensured huge hits at the box office. Another factor was the growing sense of mutiny among the ranks. Despite the sell-out tours, the Top 3 albums, singles, and all the media attention, The Spiders were still receiving almost the same measly wage they had been on when Ziggy was an unknown. When they discovered the fee Garson was commanding as a newcomer to the band, they understandably felt very aggrieved. Woody was soon to be married, and Trevor had a wife and family to support. Just before the Japanese tour, the band revolted and sent word to Defries that they were withdrawing their services forthwith. Eventually a compromise was reached, but Bowie felt threatened by the affair. It was obvious that The Spiders, having provided such a hardworking and electric backing for Bowie, would no longer be content with being sidelined financially.

Ronson had become something of a huge live draw in his own right on the Bowie tours, and had his own fan base. With Bowie exhausted and off the road, in the second half of 1973 Defries turned his attention from Batman to Robin. He genuinely liked Ronson, and was also genuine in his appreciation of the Yorkshireman's talents. So began the process of grooming Ronson for solo superstardom. Briefly, Bowie, worn down by the constant touring, was peeved at the prospect of his sideman taking centre stage, although his annoyance wasn't so much directed at Ronno but at the nature of the situation in which one rock star was being launched on the back of another's (Bowie's) initial success. Privately Bowie may have thought that he was the *main* man in MainMan, and was somewhat taken aback when he saw Defries putting quite a lot of effort into Ronson's career.

None of The Spiders took particularly well to the craziness of the rock'n'roll lifestyle, unlike Bowie himself, who revelled in all the attention. Indeed, band members, particularly Ronno, were fazed by the adulation and the sexual chaos. As working-class lads from Hull, their idea of a good time was a packet of crisps and a pint, not three-in-a-bed sex and a discussion about Genet and Isherwood over the post-coital fag. Ronson was pleased to get the girls, however, and used to take a certain vicarious delight in the fan mail which started to pour in for him alone. But on one particular occasion, he was not altogether happy with the attention. Ken Scott: 'Ronno was reading some fan mail to David and me. The letter was all about this person, and what this person wanted to do to Ronno in a sexual way. Ronno was loving it, he was totally getting off on it, but by the time he reached the end of the letter it turned out that it was from a guy. Well, Ronno completely freaked out, saying, "Oh, that's disgusting, that is – eurch!" David and I thought it was hysterical, though, as we had both suspected that it was from a bloke. It was suddenly very dirty for him, whereas before he'd been getting turned on by it. But that was the kind of thing you had to expect in the Bowie camp, because that kind of situation was being pushed and pushed.'

Finally, and most tellingly, Bowie was tired of the sort of music he was making with The Spiders. Despite all the hyperbolic copy from journalists about his calculating nature, it seems that what actually drives Bowie more than anything is not so much premeditated attempts to colonise markets, but a real hunger for musical experimentation. On *Aladdin Sane*, Bowie had already begun, with Garson's jazzy piano, to break free from the standard pop/rock format. Songs such as 'Panic In Detroit' hinted at a more obvious R&B/soul future. Bowie was, and still is, into all sorts of music, and by the middle of 1973 it was simply time for a change.

Aladdin Sane had seen him move away from conventional pop, and his next planned project, an adaptation of George Orwell's tale of totalitarian terror, *1984*, would enable him to broaden the base of his music even further. Bowie wanted to move into more serious intellectual territory outside of the band format.

First, though, there was a record company to appease. Bowie was now at a commercial peak. In the week beginning 23 July, five of his six albums were in the Top 40, three of them in the Top 15, an unprecedented feat for a solo artist. His next record, *Pin Ups*, a collection of covers from the 1964–67 London club scene, was something of a stopgap. Bowie had always enjoyed covering the work of others but had previously been dissuaded by his publishers from recording and releasing too many covers, as they wanted to earn money from his self-penned songs. Certain that the next project did not need The Spiders, he was unsure of how to break the news that not only were they out of the picture as a live backing band but that studio projects would not concern them either. Woody had already left (or been fired, according to another version of events), and although Ronson was asked to take part in the sessions for the new record, Trevor Bolder was only brought in as a last-minte replacement when the first choice, Jack Bruce, turned out to be unavailable.

Bowie had made it a rule to include one cover version on each of his albums, so, conversely, on this all-covers album he intended to include one self-penned song. Ken Scott remembers Bowie telling him it was to be an old Bowie track, 'The London Boys', but the track was never rerecorded, or at least not during these sessions.

Studio time had been booked at the Chateau d'Hérouville outside Paris long before the Hammersmith gig, another indication that the 'retirement' was just another piece of artifice. There was a definite atmosphere during those sessions. Ken Scott had been informed by his management company, formed with the owners of Trident Studios in London, not to do any work on the album as Defries had once again defaulted on royalty payments. He was also told in no uncertain terms not to work on a sideline Bowie had scheduled to take place during the *Pin Ups* sessions. Showing his talent for bizarrely incongruous mismatches, he had decided to record with the pint-sized but perfectly formed Scottish belter, Lulu. Lulu had been seriously hitless for more than a wee while (in fact, since 1969, when she was advocating the joys of 'Boom Bang-A-Bang'), and her career had slipped into the variety twilight zone of guest slots on the *Morecambe and Wise Show* and suchlike. To their credit, Bowie and Ronson did a brilliant job. The resulting single, a fine reworking of 'The Man Who Sold The World', in a sleazy, almost Berlin-cabaret style, with Bowie on backing vocal and sax, actually matched the original. To promote the single in early 1974, Lulu cross-dressed, wearing a suit and trilby like a 1930s 'Unter Den Linden' chanteuse in a largely unremembered piece of female gender-bending ten years before Annie Lennox's video-age Thin White Duke homage on 'Sweet Dreams Are Made Of This'. As an aside, though an interesting one, a version of Lulu singing 'Can You Hear Me?' was also made, in April 1974, but the track, which was played to Visconti around the time of the song's official recording later in 1974, joined the many others locked in Bowie's groaning vaults.

Ken Scott, then, was left in the bizarre position of having to vacate the studios every time Lulu walked through the door. And that wasn't all. For Ken Scott, Bowie had always been the model professional in the studio, hardworking and pleasant with it. However, by the time of *Pin Ups*, cracks were starting to appear in this facade. Bowie was becoming a little more snappy with those around him. 'The success was changing him. Bowie began believing that all the trappings of success which Defries provided, the limos and that kind of thing, had to be there. In fact, they weren't trappings any more but necessities.'

The resulting album is uneven although beloved by many, and a massive-selling hit to boot. Released in October 1973, it was a UK Number 1 for five weeks, as *Aladdin Sane* had been, and rode the crest of the wave of Bowie's enormous UK popularity at the time. Advance orders were 150,000 copies, 50,000 more than for *Aladdin Sane*. But the new album was pretty perfunctory. Bowie's still reedy vocal was unsuited to the rock attack of The Who's 'Anyway, Anyhow, Anywhere', and he was even less at ease with the hip R&B revivalism of The Mojos and The Pretty Things. When he moved on to more whimsical pop, as on the cover of The Kink's 'Where Have All The Good Times Gone', or the powerful neo-classical version of Pink Floyd's psychedelic anthem, 'See Emily Play', he was on safer ground. The album's highlight is, of course, his cover of The Merseys' 'Sorrow', the only time when he vastly improves on the original. Bowie was again aping those around him, and this time it seemed to be Bryan Ferry. Although he never explicitly admitted to impersonating

Ferry's richer, mannered croon, it was obvious to Scott and Ronson that this was the intention, and it was one thing they didn't altogether welcome with open arms. The album's only single release, 'Sorrow', justifiably became one of his biggest hits, reaching Number 3 in Britain, and staying in the charts for fifteen weeks, well into 1974.

Perhaps more inspiring than the music was the startling cover (the photo was actually taken during a Vogue photo shoot, and intended for the magazine's front cover, but apparently was never used because Vogue thought that having a man on the cover would reduce sales): Bowie, naked again, his spiky hair now dyed a deep brown, his face, outlined in black pencil, a blank, staring mask. Next to Bowie, head on his shoulder, is that personification of mid-60s cosmopolitan chic, Twiggy. Both look more like wind-up dolls than beings made of human flesh. The overall effect was that of a startling piece of artifice: the human condition reduced to (a conveyor-belt of) simulacra.

What's also important about *Pin Ups* isn't just the music itself, but the fact that it's there at all. By 1973 pop had entered its 'post-modern' phase. It had a history, and the smarter acts knew how to raid the past to enrich the present. On the one hand there was Roxy Music and their re-evocation of 1950s cinematic glamour. And on the other there were acts such as Gary Glitter, Mud and Showaddywaddy, who were busy turning 1950s rock'n'roll into pop/cabaret. It was no surprise that in April 1974 Bill Haley was in the UK Top 20 again, offering no solution to the oil crisis other than to rock around the clock. So *Pin Ups* came at a time of uncertainty, a time when many cast backward glances as pop entered its first retroactive phase. Like Bryan Ferry's *These Foolish Things*, which entered the charts on the same day as *Pin Ups*, 3 November 1973, it began an era of pop archaeology.

Indeed, Ferry had started *These Foolish Things* before Bowie had begun his own cover-version project. 'I used to say songs were a bit like ready-mades. I would take another song from another period and do my interpretation of it,' says Ferry, who seems to remember Bowie phoning him and telling him about his own project. 'At first I was a bit apprehensive, but Bowie's record turned out to be very different. I myself was always very anxious to be different from other people,' says Ferry, 'and to forge my own furrow.'

* * *

The fact that *Pin Ups* stayed at the top spot in the UK for five weeks was testimony to Bowie's broad commercial appeal and his ability to produce mainstream pop, while projecting an image so cool and so startling that it was instantly attractive to those on the fringes. By 1973 there was a recognisable Bowie cult in the UK, as 'Bowie Boys' and 'Bowie Girls' roamed suburbia.

Although Bowie's records were being bought by everyone from teens to mums and dads, his hard-core following, those that actually took to the streets in make-up and glitter, seemed to consist of two types. First, Bowie had a huge following among teenage girls. For about eighteen months his records were bought in their hundreds of thousands by the same constituency that had bought T.Rex or even Sweet and Slade the year before, and who would buy Bay City Rollers records a year later. Bowie was pop. His singles, if not his album cuts, were almost as melodically conventional as those of any other teen idol. Second, there were those arty suburbanites, the sexual experimenters, the bedsit gloomsters, who were drawn to Bowie's cleverness and his love for arty cross-referencing. It was perhaps these fans, the pop stylists, who would follow Bowie right up to the *Let's Dance* era. These fans were a jealous elite. Sociologist and writer, Simon Frith, wrote: 'Bowie-ism was a way of life – style as meaning – and no other idol has had such an intense influence on his fans as David Bowie. His example of self-creation was serious and playful – image as art as image, and his tastes, the selves he created, were impeccably suburban: he read romantic literature; he was obsessively, narcissistically, self-effacing ... Bowie was youth culture not as collective hedonism but as individual grace that showed up everyone else as clods.' In fact, as Frith points out: 'As a star, Bowie never pretended to "represent" his fans, but he did make available to those fans a way of being a "star" ... Glam rock dissolved the star/fan division not by the stars becoming one of the lads, but by the lads becoming their own stars.'

For Bowie, the music business had to be debased and radicalised, if only to reflect the attitudes and lifestyles of the fans themselves. In 1974 he told *Rolling Stone*: 'You see, trying to tart the rock business up a bit is getting nearer to what the kids themselves are like, because what I find, if you want to talk in terms of rock, a lot depends on sensationalism and the kids are more sensational than the stars themselves. The rock business is a pale shadow of what the kids are usually like ... People are not like James Taylor. They may be moulded on the outside, but inside their heads it is something completely different.'

For some Bowie fans, style became everything. A scene from the BBC 1 *Nationwide* documentary made in May 1973 by Bernard Falk, remarkable as much for Falk's slightly disbelieving, Liverpudlian put-downs of the Bowie 'circus' as it was for the shots of the fans themselves, showed a cohort of Bowie fans outside the Winter Gardens in Bournemouth waiting to touch their Messiah as he made his way from his limo to the gig. The programme recorded scenes of mass hysteria, screaming teenies and boys and girls with dyed hair, glitter and the modish Aladdin Sane thunderbolt felt-tipped across their faces. This was the beginning of Bowie's immortality through style, and, for the fans, it was this sense of sartorial danger which magnetised them. For some people, the sudden appearance of a contingent of Bowie clones was most odd. Ken Scott: 'It was amazing driving to the gigs and seeing all these people on the street with this very short, dyed-orange hair. It blew me away when I first saw that. Seeing both men and women dressed almost exactly the same was very strange indeed.'

Bowie was freakish and other, and he presented the blueprint for all those bored suburbanites. Cultural critic Paul Willis wrote in 1990: 'Clothes signify more than just musical tastes . . . Young people learn about their inner selves partly by developing their outer image through clothes. Clothes can make people feel differently in different contexts. For some young people, and especially young women, the clothes they wear on any particular day will influence the way they talk, behave and present themselves.' The adoption of short hair by Bowie boys and Bowie girls had a social and political resonance. Bowie fans indicated through their hairstyle and dress a desire to distance themselves from the communality of the hippies, tapping into Bowie's own narcissism and his rejection of the motifs of the counterculture. Short hair became a badge of difference, a way of asserting individualism, a way of being noticed. Leslie, a Bowie fan since the 1970s, remembers, 'In 1974, when I was fourteen, I took a picture of Bowie with me to the barbers and said, "I want my hair cut exactly like that," which he did, and made a good job of. It was a Ziggy picture circa 72, when his hair, although spiky, was short at the back. I was quite proud of my little haircut, everyone else had long hair and there I was, quite different to everyone else. I did not know any other Bowie fans so I stood out, plus I had a first in Lancaster, spiky hair before any of the punks.'

Paul Woods, a fan and collector since the early 1970s, says that being a Bowie fan involved much more than merely following the latest glam-rock fashions: 'In the early 70s when I was fifteen or sixteen, the fashion was glam-inspired, with Bowie playing a major part in what was an amazing feat of getting young men to look like drag queens on their night off, and it being acceptable! The more intense fans such as myself wanted more to be recognised as Bowie fans than just glam fans, and the bravest step was the hair. I always dreamed of a flame-red Ziggy cut, but compromised by having some blond highlights put in by my sister, a trainee hairdresser. I've always felt inspired by Bowie, rather than feeling the need to be Bowie. I was trying to be as cool as him.'

Bowie was acting as a cipher. He was as much created by his fans as self-created. He started off Ziggy for his fans to complete. Soon there were thousands of other Ziggy Stardusts, simulacra of the real thing, up and down the land – a cult of Bowie. Just the very act of having one's hair cut short and spiky made one different. Having it dyed red and applying make-up made you your very own suburban Ziggy. At the heart of showbiz is an ecstatic core. For writer Rogan Taylor, Bowie, like the best popular entertainers, had all the right tools to release these Dionysian forces of excess: 'What you need to crack it open is an audience that is able to open it. In a sense it's always been there in the performance. The audience controls the show by what they're able to read from it.'

By the early 1970s, British youths were demanding something altogether more stylishly rebellious to articulate their emotional dispossession. In the mid-60s the Stones had represented this sense of taboo-breaking, but their misogynous credo of womanising and anti-Establishmentarianism seemed tame by the standards of the early 1970s. The first half of that decade saw the first real crises of confidence since 1945. Everyday life was seemingly filled with phoney substitutions and this manifested itself throughout the land, as consumer society became bloated with keg beer, oppressed by the uniform blandness of the new housing estates, and surrounded by plastic. A new nihilism bred on this surface artificiality and became the new *Zeitgeist*. Bowie, with his brand of self-absorption, his anti-countercultural poses and his revelry in the surface trappings of glitz and artificiality, was the supreme expression of this new era of post-hippy, pre-punk questioning.

By the end of 1973, Bowie had extricated himself from The Spiders and was about to bring his professional relationship with both Mick Ronson and Ken Scott to an end. Bowie kept Ronno on for one last hurrah, however. Between 18 and 20 October, as the rest of the male population of the UK was still crying into their Double Diamonds after a certain Polish goalkeeper called Tomaszewski had clowned his way into footballing immortality by restricting the English football team to a draw and thus eliminating them from the World Cup, Bowie, who was never either a new or an old lad, had other things to occupy him.

The punningly titled 'The 1980 Floor Show', part of the *Midnight Special* series for NBC, was filmed at the Marquee in London. Again, MainMan's intention of breaking into the US market was clear as, much to Bowie fans' eternal annoyance, the special, which was broadcast in the US on 16 November 1973, was not aired in the UK. Bowie performed songs from *Pin Ups* and *Aladdin Sane*, employing sharply choreographed mime and dance routines to augment them. Bowie premiered a new song, a segue of 'Dodo'/'1984' which was, in fact, the last track recorded with producer Ken Scott. To reinforce his impeccable credentials as a mainstream corrupter, Marianne Faithfull appeared dressed in a nun's habit, to duet with Bowie on Sony and Cher's 1965 cheesy 'classic', 'I Got You Babe'. Ken Scott, who was mixing the show, reminisces:

The Marquee had a club on Wardour Street, and behind it was a recording studio and control room. For the purposes of recording the special, the actual performances were to be filmed in the club. The studio was the dressing room and we recorded it in the control room. The MC he was using then, Dooshenka (soon to be Amanda Lear), was changing in the studio and she stripped off in front of the control room. David was sitting next to me, and I was just staring at this incredible body. David leaned over and said, 'She's not bad, is she?' I said, 'Too bloody true, she's great.' And he said, 'Would you believe a couple of months ago that she was a man?' I tell you, I almost lost it over the console.

I also recollect the TV company being very scared about Bowie's costumes. One of the costumes was open down the front and I believe on one shot you could actually see his pubic hair, it was so low cut. Musically and recording-wise, this particular sequence worked well, but NBC wanted to do it again, so they made David sew up the garment a bit. Well, David did just about everything he could to keep the original take and proceeded to do his best to mess up the retakes. I think in the end they intercut between the two, but they did it really badly and it's noticeable on the final version.

This was the last time Ronson and Bowie would share a stage for ten years. Ronson's solo career would be launched by Defries, to mixed results as it turned out, with the *Slaughter On Tenth Avenue* album, a Number 9 hit in the UK in March 1974. A solo tour featuring Ronson and The Spiders played to sold-out venues. A second album, *Play, Don't Worry*, followed in 1975 and included the classic 'Billy Porter'. Ronson briefly joined Mott The Hoople, had a hit with Ian Hunter in 1975 on 'Once Bitten Twice Shy', and then toured with Bob Dylan. In 1980, the Human League would bring Ronson back into the public eye with a cover of 'Only After Dark'. However, he never came close to recapturing his early fame. Woodmansey and Bolder kept the name The Spiders, and hooked up with guitarist Dave Black and vocalist Pete McDonald for the cunningly entitled *Spiders From Mars* album in 1976. It's worth checking out, if only for the sleeve notes by *Melody Maker*'s Chris Welch. Here's a sample: 'Born from the rib of the rock god Bowie, The Spiders have an honoured name on the tablets of rock ... But a Martian Mystery still prevails. Who are these men who bombarded our planet with an intergalactic rhythm? As their cosmic telephone rings, should we answer? It would be a shame if the world chose to ignore The Spiders, for they have immense power, a wide spectrum of ideas is at their command and we Earthlings could well benefit from their superior knowledge.' Unfortunately the phone rang and rang and The Spiders' intergalactic mission never got off the launch pad. However, most Bowie fans cherish the days Woodmansey, Bolder and Ronson provided the no-nonsense, punky pop-rock framework for Bowie's ideas. For many a fan, their passing marked the end of David Bowie's golden age.

An underrated musician (some of his bass work on those early Bowie albums is memorable), Trevor Bolder, the man with the grooviest and largest sideboards in glam-rock history, went on to play with Uriah Heap. Woody formed Woody Woodmansey's U-Boat and later played live with Art Garfunkel and Paul McCartney as well as recording with Dexy's Midnight Runners. Woody is still an active scientologist. An account of Trevor and Woody's time with Bowie, to be co-authored by them, was mooted in the 1990s, but Woody eventually backed out.

There appears to have been no falling out with Ken Scott. Scott and Bowie were friendly, but their relationship was always a professional, rather than a personal one. When Scott left Trident Studios after mixing 'Dodo'/'1984' with Bowie, he had no inkling that their professional partnership was at an end. With hindsight, however, he concedes that maybe the rich vein of creativity which had endured for so long had in fact been exhausted: 'We had done four albums together and we'd probably both reached that point where we needed to work with other people to learn.' Scott immediately began work on the album which he considers to be his finest production achievement – Supertramp's *Crime Of The Century*.

Bowie has called Ken Scott his 'George Martin'. Like Martin, Scott was no auteur in the mode of a Phil Spector. He regarded his primary function as to collaborate on, not co-opt, the recording. It was all very much fifty-fifty when they recorded together, with Scott bringing out Bowie's natural melodicism. Scott's production on Bowie's work has tended to be underrated but, listening to those albums now, it's hard to see how any of them could be improved. The end of Bowie's working relationship with Ken Scott meant a shift of focus to more experimental techniques and arguably greater musical daring, and an end to the 'classic' pop period of David Bowie.

Without question, 1973 will go down in the rock annals as Bowie's year. On New Year's Eve, RCA presented Bowie with a plaque to commemorate having five different albums in the chart simultaneously for a nineteen-week period. RCA announced that his total UK sales were now 1,056,400 albums and 1,024,068 singles. On the domestic front, Bowie had moved out of his rented Haddon Hall accommodation after being hassled by overzealous fans. After a period living in a hotel, he swapped the Haddon Hall landlord, Mr Hayes, for the rather sassier landlady, actress Diana Rigg, who rented out an apartment in Maida Vale to the Bowie family. From there, they moved into a bigger residence in Oakley Street, Chelsea. Bowie lived there with Angie, Zowie, Daniella and Freddie. A nanny called Marion would help Angie. Initially, this move was blocked by Defries, who told her it was 'too extravagant'. According to Defries, Bowie's record sales had still not earned back RCA's advances. Bowie was famous, but he certainly wasn't rich.

Bowie's (and originally Angie's) friend Ava Cherry, a striking, black woman with short, platinum-blonde curls, perhaps several inches taller than Bowie himself and quite probably almost double his weight, also stayed *chez* Rigg. Bowie had met Ava in New York at the time of his Radio City Music Hall gigs in February 1973. Ava was a waitress at a party and Bowie soon had her earmarked as a future singing star. She followed Bowie back to Europe and was present during the summer recording of *Pin Ups* in France. Bowie promised to make her a star, saying that she could be 'the next Josephine Baker' and promptly pulling strings to get her a recording contract with MainMan. Cherry would now also be a regular backing singer for Bowie, and the two would be romantically linked. For good measure Angie's then boyfriend, Scott Richardson, was also on the scene. As an added bonus, Mick Jagger lived just up the road, as did Amanda Lear, the master of ceremonies for 'The 1980 Floor Show' and cover star of Roxy Music's first album. Allegedly Bowie was conducting an affair with her, too. As for Haddon Hall, it is, sadly, no more, having been demolished in 1981.

Bowie tried to launch Ava Cherry through the subsequently abandoned Astronettes project of the autumn of 1973. The Astronettes were Ava herself, Jason Guess and Geoff MacCormack. Many of the tracks laid down for these sessions were later reappropriated by Bowie for his own solo work. 'I Am Divine' went on to become 'Somebody Up There Likes Me' on *Young Americans*, and this was recorded in France during the *Pin Ups* sessions, while 'I Am A Laser' became 'Scream Like A Baby' on *Scary Monsters*. According to some sources, Bowie himself recorded two versions of 'Laser' – one in 1974 and one in 1980. The title of one of the songs on the Astronettes album, 'People From Bad Homes', would later be used for 'Fashion'. The rest of the tracks recorded at Olympic Studios in November 1973 included a version of 'God Only Knows', featuring Bowie on saxophone (Bowie's own 1973 version remains unreleased) and McHugh and Fields' 'I'm In The Mood For Love', which was performed in 1974 by The Mike Garson Band, who opened for

Bowie on the *Young Americans* tour. The quality of the material is uneven but the sound is intriguing – a sort of glam-soul music – and it was a direction Bowie was to build on in 1974. The Astronettes album was eventually given a release in 1995, over twenty years after recording.

Bowie's musical obsessions were changing, and changing fast. Ken Scott remembers that he was very taken with the work of Barry White. And, perhaps more surprisingly, Scott reveals that Bowie was very much enamoured of the first Styx album too! What is for certain is that, by the end of 1973, Bowie was already on the road to a more soul-inflected future.

Bowie was also working on a brand-new solo project. *Diamond Dogs*, recorded in late 1973 and early 1974, shows him at both his most indulgent and his most creative. He wrote some of the material for the album while on holiday in Rome after the *Pin Ups* sessions, and recording took place at Olympic Studios, Barnes, London.

Although never really a critics' rave, the album remains one of those most admired by his hard-core following. A truly audacious work with gorgeous melodies throughout, it's the closest Bowie has ever come to the ideal of a totally theatrical pop music, with hugely ambitious song structures and vocal performances which add a new dimension to Bowie's oeuvre in their huge showboating audacity. It's the closest Bowie has got to creating a total sonic environment which overcomes and entraps the listener. The final chant sequence, which segues out of 'Big Brother', is pure mantric oblivion. Martin Kirkup, reviewing the album for *Sounds* in 1974, commented: 'Where *Aladdin Sane* seemed like a series of Instamatic snapshots taken from weird angles, *Diamond Dogs* has the provoking quality of a thought-out painting that draws on all the deeper colours.' This was Bowie at the beginning of his painterly phase, using the studio as an instrument, applying sound like washes of paint in waves, drones, multi-rhythmic pointillistic detail, echoes and oddly formed collages.

Produced by Bowie, and engineered and in part mixed by Keith Harwood (sadly now no longer with us, killed when his car hit the exact same tree as the one which Marc Bolan hit in his fatal crash), it shows Bowie taking on the role of lead guitarist, while pianist Mike Garson is once again on hand to add a touch of eccentricity. Alan Parker, formerly of Blue Mink and today a successful composer in his own right, was on hand to play lead guitar, and Herbie Flowers, one of Britain's best bassists, also featured. Bowie's long-standing mate, the vocalist and dancer Geoff MacCormack, now going by the name of Warren Peace, was on backing vocals. Two drummers would work on the sessions: Aynsley Dunbar, who had taken Woody Woodmansey's place for *Pin Ups*, and Tony Newman, Herbie Flowers' buddy and already one of the most experienced drummers doing the rounds. Bowie had lost The Spiders, but he had constructed a powerhouse of a band to take their place, albeit on a less permanent basis. Speaking in 1976, Bowie explained that he felt more relaxed about the 'hired hand' situation. Now free to pick and choose a constantly evolving line-up of musicians to work with, in one respect the arrangement freed Bowie up: 'The nicest thing about that particular way of working is that they don't feel that they're my band. The Spiders looked to me to supply them with new identities. And I said, "Look, there really isn't a band in the next concept; the next concept is Aladdin Sane, on his own, and having done that, I want to write about the cities that Ziggy comes from, the *Diamond Dogs* thing, and there's no band in that." '

So, *Diamond Dogs* was, in essence, a clenched fist of defiance from Bowie. On the album he was to conclusively prove his genius, not only as a songwriter, but as producer, player and arranger too. Without Ken Scott, without Ronno and The Spiders, he was still able to produce work of real quality.

Diamond Dogs was also important in that it saw him working again with then ex-chum Tony Visconti, who had just ended his long and fruitful professional relationship with Bolan.

Visconti claims never to have had the same deep friendship with Bolan as he had with Bowie: their relationship was conducted more on a professional level, their way of working almost telepathically speedy. But, by 1973, it was clear to Visconti that Bolan was, to a degree, played out: 'Marc and I had developed a formula which had crystallised by the album *The Slider*. It was still exciting to make a T.Rex record then. By *Tanx* we were getting better at the formula, but nothing new was being put in. By the next album, *Zinc Alloy*, the formula was tired and Marc would not take time off, at my suggestion, to get some new musical influences.'

During the time Visconti was concentrating on Bolan, he was watching Bowie's career unfolding: '*Hunky Dory* made me jealous. I had nothing to do with it, but I asked myself, Where were songs like that when I was producing him? I thought the album was wonderful, but we still hadn't contacted each other since the split-up. When *Ziggy* came out, with its huge success, Marc had begun to watch David closely. If he said anything about *Ziggy*, it was usually condescending. It was also apparent that although Marc was probably the first major glam-rock star, David had taken the concept a quantum leap ahead with the invention of Ziggy. I thought Ziggy was very inventive and wondered if it was really David under all that make-up. I enjoyed the albums he made with Ken Scott. Ken was one of my main engineers in those days, a very talented and likeable man. I found the albums sonically thin and would've loved to have had a hand in both the arrangements and the engineering. But those albums are classics and I admire them for the ground-breaking works that they are.'

It was a good time to hook up with Bowie again. However, Visconti was surprised when he received a call from him during the summer of 1973.

David called me in the middle of the night some months before the mixing of *Diamond Dogs*. I could tell he was on something, probably cocaine, because he was speaking quickly, rambling really. He said he was up all night calling friends he hadn't spoken to in years. He said he realised it was really late, but could we get together soon? I mumbled 'yes' and never heard from him again until he called me at a more normal hour several months later, about mixing *Diamond Dogs*. He said he'd produced it himself and couldn't get a decent mix anywhere. He was just asking for advice on selecting a studio, not suggesting we should work together. I suggested he try my place. I was setting up a state-of-the-art sixteen-track studio in a house I'd just purchased but hadn't yet furnished. I had just bought all the latest digital devices as well as the 'classic' equipment. All I lacked was studio furniture, but David said he had to try it immediately. He arrived early in the afternoon the next day and we played around with the title track. Still having no furniture, we mixed sitting on a couple of carpenters' sawhorses. He took a copy home and called me that night saying it sounded great everywhere he played it, then booked my studio for the next two weeks. Before he came the next day, a huge van showed up from Habitat. David had bought me chairs for the studio and a dining table and chairs and all manner of cutlery and china for the dining area as a present. We mixed the entire album there, although he preferred his original mix of 'Rebel Rebel'. With this album, we resumed our working relationship and friendship.

David was using a little bit of coke and that wasn't unusual, since everyone in music and the media was carrying around little bags of coke in those days. I was using it, too, so we both had another thing in common which we discovered independently of each other. Although it was present at these mixing sessions, we hardly used any. The purpose of the dining table was because David had wanted to sit down to a fine meal each night and had French cuisine delivered to the studio.

Visconti mixed the album and also 'added some special effects and mixing ideas that were very germane to the lyrics and the mood and concept'. 'I always do that,' Visconti said in 1999. 'I don't make strange sounds just for the sake of it. They have to underscore something in the song. David appreciates this very much.'

Bowie had originally intended to produce a musical of the classic George Orwell novel.

Speaking in 1993, he had this to say about his original intentions:

It actually was a stone-cold version of *1984* as a musical. And it was in fact the first time that I was rejected by a literary figure. My office approached Mrs Orwell, because I said, 'Office, I wanna do *1984* as a musical, go get me the rights,' and they duly trooped off to see Mrs Orwell, who in so many words said, 'You've got to be out of your gourd, do you think I'm turning this over to *that* as a musical?' So, they came back and said, 'Sorry David, you can't write it.' And I said, 'What do you mean, it's impossible, of course I can write it!' And they said, 'No, she won't let you, you see, she won't give you the rights. She won't sell you the rights for any amount of money in the world. She said she's seen one film of it, and that that was such a disaster that she'll never let it out of her grasp ever again.'

I really had to turn around on a dime, 'cos I was already in the studio putting bits of it down and I thought, *oh no!*, I kind

▲ A sixteen-year-old Davy
Jones in his first professional
band, 1963
(London Features)

► Bowie and lover Hermione Farthingale performing in his mime troupe, Feathers, 1968 (Ray Stevenson/Retna)

◄ Frock'n'hell! Bowie on his first major US promotional tour, snapped here with Rodney Bingenheimer, 1971 (Julian Wasser/SIN)

◄ Bowie's eerie, mausoleum-like Doheney Drive residence, the site of his mid-1975 psychic collapse (note the sphinxes patrolling the exit)
(Spencer Kansa)

► The original, punky Ziggy look. Bowiemania kicks in, 1972
(Chris Foster/Rex)

David BOWIE triumphant arrival into Victoria Station, fresh off the boat train, was greeted by screaming fans and watching film crews.

Ph. AULIAC 1976

Philippe AULIAC take his first David BOWIE picture at this place.

The photographer caught me in a mid-wave I was not giving a Nazi salute
David BOWIE

▲ Bowie arrives at London's Victoria Station, May 1976, scene of the alleged stiff-arm salute
(Philippe Auliac/Andy Kent)

▲ The inimitable Iggy Pop, Bowie's Berlin chum, snapped in 1977
(Philippe Auliac)

▶ Bowie in Paris, 1977, around the time of the filming of the 'Be My Wife' video, his weirdest televisual moment to date
(Philippe Auliac)

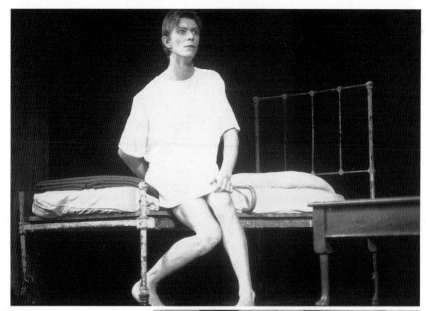

▲ Bowie on Broadway
as John Merrick, the
Elephant Man, 1980
(Michael Putland/Retna)

► Bowie at the Claridges
press conference to
announce the *Serious
Moonlight* tour in March
1983; the normalised,
besuited, businesslike rock
pose turned Bowie into a
false clone of himself
(Peter Anderson/SIN)

◀ Bowie transmogrified into the rocker he never was; macho, middle-aged angst in Tin Machine
(Dave Hogan/Rex)

▼ Taking time off from the *Sound +Vision* tour; Bowie and guitarist Adrian Belew at the shoot of the video for 'Pretty Pink Rose', 1990

▲ Nile Rodgers, co-producer of Bowie's biggest album *Let's Dance*, with Bowie in 1993 promoting their second collaboration *Black Tie White Noise*, subsequently Bowie's eighth UK Number 1 album
(Peter Gabriel)

▲ Trip-pop specialist
Mike Garson, Bowie
pianist from 1972-75
and then from 1993
onwards; his skewed,
jazzy/Broadway style
has made for some
deranged musical
episodes
(Shannon Treglia)

◀ Uncle Fester in a
kilt; Reeves Gabrels
scares the audience
on the *Earthling* tour,
1997
(Tom Zuback for Crankin' Out!)

of have to go somewhere else with this. Which was fairly easy because I was working with this real freewheeling guy called Keith Harwood. I was kind of in awe of him, because he'd worked on three Stones albums, so he was really a professional rock'n'roller. He was one of the first people who was, like, down-and-out rock'n'roll. He had the greasy hair and the boots and the leather jacket. I'd been used to engineers and producers like Ken Scott, who goes home to his wife at night, tie and shirt and all that, a very professional person – sort of my George Martin in a way. Keith was like heavyweight, cocaine and grease, and 'hey, rock and roll!' And it was only really me and Keith in the studio, because I'd got this thing, my usual thing, well, I don't need a band, I'll play all the instruments, it's as easy as that. I did end up using proper drummers and bass players and things, but a lot of the overdub stuff, the guitars and the saxophones and the keyboards, was me.

Bowie replaced Orwell's Oceania with his own future urban nightmare environment, Hunger City, a sort of post-nuclear, technologically primitive hell populated by tribes of proto-punks looting their way through the city. Again, as with Ziggy, the actual narrative remains underdeveloped. Like all of Bowie's best work, there are plenty of unanswered questions, gaps and contradictions to allow the listener to construct his or her meaning of events.

Part of the inspiration for the creation of Bowie's dystopia came from a trip behind the Iron Curtain earlier in 1973. Bowie had already begun to suffer from his well-publicised flying phobia and so had decided to travel back to Europe by train from a concert tour in Japan, accompanied by Geoff MacCormack. It was a stark introduction to a political system new to both men. MacCormack explains: 'We came back via Siberia, through China, Russia and Poland. I think it must have stirred his imagination. Here was an insight into another system, quite a shocking insight in many ways because culturally it was so different, especially coming from Japan, which we had both fallen in love with, and where the different cultural shocks were all pleasant shocks. They were lovely people in the Eastern Bloc, but it was still then in the 70s a harsh system; you felt like you were being noted, if not watched.'

The themes of urban decay, decadence and the apocalypse, which are the main ideas on the album, are given a psychosexual twist. This was Bowie's never-to-be-staged rock opera, although an animated short film was made. He envisaged a world in which snaggle-toothed ragamuffins dressed in looted furs and diamonds (hence the Diamond Dogs) took over the city. The principal character, Halloween Jack, and his gang live on top of deserted skyscrapers and travel around the city on rollerskates (there are no forms of fuel or power to be had). With hindsight, Bowie commented, 'They were all little Johnny Rottens and Sid Viciouses, really . . . In a way it was a precursor to the punk thing.'

Bowie says he drew inspiration for the characters of 'Hunger City' from a story told to him by his father, who worked for many years for Dr Barnado's. In the late nineteenth century, Lord Shaftesbury inspected London's poorest areas and found hundreds of urchins living on top of the roofs of slums. Bowie had this image in mind when writing *Diamond Dogs*.

The album begins with the track 'Future Legend', a spoken narrative describing a future urban apocalypse: 'Fleas the size of rats sucked on rats the size of cats', whilst humankind are merely 'peoploids split into small tribes' who roam the city 'like packs of dogs'. Here, perhaps, Bowie was echoing the writing of American author William Burroughs. In terms of method, Burroughs' use of 'cut ups' would inform Bowie's way of working from around 1973 onward. 'I have this memory of David taking lyrics and, with a scissor, cutting them up randomly and pasting them together,' says Mike Garson. 'I got the feeling that there was some lyric-writing and arranging on the spot.' 'As we played, other things would develop,' recalls Tony Newman.

Burroughs provided a resonant paradigm for Bowie. His books were nightmarish visions of a society populated by desensitised mental and physical cripples – his was a world full of drug addicts, criminals and sexual 'deviants'. Very often, his narrative would swing from intricate and truthful discussions of drug-induced mental states to demonic flights of fancy. What Burroughs did was to try and incorporate a different realm of experience, the experience of low-life culture, into the mainstream. Science fiction also fascinated Burroughs and the idea of aliens exerting control over humans through a parasitic relationship became a dominant theme. His novels thus centred on many of the themes Bowie was later to appropriate. Writing on the science-fiction trilogy of *The Soft Machine* (1961), *The Ticket That Exploded* (1962) and *Nova Express* (1964), his biographer

Ted Morgan comments: 'The result is a fantasy world peopled with cartoon figures rather than characters, and dreamlike episodes rather than a plot.'

'Future Legend', a portrait of a city environment on the point of collapse, and its view of a dehumanised humanity, are indicators of Burroughs' influence. Stylistically, it borrows from Burroughs' writing, too. Bowie describes the vista of urban degradation through a series of impressionistic snapshots, a shopping list of ever more sordid sights and sounds. In *Naked Lunch*, Burroughs had dealt with similar themes. He describes the junkie population as 'a baying pack of people', and his descriptions of American city life and of a country weighed down by an immutable original sin have the same apocalyptic vision as Bowie had on *Diamond Dogs*.

Two years earlier, Bowie had rumly told the press: 'People like Lou Reed and I are probably predicting the end of an era . . . and I mean that catastrophically. Any society that allows people like Lou and I to become rampant is really pretty well lost.'

In fact, in November 1973, as the project was taking shape, journalist Craig Copetas arranged a meeting between Bowie and Burroughs for an article in *Rolling Stone*. Geoff MacCormack recalls: 'I remember William Burroughs turning up one day. He was a quite awesome-looking guy. He had these tiny little black eyes, and you didn't quite know what his look was portraying, it was kind of an empty stare. He wasn't the kind of guy you would bound over to and say, "Hi man, how ya doin!?" '

There was, undoubtedly, a different atmosphere during the recording of *Diamond Dogs* than on previous Bowie records. 'I recall Olympic Studios. It had a very heavy vibe,' says Mike Garson. 'The studio played me as I played it!'

'The studio was very dark,' agrees Tony Newman. 'The whole thing was black, apart from David's lights. When he's in the studio, he's illuminated. It was like he was singing the song, and there was an aura about him, because that's exactly how I remember him singing "Sweet Thing".'

Diamond Dogs is a trip into grotesquery and seedy lowlife. The title track references Tod Browning, the maker of the then banned 1932 film *Freaks*, one of the most controversial movies ever made, starring, as it did, men and women with real-life deformities and rare medical conditions. The underrated 'We Are The Dead', with its creepy electric-piano opening, funereal pace and house-of-horrors imagery, is likewise graphically Gothic. But it's the brazen drug-referencing that is most evident: 'Is it nice in your snow-storm, freezing your brain?' Bowie inquires in 'Sweet Thing/Candidate/Sweet Thing (reprise)', before adding, 'Do you think that your face looks the same?' Earlier he suggests: 'We'll buy some drugs and watch a band/Then jump in a river holding hands'.

In fact 'Sweet Thing/Candidate/Sweet Thing (reprise)' is the real masterpiece of the album. It's in moments like this, rather than in the big hit singles or the radio-friendly songs, that Bowie's reputation as a true pop genius resides. Not only is it a bravura performance from Bowie, with the seamy, low register of the beginning building to some bracing showboating, but the music itself twists, turns and tumbles, part pop, part show-tune, part avant-garde experiment. For the middle section, when Bowie smells 'the blood of *les tricoteuses*', he asks Tony Newman to play in character: ' "Sweet Thing" is where I become the young French military drummer watching his first guillotining. David and I were talking about atmosphere and vibe, and that was one of the scenarios I had to play for him.' Newman's militaristic paradiddle captures the mood perfectly.

This highpoint of creativity aside, there are several other moments on *Diamond Dogs* that are almost as chillingly effective. For '1984', Alan Parker plays a brilliant *Shaft*-inspired riff, as Bowie warns 'Beware the savage jaw/of 1984'. The ending of the album is also quite brilliant. 'Big Brother', replete with fake horns, strummed guitar and a massive wall of sound, builds to an astonishingly overwrought climax which echoes some of Bowie's earlier work on *The Man Who Sold The World*. Then the song dissolves into the astonishing 'Chant Of The Ever-Circling Skeletal Family', a truly mesmeric and frightening chant in five/four time. It's one of the greatest moments Bowie has ever committed to tape.

The music on the album is densely packed, with piano, strings, sax, synths and guitars melding together beautifully. *Melody Maker*'s Chris Charlesworth noted that, 'For most of the tracks, he's adopted a 'wall of sound' technique borrowed not a little from Phil Spector.' Charlesworth himself was having to overcome a variation on the wall-of-sound technique when asked to review the album by MainMan in an exclusive for *Melody Maker*. This is what Charlesworth remembers of the Bowie entourage at the time:

They weren't pleasant. They were all behaving like a bunch of little Hitlers actually. Most of them were overtly gay. I've nothing against gay people but there are nice gay people and nasty gay people and these were nasty gay people. They were overly protective of David when I was asked to review the *Diamond Dogs* album for *Melody Maker*. I remember going over to MainMan's office in New York and listening to it, and I wasn't allowed to take notes or record the album or take it away to listen to it at home. I had one listen to it in this office, during which time there were people wandering in and out and making telephone calls and general clutter. I couldn't really hear the lyrics very well. And I thought, 'Well, it's a joke.' I sort of rushed home and tried to make some notes of what I could remember and I had to write this huge review. What annoyed me was that it was so unnecessary. Why did they behave like this? Because they wanted to throw their weight around and because they were a bunch of little Hitlers, that's why. And they didn't like me because I wasn't gay – didn't like my hairstyle probably.

Aside from these moments of grand experimentation in sonics and theatricality, *Diamond Dogs* also contained two of Bowie's best ever pop songs. 'Rock'n'Roll With Me', the single that never was, pointed, ever so slightly, towards the more soulful future that would be the *Young Americans* period. Geoff MacCormack remembers helping Bowie with the music.

'We wrote it in Oakley Street [Bowie's London home at the time]. 'I'd just popped round to hang. David was fiddling around on a tiny piano. He got up, and I started fiddling around with a chord sequence and stuff that I had just written. David said, 'Hang on a minute, play that again!' So, it was very much accidental. My contribution was round the verse parts. I wouldn't have dreamed of sitting down and saying, 'Oh, let's write a song together.'

And what's the song actually about? Geoff MacCormack can shed some light: 'I've never asked David, but it is my understanding that the content is the relationship between artiste and audience.'

And then there's 'Rebel Rebel', which reached a surprisingly lowly Number 5 after crashing into the Top 40 one place below that in the first week of release (a major reason was Bowie's manifest lack of television support for the single). The last of his bona fide glam singles, it was a manifesto for all the Bowie Boys and Bowie Girls: 'You got your mother in a whirl/She's not sure if you're a boy or a girl' sums up early-70s gender-bending perfectly. Arguably Bowie's greatest-ever riff, it was a brilliant taster for the album proper.

Bowie performed the new single on the Dutch show *Top Pop* in February, whilst in Holland for a few days to work on the new album at a studio in Hilversum. With an added eye patch (he had gone down with a bout of conjunctivitis), the Aladdin Sane meets pirate man look was the last time (with the exception of the cover artwork of the upcoming album) we would see the full crimson spiky Bowie haircut. Those looking for indicators for the end of glam rock might take this piece of sartorial evidence into account. The haircut that defined the glam era was, by the beginning of 1974, on its way out.

Intriguingly, Bowie's demo material for the material hinted at a more soul-inflected future. 'Take It In Right', a demo for the song which would eventually be recorded for *Young Americans*, and 'Dodo', later issued officially, showed Bowie, like Marc Bolan on his then current *Zinc Alloy* record, in transition. Unlike Bolan, however, who was never able to successfully integrate soul into his music, Bowie would make the complete transformation into blue-eyed soulster.

However, it was the demo for 'Candidate', first released by Ryko on their reissue of *Diamond Dogs* and now to be found on EMI's thirtieth anniversary edition of the album, that astonishes. 'Inside every teenage girl there's a fountain/Inside every young pair of pants there's a mountain', sings a cheeky Bowie over a brilliant piano melody. Bearing no relationship to the 'Candidate' squeezed in between two 'Sweet Things' on the album proper, except for the phrase 'pretend I'm walking home', this demo is a great Bowie song in its own right, and deserves elevation to the overcrowded pantheon of classic Bowie songs.

With the album ready for release, Bowie set about finding a suitable sleeve design. One of the shots from the session featured Bowie in a cool sombrero with a huge, jowly, snarling hound rearing up in bollock-biting mode. However, in the end he decided to go one better than his mate Jagger, who had recently commissioned Belgian artist Guy Peellaert to do the cover of their upcoming album, *It's Only Rock'n'Roll*. Bowie hastily commissioned the same artist to do the cover for *Diamond Dogs*, which hit the racks three months before the Stones' album. The resultant artwork had to be retouched, thus slightly delaying release of the album, when it was discovered that the half-man/half-dog Bowie, which adorned the full sleeve, had its doggy donger in full view. This did not detract in any way from the final effect of one of Bowie's most dramatic, and definitely most seedy, covers, which had Ziggy ending his career transmogrified into a half-canine mutant.

Diamond Dogs brought the first phase of Bowie's career to an end. Released in April 1974, *Diamond Dogs* not only closed down Bowie's glam-rock period, but became glam-rock's epitaph. The American group, Sparks, revitalised glam in the summer of 1974 with an astonishing performance on *Top of the Pops* for their Number 2 single, 'This Town Ain't Big Enough For Both Of Us', Russell Mael firing a shotgun, Ron Mael fixing camera three with a glass-eyed stare from behind his synth, half Hitler/half Chaplin. Cockney Rebel's 'Judy Teen' was similarly cool and arch. But by the end of the year Bolan was washed up, Roxy Music were in slight abeyance, and even Gary Glitter, Slade and Wizzard were being superseded by the 50s pastiche of Showaddywaddy and Mud and the hammy prog-rock glam of Queen. Indeed, one of Bowie's last (non) acts was to be responsible for breaking Freddie and the lads in the UK. Bowie was booked to perform 'Rebel Rebel' on *Top of the Pops*, but pulled out at the last moment, giving Queen, who were one of the chart 'breakers', a chance to perform in the vacated slot with their nicely quirky 'Seven Seas Of Rhye'. By early 1974, the era of The Bay City Rollers and The Wombles was upon us, and glam rock began fading from view.

That spring of 1974 was a watershed in Bowie's artistic life. In the sort of move which would come to define his career, Bowie jumped the glam-rock ship just in time, before it drifted into a blank parody of itself. Eighteen months earlier, Bowie as Ziggy had set sail for the States, but the outcome had been uneven. When he left the UK for the US in April 1974, the version of him on show was, on first inspection, a sartorially toned-down presentation. The era of glitter and stack-heeled boots was indeed over, but the man himself was entering the most paranoid and out-there period of his life, a three-year period of chill, supercharged creativity. He redesigned his Ziggy cut into an epic flame-coloured parting, packed away the kabuki garb and reinvented himself as a sharply dressed soul boy in a suit. The gouster was born.

Part II

1974–1982

6. SHILLING THE RUBES, 1974–1975

I said, 'Damn, you look like shit!' Look, he was 98 lb and pasty white. He looked like a fuckin' vampire, come on.

CARLOS ALOMAR REMEMBERING FIRST MEETING DAVID BOWIE

Like a huge army in the Middle Ages that had to keep on fighting to justify its existence, so the touring circus of MainMan had to keep partying in order to preserve its *raison d'être*. As we have seen, Bowie had made several previous attempts to crack the States. This time all of MainMan's efforts would be concentrated on selling the former glam-rock star into the mainstream US audience. It would be a tough job. True, some of the Ziggy shows had been spectacular successes, a re-released 'Space Oddity', now complete with a newly filmed promo, did make it up to Number 15, and *Aladdin Sane* and *Pin Ups* had also reached the Top 30. But he was far from being a household name.

Bowie himself loved the contemporary black music of the day, and was also intrigued by the Latin music emanating from the clubs of New York. Although he would famously dub his own version of it 'plastic soul', his enthusiasm was genuine. He was obviously tiring a little of the rock scene and, since he'd never really considered himself a rocker in the first place, he began to immerse himself in American popular culture; to educate himself, to try and understand how it operated and what he could do with its music. And he had the perfect escort to help him.

In spring 1974 Bowie met a man who would act as his guide to black music, and would also be his band leader for the next fourteen years: Carlos Alomar, a New Yorker of Puerto Rican extraction. At the time of their meeting, Alomar was a self-taught funky rhythm guitar player. He was the son of a Pentecostal minister – 'Which is what we call in America "holy rollers",' Alomar says. 'People who actually experience the Holy Ghost and flip around all over the floor in a kind of purging exercise.' After a period on the Upward Bound programme for underprivileged youngsters (when he met Luther Vandross, also enrolled on the programme), Alomar became a jobbing musician. Eventually he became the youngest guitar player in the house band at the Apollo Theater. His substitute guitar player was Nile Rodgers, later the co-founder of Chic. Alomar played with the likes of James Brown, Chuck Berry and Wilson Pickett, who would drop into town for a gig and take on local musicians and guitar players for one night. Thus, Alomar had the best possible schooling, honing his funky rhythm guitar style with some of the greats of soul and R&B. 'This was about 1971/1972,' recalls Alomar. 'I was about sixteen then.' One of his bit jobs was as a musician on one of the first episodes of *Sesame Street*, along with Luther Vandross, singer Robin Clarke (Alomar's future wife), and Fonzi Thornton, later of Chic. Alomar also played as an (uncredited) session musician on numerous recordings, including albums by Martha Reeves. While working at the Apollo, he also had a day job, and often played in after-hours' joints once his stint at the theatre had ended.

By 1973, Alomar had a regular gig in a band, The Main Ingredient. 'One of the guys in the band, Tony Sylvester, had already got me in as one of the house musicians at RCA recording studio on 6th Ave,' remembers Alomar, 'and he asked me to do a session for a producer named Bowie, who was producing Lulu. Now Lulu I remembered from "To Sir With Love", so I was very anxious to do the session. You have to remember that, as a young kid, I was anxious to get my name associated with as many people as possible so that I could have a list of credits that would do me justice when I asked for my price. I did the session at RCA Records in New York, Studio A. I thought it was "The Man Who Sold The World" but it could have been an early version of "Can You Hear Me?" ' Alomar had never heard of David Bowie before, but they hit it off instantly. Alomar was good-humoured, calm, jokey and light. He was the bridge between Bowie's pop/rock glam phase and the 'plastic soul' of the mid-1970s. The two formed a working partnership which would be almost unbroken for the next decade and a half.

To Alomar, though, back in 1973/74, Bowie was an alarming creature to behold: 'You've got to understand I'm a Puerto Rican man living in Harlem doing black music. When you see a man so pasty white with red hair, don't you think that's strange? The glam rock that he was known for was a completely different circle than that he was putting himself into. So, when he had gotten to America, his conversation was a lot about all the things that he had read about, but not seen: the Latin scene, the R&B scene. I was living this. He was interested in anything and everything that was to do with the New York experience. I was very much impressed with him. He came across as a very kind man, extremely humble, just a very nice person. I told him, "What you need is to come to my house and my wife can make you some nice chicken and rice and beans and put some meat on those bones!" And, surprisingly enough, he said, "Sure". So he got a limousine parked right in front of my apartment house in Queens and we got together and hung out. I had some gold albums on my wall even then. It looked good; I had my gold albums before he had his!'

Although Alomar and Bowie were getting on great, and frequenting the local bars and clubs to provide Bowie with an authentic hit of black music in all its various manifestations, Alomar soon found out that dealing with Bowie meant dealing with Bowie's business people, too. Bowie asked Alomar, who was still working with The Main Ingredient at the time, to tour with a new band he was assembling for an ambitious American tour. Alomar, who had hitherto hustled his fee out of the local black circuit, knew that he needed a big-hitter to represent him in the white-dominated rock world. 'At that point, I was introduced to Tony Defries. I also got myself a white manager, as I thought that I was entering an area that was a little bit whiter than I was used to, for lack of a better term. Because, to me, this was rock'n'roll, not R&B, and obviously in R&B I was used to working with "niggers". I'm not talking about working with black people, I'm not talking about working with Afro-Americans, I'm talking about niggers, which is a black man *or* a white man who messes with your money, carries a gun, and tempts you to do something about it. So, I got my manager to talk to Tony Defries in his office about my rate. Now Defries offered $250 a week for my services and I'm already making $800 a week! So I said, "If you can't match it, forget about it." And they said, "No, I don't think we can match it." So I said, "OK, goodbye," and I left. So he got someone else to do the tour, and that was Earl Slick.'

Alomar was less than impressed with Tony Defries, and this is putting it mildly. 'He was an extremely large man with a gigantic fur coat. He was extremely intimidating. I liked Tony Zanetta at MainMan. He was a very flamboyant kind of guy and I liked that. He was fun. Defries was not fun. In my business, you meet a lot of them. Defries was a guy who would try to pull the wool over your eyes. He was also non-moving. He was not giving in any negotiation. I didn't like Tony Defries at all. It's not good when you can get that feeling from the very first meeting.' However, according to guitarist Earl Slick, Defries was absolutely the industry norm at the time: 'Those people were very old school. Back then he was the prototype for any manager in the business. He was nothing out of the ordinary, he was the standard.'

Alomar would prove integral to the Bowie sound for the next fifteen years, as would his new personal assistant. Bowie befriended Corinne Schwab (known as Coco), a bright, energetic and confident New Yorker of French extraction who originally worked at MainMan's London office before leaving with Bowie for the States in spring 1974. Her father was a photojournalist who was a war correspondent during World War Two, and her mother a psychotherapist. Businesslike and bustling, she could speak four foreign languages and would become one of Bowie's best friends. The two are still together in a professional capacity, over thirty years later. Coco met Bowie for the first time in Haddon Hall in 1973 at a welcome-home party for Bowie and Geoff MaCormack, who had just returned on the Trans-Siberian Express from Japan. 'I got started working with David by answering an ad in the *Evening Standard* in London asking for "girl Friday needed for busy office', said Schwab in BowieNet Q&A in 2001. 'When I was ready to leave MainMan six months later, David called and asked me why I was leaving. I explained about this Greyhound bus tour of America thing. He paused for a minute and said, "How about a limousine tour of America?" I paused for about a nanosecond and said something like "Uh, OK."'

With Angie back in London, enjoying the glitterati of the Chelsea scene with the aid of PMA (a newly synthesised drug known as Pamela and a close kin to ecstasy), Bowie turned to Coco for both friendship and help. At this time, 1974, Bowie's coke addiction was worsening. Bowie's drug use became very excessive very quickly. One of the reasons was possibly the complete change in environment between London and New York. It was partly also some sort of rite of passage into the entertainment business in the USA, almost as if Bowie had to do this, because drugs were somehow fashionable rather than a real need. So Bowie's drug use mirrored his personality: he went from 0 to 100 very quickly. As with his other enthusiasms, Bowie became entrapped and besotted by his current obsession. Angie Bowie claims in her second autobiography that he moved to New York simply to be close to his dealer and regular supplies of the drug, rather than for any professional or creative reason. Coco was Bowie's nurse. 'When I needed soul revival/I called your name,' sang Bowie much later in 1987's 'Never Let Me Down', a song for Coco. She proved an extremely competent chargé d'affaires, who did in fact help keep him alive during those days of coke-driven paranoia – days which would turn into weeks, then months, and, finally, years. Tony Visconti: 'Coco has been a very loyal, competent assistant to David. She was well educated and multilingual, and she simply did her job very well. She became David's PA during the mixing of *Diamond Dogs*. I can't remember David's assistant's name at the time, she was a black British lady. She kept showing up late or not at all, and getting David's requests wrong. She was fired, and Coco, who was in the typing pool at the time, replaced her temporarily, but obviously did so well that David kept her in that position permanently.'

Slowly but surely Coco began taking on more and more responsibilities. She became the gatekeeper, sometimes savagely restricting access to the superstar, and began hiring and firing and organising Bowie's diary. It wasn't long before a number of people were left aggrieved, so aggressive was her protection. Coco seems to be totally absorbed in David's affairs in every way. One Bowie insider put it like this: 'Her whole life revolves around David Bowie's affairs and it's a full-time job. She never seems to have anything outside going on much. People around David start to wonder, why does he have this person, who's fairly abrasive and causes trouble to the people working with him? I guess it's a kind of good-cop, bad-cop scenario that some businesses like to have. Most people who have been around David will have something negative to say about Coco because that is essentially her role.'

Intimidating and unyielding Tony Defries may have been, but this 70s remake of Colonel Tom Parker was a brilliant strategist and had a clever legal mind. He was also committed to his artist. He was determined to make Bowie a superstar in America and, within six months, he had succeeded. The first stage of the operation was the launching of *Diamond Dogs* in the spring of 1974.

First of all, 'Rebel Rebel' was reworked for US single release in New York during April 1974. 'We travelled from Cannes on the SS *France*, and when we got in to New York, it was one of the first things we did,' recalls Geoff MacCormack. 'I put the congas down on that version of "Rebel Rebel", probably in several takes!' Then began a massive MainMan-directed promotional campaign. A copy of the *Diamond Dogs* front and reverse cover, carrying the legend 'The Year Of The Diamond Dogs', was placed as a double-page spread in the majority of the most important music trade and consumer publications. Defries also produced two newsletters, which were sent out by MainMan to over 5,000 names. The idea of enclosing a black-and-white photograph of the *Diamond Dogs* sleeve, instead of the normal artist's photograph, also paid off. Within days, the photo was reproduced in music columns throughout the world, providing much free publicity for the album. A huge poster campaign was also organised for buses, underground railway stations and flyposting. Billboards were erected in Times Square and on Sunset Boulevard, and limited edition 'Diamond Dog metal dog tags' were produced for souvenirs. Bowie made both TV and radio commercials to promote the tour and the album which were aired in each city prior to the tour's arrival. Even boxes of Diamond Dogs matches were planned. This was a new form of rock'n'roll promotion, more akin to selling a would-be presidential candidate at a primary than selling a pop star.

Stage two of MainMan's 'Operation Bowie' was, of course, the tour itself. The *Diamond Dogs* revue turned out to be the most theatrical rock tour ever mounted. In fact, in its daring and visual audacity, it has probably never been rivalled since. The tour set was conceived by Bowie and designed by Michael Bennett, John Dexter and lighting designer, Jules Fisher.

For the show, which toured across North America in the late spring and summer of 1974, Bowie would play the role of Halloween Jack. This was basically a one-man show, with just two dancers, Gui Andrisano and Warren Peace, to provide on-stage action. During 'Diamond Dogs' the two dancers, who doubled as backing singers, lassoed Bowie. For 'Time', Bowie sang enclosed in a gigantic hand, which opened as the song started. For 'Sweet Thing', he sang atop a bridge, whilst, for 'Space Oddity', he seemed to have discovered the gift of flight. Hunger City, a crumbling post-nuclear holocaust city with atomic bomb-blasted skyscrapers of molten steel, would be recreated at huge expense for an astonished public. *Melody Maker*'s Chris Charlesworth, who saw the show, remembers the impact:

I was in Toronto to see the show and I was genuinely impressed. Again, in hindsight, I see now that DB had effectively turned his new album and other songs into a musical starring only himself, but being as how I was largely ignorant of musicals (of the Rodgers & Hammerstein/Lionel Bart variety) and also unimpressed by them (they weren't cool), Bowie's props and presentation were something new for me and very striking. I suppose, in a way, Alice Cooper was doing the same thing, only cruder.

'It was a scream' is how Bowie put it in 1993:

I'd have these flats on stage. The band would be positioned behind these flats, and I'd be working through the show and, unbeknownst to me, they'd all edge out, and every time I turned round, they'd go back in again. So it was like, 'he's behind you!' like this pantomime show. It ended up with them all coming on stage with me. But the first two or three shows, I really got them behind the screens and it was like this real stark, one-man show.

We had this cherry picker, and it had this secretary's chair affixed to the top of it. I'd start off doing 'Space Oddity' sitting in the chair, on the telephone, and, during the course of the song, the arm of the cherry picker would come out of the window, but it was lit in such a way that you didn't see the cherry-picker arm. All you saw was this arm coming out over the audience, and I was about twenty-foot out over the audience, over their heads, singing, and, of course, the nights when it wouldn't go back in and I was bloody stuck out there, God, I had to sing three or four songs until they got me back in. That in itself was so totally Dada because I'd be singing three or four songs into a telephone, it was so ludicrous. And one night I had to actually climb back on the pole to get back into the window because it just wouldn't come back in again. Never work with props. We had a bridge that used to go up and down and a bridge that went from one building to another, the full span of the stage, going asymmetrically from one side to the other. Occasionally that would go plunging down at the speed of light, and I would jump off it when I assumed it would hit the bottom, and I would be in the air so that I didn't come to some catastrophic end.

It was quite an unbelievable, unbelievable headache, that tour, but it was spectacular. It was truly the first real rock'n'roll theatrical show that made any sense. A lot of people feel that it has never been bettered. I mean, it was such an extravaganza, and it was so weird, it just came from such a strange place. It really did look like one of those expressionist movies come to life, it was like *Metropolis* meets *Caligari*, but on stage, in colour and it had a rock'n'roll soundtrack to it. It was something else, it really was.

As with anything radical and new, there would always be teething problems. One night it would be the set, the next Bowie would have to deal with a certain disgruntlement from the players themselves. Here's Bowie, speaking in 1976:

I started thinking about how hard it is for musicians to take part in rock theatre, and that's when I tried to lose musicians on the *Diamond Dogs* show; and that failed dramatically, because everyone complained. They kept saying, 'We don't like playing behind these bleedin' screens,' and I said, 'Well, you've got to, because I haven't got any parts for you. I don't want people to see you playing, because it doesn't look like a street if there's a bass amp stuck in the middle, but it was very hard to convince them about that. So, they all left me, and the show sort of gradually fell apart, which it should have done, because it was about a decaying city, so it was quite apropos that it should have fallen down in the middle of the tour.

Bowie planned a film version of the album, but the plan was never realised. 'Diamond Dogs is the last rock'n'roll group,' Tony Visconti told Radio 1 in 1976. 'In one version of the song, the dogs actually eat people, or they kill people on stage, or they shoot machine guns back into the audience. He has these horrible visions of the apocalypse, the end of civilisation as we know it.'

It was Bowie's most difficult performance to date. Bowie was a soloist, with the band acting rather like an orchestra. He did not have the fall-back position of a rock band structure and could not be subsumed within that structure at times of frailty. The ability to project both a technically proficient and engaging vocal was more important than ever, and around this time Bowie developed a new, richer, full-throated vibrato.

The ten-piece band itself was the most fluent, professional and nuanced Bowie had hitherto assembled. Tony Visconti: 'It was one of the best rock shows I've ever seen. The set was gorgeous and technically brilliant, with the drawbridge, the diamond-studded hand opening and the cherry picker going out over the audience's heads. The band was large and well rehearsed. It is one of the best things David has ever done on stage. I was never a member of the entourage, so I can't tell you what the tour itself was like. Michael Kamen, the renowned film composer, played second keyboard (to Mike Garson) and oboe on that tour.'

Perhaps the hardest task fell to Mick Ronson's successor in the lead guitarist's spotlight. Keith Christmas was originally auditioned for the part of lead guitarist, but when that didn't work out, Bowie went for an unknown for the daunting task of replacing Mick Ronson on stage. Enter Earl Slick. Slick was born in 1951 in New York City. By the early 1970s, he was a regular jobbing musician around town, having his own band and writing his own material. 'I was playing in a back-up band for an off-Broadway touring company of Hair, so I was used to the wacky New York artist scene already. It was entertaining, to say the least. I was meeting a lot of strange people. I remember meeting Andy Warhol, Lou Reed, all these people who were in that artistic glitter-rock movement.' Slick was brought to Bowie's attention through Michael Kamen, the Bowie tour's musical director, who had worked with Slick previously. Kamen himself was a classically trained graduate from the Julliard Music School in New York City and, at the time, was playing in a hybrid rock and classical band.

Slick auditioned for Bowie in RCA's studios in New York. 'He was mixing *Diamond Dogs*,' recalls Slick. 'It was an audition, but it was a strange audition because there was no band there. I turned up with a guitar, met David, who was in the control room, and I remember distinctly that he was in dark clothes, dark glasses and a fedora. I came in, went in the main studio (they had already set up an amp that I had requested) and I put the headphones on. They played me a couple of tracks from *Diamond Dogs*, took the guitars out of the mix, told me what key it was in and told me to play! I was a cocky little bastard though! I remember being in the studio by myself and looking into the control room which was almost black, just having a sense of, Boy, this is a weird situation. He then came in the studio with a guitar, we started talking, he plugged the guitar into the amp and we jammed around for a little while and that was it. Coco said that they would call me in a week, because they had other people to listen to. I got a phone call the next morning. Then I shot up to the hotel, we talked, and that was it.'

Although Slick was delighted with the gig, he was less than delighted with the money on offer. In fact, it was not actually on 'offer' at all. 'I took the shitty money – $300 a week. Basically, the way it worked out for me was, here I am, I'm 21 years old, I'm working my ass off, I'm playing in a number of bands. Suddenly, I get a gig like this. The money was disappointing. I was making more money playing bars at the time. But it wasn't negotiable. And money wasn't the motive for doing it. The motive for doing it was playing in a really big act. I'm a player and to be able to land a gig like that I instinctively knew that something was going to come out of it. It took me up many levels.'

Bowie was dealing in big, bold, theatrical dramas, while also turning the spotlight on himself as a soloist. The older glam-era Bowie material was savagely restructured. 'Aladdin Sane' became a jazz-Latino rumba, 'Rebel Rebel' and 'Jean Genie' were reinvented as cabaret blues numbers, and 'All The Young Dudes' and 'Rock'n'Roll Suicide' were more bizarre still, redesigned as schmaltzy ballads. 'Cracked Actor' was completely rebuilt, and turned into a sleazy, sax-driven epic. The new version of 'A Width Of A Circle' with oboe, sax and Slick's decibel-shattering lead guitar, improved in intensity on the original in its lovelorn decadence.

The band itself was positioned in something approximating an orchestra pit. Bowie demanded that his band members toe the line in terms of stagewear, but there was the odd revolt. Earl Slick: 'The only thing that was constant was Tony Newman and Herbie Flowers. There was always something going on between them. They were like Laurel and Hardy, the practical jokes between them. I had really, really long hair when I met David and he had it all cut off for the tour because it was part of the show. We had these outfits that David had made for everybody. I had like a 40s-style suit – it was pretty cool stuff. And Tony hated his, so one day he came out covered from head to toe in tape, like white tape like a mummy, and he got on his drums like that. Another night he came on stage and he had shredded his clothes, his shirt was torn up. Tony didn't really give a shit about anything; he made his statements in his own way.'

It took a massive operation to transport the set from city to city across vast distances. The $400,000 stage set took 30 men a complete day to erect, and was transported in three 45-foot trailers. The tour opened on 14 June at the Montreal Forum, Canada. There then followed a gruelling 37 shows in 37 days (from 14 June to 20 July) with one day off and one matinée performance in Toronto. Following a road accident after the gig in Atlanta, the tour continued with only half of 'Hunger City', as the set had been damaged (a suitable irony given that the whole show was about a crumbling city). Two shows were actually filmed by MainMan: the performances of the 19 and 20 July in New York, at the Madison Square Garden. These treasures have yet to be given an official release, despite frequent urgings on fan websites.

The high point of this, the first stage of the *Diamond Dogs* tour, came with a residence between 8 and 15 July at the Tower Theater, Philadelphia. It was during these gigs that RCA and MainMan recorded material for a live album, Bowie's first. The band were not best pleased when they found out that they would be paid the same rate as for the rest of the tour, even though their performances were to be recorded for a live album. Bowie was caught in this crossfire of antagonism. Earl Slick: 'They didn't even tell us ahead of time that they were recording the shows. Herbie Flowers put two and two together when we got to the gig. He confronted them; they made us an offer at that point which was insulting. Then Herbie got us all together and said, basically, that we shouldn't do any shows unless they came up with something reasonable. Eventually, they negotiated a figure and we went on, but not before things had got ugly, very ugly. On top of that, we still didn't get paid. In the end, we had to sue David, and that was when we were still on the road with him.'

'Herbie Flowers happens to be a big member of the English Musicians' Union now,' says Garson. 'I was there, and he was standing up for his rights, and probably they were ripping the band off. But it could have been done a little nicer.'

Bowie himself was having massive financial problems of his own. He found out in July, much to his utter horror, that he did not, in fact, own half of MainMan, as he had thought all along, and that his stake in the whole Defriesian empire amounted to a pittance. Bowie was financing the tour out of his own income and, with such a wildly ambitious set design and a huge army of musicians and technicians to feed, water and keep happy, the pressure was on. 'I don't know how MainMan worked,' says Visconti, 'I wasn't part of it, except that they had more employees than they needed and lots of the running costs were charged to David, not Defries. This is what ended their working relationship.'

It was during this summer and autumn of 1974 that Bowie sank into cocaine addiction. He was starting to keep reversed hours, working by night, sleeping by day, but the coke would often keep him awake for days on end. Only his incredible natural physical stamina kept him going. Cocaine is a powerful appetite suppressant, and weight was tumbling off Bowie; he was perhaps now a little over 80lb. His mauve veins looked swollen beneath his skin and bone. When he smiled, his gaunt face erupted into wrinkles. In some ways, Bowie was 'lucky' to have become addicted to cocaine, a drug, unlike some others such as heroin, which seldom leads to a fatality if taken straight. At first, it gave Bowie a terrific rush of energy and allowed him to keep awake in order to remain alert when he was recording and working, but very soon abuse of the stimulant resulted in a paranoid, semi-narcoleptic state, the initial euphoria replaced by a horrible emotional emptiness. Unable to feel, divorced from his emotions, utterly unable to enter into 'normal' relationships, Bowie's world was now one of blank pain. He was also convinced that he couldn't write or record unless coked up; that the drug was a wonderful creative tool. So he kept taking it, and more and more of it. Coke had a glamour and mystique which heroin lacked. Heroin users were junkies, coke users were cool. It was the drug of the entertainment industry. By the mid-1970s, it was estimated that 90 per cent of the total cocaine consumption in America occurred in the film and pop industries. Bowie was just another pop star making sure that statistic remained a reality.

David Bowie began living more and more in an abstract world. He had informed MainMan and RCA that he was dropping the 'David' part of his name for the *Pin Ups* album and this continued throughout 1974. In interviews he would sometimes refer to himself in the third person, and make comments about how divorced he found himself from the 'real' David Jones.

For his part, Defries became increasingly perplexed by his singer's behaviour. Bowie started looking to the skies for signs of extraterrestrial life, each flashing, moving object a potential UFO. Any day now, an alien invasion was a possibility. Ufology, which, back in the 1960s, was more of an adolescent hang-up, now became a real, all-consuming passion. The new, 'normalised' soul boy Bowie was the least normal version of his career to date – but even more terrifying psychic states were to come.

It wasn't just Bowie who was beginning to succumb to addiction either. 'I was a very willing person,' says Earl Slick. 'But I didn't become good friends with David. Everyone was so drugged-out drunk and busy all the time I don't think you knew who your friends were.'

This paranoia infused the Bowie operation for the next two years. 'That was when the excess started to come into the picture, and I think a lot of stuff David did during that time, he doesn't have very good memories of. It was a real upside-down time for him. It is because of that, the amount of coke that was going down, and it's not a good time of his life. I was a mess, I was on a roll, and I was living the life of what a rock'n'roll guitar player was supposed to do. I was doing everything. It was way out of hand.'

It was during the summer of 1974 that Alan Yentob and a BBC film crew tracked Bowie down in America. The resulting documentary, shown the following January and entitled *Cracked Actor*, is a masterpiece and a landmark piece of television journalism. It contains scenes as haunting and mesmeric as any David Bowie song, stage performance or promo. The scene featuring Bowie, painfully thin, sipping a carton of milk, his cheekbones looking as if they are about to break through his skin, is one of the most startling images in rock history. Likewise, the shot of him edgily sniffing and snorting in the back of a limo being driven through the streets of LA, terrified by the wail of a police siren he suspects is tracking his chauffeur-driven car, is an image of terrible potency. It was at this stage that his fans, at least those old enough to read the signs (and this one wasn't quite yet), realised that Bowie was a drug casualty of the first order.

It's hard not to appreciate what Bowie meant when he said that he 'couldn't help but soak it all up'. Somehow, the Tower Theater Philadelphia and the Los Angeles Universal Amphitheater had rather more romance than the Romford Odeon and the Bridlington Spa, venues he had played the previous year. Bowie was Americanising his Englishness but, as ever, he couldn't quite get it 'right', couldn't quite pass as a bona fide soulster. This, of course, is where his charm lies – in the synthesis, rather than in any authentic vision. The next phase of this transposition into Americana came at the home of Philly Soul itself.

In a six-week gap in the *Diamond Dogs* tour, Bowie decided to cut another album, his fifth in just over three years (a pace which no artist of Bowie's stature today could even dream of matching). Just four months after the release of *Diamond Dogs*, and with that album's promotional tour to resume on 2 September at the Los Angeles Universal Amphitheater, Bowie decamped to Sigma Sound in Philadelphia and, in a frantic spell of writing, tuned in and turned himself on to black American hit radio. The album went on to become one of the most influential records of the decade – *Young Americans*.

Although not yet on tour with Bowie, Alomar was called in for the Sigma session, after MainMan agreed to meet his fee. In fact, Alomar was integral in assembling the rest of the musical team: 'He called me and said he was going to Philadelphia and that he had been studying the TSOP sound a lot and Gamble and Huff. I brought my bass player, Emir Ksasan, and my drummer, Andy Newmark, and Willie Weeks. I said to my wife, Robin Clarke, why don't you come with me and bring Luther Vandross? You know how it is when you're in the studio and they're playing stuff back in the control room, and Luther and Robin were kind of singing along with it, making up new parts and laughing. Bowie heard it and said, "Weyhey! You go into the studio and do just that." They weren't hired initially, they just came to be my friends and be with me on the session.'

If Alomar was crucial in mustering this powerhouse of a band, then Tony Visconti was equally crucial in making sure it all got down on tape. Was Visconti at all sceptical of Bowie's motives? Was this a cynical attempt to break the American market, a shrewd business calculation? Visconti thinks not: 'He was in love with the black music of that period and he wanted to "get down". I was all set to "get down" too by the time I got off the plane. The funny thing is that although we were meant to record at Sigma for the vibe and the musicians, we never used a musician from Philly in the end. David had imported his own. That rhythm section certainly had credentials. I was overwhelmed with joy to be working with Willy Weeks, one of my bass idols, and Andy Newmark from Sly And The Family Stone, a legend of a drummer. The line-up was a perfect mixture of black and white musicians, who could play "soul" as good as anybody. David sang well over the band, but had to be the most inauthentic artist involved in the project. I mean, you could argue that Eric Clapton plays "plastic blues" by the same criteria.'

Sessions for the album went on at a terrific pace, with Bowie insisting on singing live against the groove of the band. For Visconti, being saddled with primitive recording equipment at Sigma Sound would test his technical know-how to its limit. He arrived from the airport jet-lagged, but Bowie was on a roll and wanted a new song, 'Young Americans', the first song to be recorded for the album, to be cut immediately. Visconti: 'The sessions were pure joy. I set up the room so that everyone had eye contact, and small, movable walls (gobos) provided enough separation for satisfactory mic placement. However, David threw me when he announced that he wanted to sing live, in the same room as the band, and wanted me to keep his vocals. His vocals were so perfectly sung and so heartfelt that we hardly had to replace any lines. I would say that eighty per cent of the vocals are live takes, with the band playing at the same time. That's the time-honoured way most earlier soul records were made.'

For Alomar, Bowie was a brilliant, emotive singer: 'Let me tell you, from the very, very beginning, David Bowie is a singing fool, make no doubt about it. That means he's got chops galore. This dude can wail – that's the best compliment I can make. This man was doing all the inflexions and he was doing all these kind of low Newley imitations and then he goes up into a sort of falsetto, way up there. These cuts were so good. "John, I'm Only Dancing", when he goes up into the falsetto, that stuff is amazing! I mean, can you hear how well he's singing?'

The recording of the album was a blast, too. Philadelphia had always been a Bowie stronghold. Back in 1972, it had been one of the first American states to embrace Bowie's glam rock and, with such a strong fan base, it is perhaps no surprise that the arrival of Bowie and his entourage to actually record there created something of a stir, at least among his hard-core fans. What followed, however, was nothing short of a marathon of devotion, as a tribe of Bowie supporters decided to shadow his every move. There was a sort of levelling of the star/fan relationship. Soon the fans became friends, were granted illicit sneak previews of work in progress and got to speak to the man himself. In return, the fans would do favours for those on the project. Bowie and his musicians started to feel a certain responsibility for these fans, too, dubbed by Bowie his 'Sigma Kids'. Patti Brett was one such fan, and remembers the lengths she and her friends went to just to be with their idol:

We started a rotation. Every once in a while someone would drive by to see if we saw a car, and one night someone did see his car. I think that at the time he had a blue Cadillac limousine. We found out he was staying at the Berkeley Hotel, and what we would do would be to wait for him until he came out. He would come out any time between four and six o'clock in the afternoon to go over to the studio and he would talk to us on the way out. We would jump cars, run every red light to get to the studio before he did, and he'd pull up in front of the studio and we'd be there yet again. He'd get out and he'd talk to us some more, get into the studio, do what he was doing up there, and we would wait every night for him to come out and do the same thing – talk to him, rush back to the hotel and talk to him some more. They were here for about two weeks. It was August 1974. Because he was just constantly there, we got to be fairly friendly with everyone. We also sent Carlos into the studio with a Polaroid. We also got the engineer, Carl, whose window was behind the soundboard, to open it so we could hear it! We used to hang out in Carlos' room. He would play stuff that they had done that day. We would take band members around town if they needed to go somewhere. We would take them shopping. I even gave Tony Visconti a lift to the studio when he couldn't get a cab.

Bowie was working at a frantic speed. 'Young Americans' was already in the can. The songs which were being developed for the album included a funked-up version of 'John, I'm Only Dancing', a song which had yet to appear on any Bowie album, with completely rewritten lyrics; 'Who Can I Be Now?' and 'It's Gonna Be Me', two huge, lush ballads quite unlike anything Bowie had ever written; 'Can You Hear Me?' a reworking of a track demoed with Lulu; and a track, 'Somebody Up There Likes Me', based on a song, 'I Am Divine', from the previous autumn's session with The Astronettes.

Bowie was still dating Ava Cherry, who was singing on the sessions, although Visconti remembers that 'there was no romantic bonding between them. I can only assume that they were sleeping together. I think Ava was a very unusual person and David was very interested in marketing her talents and appearance. I thought she sang very well, had a style all her own.' Angie was not really on the scene very much at all. 'I heard she showed up one night, trashed his hotel room and left,' Visconti remembers. 'I should think this affected his working practices very much, but in a positive way. He was very involved in the making of *Young Americans* and *Low*, two albums that were made during his slow separation from Angie. He didn't talk about her much, or their problems.' After Angie found out the extent of the Bowie/Cherry relationship, she flipped. MainMan's Tony Zanetta wrote in his Bowie biography, *Stardust*, that he had to 'wrestle her to the ground' to prevent her from jumping out of the open window.

Despite this emotional turmoil, the fans were kept happy. 'Actually, everyone was incredibly nice to us,' stresses Sigma Kid Patti Brett. 'You know, I find it incredibly difficult when I hear bad things about Angie, because she was just so nice to us when she came to visit. David would, from time to time, make sure that we had money to get home that night or, if they'd ordered food, they used to see if anyone was hungry. He was always worrying about us, late at night, sitting out on the sidewalk.'

With the tour about to resume in early September, the Sigma sessions had to be drawn to a close. On the last night of recording, Bowie had a special treat for the Sigma Kids. Patti Brett:

So, what happened was that he went into the studio one night and he said, 'You've been so supportive, and so wonderful during our stay here, we're gonna finish putting down some tracks and we want you to come and listen to it.' It was a Thursday evening, and he said not to tell anybody that's not there. He sent somebody down to let us into the lobby, as it had started to rain. He invited us upstairs and he was behind the soundboard and he said, 'This is what we've done. Listen to it and let me know what you think.' He went and sat at the back of the studio and looked nervous. During the first run-through, I think everyone was wondering, 'What's this!?' We were pretty curious. The album played through and at the end someone said, 'Play it again!' and then everyone got up and started dancing and it was wonderful.

The title at that time, remembers Brett, was Shilling The Rube(s). This was meant as a sort of joke and an ironic comment on Bowie's quest for a hit album in the States with his ersatz version of soul music. 'Shilling the rubes' is an old American term, meaning planting an accomplice in the crowd to drum up enthusiasm for a dodgy product being offered for sale by a charlatan. 'Shilling' meant 'conning'; 'rube' was a name for a country bumpkin. So Bowie's new album was basically to be called Conning The Suckers.

Unfortunately, he rejected the title after being persuaded that his audience might not see the funny side. By the time Visconti took the tapes back to London that autumn for mixing, the boxes had 'The Gouster' written on them. A gouster was a streetwise, sharp-talking, coolly dressed all-American dude. This fitted in perfectly with Bowie's new soul-boy image, part authentic hipster, part dandified Edwardian gent. The album was mixed, a full string section for 'It's Gonna Be Me' constructed by Visconti, and readied for release. Artwork was produced, too, featuring a black-and-white shot of Bowie in black waistcoat and white shirt, a forerunner to the Thin White Duke persona.

The track listing for The Gouster was as follows: 'John, I'm Only Dancing (Again)', 'Somebody Up There Likes Me', 'It's Gonna Be Me', 'Who Can I Be Now?', 'Can You Hear Me?', 'Young Americans' and 'Right'. This was a very different record from the album eventually released as Young Americans in March 1975. No 'Win', no 'Fascination' – they were, in fact, recorded at a later session at Record Plant Studios in New York in 1974 after the end of the tour, whilst 'Fame' and 'Across The Universe' were recorded at the same venue in January 1975 and feature John Lennon, who was then mixing his covers album *Rock'n'Roll* in the next studio and had started hanging out with Bowie. Tapes of three songs – 'Right', 'Can You Hear Me?' and 'Somebody Up There Likes Me' – have been in circulation for many years among Bowie fans, and it has always been thought that they were from the shelved The Gouster album. They have a far more basic, 'blacker', sound, with different vocals from Bowie. Tony Visconti, however, claims that these were simply rejected versions which hadn't yet been overdubbed. Whatever, the original album was a far more soul-inflected album.

With an album in the can, Bowie resumed his *Diamond Dogs* tour. The *Diamond Dogs* album had finally broken into the upper reaches of the US chart, peaking at Number 5. The tour itself was constantly morphing as each week went by. Bowie's lover, Ava Cherry, and superstar-in-waiting Luther Vandross were among those called in to add some soulful backing vocals, and Carlos Alomar had been drafted in to provide some seriously funky rhythm guitar. 'Young Americans', 'It's Gonna Be Me', 'John, I'm Only Dancing', 'Can You Hear Me?' and 'Somebody Up There Likes Me', as well as covers of R&B staples 'Footstompin'' and 'Knock On Wood', gave the rock show the air of a soul revue, too.

By the October, Mike Garson had become musical director, and his band opened for Bowie with some good-time soul and jazzy flourishes. The final song of this set was a reworking of Bowie's 1969 song, 'Memory Of A Free Festival' and as the congregation sang, 'The sun machine is coming down, and we're gonna have a party, wohoho yeah,' Bowie took to the stage like a stick insect in a suit, his features ashen, his hair dyed crimson and blonde, a one-man living contradiction, part post-glam decadence, part Latino soul boy.

By the time of *David Live*'s release in October 1974, it was already largely out of date. Recorded just before the full-scale soul kick, *David Live* itself is a decadent, empty record, possibly the most deranged of his career. The tracks positively reek of paranoia and desperation. Some of the performances are as epic as any live Bowie material. Slick's guitar work, piercing, savage and high in the mix, is superb, and the actual musicianship is intricate and fluid, with beautiful surprise flourishes – a barking-mad piano trill, a rattling castanet, a lone oboe line – it's all glitzy, yet oddly formed and compelling. And, warts and all, it does sound like a live recording, even though some parts had to be redone in the studio. Virtually all the backing vocals had to be resung because of 'loss of mic contact', a euphemism for inaudible or breathless vocals delivered by backing singers dancing around too much. Through necessity, singing was coming a poor second to show.

As the cover shot for the *David Live* album shows, Bowie was deathlike and painfully thin; a skeleton in suit and braces. When Bowie remarked that the album ought to have been called 'David Bowie Is Alive And Well And Living Only In Theory' (a waggish appropriation from one of his singing heroes, Jacques Brel, whose musical, *Jacques Brel is Alive and Well and Living in Paris*, was a Broadway musical and film), he wasn't far off the mark.

Bowie's appearance on *The Dick Cavett Show* on 29 October was a portrait in televisual weirdness, with an almost incoherent pop star sniffing his way through the interview, punctuating his disconnected sentences with sharp taps on the floor with that most essential of rock-star accessories, a cane. Bowie then got down to '1984', 'Young Americans' and a version of 'Footstompin'', with Ava Cherry dancing on top of the piano! Alomar had tipped off Patti Brett and the Sigma Kids that Bowie was doing the show. 'I knew he was doing drugs, but I didn't pay that much attention to it until he did *The Dick Cavett Show*,' recalls Patti Brett. 'For me that was the first time that it hit me that he was doing way too many drugs, because he could hardly speak, he was such a mess. There was lots of nose sniffing and nose rubbing, but I was in denial!'

By the October of 1974, Bowie's stage presentation was stripped down and stark. Out went Hunger City and its appurtenances. In came a simple soul review with Bowie backlit, his shadow towering above the performers on a screen at the back of the stage. For Carlos Alomar, it was a great experience: 'I was finally on the road with my wife and friends, and making money!' However, the band itself was not altogether solid in its mutual appreciation, as Alomar goes on to say. 'I remember that, one day, Pablo Rosario, the conga player for the *Diamond Dogs* tour said, "Hey yo brother man, this dude Earl Slick hates your guts because he thinks you're here to take his gig." And I said, "Hey, I'm not here to take anyone's gig, I'm here to do my gig." The problem was that a rock'n'roll tour was coming face to face with an R&B

review. It's an intimidating factor because you know that, sooner or later, one of you is out of a gig. I like Earl Slick. He played on the bottom half of the guitar and I played on the top, so we never conflicted. I'm used to working in R&B groups where there are three or even four guitar players playing at the same time, so you've got to know how to lay your groove next to the guitar players with you. For me to get together with Earl Slick was absolutely nothing, but it was extremely something for him, because I don't think he dug any of that.'

The major problem for Slick was that in his eyes he was subjected to a campaign to get him off the tour: 'When he [Alomar] went in to finish off the Sigma sessions, I got this kind of insulting phone call from a guy called Pat Gibbons, Bowie's tour co-ordinator. He said that I probably wouldn't be doing the tour because they'd found Carlos. But, as it turned out, I was called in to do the tour because what nobody was probably thinking about at the time was that Bowie couldn't just go out and play eight new songs from *Young Americans*. They needed me for the rock material. But when I did come back in after the Pat Gibbons phone call I was always looking over my shoulder thinking they were going to fire me. But Carlos to me was the perfect team member for when we went out live because there were different styles that needed to be covered. We covered all the bases; we were a very good guitar team.'

The *Young Americans* tour was daring. This latest version of Bowie struck some hard-bitten journalists as disingenuous though. Lester Bangs wrote: 'Bowie has just changed his props: last tour it was boxing gloves, skulls and giant hands, this tour it's black folk.'

Whatever else, this draining tour-record-tour-record schedule was at least paying off for Bowie. That autumn, *David Live* also hit the US Top 10. The downside was his lack of visibility back home, and the concomitant downswing in his fortunes on the domestic front. True, *Diamond Dogs* was an instant Number 1 and stayed at the top for a month. *David Live* only reached Number 2, though, the first Bowie album for two-and-a-half years to miss the top spot. RCA, in a dosh-catching exercise, had followed up the 'Rebel Rebel' single with the distinctly un-poppy 'Rock'n'Roll Suicide', then almost two years old and a track which most Bowie fans already had, and it stalled just outside the Top 20, as did 'Diamond Dogs', a poor choice as a single, released in the summer. 'Knock On Wood', a live version of the Floyd/

Cropper Stax classic, put him back into the Top 10 later in the year but, by the end of 1974, it was clear that after the huge success of his glam-era records, Bowie had peaked commercially in the UK. Promoters, who feared that the mooted price of £7 for a ticket would be too much for the punters, turned down the *Diamond Dogs Revue*, scheduled for May 1975 at Wembley Empire Pool. The UK never got a chance to see Bowie's most theatrical tour to date.

Bowie himself was constantly at work and constantly at play. His latest (and strangest) liaison was a brief friendship with fading Hollywood celebrity Elizabeth Taylor. Taylor, who had not acted in any film of note for years, was famous just because she was Elizabeth Taylor. Bowie found her fascinating. This very odd couple, the twenty-something rock star and the forty-something celebrity, were shot by *People* magazine staring gently into each other's eyes. So began an era of celebrity chum-ups. Cher and, most famously, Bing Crosby would follow. As Bowie became personally more dysfunctional, his public appearances were designed to make him fit for family entertainment. Throughout the next two years, Bowie would be sold in the States as a friendly, cool, though eccentric, pop star. His public persona could hardly have been more different from his private self.

In November 1974 Bowie returned to Philadelphia, where he is rumoured to have cut a version of Bruce Springsteen's 'It's Hard To Be A Saint In The City'. A DJ called Ed Sharkey had introduced them the previous August, and Bowie's interest in Springsteen must stand as one of the oddest aspects of his career – Springsteen homespun, undecorated, telling tales of American blue-collar wisdom, Bowie flamboyant, epicene, a musical dabbler. As their careers developed, Springsteen would be Bowie's polar opposite, revving his audience up with honest emotion, sweat pouring down the mic stand, his music all big, bold flourishes, Bowie's all about subterfuge. Like Iggy Pop and Lou Reed, Springsteen, if only initially, fascinated Bowie with his streetwise music. Again, he was the 'authentic' pop star Bowie could never (and never wanted to) be.

After the gig at the Convention Center in Philadelphia, Bowie threw a backstage party in a bar. The Sigma Kids were there in force, some of them underage. The party was eventually broken up after a police raid, and Bowie was almost arrested. Patti Brett remembers the farcical nature of the police bust: 'The bars close at 2 a.m., and it was a quarter after three and we were still in the bar. It was a private party, but the police raided it and started taking David away! There's actually a photograph of all the cops in leather jackets leading him down the steps. He had this big green mohair fur coat and this little red beret and sunglasses – he looked like a little Christmas tree! He was very calm. Everyone else in the place was freaking out. They were arresting everyone in the bar and the bar staff were sneaking people out the back door. Nothing ever came of it, though. He wasn't charged and I think they were doing it more for show. It was just so funny to see these tons, and I mean tons, of police come in as if we were these horrible people who needed controlling, and then them escorting him down the steps.'

Another added bonus in January 1975 was an opportunity for Bowie to hook up with the 34-year-old ex-Beatle John Lennon. Lennon was estranged from his wife, Yoko Ono, and in the middle of his 'lost weekend'. This 'lost weekend' was in fact a fifteen-month brandy bender, which saw Lennon regress into a boorish, unreconstituted lad, and hell-raise it up like pop's equivalent of Oliver Reed, drinking himself comatose with singer Harry Nilsson, ex-Beatle Ringo Starr and loony drummer Keith Moon. His assistant May Pang, it is alleged, was told by Yoko not to reject Lennon if he made any amorous advances, and soon Pang and Lennon were lovers.

Bowie and Lennon clicked immediately (as did Tony Visconti and May Pang, who eventually married) and they were soon fooling around in a New York studio with Carlos Alomar. Here's Alomar's version of how he, Bowie and Lennon tore down one song and, through a process of trial and error, built a future US Number 1 out of the damage:

Bowie was doing a song called 'Footstompin'' on tour which we really liked. I immediately started playing to that song (the 'Fame' riff). So we went into the studio to record it at Electric Ladyland in New York. But it just didn't record well. It just sounded like a plain stupid old rock'n'roll song. David didn't even like it. So what he did was just cut it up into blues changes, which is one-four-five-four, which is what 'Fame' is. He cut it up so he just had drums, bass and that one guitar line, and while he was doing that he found out that Lennon was in town, so he invited him to come down. They had some conversations, and I was basically waiting for him to stop talking to Lennon so we could get on with the damn thing. The next thing, Lennon is picking up one of my guitars and he's going into the recording booth to play a little acoustic on it. So we're playing everything and everything's cool. We finish recording and play back the tape. Everyone's listening to it, and we keep hearing this thing on tape what we now know as the 'Fame' noise. 'What the hell is that?' David said. Lennon was playing acoustic guitar and it seems that he put his chin on the acoustic guitar when he played and just the breathing he did produced that funny noise. David thought he was saying 'Fame'. 'He's saying "Fame", I'm telling you!' Then he and John left and I stayed with the engineer, Harry Maslin, to work out some overdubs and ideas for the song. Going back to the whole James Brown period, where you had four or five guitar players playing at a time and it was no big deal, I started laying down all these other guitar parts. David came back some time later and I said, 'Hey David, you've got to hear this, it's cool.' He heard it and said, 'That's it, it's done, it's finished,' and then he took it home, wrote the words and came back the next day and did the vocals.

'Fame' was born out of a series of lucky flukes and inspired improvisation. Bowie stepped in and went for the kill when he knew the song was turning into something great and also called a halt to the music just as it was ready. Despite what most rock biographers have said, Alomar denies that the song was based on Shirley And Company's 'Shame Shame Shame' – 'Absolutely not, that song never came into the picture. Unless David had heard it and had it in mind when he did the vocal. When it comes to words, those are all David's words, so if he was inspired by anything, then I would never know. But that reference never came up. When he came back with the lyric, it fell in exactly the same place. I think it was coincidental more than anything else.'

There's a sly nastiness in the lyric, which is an anatomy of the perils of rock superstardom. When Bowie sings: 'Fame, puts you there where things are hollow/Fame – what you need you have to borrow', it's a more-or-less direct attack on the MainMan-created entertainment charade, depicting Bowie inhabiting a world of hollow emotion, living on hand-outs. 'Fame' is, lyrically, the antithesis of the optimism of a song such as 'Star', in which Bowie, the would-be star, wishes for a life of riches and plans coming on 'like a regular superstar'. Now he's jaded and wants out. Musically, 'Fame' booms and echoes, with Alomar's tele-phone-trill-like rhythm guitar (the sound of constant demand, engagements being made, people calling nonstop for a piece of the star) punctuating the spaces in the music. A backward section at the beginning and some speed silliness at the end, with Lennon and Bowie's voices tumbling down the octaves from unsingable high to unsingable low, create one of Bowie's funkiest and most schizoid moments.

When he found out that he had missed the session, Visconti was downcast: 'I certainly wish I'd been there for the John Lennon dates. I stayed up all night with John and David a couple of nights before I went back to London to mix the album. I would've jumped on Concorde at my own expense to be there for "Fame". David claims it happened too spontaneously to call me back, and it was only an experiment.'

Visconti's disappointment turned to near-mortification when he discovered, on hearing the new album, finally released the following March, that it had been completely repackaged, retitled and reshaped. Suddenly, some of Visconti's favourite tracks, such as 'It's Gonna Be Me', were nowhere to be found, while two new, non-Visconti-produced songs, 'Fame' and 'Across The Universe', had been inserted. The latter, a cover version of a 1970 Beatles song, sounded like a lacklustre filler, and its inclusion was a mystery given the sort of material taken off at the eleventh hour.

By the end of 1974, Bowie was living in a small house in the Chelsea region of Manhattan with the rent paid by MainMan. He was working with video producer John Dove on a *Diamond Dogs* screenplay and film. Dove arranged for private tuition in film history from a local academic and Bowie would spend days watching and rewatching cult films from the 1920s, such as Fritz Lang's *Metropolis*. Ever the autodidact, Bowie took research for his projects extremely seriously.

Bowie was still dating Ava Cherry and it has been reported that he was planning to divorce Angie to marry her. He was also in the process of divorcing himself from Defries. Bowie had finally lost patience with him and, with the help of lawyer Michael Lippman, spent the first months of 1975 trying to begin the process of extricating himself from the MainMan empire.

On 29 January Bowie visited RCA Records in New York, demanded an advance of money against *Young Americans* and told them he was splitting from MainMan. Defries was informed by letter of Bowie's decision the next day. The release of *Young Americans* in the States was then delayed after Tony Defries issued an injunction and both MainMan and RCA haggled over the ownership of the new album. On 1 April, after a 48-hour round of negotiations between Bowie, MainMan and RCA, a deal was struck, the terms of which were so punitive to the Bowie camp that allegedly the singer broke down at the conference table and was in shock for a week. MainMan would have a direct stake in Bowie's future until September 1982. Not only was Defries now entitled to half of Bowie's earnings on all records from *Hunky Dory* through to *David Live*, he was also entitled to a huge sixteen per cent gross share of all Bowie's earnings until 1982.

The main reason behind the split was not primarily Defries, or the circus that was MainMan, but Bowie's own sense of self-loathing, stoked by cocaine abuse. It is undeniable that the terms of Bowie's MainMan contract basically meant that Bowie slaved for nothing other than advances and credit, while Defries made himself extremely rich. Bowie, producers, record company people, assistants and musicians alike were all abusing themselves chemically and the result, by 1975, was that ordinary lines of communication had collapsed. Defries himself was completely straight and viewed Bowie's addiction with increasing horror. Bowie was not hiding his drug intake now. Invited round to meet Ava Cherry's mother and father, Bowie finished off his meal by bringing out a phial of coke and snorting right in front of them. Defries was running out of patience, and running out of enthusiasm for an artist who appeared intent on killing himself.

'When I found out that the management company MainMan had virtually despoiled me of any financial worth that I had, and that I was really virtually broke, I was momentarily devastated,' said Bowie in 2000. 'But, believe it or not, it wasn't completely crushing because I had such reliance on the fact that I was a good writer and a good performer that I didn't see myself having a problem of pulling myself back out of it in the future. That was just a monumental self-confidence in my own talents. I was determined I wouldn't be sunk.'

Just as he broke with MainMan, Bowie finally became the superstar in the States Defries had worked so long for. A whole empire might have been founded on the back of Bowie's talent, but Defries had helped make Bowie one of the biggest acts on the planet. His achievement, and that of MainMan, was considerable. *Young Americans* solidified it.

The record finally hit the shops in April 1975 in the US, reached Number 9, and stayed in the American charts for a week short of a year. In the UK, it was, by Bowie's standards, only a moderate success, reaching Number 2 but not coming close to matching the sales of *Diamond Dogs*. The first single, 'Young Americans', now the album's title track, confirmed the downturn in Bowie's support, reaching only Number 18 in the UK charts that spring.

The UK was largely resisting Bowie's American acclimatisation. Although tracks such as 'Panic In Detroit' from *Aladdin Sane* and '1984' from *Diamond Dogs* had presaged a groovier future for Bowie, *Young Americans* was a huge shock for those fans who were still bewitched by his glam-rock records, some of which were barely a year or two old. One UK review of the album ran: 'Bowie Takes Time-Warped Weirdness To The Cleaners', while some critics welcomed the more directly emotional music on the new album. However, the dread word 'sell-out' was seen on the letters pages of the likes of *Melody Maker*. Had Bowie relinquished the serious sophistication of rock and sold out to a 'lesser' genre of music?

Nevertheless, *Young Americans* would prove to be one of Bowie's most influential records. There had always been an interface between some of the arty set of glam rockers and the smooth soul boys and girls (same style fetishism, same mistrust of the rock orthodoxy) and *Young Americans* united the two factions. The common connecting locale for both sets of fans was gay subculture in general, and the disco in particular, a safe haven for both straights and gays in its eclectic mix of music and lack of stuffiness. Disco appealed to the dispossessed – whether they be gays, blacks or women – in much the same way Bowie's glam-era music had harnessed the discontent of the out-of-place adolescent, the bedsit intellectual and the sexually confused. It was no surprise that at this time straight soon-to-be punk rocker John Lydon was frequenting gay discos, to feel comfortable and to listen to some decent music.

Young Americans was released just after disco had hit the pop charts with George McCrae's transatlantic Number 1, 'Rock Your Baby', and The Hues Corporation's 'Rock The Boat'. By the end of 1974 the disco genre was already sending itself up in the guise of Disco Tex And The Sex-O-Lettes and 'Get Dancin'' which featured the lead vocals of Joseph Montanez Junior, owner of a chain of hairdressing salons. Scotland's Average White Band were enjoying a huge hit with their funk hit, 'Pick Up The Pieces', and just as the Bowie album came out, Shirley And Company's 'Shame Shame Shame' also entered the charts.

With hindsight, *Young Americans* is a curious album. It's certainly not an authentic soul record. 'Somebody Up There Likes Me' uses call-and-response structures, but the lyric itself, with its stream of consciousness and almost list-like rant was more like 'Cygnet Committee' than an authentic soul song, and also a sort of slowed-down white version of the proto-rap developed by Bob Dylan on his 'Subterranean Homesick Blues'. *Young Americans* sounded absolutely nothing like previous Bowie albums either. There was some sort of progression from 'Space Oddity' to *Diamond Dogs*, but on *Young Americans* the writing is far more personalised. The title track may be a piece of reportage, an expressionistic tumble of words rather cynically depicting young American love, but 'Win', 'Can You Hear Me?' and 'Fascination' are written in the first person, and are direct and emotive. In particular, 'Can You Hear Me?' written in 1973, most probably about and for Ava Cherry, is a direct, emotional love song, quite unlike any other recent Bowie song with the possible exception of 'Lady Grinning Soul': 'I need love so badly, I want you most of all'. It's almost impossible to decide whether Bowie was simply mimicking the sort of lyrics he was hearing on black American radio or actually, for one of the first times since songs such as 'A Letter To Hermione', coming clean with his 'real' emotions, desires and wishes.

Bowie never wrote love songs, finding the topic rather false, less engaging than tales of apocalyptic breakdown and psychic disturbance. Now he was at least making a good attempt at faking basic human emotional responses, even if his own personality was akin to that of a zombie.

Dubbing the album 'plastic soul', Bowie said later that year: 'It's the phoniest R&B I've ever heard . . . If I ever would have got my hands on that record when I was growing up I would have cracked it over my knee.' Talking to Radio 1 in 1993, he added, 'There was no point doing a straightforward take on American soul music because that had been done already . . . You couldn't envisage any American soul artist doing those songs. But they paid homage to the soul sound . . . Things like "Win" – the chord structures are much more of a European thing than an American thing . . . I got these pretty heavyweight American soul musicians working on it that gave some sort of a kind of fake authenticity to it. It really was a "plastic soul" album.'

'Win' is the album's standout track: lush, swooning, with one of the most gorgeous melodies Bowie has ever written. Bowie sings wonderfully well, neither hamming it up nor straining, and the moment when the music swirls up a key towards the end is genuine beauty. Bowie is out of breath on the title track, its swinging Latino beat drowned out by Bowie's almost demonic rant, like a preacher possessed. However, if Bowie is a preacher, he is rehearsing, not feeling, the fire of his words. There's nothing in Bowie's belly but the emptiness of desensitisation: 'Ain't there one damn song that can make me break down and cry?'

Next up is 'Fascination', co-written with the then unknown Luther Vandross. Not only does it have the best riff on the album but it also funks up the 'strange fascination' motif of 'Changes'. If 'Fame' is a wearied statement of disenchantment with the rock business, then 'Fascination' reaffirms a compulsion to keep doing, questing, acting, asking, originally set out in 'Changes'. Beneath the drugs, and the depression, and the financial and business calamities, his artistic will was still awesome. 'Somebody Up There Likes Me', with its long, languid sax introduction, was another song about the power of the media to reduce human beings to empty visions of the real thing: 'There was a time when we judged a man by what he'd seen/Now we judge them from the screen, what they look like, where they've been'. Again, as on 'Fame', this is Bowie musing about the lack of humanity within stardom itself. Again, it's evidence that he is one of the few pop stars with the ability to stand aside from his situation; to objectify that position and comment on the inside from the outside. As on *Ziggy Stardust*, although now with more lyrical sophistication and irony, Bowie is providing a vivid analysis of stardom itself while simultaneously acting out that stardom in real life.

Young Americans' influence on contemporary pop was major. Bowie developed, vocally, a sort of 'white hysteria'; a white European take on black music. He made it possible for 70s and 80s white musicians, who might never have played a funky bass line in their life, to appreciate contemporary black sounds. Bowie was taken very seriously as a musician and as a weather vane of good taste within British popular music. If he did it, and if he did it well, others would, too. It now seems remarkable that one man's vision would have counted for so much, but it did.

One of the major effects on Bowie's own career was that his singing and writing style would never be the same again. Bowie would almost always have some sort of a groove in his solo songs, if not his instrumentals, from this point on. Furthermore, his voice lost that haughty 'head' tone and developed into a big, booming, colourful, almost operatic, baritone vibrato. According to Bowie biographers Zanetta and Edwards, Bowie deliberately tried to 'lower his voice so that it would sound dark, husky and black'. The Ziggy-era vocal style was unmistakably English, with none of the Americanisms of Rod Stewart, Elton John or Mick Jagger. It was also slightly fey and shrieking, and this odd delivery, as if he were singing with a clenched jaw in a proud, affected manner, set against the hard-rocking style of The Spiders From Mars, would influence The Smiths in the 1980s and Suede in the 1990s. On *Diamond Dogs*, Bowie had perfected the technique of 'octave doubling' on tracks such as 'Big Brother'. By recording two vocal lines an octave apart, he was able to give much of his subsequent music an eerie, disembodied aura. By the time of *Young Americans*, Bowie's vocal was altogether much lower and resonant, and was placed higher in the mix, thus creating an illusion of intimacy. The full-throated vibrato which he uses so much now, and which has far more in common with non-rock singers such as Bill Medley and Scott Walker than it does with standard rock singing, was developed first on *Young Americans*. Trevor Bolder has said that, although the 'control he had over his voice was stunning', 'there's no way he's a rock singer'. Yet there was, to some ears, still something rather odd about the new, richer, seemingly more committed style. Writer and broadcaster Paul Gambaccini put it like this: 'You know he's distant from a soul singer in the way he sings: "Ain't there one damn song that'll make me break down and cry?" It's strangely removed from what you would consider to be a "break down and cry" song.'

Bowie could be ironic when other singers – Elvis Presley, for example – could not. Presley wasn't able to distance himself from the pose he produced, and, consequently, in the 1960s and 1970s he slipped into self-parody. Writer John Shepherd says: 'When Elvis was doing an imitation, he was doing an imitation of himself. Bowie isn't doing an imitation of himself because it's not clear who Bowie is, and that's the big difference.'

Young Americans was important, although its true significance was, perhaps, only slowly revealed as the 70s turned into the 80s. As a white artist crossing over into disco/soul music, he paved the way for the greater commercial success later in the decade of The Bee Gees. Just months after Bowie's work at Sigma Sound, Elton John, who had already tracked Bowie's 'Space Oddity' with his own 'Rocket Man', recorded 'Philadelphia Freedom'. By mid-1975, funk and disco had become hugely alluring for many a rock act. Roxy Music devised their own funky bass line for 'Love Is The Drug' and 'Both Ends Burning'. The funkiness of the art-rock of Talking Heads later in the decade was also in this tradition. As the 1980s unwound, the Bowie model of white, blue-eyed soul was rehashed, with ever-decreasing dividends, by the likes of ABC, Spandau Ballet and Simply Red.

Bowie pioneered the 'wedge' haircut for that album's cover and traded in the glitter trappings of the early 70s for a version of American cool, as Peter Yorke noticed in his almost contemporaneous 1980 book, *Style Wars*: 'Bowie's [latest] incarnation . . . baggy Aladdin pants, Snob sweat shirts, hair parted to the left in that heavy bob, is the basis of a whole group's style: the soul boys. The Fiorucci baggy jeans, white socks, sneakers, and The Wedge, the haircut Bowie had in *The Man Who Fell To Earth*, and on the cover of *Low*; the most persistently influential haircut of the decade.'

The *Young Americans* look thus provided a focus for a 'white' expression of affinity with and admiration for a perceived 'black' musical form. What Bowie did in 1975, the journalist Robert Elms argued in an article in *The Face*, set the tone in British popular culture for the decade that followed. Looking back in 1985, Elms suggested: 'Now, exactly ten years later, it's all come true. We're a nation living in a disco, everybody's a soul boy, everybody's a trendy. There's black music in the charts and in the clubs that everyone goes to and there were Wedges on the miners' picket lines and on the pitch at Luton . . . When Bowie performed 'Golden Years' on *Soul Train* all those years ago he was the first English artist to tart up black music and sell it back to the Americans since The Beatles did it in 64. In the 80s doing precisely that has become one of the cornerstones of our national economy.'

If all David Bowie was doing was 'tarting up' soul and selling it back to whites, he was simultaneously gaining the respect of some black artists, too. And they don't come much bigger than the godfather of soul himself, Mr James Brown. In the 1980s and 1990s, Brown was sampled more times than any other artist, but in the mid-1970s, well before musical theft was legit, he was caught red-handed nicking a song from a most unlikely source. Carlos Alomar: 'We found out that James Brown had decided to cover "Fame" and he renamed it something different ["Hot" – a single issued in January 1976] and what's worse is that I knew some of the musicians on that track. [David] said to me, "Carlos, let's just wait." First of all, he was extremely flattered that James Brown would take one of his songs. "Let's just wait and see if it charts. If it charts, then we'll sue him." But the record didn't do anything, so we left it alone.'

Despite the adulation and attention of the white mainstream rock and soul audience, in the States Bowie was still finding it nigh on impossible to throw off the gay tag. A crushingly embarrassing moment came when Bowie was asked to present the 'Queen of Soul', Aretha Franklin, with a Grammy on 1 March 1975. Bowie gave a genuinely funny introductory speech to the assembled dickie bows in the audience before presenting the award to Franklin, who promptly told the viewing millions, 'I'm so happy, I could even kiss David Bowie.'

But the gouster act had made David Bowie a star in the biggest market in the world and, for the next eighteen months, he was bigger across the pond than in any other territory. He was by now resident in Los Angeles, but desperately unwell and unhappy. With a mind already confused by cocaine, Bowie was about to mutate on a film set in New Mexico, into his craziest and most sinister persona yet. The Thin White Duke was about to make his debut.

7. MAKING SURE WHITE STAINS, 1975–1976

I went to the Academy Awards in 1975. Bowie was there and so was John Lennon. Bowie's got the huge Black Spanish hat, he's got the cape – it's like The House Of Wax. He's like a duded up version of Vincent Price. He looks fuckin' dramatic, he looks dynamite, like the ultimate gigolo. There's this party going on and he's unquestionably in character. He's surrounded by eight tonnes of charisma and everyone is gasping. I haven't seen him for six years, I'm sitting having a drink, and I'm thinking, 'bloody hell, can you believe it'. He wanders over and sees my wife and me and goes, 'God, bloody hell, how are you?' The Thin White Duke disappears and a completely different bloke appears. He gives us a hug and a kiss, and he sits and talks to us animatedly for fifteen minutes or so. And when he gets up to leave and on goes the hat, here comes the charisma, and he's immediately The Thin White Duke again. It was like that film, The Mask. What a star!

GUS DUDGEON, 1998

The Thin White Duke was Bowie's nastiest pop facade – a heartless, under-emoting, amoral zombie of a figure developed during the second half of his American sojourn. Bowie himself referred to the creation as part and parcel of a wish to get back to Europe. His creation embodied what the Germans call *kalte Pracht* (cold splendour) while also echoing the surrealistic silent film greats of the 20s such as Keaton. 'There's a lot of Buster Keaton in everything I do,' conceded Bowie a few years later in an interview with *Rolling Stone*. Just as Keaton was the great stone face, or like the mime, clown or kabuki artist whose features have become so fixed that they become stuck in a permanent grin or grimace, so Bowie himself suggested everything and nothing. He provided his fans with an image so devoid of emotion that they could read anything into those frozen features. Just where the Thin White Duke ended and Bowie began is a moot point. If one agrees with Bowie's own analysis in interviews, then these invented personae governed the real-life David Jones and made him act in accordance with their character. But how much of this is a smokescreen to cover up, or excuse, huge lapses in taste, half-baked intellectualising and coke-driven madness? All of these character traits were displayed by Bowie over the next eighteen months – paradoxically, one of the most creative periods of his life.

It was on the set of his first major film role, as alien Thomas Newton in Nic Roeg's sci-fi classic, *The Man Who Fell To Earth*, that Bowie's off-screen unhappiness fused with the alien morphology of the Newton character. Bowie became a frozen addict – part media creation, part human being. Throughout the Thin White Duke period, he was in a state of psychic terror. In 2000, Bowie called Roeg a 'marvellous man' but added: 'I find it very sad, because I look at a younger me and I feel almost protective because I can see an incredible amount of pain and isolation that I was putting myself through with my drug abuse and I just feel quite sad for that person. Nic [Roeg] had a knack for being able to create a chemistry between the off-screen personas of the stars, and the on-screen characters they were playing. You might say that he was abusing my psychological state at the time. But he did pay me for abusing me!'

By mid-1975 Bowie's cocaine intake was astronomic. He was still married to Angie but she spent a good deal of her time back in the UK, while Bowie stayed in the States. Neither Bowie nor Angie were ever faithful, but the premise on which their relationship was originally based, i.e. that of an open marriage, had simply collapsed into what Bowie himself now calls promiscuity. Divorced from Tony Defries, he promoted lawyer Michael Lippman to manager, both MainMan's Tony Zanetta and Angie Bowie herself having been suitors for the role. Bowie had relocated from New York to Los Angeles, once again to rented accommodation in Doheney Drive, LA: a comparatively small, cube-shaped house with an indoor swimming pool, it had two white sphinxes in the garden (symbols of the occult and bisexuality) and was full of occultist Egyptian *objets d'art*. Bowie would sit for long hours in his bedroom, the searing sun blocked out by drawn curtains. As black candles burned, the pop star would draw pentagrams on huge sheets of paper or the walls. Bowie's paranoia was entering a new, even more sinister phase. He was not able to make any records in this state of oblivion: his last trip into the studio of any note had been months earlier with John Lennon to record 'Fame' and it would be another six months before he would record again. Amazingly, however, Bowie gathered himself together sufficiently for his debut big-time acting role.

The colonisation of film by Bowie was a logical and wholly expected move – after all, his stage shows and songs had a cinematic quality. He was also supremely photogenic, and had, way back in the 1960s as we have seen, made some tentative forays into film acting as part of ex-manager Ken Pitt's vision of him as entertainer. In addition, Bowie was hugely interested in film as a medium, kept an extensive library, particularly of pre-1930s expressionist films, and wanted to know about the mechanics of direction and production. Bowie had also begun work on, and then abandoned, two possible film projects. The first was a *Ziggy Stardust* musical and stage show, the second, an adaptation of *Diamond Dogs*. In early 1975, according to Tony Visconti, 'Bowie busied himself creating a film, set in Hunger City, using primitive video techniques. I remember helping him to construct a miniature *Diamond Dogs* set in his hotel-suite living room, and to film him walking electronically through the set. The script was actually the videotape itself at one point. I've never seen it written down on paper, although I'm sure it exists in that form by now.'

The role in *The Man Who Fell To Earth* was originally intended for Peter O'Toole, with actor and novelist Michael Crichton, all six foot nine of him, another option. The alien in the William Tevis novel was a simulacrum of a human being, but a very tall one, and Nic Roeg needed a Robert Wadlow of an actor. Bowie, who claims to be five feet ten, was on the titchy side for the role. Nevertheless, he had something that O'Toole and Crichton didn't have – real-life weirdness. Roeg had been captivated by Alan Yentob's Bowie documentary, *Cracked Actor*, aired that January on the BBC. Edwyn Collins, lead singer with Orange Juice in the 1980s, once dryly remarked that the only thing to match Bowie's complete freakiness in this documentary was Princess Di's exclusive BBC *Panorama* in 1995 (with Martin Bashir). Anyone who witnessed her manic, glazed stare and disconnectedly earnest behaviour will know exactly what he meant. So it appeared that Bowie wouldn't actually have to do very much acting at all, so extraterrestrial was his terrestrial demeanour. Roeg was also attracted to Bowie because of 'his sense of mime and movement' on stage: Roeg had, of course, used a pop star, Mick Jagger, for his 1970 film, *Performance*, and would later use Art Garfunkel in *Bad Timing*. His then latest movie, *Don't Look Now*, an adaptation of the Daphne Du Maurier short story set in Venice, remains unsurpassed in its psychological terror, and did absolutely nothing for the sale of red duffel coats to parents of the under-fives either. In short, Roeg was exactly the right sort of director for Bowie: unconventional, visually daring and cutting edge.

Roeg went to see Bowie in New York. His appointment was for 7 p.m., but Bowie only remembered about it at 8 p.m. and, figuring Roeg would have long since departed, decided to get on with other things. Manfully, Roeg stuck it out for eight hours, sitting in the Bowie kitchen until his return. The two got chatting and it was clear to Roeg that he had found his alien. Roeg later commented to journalist Tony Parsons, 'Usually an actor comes for a part but on other occasions the part seems to go towards one actor. That was the case with David and *The Man Who Fell To Earth*.'

The film itself dealt with Roegian themes of weird sex, alienation and space-time fission, rather than the standard currency of sci-fi/fantasy light entertainment. For most of the film, Roeg's alien was to be Bowie as he was, not Bowie dressed in a fright costume and ten tonnes of green slime. Bowie's alien, Thomas Jerome Newton, journeys to Earth in search of resources for his dying planet and becomes corrupted by mankind. The film works on two levels. As a superior sci-fi film, it is full of genuinely shocking moments, such as the scene, which had to be edited out when the film was first released in the US, where Bowie reveals his true alien physiognomy, with its almond-shaped eyes and hairless body, to his girlfriend Mary-Lou (played by Candy Clarke), who promptly responds by wetting her knickers. There are also extraterrestrial sex scenes portrayed in voyeuristic flashback as we get a glimpse of alien intercourse – all oily, smooth, fluid and slimey. Second, it is a sort of parable. Newton is the

Everyman figure, or Christ figure, who comes down from the heavens only to be 'sacrificed' in the final scene. His fall from grace (by the end of the film Newton is corrupted by the media, big business and booze, and is unable to return home to save his planet) is meant to be read allegorically as a modern-day morality play. One scene, showing Newton overdosed on television, provides a vivid glimpse of the future – 1990s information overload and *Zoo TV* wrapped into one stylish whole. As journalist Neil Spencer wrote: 'Roeg's kaleidoscopic approach to film-making is neatly caught by the image of Bowie, remote control in hand, sat before a bank of TV screens, absorbing a simultaneous barrage of old movies, pop songs, nature documentaries and news flashes. The post-modern age, one feels, started right here.'

Bowie was defensive about his acting ability: 'I'm not a good actor; too much of a ham' – but during shooting that summer he was the model professional. He arrived on the set two days early, and watched Roeg like a hawk, constantly picking up film-making tips. He was diligent and hardworking. 'He's got fantastic concentration,' Roeg told *Creem* in 1975, 'and he's also got an amazing self-discipline.'

Bowie made it a condition of his appearance that he would be allowed to choose his own wardrobe, and his '75 look – crimson and blond centre-parted hair, jacket and fedora – was essentially that of Newton's. He passed his time on the set writing short stories, lyrics and the music which he had been asked to produce for the album's soundtrack. Bowie commented to journalists later in the 70s that, after a day's shooting, his face would positively ache, so expressionless and unsmiling was the character he had portrayed.

Producer Nic Roeg told the rock star that there was a high probability that the role would stay with him long after filming had ended. This is indeed what happened. Not only did Bowie leave with Thomas Newton's frozen demeanour and otherworldly starkness; he also took with him the clothes and the haircut he had devised for the role. The Thin White Duke, Bowie's last and most desensitised alter ego, had been born. Just as Newton was an outsider, corrupted by contemporary mores and utterly rootless, his sense of self debased, so for his next recording project, Bowie, a spiritually debased shell of a man, traded on these fictionalised emotions and created an astonishing piece of work.

That Bowie's remarkable follow-up to *Young Americans*, originally titled *The Return Of The Thin White Duke*, turned out to be the masterpiece of invention it did was against all the odds.

In a prophetic moment in 1975, long before cultural commentators made capital out of such headlines, and a generation before Marilyn Manson said the same thing, Bowie famously pronounced rock dead. 'It's a toothless old woman,' he cried, 'I've rocked my last roll.' Despite having wallowed in all the trappings of rock superstardom, Bowie never really considered himself to be much of a rocker in the first place. He was now leaving rock behind, initially for his own idiosyncratic take on black American styles, and later for the rich vistas of European experimentalism. His assessment of his own legacy was surprisingly harsh. A few months later he told Cameron Crowe:

> It's interesting how this all started. At the time I did *Ziggy Stardust,* all I had was a small cult audience in England from *Hunky Dory.* I think it was out of curiosity that I began wondering what it would be like to be a rock and roll star. So basically, I wrote a script and played it out as Ziggy Stardust onstage and on record. I mean it when I say I didn't like all those albums – *Aladdin Sane*, *Pin Ups*, *Diamond Dogs*, *David Live*. It wasn't a matter of liking them, it was 'Did they work or not?' Yes, they worked. They kept the trip going. Now, I'm all through with rock and roll. Finished. I've rocked my last roll. It was great fun while it lasted but I won't do it again.

By mid-1975, Bowie was living a cocooned existence, disconnected from the real world and from his own emotions. Roeg told Tony Parsons in 1993: 'What I found so difficult was that he was so hard to reach – not emotionally, just on a purely physical level. There are barriers, a filter system, around every star, of course, but they seemed particularly strong around Bowie.'

Bowie wanted out, but, as yet, couldn't find the way. What was worse was the weight of expectation from a public who viewed him as synonymous with shock and outrage. How could Bowie pull back when his *raison d'être* was to keep pushing at boundaries of the abnormal? The fact that he came from a family with a history of mental illness, coupled with the fact that he was drawn to eccentric, erratic and, some would say, borderline psychotic personalities (Iggy Pop being a prime example at the time), meant that Bowie found madness, real and imagined, all around him.

Under this weight of emotional pressure, his mind was beginning to fracture. He was well under seven stone and survived on a diet of red and green peppers washed down by milk straight from the carton. 'I would keep a fridge fully stocked with this stuff,' Bowie remembered in 1998, 'and when I wasn't hallucinating I was sitting on the floor in the dark, lit by the little light inside the door, cutting up peppers with my knife and cramming them into my mouth . . . Meal times were 4 a.m. and 5 p.m. . . . The curtains were always closed. Didn't want the LA sun spoiling the vibe of eternal now.' A terrified Coco would try and get some proper food down him, and would help him through his more alarming coke binges, but there was little anyone could do for him. It was a story of utter abjection. 'The one thing I remember Coco telling me,' says producer Hugh Padgham, who worked with a saner Bowie much later, 'was that she would get up in the morning and find David slumped somewhere and would use the mirror that had the coke on it to put in front of his face to ascertain whether he was breathing or not. She would put the mirror in front of his nose so that it would steam up with the breath.'

The occult and numerology-fixated Bowie allegedly began storing his urine in the fridge so that no other wizard could use his bodily fluids to enchant him. Bowie was also indulging an interest in Kirlian photography, a technique developed by the Soviets which purports to measure the flow of animal magnetism in the human body. The technique was a reactive response to the Hindu occultists and Tibetan yogis, who had for centuries known how to control energy flows. An *Arena* Bowie special of 1993 reprinted a Kirlian photograph of the magnetic field surrounding his fingertip and his crucifix before and after consuming coke. The photograph, or one very like it, dated April 1975, was to be used over two decades later for the inside sleeve of *Earthling*.

'Every day of my life back then I was capable of staying up indefinitely. My chemistry must have been superhuman. I'd stay up for seven or eight days on the trot!' says Bowie in the 1990s. 'Of course, every day that you stayed up that long, the impending tiredness and fatigue produce that hallucinogenic state quite naturally . . . well, half-naturally. By the end of the week my whole life would be transformed into this bizarre nihilistic fantasy world of oncoming doom, mythological characters and imminent totalitarianism. Quite the worst.' He added, 'I was in LA with Egyptian décor. It was one of those rent-a-house places, but it appealed to me because I had this more than passing interest in Egyptian mysticism, the cabbala, all this stuff that is inherently misleading in life; a hodge-podge whose crux I've forgotten. But at the same time it seemed transparently obvious what the answer to life was. So the house occupied a ritualistic position in my life.'

Bowie was surrounded by post-hippie occultism. The Sunset Boulevard of the mid-1970s was over-running with occult shops. Bowie, searching for spiritual unity (it was around this time that he first began wearing a crucifix as a sort of talismanic protection against evil forces) soaked it all up like a sponge. Bowie became particularly interested in the teachings of theosophist Madame Blavatsky, notions of the esoteric and other occultist and cabbalistic works. But his interests, in part motivated by genuine curiosity, started to obsess, trouble and haunt him. 'I demonised myself and created many psychic wounds that took many years to heal,' said Bowie in 2002.

On one occasion Bowie rang his wife Angie in London, claiming he was being held somewhere in LA against his will by witches who wanted his semen in order that they might be impregnated on the Witches' Sabbath on 30 April. It transpired that he was merely spending time with some female fans but was so coked out he began to have paranoid, semi-hallucinogenic anxiety fits. Matters came to a head when he had his Doheney Drive residence professionally exorcised. According to Angie, the image of the devil was burned into the bottom of the indoor swimming pool after the event. Bowie needed help. He had obviously undergone a nervous breakdown after the final days of MainMan and needed urgent help for his addictions and for what was probably a state of near-anorexia. But none was offered and if it had been, Bowie would not have undergone a series of treatments willingly, so focused was he still on his various projects.

Perhaps most alarming during this deeply unhappy time for Bowie were his less than veiled public statements of appreciation for the theatricality of Hitler and the Nazis.

In an interview with Tony Parsons in 1993, Bowie spoke at length about the way in which his fascination with Nazism and mysticism grew out of control:

Goebbels intrigued me more than any of the other Nazis because of the way he used the media. He was an extraordinary guy ... And my other fascination with the Nazis was their search for the Holy Grail. There was this theory that they had come to England at some point before the war to the Glastonbury Tor to try and find the Holy Grail. It was this Arthurian need, this search for a mythological link with God.

But somewhere along the line it was perverted by what I was reading and what I was drawn to. And it was nobody's fault but my own. I was never turned by some satanist. It all happened in LA. There was something horrible permeating the air in LA in those days. The stench of Manson and the Sharon Tate murders ... And I was interested in the symbols of the Nazis. I think they had the most powerful set of symbols that have ever been invoked in terms of political history. The swastika. They took a Buddhist symbol, the Eastern symbol of the sun, and turned it around so that it became a symbol of the dark. That intrigued me about the Nazis. Who was the magus? Who was the black magician?

Looking back, it is clear that Bowie had always had an interest in the occult combined with a fascination for superhero figures. A song such as 1970's 'The Supermen' is an obvious example. In 1976, Bowie told Radio 1's Stuart Grundy, 'I was still going through the thing when I was pretending I understood Nietzsche ... A lot of that came out of trying to simplify books that I had read ... And I had tried to translate it into my own terms to understand it so "Supermen" came out of that ... It's pre-Fascist.' In 1971, on 'Quicksand', he sang: 'I'm not a prophet or a stone-age man/Just a mortal with potential of a superman'. Likewise, 'Oh You Pretty Things' carried the message: 'Let me make it plain/You gotta make way for the Homo Superior'. Also in 'Oh You Pretty Things', Bowie sings: 'We're a part of the Coming Race'.

The phrase 'the coming race' refers to a nineteenth-century novel of the same name by Bulwer Lytton. According to JH Brennan, author of *Occult Reich*, Lytton believed in the existence of the 'vril', 'an enormous reservoir of universal power, some of which could be concentrated in the human body'. In *The Coming Race*, Lytton describes a subterranean nation of supermen who have gained control of the vril and used it to work miracles.

And again, on 'Quicksand', Bowie sings: 'I'm closer to the Golden Dawn/Immersed in Crowley's uniform of imagery'.

The Hermetic Order of the Golden Dawn was instituted in 1888. Bram Stoker and WB Yeats were original members. JH Brennan points out that the Golden Dawn had a hierarchical structure, its leaders guided by mysterious secret chiefs, men who were at the top of the evolutionary tree: supermen.

Together with a rhythm section consisting of Carlos Alomar, Dennis Davis and George Murray, The E-Street Band's Roy Bittan on piano and whiz-kid Earl Slick on lead guitar, Bowie began work at Cherokee Studios in the early autumn of 1975 on what some critics would argue, perhaps unfashionably, is his finest record. Bowie himself admits that he cannot remember very much about recording the album at all. One of his only memories is standing with Earl Slick in the studio and asking him to play a Chuck Berry riff in the same key throughout the opening of 'Station To Station'. Apart from this little nugget, his mind is a complete blank. 'I have only flashes of making it,' Bowie would say much later. 'I have serious problems about that year or two. I can't remember how I felt; I have no emotional geography.'

When he began work on the album, his commercial stock was at its highest – higher even than during the heyday of his glam records. Within six weeks, he was to have Number 1 singles on both sides of the Atlantic. 'Fame', the second single from *Young Americans*, reached Number 1 in the United States, but was then knocked off by John Denver's 'I'm Sorry' before promptly regaining the Number 1 spot the week after. RCA responded to the moderate success of 'Fame' in the UK, where it only reached Number 17, by ransacking their back catalogue. In the autumn of 1975, 'Space Oddity', backed by that hardy perennial 'Changes', and a track from the *Ziggy* sessions, 'Velvet Goldmine', were released as a maxi-single. Bowie was furious when he found that 'Velvet Goldmine' had been resurrected (and remixed) without his permission. However, 6 years and 63 days after first entering the charts back in 1969, in November 1975 the reissued 'Space Oddity' finally gave Bowie his first UK Number 1 single after a succession of near-misses, dethroning Art Garfunkel's catatonically paced 'I Only Have Eyes For You'. It was the 27th UK single release of Bowie's career.

Surprisingly, Tony Visconti was not called in to record the new album with Bowie. Visconti claims that there was no falling out between Bowie and himself after Bowie's 'tampering' with The Gouster, but does admit to being disappointed. 'David later explained that he had to cram *Station To Station* in between shooting scenes for *The Man Who Fell To Earth*, and there was no set schedule or method of procedure. Like most of his albums it started as a collection of demos in the studio and, at a certain point, became an official album. He was also composing and recording music for potential use in the film. I was 6,000 miles away, recording someone else. Things just worked out this way. As for *Young Americans*, of course anyone in my position would get upset after such hard, meticulous work, but all the emotions were duly communicated and no falling out occurred.'

Alomar remembers the *Station To Station* sessions with obvious delight: 'It was the height of our experimental time. It was one of the most glorious albums that I've ever done, and it was one of the longer ones. I think it might have taken two months. We experimented so much on it.' According to Alomar, there was still some tension between himself and the recalled Earl Slick, though: 'Earl Slick was back. I had to calm him down a bit and say, "Look, man, we're just two working musicians. I'm in. Stop even thinking about me. I'm not going anywhere and unless you wanna lose your gig, chill out."'

But the sessions went well and according to a pattern which would endure until *Scary Monsters* four years later. Alomar, Davis and Murray would lay down a solid rhythm section, with Alomar often putting down the lead guitar lines at the same time. Then the overdubs would be done: a lead guitar line sometimes following Alomar's guide line, which would then be deleted, a saxophone part, synths, piano or strings. Only then would Bowie lay down his vocal. Finally, it was time for those little extras or sweeteners to weirdify the whole musical structure. Bowie was the originator of the material of course, writing both words and music, but Alomar was a key figure in terms of providing versions of the songs for Bowie to select from. This system helped to produce some of the finest pop music of the 1970s.

On *Station To Station*, the musical mix was very unusual. Alomar's funky guitar and Slick's heavy lead lines compete for attention with Bittan's piano (this album had more lead piano overdubs on it than any album since *Ziggy Stardust*). The result was a combination of rather straight, conventional instrumentation and experimentalism, particularly on the epic title track.

'That album's a little fuzzy – for the obvious reasons!' says Slick. 'We were in the studio and it was nuts – a lot of hours, a lot of late nights. We didn't start a lot of times till one or two o'clock in the morning. I like the album very much, but the recording process was very vague. I don't remember a lot about it.'

Alomar explains the whys and wherefores of cocaine and its role in the creative process:

What happens is that when you're trying to do something, the most disturbing thing that can happen in the studio is to have to go to sleep if you're on a roll. Let's say, you're doing this song and you've laid down the basic track. After this you do what they call a sweetening session – you put in all the little extras, something on top. Now for the sweetening sessions, you really have to be off on a tangent somewhere so that you can hear things a little bit different. You wanna change your perception. This is kind of like what drugs do. If I wanted to do a session and I had all the stuff already laid down but I wanted to get kind of weird about things, I might smoke a jay. If I smoke a jay I'll start thinking about stupid stuff, and suddenly I'll be playing something that I wouldn't ordinarily play. Say I have a guitar line that I have to do. David is doing some work on some other thing, and I have to wait around until he finishes that. When we were working on *Young Americans*, David was writing in the studio – he might be working on a line in the studio for three hours. What are we gonna do? Sleep in an armchair? Now at 3 a.m. he says, 'Well, it's time for you to start your guitar part.' Now if there's a line of coke which is going to keep you awake until 8 a.m. so that you can do your guitar part, you do the line of coke, because it basically just keeps you up and keeps the mind bright. He was doing far too much on *Station To Station*, but the coke use is driven by the inspiration. You're not going to stop doing it halfway through the album when everything you've done so far has been so fabulous! It doesn't make sense.

The first track to be cut was 'Golden Years', the lead-off single from the album. According to some reports, it was offered to Elvis Presley to cover, although it would appear that this did not actually happen. However, there was talk of collaboration around that time. 'Apparently Elvis heard the demos, because we were both on RCA, and Colonel Tom thought I should write some Elvis songs,' says Bowie. 'There was talk between our offices that I should be introduced to Elvis and maybe start working with him in a production-writer capacity. But it never came to pass. I would have loved working with him. God, I would have adored it. He did send me a note once, "All the best, and have a great tour." I still have that note.'

'Golden Years' turned out to be one of Bowie's greatest singles. Dripping schmaltzy, ironic cool, Bowie's vocal went from a low, almost mumbled vibrato to hep-cat white rap to falsetto and back again. Written, according to some sources, for Angie, the lyric was very filmic, telling the story in affected American jive of glamour and stardom through the eyes of nostalgia. The opening riff was a killer too, and has the listener hooked before the entry of the Bowie vocal. Even the whistling section at the end was quite cool. Alomar remembers that the genesis of the song came when Bowie was fooling around with some chords on the piano, trying to recreate a glitzy 'On Broadway' vibe: 'David goes to the piano and plays, "They say the neon lights are bright on Broadway ... Come de dum ma baby . . ." That's the kind of vibe he wanted. I said, "How about this?" and then I said, "How about this?" I play the opening guitar riff and he says, "Yeah, yeah, yeah, like that, do that, do that." Once you've got the original vibe of what you want, then the band just kicks in and you have fun.'

During Alomar's long time with Bowie, one of the most important things he did musically was to help create unforget-table, classic openings for songs: 'This is one of the things I've always specialised in and David's always known me for this. You've got to have a classic guitar line at the beginning of a song. The presence of the guitar means that you can play something and before the lead vocalist has got to come in, everybody's already gone crazy. This is something that I felt was evident when I was young, when I heard "Satisfaction". The moment you hear that, that's it, you've gone crazy. The guitar has the ability to set up the song with a fabulous introduction, and during the heyday of rock'n'roll the signature guitar line was the most important thing you could put on a record. I always wanted to make sure that each song had a signature guitar part so that you'd know that Carlos Alomar was on the scene! "Golden Years", "DJ", "Scary Monsters", "Stay" – that's what I specialised in.'

Indeed, 'Stay' was a riff and a guitar solo first and a song second. But what a killer riff! Alomar recollects, ' "Stay" was fabulous! We had a field day with that one. That was recorded very much in our cocaine frenzy. "Stay" was basically done with the rhythm section. It was pretty funky and pretty much straight ahead. I wrote out a chart and said this was pretty much what we wanted to do. That song I think David did on the guitar. He strummed a few chords for me, and then we gave it back to him. The rhythm section really liked that one, and then Earl Slick covered some of the lines I had laid down with a thicker sound.'

On 'Stay', Bowie's emotions are pure shellac, brittle, yet simultaneously claustrophobically contrived and alienated. Ostensibly about the uncertainty behind sexual conquest ('Cos you can never really tell, when somebody wants something you want too'), the song contains a vocal that remains one of Bowie's most insecure and helpless performances to date.

Perhaps even closer to the precipice of emotional collapse is 'Word On A Wing'. Here Bowie is seemingly reaching out for catharsis in the form of a spiritual experience, for the song is essentially a hymn. Starting with a simple piano line against a gentle wash of synths, a trademark ascending guitar riff carries it through to Bowie's soft, conversational entry. Building all the time, the song explodes into life halfway through, with Bowie prostrate on the altar steps, offering himself up to Christ. 'Lord I kneel and offer you/My word on a wing/And I'm trying hard to fit among/Your scheme of things'. The song dutifully ends with an organ and choir, as we leave the church. Bowie is so emotionally unstable, he is possibly hovering near some sort of rebirth scenario. 'I wrote the whole thing as a hymn,' Bowie told *Melody Maker* in February the following year. 'Yes, I do feel like I am starting over again in a way.'

'TVC 15' is deliberately jokey and good-time, yet it is the weak link on the album. Whereas 'Word On A Wing' has only had one live outing since 1976, 'TVC 15' has featured on four major world tours and at Live Aid. As a single, it flopped at Number 33 in the UK charts in 1976. The lyric, undoubtedly motivated by Thomas Newton's goggle-eyed scene with the cathode-ray tubes, is about a sort of trans-human interface between a girlfriend and a television set. But the song is somehow slightly substandard for the time, all groove and self-conscious funkiness. Alomar: 'Well, he didn't want it organised at all, he really wanted it fucked up like when we did "Boys Keep Swinging", kind of loose and stupid.

But then when we got to the end, he really wanted it to drive home. During those times the drones of music was starting to get a bit vampy. By that I mean the music would stay in one place and just keep going. So, towards the end of the song, that's what he wanted – "Oh my TVC 15, oh oh, TVC 15". So we were just playing the rest of the song just to get to the end!'

Bowie liked to put a cover version on most albums, to test himself and to see if he was as good an interpreter and singer as singer/songwriter. 'Wild Is The Wind', a song by Dimitri Tiomkin, and covered by both Nina Simone and Johnny Mathis, is a big, powerful ballad. Bowie claims that this song, more than any other from the era, showed his true singing voice. It is, in fact, a fantastic vocal performance, with its deep, rich vibrato. The song itself builds and builds with crashing waves of acoustic guitar, like a more soulful arrangement of Ken Scott's overdubbed acoustic guitar on 'Quicksand'. Here Bowie's singing is deliberately overblown, with each syllable stretched out to preposterous lengths as he strangles each note on the song's title in the final section – more Bassey than Bolan. Carlos Alomar: 'He wanted "Wild Is The Wind" to remain a classic song, not to be trifled with to the point of it not being recognisable. He loved the richness of his voice at the time and I was discovering different tones to his voice, too, all that time.'

It is the title track of the album that shows Bowie entering a new era of experimentalism. It was definitely the most ambitious song he had yet attempted and arguably his finest recorded moment. Musically, it shows Bowie filtering Krautrock and the robotic motorik of Kraftwerk, then about to bubble through into the mainstream and invent techno in the decade to come, into his funky dance-rock. The opening section was, in part, developed from Bowie's ideas by Alomar, who layered and layered more guitar parts and, after a suggestion from Bowie, added arpeggiated figures on guitar as the opening section developed. 'The opening is all melody and counterpoint. The rhythm section had already done their stuff and we were watching him with Earl Slick, trying to tell him what was going on: "I know it's long – just keep playing!" He was trying to hold this note for about two minutes for that opening section. And we were saying, "How the hell is he going to hold this note any longer?" "Plug in another amplifier! Just keep the chain of amplifiers going until the sound just keeps going." '

The first part of the song is a slow-tempoed mantra in which Bowie delivers a line-by-line incantation. It's Bowie's own 'Sympathy For The Devil', as his eerily double-tracked vocal outlines a present pregnant with occultist imagery: 'Here am I, flashing no colour/Tall in this room overlooking the ocean/Here are we, one magical movement/From kether to malkulth' ('Station To Station', 1976)

Although Bowie was obliquely referring to the 'Stations of the cross' from the New Testament, 'Kether' (crown) and 'malkulth' (kingdom) are Hebrew words and are part of God's ten creative emanations or stations called sephiroth found in the 'Tree of Life', the basis for the tarot. According to writer Peter R. Koenig in his essay, 'The Laughing Gnostic: David Bowie and the Occult', 'To travel from "Kether to Malkuth" (as Bowie sings) equals the descending of/from God to the physical level which makes Men one with the Divine.' A fixation with black magic is also referenced in the lines: 'The return of the Thin White Duke/Making sure white stains' ('Station To Station', 1976).

The phrase 'white stains' has three meanings. First, it has obvious sexual associations. Second, it highlights the racial purity of the character. Third, it alludes to a collection of poems by the diabolist Aleister Crowley, the self-styled 'wickedest man in the world'. Crowley provided Bowie with an intriguing role model and his doctrine of moral code-breaking and experimentation struck a chord. In 1971, Crowley's biographer, John Symond, wrote: 'Unexpectedly, the tide has turned in Crowley's favour. The doctrine of "Do What Thou Wilt", with its encouragement to trample the Gods under foot and to take one's fill of love, wine and "strange drugs", has seized the imagination of this restless world.' Bowie would later joke that the entire record was 'Black Magic – the musical!' In its charismatic, spell-like intensity, the first section of the song is unquestionably one of Bowie's most brilliant moments on record.

'Station To Station' then changes gear mid-song. Bowie sings 'got to keep searching and searching' – evidence of his unstoppable enthusiasm for new ideas and a restatement of 'Word On A Wing''s theme of the grand quest for an absolute, a spirituality to underpin a hollow life. Bowie's cry, 'It's not the side effects of the cocaine, I'm thinking that it must be love' is an open admission of drug dependency. The music then kicks into a vamp – 'It's too late, to be hateful. The European canon is here!' The song, which starts as a black-magic ritual, ends in a plea for a return to Europe. A hugely powerful and audacious piece of music, it encapsulates all the drama and musical flamboyance of Bowie at his very, very best. In essence, Bowie's next two albums, *Low* and *"Heroes"*, were an extrapolation of the sonic daring of this one track.

Bowie was pleased with the album, although he later said that he chickened out on the mix, giving it a more commercial sheen when he really ought to have left it slightly uncompromising. He told *Creem* magazine the following year that, while *Young Americans* had a sort of 'pathetic dignity', the new album was 'devoid of spirit, very steely. Even the love songs are detached, but I think it's fascinating. It's very much like me, or very much like I want to be.' Today, Bowie says that at times he found the entire album 'beautiful' at others, 'extraordinarily disturbing'. What is certain is that it is yet another quite brilliantly realised work.

In the late autumn of 1975, Bowie also busied himself with the soundtrack to *The Man Who Fell To Earth*, which was being edited at the time. As a collaborator, Bowie chose the classically trained Paul Buckmaster, who had played on, and arranged, 'Space Oddity' six years earlier, and the two hooked up in Bowie's rented house in Bel Air. They recorded using a TEAC four-track tape recorder, and they also had some of the first nonprogramm-able drum machines in the shape of some Japanese rhythm boxes. Bowie used a Rhodes Fender guitar and Buckmaster took along his cello. The two were very interested in the new music of Kraftwerk, particularly *Autobahn* and the recently released *Radioactivity*. 'I was fascinated and tickled and amused by them,' remembers Buckmaster. 'We both enjoyed their records very much indeed. We kind of took them seriously, but we kind of laughed as well. Not at it, but because the music had a kind of innocent quality which was very fetching, and a deadpan humour as well.'

The major problem throughout the five weeks they worked on material was that both musicians were serious coke users. 'I'm very loathe to talk about it because it's so personal,' Buckmaster said in 1998. 'A lot of people across the whole spectrum of the entertainment industry were using coke at the time. It was relatively cheap and readily available. We were all trapped by this siren seduction. It's a hideous drug and I decry it totally. Thank

God that I got away from it, and I know David did too. At the beginning, it created so much energy. It's a powerful stimulant; it gets your energy and enthusiasm up. But it's a false enthusiasm. Soon it disconnects you from yourself, from your life, from your heart, your soul and your spiritual life. It turned me into a false clone of myself.'

In the end, the music created by Bowie and Buckmaster did not make the soundtrack of the film. Just why this was so is still something of a mystery. However, at the end of 1975, Bowie fired Michael Lippman, his first (and only) post-Defries manager. He had intended to spend New Year in Jamaica rehearsing for his upcoming world tour, but had to relocate to Keith Richards' house when he found that no arrangements had been made for his stay. He phoned Lippman to give him the sack, but this was just an excuse. Bowie had been none too pleased that Lippman had failed to get the Bowie/Buckmaster tape soundtrack used (when in actuality it was possibly unusable).

However, in Buckmaster's assessment, the real reason it wasn't used was that Roeg simply didn't like what he heard and didn't think the music was up to scratch. 'I think Roeg got cold feet about it. I considered the music to be demo-ish and not final, although we were supposed to be making it final. We also didn't have a producer at the time and we were trying to hammer it out together. All that produced something that was substandard, and Nic Roeg turned it down on those grounds. That is my honest opinion. You also have to remember our respective biochemical conditions, and these got worse as the weeks progressed. In fact, at one session – it may have been one of the sessions for *Station To Station* – Bowie had to be helped out because he had gone too far. I have to say I wasn't much help, being in the same boat. We both encouraged each other simply by our behaviour. It's all rather shameful and I don't like to recall that part of it. It's healthy to remember that one makes mistakes like that; some serious mistakes. Some people might call it a crime, but I don't know if I could go that far . . .'

What makes Bowie and Buckmaster's collaboration important is that, in writing moody, instrumental music for a soundtrack album which, in the end, never was, Bowie had inadvertently presaged, or at least shadowed, the work being carried out by a certain Brian Eno. When Bowie and Eno got together the following year, Bowie was not so much converted to ambient and mood music as the media at the time liked to portray it. Rather, what they did was a logical progression from an earlier project. Unfortunately, the public at large will have to wait to hear just what this progression involved. A DAT tape of the soundtrack remains in Buckmaster's archive awaiting future release. Only a backwards bass line recorded for the soundtrack would eventually find its way on to vinyl, as part of the instrumental that would be used on 'Subterraneans' on Bowie's next album, *Low*.

On 27 January 1976, Bowie brought a $2 million lawsuit against Lippman, claiming that the latter had taken 15 per cent instead of the customary 10 per cent commission and had withheld $475,000 after being dismissed. Lippman in turn sued Bowie for $2 million. In the end, Lippman won after a meeting in Paris in the summer of 1976, but settled for less than his hoped-for $2 million. Again, Bowie was losing money hand over fist. He was probably almost unmanageable by this stage. As for Lippman, he later went on to manage one of the biggest names in the business: George Michael.

In between not inconsiderable recording commitments at the end of 1975, Bowie was making a last bid for mainstream American acceptance. That autumn he appeared on two prime-time TV shows. He recorded a slot for the high-rating *Soul Train*, messing up the words to his new single, 'Golden Years'. Legend has it that he had had one too many drinks, so nervous was he about performing on a show pretty much the preserve of authentic black music. When the backing tape reaches the point where Bowie's vocal appears, Bowie lurches back to life as if he'd just nodded off on his feet. 'I do remember not knowing the words,' said Bowie in 2000:

I wasn't even buoyant enough to feel apologetic. I mean I really was a little shit in that way, I hadn't bothered to learn it. And the MC of the show, who was a really charming guy, took me to one side after the third or fourth take and said, 'You know there are kids lining up to do this show who have fought their whole lives to try and get a record and come on here.' And I know that at the time it made no impression on me, his little speech, which was absolutely necessary. And I just screwed up the lyrics.

In the same month, he sang live to 'Fame''s backing track on *The Cher Show* and, in a sequence which almost rivals later collaborations with Bing Crosby and Tina Turner for inappropriateness, he duetted with the show's host on 'Can You Hear Me?' before getting down on a 'Young Americans' which segued into the all-American light-entertainment delights of 'Song Sung Blue', 'Wedding Bells', 'Da Doo Ron Ron Ron', 'Daytripper', 'Blue Moon', 'Only You' and 'Young Blood' before reprising 'Young Americans'. Then, in January 1976, Bowie appeared with Henry 'The Fonz' Winkler on *The Dinah Shore Show*, singing 'Stay', a new song from the upcoming album, and a powerful version of the stunning *Ziggy Stardust* track 'Five Years', then being rehearsed for the tour.

Bowie had chosen a satellite interview with Russell Harty, broadcast by London Weekend Television the previous November, to announce that forthcoming tour. Moments before the interview was recorded it was announced that the Spanish leader, Franco, had died, and Bowie was asked to give up booked satellite time in order to break the news. He declined. What followed was a startling exchange between Harty and Bowie. Whether it was the slight delay caused by the satellite link, or Bowie's huge intake of cocaine, or both, the singer made hardly any sense at all throughout what was quite an extensive interview. His hair slicked back in the new Thin White Duke style, Bowie looked completely disconnected and was hardly able to utter a coherent sentence. 'I'm coming home in May to play shows, look at you and be English again.' 'He'll be lucky if he gets through rehearsals, much less a six-month tour,' said one unnamed rocker who saw Bowie that Christmas.

'Golden Years', the first single off the new album, was a transatlantic Top 10 hit and, early in 1976, *Station To Station* became his biggest American success to date, going all the way to Number 3. The release of the album was delayed slightly when Bowie scrapped the original colour cover for a black-and-white version of the same shot, as this fitted in rather better with the expressionist stage show then in production. In fact the cover depicts Bowie entering an anechoic chamber in which all ambient noise is absorbed, rendering the activity of the heart and brain audible to the human ears in the form of a pumping noise and the crackle of electric currents.

Bowie took the stage for the first date of the *Station To Station* tour, or the White Light Tour as it is now better known, in Vancouver on 2 February. For the tour, Bowie christened his new band Raw Moon. He retained the rhythm section of Alomar, Davis and Murray. Tony Kaye, who had worked with Yes, was this year's keyboard maestro, and an inventive 21-year-old Canadian, Stacey Haydon, replaced Earl Slick on lead guitar after a misunderstanding between the hot-tempered guitarist and the representatives of the temperamental singer just before the tour kicked off. Earl Slick:

There was so much chemical abuse going on that communications kind of fell apart. Somehow, David and me ended up having a falling-out. I left the band early in '76 and that was based on a conversation I had had with Pat Gibbons. David had gone to Jamaica. We were supposed to rehearse there, but I couldn't get in touch with him. The last time I'd seen him he wasn't in the best of shape, and I was trying to get details about finances. You know, what we were going to get paid. Pat was very vague with me, and I said, 'Look, I need to talk to David.' 'Well, David's busy. I can't get through to him. He's not taking calls.' I was doing my solo career at the time, with David's blessing, and when I decided not to do the '76 tour, Bowie took that as an indication that I was putting my solo career above playing on his tour, which was not true. The main reason was this Pat Gibbons guy, who was playing games with everybody. He used to do the payroll and as soon as David and Lippman had a falling out, Pat was in a position of taking care of David's daily business, which I'm sure he wanted all along.

My relationship with David just vaporised. I wasn't in the best of shape either, so I wasn't making rational decisions at the time. I just think everyone had a hand in messing up. I'm not going to point my finger at anyone in particular. I think we were all equally guilty of being a bunch of assholes at the time, myself included.

Despite all this unrest, the tour itself was a huge triumph for Bowie artistically. Although the stage was largely devoid of props, gadgets and visual chicanery, the tour was still every bit as theatrical as any Bowie tour before or since. Bathed in blinding white light, with crimson and blond hair centre-parted and swept back in the wedge hairstyle which would be aped by young people well into the 1980s, Bowie, dressed in white shirt, white gloves and black waistcoat, like the barman from hell, played the Thin White Duke to audiences on the verge of hysteria as the tour progressed through the States. If 1973 was Bowie's high-water mark in the UK, then the American tour of early 1976 performed the same function for the States. As writer and broadcaster Paul Gambaccini said of one concert: 'It was the finest performance by a white artist I had ever seen.'

On a few dates Bowie revealed one new song, 'Sister Midnight', which he later gave away to Iggy Pop. A funked-up song with a great tumbling riff by Alomar, it possessed a crunchingly mechanistic, walking-paced groove. This, in microcosm, was Bowie's objective for the tour: to marry funkiness with the disciplined experimental beats emanating from Germany that he loved so much. *Melody Maker*'s Michael Watts, reviewing Bowie at Wembley that May, had this to say about the music: 'It's undoubtedly funky, but it remains somehow mechanistic, ferocious in its loudness and intensity, and quite unlike soul, white or black.' By the end of the decade a whole range of both black and white artists, from Talking Heads to Afrikka Bambaata, would be making music which jumbled up musical styles in a way Bowie had pioneered. Punk would get funky, funk would get punky.

Bowie did not short-change his fans, though, and even the biggest die-hard traditionalist would have much to savour. Included in the eighty-minute set were 'Queen Bitch' and 'Life On Mars?' from 1971, an awesome 'Five Years' and a rum 'Suffragette City' from 1972, 'Panic In Detroit' (with a drum solo allowing for pees and refreshments) from 1973, 'Rebel Rebel' and 'Diamond Dogs' from 1974 and 'Fame' from 1975.

However, the latter was the only track from the *Young Americans* album, then less than a year old, to be played live. With a typical perversity, his then current chart single, 'Golden Years', which Bowie found difficult to sing live in the key in which it had been recorded, was removed from the set list after a couple of dates. A very fine and funky version of The Velvet Underground song, 'I'm Waiting For The Man', did make the shows, however, as did most of *Station To Station*, including the heroic title track which was the concert opener.

This was Bowie's valedictory tour as far as Americana was concerned. His musical obsessions at the time included Fripp and

Eno's *No Pussy Footing*, Lou Reed's *Metal Machine Music*, and Kraftwerk. Indeed, Bowie considered having the quartet from Dusseldorf as the tour's opening act until he realised that they needed a whole bank of synths and keyboards – in other words, too much equipment for a run of short one-nighters. Instead, before he took the stage, Bowie had their latest offering, *Radioactivity*, played together with an excerpt from the Salvador Dali and Luis Buñuel classic surrealist film, *Un Chien Andalou* (1928). The image of an eyeball being severed in two was intended to unnerve and shock and was made increasingly bizarre by both the musical accompaniment and by its positioning as an opener for a rock concert. A mood of both futurism and nostalgia flooded the arena even before the Thin White Duke made his entrance.

But the overriding atmosphere of the 1976 tour was its starkness; the affirmation that theatricality lay in less not more. Although this time the band inhabited the same space as Bowie on stage, their visual impact was virtually zero, as journalist Lisa Robinson spelled out: 'This band stands behind Bowie but are so unimportant that they might as well be behind a curtain . . . I love it when Bowie stands to one side of the stage to watch the solos of Carlos Alomar, Dennis Davis and Tony Kaye, and nods his head like he's really digging it. Aside from admiring such fine acting, it makes one long for the star's speedy return.'

Bowie used light like paint, showering the stage with different intensities of white light, the performance the equivalent of chiaroscuro, the artistic distribution of light and dark masses. The blistering light was almost painful to the eyes, and deliberately so. The intent was to confound audience expectations. Michael Watts again: 'The staging of the performance was inspired. Using an overhead bank of neon lights, and the auxiliary power of Klieg, he exposed the stage in a brilliant glare of black and white expressionism that emphasised the harshness of the music and reflected upon his own image as a white-shirted, black-suited creature of Herr Ishyvoo's cabaret. It was, I think, the most imaginative lighting of a rock concert I have ever seen.'

The origins of the technique as far as pop was concerned lay in the early Andy Warhol-directed shows of The Velvet Underground's first tour. Later, at the Hammersmith Odeon in 1979, Lou Reed deliberately left the house lights on throughout the entire concert, in order to put his audience on edge and to strip away the usual balance between hidden audience and lit star. Bowie himself states that the most direct influence he had had in this area came from a production of *Cabaret* he had seen in the mid-60s which starred Judi Dench. In Brechtian theatre, the intention was to make the actual lights themselves visible and intensely bright in order to destroy the illusion of 'natural' lighting in a play. Again, Bowie was using a tradition of artifice to befuddle a rock audience more used to being lost in the theatre of a rock event.

During 1976, Bowie was at his most disconnected on stage, using stiff, jerky, choreographed karate kicks one moment, fumbling intentionally for his pack of Gitanes during 'I'm Waiting For The Man' the next. At 29, he had reached a new peak as a performer. Sadly, no official footage has ever been released of the tour and so, as a touchstone for Bowie's greatness in the 70s, it is always the Ziggy Stardust era that is remembered by the media and the public in general. The odd snippet of live action does exist among collectors, as does a good-quality film of the tour's rehearsals, which shows Bowie in a light-hearted and good-natured mood, forgetting lines and fucking up.

The tour worked its way through the States in February. On 6 February, Bowie triumphed at the same venue, the San Francisco Cow Palace, where three years before he had drawn a pitiful crowd. The guest list for his Los Angeles Inglewood Forum shows on 8, 9 and 11 February included David Hockney, Christopher Isherwood, Patti Smith, Elton John, Rod Stewart and Britt Ekland, Herbie Hancock, Ray Bradbury, Carly Simon, Henry Winkler, Alice Cooper, Ringo Starr and Linda Ronstadt. Bowie's critical and celebratory star had never shone harder, despite his parlous mental state. He was a mainstream star, feted by the glitterati of the film and TV worlds. Yet, he was also undeniably considered seriously as an artiste, hence his attraction to the literati like Isherwood and Bradbury. This was a remarkable state of affairs and quite unprecedented for a rock musician to have such a fascination for representatives of both high and low culture. In fact, Bowie was breaking down these cultural divides by the year. By 1976, Bowie was in a unique position, both a hugely successful pop star and a heavyweight, cultural pop icon. He would never have such huge kudos in equal amounts at the same time again.

The most famous gig on the tour as far as Bowie fans are concerned took place on 23 March in New York, at the

(Uniondale) Nassau Coliseum. This gig was broadcast on FM radio and, later, excellent-quality bootlegs circulated among the Bowie hard core. Along with the gig in 1972 at the Santa Monica Civic Auditorium, it would be the most admired live recording never to be given an official release. For sheer musicality, the Nassau gig made both *David Live* and the later *Stage* sound slightly flaccid by comparison.

A few dates into the tour, Iggy Pop became Bowie's constant companion. The two would stay together for the next year and a half. At the time, Iggy was still feeling his way back after his voluntary stay in a mental hospital, so when he was given the chance to test his stamina as backing vocalist on the tour he eagerly took it. In fact, during his hospitalisation in 1975, Bowie was his first visitor. 'If I remember it right, it was me and Dennis Hopper,' Bowie told Clark Collis in 2002 (two years earlier he told *Q* it was actor Dean Stockwell who accompanied him). 'We trooped into the hospital with a load of drugs for him. This was very much a leave-your-drugs-at-the-door hospital. We were out of our minds, all of us. He wasn't well; that's all we knew. We thought we should bring him some drugs, because he probably hadn't had any for days!'

By 1976, Bowie's management team had been severely slimmed down. Pat Gibbons was Bowie's acting manager; Coco was ever more dominant. 'My office is a suitcase that stays in my room,' he said that March. 'It's far better than before when I never knew what was going on.' Bowie was still, perforce, extremely isolated as an individual. Another ever-present person was his bodyguard and driver, Tony Mascia, a burly middle-aged Italian from the Bronx who used to be the great Rocky Marciano's sparring partner. Mascia was a part of the Bowie entourage until his death in 1991. He was a surrogate big brother to Bowie, and would tell him tales of derring-do in the boxing ring.

Financially, though, these were troubled times. Chris Charlesworth, who interviewed him for a *Melody Maker* exclusive in 1976, remembers: 'He had firmly grasped the basics of how to give a good interview, unlike most rock stars. He knew that it was advantageous for him to utter controversial statements. He followed in a long tradition here, because I think he learned this from John Lennon. Lennon was the same – he gave great interviews, as did Pete Townshend. From the point of view of headline-grabbing, the most important thing he said was that he was broke and that he had lost all his money because he had been ripped off by his management. This is what he implied. He knew full well that "Bowie broke" makes a great headline. He didn't just waffle on about the difficulties in recording "TVC 15" and how he had to double-track the guitar because the first track wasn't working properly. That might be interesting for fans who liked his music, but from the point of view of grabbing headlines, "TVC 15 double-tracked guitar" doesn't look too good, does it, at the top of the page? If you got him in the right mood, he'd talk for hours. Coke makes you talk a lot; makes you babble.'

However, before Bowie could return to Britain that May, the new slimmed-down management team was rocked by two huge PR calamities. The first was a high-profile drugs bust on 21 March after the show at the Springfield Civic Center in Massachusetts. Bowie, along with Iggy Pop and two friends, was charged with possession of 8 oz of marijuana. Released on $2,000 bail, with no charges being pressed, he had had a very lucky escape, given his hard-drug use. Then, in early April 1976, returning from Moscow with Iggy Pop, Bowie was detained by customs officers on the Russian/Polish border when a cache of Nazi memorabilia was found in his possession. Fatefully, a couple of weeks later after a gig on 26 April in Stockholm, Bowie was reported in the press as saying, 'As I see it, I am the only alternative for the premier in England. I believe Britain could benefit from a Fascist leader. After all, Fascism is really nationalism.'

In an interview in 1975 Bowie had commented, 'I think that morals should be straightened up for a start. They're disgusting.' He added, 'There will be a political figure in the not too distant future who'll sweep through this part of the world like early rock'n'roll did. You probably hope I'm not right but I am ... You've got to have an extreme right front come up and sweep everything off its feet and tidy everything up. Then you can get a new form of liberalism.'

Bowie saw in Hitler all the attributes which made rock stars tick. In an interview conducted with Cameron Crowe for *Playboy* in 1974, Bowie had said, 'Adolf Hitler was one of the first rock stars. Look at some of the films and see how he moved. I think he was quite as good as Jagger ... [Hitler] was no politician. He was a media artist himself. He used politics and theatrics and created this thing that governed and controlled the show for those twelve years. The world will never see his like again. He staged a country.' This story was reactivated in the tabloids after Bowie's ill-judged comments in 1976.

All this was cast-iron evidence that Bowie was losing the plot, particularly when he remarked to one journalist that he would make a great prime minister in the UK since he would be dictatorial and quite mad. According to rock legend, Bowie also visited Hitler's bunker and had photographer Andy Kent snap him with his arm outstretched in a Nazi salute. Allegedly, Kent had to swear never to release the photograph to the press.

However, the day that has gone down in Bowie folklore is 2 May 1976. Bowie arrived at Victoria Station, where he was to be picked up by an open-top limo, one which had, in fact, once belonged to a South American dictator who had been assassinated. Shaky archive footage exists of Bowie waving and smiling to a huge crowd of fans, a few giving him the victory sign and screaming their adulation, having assembled to greet him after his two-year American 'exile'. The film then shows Bowie standing in the back of the limo and, for a split second, raising his hand in a furtive but straight-armed manner. It might have been a Nazi salute; it looked a lot more like a little wave, or even a sort of John Lennon, right-on brothers, left-wing air-punch.

Bowie was mentally disturbed enough to have given a Nazi salute that day at Victoria Station, but the evidence is by no means clear cut. According to an article by Bowie fan David Burbidge in the Bowie fanzine *Zi Duang Provence* [sic], none of the tabloid newspapers that reported Bowie's arrival made any mention of the infamous gesture (although the *Daily Mail* does say that he saluted the crowd with a clenched fist). In fact, the story started at the *NME*. It printed a photograph of Bowie (under the heading 'Heil and Farewell') showing him, according to Burbidge, 'with his arm in the air, in a position vaguely resembling a Fascist salute – except that the fingers are loosely cupped and relaxed, not straight and stiff'. *NME* did not actually say anything about a salute in the accompanying text. (Bowie always claimed that the photographer merely caught him mid-wave.)

In the crowd that day was the seventeen-year-old Gary Webb, soon to be pop star Gary Numan. 'I didn't actually see him because there were too many people. But Bowie had just come back from Germany, and I'm sure the press was looking for something. You're standing up at the back of the car and you're waving at this massive crowd that's some distance away. Think about it. If a photographer takes a whole motor-driven film of someone doing a wave, you will get a Nazi salute at the end of each arm-sweep. All you need is some dickhead at some music paper or whatever to try to make an issue out of it and it looks bad. But I'd be amazed if he'd done a Nazi salute. When I was there I didn't see anyone, there were thousands of people there, and I didn't see anyone walking around saying, "What a wanker, he did a Nazi salute". No one. People just thought he was waving at them, and I'm sure he was.'

Regarding Bowie's pro-Fascist statements to the media, playwright, songwriter and *Times* writer Alan Franks, who interviewed Bowie during the summer of 1995, puts it like this: 'At the time, in the words of a much later song, he was indeed "deranged". He had some very bad experiences with hard drugs and indeed with alcohol, and I think the stories about his suicidal tendencies probably had some truth in them. I imagine he was as depressed as hell. I think he has really known addiction. That behaviour, with the Nazi salute, was probably in the teeth of that dependency. We all say and do reckless and stupid things. That particular incident was the result of an external agency, and I'm talking of mood-altering chemicals which did make Bowie into something other than he was. This is quite a crucial point because however many ch-ch-ch-changes he's gone through, I don't think they were the result of mood-altering chemicals but of something like a kind of natural evolution of a bloke who's really into his art and forms of self-expression.'

In 1993, Bowie himself drew attention to his own naivety (and, some would say, stupidity): 'Politically, I equated Fascism with Communism, or rather Stalinism. On my trips through Russia I thought, well, this is what Fascism must have felt like. They marched like them. They saluted like them. Both had centralised governments. It's hard to see that you could get involved with all that and not see the implications of what you were getting into.'

Some pop stars have mined rightist imagery and iconography to make visually bold and shocking statements, and Bowie was certainly in this tradition. The Nazis did have a very potent and commanding visual aura and it's an aura which has been deployed in the most unlikely of spheres. In 1975, a *Dr Who* story, 'Genesis Of The Daleks', was criticised for the Fascistic overtones in the black-shirted, mass-murdering cronies depicted as the daleks' aides. In 1999, the editor of men's magazine *GQ*, James Brown, had to resign after the magazine placed Goebbels in a Top 200 of the most stylish men of the last 2,000 years. Many journalists witnessing the 1976 Bowie tour remembered old footage of the Nuremberg rallies and the dramatically creative use of white light to illuminate *der Führer*, and drew obvious parallels. Bowie's then well-publicised interest in the occult merely stoked the fires of outrage, particularly since there was a more or less direct link between Hitler, Nazism and occultist practice. Even parts of the Bowie iconography itself had unwittingly tapped into Fascist iconography. Bowie's most recognisable insignia, the *Aladdin Sane* thunderbolt, originally designed by photographer Brian Duffy, who quite innocently saw the design on a Panasonic kettle, had its roots in Nazi iconography. According to Brennan, 'Himmler adopted the sig or "S" rune, which looks like two tiny lightning flashes, as the special emblem of his order.'

By 1977, Bowie had seen the very serious error of his ways as a pop star with the power to influence millions. 'I am totally apolitical . . . It is not my position for the kind of artist I am, who tries to capture the rate of change, to adopt any given policy or stance politically because my job is an observer of what is happening and any statements made in that direction [vis-a-vis Fascism] were a general reaction and a theatrical observation of what I could see happening in England.'

Bowie thus explained his comments as a piece of imaginative theatricality – another pose to be adopted for the purpose of his art. As he himself commented recently, what people really want to know is not so much if Bowie is a Fascist, but if he is a racist. In his defence, it has to be pointed out that Bowie has never uttered anything to the media which could be deemed a racist statement. He has played 'black'-inspired music with black musicians since the mid-70s, has dated black girlfriends, employed black men and women, and is now married to a Somalian. In 1992, Iman and Bowie contributed to *The Face*'s anti-racism issue, and songs such as 'Black Tie White Noise' are deliberate celebrations of racial difference. Of course, this evidence taken by itself is not one hundred per cent conclusive: misogynists date, employ and marry women. Nevertheless, it is highly improbable, taking into consideration all we know about Bowie and his art, that he harbours racist sentiments. Virtually every interview Bowie gives eventually turns to the subject of his alleged Nazism, and, every time, Bowie graciously gives the same reply, year in year out.

There was no doubt that Bowie flirted with the symbols of Fascism in a very dangerous way. However, in reality, all he was doing was performing a function he so often performs. Bowie's unique ability is to distil an essential 'now-ness'; to provide us with the quintessence of what it's like to live through one particular period. This has always given his work not so much the aura of prophecy, rather a sort of surrealist diary-maker's take on existence. Where other pop writers (Dylan, Lou Reed, Neil Young, Elvis Costello) capture the present primarily through language, Bowie summons it up rather more abstractly with images, textures, feelings. This is not to exonerate him from some of the things he has said but, to explain these comments away as the product of a druggy oblivion, is not the whole picture either. Rather, Bowie was picking up on the *Zeitgeist* and theatricalising it through his art. Three years after his proclamation, the United Kingdom elected the most right-wing government in its history; while in the USA, right-wing Republicanism was soon back in vogue.

In the mid-70s, Britain witnessed a growth in support for extreme right-wing organisations such as the British Movement and the National Front, organisations that worked within the socio-economic context of mass unemployment and youth discontent. Bowie was praised in the neo-Nazi paper *Spearhead* for rejecting the flower-power styles of music so hated by the extreme right, and for championing Nietzsche. Here is a short extract from the article, 'Don't Condemn Pop', published in 1981: 'It is this old 60s Flower Power music with its inclination to drugs etc. which more than anything constitutes the strong feelings many radical nationalists have against pop music in general. However, in the early 70s emerged David Bowie whose total rejection of this style of music is wonderfully indicative of his brand of pop music. He became a breath of fresh air on the music scene – indeed the influence of Friedrich Nietsche [sic] is plainly evident in Bowie's songs such as "Starman", "Changes" and the excellent "Quicksand".'

Bulldog, the paper of the Young National Front, called Bowie 'the Big Daddy of Futurism', who, on *Hunky Dory*, 'started the anti-Communist musical tradition which we now see flourishing amidst the new wave of Futurist bands'.

There were other cases of pop racism, such as when Eric Clapton made a racist comment at a gig in Birmingham while out of his head on drugs. But Bowie had unquestionably let both himself and his fans down, as Paul Du Noyer, an *NME* writer in the late 70s, and later founder of *Mojo* magazine, comments: 'His escape clause has always been, "Well, I took so many drugs in those days." For a man who was always so sure-footed up until 1976, things went disastrously off the rails for a while and I think he quickly realised that he had alienated precisely that part of the world that he needed most in terms of support.'

According to band leader, Carlos Alomar, Bowie was never a Fascist, or a Nazi. It was just so much verbiage: 'It was all just talk. He is what he reads and at that time in his life, he was reading so much bullshit. We're both kind of preachy. I'm more preachy on the religious side, he's more an expounder of information. He'll pick a subject no one knows anything about and expound on it for about an hour so that you're not interrupted. Those types of conversation – Nazism, baroque, and architecture of the turn of the century – that's David talking. I don't put too much weight on any of that; he likes to talk. If he considers himself an intellectual then that needs to be proven amongst other intellectuals. He is undoubtedly well read, but if you're picking a subject no one else knows about, I don't think that's conversation.'

Returning to matters Terpsichorean, the six shows between 3 and 8 May at Wembley Empire Pool, Bowie's first in the UK for almost three years, were hugely successful. Long-standing Bowie fan Paul Woods remembers that 'the audience was as eye-catching as the show (almost!), with a spattering of Ziggys and multiple versions of Bowie's style to date. The up-to-the-second greased hair and black-and-white outfits impressed the most, I recall. The lighting was definitely the thing which set the show apart from any other I'd seen. It was stark rather than blinding, giving the stage the atmosphere of an old black-and-white movie or theatre production of the 1930s. This was the backdrop to some of the most futuristic and powerful music I'd ever heard. I recall the opening moments to "Station To Station", which sounded like a train running headlong through the auditorium, and being stunned, amazed and excited all at once.'

THE EXILE RETURNS TO A MESSIAH'S WELCOME ran *Melody Maker*'s headline for their live review. In a rare emotional moment, Bowie left the stage in tears that first night at Wembley, so rapturously received was his homecoming. Bowie fan and writer Kevin Cann puts it like this: 'It was beyond words, amazing, absolutely amazing. You didn't want it to finish, it was a great show. The power coming off that stage was incredible. He'd been away for so long, and everyone was so desperate to see him live. It was his best show without doubt. The Arena was considerably darkened, so, when those really big white lights came on it, was like WOW!, especially if you were close to the stage.' 'The *Station To Station* Tour was the point at which I thought he was at his greatest,' says writer and long-time Bowie watcher Paul Du Noyer, who also attended one of the London gigs:

It was the point at which the music and the style came together most effectively. There was no longer anything self-consciously freakish about his appearance as there had been during the Ziggy and Aladdin Sane times. As much as I liked all his music prior to that, there was something thrillingly innovative about the music that was coming through now. One was vaguely becoming aware of European music, electronic music, and one was becoming aware of a possibility of a crossover between white European electronic music and black American funk music, which in due course would be one of the most significant developments of the next twenty years. In fact I think it continues to dominate music to this day, actually. But *Station To Station* was one of the first premonitions one got of this impending sea change, and I think that was part of the excitement, something absolutely new. Nothing in pop had been absolutely new probably since Elvis Presley in the 1950s. Much of it had been superlatively good, but there hadn't been such an element of utter strangeness to it.

Gary Numan was once again in the crowd for one of the Wembley gigs, which he remembers as one of the most thrilling moments of his life. 'The whole thing is kickin' off, it's totally brilliant and I'm up on the balcony on the right as you look up from the stage, about halfway up.' Numan led a mass cavalry charge of fans, knocking over a rather long-in-the-tooth security guard, to jump down from the top tier of the auditorium. After climbing along the backs of the chairs nearest the stage, Numan led his throng

Pied Piper-style to the front of the stage. 'I threw my little luminous green stick at him and it hit him during "The Jean Genie". He bent over and picked it up,' recollects Numan. 'I thought I was going to wet myself! Up to that point, it was the greatest moment of my life. It completely blew me away, and I nearly got beaten up at the end because one of the crew gave it to somebody else and I just lost it and started screaming and shouting at him. I just couldn't believe it. The man had touched it and they gave it to somebody else!'

The tour ended in Paris on 18 May. Against all the odds, Bowie had not only survived it, but had turned in some of the best live performances of his career. However, he was profoundly uncomfortable as a rock musician, on any level at all.

Bowie, who was currently enjoying a transatlantic hit album with the compilation *ChangesoneBowie*, was a rocker without any of the trappings rockers were supposed to have. He wasn't animalistic, he wasn't macho, he didn't play straight rock'n'roll and he wasn't in the slightest bit interested in performing according to the rules of the grand rock spectacle. He also knew that he had to break away from the States, and from the regular and easily obtained supplies of the cocaine that was probably killing him. Without seeking professional medical help, Bowie determined to kick his drug habit, with his friend Iggy Pop back in Europe, and to find a new way of relating to the rock business. His Berlin years awaited. By mid-76, Bowie had decided to leave his old rock-star self back in a darkened room in LA.

8. THE NEW SCHOOL OF PRETENSION, 1976–1977

Art is the one place where we can crash our plane and walk away from it.

BRIAN ENO

When Ziggy fell from favour and lost all his money, he had a son before he died . . . Johnny Rotten!

BOWIE TALKING TO JOURNALIST PHILIPPE MANOEUVRE, JULY 1977

The two-and-a-half years of New York then LA insanity had reduced Bowie to a state of emotional collapse. He would later admit that the entire '76 tour was undertaken under duress; that his mind had fractured under the pressure of substance abuse. After wishing for a European future on *Station To Station*, he resolved to turn the fiction into reality. By the summer of '76, Bowie officially lived at Clos des Mesanges, a villa near Blonay on the north side of Lake Geneva, which he shared with Angie, Zowie and household staff. Angie had selected the house as a bucolic retreat from LA madness. Neighbours were Charlie and Oona Chaplin, and the elderly maverick painter, Balthus. There were, of course, sound financial reasons for taking up Swiss residence: after five years of being fleeced, Bowie determined to domicile in a country with advantageous tax laws. His main motivations for the move, though, were both personal and professional: he knew that he had to rid himself of the circle of dealers, pushers and hangers-on that had attached themselves to him in the States. Approaching thirty and with a five-year-old son, he was beginning to realise that his parental responsibilities were moral obligations, not optional extras. It would take months for Bowie to kick addiction, but years for him to kick drugs.

Professionally, mainstream success and the huge expectations being placed upon him wearied Bowie. He was less artist, more product, and for his next project he resolved to regain his single-minded, fuck-the-lot-of-you mind-set of the early 70s. The result was arguably the most important record of his career.

After a short break following the White Light tour, Bowie and Iggy moved to the Chateau d'Hérouville, the venue of *Pin Ups* and some of Elton John's recordings, ostensibly to continue their holiday and with no real plans to record together at all. However, much of Iggy Pop's *The Idiot* was recorded there during that summer. Bowie and Iggy worked through July on the album in France, then relocated first to the Musicland Studios in Munich and finally to the Hansa Studios, Berlin, to complete the work.

Bowie also had plans for a radical artistic move for his own work. His interest in Kraftwerk has already been documented, but equally, if not more, important to Bowie were the works of other Krautrock acts, including Neu!, Edgar Froese, Can and Cluster. Bowie was embarked on a radical programme of fusing these novel sounds with the rhythms and energy of both rock and, more importantly, black music. It was a programme which helped define the very trajectory of modern music, and its influence is still being felt today. Immediately after the *Station To Station* tour, he called Tony Visconti and his future chosen collaborator, Brian Eno, who he had met at one of the Wembley gigs that May. 'What I think he was trying to do was to duck the momentum of a successful career,' Eno later said. 'The main problem with success is that it has a huge momentum. It's like you've got this big train behind you and it wants you to carry on going the same way. Nobody wants you to step off the tracks and start looking round in the scrub around the edges because nobody can see anything promising there.'

Eno's post-Roxy Music work had already established him as left-field experimenter *par excellence*. His main contribution had been his 'invention' of ambient music. Recovering in bed after being knocked down by a car, he was listening to a piece of music when the speaker malfunctioned and the music became almost inaudible. Too ill to turn the music back up, or to fix the fault, he discovered that this peripheral music was providing a background ambience and mood which he liked very much. Herein lies one of the origins of ambient music, and Eno began exploring this new musical language in the mid-70s. Bowie spotted that he represented a future he wanted to be a part of.

Eno's *Another Green World*, released in 1975, with its short, pastoral instrumentals and quirky post-prog-rock-styled songs, was an obvious influence on Bowie's next move. One can hear the future on this album, the slap-based funk of Japan and Talking Heads and the modernist music of Bowie's *Low* and *"Heroes"*. This was music with a sense of environment, a sonic space outside of the traditional dialogue between vocalist and guitar backing, a new way forward that meant the synth rather than the stratocaster.

Eno was yet another in a long list of inspired choices by Bowie. His new studio workmate was born Brian Peter George St Baptiste de la Salle Eno on 15 May 1948, in Woodbridge, Suffolk, England. He attended art school in Ipswich and then Winchester, and had developed an interest in 'systems' music and the aleatory methods of John Cage. He was famously co-leader of the bipolar Roxy Music with Bryan Ferry until a power struggle forced him to leave the group in 1973. On first inspection, Eno had been as personality-driven as Bowie had back in the early days of Roxy Music. He stood at the side of the stage, a balding man with long hair, make-up and feathers, rivalling Ferry as the centre of attention, twisting and treating the music with his various electronic gizmos before it hit the audience.

After his split from Roxy in 1973, Eno started the cult of the non-celebrity. His whole rationale was to destroy the authorial figure within the pop process. While Bowie was the great photogenic pop icon, his work about characters and masks, Eno's art was in disappearance: '. . . Eno's object was to eliminate himself from his work, to minimise his "degree of participation", to cleanse his art of the idea of the individual artist,' wrote Simon Frith and Howard Horne in their book *Art Into Pop*. Eno was interested in systems music, music that almost played itself and followed repetitive patterns. Bowie was interested in dramatic gestures and melodic sweeps. This created a great tension in the Bowie–Eno axis; the one a maverick pop star, the other resolved to eradicate himself from the pop world completely as an image. They were intriguingly mismatched.

What renders the three Bowie albums made with Eno (with deliberate pretension called 'the triptych' by Bowie) so interesting is this tension between Bowie the impulsive pop superstar learning a new musical language (and learning it very quickly), and Eno, naturally minimalistic, intensely resourceful, deliberate, cranky and keen to create the correct environment for music to take place and with a clear idea of how music might be used by the listener.

As Visconti put it, Eno was Bowie's Zen master. He would arrive at the studio brimming with stratagems and tricks, a notebook chock-full of possible routes to take if recording hit a creative dead end. One of the most unusual features of the recording process was the use of his Oblique Strategies cards. Eno had developed these with Peter Schmidt in 1975. They formed a sort of musical tarot ('over one hundred musical dilemmas', according to their author), each card containing a little aphorism suggesting a possible route to the next creative plane. Such random processes appealed enormously to Bowie, who had already chanced upon the work of Burroughs and cut-ups. Eno's cards contained such directives as 'Listen to the quiet voice', 'Fill every beat with something', 'Emphasize the flaws', 'Mute and continue' and 'Use an unacceptable colour'. One of Eno's most apposite maxims was 'Honour thy error as a hidden intention'. During the recording of the Bowie/Eno triptych (*Low*, "*Heroes*" and *Lodger*), mistakes, chance and random influences were to be built into the compositional processes as if they had been intended. Bowie and Eno used the recording process to plan accidents and then react accordingly.

Bowie, in 1978, said that Eno 'got me off narration which I was intolerably bored with ... Narrating stories, or doing little vignettes of what at the time I thought was happening in America and putting it on my albums in a convoluted fashion ... Singer-songwriter-askew ... and Brian really opened my eyes to the idea of processing, to the abstract of communication.'

So began the high-water mark of Bowie's cut-up phase. Randomness and juxtaposition were to be the guiding principles in his work in the second half of the 70s. He had started using the cut-up technique pioneered by William Burroughs and Brion Gysin when writing the lyrics for *Diamond Dogs*, and found that by applying the same procedure to other literary matter, such as old diaries, it would often tell him something about the past or predict the future. The sense of randomness appealed greatly to

Bowie. He would write a song both in the first and third person and then randomise these two perspectives to create a 'new' subjectivity.

Bowie said in 1993, 'We would devise systems where I would put down a piano part, say, and then take the faders down so you could only hear the drums and he only knew what key it was in. Then he would come in and put an alternative piece in, not hearing my part but knowing what the key was. Then we would leapfrog with each other, each not hearing each other's parts, and then at the end of the day put each other's parts up and see what happened.' Bowie and Eno would then choose which piano parts they wanted to form the basis of a particular song – 'really musically cutting up'. This can, of course, make for a difficult listening experience. One Bowie fan, Steve Lowe, now a record engineer, puts it like this: 'For me the studio albums from *Hunky Dory* to *Young Americans* work the best musically. When I listen to the albums from *Low* to *Scary Monsters* my ear's distracted and I find I'm listening to the way the song's been recorded.'

Nevertheless, these albums pushed pop into a completely new area. Bowie called himself a 'generalist', not a musician, while Eno tried to get the occupation 'non-musician' stamped on his passport (a request refused by the Home Office). Bowie told the press his painting activities were just as important to him as his music. His work with Eno formed 'a new school of pretension', an idea dropped into media conversations wherever possible by Bowie as the 70s drew to a close. This was pop with a pretension to be art, a self-conscious low-cultural appropriation of high-cultural forms. It lost Bowie sales and support. However, it would ultimately win him huge respect.

Recording began at the Chateau d'Hérouville studio near Paris on 1 September 1976. When the team assembled, it was by no means clear whether the experiment would ever even be released. 'I think David just felt that he had a little time to experiment with new concepts before he made up his mind to make another "official" album,' recalls Tony Visconti. 'I remember the night, about two-thirds of the way through the sessions, when we rough-mixed everything that we had on tape and gave David a cassette copy. He was waving it in the air, saying gleefully, "We've got an album!" over and over. That was the transition from experiment to a real album.'

The chateau itself was beautiful and secluded. Bathed in a quiet solitude by day, by night it was a Gothic freak show. 'It was a very friendly environment out in the French countryside,' recollects Alomar. Unlike the set-up for the previous two albums recorded in the States, 'there was no stimulation, no outside influence, just the castle. I remember that the menu got a little repetitious, meat, meat, meat, so I asked for some fish and we got served prawns with their heads on! All those little eyes looking back at you from the side of the bowl! We (the rhythm section) said, "We can't eat that, we're New Yorkers!" In fact, after work we were bored out of our minds! So David got some wine in and we would always end the evening by watching a video of *Fawlty Towers*!'

'What a peculiar and lovely place that was,' Visconti remembers. 'It was chosen because it was an idyllic setting to make music. David had done *Pin Ups* there, I recorded *The Slider* there with Marc Bolan, and, of course, Elton had recorded there too. When we made *Low*, it was during the summer holidays. We could hardly believe that we were left with only two people to run the place. We suffered food poisoning, and infiltration from the French press during that month, which revealed our daily life there and reported on our conversations. I took the master bedroom because David refused. We heard about the ghosts of Frédéric Chopin and George Sand haunting the place. I must admit that room was weird. There was a corner of the room that just seemed to suck in light. It was cold and could never be illuminated. But Brian Eno stayed in another wing of the chateau and claimed that every night he was woken up by a firm tap on the shoulder. When he woke up, no one was there.'

Low was yet another Bowie album conceived in an atmosphere thick with disorientation. *The Man Who Sold The World*, *Hunky Dory* and *Ziggy Stardust* had been written, partly, in a haunted house (Haddon Hall); *Station To Station* was infused with LA black magic; and now *Low* was another album conceived in a house where spirits roamed the landing. It is little wonder that such records entrap a magical, otherworldly set of ideas and allusions.

Eno's arrival meant the (temporary) eclipse of Carlos Alomar. Whereas, on *Station To Station*, Alomar took the leading role in translating Bowie's musical ideas into actual forms, now he felt his role to be minimalised by the minimalist. Although Alomar liked Eno a lot on a personal level, he was not altogether sympathetic to his approach in the studio:

> Brian Eno had come in and he had these cards that he had made and they were supposed to eliminate a block. Now you've got to understand something. I'm a musician. I've studied music theory, I've studied counterpoint and I'm used to working with musicians who can read music. Here comes Brian Eno and he goes to a blackboard and then starts writing chords on a blackboard. He says, 'Here's the beat, and when I point to the chord, you play that chord.' So we get a random picking of chords. I finally had to say, 'This is bullshit, this sucks, this sounds stupid.' I totally, totally resisted it. David and Brian were two intellectual guys and they had a very different camaraderie, a heavier conversation, a 'Europeanness'. It was too heavy for me. He and Brian would get off on talking about music in terms of history, and I'd think, 'Well, that's stupid – history isn't going to give you a hook for this song!' I'm interested in what's commercial, what's the beat, what's funky, and what's gonna make people dance! When Brian is around, Brian is in control, make no mistake about it, even more so than David, because he controls David's mind as well as David's direction. I had no control or say in any of that stuff . . . and preferred it that way.

However, sonically, perhaps, the biggest contribution on the album came from Tony Visconti who was, according to Alomar, 'very much a fifth member of the band. The sounds that Tony Visconti was getting at this time were the sounds that later would become the signature sounds of snare drums. Snare drums with gates and reverb on them weren't usual at that time.'

Indeed, the drum sound was extraordinary, brutal and mechanistic. Visconti says, 'I was always interested in the latest studio "toys" and I leaped to buy the second Harmonizer, made by a company called Eventide. I heard that it could change the pitch of a sound without changing the speed. My brain nearly exploded when I found what I could do with drums. By lowering the pitch of a live drum, then feeding it back, I got a sort of infinite dropping of pitch, ever renewing itself.' The end results were revolutionary. The effects on 'Speed Of Life', 'Breaking Glass' and particularly 'Sound And Vision' are stunning.

However, Eno was not going to be upstaged in the sonics department. A weird noise was his calling card; a sonic boom his party trick. 'He brought his wonderful EMS synthesizer in a briefcase,' Visconti recalls. 'It had no keyboard, just a joystick, and he came up with wonderful sounds you can hear all over the album that weren't produced by conventional instruments.'

Alomar and the rhythm section had a few neat tricks of their own up their sleeves too, particularly on 'Breaking Glass'. 'Dennis Davis had a lot to do with that,' remembers Alomar. 'I wanted to ape a Jew's harp, just a drone. We were just having fun! If you listen to all the quirks in the music – the call and response stuff between bass, guitar and drums – that was just done with three members of the band.'

'Breaking Glass' is more like a scion of an unfinished (and hidden) whole, a fragment of a song. 'The feeling around was that we'd edit together . . . and turn it into a more normal structure,' said Eno, 'and I said, "No, don't, leave it abnormal, leave it strange, don't normalise it . . . If it's like that, and you like it, keep it. Why fix it? It's not broken." ' The lyric itself is an extension of the occultist imagery to be found on 'Station To Station'. Bowie sings, 'Don't look at the carpet/I drew something awful on it. See.' A year earlier, Bowie had been photographed drawing the 'Tree Of Life' from the cabbala on the floor. He now admits that this line refers to 'both the cabbalistic drawings of the "Tree Of Life" and the conjuring of spirits'.

The songs that would eventually be grouped together on side one of the album took time to emerge in the form we know. Visconti: 'When Carlos was there for the backing tracks, there was hardly a lyric written yet and the songs were very loose structures. Lyrics and melodies were written at the last possible minute. The band just played loosely structured chord changes and rhythm grooves. After about five days we had enough rhythm tracks and only Carlos and Ricky Gardiner the lead guitarist were retained to do some guitar overdubs, again not knowing what the melody or lyric would be. All the songs had working titles, different from their final titles. Tracks one and seven on side one were meant to have lyrics, but they seemed to evolve as instrumentals and we went with the flow. Finally, Brian added his EMS synth where he felt it would make sense (or no sense) and David wrote his melodies and lyrics after everyone was gone. Even the doo-doo-doos on "Sound And Vision" were recorded before there was a lyric, title or melody.'

Those 'doo-doo-doos', sung by Visconti's then wife, singer Mary Hopkin, were the only obvious nod towards conventional pop to be found on the whole album. 'Sound And Vision', however, was no conventional pop song. An introduction of 1 minute 45 seconds before the first line was certainly something of a radical departure for a pop song, but the music was stunning – a mixture of almost Mantovani-style melody played with the synth, a great mechanistic guitar part and that huge gated snare topped off by one of Bowie's bleakest and blankest vocal performances describing a scene of emotional crash, his senses shut down. It's Bowie's LA drug hell reduced to monosyllabic, primal collapse: 'Pale blinds drawn all day/Nothing to do, nothing to say/I'm gonna sit right down/Waiting for the gift of sound and vision'.

Visconti remembers too that 'there were more verses, but we honed it down during the mix to what you've heard'.

The two short instrumentals on side one, the brilliant opener, 'Speed Of Life', and the closing 'New Career In A New Town', are also haunting. The unsung hero of side one of the album was the lead guitarist, Ricky Gardiner. 'I had met Ricky Gardiner and his talented singer/writer wife, Virginia, just before the album and I was recording demos of their songs,' says Visconti. 'I was flabbergasted with Ricky's playing and told David.'

If the songs which would form side one of the album were a radical departure from *Station To Station*, then the music of side two inhabited a different planet altogether. It was side two, consisting of four longer instrumentals, which was reported to have given RCA a collective coronary in the autumn of 1976. Despite the assertion by some critics at the time that these instrumentals show Bowie slavishly aping Eno's style, they are, in actual fact, very different from Eno's work up until that time. The instrumentals on *Low* demand to be listened to. They make the most obtrusive ambient music imaginable. According to Eno, 'Ambient music must be able to accommodate many levels of listening attention without enforcing one in particular; it must be ignorable as it is interesting.' Bowie's music on *Low* and *"Heroes"* unquestionably fails to accommodate these levels of listening.

But Eno was no bit-part player. 'Side two was where Brian really came into his own,' recalls Visconti. 'All the tracks on side two (except "Subterraneans") started with a metronome making a click track. It wasn't necessarily done in a particular time signature; we just needed a "pulse" to hang the music on (later, Philip Glass had to convert this music into time signatures and actual bars of music for classically trained musicians playing the *Low* symphony). After about seven minutes of clicks had been laid down on tape, one of us had to count the clicks. I was elected and my voice was recorded on another track, next to the click, droning 1–2–3 . . . 203–204–205, etc. Then David and Brian started to improvise over the click. Once a bed of "ambient music" was laid down they would start a new section, say at click 59. That's how the Bowie/Eno side two pieces were created. We had several keyboards in the studio from Roland and Yamaha, plus David's unique Chamberlain. It was a more advanced Mellotron. We also used conventional piano and guitar, but highly treated electronically by myself.'

'Warszawa' is the most startling piece of music on the album. Bowie fans might have thought side one a bit odd, but four minutes into this opener on the second side, as Bowie starts singing a totally invented language, they may reasonably have lost the plot altogether. Tony Visconti reveals that this invented language, sung with such conviction as to sound authentic, was in fact based on a real one. 'I loved it when David did the quasi-Balkan singing. He had an old recording of a boys' choir from one of the Balkan countries and he played it for me at some earlier date (on reflection, this record was not unlike the female choirs of Bulgaria that eventually won a Grammy in the 80s).

' "Warszawa" reminded him of that recording and he went in front of the microphone to try and re-create it. To make him sound like a boy I slowed the tape down about three semitones and he sang his part slowly. Once it was back up to speed he sounded about eleven years old! I can't tell you how much fun the three of us had recording side two – it was more fun than side one.'

For 'Warszawa', Bowie wanted to musically re-create a sense of place – on this occasion the Polish countryside and the city of Warsaw. The other three long instrumentals also dealt with a specific environment. The unnerving (and punningly entitled) 'Art Decade' saw Bowie trying to capture the ambience of West Berlin, 'cut off from the world, art and culture, dying with no hope of retribution'. The self-explanatory 'Weeping Wall' is beholden to Philip Glass' neo-classical accumulative work. Bowie plays all instruments and sets the shiny but 'real' timbres of the xylophone and vibraphone against the synths.

It completes the trilogy of instrumentals about Berlin, this time focusing on the East. Bowie later commented that it was 'about the people who got caught up in East Berlin after separation – hence the faint jazz saxophones representing the memory of what it was'.

Low was about purging. The sounds have a clear, clinical feel, a sort of musical catharsis, but Bowie was in an embattled state of mind during the making of the record. He had to leave the studio for several days to make a deposition in a Paris law court in the Michael Lippman lawsuit. Visconti accompanied Bowie there to give him moral support.

It was also around this time that Bowie made a conscious decision to take firm control over his family affairs. 'Zowie was with him there,' recalls Alomar. 'He was very much into having his kid with him. When I was leaving the chateau, Zowie was looking out of the window and I remember him saying, "Carlos, you won't forget me, will you?" And I said, "Of course I won't forget you." A little later on David told me that he wanted to take some time off the road to take care of his family situation and that he wouldn't be calling me because of that. I was home and I had my own baby at the time so it made sense. We had that conversation at the chateau. He's serious about his son; he will sacrifice anything for Zowie.'

A year later Bowie told *Melody Maker*, 'I think having a son made an enormous difference to me. At first it frightened me, and I tried not to see the implications. Now it's his future that concerns me. My own future slips by.'

According to Angie, Bowie disliked his new Swiss residence and spent most of the next eighteen months in Berlin with Iggy Pop. Contrary to popular myth, Bowie was not roughing it in Berlin, but did live in a relatively modest flat over a car shop at Hauptstrasse 155, a tree-lined dual carriageway in the Schonberg district of West Berlin. It was just a quarter of an hour's walk from where the writer Christopher Isherwood stayed in the early 1930s, his own portrait of proto-Fascist gay samurai icon, Yukio Mishima, hanging over his bed. Bowie would breakfast at the gay bar, Anderes Ufer, next door. Then he would spend his time overloading his febrile imagination with ghoulish remembrances of the city's grand decadence, exploring East and West Berlin by bike, visiting the Brucke Museum and wandering around Kreuz-berg, the gay area which also housed many of the city's other dispossessed – the Turkish immigrants, the homeless, the artists and the punks. According to the *Independent*'s Steve Turner, who wrote an excellent article on Bowie's Berlin in 1991, 'Friends remember him being particularly interested in anything to do with Hitler.' Bowie and Iggy ate well and cheaply on Turkish food in many of the small restaurants in the city. Berlin was in-between: neither wholly east nor west, a city of minorities, ethnic, cultural and sexual. It appealed very much to Bowie's innate outsiderdom.

He was still not in good shape. In the autumn of 1976, he collapsed at his apartment in Berlin after a row with Angie, allegedly over Coco. This might have been an overdose, or an anxiety attack, or a mixture of both – the real reason has never been revealed. It was not the suspected coronary reported in the press at the time: the medical staff merely concluded that Bowie had overdone things and had too much to drink.

Iggy, trying to kick his heroin habit, and Bowie were on a self-administered rehab course which was not running altogether smoothly. By his own admission, Bowie was drinking (mainly König Pilsner beer) quite heavily in those first few months in Berlin, a regular night-time visitor to a bar called Joe's Beer House. Berlin was also, as they soon discovered, and as Bowie dryly remarked many years afterwards, the heroin capital of Europe. With his closely cropped, undyed hair, moustache, checked shirt, blue jeans and cap, he frequented the streets of the city with Iggy and Coco, almost unrecognisable from the glam-era pin-up of yore. Driving a clapped-out 1950s Mercedes around town, he had, in effect, turned himself into a native Berliner. Once again, Bowie had become his environment.

Although his cocaine use had been scaled down, Bowie himself admits that he was to have 'lapses' for a good ten years after the mid-70s. Iggy Pop said, in 1999, that they would be good boys for most of the week, then binge for two days. Alomar: 'It lasted a few albums, I guess, until after the Berlin time and "*Heroes*". The tightest period was at the end of *Young Americans* and *Station To Station*, and after that it kind of tapered to a little bit here, a little bit there. It wasn't part of what he needed to get his work done. Of course, he could lapse, but, hey, man, going into the bathroom and doing a few nails is not the same as walking in with a bagful of cocaine. It's not in the same conversation. But do you really think he's gonna do all that synthesizer music without being high? When you move into those areas like Paris and Berlin, you can't readily get all that stuff that you get in America; it's a more dangerous situation. You have to remember that Eno had a very clear-headed influence. Brian was straight as a nail and his influence was just that – sobering.'

Angie Bowie disliked Berlin and was seldom in the city with her husband, preferring to stay in Switzerland. His off-on relationship with Ava Cherry seemed to be over (she was slated to accompany Bowie on the White Light tour as one of the backing vocalists but was dropped at the last moment) and Bowie was dating trans-sexual Romy Haag, the owner of the transvestite revue at the Luttzower Lampe and a local celebrity in Berlin. Their affair ended when Haag spilled the beans about their relationship to a local newspaper. Bowie demanded privacy in his new life away from the media.

Bowie was also having a hard time convincing his record company, RCA, that his new album, then titled *New Music Night And Day*, ought to be released at all. It was the first major bust-up between artist and record company, and from this period on, Bowie's relationship with RCA would be in a slow, inexorable decline. Visconti: 'I am not sure of the details. Although he and David had parted company, Defries still had a personal stake in Bowie's releases until 1982, to the tune of sixteen per cent. He heard an advance copy of *Low* (we didn't send him one) and thought it didn't sound like a Bowie album. He was afraid it wouldn't be successful, so he implored RCA to block it. He had his sympathisers at RCA, and one nameless executive there remarked how he'd like to buy Bowie a house in Philly so he could record *Young Americans II*.'

For Bowie, personally, it was a very important album. First, it was released just after he had turned thirty and, in the climate of punk, he was superannuated. Indeed, at that stage, there were very few pop stars around and in the charts who were significantly older than Bowie. It was by no means certain that it was possible to sustain a career in pop after the age of thirty with any real conviction. Most of those older than Bowie were regarded as 'boring old farts' (Clapton, Jagger, Richards, Townshend, McCartney – though significantly not Lennon), while all those over, say, forty and still on the road were either original rock'n'rollers (Presley, Berry, Little Richard) or from the jazz, country or blues traditions. Bowie was entering uncharted waters. Could a thirty-something pop star still speak to 'youth culture'? It was obvious that *Low* had, in an unconscious way, already addressed the problem. Bowie was dropping out of generational pop politics and seeking to create a new 'adult audience'. In addition to this, Bowie's youthful charisma, stylishness and danceability meant that he still kept hold of some of his teenage and twenty-something audience too, something other artists did not.

Released as punk was becoming significant (The Sex Pistols had just had their first Top 40 hit with 'Anarchy In The UK'), on the surface *Low* stood as punk's very antithesis. At a time when punk rock was noisily reclaiming the three-minute pop song, Bowie almost completely abandoned traditional rock instrumentation and embarked on a kind of introverted musical therapy. The most obvious parallel is with John Lennon's post-primal therapy album, *Plastic Ono Band*, released in 1970. If *Station To Station* is desperate, then the songs on *Low* show an individual almost beyond hope, with Bowie reduced to the simplest of pleadings for some sort of human connection on 'Be My Wife'. Bowie sings like a man in genuine pain: 'Please be mine/Share my life/Stay with me/Be my wife'.

This rather wonderful song was chosen as the second single off the album in May 1977, but missed the charts totally. The promotional clip, shot in Paris that spring, is a portrait in absurdity. As with the earlier 'Life On Mars?' video, Bowie is filmed against a stark white studio space. But whereas, on this video, he at least looks part of humankind underneath all the mascara, on 'Be My Wife', he is totally freaky, singing to camera, his features twisted in expressions so mannered and unnatural that the effect is rather shocking, all the more so given that he is projecting this artifice almost straight (little make-up, no costume, no special effects).

The songs on *Low* also show a new aspect to Bowie's vocal style. On *Station To Station*, he had summoned up a white hysteria for 'Wild Is The Wind' and 'Word On A Wing', a mélange of *chanson* and soul. But on songs such as 'Sound And Vision', 'Always Crashing In The Same Car' and 'What In The World', he presented a new, chill, blank facade, the lines sung in a quiet, lobotomised stream of consciousness. Short, verbally undernourished sentences were delivered monosyllabically over a robotic rhythm section, and this sense of blanked-out isolation fitted the lyrics well. This technique was borrowed most notably by Gary Numan in the late 1970s and, more recently, under the auspices of Brian Eno, by U2 on 'Numb' in 1993. Under-emoting became part of the mainstream. 'The emotions on it are those rarely touched by writers, I think,' concluded Bowie, his work not concerned with 'general, emotive terms: love or anger, or whatever'.

However, in many ways, *Low* was also incredibly punky. After a decade of prog-rock noodling, when the synthesizer had the terrible reputation of being played only by highly proficient boffins displaying their prowess in seventeen-minute song sequences, *Low* helped redeem the synth as an object of cool. There had been very few mainstream pop songs which had used the synth to any great effect, and those that had – like The Peppers' 'Pepper Box' and Hot Butter's 'Popcorn' – were more novelty records than anything else. *Low* was released just at the time when synths became affordable and, more importantly, programmable. Back in the UK, The Human League, Cabaret Voltaire, Joy Division (originally called Warsaw after 'Warszawa') and, a little later, Ultravox, Gary Numan and Orchestral Manoeuvres In The Dark all walked in the shadow of *Low*. The synth overtook the guitar as the instrument par excellence for the man or woman with big ideas and great tunes but minimal conventional musical wisdom or proficiency.

RCA finally relented and released the album on 14 January 1977. 'When I got the album I rushed home and treated it like a classical record,' says Alomar. 'I put side two on which had all the nuanced stuff, turned off all the lights and played it and I was in such heaven!'

The cover, a striking shot of the duffel-coated Thomas Newton in side profile set against a discordant vivid orange wash, was meant as a visual pun – 'low profile'. Not many got the joke until Bowie pointed it out in an interview later. Against all the odds, and with no promotion from Bowie at all, *Low* reached Number 2. The first single off the album, 'Sound And Vision', was making a slowish, but inexorable rise up the charts, and eventually reached a lofty Number 3, his biggest hit with new material since 'Sorrow' way back in 1973. Although no promo was made for the song, the single picked up considerable airplay, and was even used by the BBC as the background music to their continuity announcements. Surprisingly, it was the first Bowie single co-produced by Tony Visconti to reach the UK Top 10.

Bowie decided to tour that spring. However, with typical perversity (and presumably with the intention of antagonising a record label which he deemed unsupportive of his career), the tour would not be to promote his own new album, but someone else's.

That someone else was, of course, Iggy Pop. A single, 'Sister Midnight', was already in the shops, with a second, 'China Girl', to follow in support of a tour in March 1977. Neither charted but, that spring, the album, *The Idiot*, with the cover photo shot by Bowie himself, became Iggy's first Top 30 album in the UK. Bowie toured as Iggy Pop's piano player.

Iggy Pop is a man of incredible extremes. According to one Bowie fan's testimony, one minute he would barge straight through someone walking arm-in-arm down a corridor with a band member of a Bowie tour or scream 'Burn me, burn me!' through a hotel lobby if he saw someone smoking. The next he was your regular, friendly weird guy. Tony Visconti noticed a big change in Iggy as an individual: 'On a personal level, I really liked Iggy. He was not the notorious member of The Stooges any more. I was amazed how fit he was and what good friends he and David had become.'

One thing for certain is that he has one of the most distinctive voices in pop history. Low, crunching, gnarled, wrecked, it reaches bottomless pits of anguish in just one syllable. *The Idiot*, viewed from the perspective of a quarter of a century later, now sounds closer to the sound Bowie was perfecting on his own White Light tour than *Low* itself does. It's a funky, robotic hellhole of an album, full of droll conceits (such as the least appropriately titled song of the set, 'Funtime') and great melodies (nowhere better displayed than on the original 'China Girl', a more unstable, yet somehow more charming, version than Bowie's more famous remake). On 'Nightclubbing' we're right there with Bowie and Iggy in Berlin, plodding along the Kurfurstendamm in the rain, passing the seedy night joints, rolling along with that wonderful tumbling piano line. 'Sister Midnight' is not quite as Bowie would have made it had it remained one of his songs, but Alomar's riff is still a thing of rare funkiness and the song is sublime. It was not, in truth, the best recorded of albums, however, and it certainly had no FM radio sheen. Visconti was brought in at the end to mix the album: 'I just remember the mixes being really hard, because the master tapes weren't recorded very well. It was more of a salvage job than a creative mixing.'

But Iggy had a mostly fine album to promote, and he had a great band too, including a young, dynamic rhythm section of Ricky Gardiner on lead guitar, Alomar on rhythm guitar and Hunt and Tony Sales, sons of US comedian Soupy Sales, on drums and bass. Bowie played the joanna. The opening night of the tour was at Friars Aylesbury, where Bowie had decided to form the band that would become The Spiders From Mars back in 1971 and, in 1972, had played there as Ziggy. The venue's owner, David Stopps, welcomed Bowie back: 'I knew David was going to be the keyboard player, but nobody else did. I remember the band turned up really late and David saw the queue outside and said, "Just let them in. We'll forget the sound check." I'll never forget him doing that. It was incredibly noble of him. He said it was more important that they came in out of the rain or whatever it was, rather than keep the audience out while they did the sound check. I remember that when people realised that David was the keyboard player, the entire audience shifted to one side of the venue! It was the first time I'd ever looked from the balcony and seen an unsymmetrical audience. Quite extraordinary, really. Bowie hadn't changed. He was always very friendly, very outgoing, very gregarious. He'd always talk to you; he never played the superstar thing. He was very friendly, fairly chummy and always very approachable. Iggy was a very much moodier character altogether; a tougher character to deal with for a promoter. Wouldn't say I didn't like him, though.'

The Iggy Pop tour would have quite a marked effect on Carlos Alomar. By pushing him to the forefront it made him more assertive and dominant on stage: 'I was brought in to do the tour and that's the first time I really met Iggy. I liked him – he was crazy! Now, when I'm with Bowie, I'm back there on the microphone, singing "la la la". Everything's great with the world and I'm being paid large. Here I am, here's David, hi everybody. Now, with Iggy Pop, you're in the front line. If he's getting spat at, you're getting spat at. If he's getting beers thrown at him, you're getting beers thrown at you. It's a very aggressive, in-your-face, everybody's-the-star-let's-kick-everybody's-ass kind of tour. It really put me more aggressively to the front, so when I came back to the Bowie tour I wanted to be more upfront. At that point, I was a little bit more resentful of the other guitar players when I had to show them the lines. They were playing my lines! I wanted be a lead guitar player. I was resentful of the fact that I had taken a back seat to any of the guitar players working with Bowie. At that point it was a bit more like, "I'm David's guitar player, who the hell are you?" But soon all that fell by the wayside too!'

Iggy and the band played six shows in the UK before a nineteen-date tour of North America. Another Iggy Pop album, *Lust For Life*, was released in September 1977. This was another collaborative effort with Bowie and Iggy writing and recording together in Berlin, and production overseen by Colin Thurston, a Visconti protégé who was to engineer Bowie's next solo album. An astonishing cover shot on the sleeve, showing a maniacally smiling Iggy, housed an album which was far more raucous and guitar-based than *The Idiot*.

The title track, given a fresh lease of life through its inclusion in the soundtrack for the cult hit *Trainspotting*, is all cavernous, rebounding drum figures. Iggy Pop: 'David Bowie wrote that one in Berlin, in front of the TV, on a ukulele … He cribbed the rhythm of this army forces network theme, which was a guy tapping out the beat on a Morse code key. Ever the sharp mimic, David picked up the nearest available instrument and started strumming.'

Lust For Life was to provide Bowie not only with the title of a future album, but also the basis of his first real band since The King Bees, for it was drummer Hunt Sales and bassist Tony Sales who would form the rhythm section for Tin Machine over a decade later. Also on the album was the Ig's calling card, 'The Passenger', co-written by Pop and Ricky Gardiner, and possessed with one of the greatest riffs of all time. While *The Idiot*, like the Bowie-produced *Blah Blah Blah* ten years later, sounds closer to Bowie's albums, *Lust For Life* is trademark Iggy Pop, more groove-based, looser and rockier.

Although Iggy had just made the two best albums of his career, his move into the Bowie camp lost him credibility as an artist, particularly among a wing of uncompromising critics in the music press. In their eyes, Pop had allowed himself to be co-opted, the vampyric Bowie merely feeding off the Ig's purer rock vision. Iggy was now just a small part of the Bowie empire. Again, Bowie was the fall guy, his honest intention of making great music with Iggy trashed as another piece of unwanted colonisation.

During this period, in Berlin, Bowie slowly, but surely, began to feel less like a paranoid freak, more like a human being.

According to Tony Visconti, Bowie was becoming a more stable and happier individual: 'He was very upbeat. Besides the recording sessions, he had a life! He had new friends, Iggy was there and he had the support of Coco, who lived in another flat in the same building. I remember going to some great clubs and just having a few beers and a great time. Not one of us was getting out of our skulls. We met several painters and musicians, including Edgar Froese of Tangerine Dream. We made a few trips through the wall at Checkpoint Charlie into East Berlin, did some sightseeing, and went to the Bertolt Brecht theatre. We would often go to fine restaurants too. Iggy was keeping fit walking about ten miles a day and David was painting and recording.'

However, life was still not without its little surprises for the former Thin White Duke. 'I would have days where things were moving in the room – and this was when I was totally straight,' said Bowie in the 1980s. 'It took two years in Berlin to really cleanse the system.'

Bowie was living a less-cocooned existence now, but his 'normality' was more a new angle to give to journalists, a new selling point, than anything else. In the late-70s, Bowie interviews, such as Charles Shaar Murray's 'Who was that (un)masked man?' for the *NME* in 1977 and Jean Rook's piece, 'Bowie Reborn', for the *Daily Express* two years later, took the new, unfreakish Bowie for granted. It was this idea of Bowie finding himself, stopping the play-acting and generally learning how to be part of humankind that began to dominate. He told Jean Rook: 'Every day I get up more nerve, and try to be more normal, and less insulated against real people,' and added, 'When I thought I was coming to the end of my tether I considered everything as a way out.'

Bowie's move to Berlin was crucial. He pulled himself away from addiction, and regained his enthusiasm for music. More than most other pop writers, Bowie functions best in strange environments. London, New York and LA had become uninspiring through overfamiliarity. Of Berlin in the late 1970s, Bowie commented: 'I like the friction. That's what I look for in any city. West Berlin has the right kind of push. I can't write in a peaceful atmosphere at all, I've nothing to bounce off. I need the terror, whatever it is.'

Bowie was no recluse, just as his friend John Lennon, in the second half of the 70s, because he was not courting the media and was not making records, was equally no recluse. Berlin, a sombre, schizoid city with a charge of negative energy, gave Bowie and his music a completely new focus. For his new record, Bowie was to capture the sound of the Wall itself.

Bowie reconvened an almost identical personnel for the second collaboration with Eno, "*Heroes*", recorded during the summer of 1977 at the Hansa Studios in Berlin.

The tone of the album, according to Visconti, was more optimistic, more positive. 'I think it was assumed it would be more of the same but a progression, because Bowie, Eno and I suffered from a low boredom threshold. We were certainly more confident on this one, due to *Low*'s reception (we only read the good reviews). The studio was better than the last one and the city was magic! We were all on a creative high. Even the rhythm section, who hadn't been sure of the musical merits of *Low* while they were recording it, knew that this one was going to turn out to be a killer.'

However, despite this air of positivity, there is a gloominess to "*Heroes*". The music is cluttered and troubled, the singing mannered and unstable. Take 'Joe The Lion', for example, a wild, dissonant mixture of distorted guitars and Bowie's vocal veering between conversation, screams and grand melismatics. According to Visconti, 'The melody and lyrics and final vocal took less than an hour.' Part of the lyric deals with an Australian performance artist, Chris Burden, who had himself nailed to his Volkswagen car back in 1974. This was an event not unnoticed by Bowie, who would revisit Burden and performance art more fully in the 90s. 'Blackout', a song about Berlin night people, sees Bowie snarling, his vocal distorted and discordant, the backing verging on industrial. 'Sons Of The Silent Age' is another futuristic nostalgia song, doomy sax-driven verses set incongruously aside cheesy choruses.

The site of the record's production, Studio 2 at Hansaton Studios, within walking distance of Checkpoint Charlie, gave the sessions a decadent grandeur not possessed by any other Bowie record. Carlos Alomar:

David has this thing of taking everybody out of their environment so that all they can think about is their own material. The studio itself was a relic. My first impressions were of the curtains surrounding the studio, and the darkness in the studio.

It was not foreboding, just that the air was thick with a darker vibe. You have got to remember, we're painting a picture based on our emotional disposition and you're thinking: Germans, Nazis, the Wall, oppression. These things are hanging in the air, and when things get darker physically, you kind of think of darker themes too. Berlin was a rather dark, industrial place to work. There was one point when we wanted to see a bit of light and we asked them to open the curtains. There were these gigantic, heavy curtains and when they did that we saw the walk where the gunner is and that was a rather rude awakening. Although it gave us a cold slap in the face as to where we were, it also gave us a heavier resolve about the intensity of what we were doing.

The intensity of the moment wasn't exclusive to the studio environment. We would go out at night to the darker elements of the city, to the underground subway red-light districts, just to walk around and check out all the decadence. I would say that his mental stimulation was at an all-time high at that point. It was actually a very good period; there was a lot of clarity to David at that point, in that he was back to being a literary person, very interested in the politics of the day, knowing the news, which I found amazing because he never cared about that. Obviously, there were other things on his mind than doing his record.

It was also a fantastically adventurous time for producer Tony Visconti. He loved working at Hansa. Studio 2 was a converted first-floor concert hall which, during the war years, had been used as a ballroom by Gestapo officers. 'In the basement they had boxes of old valves that you put in the old valve microphones which had swastikas on them,' says Tony Visconti. The studio had a stage for a full choir which could accommodate up to 120 musicians. According to Visconti, in the 1930s and 1940s, Hitler had some of his inspirational music recorded there. It was a huge space for recording an album and Visconti would utilise the ambience of the room in the recording sessions themselves. According to journalist Steve Turner, 'Bowie called it "The hall by the wall" and the name stuck.'

'It was one of my last great adventures in making albums,' Visconti now says. 'The studio was about five hundred yards from the wall. Red Guards would look into our control-room window with powerful binoculars. Berlin was then a modern Gothic city, full of surprises and lovely people. The drag clubs like Romy Haag's and the Luttzower Lampe were lots of fun, because they weren't gay clubs per se. Entire German families – mom, dad, teenage sons and daughters – would be in the audience. Drag clubs were high humour then. It was fabulous entertainment. Romy Haag could get as many as fifteen people on a stage about ten feet wide, miming to a playback of a popular song at twice the speed. The next day in the studio we'd remind ourselves of how cool the cabarets were.'

Robert Fripp, who had made his name with the art-rock band King Crimson and had recently worked with Brian Eno himself on two collaborations, was brought in to add his distinctive guitar work. Robert Fripp was an inspired choice. His solos were often composited; that is, one guitar part was formed from editing together several 'rushes'. Visconti: 'Fripp was there for two days, at the end of all the rhythm-section playing. He played so easily and quickly, he kept us amused the rest of the time with some ribald humour. I never worked with a more competent guitarist.'

Eno was astounded by Fripp's virtuosity: 'We put the songs on. These were songs he'd never heard . . . He didn't know what the chords were going to do, what the changes were going to be . . . He would just launch into them at full speed and somehow navigate his way through them.'

The title track itself has gone down as one of Bowie's finest. Visconti tells the story of how a rock standard was produced out of wild improvisation and brilliant studio craft:

David was always willing to try any new recording techniques I wanted to experiment with. In a studio so full of reverber-ation, it is common practice to seal off a singer between four movable walls. Instead, I wanted to use it. So I set up three mics with electronic 'gates' on them. The gates wouldn't open until David sang above a certain volume. It took about half an hour of David alternating between shouting and whispering, but it came off beautifully when I got the levels just right. The reverb you hear on "*Heroes*" is the natural but gated reverb of the room he sang it in. David's take was also his lyric-writing take. He wrote, or modified a prewritten verse, as he sang it, asking me to stop the machine while he amended a line or two. At the end of two hours, we had a final vocal take and a final lyric, which happened almost simultaneously.

Afterwards David and I sang the backing vocals, embellishing and answering certain lines. You can hear my lovely Brooklyn accent on lines like, 'I remember' and 'By the wall'. It has been erroneously written that Brian Eno and David sang back-ups on "Heroes", but the album credits clearly state that they were sung by David, myself and sometimes Antonia Maass, a singer we met in a club in Berlin. Yes, Antonia and I were interested in each other, and we left David alone that afternoon, so he could have some quiet to write lyrics to the title track. We stopped by the wall and kissed. David saw us from the control-room window and that inspired a verse for the song.

"Heroes" is David Bowie's 'River Deep Mountain High'. It is a huge wall of sound; a droning, repetitive, oncoming, unstoppable, mechanical block of sound. The image of Bowie standing in the Hansa Studios, with its cold decadence, blowing Visconti's gated mics to smithereens, was one of his finest moments. The little pieces of dramatic repetition ('I, I will be king') are in the tradition not of the pop song but of big light-entertainment ballad singing (such as Shirley Bassey's, 'I, I who have nothing').

Broadcaster and writer Mark Radcliffe captured the essence of the song perfectly when he wrote: 'There was a sense that everybody was playing a different song at a different speed at the same time, and yet somehow creating something effortlessly glorious.' Recently, Bowie himself has revealed that the 'plodding tempo and rhythm' were inspired by 'I'm Waiting For The Man'. The result is possibly Bowie's most universally admired song.

The instrumentals on the second side of "Heroes" have a dark, forbidding gloom about them, the clear, crisp timbres of the Low album replaced by sax, drum kit and lead guitar on 'V-2 Schneider'. On this track, in part a tribute to Florian Schneider-Esleben of Kraftwerk, Bowie had begun his sax part on the wrong beat, but decided he liked it better and finished off the take. It's a piece of music which has sucked in Berlin's history. One can almost see the Nazis parading past the control room of the Hansa Studios as the music – insistent, militaristic – tumbles out of the speakers. 'Sense Of Doubt' is chill and frightening, a four-note piano phrase set against an eerie synth line like a scrap of sound from a silent expressionist-era soundtrack. 'Moss Garden' is tranquil and passive, evolving so slowly as to be almost change-less. Here are Bowie and Eno at their most painterly and abstract.

Like one of Eno's art installations from the 80s, like an almost static collage of slowly evolving shapes and sequences of patterns, the receptive elements in 'Moss Garden' form a patchwork which floods the listener. The intrusion of a cyborg dog yelping at the back of the mix, or Bowie's koto, come as novel surprises.

'Moss Garden' segues into 'Neukoln'. Again, the listener is enveloped in sound. There is a very unsettling tone to the music, and it is less deliberately portentous or obvious as 'Sense Of Doubt' as Bowie sketches in his impressionistic slabs of melismatic sax. The sense of disquiet and unease created by the music mirrors the sense of not belonging and dysfunction felt by the newly arrived Turkish immigrants who lived in the Neukolln area of the city. The end section has Bowie's sax booming out across a harbour of solitude, as if lost in fog; the final death throes of an instrument ending in one furiously rebounded note.

'The Secret Life Of Arabia' is a great song, but its position on the album spoils the dramatic effect. Although the last note of 'Neukoln' really ought to have been the last sound on the album, Bowie ends the set with a more conventional pop song. There's a huge groove which spirals on and on through the song, and Bowie, once again, is the hero in a movie played out in sound. The lines 'You must see the movie, the sand in my eyes/I walk through a desert song as the heroine dies' return to the camp theme of real life merely being a B-movie.

The imagery of the Berlin Wall dominates "*Heroes*" (and the second side of *Low*). The Wall wasn't just a symbol of disconnection or even of tyranny or political division for Bowie. What the Wall represented was his past life as a rock icon. The Wall was the 1970s. The other side was a new, less addictive and less obsessional lifestyle for Bowie. When he sang, 'We can be heroes, just for one day,' it was an acknowledgement that the future didn't just belong to him any more. It belonged to everyone. Just as Warhol had predicted fifteen minutes of fame for everyone back in the pop-art 60s, so Bowie, like punk rock itself, was predicting a future of heroism for all, not just for an elite. The same month Bowie was on *Top of the Pops* singing "Heroes" (only his second live appearance on the show), new-wave group The Stranglers reminded us that there were 'no more heroes any more'. Heroism was for everyone, Bowie was saying. Be your own hero, the age of mass idolatry was over.

With "*Heroes*" Bowie retreated even further from the role of rock icon: 'I feel incredibly divorced from rock and it's a genuine striving to be that way,' he told *Melody Maker* soon after the album's release. According to his friend Carlos Alomar, 'The internal politics of record companies had ravaged his career and taken their toll, so he wasn't really concerned with what would be considered commercial. He was instead trying to make a statement about where he was, why he had gone there, and what he was bringing back. What he was bringing back was more a piece of himself.'

Bowie had refused all contact with the press for *Low* but "*Heroes*" saw him on a conveyor-belt of media meet-and-greets. The title track was chosen as the lead-off single but in severely edited form (in the hope of radio play) it lost some of its dramatic appeal. Despite its now legendary status, at the time it was a relative underachiever, reaching Number 24 in the British charts, but staying in the Top 40 for an impressive eight weeks. The video featured Bowie in a cool leather jacket, backlit, twitching and contorting his body as if he were undergoing shock therapy.

Bowie also reaffirmed his new Europeanism by recording both German and French versions of the single (the former was even more intense than the English version). He also agreed to perform the song at short notice on the last of a series being shown by Granada Television called *Marc* – a showcase for the music of former glam king, Marc Bolan. His own single, 'Celebrate Summer', with the rather unpromising lyric, 'Summer's not a bummer/It's a stunner/And it's now – Summer is heaven in '77', captured absolutely no *Zeitgeist*, for summer 1977 was cold and wet in the UK compared to the almost Mediterranean 1976, and the country was in no mood for such hippy-drippy frivolity. This was the summer of punk, of 'God Save The Queen' sticking two fingers up at the monarchy, of The Clash, The Stranglers and The Damned. The new wavers may have admired Bolan, but his new music sounded antiquated.

Bowie agreed to appear on the show but, on arriving at the Manchester studio, was none too pleased when he found out that Marc's bass player was none other than Herbie 'everyone out' Flowers. He was the man who had (quite rightly) shop-stewarded the backstage revolt at The Tower, Philadelphia back in 1974, when it was clear that Defries had put the mockers on some extra dosh for a live album.

What's quite funny about Bowie's late '77 performances, including this one, is the gap between Bowie the man and Bowie the clothes. Whereas Bowie the man is all rolling eyes, frozen features and glum elitism, the clothes are extraordinarily normal – checked shirts, jeans, plain suits. It's as if Bowie was attempting to wish himself into a saner future, hence the casing of normality, but his expressions and contortions scupper the overall sartorial effect. Perhaps also, in the wake of punk, Bowie was keen not to 'come on like a regular superstar'.

After performing "Heroes", Bowie jammed along with Bolan on a new song, 'Standing Next To You'. Bolan then promptly fell off the stage while the cameras were still rolling (allegedly worse for wear after overindulgence in hospitality before the show). Since the show was running over and the production crew were rather uncharitably refusing to work overtime, the song was not reshot and the first (and last) TV appearance of Bowie and Bolan together ended in tears. The two then spent some time writing and demoing a new song, 'Madman', later actually recorded by new-wave act The Cuddly Toys in 1980, after Bolan had leaked copies of the song on cassette to his fans.

Two days later Bowie put his career on to a new level of downright weirdness: he arrived at ATV's Elstree Studios in London to appear on 'Bing Crosby's Merrie Olde Christmas TV Special'. For this, surely one of the most surreal events in pop, Bowie had agreed to perform a duet on a segue of 'Peace On Earth'/'Little Drummer Boy'. The sight of the 30-year-old former cross-dressing, cocaine-snorting, bisexual rock god singing counterpoint to the bumbling cardigan that was Bing, 44 years his senior, made for one of those moments so irregular you had to blink hard a few times just to make sure you hadn't been whisked off to a parallel universe when it was aired later that year. Bowie also sang "Heroes", but after such a rum do with Bing, what did that matter? Bowie would later comment that Bing himself was a funny orange colour, an observation which is backed up by the promo!

Within six weeks both Bing and Bolan were dead, of course. In a rather macabre coincidence, Bowie had symbolically administered the last rites to both performers and the eras they represented. Crosby, already quite an elderly chap, died of a heart attack while playing a round of golf, the game he loved. Bolan, just 29, was killed in a car crash in Barnes, southwest London, just a week after recording the final *Marc* show with Bowie. Bowie attended Bolan's funeral, at The Chapel, Golders Green, on 20 September, along with Tony Visconti, producer of all of Bolan's finest work. Bowie was distraught.

The month of October 1977 was spent relentlessly promoting "*Heroes*". It was already Bowie's twelfth studio album and his ninth in less than six years, a work-rate no modern-day pop star could dream of matching. What's more, with the exception of *Pin Ups*, all of these studio albums, from *Hunky Dory* onwards, are now regarded by various media commentators and to varying degrees as 'classic' pop records.

However, Bowie's impact was not simply confined to music. In terms of style and fashion, there were little Ziggy Stardusts everywhere. Of course, they were more like Ziggy rejects – false Ziggy clones who replaced Bowie's beautiful kabuki costumes with ripped T-shirts, safety pins, kettles for handbags and bondage gear. But the standard punk haircut, spiky, dyed orange and then messed up, would have been inconceivable without Bowie's 1972 Ziggy look. Punk merely took the Bowie model and inverted it, sabotaging the pulchritude of the original, making it into a hamster-chewed topping. The punk penchant for silly, subversive and provocative noms de plume (Rat Scabies, Jet Black, Johnny Rotten, Poly Styrene, Sid Vicious, Ed Banger, Ari Up) was in the long tradition of show-business remodelling. But the glam era, with Alvin Stardust, Gary Glitter and Ziggy Stardust, provided the most recent, and therefore most visible, examples.

The transition from Bowie-worship to punk was rapid. The Bromley Contingent (which included such future pop stars as Siouxsie Sioux, Billy Idol and Steve Severin), a coterie of middle-class kids who would inject much of the subversive style fetishism into punk, were mostly Bowie and Roxy Music fans first, punks thereafter. The 'punk revolution' of the mid to late 1970s also traded on the nihilism of glam rock; their world was *Diamond Dog*'s Hunger City made real. The original impetus for punk came from the English love of stylisation, not from dole-queue blues. Bowie fans were the central conduits for this flow of information.

Throughout the rest of the 70s, both Bowie and his fans had a huge influence on youth style. The growth of 'casual styles' was another legacy of this stylistic redefinition, one with a greater affinity to working-class youth culture and 'laddish' styles of dressing. The duffel-coated Bowie of the 1976 film, *The Man Who Fell To Earth* (also found on the cover of the *Low* album in 1977), taken together with the elements of star iconography already in place (the sexual ambiguity and the science-fiction references), provided a stylistic model which was 'proletarianised' and which found its way, for example, into the dress styles of football supporters.

Bowie's quick-fire changes of style provided a protean image for youth culture to assemble around. In fact, Bowie Boys and Bowie Girls were perhaps emblematic of a new type of youth formation altogether. Bowie's impact on youth culture has been to show that personal style is always in flux. Before Bowie, most rock icons came to be associated with one particular look, whether it was Presley's quiff or Lou Reed's leathers and shades. Indeed, most youth cults jealously defined themselves sartorially. The mod, rocker, skinhead or suedehead look became rather like a uniform, essentially changeless over time. Bowie fans and almost all youth groupings following in their wake showed, in contrast, that the boundaries could be fluid and that styles could merge. Peter Yorke, writing in 1980, concluded that, after Bowie and punk, 'Kids are dressed in confusing ways because the language of teen style has been subverted. For every real teenage style group, every one that bites, there's a shadow group – somebody knocking it off, picking it up, doing it ironically, styling it up, people who don't have the thought to go with what they're wearing.'

Although he had tried to institute a 'new school of pretension' with Eno, Bowie was charitable to his little punk children. 'I totally sympathise with the new wave's indignation,' he told *Melody Maker* in the October of 1977. However, while the cult of Bowie spoke the language of individualism and difference, punk stood for a collective action that the singer thought crass: 'The sad thing about it all is that it's being called a movement. I wish the people involved were being treated as individuals. I'm so worried for them. I'm dissatisfied with them because I can't tolerate people who either want to form, or be part of, movements.'

Likewise, Bowie was keen to plough his own furrow, to distance himself, at least in part, from the work of others in the broad field of electronica. Although keenly interested in the work of other musicians, there was, according to Bowie, never a chance during his stay in Germany that he would actually collaborate with any of the leading Krautrockers of the time. Bowie later told *Uncut* categorically that no attempt was made to actually collaborate with any of these musicians. 'I knew Edgar Froesse and his wife socially but I never met the others as I had no real inclination to go to Dusseldorf as I was very single-minded about what I needed to do in the studio in Berlin.' Later, in 1977, a collaboration was mooted between Bowie and Michael Rother of Neu!, but, as Rother himself confirmed on his website, wires were crossed: 'The story is this: Both David Bowie and I were tricked into believing that the other had changed his mind about our collaboration in 1977. I was surprised to read Bowie saying in an interview in a British magazine some years ago that I had declined to work with him. This isn't true. David called me in summer 1977, invited me to join him and Brian Eno in the studio in Berlin and we both were absolutely eager to do recordings together. However, some days after our conversation I received a phone call from somebody speaking for David (it may have been his management, I can't say for sure) telling me that he had changed his mind about our collaboration and that I needn't come to Berlin. And David was obviously told that I had changed my mind. We only found out about this trickery when David and I exchanged emails in 2001. It's up to speculation why somebody didn't want our collaboration to happen but it is known that David Bowie's more experimental albums in the 70s didn't do so well commercially back then ... Anyway, the short answer to your question is: I didn't turn David Bowie down at all.'

In late 1977, the *Sounds* weekly finally put a name to the music that would come to replace punk and would become the font of ideas for almost every arty band of a certain intellectual persuasion up to and including the likes of Franz Ferdinand in the Noughties. As Jon Savage recalls, the term 'New Musick' was coined to describe what perhaps now might be dubbed 'post-punk' music, or at least a subsection of it. 'The term originates from a big two-issue article that we did at *Sound*s on 27 November and 3 December 1977,' he says. 'Alan Lewis had asked his punk correspondents – myself, Jane Suck, Sandy Robertson and features editor Viv Goldman – to do an "Images of the New Wave" part 3. Having already decided that punk was old hat, we collectively came up with the idea of celebrating the new electronic and futuristic music that seemed much more interesting than old pub rockers banging out three chords. Jane Suck and I did the editorial in the first issue. Over the two weeks, Steven Lavers wrote about Kraftwerk, Viv about Dub and Siouxsie, Davitt Sigerson wrote about disco, Sandy Robertson wrote about Throbbing Gristle, and I wrote about Devo and the Residents. Obviously Bowie and Eno were a big reference, cited in the editorials.'

At the time Bowie himself was taking an interest in American new-wave group Devo. He was scheduled to co-produce the group with Eno, but had to back out when it was decided that, in 1978, Bowie should again tour the world. Although in better shape both mentally and physically, Bowie was still a far from happy individual, and looked upon the prospect of spending most of the next year living out of a suitcase with grim determination and gritted teeth rather than with any enthusiasm.

If 1977 was the Year of Punk (it was also, we should remember, the year of disco, and Fleetwood Mac, and The Eagles), it was very much Bowie's year too. *Low* and "*Heroes*" would ultimately prove as influential as any punk record made that year. "*Heroes*" was a moderate commercial success by Bowie's standards, reaching Number 3 in the UK and Number 35 in the States, but his place in rock legend was already assured. The album was promoted in the press with the banner: 'There's Old Wave, there's New Wave, and there's David Bowie.' Part of pop culture and yet with a very distinctive take on it, for the rest of the 1970s and the beginning of the 1980s, Bowie found himself slowly but surely being sucked back into a mainstream he had helped create.

9. AN AXE TO BREAK THE ICE, 1978–1982

*It's difficult for me to explain what it's like to be with him, but there's
some sort of halo around David Bowie. I was thrilled by the experience.
It motivated me to want to do the best work I could for him.*

AWE-STRUCK GUITARIST, ADRIAN BELEW, ON WHAT IT'S LIKE BEING ON TOUR WITH BOWIE

*I was writing my first songs when I was in my late teens. I was living at
home, probably had had sex with two different women and was
desperately trying to make myself more interesting. I was pretending
that I was really strange and interesting, and I wasn't any of those
things. I was still sitting upstairs, probably miming to David Bowie
records in front of the mirror, which most of my teenage years seem to
have been spent doing really.*

POP ICON GARY NUMAN ON HIS BOWIE-FIXATED TEENAGE YEARS

It was now five years since the killing of Ziggy Stardust and
almost a decade since his first hit, 'Space Oddity'. Bowie had
become an institution. After twelve studio albums in ten years,
Anglo-American success and artistic kudos for his acting role in
The Man Who Fell To Earth, his place in the pantheon of rock
legends was already assured. However, each of his new releases
saw sixteen per cent of the profits siphoned off to Fleur Music,
Defries' company set up to deal with his share and parent
company to Bowie's own Bewlay Brothers. After fourteen years in
the business and huge international renown, Bowie was still a
considerable way short of being able to retire and live in rock-star
luxury. It's probably true to surmise that the 1976 tour was the
first which saw the singer make money for himself. The 1978 tour

was another step towards financial security for Bowie, while at the same time a chance to introduce his audience to the experimentalism of *Low* and *"Heroes"*.

Christmas of 1977 saw the final break with Angie. A disastrous pre-Christmas Swiss rapprochement led to Bowie leaving to spend the holiday and the first weeks of the New Year with Zowie and his nanny, and in Berlin, where he was filming *Just A Gigolo* with David Hemmings. Angie jetted off to spend Christmas with friends in New York. In the full knowledge that her marriage was over, she spent parts of January in a state of drug-induced stupefaction (it may have been a cocked-up overdose attempt) and, desperate for dosh, sold her story to the *Sunday Mirror* in January 1978. She claimed that Bowie had unlawfully taken away her pride and joy. There then followed the usual, unseemly rock star and wife break-up, a protracted affair, which finally resolved itself in March 1980 when the Bowies divorced.

In 1978, Angie, still only in her late twenties, had again tried to commit suicide. On one occasion, the paramedics arrived to carry her, comatose, from the bathtub to the ambulance and dropped her down the stairs, breaking her nose. It was a tragicomedy of an ending for an eccentric, friendly, individualistic woman, who, some would say, had gone too far, too soon, on the back of another's success.

Angie Bowie did not create Ziggy Stardust, nor did she turn David Bowie into a star. However, she was an important influence in the glam-rock days and undoubtedly imposed part of her flamboyant vision on her husband. Today, Angie's ex-husband rarely talks about her in interviews, and, one suspects, there are very strong feelings of bitterness towards her. The problem was that she never progressed beyond the glitz of glam-mania and, like Ken Pitt, Ronno and Tony Defries, did not change either personally or professionally at the velocity of her husband's muse. Since it was never based on emotional or sexual fidelity, their marriage had been collapsing over a period of ten years.

According to the terms of the divorce settlement, Angie was barred from talking to the media for a decade; Bowie was awarded custody of his son, and had to pay Angie alimony of just $750,000 over a ten-year period. The final nail in Angie's coffin allegedly came when the Bowie camp produced as evidence an unseemly shot of his wife in an intimate pose with another woman, a heroin dealer according to biographer George Tremlett.

Angie was granted restricted access to Zowie, now calling himself Joe. By the end of the 1980s, he had decided not to see his mum any longer. Joe and his dad were by then inseparable and, despite Bowie's career, the two spent more and more time together. In the 1980s, Joe attended a private boarding school, Gordonstoun, in Scotland (in contrast to Paul McCartney, who sent his children to state schools). Bowie even endured his son's brief fascination with the Electric Light Orchestra with good grace. Angie herself achieved nothing of note herself in the 1980s and 1990s and only hit the tabloid columns when she dished the dirt on her husband's infamy. It was a sad and undignified slip into the role of media assassin for a woman who was well liked by many, and a cultured, funny and glamorous player on the glam scene. In the Noughties, Joe, by then going by the name of Duncan, has apparently resumed limited contact with his mum.

Bowie began 1978 back in Berlin cuddling a piglet in David Hemmings' ill-starred film *Just A Gigolo*. More importantly, and considerably more impressively, he was back on the road. It would be his last world tour of the 1970s, and the last time his fans would see him in concert for five years. He had a new lead guitarist for the tour too, and the manner of acquisition was suitably unorthodox.

Bowie again went for an idiosyncratic talent, this time in the form of 28-year-old Adrian Belew from Kentucky. 'I was on tour with Frank Zappa in early 1978,' Belew recalls. 'Brian Eno came to our show in Cologne. He knew that David Bowie was looking for a new guitarist and David came to our show about a week later in Berlin. He was standing by the side of the stage by the monitor board with Iggy Pop during the concert. There was a part of the show where Frank took an extended guitar solo for about fifteen or twenty minutes and some of the members of the band, including myself, would leave the stage at that point. I went over and I thought, Well, here's my chance to say hello to David Bowie! I said, "Hi, David. I really enjoy your music and I just wanted to say thank you." And he said, "Well, great, how would you like to be in my band?" '

It's a bizarre picture: Zappa halfway through some amazing feat of technical excellence, and his lead guitarist being poached by another rock legend just a few yards away. The main problem, of course, was how Bowie and Belew were to get into bed together. Bowie suggested an after-show meal and a chat, and the two hit Berlin for a spot of serious ligging. Belew, for his part, was over the moon:

> Of course, I jumped at the chance because I was very familiar with David's music and a big fan. I had played different songs of his in cover bands I had been in. Bowie was very secretive because I guess he didn't want anyone to know that he was wooing me. And so we were secretly meeting after the show. Well, can you imagine this? We decided on going to a restaurant, one of the thousands in Berlin. We walked in and there was Frank Zappa and several members of his band! So, the game was up. It was obvious that something was afoot. We sat with Frank and instantly Frank knew that David was trying to get me into his band, so it was a very uncomfortable situation. David tried to be friendly to Frank, but meanwhile Frank was very unfriendly to David. He sort of told him that he didn't want anything to do with him and kept calling him 'Captain Tom' ('I don't care what you think, Captain Tom. Leave me alone!'). I managed to smooth things over with Frank later. He said, 'Yes, I understand. You wanna go off and play with David Bowie.' I really did want to go and play with David Bowie. He was a major figure for me, second only really to playing with The Beatles.

Belew finished the Zappa tour, then immediately went into rehearsals for the Bowie tour, scheduled to start in San Diego two weeks later. 'It was like two different worlds,' recalls Belew. 'Frank's music was completely created by him and the idea was for you to play it consistently and correctly. The idea was not to add something to it. The idea was to play it right, or sing it right. With Bowie, the idea was entirely different. He gave me full rein to be his guitarist and to add a lot of colours and sounds; to play solos and to be involved in the shape and form of the music itself. Songs like "Stay" stick in my mind. It's a big guitar solo with some vocals thrown in! To be honest, at the time I was with Frank Zappa, I needed the kind of discipline and education that he offered. So they both worked for me. It was kind of like going to college with Frank Zappa and then kind of graduating in David Bowie's band.'

What Belew had was a quirkiness and a sense of naivety. He didn't sound like your average rock guitarist. As Bowie told the pianist for the tour, Sean Mayes, a little later, 'I'm very suspicious of virtuosity. I like people who play with an original style.'

By now the Alomar/Davis/Murray rhythm section were always first on the team sheet. Bowie added Simon House on electric violin, Sean Mayes (whose band Fumble had actually opened for Bowie back in the early 70s) on keyboards and Roger Powell on keyboards and synths. Rehearsals were held in Dallas with Alomar taking the band through their paces from 10 a.m. in the morning till 9 p.m. at night for a solid fortnight, with only one morning off. Bowie arrived midway through, after a holiday in Kenya. He looked tanned and, at around 130 lb, in better condition than he had for five years.

Alomar led rehearsals, arranged the music and acted as go-between for Bowie and band. He also produced all the sheet music for publishing. 'Anyone watching would think Carlos was in charge,' reported Sean Mayes. 'David seems like a kid who's been allowed to sing with the band, but doesn't think the musicians are going to take him seriously ... I know he is naturally shy and probably doesn't like directing a group of people ... He hardly ever tells us what to do, but suggests different things – how about this ... let's try that ... He allows us great freedom and encourages us to be creative, but it is still very much his music.' Bowie pogoed up and down to the ending vamp section of 'Hang On To Yourself' in rehearsals: perhaps he was relieved that at last a dance had been invented for the song he wrote way back in 1971.

One evening during rehearsals, the band crowded into Bowie's hotel room to watch Neil Innes and Eric Idle's brilliant Beatles spoof, *The Rutles*. Bowie had the soundtrack taped and played through the PA system on the tour. Incidentally, Bowie and Idle have remained chums. Idle is Joe Bowie's godfather and Bowie later appeared with a shark's fin protruding out of his back in a cameo in the Monty Python/Marty Feldmann side-project *Yellowbeard*.

For the 1978 world tour Bowie wore costumes designed by Natasha Korniloff (who had worked with Bowie and Lindsay Kemp a decade earlier), including huge ballooning white pants, T-shirt and sailor's cap for one show, a fake snakeskin jacket for another, and a long, plastic frockcoat for a third. With his hair cut short and with a side parting, he looked healthier, if noticeably older; a little heavier and rather less icy. His voice, now rich and powerful, had never been finer.

The rhetoric around this tour was that Bowie was playing Bowie, no characters around this time thank you very much. Now he was able to play the rock star without the rock star playing him. Despite this, Bowie still filled his performance with ample doses of clinical showmanship and stage-dominating poses: huge high-kicks; mimelike bends and twists; stares, sways, shimmies and glares were all part of the Bowie repertoire. At the end of 'Hang On To Yourself', Bowie would stretch out both hands as if to touch the heavens, his eyes half-closed, his face contorted in an almost ruthlessly haughty pout. This was still a hugely powerful theatrical performance.

This would be Bowie's first tour for five years in which he had probably not anaesthetised himself with copious quantities of cocaine before taking the stage. Perhaps as a result, touring became more and more of a chore. According to Belew:

David was distant. I was anxious to get to know him and I did to a certain degree, but, at the same time, there was always this buffer of people around him who really overprotected him. So, unfortunately, I came away from that experience feeling somewhat disappointed that I didn't get to be a better friend of David Bowie. He didn't always look well on the '78 tour. Whether he was using drugs during that period was kept from me. All I can say is that the flare-ups and behind-the-scenes cacophony that occasionally happened with the people around him might have had something to do with that. I didn't feel it was a great time in his life. This might have been one of the reasons why I just naturally wanted to reach out to him and try and become a friend.

That was the main problem for David Bowie in the late 1970s. He needed a friend. More than ever, he had become the sort of individual his music had traditionally always spoken to and for: the depressive, disconnected, lonely individual. Without the oblivion that drugs had brought, he was now in a healthy enough mental condition to want to make friends. But it was so long since the days when he was used to making friends that he appeared shy, recalcitrant and awkward in company. Apart from Coco and his son, he felt comfortable with very few people. Rebuilding his shattered personal life would take Bowie over a decade to sort out.

Bowie was also becoming less accessible to his fans. Patti Brett, one of those Sigma Kids, recalls, 'On the *Stage* tour we were downstairs in the lobby of the hotel he was staying at and he came down to talk to us. He was a little afraid and he started to get very distant. He would come in and talk for a few minutes, then off he'd go.'

The shows themselves were often superb. 'That was a wonderful band,' said Alomar. 'You wouldn't normally find a band that would have a violin player, a lead guitar player and a synth player and a piano player – these are all soloist instruments.'

Simon House's violin and Belew's guitar interwove beautifully on the resurrected Ziggy Stardust-era tracks showcased in the second half of the live set: 'Hang On To Yourself', 'Soul Love', 'Five Years', 'Suffragette City' and 'Ziggy Stardust'. The decision to play so much from Bowie's then best-known album was, perhaps, a defensive, even audience-pleasing attempt at a palliative, as the rest of the set was overwhelmingly culled from the more recent Eno collaborations. 'Warszawa', the long, solemn piece of music found on the second side of *Low*, was the concert's opener. Bowie walked on stage as a band member positioning himself behind his synth, while Alomar conducted the band through the number. Alomar claims that the band had to be conducted because the piece had no formal bar structure, although to some it seemed like supreme artifice – a pop artist trying to create a 'serious' atmosphere by aping the patriarchy of the concert hall. However, Alomar enjoyed the role: he bought himself some batons and liked the musical credibility these bestowed. To select 'Warszawa' as an opener to a rock show was either monstrously foolish or incredibly brave. Whatever, by the show's second number, "Heroes", played in its proper full-length version, the audience were basking in Bowie's romantic grandeur and we were back at a pop gig.

The rest of the set included recent songs such as 'Blackout', 'Beauty And The Beast', an extended (and hence rather less eccentric) version of 'Breaking Glass', a reggaefied 'What In The World', 'Be My Wife' (although, perversely, 'Sound And Vision' was only played once on the tour) and the instrumentals 'Sense Of

Doubt', 'Speed Of Life' and 'Art Decade', which were given a heavier, more positive sound by Alomar and Bowie. 'Fame', 'Rebel Rebel' and 'The Jean Genie' were concessions to crowd-pleasing (and the only hit singles played on the tour). 'Station To Station', 'Stay' and 'TVC 15' endured from the White Light tour, while Bowie's reading of Kurt Weill's 'Alabama Song' (a piece perfectly suited to Bowie's mannered vibrato) added a touch of high Weimar-era dramatics to the proceedings.

The set design was simple but effective. The bars of white light from the '76 tour were retained in modified form and appeared in banks lined at the back of the stage, forming cages of light that flashed maniacally at the dénouement of 'Hang On To Yourself'. However, the starkness of the '76 tour was washed away by the use of greens, reds and blues, and the whole effect provided a warmer, less forbidding visual experience.

This was not, however, an altogether happy bunch of musicians on the road. 'I didn't particularly get along well in that band, and I felt sometimes that we weren't doing our best,' says Adrian Belew. 'I think I disagreed with Carlos a few times because I felt at the time Carlos wasn't doing as well as I wanted him to. I kept getting into trouble for making suggestions.' Alomar himself admits that, after his time on the road as guitarist with Iggy Pop, he wanted more of the limelight for himself: 'It was to do with the fact that you constantly hear your guitar parts being played in a different mode, and then you hear your own guitar part and it's a little chintzy guitar and the other guitar player has this big wide fabulous sound. That was bumming me out.' In addition, as on the '73 and '74 tours, pay, or lack of it, was a problem: 'One thing that's terrifying in a band is if everyone is on a different pay scale,' says Belew. 'Once that comes out, which it did, there is a lot of resentment.'

Belew in particular felt increasingly under pressure from Coco, who thought his onstage antics were drawing attention away from the man himself: 'Coco thought I was trying to upstage David! She constantly nattered on about it, saying, "Don't do that", "Don't do this", "Don't move over there", "Don't move around so much". "You're trying to upstage David." This is a ridiculous idea because I knew it was impossible to do that. At the same time David was saying, "Come on, jump around more, play with me, let's put on a little bit of a show here!" So every night I'd have David on stage encouraging me and Coco off the side glaring at me, so it became a little bit schizophrenic for me and I felt somewhat ostracised because of her. I felt just like a hired hand.'

Despite an unhappy singer and other interpersonal conflicts, the tour was a success. The North American leg of the tour ended with two triumphant concerts at Madison Square Garden in New York. Adrian Belew remembers the crazy, almost surreal nature of the time there:

During the sound check I'm on stage and I'm trying to get my guitar out. Suddenly I hear behind me the trumpeting of elephants. I turn around and there are four elephants standing behind me! Apparently, the Ringling Brothers Circus was being housed in Madison Square Garden and they would bring up their elephants, of which they had thirty or so, four at a time to feed them. Later in the day we were standing in the buffet room and there's this long buffet table full of food, and suddenly the door opens and in comes this chimpanzee in a bright-coloured hound's-tooth suit on rollerskates. As he's skating around the table he's being chased by some of the kids. I guess one of them would have been Simon House's little boy. Suddenly the door opens and the chimp's manager, in the exact same hound's-tooth suit, comes in and starts passing out flyers about the chimpanzee. Then there's the show itself. In the audience there's Dustin Hoffman, Talking Heads, and over to the side of the stage with his own little entourage is Andy Warhol. That's what it was like to be around David Bowie. It was an amazing circus of important, interesting people.

With just a five-day break, Bowie began the European leg of the *Stage* tour in Germany in the Frankfurt Festhalle. On 16 May, Alan Yentob, the BBC producer who four years earlier had shot the skeletal Bowie entombed in a hearse-like Cadillac in Hollywood, interviewed him in Berlin. Bowie sat framed against the skyline in smart, almost regimental short-sleeved shirt and tie, his hair now its natural mousey colour. He looked nervous and edgy. His voice was mannered, upper class and crisp, and the paranoia of the *Cracked Actor* documentary was still faintly visible despite his protestations that he was now entering calmer waters. Later that month, during the band's stay in Germany, a television special was filmed for the *Musikladen* series.

By the time Bowie reached the UK he was being feted in the rock weeklies like never before. Although the craziness of Ziggy-mania had abated, he still had an intense relationship with the cult of Bowie. Adrian Belew:

On the 1978 tour, he still had the more rabid, highly influenced audience, people who would still come dressed like him. The lobbies of the hotels were filled with people like that. There was a time in Philadelphia, which of course is one of David's strongholds, when we came to the hotel and in the lobby were people everywhere, on every floor. You couldn't eat breakfast without a table full of people around you. Of course, it was very exciting and I enjoyed it!

There was a crew of young kids who wore make-up and looked like David, and they would be everywhere we went. We flew to Oslo, Norway, and if you've ever flown to Oslo, you'll know it's an exasperating trip because you have to take several different flights, ending in a small aeroplane which finally arrives in Oslo. When we arrived at the hotel they were there, ahead of us, waiting outside the hotel, and we were totally amazed. Often these people would follow David around, show after show, and gradually you could tell that they really didn't have the money to do this. Carlos often invited them to use his room to shower or clean up. After a while you felt like you had an affinity with these people.

However, many of his fans were now in their mid to late twenties; they were growing older with their man. One Bowie fan had this to say about the show at Stafford Bingley Hall: 'The crowd was very civilised, which I wasn't used to in those punk days, and I remember walking in, and going straight to the front and standing about a dozen rows back. I also remember the audience was quite old – probably in their mid-twenties. It was the first time I had seen a really big rock show and I was impressed by the huge stage and the deafening sound and brilliant lights. I especially remember the flashing white neon lights in "Star" and the coloured lights sweeping the crowd during "Sense Of Doubt". With the benefit of hindsight I always say that the 1978 tour was the best because he had such a good band – very clear sound, but distinctive with the violin, and very tight with it. The *Ziggy Stardust* material was superb as well. The *Stage* album doesn't do it justice.'

David Hemmings filmed one of the shows at Earls Court for future release, but the project never got off the ground. It was rumoured that after the *Just A Gigolo* debacle, a film which Bowie called his '32 Elvis movies rolled into one', Bowie was so upset that he refused to speak to Hemmings for years. Janet Street-Porter interviewed Bowie for a 'London Weekend Television Special' at the second Earls Court gig, the venue, five years earlier, of a near-riot and an acoustic collapse. But the British tour did little to boost sales of either *Low* or "*Heroes*".

Bowie's next move was to plug a gap in the touring schedule with some sessions for a new album. Four years earlier he had frightened the entourage of Sigma Sound with his pre-plastinated state and agonised falsetto. Now, he was ready to start the recording of the final stage of his trio of albums with Eno, eventually to be called *Lodger*. Whereas "*Heroes*" had been recorded in Berlin, a city brimming with artistic life and internal social and political polarities, the new Bowie album was to be created in the regimented beauty of Switzerland.

Carlos Alomar was none too impressed with the transition from zany nights at transvestite revues to the antiseptic climate of an Alpine retreat at Mountain Studios: 'It was a very nice studio, but it was very Swiss, uneventful. I prefer the Hansa Studios. Switzerland is Switzerland – pretty boring. Who cares about pretty? Give me excitement!' However, the record that was fashioned there, and later finished off in New York, is probably Bowie's most underrated work.

The studio itself was built on the site of a previous studio which had famously burned down during a recording session involving Frank Zappa – Deep Purple's 'Smoke On The Water' consummated the event in the annals of rock. The new building was a multimedia centre, built out of concrete with long concrete corridors and winding stairways. All in all, it was rather bunker-like and in complete contrast to the Hansa Studios in Berlin with its cavernous decadence. The control room was on the first floor, and the actual recording room on the second. The musicians themselves couldn't see the control room when they were playing, but they could be spied on by short-circuit television from there. This led to a mildly voyeuristic, and slightly disquieting, vibe. The band were housed in a hotel overlooking Lake Geneva. Every morning Belew remembers being woken by the sound of Visconti's wife, Mary Hopkin, doing her early morning vocal exercises at an open window!

'The title for the album at the time was Planned Accidents, which I think was an Eno idea,' says Belew. 'What they wanted to do was to elicit accidental responses from me. They said to me, "We're not going to let you hear the songs first. You won't have any idea of what the chords are, or what the tempo is, or anything. You're just going to hear the count-off in your headphones and then you start playing something." They would allow me to do this maybe three or four times. By the third time on each of these tracks, I might start to actually know what I was doing. I might even have some idea of the chord changes by then. The next thing they would do was that they would take my three guitar tracks and do something called compositing. That's when you take the best bits of each guitar track and edit them together, to make one guitar track. So really, everything that I played on that record was, for the most part, not actually played as it sounds. For example, on "Red Sails", the guitar part is jumping all over the place in a somewhat impossible manner. That's because the tracks are edited together. They might be going from one note to another that you couldn't actually have played. That made for a very interesting way of doing a record, especially since they did that particularly with the lead instruments, the violins and the guitar solos. On "DJ" the guitar solo goes through a whole mismatch of different guitar sounds almost like you're changing channel on the radio and each channel has a different guitar solo on it.'

The Lodger album would be finished off after the tour. It was during a week-long stay chez Bowie to work on the Hemmings-directed, and aborted, live documentary that Bowie gave Belew a crash course in his cultural passions. 'He played me "Mars" by Holst and The Plastic Ono Band album. He tried, in essence, to give me a brief education about those things from the music world, the art world, the fashion world and movies, to show me where he came from,' says Belew. 'Bowie also indicated that he was unhappy with his career on a number of interconnected levels. There was definitely a feeling in the air that he wanted to change direction. He was very unhappy with RCA. He was planning to move his career forward in lots of ways. I think his relationship with Eno was winding down. They didn't quarrel or anything uncivilised like that; they just didn't seem to have the spark that I imagine they might have had during the *"Heroes"* album.'

However, in the September of 1978, Bowie made (or was perhaps cajoled into making) a public statement defending RCA and quashing rumours that he was seeking to move to a new label. Despite this, it was obvious that there was something afoot. A new live album, *Stage*, was delayed several weeks. The official reason was that there had been a hiccup with the artwork. The real reason seems to be that Bowie wanted this live double album to count as two albums towards fulfilling his contractual commitments, while RCA insisted that it could only count as one.

Stage was eventually released on 25 September to a largely indifferent critical response. It performed moderately in the UK, reaching Number 5, but relatively poorly in the USA, where it peaked at Number 35. Tony Visconti had decided to mix the audience level way down, especially on the instrumental tracks (according to Visconti there were audible boos on 'Sense Of Doubt'). The material was grouped chronologically, starting off with the *Ziggy* material and ending with the recent *Low* and *"Heroes"* work. This decision, approved by Bowie, essentially killed the pacing and the drama of the stage show itself, and with the audience reduced to some far-off, slightly disembodied mutter way back in the mix, the result was disappointing. According to Sean Mayes, the band was even asked to play a little slower for the Ziggy numbers. The cover packaging itself, showing an unflattering picture of Bowie, replicated both in the fold-out sleeve and on the back cover, was Bowie's first unresonant album cover of the 1970s. Adrian Belew was succinct: 'I hated that record. It might have been that the tracks just couldn't be recorded properly, but the sound is thin and awful.'

By now the tour had reactivated itself in the Far East and Australasian markets. For really the first time in his career, Bowie was playing larger, outdoor venues. One of the highlights of this, the tour's third leg, was a show played in torrential rain at Melbourne Cricket Ground on 18 November. 'Oh, that was an incredible show,' enthuses Belew. 'There was a huge expectation and everyone's waiting for you to come out and finally you do come out and there's this concern whether everyone will be electrocuted!' The band played a tremendous gig, with mascara and make-up dripping down their faces, and the threat of a rather terminal end to the show an ever-present possibility.

Next up was that Bowie stronghold, Japan. In order to get these rather stately and subdued fans bouncing in the aisles, Alomar elected to hit them hard with a rearranged, high-energy set: 'The Japanese have a tendency to sit in their seats – a very calm, contained audience. When we first went to Japan all the crowd had binoculars! We stared out into the audience and all we saw were these reflections. It was somewhat disturbing.' He continues: 'Normally a rock show is conducted in such a way that it goes in a wave. You don't want to hit them with too much intensity, because you'll frazzle them within the first thirty minutes. Usually you have certain songs that allow for a release so you can go even higher a few songs later. Our intention was to disturb the Japanese, to make them get off of the seats and to create a certain amount of chaos to see the Japanese police try and gain control over the audience, which they never can once it's out of control. We wanted to be very disruptive of the way they normally behave at a concert. We just kept it fast and furious.'

Bowie was quite at home in the Far East, as rooted as he could be anywhere in the world. The Zen tranquillity mixed with garish formality was an instant turn-on for him. Belew remembers walking through the streets of Tokyo late one night in search of a meal, with Bowie as his guide: 'Invariably David would find these very strange out-of-the-way places that probably only the local people knew about. Usually he would order the most experimental types of food. David is an experimenter in his eating habits, just like David Byrne from Talking Heads.'

Bowie attended the premiere of his latest movie, *Just A Gigolo*, in Japan (suitably attired in a kimono and with a Japanese date), spent Christmas 1978 in Tokyo, and holidayed thereafter in Kyoto with his son, Joe. In March 1980, he even made a commercial for Japanese television promoting a brand of saki called Crystal Jun Rock.

One of the concerts in Japan that December 1978, the penultimate date of the tour at the NHK Hall, Tokyo, was filmed for an edited hour-long special. The final night was at the same venue on 12 December 1978. It would be Bowie's last concert performance for four and a half years.

Bowie's new album was finally released on 18 May 1979. It was the longest gap between studio albums since the interval between his Deram debut and his *Space Oddity* follow-up in the late 1960s. Then the gap could be excused because Bowie couldn't find a deal. Now it was obvious that, even without touring commitments, Bowie's rocket-like pace of work as a studio artist was beginning to slow down. *Lodger* is not regarded as a substantial Bowie album in the overall scheme of things. Bowie himself was reported to be quite down after handing in the tapes to RCA, and Eno has stated in numerous interviews since the late 1970s that he thought the rich vein mined in the first two collaborations had been largely exhausted. Eno had just released the hugely influential, decidedly non-rock album, *Music For Airports*. The rock business with its album/video/tour promotional merry-go-round both bored him and was superfluous to his music. He made albums then looked for companies to release them, and was pleased with relatively modest commercial reward. But all was different on planet Bowie.

According to Eno, the need to get the product out overrode curious artistic investigation. Looking back on the album, Alomar, too, comments on the disappointment felt by some: 'I think people had by that time understood that they were due for a trilogy. You see, when you don't know, and you're anticipating something, it's somewhat different than when you know that the last instalment is due. I think it kind of jades things.'

The main problem with *Lodger* was that it sounded as if the instruments had been recorded through soup. Visconti says that he was having 'sonic problems' during the mixing stage in New York, where studio craft lagged behind that of Europe. The studio itself in Switzerland also had none of the huge acoustics of Hansa.

Nevertheless, *Lodger* is a very fine Bowie album. Side one contains Bowie's tales of derring-do, a sort of international rock star's tour round the world using the currency of sound. If Fripp was the star of "*Heroes*", then Belew's contributions provide *Lodger*'s one point of coherence. Where all else is based on a shifting terrain of ambient, proto-techno, ethnic and ballad styles, Belew's playing is consistent, and consistently inventive, throughout. The wailing, slightly off-centre and off-key blasts of noise Belew fashioned on 'Red Sails', 'African Night Flight', 'DJ' and 'Repetition' became the trademark Bowie guitar sound.

After the jagged, ominous music of "*Heroes*", *Lodger* starts off with a surprisingly delicate song, 'Fantastic Voyage'. The song signals the beginnings of a certain political awareness in Bowie's work, dealing as it does with the threat posed by the 'depression' of our Cold War leaders. Incidentally, Bowie said that the song had exactly the same chord sequence as 'Boys Keep Swinging', showing that even then he was already ripping himself off. 'I remember Tony Visconti did a written arrangement for the mandolins on "Fantastic Voyage",' says Belew. 'We had three mandolin players playing the same parts. We tracked them three times so we had nine mandolins playing the same part.'

'Repetition' switched the focus from public to private space. This description of domestic violence told by Bowie as narrator in short, prosaic, descriptive lines is minimalistic and deliberately under-emoted. The music, with its insistent and very odd bass guitar riff, repeats the blows by the man on his wife with such detachment that the result is Bowie at his most chilling.

On 'African Night Flight', Bowie's vocal is delivered at breakneck speed. In fact, with hindsight we might call it rap, if a very white, middle-class version. Bowie had always had a liking for fast-talking and quick-moving tumbling flows of words. 'Young Americans', recorded in 1974, is another close cousin. Bowie uses a Swahili chant which, with Eno's 'prepared piano and cricket menace', produces a collage of textures that presciently deal with what in the 80s was called 'world music'. According to Tony Visconti, the music was influenced by the 1957 swamp-rock classic 'Suzie Q' by Dale Hawkins. 'All we kept was the beat,' he said in 1999.

Two other songs carry on the travelogue, sketchbook motif. For the never-was-but-should-have-been single, 'Yassassin' (Turkish for 'long life'), Bowie took a reggae riff, itself a parody of Carlos Alomar's riff for 'Fame', and overlaid a violin part which could have come straight out of traditional middle-European folk song. Bowie's singing is fantastic too, melismatic and cool.

In 'Move On', Bowie is 'just a travelling man' and croons, 'Cyprus is my island/When the going's rough/I would like to find you/Somewhere in a place like that.' The music was arrived at quite by accident. Tony Visconti: 'David played a tape of "All The Young Dudes" backwards and liked the inverted chord changes. Carlos wrote out the inverted chords and the band learned it and recorded it. To sing the back-ups, we flipped over the multi-track tape of the band recording and there was "All The Young Dudes" again, and David and I sang the melody. Then we flipped back the tape and you've heard the results.'

'Red Sails' is one of Bowie's most eccentric songs of any era; a deliberate attempt to ape the ambient rock of the likes of Neu!

'Here we took a German new music feel and put against it the idea of a contemporary English mercenary-cum-swashbuckling Errol Flynn, and put him in the China Sea. We have a lovely cross-reference of cultures,' said Bowie. 'I honestly don't know what it's about.'

'DJ' was jaundiced, the role of the DJ dehumanised and reduced to the logic of his own performance ('I am a DJ, I am what I play'). In 'Look Back In Anger', Bowie encounters an angel of death come to claim his soul. It has one of the best mid-song guitar solos of any Bowie record: 'He wanted me to play something in the middle, but he also wanted something like that break in "Young Americans",' recalls Alomar. 'There are times when I want to take a solo, but I don't want it to be a lead-guitar solo – that's always so played out. During that period we had a lot of those lead guitarists on the hill, the wind machine blowing their hair. Come on, give me a break! So, if I am going to take a solo, I'm going to take a rhythm-guitar solo. In this, John Lennon influenced me. I really appreciated what he did with rhythm guitar.'

'Boys Keep Swinging' was the last in a long line of Bowie songs which targeted and addressed his old constituency of good-time groovers. 'David did the whole lyrics and vocals for the album in about seven days in New York,' remembers Belew. 'I came to the studio to see what he was doing and he said, "Boys Keep Swinging' is not really about you, but in the spirit of you. It's for you, Adrian, because you're sort of boyish and naive and you're the world-is-your-oyster kind of guy." I thought that was a very nice compliment.' Alomar vividly remembers recording the track: 'We started doing "Boys Keep Swinging" with everyone playing their instruments. David said, "It's OK, it's right, but it doesn't sound like young kids in the basement just discovering their instruments. It sounds like professionals!" So, to that end, we all switched instruments to see if we could capture that feeling and, hey, look, I can't play drums. I'm the worst, as evidenced by the performance given on that song. Dennis Davis went over on bass and ended up getting the sound that was the best-sounding horrible young-teen punk-band sound you ever heard and we really liked it.' The motivation behind the instrument switch may also have come from a rather more intellectual source. Two of Eno's Oblique Strategies cards said 'Change instrument roles' and 'Use unqualified people'.

Lodger repays repeated listening. Its stature grows with each passing year; each new listening reveals some hidden shading. Adrian Belew, like many others, found the album very hard going on first hearing: 'I got the record the next year. I was at home and I hadn't seen David in a long while. I listened to it for the first time and I was thoroughly disappointed. In fact, I hated it. I listened to it over and over, and by the fifth time I got it. It's avant-garde pop music. Personally, for me, that's the greatest thing David Bowie has given the rest of the world.'

In April and May 1979, Bowie came out of hibernation for a brief round of media meet-and-greets. He now affected a waggish charm. Dressed in a thin tie and smart jacket he looked like a member of a new-wave pop band like The Jam. He was also armed with a rediscovered sense of humour. Most peculiarly, Bowie recorded a slot for *The Kenny Everett Video Show*, a pre-MTV collection of Everett's zany, visual gags interspersed with pop and the throbbing torment of Hot Gossip, a 'risqué' all-girl dance troupe.

Bowie performed his new single, 'Boys Keep Swinging'. At the end of the show Bowie chased the former Maurice Cole round a mock-up of a rooftop, the comedian in his Angry Of Mayfair garb (suit and bowler hat at the front, kinky knickers and suspenders from the rear), and Bowie fencing him with a violin bow. 'I fought in the war for the likes of you. And I never got one!' shrieked Everett. To see the arty and aloof pop star trading in such horseplay was odd and slightly stilted. Bowie was impressed by the show's producer, David Mallet, and hired him to direct his next video, for 'Boys Keep Swinging'. It was a working relationship that would go on to produce some of the greatest pop videos ever.

Bowie also acted as guest disc jockey on Radio 1's *Star Special*, where each week a guest celebrity would spin two hours of their favourite music. Bowie was by far the biggest star ever to agree to appear on such a programme. Never one to look a gift horse in the mouth, Bowie, in an endearing display of gross self-publicity, decided to plug two tracks from his upcoming *Lodger* album as well as have his own instrumental, 'Speed Of Life', as the lead-out music. Other tracks played (including some with no Bowie connection) included 'Love Street' by The Doors, 'TV Eye' by Iggy Pop, 'Remember' by Lennon, 'Trial Prison' by Philip Glass (almost certainly the first time that the majority of Bowie fans had heard anything by him), '20th Century Boy' by T. Rex and '21st-Century Schizoid Man' by King Crimson. He also found airtime for two numbers each by Roxy Music and Talking Heads, as well as a classical piece by Elgar (dubbed 'punk' by Bowie), and 'Inchworm' by Danny Kaye. It was an intriguing two hours, and a great insight into Bowie's left-of-centre, though quite poppy, record collection. Millions of Bowie fans, desperate to get a glimpse of the Bowie record collection, tuned in. After years of being divorced and aloof from his fans, Bowie was beginning the process of opening up to his audience.

These two shows were the first attempts to present a new image for David Bowie. As the 1970s turned into the 1980s, Bowie's personae would become less freakish, more mature; his influences and his obsessions talked about and analysed by the man himself. He was becoming, slowly but surely, a different type of rock star, perhaps a more conventional one. The huge secrecy and charisma surrounding Bowie's image was being demystified; Bowie was becoming known to his fans. It was also around this time that we began to get the tabloids contrasting the old 'outrageous' Bowie with the new besuited and 'nice man' model they wished into place. Jean Rook's article 'Bowie Reborn' for the *Daily Express* is typical: 'Bowie has seen it all, and done most of it. When I interviewed him three years ago, he was terrifying to look at. Chalk-skinned, bloodless, and apparently dying, if not un-dead. Today he looks seventeen. His undyed hair is pale brown, with a short back and sides. The unmade-up face is guiltless and spotless. In grey flannel bags, grey shirt and tasteful tie, he looks like a public schoolboy. Or, like Edward before he met Mrs Simpson.'

Also in April 1979, *Melody Maker* revealed one of the most unlikely personae yet adopted by the Thin White Duke; namely, Bowie the boxer. Allan Jones reported the fisticuffs and theatrical temper tantrums between our man and the king of sex, drugs and perversion, ladies and gentlemen, in the blue corner, Mr Lou Reed. Bowie and Reed were dining together, toasting each other and generally being buddies in a rock'n'roll type way after one of Reed's London gigs, when Reed appeared to take exception to something Bowie said and gave him a sound spanking. Allan Jones, an eyewitness and *Melody Maker* editor for twelve years, picks up the story: 'The next thing I know, Lou is dragging Bowie across the table by the front of his shirt and fetching him a few smart slaps about the face ... "I told you NEVER to say that,"

Lou screeches, fetching the hapless Bowie another backhander . . . Lou looks like an irate father boxing the ears of a particularly recalcitrant child for pissing in his slippers. He gets in a few more whacks before the minders haul him away from Bowie.'

From what Jones gathered, the episode was not an elaborate stunt for Bowie's new single 'Boys Keep Swinging'. Apparently the two had talked of Bowie producing Reed's next album and Bowie had made the singer's cleaning up of himself and his act a prerequisite (which didn't go down too well with his old, and now ex-, buddy). Bowie himself was still hardly a drugs-free zone. His producer reports that after work on *Lodger*, 'coke was consumed'. It was all part and parcel of the first attempts (a trend which would reach its apotheosis around 1983) to present a man who was now a stable and aware individual. While Bowie had indeed become a partly reformed character, his muse was still trading on the themes of alienation and disconnection as it had done for the entire decade.

All this exposure helped 'Boys Keep Swinging' recover from a mid-chart slump (it had actually started dropping down the chart for a week before Bowie's TV and radio plugs), and the single finally ended up at Number 7, his first big hit since 'Sound And Vision', although nowhere near as high as it ought to have been.

Bowie was to make three videos for the album. 'Look Back In Anger' was a pastiche of Oscar Wilde's *The Picture of Dorian Gray*, with Bowie as the song's angel of death, gazing at his self-portrait in an artist's studio before his skin begins peeling away in globules of paint. For 'DJ', Bowie cast himself in the title role, smiling gleefully as he delivered the song's opening lines: 'I'm home, lost my job/And I'm incurably ill'.

Shots of Bowie destroying a turntable and recording equipment are intercut with film of him walking down the street being mobbed by fans. One man plants a kiss full on his lips.

The most successful of the three videos was undoubtedly 'Boys Keep Swinging'. Bowie used the set from an earlier TV performance on *The Kenny Everett Video Show* as the basis. The lyric itself parodied the Village People's 'YMCA' (a then recent UK Number 1, US Number 2), which exhorted all men to 'pull together', and listed all the pleasures available at the YMCA: 'You can have a good meal', 'You can hang out with all the boys' and 'You can do whatever you feel'. Bowie re-heterosexualised the lyric, but in the video turned the logic on its head.

Twisting and posturing to the backing track, Bowie sang the opening verse dressed in what looked like school uniform. The video then cut to the backing singers – three women – except they were not three women but three Bowies in drag. For the first he wanted 'a 50s-type girl from the Midlands, a gum-chewing, working-class "tart".' The second was a 'Lauren Bacall' clone, all flowing locks and red lipstick encased in star-spangled splendour. The third was a 'Dietrich–Garbo' cross-pollination, portrayed in old age. At the song's dénouement, the first two singers walk along the catwalk, parodying the 'Disco Queen' strut, face the camera, then tear off their wigs and smear lipstick across their faces in a violently stylised gesture. This was to become a self-referential motif in Bowie's videos. In fact, Bowie had borrowed the idea from German artist Romy Haag, whom Bowie had seen perform in 1976 and had temporarily befriended. Bowie biographers Zanetta and Edwards: 'At the end of the show Haag sang "My Way". She ripped off her wig and her beautiful long hair tumbled to her shoulders. Then she took her hand and rubbed it across her face, smearing her painted red lips until her face resembled an open wound. As the audience gasped at the image, Haag fled from the stage.' When the video was played on *Top of the Pops*, it undoubtedly challenged the early Ziggy performances in terms of shock value (apparently the BBC phone lines were jammed with complaints from irate viewers). It was Bowie's first great pop video. There would be many more to come.

Lodger performed respectably enough, reaching Number 4 in the UK, and Number 20 in the States, and Bowie was at least steadying the ship after the commercial slump heralded in by *Low*. Unlike *Stage*, this time the packaging was good. *Lodger*'s postcard cover portrayed a blurred Bowie stretched out on the bathroom floor/mortuary slab, his nose smashed at right angles, his body broken and contorted like a swatted daddy-longlegs.

Meanwhile, Bowie was for the first time being out-Bowied. With a fitting irony, one of his 'children' was about to launch a career by cutting the ground from under Bowie's feet.

Bowie's retreat from pop had opened up the field for competitors from a variety of stables and of a variety of pedigrees. In the hiatus between the release of "*Heroes*" in October 1977 and *Lodger* in May 1979, popular music had undergone something of a sea change. Punk rock, never anything but a spit in the face of the Establishment, had been superseded by a new age of pop iconography and a new-wave era of photogenic pop stars. In 1978, Blondie and, perhaps more specifically, 32-year-old Debbie Harry, had almost single-handedly brought glamour back into pop. She was the first female pop superstar of the video era, her longueurs to camera laying claim to the peroxide Marilyn Monroe look over five years before the material girl was to do so herself. Blondie, although a pop act through and through, would (like Bowie) later help make the mainstream a wider receiver. 'Heart Of Glass', their huge 1979 single, was the first perfect marriage of punky pop and disco, and 'Rapture' in 1981 was the first white rap hit.

The video age was definitely dawning. Pop acts such as The Kinks, the Stones, Dylan and The Beatles had been making very fine promos since the mid-1960s, but the real era of video came not, as the textbooks say, with Queen's 'Bohemian Rhapsody' but a couple of years or so later, when the new wave became star-rich. In March 1978, eighteen-year-old ex-Lindsay Kemp mime student, Kate Bush, had hit Number 1 with 'Wuthering Heights', still a remarkable record. The video saw her cascading and tumbling in a highly stylised mime sequence and just hinted at Ziggy, despite its wistful prog-rockness. The new-wave era proper was brought to an end by Bob Geldof's Boomtown Rats, who increasingly played an inauthentic, 'Springsteenised' version of punk. Their single, 'Rat Trap', was new wave's 'Bohemian Rhapsody'; meandering, overlong, a mutant form of punk, just as the Queen single was a mutant form of glam rock. By the time of the Boomtown Rats' video for 'I Don't Like Mondays' (produced by Bowie's producer David Mallet), video was as important as music.

But also by 1978, a new type of pop music was being developed, and one that sounded like it had been forged out of the same stuff that had made Eno and *Low*-era Bowie. This year saw the release of a set of quirky, three-minute rants from Devo, whose *Are We Not Men? No: We Are Devo!* was part-spoof/part-serious retake of Bowie's android future, predicted as far back as *The Man Who Sold The World*. By the end of the same year, in the UK a new school of pop-orientated synthesizer groups would also display grandiose designs with minimal conventional technical ability. Bowie himself was rightly very much taken with a group from Sheffield called The Human League, whose experimental pop later gave way to the chart success of 1981's *Dare!* Bowie went to see them in concert in February 1979 at the Nashville. 'He was very complimentary and very nice,' recalls the League's Adrian Wright. When he saw our visuals he said something like, "Oh bugger, I was going to do something like that on my next tour"!'Also in the audience that night was a certain Gary Numan. 'I saw Bowie there. I fluffed up his hair as he walked past! When I was nineteen, twenty, I was still acting like a schoolgirl when it came to David Bowie.'

It's hard to picture it now, but that year, 1979, witnessed the first real sustained challenge to Bowie's natural constituency. In the late 1970s, Bowie had played down his role as 'other'. He neither looked like the alien pop star he was up until 1976, nor was he really able to break his new music into the pop market itself ('Sound And Vision' excepting). For the very first time since *Ziggy Stardust*, there was a gap in the UK marketplace, a need that was not being met. In 1979, Gary Numan emerged as claimant to the throne of that territory of sci-fi futurism and outsiderdom which Bowie had always thought his own.

Even his surname, Numan, came about directly as a response to Bowie. Plain Gary Webb actually found his name by running through the electricians in the Yellow Pages one day and chancing upon the name 'Neumann'. Not liking the name's Germanic origins, Webb changed it to Numan and a snappy stage name was born. 'It was round about the time when Bowie was doing his Berlin bit and I just thought it would probably be a mistake to call myself Neumann because of the Bowie thing,' recalls Numan. Ironically, although Webb thought he had anglicised the name, he had, in fact, 'dutchified' it by mistake.

Numan was a huge Bowie fan, and passed the 'Santa Monica Test' (if you were a proper Bowie fan you had to have this bootleg). He was also instrumental in starting up a Bowie Night in a club he frequented: 'We convinced the people at a club in London called Crackers to start a David Bowie night. I think it was held every Friday and Saturday night and it was really popular. This was around '75, '76. For about a year I tried to look like Bowie, but it never happened for me, unfortunately. For a very short period I had the Thin White Duke look. I used to wear the waistcoat and I had the blond bit at the front of my hair.'

Fast-forward to May 1979, and Tubeway Army's 'Are Friends Electric', Numan was Number 1 in the UK charts, and deservedly so. On record, Numan did borrow a certain amount from Bowie. On *Telekon*, released in 1980, Numan recounts how he got the Bowie piano effect to a T. 'I can't play like Mike Garson, so what I used to do was just shut my eyes and hit any notes that my hands touched. On "Sleep By Windows", there's like a synthy thing towards the end of it, and I swear to you, I'm sitting in front of it and have my eyes closed and I'm just hitting whatever notes come to hand!' What he also adopted from Bowie was his singing stance: 'I just used to find it really irritating to hear British people singing in an American accent. It used to irritate the fuck out of me, and it still does. I noticed that David Bowie would have a very definite London accent and I just used to think that was honest. That's where he's from, so that's how he should sing.'

On stage, Numan was one of Bowie's children. On those first TV appearances he was frozen and unsmiling (and incredibly nervous), his movements jerky. He had Bowie's stare, sway and sneer down to a T. 'Certainly, the use of image to help project lyrical content and atmosphere was entirely down to Bowie,' says Numan. Later in 1979, he would update the *Station To Station*-era lighting and design a lavish stage set with bars of neon white light. This essence of Bowieness found plenty of admirers. Too young to get a hit of the Bowie tour in 1976, the likes of Billy Corgan, Trent Reznor and Marilyn Manson were just old enough to catch Numan in his pomp in the late 1970s and early 1980s.

Numan was the biggest-selling solo artist in the UK in 1979. The music, now totally guitar-free, was stark and filmic, driven by cascading drum rhythms and stirring synth figures ('Cars', 'Metal'). By the autumn of 1979, Numan was massive while Bowie's second *Lodger* single, 'DJ', only reached the lower end of the Top 30 in the UK.

Numan's rise to stardom largely antagonised Bowie fans, who dubbed him a third-rate copyist. Bowie himself was far from flattered and certainly felt slightly threatened by Numan. In an interview with Paula Yates for *Record Mirror* he said of him, 'I've seen some of his videos. To be honest, I never meant for cloning to be part of the 80s. He's not only copied me, he's clever and he's got all my influences in too. I guess it's best of luck to him.'

Speaking in 1999, Numan remembers the upset:

I lost my whole thing for Bowie within five seconds of reading what he had said. The man had been, outside of my family, the biggest thing in my life. I'd had fights over him, I'd got beaten up because of him. If there was a Bowie influence running through my songs, it wasn't intentional, although I would be stupid to deny it because he was such a big part of my life. To have someone who you hold in such high regard say something so dismissive and so petty about somebody else's life I thought was pathetic, really. I understand it much more now because I'm forty years old and I've had my ups and downs and I can understand much more what was going on in his mind. That would have been about seven or eight years into his fame. If I'd gone back to when I was seven or eight years into mine, I guess that I might have had similar problems if someone had come along in the mid-1980s who had a really big electronic hit. It didn't actually happen, but if it had, I might have felt a bit bitter about it, and I might have said something a bit scathing in an interview.

Around this time, Numan was asked to perform on a Kenny Everett New Year's Eve special. Producer for the show was a certain David Mallet, Bowie's video producer. Numan:

I'd done my bit, then Mallet said, 'Bowie's going to be here next week. Do you want to come and see him?' Can you imagine? You'd just got famous yourself and all that was brilliant in your life and the next thing you're actually going to meet David Bowie! Short of flying to the moon and back I couldn't imagine anything else I would rather have done. So, I go along, and there are a few other famous people there like Bob Geldof and Paula Yates, and I am shy. There's a little side room and we are allowed to look through a doorway and I'm right at the back of the room and bugger me if Bowie didn't see me! I am sitting at the back of this room, trying to keep out of the way, and totally in awe. So recording stops and it's all awkward for a bit and nobody's sure what is going on. Obviously, something's happened because Bowie's not happy. Mallet comes over to me and says, 'Can I have a word?' So he takes me outside and says, 'David Bowie's spotted you. He's not very happy about it and doesn't want you in the building.' And that was it! So I'm thrown out! If Bowie said, 'Look, Mallet, I want that bloke off,' then you were off because Mallet had a huge financial incentive to want to stay doing Bowie's videos. The next thing I know is that about three or four days later we get a call saying unfortunately it's not possible to have your song on *The Kenny Everett Show*, it doesn't fit the schedule, or some other fuckin' stupid excuse. So that was it! Out of the building and off the programme!

Bowie was obviously not enjoying having a man who was regarded as some sort of clone of himself suddenly sharing the limelight with him. Bowie throwing Numan off was the equivalent of, say, Bowie being kicked off an Anthony Newley special in 1967. This showed Bowie to be emotionally fragile. However, speaking in 2000, Bowie refutes Numan's account of what actually happened, calling it 'apocryphal'. 'If he were asked not to come onto the set, it would have been during rehearsals. I do remember having told the studio people that he was welcome to come to the actual shoot. He never appeared.' And it should also be pointed out that Bowie added in the same interview for *Q* in 2000, 'I think he's written a couple of the finest things in British pop.'

In 1981, Numan famously quit live performance. The parallels between his decision and the retirement of Ziggy in 1973 were there for all to see, although Numan protests that he wasn't attempting to ape the Bowie story in this final respect. He claims that media hostility forced him to bow out and that the Bowie-copyist tag 'didn't help'. But Numan has endured, and proved massively influential in his own right, far more than any *Stars In Your Eyes* version of the real thing.

Numan's fame, if perhaps only indirectly, shook Bowie into some serious pop action. His next project was both more accessible and involved a noticeably redesigned, more telegenic image. Before returning to New York in February 1980 to record the new album, the first since *Station To Station* without Eno, Bowie recorded two important sessions. For the Numan-less Kenny Everett New Year's Eve show, he sang an acoustic version of his 1969 hit, 'Space Oddity'. It was a stark, stripped-down rendering, with acoustic guitar, drum and bass. He also did a remarkable three-song set for *Saturday Night Live*. Bowie and his band (which included Jimmy Destri on keyboards on a sabbatical from Blondie) were augmented by performance artists Klaus Nomi and Joey Arias. Bowie was hip to the new video age and designed a distinct look for each song. For a musically fairly faithful 'Man Who Sold The World', Bowie was carried to the microphone encased in what looked like a cardboard coat. He was in fact trying to re-create the sort of performance given in the 1910s by Hugo Ball at the Cabaret Voltaire in Zurich, who would be carried to the front of the stage in a tube. 'I combined the tube device with another Dada costume, that of a highly stylised men's evening dress with huge shoulders and bow tie,' wrote Bowie in 1999. For 'Boys Keep Swinging', television trickery was used to graft a puppet's body on to Bowie's head, with hilarious results as he flopped around performing impossibly loose-limbed acrobatic feats. Bowie got the idea for this from fairgrounds in Germany: 'Standing in a kind of Punch and Judy booth, the performer, dressed in black, would attach a small body puppet (just trunk and limbs) below his chin. This gave the effect of a human-headed marionette.' For 'TVC 15', Bowie wore drag on stage for the first time in eight years, wearing a uniform which was supposed to give 'the impression of a Chinese airline stewardess outfit'. A pink poodle with a TV monitor in its mouth relayed the song as it was played – a sort of half-machine, half-animal interface, and a neat touch.

At Christmas 1979, Bowie was also back in the UK charts with the old Sigma Sound out-take, 'John, I'm Only Dancing (Again)'. This was followed up early in 1980 by his reading of 'The Alabama Song', recorded in 1978. The new acoustic 'Space Oddity' was the B-side. On the vinyl single next to the run-out groove were scratched the words 'Sorry Gus'.

Bowie was altogether less haphazard with his next project, and without Eno he became more craftsmanlike and song-based. In February 1980 he went to the Power Station Studios in New York to record a piece of work which has become the benchmark for every subsequent Bowie album and which is rightly regarded by Bowie's hard-core fans as one of the best albums he has ever made. It was also, according to Tony Visconti, his first attempt to record a more commercial album.

Bowie now had a solid, stable, musical line-up with Alomar, Davis and Murray the indomitable spirit of each Bowie band. 'That rhythm section, though, was the best he ever had,' says Alomar. 'Dennis Davis is a congenial, jovial jokester, a prankster. He was totally off the wall. There was never a dull moment and never a serious moment. George Murray was extremely moody, quiet and shy, but a sweet man.' In fact, by now, Alomar and Bowie were neighbours, augmenting a home in Lausanne, Switzerland, and a rented London apartment with a chic New York loft. Alomar recalls:

It was on 26th Street across the street from FIT [Fashion Institute of Technology of New York]. It was called a Chelsea loft and it was great. Even then, I just didn't call David out of the blue, he calls me. After a while you get used to it, but at the beginning it would sort of bother me, because I don't have friends like that. You go with the relationship the way in which the superstar makes the relationship. That was the way he operates, so you just work under that. It never bothered me. One of the things that I feel kept me there for so long was that others were sticking their claws into him, saying he owed them. I did the last tour, why didn't you call me? What's this someone else playing guitar? That's something David has always known. If you call me for the next session or doing another tour, I'm always in shock. And if he called me tomorrow and said, 'Carlos, would you go on tour with me?' I'd probably go. We have a very close relationship and it might be unusual, but it's not a strange relationship, nor is it complex.

Even someone like Alomar, who had been the linchpin of the Bowie sound for half-a-dozen years and who was a close friend and neighbour, never knew from one album or tour to the next whether he was to be called upon. Just as Bowie dropped in and out of musical styles, so he dropped in and out of people's lives too. Take Adrian Belew:

I assumed that, when the 1978 tour was over and we had done *Lodger*, I had a place in David's future. They gave me an advance for the next record. Well, months and months went by, I did other things, and I never got a call from David. Suddenly I heard that *Scary Monsters* was coming out and that he'd got Tom Verlaine and Robert Fripp on it, and it stunned me because I thought, That's interesting – I got paid to do this record! I was on tour with Talking Heads and maybe he wanted someone for a longer period. What I eventually heard was that he worked for a long time with Tom Verlaine, but that it didn't work out and, at the last moment, they brought in Robert for the day and Robert did all his parts in one day and left. It's not surprising for artists like David to do that; someone who's ever changing and moving forward. Obviously, you change your mind. I respect that, of course, but at the time it was a big disappointment.

Verlaine, in fact, was just one of four guest guitar soloists on the album along with Fripp (whose playing is superb), guitar synthesist Chuck Hammer, and Pete Townshend. The songs on *Scary Monsters* took several months to evolve. Cassettes in Visconti's archive dated 11 March 1980 include songs for the new album such as 'People Are Turning To Gold' (later 'Ashes To Ashes'); 'It Happens Everyday' (which later became 'Teenage Wildlife', and on which instead of singing, 'Not another teenage wildlife', Bowie screamed, 'It happens everyda-ay'), and 'Jamaica' (which was nearly left unfinished until Bowie turned it into 'Fashion'). A backing track for a cover of Cream's 'I Feel Free' was started (according to Bowie writer Nicholas Pegg this track appears on bootlegs as 'Is There Life After Marriage'), whilst Bowie also recorded 'Fuje Moto San' (an instrumental piece written for a Japanese saki advert and later retitled 'Crystal Japan'). Unusually, Bowie asked for time to work out melodies and lyrics rather than make them up on the spot; when he returned he presented Visconti with some of the most innovative melodies of his career.

Scary Monsters was finished off during spring 1980, and to promote it, a single, backed by Lodger's 'Move On', hit the shops in early August. It was obvious from the Duffy-designed multiformatted sleeve (the single came in three different though similar designs showing Bowie as a Pierrot figure) that the new David Bowie was a far more glamorous affair than any since the *Ziggy Stardust* days. The new single, the sublime 'Ashes To Ashes', was a sequel to his very own 'Space Oddity', and the accompanying video showed Bowie in more lipstick and make-up than ever before. As a package of song and video, it was unsurpassable: Bowie's best ever video with arguably his best ever single. The song's melody, its incantatory quality (with the almost inaudible voices drifting in and out of the mix) and quirky rhythm (based, according to Bowie, on an 'old ska beat') make for a collision of astonishing musical textures.

After a week in the shops, it was Number 4 in the UK charts. After a *Top of the Pops* showing of the video – at £250,000, the most expensive which had ever been made – the song was at Number 1, deposing Abba's 'The Winner Takes It All' and becoming the fastest-selling Bowie single up to that point. In a way, it was Bowie's first ever 'real' Number 1 in the UK. It was a new song, not a reactivated oldie like his previous Number 1, 'Space Oddity'.

Updating the story of 'Space Oddity''s Major Tom, this song made overt references to the drug use which was only implied in 'Space Oddity''s lift-off section: 'Ashes to ashes/Funk to funky/We know Major Tom's a junky'. Bowie turned the song not simply into a comment on his own period of addiction but also on his career, using a rather sarcastic piece of self-deprecation: 'I've never done good things/I've never done bad things/I never did anything out of the blue'. The next couplet is also a comment on Bowie's career, and with hindsight looks like a public announcement of a desire to move his career into less experimental and more 'normalised' terrain: 'I want an axe to break the ice/I wanna come down right now'.

The video was shot in May 1980, partly on location in Hastings. And no, the elderly lady playing Bowie's mother in the video is not his real mother. In the four-minute video Bowie plays three characters, all variations on the outsider theme of the song. The first is a Pierrot figure based on a commedia dell'arte Renaissance costume, the second an astronaut and the third an asylum inmate. Bowie appears to be summoning up these archetypes, archetypes that had pervaded his writing in the past decade, in order to kill them off and lay to rest the ghost of impersonation.

The format of the video also acts out the psychoanalysis of the song. The writer Michael Shore in his book on pop video points out 'the stunningly elegant self-referential video-within-video motif, wherein each new sequence is introduced by Bowie holding a postcard-sized video screen displaying the first shot of the next scene.' 'Ashes To Ashes', like most of Bowie's videos, has no real story. It is full of incongruous images, as if we are being given direct access to a dreamlike mental state. Four Slavic figures walk in front of a bulldozer in a recurring image of oncoming violence. Bowie, as Pierrot, sinks into a lake, as if drowning in his own subconscious, an image re-used by Peter Gabriel in his 'Shock The Monkey' video two years later. At the end of the video, Bowie, a black sky above him, walks along the beach being lectured by his mother. Bowie gives the song and the video an Edwardian queasiness, portraying a world of nostalgia, childhood reminiscence and distant memories. It is also significant in terms of production values. Bowie storyboarded it with David Mallet, whose contribution was, as Shore concludes, very important: 'Most impressive is Mallet's deliberately overloaded direction – demented, horror-movie camera angles, heavy solarisations, neurotic cuts from supersaturated colour to black-and-white.' Bowie asked Mallet if he could turn the sky black for the video and Mallet duly obliged.

Perhaps, as Mallet would later claim, pop video arrived just too late for David Bowie. When Bowie was most interested in the medium during the early 1980s, when he was at his peak commercially, pop-video techniques were relatively unsophisticated. That said, 'Ashes To Ashes' still stands as the defining early music video, an astonishingly surreal four minutes which has some claim to represent Bowie's highpoint as an artist.

This video was also the first time that a mainstream pop audience had been confronted with new romanticism. Just as a new neo-glam rock movement was happening in the clubs in London, Bowie introduced it to the rest of us. The video featured Steve Strange, singer with Visage and one of the leading lights of the new romantic scene. Bowie had gone headhunting in clubland for bit-players and had spotted Steve Strange, transvestite pop singer and ligger Marilyn (who promptly sat on Bowie's lap), and Boy George (whom Bowie likened to Klaus Nomi and, much to George's dismay, did not pick for the video shoot).

The new romantic scene had Bowie's fingerprints all over it. Whereas punk had ransacked every significant post-teddy-boy look, subverted it and angrily gobbed it out, new romanticism looked to glam rock and reconstructed its self-preening narcissism for the 1980s. Initially a London-based phenomenon, it was also a club-based movement. 'Bowie Nights' were started by Rusty Egan and Steve Strange in clubs such as The Blitz in London, and the whole new romantic movement was essentially an early 1980s reconstruction of Bowie and Roxy Music with a disco beat. Soon 'Bowie Nights' were being held up and down the country. One Bowie fan describes the late 1970s and early 1980s club scene in the north of England like this:

For us, there was an obvious link from Bowie to punk and we embraced both. The punk scene was heavily geared towards live gigs so on the weekends when there were no live bands we looked for something else to do. The only nightclubs in those days were the usual meat-markets playing *Saturday Night Fever* disco and we were invariably not allowed in due to henna-ed hair, ripped jeans, etc. Leeds and Manchester were the two nearest big cities where there was any sort of nightlife, so we used to cadge lifts off the older lads who had cars and go to Bowie nights in pubs and clubs there. Manchester had a huge club called Pips which had three floors – one for the usual disco, one for northern soul and the top floor for Bowie fans. It was always packed and full of the weirdest people from all over the north of England in their plastic sandals, floppy fringes, fedoras and peg-leg trousers. Some of these were truly radical and wore make-up – not a sensible thing for a man to do in Manchester on a Saturday night! The music was always the same – any Bowie (but mainly *Young Americans* and *Station To Station*) with Roxy Music, Iggy Pop, Lou Reed and The New York Dolls as well. There was also a place called the Ranch Bar where we used to go in Manchester and I always remember this because the two bouncers used to wear SS uniforms!

Another Bowie fan, Steve Lowe, remembers that he and his mate were often better served at gay clubs for their fix of Bowie: 'In gay clubs you'd find Bowie music any night of the week. As a sixteen-year-old heterosexual, it took me a while to get used to people thinking we were an item! Eventually going into gay clubs didn't bother me, as the general atmosphere was more welcoming and less violent than at Pips, for example. Being a Bowie fan in the 1970s was a dangerous occupation. Even at school I suffered regular taunts and the occasional beating or two just for being different from the other twelve-year-olds and for reading magazines such as *Fab208*, *Jackie*, *Popswop* – in fact, any mag featuring Bowie articles.'

'Sequential artist' David Gough describes Liverpool's club, Planet X, in the early 1980s in a short article he wrote about his life as a Bowie fan. Bowie Nights were for the 'kooky and the jaded' and for 'pasty necro-punkettes in fishnets and kohl eyeliner, dancing to the celebratory beat of drawing pale blinds. These were people I never knew beyond the same iconoclastic revere and the compelling nature of the outsider in all of us. Glitter kids and style boys, procuring their alter egos carefully for tonight, only to return to irksome acned little waifs in the morning. Of course it wasn't all Bowie. The tide had already begun to turn, heralded by a new wave of Numans and Durans, and we listened and bought their records anyway because we knew that they were only paying lip service to the godfather – it seemed right, and years later when the same kids abandoned Bowie for their Genesises and Smiths, I never lost my faith – even when he did. Besides there was still always *Low*.'

'Ashes To Ashes' stands as a Bowie landmark therefore not simply because it was technically brilliant but because it encapsulated 1980 perfectly. By creating a video with all the garishness and mock grandeur of the new romantic movement, Bowie popularised an underground cult centred on appropriating his own, and glam's, visual heritage. He was, in a sense, helping to relaunch a part of his artistic past. One reviewer would later comment that on *Scary Monsters* David Bowie 'ate his young'. By jumping on a bandwagon full of Bowie clones (if only for one video) he was copying a copy (new romanticism) of a fabrication (glam rock, Ziggy) of the real David Jones.

Bowie was absolutely perfect for the video age: his songs always carried some sort of expressive element and he never regarded pop as a purely sonic experience. He tried to make his videos freestanding from the lyric of any particular song with a weight equal to the song itself; he wanted a video to offer a parallel piece of information. He was also never happier than when layering as much visual information on to the screen as possible. Videos had to stand the test of repeatability, and it was a challenge Bowie met with gusto. For Bowie, video was just another format to express the dialogue between music and images which was going on all the time in his own brain. In an interview with *NME*'s Angus McKinnon that September, he said: 'The chauvinism between various art forms – theatre, film and music – it's all so silly because the creative force is operative in all these things. I think it might be evident that I never completely leave one for the other – there's no barrier.'

For some, video was a constraining factor in the promotion of pop, and less videogenic performers suffered. Every new band was expected to have 'acting' skills as part of their armoury, and it wasn't long before a flood of clichés started to make most videos crushingly boring. But Bowie, who loved layering information, made some of the best videos of the day. Take the second single off *Scary Monsters*, 'Fashion'. The song poked fun at the banality of the dance floor and the style fascists, while at the same time framing the critique in a New York-style dance groove. The video, again a collaboration with David Mallet, is loosely based around some footage of Bowie and band in performance. The video supports the lyric's condemnation of 'style fascism' and consumerism gone ape by incorporating a direct attack on the banality of advertising in the form of two mini-adverts coinciding with the song's 'beep beep!' section. He also plays the twin roles of rock icon and rock fan during the song's most telling sequence: 'Listen to me – don't listen to me/Talk to me – don't talk to me/Dance with me – don't dance with me/No . . .'

Bowie the artist stands on stage, snarling dismissively at Bowie the fan, looking on. Bowie the icon is literally elevated on the stage, the camera, at stage level, looking up at the pop star and down at the fan. The scene encapsulates the icon–fan relationship, with its impersonality, detachment and inequality, and provides a visual statement of the quintessence of Bowie's 70s stage shows. As in 'Ashes To Ashes', Bowie's performance is closer to mime than to acting. In 'Ashes To Ashes', the funeral procession walks solemnly in front of a bulldozer. The figures touch the ground in front of them, their right hands extended in an ominous slow arc. The result is the creation of a new but blank gesture which Bowie utilised in a number of videos, 'Fashion' being one of them. In 'Fashion', Bowie scratches, twitches, sniffs and lunges in an almost Tourettic display of visual infirmity, and bends to his knees to swoop down and touch the ground with an unbent arm (rather like a cricketer's round-arm bowling action). A final note on the video: Lennon's ex-girlfriend and future wife of Tony Visconti, May Pang, is one of the 'beep-beeping' girls in shot.

'Often Copied, Never Equalled' ran the promotional slogan for the release of the new album in the wake of Gary Numan and Co. Bowie had in fact hit a new peak. He had made an experimental album that was also a pop record and which sold in impressive numbers – the perfect balance. *Scary Monsters (And Supercreeps)* made Number 1 in the UK on its first week of release. *Record Mirror*'s Simon Ludgate's impossible rating of seven out of a maximum of five stars set the tone for the album's reception. The sleeve showed Bowie as the Pierrot in 'Ashes To Ashes', the first to have him noticeably in make-up and satin and tat since *Aladdin Sane*, seven and a half years earlier. In fact, the same photographer/designer, Duffy, was brought in to do the photo shoot

(Bowie took delight in smearing the painstakingly administered lipgloss, à la 'Boys Keep Swinging' for the final shots of the session), and the cover artwork came from artist Edward Bell, who produced a series of paintings based on the original shots (also used for a Bowie calendar called Glamour a little later, now a collector's item). The back cover showed images from previous Bowie albums washed over with white paint. Indeed, the record was enormously self-referential. 'It's No Game' was a rewrite of a 1970 song, 'Tired Of My Life'; the 'beep beep' section on 'Fashion' was from an earlier unreleased song, 'Rupert The Riley'; 'Scream Like A Baby' was a rewrite of an Astronettes track ('I Am A Laser'); 'Ashes To Ashes' obviously revisited 'Space Oddity'. Bowie was either short of new musical ideas, or was being deliberately archly post-modern and deciding to recycle obscure bits from the past. Probably a bit of both.

The second single, 'Fashion', is his definitive statement on the style fascists he observed populating the new romantic movement and is a put-down of those slaves to the nuances of style. Bowie told *NME*'s Angus MacKinnon: 'I was trying to move on a little from the Ray Davies concept of fashion; to suggest more of a gritted-teeth determination and unsureness about why one's doing it, rather like one goes to the dentist and has a tooth drilled.' Despite the existence of a generation of people who were prepared to spend hours copying his various looks, Bowie now claims that fashion is something that does not much concern him. 'I rarely buy clothes,' he told the *Observer* in 2002. 'I wear them well and people give me stuff and I'm quite keen to wear it for public shows and albums and all that. But I'm not interested in fashion.'

'Teenage Wildlife', musically reminiscent of "Heroes", is the first Bowie song to show a recognition of the age gap between pop star (Bowie was then 33) and the current pop world. 'Same old thing in brand new drag/Comes sweeping into view/As ugly as a teenage millionaire/Pretending it's a whiz-kid world' ('Teenage Wildlife', 1980).

Gary Numan was almost certainly one of the intended targets of these lines. 'I was quite proud about it at the time, to be honest,' says Numan. 'Even though I'd fallen out with him it still made me feel, Wahey! I'm in a Bowie song. That's cool.'

'It's No Game Part 1' was powered by searing guitar riffs from Fripp and colossal rebounding drums from Davis. The juxtaposition of disparate information was the key strategy in this song, as biographer Jerry Hopkins explains: 'When he recorded the album's opening track, "It's No Game", he used a Japanese friend, Michi Hirota, to sing the lyrics in Japanese (as a counterpoint to his English) because he wanted "to break down a particular kind of sexist attitude about women" and I thought the Japanese girl typifies it where everybody sort of pictures a geisha girl – sweet, demure and non-thinking. So she sang the lyrics in a macho, samurai voice.'

Like 'Drive-In Saturday', 'Scream Like A Baby' looks back on a fictional future and thus comments on the present, a standard device in science fiction but hitherto seldom, if ever, used in pop. The lyric deals with the relationship between the song's narrator and the character Sammy. They are both processed and tortured, pumped full of 'strange drugs' and persecuted because of their suggested sexual 'deviance'. Bowie delivers the line: 'And now I'm learning to be a part of society' ('Scream Like A Baby', 1980) but is unable to complete the final word, stuttering to a full stop and signalling not just the fictionalised narrator's sense of estrangement. In the middle eight, Sammy's execution is described: 'But he jumped into the furnace/Singing old songs we loved'.

Bowie split the vocal in two (the splitting of the word 'athletic' into four syllables is peculiarly reminiscent of Dalek-speak) and recorded using varispeed (a technique which speeded up and slowed down the voice and set one against the other out of sync). The effect was a split personality, schizophrenia: the 'real' personality speaking to the mask; a key moment in Bowie's recorded work.

One line from *Scary Monsters* would prove almost like a premonition. On 'It's No Game', Bowie sang, 'Put a bullet in my brain, and it makes all the papers.' It was almost as if Bowie's music was anticipating the events of 8 December at the Dakota Buildings, New York City, when his friend, John Lennon, was gunned to death.

Tony Visconti told the Bowie fanzine, *Starzone*, in 1984: 'John Lennon's death certainly stopped anyone being very open with the public.' Indeed, it must have terrified Bowie and his entourage when the news came out that December. Bowie was also in New York acting in a theatre just blocks away from the murder scene. Bowie had been interviewed by Radio 1 DJ Andy Peebles a few days earlier. Peebles, who had gone to New York to talk to Bowie (a measure of Bowie and Lennon's respective standing at the time), also took the opportunity to conduct an interview with Lennon, just hours before the ex-Beatle's death at the hands of a crazed fan. The Peebles' interview with Lennon had contained compliments to Bowie and friendly reminiscences about him. Lennon's murder was the nightmare made corporeal: the obsessed, psychotic loner who identified so completely with a rock icon that he almost became him.

At the time, Bowie was working on Broadway, his first and, to date, only time in theatre. Rather than tour his new album, Bowie had taken the lead role in Jack Hofsiss' production of *The Elephant Man*. The play, with a script by Bernard Pomerance, told the tragic tale of John Merrick, born with deformities so disfiguring that he was displayed in circus freak shows. According to neurologist and writer Oliver Sacks in his book *An Anthropologist on Mars*, Merrick suffered from either Proteus syndrome or neurofibromatosis, 'a bizarre and sometimes cancerous disease that can produce huge brownish swellings and protruding sheets of skin, disfiguring the whole body'. Bowie researched the part meticulously, visiting the London Hospital to view Merrick's clothing and a body mould made after his death. Bowie, who told Tim Rice in a BBC2 interview for *Friday Night, Saturday Morning* that he always looked for characters to play who had 'either a physical or emotional limp', knew of the tale of the elephant boy from a book called *Strange People* by Frank Edwards, a pulp classic of its day full of voyeuristic items on freaks, monsters and as many limping creatures as Bowie might desire.

The show began in Denver in July 1980 before hitting Broadway that autumn. By all accounts, Bowie was splendid in the role, providing Hofsiss with performance after performance of singular artistic control. While John Hurt's film rendition released in late 1981 was a brilliantly grotesque portrayal, Bowie, through the use of mime, not make-up, suggested John Merrick's myriad deformities through illusion and allusion. By twisting and contorting his body posture and delivering his lines in a brilliantly suggestive affected voice, syllables undulating and stressed in the most bizarre fashion (he had apparently researched the diction of the handicapped), Bowie created an elephant-man role that was a triumph of suggestion, hinting as it did at the horror of deformity. Bowie thus gave Merrick over to his audience, asking them to re-create the horror of Merrick's physicality and thus at the same time making him less a freak and more a human being. That Bowie gave such a performance is a credit to his gritty professionalism. For part of the play he delivered his lines naked, seated in a bathtub, and many a night he climbed in to find that the crew had filled it with porn mags and dildos, leaving Bowie struggling to keep his face straight.

Incidentally, BowieNet subscribers can access photographs of David Bowie and John Hurt at a neighbour's indoor bowling evening in Gstaad, Switzerland, taken in February 1985. One shot shows Bowie standing next to Hurt; holding a bowl, his body is contorted in the same crushed-bone stance of his original portrayal.

Bowie left the role on 3 January 1981. Lennon's murder (together with Bowie's notoriously butterfly nature) had probably put paid to Bowie accepting the invitation to continue in the role. Mark Chapman had been to see *The Elephant Man* just days before killing Lennon, and it is rumoured that Bowie was next on his list of visible celebrities to gun down, should Lennon have been unavailable that night. Long-standing fan Patti Brett noticed that he had grown introverted and frightened of fan contact: 'I think he got really afraid after the John Lennon thing. I noticed more and more that he was less and less accessible after that happened. We went up to New York for *The Elephant Man* and even after those shows he would rarely talk to anyone. He would just run into the car after his performance.'

By early January, a new single, 'Scary Monsters', was already in the lower reaches of the UK chart and a compilation, K-Tel's mildly tacky *The Best Of Bowie*, capitalised on the increase in Bowie's commercial and critical stock. Although he promised a short tour in 1981 (with cinema screens relaying the events round the provinces), the idea was dropped, and it was the first year since 1968 in which no new Bowie album was recorded or released. Bowie's workload was lighter than ever before. In February, he appeared at the 1981 Rock and Pop Awards in London, where he picked up the award for Best Male Singer, presented to him by Lulu. He was snapped holding the plaque backstage with a boyish Tony Visconti. Bowie also provided the soundtrack culled from his recent work and made a cameo appearance in the German film *Christiane F: Wir Kinder Vom Bahnhof Zoo*, commonly regarded as a classic of its type in its realistic depiction of teenage drug addiction. In July 1981 an accidental meeting with pomp rockers Queen led to a one-off track being cut, 'Under Pressure', and Bowie adding guest vocal to a Queen track, 'Cool Cat'. Apparently, Bowie quizzed Mercury about the joys of being contracted to EMI, and Mercury promised to find an 'in' for him at the company. It seems certain that, with the terms of the 1975 settlement with Defries due to expire a year later, Bowie had already decided to leave RCA.

In August he appeared as the lead in a BBC adaptation of Bertolt Brecht's minor work, *Baal*. He also recorded a soundtrack EP at Berlin's Hansa Studios. Eventually aired in the spring of 1982, the soundtrack, backed by a full orchestra and produced by Tony Visconti, is a bravura performance. The highlight is unmistakably the Brecht/Mildowney song 'Baal's Hymn (*Der Choral Vom Großen Baal*)', his vocal dynamic, dramatic, and just possibly the best of his career. The whole thing took just one day to record, and one to mix.

At the end of 1981, Bowie was at Number 1 in the UK singles charts with a record which, although now possessed of classic status, is in fact one of his least memorable songs. The Queen/Bowie collaboration was released on 2 November 1981 during one of the few times since Queen's meteoric rise in 1974 when Bowie was actually shifting more units than them in the UK. It was Number 1 in the UK within a fortnight, but its commercial success couldn't hide the fact that it was a new type of David Bowie record, and not a terribly good one at that. Although this particular pairing dismayed many long-standing Bowiephiles at the time, it was a taste of things to come. Whereas his 1970s celebrity team-ups were often bizarre mismatches, notably the downright surreal Christmas duet with Bing Crosby, this particular collaboration seemed less like a weird joke at the expense of a hapless chanteuse like Lulu or Cher, and more like the first step towards winning mainstream acceptance.

If Gary Numan in 1979 had traded on Bowie's frozen-addict stage of the mid-70s, then a new pop star was busy with a return to the Ziggy days of satin and tat. Boy George (real name George O'Dowd, born in Eltham, Kent, in 1961) was one of the leading starlets in this new pop formation. George was one of those Bowie fans who used to hang round Haddon Hall in the glam-rock era, waiting for a glimpse of their man. In 1999 Boy George told Bowie, 'Angie opened the window and said, "Why don't you all fuck off?" We were thrilled!' Boy George's group, Culture Club, was a cultural and gender hybrid consisting of a chatty, out-gay singer, a non-out-gay drummer, a black guitarist and a white heterosexual keyboardist. Their music was a breezy, undemanding, though sometimes very fine mix of reggae, disco and Motown pop, and for an eighteen-month period they dominated the British charts. Like Adam Ant before him, Boy George became a tabloid hero; stars like him put pop stardom on a par with soap celebrity.

Boy George stripped gender-bending of its violence, and made it fun. He was a likeable, blokey tabloid queen, who once famously rated a cup of tea as preferable to sex (he must make the mother of a cuppa). It was all a far cry from the sort of psychosexual apocalypse triggered by Bowie in the 1970s. It seemed that Bowie's legacy was, if not actually being diluted, then turned into something altogether less menacing, fit for *Wogan* and other chat shows, *Smash Hits* and *Record Mirror*.

It also appeared that other pop stars were handling the absentee Bowie's legacy with none of Boy George's witty kitsch. If Bowie was about psychic reconstruction through personal style, then soul singer Michael Jackson was taking it all too literally and way too far. Jackson took home improvements literally and, by redesigning his face and skin tone, allegedly through elective cosmetic surgery, he gave the impression of being ashamed of his colour. Running through all this was a Peter Pan-esque androgyny. Jackson, with the body of a boy and the face of a strategically redesigned white/black, male/female hybrid, made a global impact in the 1980s through his plastic-surgery bisexuality. In a decade in which Western youths were subjected to increasing pressure to reconstruct their bodies through diet and exercise (with often fatal results), Jackson set himself up as the ultimate example of an individual trying to cheat nature. At a time when hundreds of thousands developed eating disorders and became ashamed of their natural size and shape, Jackson's quest for bodily 'perfection' was another signal to youth that the current orthodoxy was both righteous and right. Under the Reaganomics of the early 1980s, a figure such as Jackson rendered cruel the aspirational politics of individualism that Bowie had represented.

Annie Lennox, a long-time Bowie nut, also skilfully repackaged herself as a pop androgyne. Like Grace Jones, she was a female counterpart to Bowie. By the time of the Eurythmics' late-1982 release, 'Love Is A Stranger', Lennox was a red-haired, crop-headed girl in a suit. This was Bowie's Thin White Duke persona crossed with the image of the power-dressing executive business-woman. Although unmistakably female (except to the American authorities, who demanded documentary proof of her gender before they would allow her into the country), Lennox's white vocal hysteria wedded to the cold-fish detachment of her updated Thin White Duke pose on videos such as 'Love Is A Stranger' and The Eurythmics' breakthrough hit in early 1983, 'Sweet Dreams Are Made Of This', borrowed from Bowie, but added little new. Later the same year, Lennox logically reconstructed herself as a moustachioed greaser for the 'Who's That Girl?' video, in which she paid playful homage to the joys of cross-dressing.

In the autumn of 1982, Bauhaus reached the UK Top 20 with the single that Bowie never released, 'Ziggy Stardust'. Bauhaus' version stuck close to the original and so seemed rather pointless in its slavishness, and on *Top of the Pops* they looked more like a tribute band than anything else. Ersatz Bowie was in, and the climate was right for the 'real' version again.

But where was Bowie himself? After years of constant media attention he appeared to have almost totally disappeared from the pages of pop history. Apart from recording the music for the BBC's *Baal*, and a soundtrack theme song with Giorgio Moroder for the remake of *Cat People*, he appeared incredibly lazy. In truth, he had elected not to record again until after September 1982, when Defries' stake in his new recordings would have expired. He had also determined not to record with RCA again. After the reception *Low* had been given at RCA, the squabble over *Stage*, and the constant pressure on Bowie to maintain his hit-making potential, Bowie was weary. He filled his time by reactivating his acting career.

In the spring of 1982 it was reported that he was playing the lead in a vampire movie called *The Hunger*, to be directed by Tony Scott, brother of the then more famous Ridley. As filming progressed, alarming photos were released to the press showing a very unwell Bowie, with shards of skin for a face. For the purpose of his role, Bowie had been expected to age scores of years in minutes. No sooner had these photos been digested by the Bowie faithful than it was reported that Bowie was on location in the South China Sea with cult film-maker, Nagisa Oshima. Oshima's last film, *The Realm of the Senses*, portrayed a graphic descent into pain, pleasure and brutal eroticism. The new film, an adaptation of Laurens Van der Post's story, *The Seed and the Sower*, cast Bowie as an internee in a Japanese prisoner-of-war camp, a rather more legitimate role for him and perhaps his best chance of box-office success since *The Man Who Fell To Earth* seven years earlier. Both new Bowie films were set for release in 1983.

But there was still no sign of a new album from Bowie until nearly the end of the year. Bowie booked studio time in December for his first recording session for a new album in almost three years; Tony Visconti was told to keep the month free. Bowie was about to relaunch his pop career after a very long gap, a gap which had seen planet pop fill up with little David Bowies. In December 1982, his management company in New York announced that Bowie would be touring for the first time in five years in 1983. Nobody quite anticipated what was to happen next, though – least of all David Bowie himself.

Part III

1982–2005

10. DAVID BOWIE: SUPERSTAR, 1982–1987

'Who on earth do you think you are?
A superstar? Well, all right you are!'

(JOHN LENNON, 'INSTANT KARMA', 1970)

It was hardly surprising Bowie had so little to offer in the 80s – he'd
already lived through them.

WRITER BEN THOMPSON, THE *INDEPENDENT*, 1996

In the 1980s, simply being a pop star was no longer enough. Superstars now were expected to colonise film and video, to exploit their back catalogues and to be packaged as stars across a whole variety of different media. For the very first time perhaps, it was now also possible for superstars to become obscenely rich in the process. The era of the stadium tour was upon us. Pop music no longer spoke only to young people; the real catches were the twenty, thirty or even forty-somethings – those with the money. Rather than setting himself up as a new kind of rock superstar as in the 70s, Bowie became the superstar figure he had set out to replace. He accepted and became part of corporate rock.

Bowie was ideal for this new multimedia, multi-cash-in era. The 1980s had finally caught up with what Bowie had been doing since around 1968 – mixing media. Instead of carrying it out with panache and artistry, though, many of the 1980s superstars proceeded with deadening predictability. They were playing an old tune, and it was a song Bowie had been whistling loud and clear for a decade. With horrible irony Bowie allowed himself to be packaged blandly as this new star by big corporate rock. Instead of doing the packaging himself, he became more acted upon, more produced, more cramped by notions of industry product. He was that video star, that film star, that greatest hits machine, that man in the Pepsi ad or the Levi jeans. With the chance of becoming a multimillionaire many times over in the offing, Bowie decided it was time that his commercial standing matched his critical kudos. Bowie became branded.

In terms of the sales pitch, Bowie became one of the first stars to be sold like a brand name. His videos became slicker and less confrontational, his look became more 'parent-friendly', his choice of movies to act in became increasingly more populist, and his music instantly accessible. In 1986, with the *Absolute Beginners* film, there was a title song sung by Bowie, a pop video which intercut movie images with video footage, a range of official merchandise (including the ubiquitous T-shirt), press exposure, a documentary about the making of the film, the media hype surrounding the premiere of the film and finally, if anyone was still interested, the film itself. Like Prince, Michael Jackson and Madonna later in the decade, Bowie was a trans-generic brand name who could be used in a variety of media and sold to the public because he happened to be Bowie.

Bowie was a guarantor of a certain type of stardom. By the mid-80s he was the epitome of an almost Hollywood cool and mildly left-field artiness. Adrian Belew called him a 'rock'n'roll Cary Grant'. He became less an artist and more a transferable image. The only problem with selling oneself as a brand is that the product has to be consistently good, or else the brand becomes tainted.

Bowie's 'missing time experience' between 1981 and 1982 was a very smart career move, and a rather novel strategy in the rock world at the time. Seldom did rock stars, even hugely famous ones, stay away from the limelight so long, but it was a move others would subsequently adopt. One of the reasons behind it is to stockpile demand. Bowie had left the pop scene in 1980 when his commercial stock in the UK was at its highest since the Ziggy Stardust days. The huge success of the various one-off releases (such as the Queen collaboration) and the existence of so many pop stars making it big by trading off the Bowie legacy, all indicated a groundswell of support. The Bowie fan-market was at its busiest. Bowie Nights continued, Bowie conventions were massively popular and record shops such as Adrian's in Wickford, Essex, became specialists in arcane Bowie vinyl. The Bowie bootleg and trading scene had never been stronger, with almost two decades' worth of material to flog or swap, and a very classy Bowie fanzine, *Starzone*, edited by David Currie and featuring writer Kevin Cann, was flourishing. Bowie books became very big business too, with Omnibus Press' *David Bowie: Black Book* selling around 100,000 copies. In short, the ground was prepared for a huge comeback.

In January 1983, Bowie signed a record deal with EMI-America, who had beaten off Columbia, Geffen and his old record label RCA for his signature. The deal was lucrative. A figure of $17 million has been rumoured ever since (one biographer puts it at as high as $20 million). Bowie had probably already killed off all his MainMan debts by the end of the 1970s and, by 1983, was already a wealthy man, undoubtedly a millionaire, probably a few times over. The EMI-America deal put him into the super-rich category, although still well behind ex-Beatles or multiplatinum acts from the 70s like the Stones, Fleetwood Mac, Rod Stewart, Elton John, Queen or Pink Floyd. Unlike some of these ageing rockers, there was absolutely no indication that Bowie was creatively a spent force; *Scary Monsters* was a renaissance in an already exceptional career. EMI-America paid big because they were getting not only a bona fide superstar in his prime, but also *Let's Dance*, an album sure to set corporate-executive pulses racing on first hearing. It was cool, it was melodic, it was dancey; it was guaranteed to be huge.

Let's Dance has been accused of heralding in Bowie's new era of mainstream pop, but it was the two albums that were to follow, *Tonight* and *Never Let Me Down*, that were the culprits. On release in April 1983, *Let's Dance* was merely regarded as a *Young Americans*-type move into a commercial black sound – just another tactic and the latest product of Bowie's enduring musical fascination. It certainly wasn't regarded as being a sop to mainstream expectations. Its sound was unique. What other record mixed late-70s Chic-style dance music with rock and blues guitar, filtering the result through a contemporary New York dance groove?

Bowie recorded *Let's Dance* in the first three weeks of December 1982 at the Power Station Studios in New York. Visconti was not informed by his friend that he had been dropped from the album, and he was hurt by the manner and timing of Bowie's manoeuvre: 'I would've preferred more notice. It caused a big hole in my schedule – I didn't book any studio time, but I was inquiring about my plane tickets when I found out that my presence wasn't needed.'

With a new record label in the offing and a concerted idea of a new commercial sound in mind, Bowie wanted to start afresh with a new producer. This was the most visible signal that Bowie wanted bridges with the past burned. The fact that Bowie had struck an opportunistic blow and hired another hot producer showed Bowie's radar instinct for the new to be undimmed, but the impersonal manner of breaking the news was regrettable. Ironically, Visconti would be replaced by a producer who literally had his office next door to him: Nile Rodgers, from seminal dance outfit, Chic. 'The interesting thing,' says Rodgers, 'was that Tony was my next-door neighbour in the apartment that I lived in! I was in 28a and I think he was in 28b. We just knew each other in passing. He had an office right next door to my apartment.' In 1982, Nile Rodgers was more commercially successful than David Bowie. His band, Chic, were, globally, one of the biggest-selling bands of the late 70s. What he lacked, however, was credibility amongst white critics; something Bowie had in abundance.

As a member of Chic, Rodgers had laid down some monster grooves. Chic's ultra-cool take on dance music was sumptuous; a glamorous melody of sweet strings, with Nile Rodgers' trademark clipped funky rhythm guitar and Bernard Edwards' toe-tapping bass lines. 'I Want Your Love', 'Le Freak' and, most importantly, 'Good Times' (the song that launched mainstream rap when its bass line was sampled on 'Rapper's Delight' by The Sugar Hill Gang in late 1979) were some of the best pop singles of the late 70s. However, his record as a producer was uneven. His work on Diana Ross' 'Upside Down' was cool, his handling of Debbie Harry's *Koo-Koo* far less so. It was a bit of a gamble for Bowie, but it paid off, big time.

Rodgers and Bowie first met at an after-hours joint called The Continental in New York City during the autumn of 1982. 'It was purely by accident,' says Rodgers. 'He was just sitting there groovin', taking it easy. I had just finished chatting with Billy Idol, who almost vomited on me. I think he had had one too many and vomited and I got out of the way just in time. I happened to notice David in the corner. He was just sitting there being quiet by himself, actually, which I thought was pretty cool. We just sat down and had a very relaxed chat. It was freezing in there, we were off in kind of a loading-bay area – I guess it was considered the VIP area. We just went from one subject to the next. I'm a real fan of music history and I'm always amazed how well versed English pop stars are in music and culture and history. They're real fans of music, whereas with some American pop stars, a lot of their knowledge is somewhat limited. But David and I just went on a roll; we were talking about everyone from Louis Jordan to Henry Mancini. My historical knowledge of Iggy Pop goes way back. It was funny when David started talking about Iggy Pop, it was a joke to me because I thought, I bet I've known him longer than you! We used to be the opening act for The Stooges way back. I remember when Alice Cooper was our opening act. David is a real fan and he was telling me all these stories and I was saying, "Hey man, I know all this shit, I was there!" You have to understand that I've been a big David Bowie fan all my life. In other words, he was the one artist I always wanted to play with in his band. I was a big fan from the first record that I ever heard, which was the *Hunky Dory* record.'

Rodgers was brought in to produce a hit album and in this respect, he was surprised. Bowie told him that he wanted a hit. Bowie was out of contract, and needed a commercial record to get the biggest advance from his next label. For his part, Rodgers expected to make 'Scary Monsters Part 2', an avant-garde pop masterpiece, not an overtly commercial record. 'I stayed at his house and he either played demos or he sang the songs. He did a little performance on a twelve-string acoustic guitar,' recalled Rodgers in 1999:

He was playing 'Let's Dance' to me on a folk guitar! What he had written actually took me by surprise. In the black-music world in America, if you go against the grain, chances are, you will not get on the radio and people won't hear you. I always hear a lot of criticism of black artists saying the lyrics are shallow, they only write about sex, and you say to yourself, there's a reason for it. It's not because there isn't interesting intellectual subject matter for black artists to delve into, it's the fact that you won't get played. I get hip-hop artists now, coming up to me and apologising. They say, 'Mr Rodgers, believe me, we only write this stuff because if we don't curse and say "bitches" and "niggers" we won't get played!' Black artists are held to a different standard artistically than white artists. With Chic, the way I started to write songs was that I had read a Paul Simon interview many, many years before and I went away with this concept. When you write a song, sit down and imagine the radio station that song would appear on, and if it seems like it could fit that rotation, you've written the right record. Now as an artist, you feel that you should write from the heart and the people should accept it, but nothing could be further from the truth for a black artist in America. You have to be very commercial-minded and think of what the market is into now.

Initially, Rodgers was disappointed. Having been given the chance to work with Bowie he thought that finally he could win respect and break free from the sort of stance expected from him as a black artist. But, as soon as Rodgers was clear about his brief – to do what he did best and make hits – his task became easier:

He had a demo of 'China Girl', and my first reaction was, 'God, it's damn good to be white!' You can write an esoteric song with hidden meanings, whereas in black music if you have a song called 'China Girl' it had damn better convey some message about a girl you met in China or something. It has to be a lot more literal. David had given me very specific instructions that he wanted me to do what I do best, to make hits. If I was going to make hits, I could only use the formula I knew. Which was, you call a song 'China Girl', it better sound Asian. You call a song 'Let's Dance', you damn well better make sure people dance to it. The most nervous moment I had in my entire career of making records was when I walked into the room and picked up my guitar and played that opening riff for 'China Girl'. I thought I was putting some bubblegum over some great artistic heavy record. I was terrified. I thought he was going to tell me that I'd blasphemed, that I didn't get the record and that I didn't get him, and that I'd be fired. But it was exactly the opposite. He said it was great! It gave me the freedom to make this great record. To have someone who I still considered one of the true great geniuses of our time hire me to be that communicator, to craft his biggest record, is an incredible honour.

Bowie wanted a warm, upbeat feeling that would complement the new-found humanism of his songs. This meant getting rid of his prime musical ally of recent years, the synthesizer, and, indeed, totally removing the *Scary Monsters* sound. It was, as Bowie commented, 'the epitome of the new wave sound at the time; from bubbling synthesizers to erratic and unconventional guitar playing, it had all those elements that are, by definition, the young way of playing music'.

Many of the songs had been demoed in Switzerland in 1982 with the talented Turkish multi-instrumentalist Erdal Kizilcay. Born in 1950 in Istanbul, Kizilcay had been playing professionally since the age of fourteen and could literally turn his hand to any instrument he touched. He was called into Mountain Studios to work with engineer David Richards and producer Nile Rodgers on demos for the new album. 'I was very good friends with Jaco Pastorius and I loved the way he played the bass,' said Kizilcay in 2005. 'I always tried to play like him, and on the first version I did of "Let's Dance", I was playing a lot of fast and fancy stuff on the bass. David had a little smile on his face, and Nile came to me and said, "Erdal, that's great the way you play, but don't play that shit. I love it, but, it's not your solo album, it's David Bowie's!" So we sat down and we found that great bass lick for "Let's Dance" together, which I played on the demo.'

The *Let's Dance* record itself took only nineteen days to complete. Rodgers was amazed at Bowie's studio craft: 'The last thing David does is toil over vocals. David is much more concerned with the concept and getting the messages right. His commitment to an intellectual concept is fantastic, and I love to see his level of artistry and dedication – it's mind-boggling. And for an artist to come from the black-music scene to work on records like that is an absolute privilege. It's an honour; it's really liberating.' The first song to be recorded was 'Let's Dance' itself:

Bowie got the 'serious' bit of 'serious moonlight' from me, I think. I used to say 'serious' all the time. I would say, 'Man, that shit is serious!' meaning it's happening, it's great – it's a disco expression. In the disco everything is serious. If you take 'Let's Dance', the thing that gave it that depth and perspective was David's interpretation of it. Having the synth bass with the Fender bass, David threw in little elements like that and gave it that edge and excitement that I probably wouldn't have thought of. On a song such as Chic's 'Good Times' the most important part was the breakdown, when the instruments are taken out just leaving the bass, and then the piano, then the Fender Rhodes, then the guitar, then the solo, then the backing singers and finally back to the song. Whenever the band would go to the breakdown the audience would scream. We used the same tactic for the 12-inch version of 'Let's Dance'.

Rodgers and Bowie kept the album short – just eight tracks. They wanted it to sound fantastic, and the longer the album the less likely that the vinyl album would sound good. Much of the record's charm was derived from the ambience of the recording studio itself. 'The Power Station is famous for its great drum sound,' says Rodgers. 'And we had great players too, like Tony Thompson.'

Carlos Alomar was looking forward to playing with Nile Rodgers, a friend and, in a past life, his substitute guitar player at the Apollo Theater back in the early 1970s when they were both jobbing musicians. But, with Rodgers on hand to play guitar, Alomar was the first to feel the full force of Bowie's cost-cutting regime:

I went up to Bowie's office to negotiate the deal, and Bowie had these new people that he has hired. They said, 'Well, we don't want you to be the band leader on this. We just want you to play guitar, and we already have a producer. We're trying to save David money.' I said, 'Look, with all due respect to your newly found situation, I've played with Bowie since 1973 and my increases have been the same every year. Each time he calls me back, I take a moderate increase. And that moderate increase has brought me where I am now. If you don't have the respect to do your homework and see how much I was getting paid before, then I'm not interested.' You see, they were offering me scales. I haven't worked for scales since 1968. Scales meaning $100 an hour, which is the basic rate that you would give any musician that's coming from the musicians' union – minimum payment. I said, 'If I play one note on this record or if I play every note on this record, my price remains the same. If my name appears on that record then I need to get my money.' And they said, 'Oh, no, no.' So I said, 'Well, fine, I don't need this album.'

By offering him a lower rate than normal, it was almost certainly a ruse to get Alomar off the album without actually telling him so. The episode clearly indicated that Bowie's new 'team' would aggressively defend Bowie's 'interests'.

So Visconti and Alomar were not part of the new Bowie musical world-view, at least for the album. Also gone was the rhythm section of George Murray and Dennis Davis. Bowie was wiping the musical slate as clean as he could. He brought in Omar Hakim on drums, who shared duties with Tony Thompson, and Brooklyn-born session musician Carmine Rojas on bass.

The lead guitarist for the project, Stevie Ray Vaughan, was the bizarrest choice. Bowie had seen him perform at the Montreux Jazz Festival the previous spring and had been mightily impressed. But how could it work? Ray Vaughan was a straight-talking, 28-year-old Texan blues guitarist. He was almost completely unknown. His debut album with his band, Double Trouble, hadn't even been released yet. With his warm, bluesy, authentic sound, Ray Vaughan was about as far away from Robert Fripp and Adrian Belew as you could get. However, the choice was simply inspired. Nile Rodgers: 'Stevie was fantastic. I adored him, and he and I became soul mates almost right away. Stevie and I became almost as close as brothers. I even delivered the eulogy at his funeral. That is why I believe David Bowie is an absolute genius because he was able to see the great fusion of styles between my background, his background and Stevie Ray. David had a feeling, a premonition, that this would work, and he had faith in me and my ability to communicate with all these different musicians from different genres.'

Let's Dance is full of fantastic guitar parts (some courtesy of Rodgers himself) which sing on top of the rhythm section – aggressive on 'Cat People', haunting on 'Criminal World', earthy on 'Let's Dance'. Finally, the most noticeable change to Bowie's overall sound was brought about by a big, honking horn section. Tracks such as 'Let's Dance' were collisions of Chic-styled R&B and 30s and 40s big band. It would be that song, the one that called upon all good men and women to 'put on their red shoes and dance the blues', that would change the course of Bowie's career.

Released as a single on 18 March 1983, three weeks before the album, it was a massive international hit. A fabulously catchy single, Bowie was never able to match its instant accessibility again. At the time, 'Let's Dance' was not the obvious single choice for Bowie, as he now admits: 'The truth is, I told Nile, "Why on earth you think that's a single, I have no idea". I had serious doubts – I wanted "China Girl" to be the first single. But he said to me, "No, you're wrong. 'Let's Dance' is the one." And he was absolutely right.'

'Modern Love', the album's opener, is another classic Bowie pop song, with a glorious circular call-and-response structure. 'China Girl' is an ultra-cool reading of the 1977 Iggy Pop track, complete with a driving bass line and cod-oriental guitar figure at the beginning. Bowie also included two further covers – 'Criminal World', an excellent interpretation of a song by The Metros, and a revamped version of 'Cat People (Putting Out Fire)', originally recorded with Giorgio Moroder for the *Cat People* movie soundtrack the year before. Of the five totally new compositions on the album, only 'Ricochet', with its rebounding, ricocheting rhythm and obtuse quasi-religious lyric, carried anything of the gravitas of Bowie's late-1970s recordings.

The album was in the can by Christmas 1982 and, early in 1983, Bowie went to Australia to film videos for the first two singles; the title track, 'Let's Dance', and 'China Girl'. The 'Let's Dance' video is a self-contained world, having nothing at all to do with the song itself, with Bowie for the first time in his career positioning himself as paternal narrator rather than protagonist. It focuses on a young Aborigine couple and includes mundane shots of them visiting an art gallery, having a meal, working in a factory, doing the cleaning for a white family and walking with friends barefoot in the outback. However, these everyday scenes transform alarmingly into surrealism, the Aborigine boy being forced to drag a huge piece of machinery down a busy main road, the girl forced to clean the tarmac with a scrubbing brush and bucket of water. Scenes of Bowie, first singing in an Australian bar (where a middle-aged barfly performs a gooky dance), then playing guitar at the end of the video, move the footage back to the traditional performance-based genre. Throughout, Bowie looks incredibly detached, lyrics delivered to camera as if through a clenched jaw, acting out the song rather than singing it. There's very little in this performance to suggest, despite the rhetoric in the press, that Bowie was being very successful in breathing some warmth into his persona.

The video was also a political allegory – an attempt to articulate the clash of interests between white consumer capitalism and the

Aboriginal traditions it displaced. The video's only reference to the lyric of the song – the red shoes – becomes a potent disruptive symbol. Bowie explains: 'Firstly, they [represent] the sinfulness of the capitalist society – the pair of luxury goods – red leather shoes. Also they're the striving for success out of black music. It was always: "Put on your red shoes, baby." ' The shoes are found by the Aborigines in a shop window, a symbol of conspicuous consumption. They are then worn by a female factory boss, indicating capitalistic domination and the exploitation of labour in general and Aboriginal culture in particular. The shoes are then found by the Aborigine girl in the outback. She puts them on, only for a nuclear blast, symbolic of the twisted and corrupt result of unrestrained capitalism, to finally turn the 'red shoes' from a talisman of power, wealth and opulence into one of ill-fortune and corruption. The shoes are then stamped on by the Aborigines and left, soiled and tattered, in the outback. 'Let's Dance' champions the Aborigine cause and is a visual precursor to the white Australian critique of the same subject by Midnight Oil.

Deborah Holdstein wrote that Bowie also implicates himself in the machinations of consumerism: 'Alternating surreal images of the young man pulling heavy machinery through Sydney traffic, and the young woman trying to scrub clean the city's streets, Bowie undercuts his own stardom, his own capitalism, his own success . . . The final shot is three-part in nature. With Bowie at the center, the Aborigine couple at the left and visions of elegant Sydney on the right, the rock star visually and narratively becomes the "bridge" between the dominant and oppressed cultures, partly with the capitalists, partly with the oppressed. He reveals the multi-layered complexities of keeping one's culture while participating with another, and the essential problem of the Aborigines being able to participate at all in a white dominated world.'

'China Girl' is almost identical thematically, juxtaposing opulent Sydney with the ethnicity of the city's large Chinese community. The video's most startling scene, which depicts Bowie, dressed in top hat and tails, miming the shooting of his China girl (intentionally reminding us of one of the most horrific images from the Vietnam war, the photograph of South Vietnamese army General Loan shooting a prisoner in cold blood in 1968), was pointedly political. All this is a form of what could be termed entryism – the infiltration of the mainstream with unexpected and pointed material, in the same way that the song, with its sing-along chorus and clichéd oriental flourish, contains some of Bowie and Iggy's most contentious material. It's hard to tell whether the lines 'Visions of swastikas in my head/Plans for everyone/It's in the white of my eyes' represent a detached retelling of white imperialism or the emotional wreckage of Bowie's mid-70s Nazi flirtation. Probably both.

Most importantly, however, was that both videos were totally absorbing and activated key archetypes in the pop world. 'Let's Dance', with its little narrative surrounding the young Aborigine couple, targeted 'youth', and 'China Girl', with it's bare-bummed (and later partially censored) beach lovemaking scene (a homage to the film *From Here to Eternity*), was sufficiently sexually provocative to guarantee heavy rotation on MTV. By 1983, Bowie had emerged as one of the most important video artists of the day and, in a field not yet saturated by competition, his videos were on constant show throughout the early 1980s.

On 17 March, Bowie held the most famous press conference of his career at Claridges in London, where he announced details of his new label, EMI-America, his new album, *Let's Dance*, and his new tour, Serious Moonlight. Bowie walked into the press conference immaculately besuited, his hair washed blond after six months in warm climes, his preternatural white colour of the 70s transformed by a moderate suntan. He walked in to a round of applause from the champagne-sipping media, and, finding the chair too low for the microphone position, got his leg over and sat on the table. Even such a simple piece of expediency as this struck as grandly theatrical and totally stage-managed, and rather than looking normalised, he looked weird – like a Bowie clone. The new corporate skin made Bowie look businesslike and harsh. For the first time, he looked aristocratic, a member of the jet set. It was a difficult image for his fans to even like, let alone want to copy.

Bowie was entering what was probably the period of the most contrived imaging his career had ever seen. He was now the concerned white liberal; the anxious father; the suavely manicured, old-fashioned superstar; the song-and-dance man and the svelte son-of-Sinatra. 1983 saw a carefully managed reinterpretation of what 'David Bowie' was about. Bowie now looked almost like a copy of himself, as if he'd allowed himself to enter into someone else's vision of what a sensible, mature David Bowie should look like. Behind the suntan and smiles, he looked as frozen and as plastic as ever before. The new mask of normality represented the achievement of the most extreme artifice of his career.

In the next few days, however, his career was to scale new heights. The 'Let's Dance' video was given its first UK airing on the seminal rock show *The Tube* the following Friday, along with an interview with Jools Holland. By the time the programme gave news of shows at Wembley Arena and the Birmingham NEC, they had already been sold out. The thousands upon thousands of unlucky applicants were to be catered for by three huge open-air shows later in the summer at the 65,000-capacity Milton Keynes Bowl, although even these couldn't accommodate everybody. By the following Tuesday, 'Let's Dance' was already at Number 5 in the UK charts, and a fortnight later it was Number 1. Two weeks after that, the new album, featuring Bowie the shadow-boxer set against the New York skyline, was released. It debuted at Number 1. It was also the first new Bowie album to be issued on that functional though depressingly unadventurous format, the compact disc. The 'Let's Dance' single was played endlessly on UK radio and the following month it had reached Number 1 in .the US too, and was already a big hit in Europe.

On cue, *Ziggy Stardust*, *Hunky Dory*, *Aladdin Sane*, *Low*, "*Heroes*", *Diamond Dogs*, *The Man Who Sold The World*, *Space Oddity* and *Pin Ups* all started to chart again (indeed, the first two on the list had often inhabited the lower reaches of the chart in the early 1980s). At one point in the July of 1983, Bowie had a staggering ten albums in the UK Top 100, a figure surpassed only by Elvis Presley in the wake of his death six years earlier. In total, Bowie's albums spent an amazing 198 weeks on the UK charts in 1983. His fans had never seen anything like it. Many of them look back on the Serious Moonlight period with the fondest of memories. It was the time when, finally, they felt that their judgement had been vindicated; the year Bowie became a global superstar. One fan told me: 'Bowie's commercial success of 1983 and *Let's Dance* seems now to have heralded the end for many of his fans. But for me it was pure ecstasy – I was so proud to have been into David Bowie before the album, and the opportunity to see him live in Milton Keynes was the highlight of my life to date.'

But there were dissenting voices and disappointed fans. One American female fan later put it like this: 'I still find it amazing that many fans began their interest in David in 1983. Personally, after hearing *Let's Dance*, I actually boycotted the Bowie business for a short while (including the Serious Moonlight tour). I had really felt that David being "pop" was outrageous ... more so than any other persona he had assumed. Today I can understand why an artist needs to produce a more "public-pleasing" album in order to pursue less popular endeavours, but in 1983 I just couldn't believe that David would "sell out" to such trash.' Writer and journalist Jon Savage put his disappointment like this: 'The problem with the new mature Bowie is that everybody liked the old, shrill, coked-out artificial one. Once the mask was stripped to normalcy, there wasn't a great deal left.'

In a series of press interviews throughout the first half of 1983, Bowie gave a number of reasons for this normalcy. He was entering a new age of responsibility, an era in which he took his life more earnestly. His marriage to Angie had ended in divorce three years earlier. His twelve-year-old son, not his music, was now his prime concern in life. At 36, he was also at a tricky age – neither terribly young nor yet quite middle-aged. Despite public protestations that he felt comfortable in his skin, he was obviously bothered. The angst and Messianic sense of destiny were attitudes from the past. In interviews, he sounded lacking in motivation and confused, unsure of how he fitted in with a rock world still overwhelmingly the preserve of youth. 'I don't really have the urge to continue as a songwriter and performer in terms of experimentation – at this moment,' he told Chris Bohn in an *NME* interview. 'I feel that at the moment I'm of an age – and age has an awful lot to do with it – I'm just starting to enjoy growing up. I'm enjoying being my age, 36, and what comes with it in terms of the body ... I don't think I would want to continue performing any more if I didn't think I could do something hopeful and helpful with my music, both for myself and for my audience.'

Let's Dance's one lame moment comes on the slightly flimsy 'Without You', on which Bowie is very uncomfortable dealing in that currency of pop, heterosexual love, which dominated the genre and to which he had traditionally given a wide berth. It was, unfortunately, something of a pointer to his future direction. As a lyricist, Bowie found it difficult to make his new humanistic concerns as compelling as the tales of emotional bankruptcy described in the previous decade. Long-time Bowie-watcher and journalist Michael Watts summed up the album like this: 'His new album seems to me to be a step sideways. He's not doing anything particularly new and I suspect for the first time ever his fans are up there with him and he's not ahead of the game. He seems to have become something rather old-fashioned, which is to say, a superstar.'

During this early to mid-80s period, Bowie tried, either consciously or unconsciously, to feed misinformation to his fans via the press. Crucially, he reheterosexualised himself. He told *Rolling Stone*'s Kurt Loder in May 1983 that saying 'I was bisexual' was 'the biggest mistake I ever made'. In July the same year, he told *Time*'s Jay Cocks that his admission of bisexuality was a 'major miscalculation'. As Marjorie Garber points out in her major study, *Vice Versa: Bisexuality and the Eroticism of Everyday life*, Jagger at this time was also trying to 'in' himself, telling reporters that he had never really taken drugs and that rumours about his bisexual past were just that – rumours. Going the other way at this time were Elton John, Boy George and record boss David Geffen, who were now 'repudiating bisexuality in favour of coming out as gay'. But while it is probably true that Bowie was never gay, nor even consistently actively bisexual, it is also true that he did, from time to time, experiment, even if only out of a sense of curiosity and a genuine allegiance with the 'transgressional'. Was admitting his bisexuality really the biggest mistake he ever made? Today, Bowie takes a far more measured view of what it all meant. 'I don't think it was a mistake in Europe, but it was a lot tougher in America. I had no problem people knowing I was bisexual. But I had no inclination to hold any banners or to be a representative of any group of people. I knew what I wanted to be, which was a songwriter and performer, and I felt that [bisexuality] became my headline over here for so long. America is a very puritanical place, and I think it stood in the way of so much I wanted to do.'

Bowie now claimed in interviews that his period of excesses was well and truly in the past and that he was free of drugs. When, of course, he wasn't. According to band leader Alomar, by the early 1980s Bowie's coke use was infrequent but he was still using it. But Bowie was using his 'straightness' to sell his records, and at the same time warding people off the horrors of hard drugs. Between around 1983 and 1993, virtually every interview he gave would touch on his LA drug-crazed paranoia, and how unhappy his life had been, and how very different it all was today. He'd pulled through. Given that he was still using coke for at least the early part of this time, it was a strange act to have to pull off. But again, it made good copy.

This same year also witnessed the birth of another Bowie myth: in the 1970s Bowie was nothing more than a cult artist. Now, a cult artist would be somebody like Nick Drake, Gram Parsons, Lou Reed or Iggy Pop. Iggy never had a hit single in the US or the UK in the 1960s or 1970s; Lou Reed had just one. They seldom progressed beyond medium to small-venue shows on their tours. They were a relatively acquired taste, one for the aficionado.

Bowie was something rather different. He was a cult, of course, and his fans were incredibly partisan. It is true that at various stages during his career in the 70s and early 80s his records had been bought by a rump of hard-core fans only, but, even so, albums such as *Low* and *"Heroes"* still made the UK Top 3. By 1983 he had had three Number 1s, eight other Top 5 hits, and four Number 1 albums. Nevertheless, Bowie presumably tried to justify the large sums of money he was making out of *Let's Dance* and the world tour by constructing a mythic past of relatively small-scale financial rewards. Bowie called the Serious Moonlight tour his 'pension plan' in private, but in actual fact it made him one of the richest pop stars in the world. By claiming that he had been broke in the past, he was also hinting that he really deserved to cash in his chips in 1983.

Another myth put around by Bowie later in the 1980s to explain the sudden downturn in his creativity was that, quite unexpectedly, he had a new mainstream audience that he had to 'write for' and appease with more accessible fodder. But this overlooked the fact that he played Madison Square Garden back in 1974, Wembley Empire Pool in 1976, and huge outdoor concerts on the 1978 tour. And what were 'Starman' or a 'Rebel Rebel', if not wonderful mainstream pop records? The Serious Moonlight tour obviously did push Bowie's marketability up a level or two, but the step up was not the quantum leap Bowie later talked about. The chief problem was not just that Bowie now had a bigger fan base but that, quite simply, he wanted to make more mainstream pop.

Bowie loved the adulation and respect he gained in 1983. He was photographed willingly with Dylan, Jagger and Tina Turner in the mid-80s, and was invited by Madame Tussaud's to model for his waxwork likeness. His 'conversion' to mainstream pop star is a myth because for a start, he had always been one, playing the very valuable role of linking that mainstream with obtuse, non-mainstream cultural bric-a-brac. For most of the 1980s, Bowie simply was neither able, nor even interested in, refreshing the mainstream with anything much worthwhile from the margins. The difference was that in the 1980s it appeared that all he wanted to be was a star, whereas, in the 1970s, stardom had been the net result of a creative act designed to please himself, not others.

In addition to the mythic history he was feeding the press, Bowie had really changed. Rehearsals began in the spring of 1983 for the upcoming Serious Moonlight tour. Carlos Alomar was back as band leader and was well pleased: 'Well, not only did I get the money that I was supposed to get for the tour, but I also charged them for the album, which I did not do, and I got paid for that too! I told him myself, "You have two of us who are the same style guitar player – you're not going to lose out on anything by having Nile Rodgers on the album." I loved the album and I love Nile's treatment of the album. Nile promised him a hit and, as always, Nile delivers. But of course, David hated the fact that he had to have a hit like that and that whole period, but that's another story.'

The rest of the personnel were largely as on the *Let's Dance* sessions. However, the assertive Stevie Ray Vaughan and the equally single-minded Bowie were soon to be at loggerheads. Alomar recalls:

Bowie didn't have a temper at all, really. He was kind of wimpy, in fact, until we were doing *Let's Dance*. He brought on Stevie Ray Vaughan, who had a girlfriend or wife who was extremely forward and who was, let's say, extremely dedicated to Stevie Ray Vaughan. At one point we were doing our rehearsal and she was constantly trying to get Stevie Ray Vaughan's attention to talk to him about some nonsense. At this point David stopped the rehearsal and really bawled her out. You've got to understand that this is somebody who beforehand would take it, and take it, and take it. Then suddenly, in 1983, David was first of all taking one of those punching bags on the road, hanging out with the bodyguards and doing all these exercises in the morning to improve his stamina. I guess he was tired of being called a 98 lb weakling, which I was constantly calling him because his body had such a small frame. And he came back on this tour like, I mean, totally aggressive, which I thought was fabulous. He was more in control over all of what he was doing and that leaked out into his personal stuff.

Just a matter of days before the European tour was scheduled to open in Brussels on 29 May, Ray Vaughan was finally fired. There appear to have been a number of reasons for this. Firstly, Ray Vaughan allegedly found Bowie's 'no drinks, no drugs' dictate to be supremely hypocritical and told him so. Ray Vaughan almost certainly did have a substance abuse problem and finally kicked it a few years later. With Bowie resolved to clean up his act, Ray Vaughan's presence was intimidating. There was also, or so it was rumoured, a dispute over his fee. For his part, Bowie found Vaughan's suggestion that his band, Double Trouble, should act as Bowie's support band impractical. Bowie, however, claims that money matters were not at the heart of the dispute: 'He was rehearsing with me for about two months before going out on the road and unfortunately he had a shyster of a manager at the time so for one reason or another I decided it wasn't going to work out. Fortunately, though, we got to know each other again just before he died. Wonderful guy, wonderful player.' With supreme irony, the cavalry arrived just in time in the shape of Earl Slick, who had himself been replaced at the last moment by Stacey Haydon for a Bowie tour seven years earlier. 'I could have been the only guy around who could have done it. That's what I think, in all honesty. I knew the material, he knew I could pick it up. He also knew that once I was there I always did my shows and did them great,' Slick points out.

Slick promptly learned the whole Bowie set in 72 hours and was ready and rocking as the tour kicked into gear with dates in Brussels, Frankfurt, Munich, Lyons and Frejus. Like Bowie, he had grown up and significantly cleaned up his act. 'David on that tour was way more together,' says Slick. 'We had our moments, here and there, over the eight or nine months that we were out, but no, he was very well together. We had a great time. We got together sometime during the first week of the tour and kind of cleared the air about all the stuff that had happened in 1976. We both realised that it had been a very confusing period, and we talked about it candidly because we had to clear the air at the beginning of the tour. I think we went out for coffee in Germany during the first week of the tour. I remember sitting in an outside café and talking about all this stuff and coming out of it feeling good. I thoroughly enjoyed the 1983 tour. It was a lot of fun. We were taken care of as far as accommodation and travel were concerned. Bowie was a lot more accessible and a much nicer bloke. It was much more of a pleasure to be there. I had undergone the same type of changes as Bowie himself. I loved that tour. It was great, and I have a lot of fond memories of it.'

With a PA announcement of, 'Ladies and gentleman, on stage for the first time in five years – David Bowie and his band!', Bowie was back as a gigging rocker, on what was, to all intents and purposes, a greatest hits tour. There was 'The Jean Genie', "Heroes" (prefaced by a neat 'lavender blue, dilly-dilly, lavender green, I will be king, dilly-dilly, you will be queen' opening intro), 'Golden Years', 'Fashion' (which segued into the current biggie, 'Let's Dance'), 'Life On Mars?', 'Sorrow', 'China Girl', 'Rebel Rebel', 'Ashes To Ashes', 'Space Oddity', 'Fame' and 'Modern Love', the show-closer and future hit single. The band was warm and friendly, powered by bona fide rock guitarist, Slick. It was a relatively mainstream pop-rock sound, professional and serviceable, but with none of the quirks of the previous mid-to-late 1970s shows and with a horn section which gave songs such as the expressionistic 'Station To Station' an incongruous swing.

'The Serious Moonlight tour was my favourite musically,' says Alomar, 'because it was the first tour where we did all of the hits. And I was able to update all the material with horns and to work with Lenny Pickett. We did all these fabulous horn arrangements so that every song sounded as if it had just been recorded. David had great singers with the Simms brothers – he had a great band and it was all Bowie.' Drummer Tony Thompson, who had powered many a classic Chic track, was another integral part of the new Bowie sound. 'The strongest aspect had to be his power,' said Carlos Alomar, paying tribute to the drummer who sadly succumbed to cancer in 2003 aged just 48. 'He was one of the loudest-hitting drummers I have ever had the fortune to work with. Unlike Dennis Davis (who Tony knew very well and respected), who danced with his hi-hat, Tony was a power drummer. To that end, nicknames like "batter-head", "beater" and "pounder" would often be heard.'

Bowie took the stage as a cosmic cabaret singer, strolling through his back catalogue like a thirty-something Sinatra.

Exuding a faintly feminised, glitzy cool and dressed in a baggy suit, he was confidently tanned, his hair dyed a peroxide blond and backcombed into a lacquered frenzy. Bowie had reinvented himself as the song-and-dance man his 1960s manager Ken Pitt had always wanted him to be. Far from being stripped down to normality, Bowie was playing at being real. His look was as grandly artificial as any in the 1970s. On stage his actions became a parody of traditional showbiz performance, as Patricia MacKay wrote: 'On stage throughout the Serious Moonlight concert tour he uses every gimmick ... Carefully timing the removal of his jacket. Selecting the right moment to casually roll up the sleeves of his shirt. Nonchalantly loosening his tie. In earlier rock eras, these moves might have been in the heat of the moment. But not now. Not for Bowie. He's in control.'

An enormous, double-jointed hand, a parody of the *ET* motif, was fixed on one side of the stage, pointing blankly at the 'serious' moon on the other, which ruptured during the concert's dénouement, showering the audience with tiny helium-filled stars. For 'Cracked Actor', Bowie reused the skull-and-cloak routine from 1974's Diamond Dogs Revue, which only the US had seen. It evoked a mild air of transgression to see Bowie French-kiss a skull on stage in front of 60,000 fans in T-shirts. The whole stage show was a mix of fairground, surrealism, space age, cabaret and the exotic. It dealt in big, bold theatrical flourishes and, very importantly, it was filmed and simultaneously broadcast via Diamond Vision flanking the stage.

On 30 May Bowie played to a quarter of a million people at the US festival, San Bernardino, in Glen Helen Park in North Carolina. He reportedly received a fee of $1.5 million, then the biggest pay cheque ever for a pop singer. In stark contrast was the comparatively intimate charity gig to support his home town's Brixton Neighbourhood Community Association at the Hammersmith Odeon, almost ten years to the day since he had retired Ziggy. It raised £90,000. Next up were the three giant open-air concerts at the Milton Keynes Bowl in the blistering heat of a surprisingly hot English summer. Everywhere across the 65,000-capacity amphitheatre-like venue were fans in jeans and Bowie T-shirts – grey ones with the new Bowie logo embossed in pink, or black ones with the *Let's Dance* album figurine standing proud. It was a relatively normalised audience, the Bowie clones few and far between. Bowie remarked years later in the late 1990s that when he took the stage and looked at the faces of his new fans he often wondered how many of them had a Velvet Underground album in their record collection.

In Toronto, Bowie even hooked up again with a certain Mick Ronson. Shimmying through a rendition of the Spiders-era classic 'The Jean Genie', it was the first time they had played together on stage for ten years.

The tour was brilliantly documented by official photographer Denis O'Regan in his photojournalistic *Serious Moonlight* book published the following year; there are shots of Bowie hanging out with Keef, Tina, Jacko, Le Bon, David Hemmings and other 'A'-list celebrities, including top tennis star John McEnroe. Having always fancied himself as a bit of an axeman, McEnroe used to practise lead guitar. One evening, in what must have been one of those surreal 'you cannot be serious' moments, McEnroe met his match. He told Eamon Dunphy: 'Although I didn't know it at the time, I was staying in the same hotel as David Bowie. I was in my room strumming a Bowie tune on my guitar when a knock came at my door. It was one of Mr David Bowie's people inviting me to have a drink with the star. I was delighted and asked, should I bring my guitar? The swift reply was: you are invited but it would be best if you left your guitar in your room!'

In contrast to the 1978 tour, when Bowie appeared on occasion under pressure and tense, the vibe in the 1983 band was good. Cheekily, but not without some humour, they began nicknaming David 'his ladyship'. (Later in the 1980s, the British music press would pick up on this and christen him 'The Dame'.) Alomar and bassist Carmine Rojas became inseparable. It was at their quarters that the after-show parties would take place and where, good-naturedly, Bowie would join them to wind down after the shows. This did not please Bowie's personal assistant, Coco, and the result was a showdown between band leader and PA, the two most important cogs in the touring wheel. 'Well, I always liked Coco. Coco never always liked me!' says Alomar. He continues:

First of all, I like everyone and I have to accept everyone for who they are, which is part of my Buddhist training. Coco was definitely a force to be reckoned with, make no doubt about it. But apparently she loved David very much and she was very dedicated to him and so I could never fault her for that. She would forsake her own needs to please David, and that was one thing I worried about with Coco. What happens when you're not working with David? Where's the real Coco in all of this? When she spent some time with me at my house with my wife and family, I found her to be one of the most endearing and loving people that I have ever seen. Yet, when she came back on the road, that mask came back on. We both loved David, and that would never do, because David would have to choose between us in one type of situation or another. One time she slapped me right in the face and everyone said, 'You should have knocked her out. David wouldn't have said anything if you'd have kicked her ass.' When I saw the venom that everybody else felt towards her, it was like, Well, now I'm really not going to do anything about it because that was wrong. I was the only one who could talk back to Coco: she could have everybody else fired but I couldn't be fired and that was extremely frustrating for her.

Carmine Rojas and me were the Latino brothers. I was the older brother; he was the younger brother. We would have all the parties in our suite, where we would have adjoining rooms. We would open the door and that was where the party would be. Because I'm married I never allow myself to be one on one with any female, because that's dangerous, but we could always throw parties. The more people, the better, so there'd be no chance of anything happening. During that time, David would knock, knock, knock on the door, so we would let him in, and he would party with us. Sometimes he would do a little cocaine, and Coco didn't like that. She would say, 'You guys are a bad influence on him because I know he's doing cocaine with you.' And he was. A little bit here and there. But I said, 'Look, you can't tell me about that – you've got to tell David about that! If he knocks on my door, I'm not going to say, "No, Coco said not to let you in." Are you crazy? That's his business. You need to talk to the man.' So we had a true reason to be arguing in certain respects. I respect the fact that she was looking after his best interests.

She was the force behind every tour. David would never tell you anything bad, but if he ever said anything in intimacy to her, she would let you know what he said. It came from her, so it was true. I was the band leader; I was the one who was supposed to make sure that everyone was happy. If anybody had a problem they came to me and I would resolve the problem. If it had to do with Coco, I would put her in her place as well. Anything that would keep my band members happy I would do, to make sure that they would be on that stage in shape to do the show. I was the only one who was able to talk back to her. She hated my fuckin' guts! I had a different agenda than her. She wanted to protect David and wanted to do everything she could for David and I could never hold that against her. But after that row, when she slapped me, I thought, well, that's the end of my relationship with Bowie. Surprisingly, I was asked back and she was as sweet as she could be, so obviously David had said, 'Well, he's coming back and you just behave!'

To the outsider, Bowie seemed to be becoming somewhat overprotected. DJ John Peel, whose *In Concert* series had kept Bowie in the public domain during the interregnum between 'Space Oddity' and 'Starman', remembers his last 'meeting' with Bowie. 'I was quite touched that he turned up on my *This Is Your Life*. He was perfectly amiable. Because it was on film I didn't have the opportunity to say to him, "That's all very well, David, but the last time I saw you and tried to speak to you, it was during the time when you were going round surrounded by black American karate experts." I went over and said, "Hello, David, how's it going," or something terrific like that, and this bloke interposes and says, "Hey, motherfucker, where do you think you're going?" I said, "I was just going to have a word with David," and he said, "My ass you're gonna have a word with David!" I do think that it's possible to be famous and to do good work and still retain some basic human traits. I've seen the opposite happen so many times to so many people. They just lose all grasp on reality. I mean, you don't need, frankly, to go everywhere with karate experts. I can see that sometimes life can be complicated but it's only because you're maintaining your status and letting people know you're important. You become like that because you want to be like that. You can function in a perfectly satisfactory way and still go on the bus and still go to the pub.'

In 1983, Bowie also gave the impression that he was as likely to become a movie star as he was to continue in rock. In the Tony Scott-directed film, *The Hunger*, Bowie appeared, quite fittingly, as a vampire, alongside Susan Sarandon. Taken as a piece of comedy acting, *The Hunger* makes for entertaining viewing, although it is not Bowie himself who is the star of the show, but rather the make-up designer, who aged the 35-year-old actor by a couple of hundred years over the 72-hour period covered by the film. By the time of his demise, Bowie looks amazingly unwell and is bald as a coot, with huge shards of skin sagging round his boots. The film was only a moderate box-office success.

In the second half of 1982 Bowie had decamped to the Cook Islands, Auckland and Tokyo to take the lead role of POW Jack Celliers in Nagisa Oshima's *Merry Christmas, Mr Lawrence*, a film based on the short story 'A Bar Of Shadow' from Laurens Van der Post's *The Seed and the Sower* collection. The film dealt with the relationship between a British prisoner of war (Celliers) and a guard, played by pop star Ryuichi Sakamoto, the driving force behind electronic pioneers The Yellow Magic Orchestra. He also provided the really excellent soundtrack for the film (the eerie title song, 'Forbidden Colours', by Sakamoto and David Sylvian, was a UK Top 20 hit in 1983). The film's main message is that, despite the cruelty of Japanese martial codes, the supposedly enlightened Western ideas about fair play and honourable conduct in war ultimately alter nothing. In the end, there is always killing, cruelty and barbaric acts, victors and vanquished, glory and ignominy.

Merry Christmas, Mr Lawrence is predominantly about cruelty, violence and representations of honourable behaviour. The violence contained in the film (which at times threatens to swamp the narrative) is peculiarly stylised, as is much of the acting. After being tortured by his Japanese masters, Bowie, as Celliers, moves with an affected limp, as if miming pain and representing feeling rather than trying to create the illusion of pain itself. The film's subtext is the idea of love (in this instance, homosexual love) transcending cultures. The homosexual attraction between prisoner and guard is understated throughout, resulting in the climax in which Bowie embraces Sakamoto and plants a kiss on each cheek as one of his co-prisoners awaits execution. The scene is perfectly played and beautifully shot in slow motion, and is Bowie's best moment on film to date.

Why was Bowie turning to film in the early 1980s? At 36, and with as many albums in the can as The Beatles had produced, Bowie instinctively knew that his career in music was, if not winding down, then probably entering an antique phase. There was absolutely no reason to think that a career in pop could be sustained into middle age with any certainty. This was an era before ossified Stones and deaf Who members showed that it could be done with a little swagger. Film, on the other hand, was a credible medium for a middle-aged man and was also potentially very lucrative. It was a logical next step for Bowie. The problem was that Bowie's enthusiasm for the medium, purely as an actor, was always in limited supply. The hanging around, the endless make-up, the chitchat between scenes bored him rigid. By the end of the 1980s, he would have largely moved out of film, and back into music.

Bowie won praise for a good tour and a very fine album. Rock journalist Mat Snow doubts that the Serious Moonlight era really damaged Bowie in any significant way: 'It hadn't really pissed off the hard-core. They'd moaned that it was a bit commercial, but ultimately people were pretty pleased for him because it was a good selection of songs. Even the hair and the suits – it was a bit school of David Byrne and it was a bit odd to see him imitating one of his imitators, but even so, you didn't feel that this was any real rot setting in. With regard to the Serious Moonlight tour, years of rock journalism have shown me that when people make these commercial moves – huge tours or reunions or whatever – there is generally a divorce settlement or tax bill behind it.'

In terms of Bowie's future career, perhaps the most significant event of 1983 was the souring of relations with his long-standing friend and producer, Tony Visconti. Although dropped from the album, Visconti was drafted in by Bowie to sort out the sound on some of the UK gigs. Bowie was very pleased with the results and asked him to do the whole tour. Visconti declined. 'I was about to go on vacation and he wanted me to drop everything and mix his live show for the rest of the tour,' says Visconti. 'As I was separated from my wife, this vacation with my kids was far too important to do that!'

Bowie would not speak to Visconti for fifteen years. Later Bowie claims that Visconti had been rather too liberal with his comments about the former's relationship with his son Joe. Always ultra-protective and mindful of the dangers surrounding the offspring of celebrities (kidnapping being an unlikely, though not fanciful, possibility), Bowie studiedly kept Joe's contact with the media to an almost nonexistent level in his teenage years. The real root of the problem between Visconti and Bowie appears to be a cordial and excellent interview Visconti gave in early 1984 to David Currie, editor of the Bowie magazine *Starzone*. Visconti spoke mostly about recording with Bowie and hardly at all about Bowie's personal and domestic life, but he did make some comments about the Bowie father-and-son relationship. Visconti also agreed to be interviewed for a 1986 book, *Alias David Bowie*, the first Bowie biography to reveal the true extent of the history of mental illness on the distaff side of the family. Bowie took great exception to these interviews, so Visconti became Bowie's ex-producer, although he had yet to co-produce a dud studio album with him. There would be plenty of dud moments to make up for it in his absence.

The next release should have been a live album of the 1983 tour, as a companion piece to the two-part release of the *Serious Moonlight Live* videos in the spring and autumn of 1984. It got as far as the mixing stage, with Bob Clearmountain on knob-twiddling duty. Scheduled for release in 1984, it would have bought Bowie time to take stock and build up a body of new work for his next album. Touring always left Bowie devoid of new ideas, and he admits to finding it hard to actually write on the road. But, almost certainly down to record company pressure, Bowie was forced back into the studio the following spring in a totally unprepared state. The result – the album which was to become *Tonight* – was the nearest thing Bowie had come to an artistic disaster.

For some inexplicable reason, Nile Rodgers, who had shown true class for *Let's Dance*, was not asked to produce the follow-up. He was perplexed:

> Nothing is more guarded in the music business than an artist's image. David Bowie was on the cover of *Time* magazine on the strength of *Let's Dance*. You only get on the cover of *Time* either because you're infamous, or really successful in a positive way. And this was really successful in a positive way that had gone way beyond what he had achieved in the past. Before, he had the notoriety, he had the name, but he didn't have the big gigantic success to go with it.
>
> Here's what it looked like to me: in the early 80s I was a very prominent producer and I came from a band that was popular.

Not only had I had a hit with David Bowie, but I had my own career before I met Bowie, and my records were bigger than his. There's no one on Warner Bros or Atlantic or Elektra that had a bigger single than Chic. Journalists would start asking David questions like 'How much did Nile have to do with this?' and this is very difficult for any artist, especially someone of David's stature. I used to see the interviews, like the big one in *Rolling Stone*. I don't know if my name is in there, but if it is, it's mentioned once. All of the praise is going to Iggy, or Robert Fripp, and I'm thinking, Hey, if you're on the cover of *Time* magazine, it's not because of that shit, it's because of *Let's Dance*! It seemed to be a conscious effort to distance himself from me. Now, in the 90s, when you hear him talk about it, he's giving me credit and then almost saying, "Wow, I shouldn't have done that. That was basically a Nile Rodgers album with me participating." But nothing could be further from the truth. There's no way I could do a record like that without David. I wouldn't even attempt it. But, at the time, had he given me more credit, it would have opened doors for me. I would have loved to have crossed over and produced more rock acts like U2 or Sting or whatever.

In contrast to his experimental methods in the 1970s, Bowie was now demoing tracks at home and finishing them off in the studio. This was a relatively new way of working (one which he hadn't used much since the Ziggy Stardust days) and it turned Bowie into a more regular writer and performer. The *Let's Dance* engineer, Bob Clearmountain, was asked to work on the follow-up but couldn't, and suggested British producer, Hugh Padgham, who had already worked on successful albums by Genesis, Peter Gabriel, XTC and The Police. Padgham suggested a studio where he had recorded with The Police – Le Studio, in Morin Heights, Canada, about 100 miles north of Montreal.

Recording began in May 1984, less than five months after the end of the Serious Moonlight tour. Bowie, his hair returned to its natural mousey colour, now sported a mildly comical moustache for the duration of recording. At the suggestion of his London publicist, Bernard Doherty, Bowie had signed up for producing duties the relatively unknown Derek Bramble, who had played bass with British disco group Heatwave and who had more recently been working with soul singer David Grant, formerly of

Linx and today better known as a singing instructer on UK TV's *Fame Academy*. David Bowie's successful version of Iggy Pop's 'Don't Look Down' as a reggae song, together with the unsuccessful saccharine reggae-lite of the title track, hinted at a coherence the album lacked. Bramble 'made the album's reggae tunes possible', said Bowie. 'Where Derek can succeed is that he will leave a lot of spaces. He's not scared not to play a note.'

Hugh Padgham had produced The Police's brand of white reggae, so the opportunity was there for Bowie's 'plastic reggae' album. Bowie also had Alomar on the session as band leader and musical know-it-all, and Omar Hakim, who had played with Weather Report. The standard of musicianship and technical know-how was first class. That was the problem. It was a very un-Bowie-like team of people in a way; they were brilliant technical musicians, but in essence nothing more than 'hired hands'.

From the very outset, although the sessions went well enough, it was obvious that there was something amiss. Hugh Padgham:

At that time I had been producing, or co-producing, and had done big records for The Police, and I was a bit iffy about doing it just as engineer. But because it was Bowie, I thought, Well, Christ, I can't miss this opportunity. Now Carlos was the unsung hero – he really didn't get any of the credit that was due. He was suddenly not there for *Let's Dance*, and then suddenly he was back again. So I think there was a little bit of a vibe going on, although it wasn't noticeable, but there must have been.

I remember occasions when I had to poke my finger into the situation. I think it started when David was doing vocals and Bramble would say, 'Oh no, you've got to do it again,' for this reason or that reason. I was trying to keep quiet and I could see David going, 'Why?' Then I eventually said, 'Look, Derek, there's nothing wrong with that vocal, it's not out of tune. What are you doing?' I don't think Derek was used to anyone being able to do a vocal in one take or two takes or whatever. Eventually it did get to a bit of siding up, with David and me on one side and Bramble, the producer, on the other.

Alomar sums up the situation as he saw it with brutal honesty: 'Well, Derek Bramble was a really nice guy, but he didn't know jack-shit about producing. Hugh Padgham was excellent and he was the engineer and he was doing his best but, with all due respect, the producer was Derek.'

Padgham was incredibly impressed by Bowie's technical ability as a vocalist and his studio craft. Bowie was the model of professionalism, light years away from the previous decade, when albums were created in a coke haze. 'He would turn up looking wasted, but that would be more from being up all night with a girl!' says Padgham with a chuckle. 'My bedroom was next to his. We used to live in this house just down the road, and the walls were quite thin. In the morning you'd hear him cough terribly because he'd been smoking like a chimney. So there was that going on for bloody hours, and then he'd come into the studio looking really sort of knackered! Saying that, I don't think I have worked with anyone who was more professional as a singer, ever. Doing vocals is a real pain in the arse for some singers, whether it's because of tuning or attitude, but he would just go into the studio, do one run-through, and then you'd have the tape running and then that was probably it.'

Padgham also loved having Iggy Pop in on the sessions – that was when the creative sparks would be flying. The two had holidayed together in Bali and Java after the Serious Moonlight tour, and Bowie was keen to work with Iggy again on his next solo project. But as a taster for a more formal collaboration, Bowie invited Iggy into the sessions for his own new album. The result was 'Tumble And Twirl', an uneasy collage of horns, funky rhythms and world music which didn't catch fire, and 'Dancing With The Big Boys', with its gated snare, big beats, distinctive riff and big horn section, another near-miss almost successfully realised. According to Padgham, Iggy and Bowie wrote more songs during the sessions than the two that made the final album: 'Iggy came up with quite a lot. There were also a bunch of songs that David had written, and maybe one or two with Iggy that were more left-field or less poppy. It might have been because David was bored of being in the studio where we were, which was in the middle of nowhere, but my feeling was that he couldn't be bothered to write the lyrics and finish them off. If you found the tapes you would probably find a bunch of out-takes or songs which had, I reckon, real possibilities.'

As the sessions went on, it became apparent that the material just wasn't there. 'I was thinking, oh my God! After all those amazing records he's done in the past, what am I doing working with Bowie on this one?' says Padgham. 'I hated "Blue Jean". It was too poppy.' He adds:

I tell you what completely took the biscuit for me – the song 'Tonight' with Tina Turner. Now she was really good, but I just thought, This record is so poppy. When they decided to call the record *Tonight*, I was mortified. But I was, I don't know, about 27 or 28 and I was a little bit in awe and a little bit reticent to tell someone like that what to do. I was pretty upset and I suppose, looking back, didn't have the balls to say, 'Finish those other songs off.' He would go into the studio with Iggy and they would write lyrics together more or less when they were being sung and it was cool. I really enjoyed it when he was up there and it was really happening and Iggy was pretty clean at the time as well. Two or three songs were started but had no vocals. If you had taken 'Tonight', 'Blue Jean' and 'God Only Knows' off and put on three more left-field or more rocky tracks, the flavour of the album would have changed.

Looking back on it now, what it stinks of was that he was probably coerced into the studio before he was ready, or he thought he could do no wrong, going into the studio relatively underprepared. I think he's always been very vain, for want of a better word. To suddenly have a worldwide successful record and to be a big star was probably on his mind more than anything else. He loved hanging out with Tina Turner when she came up. If you look at that period of time with David, I bet you see lots of smart Anthony White suits hanging out with famous people, and that to me was what the vibe was. It was sort of epitomised by the fact that there were some great songs that he couldn't be bothered to finish because he wanted to get the record out.

A few weeks into the session, with Bramble having departed, Bowie asked Padgham to take over as producer. It was never quite clear to Padgham if Bramble had been fired or 'put to bed early' but he accepted the offer willingly. 'David took me aside one day and said, "I want you to mix this record and finish it off." I was left with what I considered to be in some respects a substandard album. I had exactly the same problem with McCartney soon after that, when I produced his album *Press To Play*. And the one time I said to McCartney something about one of his songs he said to me, "Hugh, how many hit songs have you written?" And it was like the worst thing someone had ever said to me and I felt like crawling into a hole, but I was also extremely angry and I've never forgotten that or forgiven him for it, to be honest. Ever since then I have learned to have the courage of my own convictions. If I was working with David now I'd probably say, "Are you trying to make a pop album or what?" But it is difficult. Who am I to say to Mr David Bowie that his songs suck?!'

Carlos Alomar was reasonably happy with the record – 'I was able to find a lot of good cuts that I enjoyed. "Loving The Alien", I love that song, and because it had to do with Major Tom, we really gave it some thought' – but the fact that this was the first album since Bowie's debut to have more misses than hits is undeniable. The record's twin nadirs came with a bathetic interpretation of 'God Only Knows' on side one and a remake of 'I Keep Forgetting' on side two. For The Beach Boys classic, Bowie was always going to come off second best. Bowie sings technically well, but it's such a staid, plodding version that it's one of the few Bowie tracks really to embarrass the listener. With Lieber and Stoller's 'I Keep Forgetting', originally recorded in an earthy R&B style by Chuck Jackson, Bowie had the reverse problem – how to make a relatively obscure song come alive for a mainstream audience. But Bowie's take on the original is so emasculated and polite that the result was wholly unmemorable.

However, the two other Iggy covers work fine. 'Don't Look Down', helped by Bramble's know-how, is super-cool and 'Neighbourhood Threat' really sears through, a punchy, poppy song. The two new songs written with Iggy were pretty lame compared with past glories, and that left just the two new Bowie songs. 'Blue Jean', later dubbed by Bowie as 'sexist rock'n'roll', and inspired, in part, by the vibe of Eddie Cochran's 'Something Else', is a fine pop song – slightly run-of-the-mill by Bowie's standards, but head and shoulders above all else save the one gem on the album, 'Loving The Alien'. Bowie sings gloriously, the music is epic, and the string section which closes the record courtesy of Arif Mardin is truly beautiful. Showing Bowie at his impressionistic best, the lyrics are a series of comments on the lies and deceits that underpin the power of organised religion and the intolerance caused by the whole ideological system. Bowie overlays this with a reiteration of the Major Tom/Ziggy myth of Christ as alien. The opening vocal refrain, which resurfaces throughout the song, filtered via Laurie Anderson's 'O Superman' from Philip Glass' 1975 work *Einstein On the Beach*, is an inspired appropriation. It was all far too daring for a pop album such as *Tonight*, and the song stands out a mile.

Bowie, deep down, was obviously extremely unhappy with the album, and this became apparent from a series of semi-apologetic comments made to Charles Shaar Murray in a September 1984 interview, the only official interview he was to give in support of *Tonight*. Publicly, Bowie told reporters that he was a happier, saner individual, but he found it impossible to redirect his muse to accommodate this new wholesomeness. 'I think because I was starting to feel sure of myself in terms of my life, my state of health and my being . . . I have relapses as we all do, but I feel, on the whole, fairly happy about my state of mind and my physical being. I guess I wanted to put my musical being in a similar staid and healthy area, but I'm not sure that that was a very wise thing to do.' It was a public relations nightmare, the artist himself virtually disowning the album on release.

The single, 'Blue Jean', reached Number 6 in the UK, massively helped by its video. ' "Blue Jean" – that was a classic Bowie single because of a classic Bowie video. That video sold that fucking song!' is Alomar's rather terse assessment of *Tonight*'s only big hit single. In its long format, the Julien Temple-produced video is a light comedy. Bowie plays himself twice: as the nerdy fan, Vic, and his doppelgänger, Screaming Lord Byron – a light-hearted piss-take of Bowie's 1970s alter egos. The club sequence, in which Mr Screaming performs 'Blue Jean' to Vic and girlfriend in the audience, is frivolous but endearing and the 'band' even has future Right Said Fred pop star, Richard Fairbrass, on bass. It's hardly 'Ashes To Ashes', but 'Jazzin' For Blue Jean' showed that Bowie was quite skilled at producing longer-format videos. In fact, 'Jazzin' For Blue Jean' was more a short film than a long video, and functioned as such on its premiere in London on 21 September as support to the feature-length *The Company of Wolves*.

The packaging and promotion of the album (despite its manifest shortcomings, briefly Number 1 in the UK chart) were worryingly third-rate too. The album cover, a sort of homage to the work of British painters and performance-art dandies Gilbert and George, was nondescript, and the Bowie image at the time – loudly clashing shirts and short-cropped hair dyed dark brown – was someone else's version of off-the-peg cool, not Bowie's own. For the first time ever, Bowie was sartorially run-of-the-mill. 'If you look at the album covers and the way he's dressed, it looks like a man who has let himself be designed by others rather than reinventing himself, which is what he has proverbially always done', is how Paul Du Noyer puts it. 'Some of those covers do look like the attack of the killer stylists!'

The final few months of 1984 and the first few of 1985 were spent on various miscellaneous projects, all of which amounted to nothing more than a severe case of treading water. Bowie was asked to sing the first two lines of a new Christmas song, 'Do They Know It's Christmas?' a hastily written charity song penned by The Boomtown Rats' Bob Geldof and Ultravox's Midge Ure. It was originally intended for Bowie to sing the opening lines, but he couldn't make the recording day and so Paul Young, the only singer with a comparable range, was given the chance to lead off the single instead. Bowie did, however, contribute a suitably solemn message for the single's B-side ('It's Christmas 1984, and there are more starving folk on the planet than ever before'), and both Ure and Geldof were delighted that an artist of his stature had deemed the record cool. The single, of course, went on to sell over two million copies in the UK alone and was a welcome reminder that at least someone in the capitalist pig-out that was the rock industry cared about the rest of humanity. Band Aid spawned countless imitations and spin-offs. Bowie, always wary of aligning himself with a political cause (being, firstly, extremely wealthy and privileged and, secondly, incredibly ambivalent towards politics in any case), kept clear of the shenanigans. At least for the time being.

With his own pseudo-Christmas single, 'Tonight', a complete flop, Tina Turner and all, Bowie recorded a new song, 'This Is Not America', with new-age jazz guitarist Pat Metheny and his group for the soundtrack to the film *A Falcon and the Snowman*. It was a toe-dipping venture into uncharted territory for Bowie. Wistful and rhythmic, the song teetered along that very thin line between classy MOR jazz and the sort of pseudo-intellectual aural wallpaper of much new-age meditative music. Stylistically it proved to be a dead end (Bowie was never to record in this style in the future), but it makes for very interesting, if totally incongruous, listening. It was also a moderate UK hit (and a huge hit in Germany), reaching Number 14 and restoring some commercial pride after 'Tonight'.

However, 1984 had been Bowie's first bad year since the 1960s' frustrations and miscalculations. He was losing the support of the mainstream audience he had won in 1983, with a mainstream album that didn't have enough hits, and he was losing support from his natural constituency too, as it began haemorrhaging away to the new purveyors of arty bedsit gloom, The Smiths and The Cure, or to Prince, the Little Richard/Jimi Hendrix mutant most critics regarded as Bowie's natural successor, then breaking big with *Purple Rain*. For the first time in his career, Bowie was yesterday's man.

There were not one, but two versions of Prince Charles at Live Aid at Wembley Stadium on 13 July 1985. There was the real one, the one with a penchant for 'Gooning' around, whose father made 'jokes' about slitty-eyed foreigners; and there was the altogether more convincing fake one, the one who deported himself like a real aristocrat and belted out "Heroes" in the best moment of the entire show.

Bowie's triumph at Live Aid was a triumph of cool and professionalism. Queen, natural stadium rockers, and U2, who had actually come off stage disappointed with their own performance, enjoyed the best press and the mainstream accolades, but Bowie turned in the best performance. He opened, rather lamely, with 'TVC 15', a song obviously dearer to him than it is to the rest of us, before switching on the juice with a great 'Rebel Rebel' and 'Modern Love', then giving the audience the best version of "Heroes" he had ever sung. He prefaced it with a peculiarly touching and poetic moment: 'I'd like to dedicate this song to my son, to all our children . . . and to the children of the world.' The moment when Bowie reached out for saxophonist Clare Hirst's hand when he delivered the lines, 'And we kissed, as though nothing could fall,' was a moment of genuine poignancy in a show of big bold gestures and stadium rock.

Bowie returned to the stage after the eighteen-minute set to introduce what was undoubtedly the most affecting moment of an uncommonly emotional day. A CBC TV film crew had gone up to Bob Geldof's Phonogram office to film Geldof in the weeks running up to Live Aid, and had spliced together graphic scenes of starving children in Addis Ababa. Having seen the film, a tearful Bowie immediately dropped 'Five Years' so that it could be aired live at the end of his set, so tight was the schedule on the day with dozens of groups competing for very limited stage time. The footage was backed by The Cars' love song, 'Drive', and made for one of the most affecting and disturbing visual and musical cut-ups ever broadcast. The amount of cash pledged on the day rocketed after the film's airing.

Bowie had also planned to sing a duet with Mick Jagger. The intention had been for the two to perform a live satellite link-up, Bowie in London, Jagger in Philadelphia. They tested it out on the telephone, harmonising to Bob Marley's 'One Love', but the technology wasn't there. A split-second delay meant that the two voices couldn't synchronise for a live performance. So, just days before the big concert, Bowie invited Jagger down to a London studio where he was busy recording the title song for his latest film project, *Absolute Beginners*, with producers Clive Langer and Alan Winstanley. They decided to record a version of the old Martha Reeves And The Vandellas hit, 'Dancing In The Street'. Alan Winstanley:

> It was a Saturday and I remember Bowie coming in and saying, 'Look, can we knock this on the head about six o'clock today? I've got Mick coming in.' Anyway, at about five o'clock we decided to routine the song. We got the Martha Reeves And The Vandellas version out, which I think is brilliant, and the band learned the chords. They started playing it and it sounded fuckin' awful! It sounded like a cabaret band. I remember I was in the control room and I had my head in my hands, thinking, What the fuck is this?
>
> Jagger's turned up by now – he didn't come into the control room, he came straight into the studio – and I'm looking through the glass and he does this 'Mick Jagger strut' with one hand on his left hip and the right hand pointing in the air. I saw our drummer, Neil Conti, at the other end of the studio. He looked up, saw Jagger strutting across the room, and went whooom! into fifth gear. Suddenly the whole band picked up. We already had a mic set up in a booth next to Bowie. At this point Bowie was singing on his own. Jagger went into the booth, started singing with Bowie, and it was one take.

'Dancing In The Street', a classic covered by two rock legends, couldn't fail to impress the media, and soon the pressure was on for it to be released as a single. The video, although dearly loved by MTV, was actually a tad cringe-inducing, and the record itself was in fact pretty ordinary. 'You're right,' says Winstanley. 'It isn't a great version, but it was better than it was five minutes before Jagger turned up! At that point it was never going to be a record – it was the soundtrack for the Live Aid video. By ten o'clock, we had a rough mix done and they took it over to the film crew on the other side of London and shot the video.'

Although 'Dancing In The Street' became his fifth, and to date last, UK Number 1 single, the song that Bowie had been working on in those Langer and Winstanley sessions, 'Absolute Beginners', was a gem. Winstanley remembers meeting up with Bowie in his penthouse suite at St James' Club, where Bowie played them the demo. 'I remember walking out of there,' says Winstanley. 'We got into the lift and me and Clive said, "Fuckin' hell, we've just been given this on a plate!" The demo sounded great. I thought it was a great song and it sounded good. I think he did it at Abbey Road somewhere. So, although we thought we'd been handed this great song on a plate, we also had to compete with this demo. I mean, he called it a demo, but it really sounded like a master. I think he's a great producer, anyway.'

Bowie has often spoken of the 1980s as some kind of 'missing time' experience, in which his creativity was abducted by the alien forces of commercialism. Did Winstanley notice any lack of commitment from Bowie? 'He didn't look washed up to me. He'd wear a suit every day, he was immaculately groomed and he looked fuckin' great.' And Winstanley did indeed have a Bowie classic in the bag. 'I thought it was the best thing he'd written since "Heroes". But with the backing vocals we were almost, in an affectionate way, parodying him! I don't know if those were on the demo, but we added them in quite deliberately.'

Bowie also had a lot of fun in the recording studio. 'While we were doing the vocals on "Absolute Beginners", he'd suddenly start impersonating people,' chuckles Winstanley. 'He'd do Lou Reed, Bruce Springsteen, Iggy Pop . . . and he sounded just like them! We had it all on tape but at the end of the session, he made sure they were all given back to him. But it was really entertaining!'

'Absolute Beginners' was finally released in March 1986. It entered the UK charts at Number 8. The following week it was Number 2 and looked set to become Bowie's sixth Number 1, his fifth of the 1980s. However, the next week it had slipped to Number 3 behind the previous week's Number 1, Diana Ross' 'Chain Reaction', and another charity record, this time for Comic Relief. There was a fitting irony to this, according to Winstanley. 'While we were making "Absolute Beginners" Clive and I were asked to do a charity record with Cliff Richard and The Young Ones. Bowie got wind of this offer and said, "You can't do that. Don't work with Cliff Richard and The Young Ones. It's gonna be awful!" So we turned it down, and that's the record, "Living Doll", that kept us from Number 1!'

The year 1985 began, however, with a personal tragedy for Bowie. Over Christmas his half-brother Terry Burns had attempted suicide. Scaling the walls of Cane Hill, the mental hospital that had been his home for close on two decades, he had made his way to Coulsdon South station and lain down with his head over the track as the express train for London approached. Just in time, Terry relented and moved his head away as the train sped on its journey. Such was his misery, he immediately overdosed on sleeping tablets and had to have his stomach pumped out at the local hospital. Three weeks later, Terry was allowed to walk free from the institution again, but this time he didn't move his head away and, although the driver saw Terry's bulky frame on the tracks, it was too late. He was just 47. There were eleven mourners at the funeral. Bowie did not attend. 'You've seen more things than we could imagine but all these moments will be lost, like tears washed away by the rain. God bless you – David,' read Bowie's card, sent with a bunch of red roses in his stead.

The media picked up on what they thought of as Bowie's heartlessness and lack of consideration for Terry's welfare during the 70s and 80s, an assessment seemingly confirmed by Bowie's decision not to attend the funeral, fearing a 'media circus'. Terry had attempted to commit suicide three years earlier, throwing himself out of his bedroom window at Cane Hill and fracturing his arm and leg. Concerned, Bowie went to visit him and this probably raised in Terry the hope that his kid brother might be around more often. But it wasn't to be and, shortly after Terry's death, a book was published which probed in a deeply personal manner into Bowie's family background.

In 1985 came the first revelatory articles by journalists Peter and Leni Gillman. The Gillmans were no fans of Bowie or his music – at least initially. During the course of researching their book, *Alias David Bowie*, they unearthed what they considered to be convincing and overwhelming evidence of a history of mental illness in his family. Bowie had been quite open about this when questioned in interviews as far back as the 1970s (he commented in 1976 to Stuart Grundy: 'Most people say, "Oh, my family's quite mad, you know." Well, mine really is.'), but the Gillmans went for the jugular, and constructed a history of batty aunts and mentally ill scions and relatives. Bowie must have been mortified to have his ancestry so painstakingly anatomised.

The Gillmans' analysis was rather reductive; even the most seemingly innocuous song was linked to the central thesis that Bowie's work was all about exorcising the 'family curse'. But the fact of the matter was that the Gillmans had done their research and had hit a very raw nerve. Post-1983, Bowie had been constructed in the media as a responsible, caring individual and a family man, his days of drugs, women (and men) part of a previous existence. Now the Gillmans' book was laying bare some of his most private moments for public consumption. Bowie also felt betrayed when he read the names of some of his former closest friends and allies in the acknowledgements section (Lindsay Kemp, Ken Pitt, Ken Scott, Tony Defries and Tony Visconti).

To compound the sense of betrayal, another book published in 1986, *Stardust*, by Tony Zanetta and Harry Edwards, painstakingly revealed the craziness of the MainMan years and Bowie's decision to 'erase' his past post-Serious Moonlight by barring access to former friends and colleagues. Again, Bowie hardly emerged in the most flattering of lights. Now a very wealthy international rock star, Bowie was paying the price for his colossal fame. Whereas in the 1970s he was adored by journalists who rejoiced in his works, now, with his muse only fitfully operational, the space had opened up for attacks on his person rather than critiques of his work.

After a three-year gap and with his musical career in some disarray, Bowie made the decision in 1985 to return to his acting career, although he turned down the chance of playing the baddie, Max Zorin, in the next Bond movie, *A View To A Kill*, a role subsequently taken by Christopher Walken. In the eventual film, Zorin's sidekick Mayday was played by Grace Jones; presumably the producers had had a Jones/Bowie teaming in mind which would have brought together two famous gender-benders in one film. Bowie did, however, agree to play a cameo role as a killer in

John Landis' spy film *Into the Night*, and followed this up with two other film parts.

The first was in the pop musical of Colin McInnes' *Absolute Beginners*, to be directed by Julien Temple, who had made the controversial 1979 punk-rock movie, *The Great Rock'n'Roll Swindle*, and worked with Bowie the previous year on 'Jazzin' For Blue Jean'. Temple had impressed Bowie with his single-minded determination and iconoclastic view of pop culture. The two would gulp coffee at the Bar Italia in London, and Temple would tell tales of the punk wars of half a dozen years earlier, a time when he was in the front line as a new-wave film-maker, and Bowie was cut adrift in Berlin. Temple's idea for a new film, to be financed by ailing British film-makers Goldcrest, appealed to Bowie's sense of pop history. Goldcrest had been responsible for films such as the ill-fated *Revolution*, featuring Annie Lennox in her only film role to date, and *Absolute Beginners* was being thought of as a make-or-break movie for the company. It would go to the very dawn of British pop culture, back to the late 1950s era of jazz cool, hep cats, conniving publicity hoaxers, star photographers and the first stirrings of the glitterati. It would also unearth the secret history of racial intolerance and the Notting Hill riots.

Bowie agreed to provide the theme tune and to play conniving, slimy ad-man, Vendice Partners, and got to tap-dance for what was the first and, one hopes, last time in front of camera. In essence Bowie's role was little more than a cameo, and the film – a grating amalgam of musical and pop video – was neither the turkey some critics have dubbed it nor the critical and commercial success Goldcrest desperately needed. It was released to much hype, but lukewarm notices, in the spring of 1986. In the end, *Absolute Beginners* was more a commentary on a certain type of 1980s' vacuity than on the 1950s' spirit of adventure and nowness.

Bowie then donned a blond kabuki wig and genitalia-hugging tights to star in Jim Henson's latest movie, *Labyrinth*. Essentially a pastiche of a number of children's fantasy themes from *Alice Through the Looking Glass* to *The Wizard of Oz*, the film was likeable enough, despite a number of rather weak songs from Bowie himself, which reduced it, like *Absolute Beginners*, to a series of pop promos. Bowie as Jareth the Goblin King is not cruel or nasty enough to give the film the sort of chill that older children would have found more to their liking, and he is just a little too scary for the under-fives. Likewise, the film fails to deliver the sort of studied disquiet hinted at in Bowie's opening scene, when he arrives unannounced in Sarah's bedroom to tell the teenager that her brother is now incarcerated in the Goblin City, and falls well short of *The Wizard of Oz* and its ability to scare, enchant and moralise in equal measure. There is a more weighty subplot, that of the awakening sexuality of the film's heroine, Sarah, played by Jennifer Conolly, who is both repulsed and attracted by the camp Goblin King as she tries to rescue her baby brother, but it's all pretty dispensable, lightweight stuff. The soundtrack album, which contained five new Bowie songs, and was puzzlingly released six months before the film (thus guaranteeing its commercial failure), is almost completely superfluous, save for a 'Let's Dance' retread entitled 'Magic Dance', and the gospel-influenced 'Underground', which was a minor UK hit in 1986 (and perhaps provided some of the inspiration for Madonna's rather better 'Like A Prayer' three years later). Bowie still hankered after that authentic bluesy sound, and to that end called up guitar great Albert Collins and veteran Arif Mardin (who had just produced the seminal dance/pop crossover album *Cupid And Psyche '85* for Scritti Politti). But the songs were insubstantial, and what might have been an interesting project floundered due to a lack of anything resembling sparkling material.

Most fans viewed his film career as a major distraction. It was no coincidence that the downswing of his musical abilities and the infrequent, almost patronising, pacing of each release (albums came every two or three years, as if the master had deigned to spoil his people with another record) came with an upswing in his film presence. One of the main motivations behind Bowie's increasingly bland music in the 1980s was his film career. In order to get big parts and be a major box-office draw, film companies had to be sure that his career as a pop star did not alienate mainstream expectations through excursions into the avant-garde or threatening. Largely, people did not want Bowie as an actor; they wanted Bowie doing what he was best at, making music. His deviations into film were made doubly annoying by the simple fact that, to a large degree, the roles he took on were worryingly unspectacular.

His transmogrification from the cutting-edge star of the 1970s to all-round entertainer was now complete, and in a series of interviews Bowie seemed almost desperate to point out that he not only accepted his new role as 'populist entertainer' but also actually welcomed it. An interview with Dave Thomas in the March of that year gives a clear indication of his moribund mind-set. On music: 'The music is so awful here . . . I've dropped out of radio. I play my old record collection'; on his own intentions: 'music starts to mellow . . . I don't have the riveting desire now to persuade people that what I have to say is right'; and finally on his audience: 'What's the point of me trying to write for teenagers? The only way I could do that would be as some kind of father figure.' Bowie biographers are wont to point out that Bowie 'found himself' in the 1980s, after years of psychic travail. In fact, the reverse is true: the mainstream pop star of the me-decade was far more of an act than any of his past manifestations. By the middle of the decade, he had lost virtually all sense of how he related to his art.

However, 1986 ended on a much more encouraging note, with the release of the Bowie-produced Iggy Pop album *Blah Blah Blah*. Iggy has since virtually disowned it, calling it a Bowie album in all but name, but this is to unfairly denigrate what is, in fact, a very fine, if uncustomarily poppy, Iggy Pop album. Bowie co-wrote five of the songs, including the absolutely superb 'Shades', a smouldering ballad, mildly psychotic and lyrically childlike (Iggy had to change the line 'It makes me come in the night' for the single release). The title track, too, with its use of sampled snippets of information as the riff, was a real innovation. *Blah Blah Blah*, together with the title track to the Raymond Briggs anti-nuke film, *When The Wind Blows*, in which Bowie sang beautifully against another great percussive figure (this time courtesy of Erdal Kizilcay, dubbed 'The Invincible Turk' by Bowie, who worked with him on his demos in Switzerland), hinted that the new album and tour promised for the coming year would see a welcome return to form. However, 1987 turned out to be a crisis year for Bowie.

Recorded immediately after the *Blah Blah Blah* sessions at the Mountain Studios, Switzerland, in the autumn of 1986, *Never Let Me Down* was co-produced with David Richards and featured Erdal Kizilcay and ex-schoolmate Peter Frampton on lead guitar. During this period, Bowie started working with Kizilcay on a regular basis, usually on Tuesdays and Thursdays, and often at Kizilcay's home studio. However, the new album contained only one song worthy of comparison with his 1970s work – the haunting 'Time Will Crawl'. Whereas *Tonight* was an entropic mess and totally unfocused, its successor possessed greater coherence but was drastically overproduced, with any number of superfluous instrumental parts cluttering the mix.

'Day In Day Out', the album's lead-off single (and a Top 20 UK hit), demonstrated this clearly. It has a busy, jumbled cacophony of guitars and horns set against a lyric about the plight of the homeless in the USA. It did, however, boast a great opening line in 'She was born in a handbag', a steal from Grand Master Flash and Melle Mel's huge rap hit of 1982, 'The Message' (which contained the line 'Living in a bag'). 'Day In Day Out' was a foretaste of the didacticism of the Tin Machine project. The rest of the album simply sounds uncommitted and contrived, although there are brief glimpses of something of a return to form. 'Glass Spider', although vilified at the time for its spoken narrative opening section, builds wonderfully well. The title track, co-written with guitarist Carlos Alomar, is a sort of homage to the Lennon ballads such as 'Jealous Guy', as well as to Coco, and is catchy enough. The equally catchy, though ludicrously tinny and toppy 'Shining Star (Makin' My Love)' pays lip service to the pop *Zeitgeist* with a rap section with actor Mickey Rourke. The remainder of the album varies, from the songs with definite unfulfilled potential ('Beat Of Your Drum', 'Zeroes'), to the superfluous ('Bang Bang') to the unashamedly mainstream 'Too Dizzy' (a song Bowie removed from his back catalogue by deleting it from the 1995 reissue of the album). Strangely, 'Julie', the catchiest song of the set, was relegated to a B-side, although it did make the reissued album in the 90s.

Band leader Carlos Alomar thought the whole album 'uninspired'. Bowie's 'new' way of working – actually coming into the studios with demos – was in direct contrast to his 70s experimentalism, and contributed to the staid, rehearsed quality of the music. More importantly, so Alomar maintains, external pressure from his record company was killing his art:

David was at a loss during the whole album. He just gave up. You cannot have a record company constantly telling you, 'Look, this is no good, give us something like this. Work with that person, work with this person, we don't want you working with that person any more.' It's bullshit. After a while the

▲ Bowie in 1967, around
the time of the release of
his debut album
(King Collection/Retna)

► The Kabuki Monster in full flight; *Aladdin Sane* in concert, 1973
(Rex)

◄ Bowie with his first wife Angie and a two-and-three-quarter year-old Zowie, early 1974
(Peter Mazel/London Features)

◀ Bowie on the *Diamond Dogs* tour, USA, 1974; possibly the most theatrical rock show ever
(Rex)

▶ The Thin White Duke, on stage in 1976
(Philippe Auliac)

◄ Bowie and Marc Bolan perform on television together for the first and sadly last time. Bolan would be dead just a matter of days after the filming of this sequence for the *Marc* show, Granada, September 1977
(London Features)

► Jaunty of cap and crimson of bathrobe, Bowie camps it up for the 1978 tour
(Andre Waszczyszyn)

▲ Bullish mood? Bowie
on the triumphant
Serious Moonlight
extravaganza, 1983
(Wolfgang Gürster)

► Celebrity Squares; Bowie
and Tina Turner all smiles
for 'Tonight', May 1984
(Hugh Padgham)

▼Carlos Alomar and Bowie hamming it up on the *Glass Spider* tour, 1987
(Retna)

▲ Bowie at prayer; the Billy Graham of pop, Wembley Stadium, April 1992
(Michael Putland/Retna)

◄ Bowie the *Earthling* in Union Jacket frock coat, a dandified blast at Britpop, 1996
(Tom Zuback for Crankin' Out!)

▲ Let's Make Up And Be Friendly;
Tony Visconti (centre) with Bowie
and Reeves Gabrels, 1998
(May Pang)

▼ Forever young; Bowie and Placebo live
on stage at the Brit Awards, belting out
Bolan's 'Twentieth Century Boy', 1999
(Fiona Hanson/PA)

Bowie: balls of steel◀
(Mick Rock   www.mickrock.com)

▲ Live in 2002 on the
triumphant Heathen tour
(Christina Radish/Redferns)

▶Bowie and Iman in
New York, April 2005
(Getty Images)

record company was saying, 'Look, you're gonna have to go into the studio to deliver another album by the end of the year or you're gonna get into trouble for non-delivery.' The man didn't want to go into the studio to record an album. When you let the political agenda of a record company infiltrate your mood, there's no inspiration.

Bowie left RCA for greater achievements with EMI. When these expectations fall short, that's a personal affront, a personal hurt. Bowie felt let down. He discussed EMI constantly and talked about how horrible they were. He's always put under pressure to make commercial records.

Bowie turned forty on 8 January 1987. *The Mirror* pictured him at a special birthday party at the Swiss ski resort of Gstaad, hurling his cake down the piste. In a later report the *Mirror* tattled on about his appearance, with three girls, at the Steigenberger Hotel: 'He grandly presented the DJ with a copy of his upcoming album . . . The crowded dance floor cleared – and the only people left dancing were Bowie and his sexy pals.'

By now, Bowie was extremely wealthy. He lived in luxury in homes dotted throughout the world. He had already made the biggest contribution to post-Beatles pop of any musician. But he was not a happy man. He had no regular girlfriend or prop in his life, no one to share his happiness or his misery. The desire to make ground-breaking music had been beaten out of him by a combination of middle-age droop and record company pressures. Like many other musicians who had first established themselves in the previous decade, Bowie found the mid-1980s to be a creative desert. He was a mainstream pop star, something he never wanted to be, and he began to hate his position and himself for having been desperate enough to go for the big-time bucks in 1983. It was with a combination of severe self-loathing and the realisation that his professional and personal life had to change that Bowie began the process of killing off his career as a pop superstar. Bowie was entering the end of the 1980s as Saint David Bowie, rock'n'roll martyr.

11. 'THE EMPEROR'S NEW CLOTHES', 1987–1990

I hated all that dancing and shit.

BAND LEADER CARLOS ALOMAR REMEMBERS THE GLASS SPIDER TOUR

EMI may have wanted Let's Dance 2 but they got World War 3!

TIN MACHINE PRODUCER TIM PALMER

Bowie's 1987 Glass Spider world tour was a vastly entertaining tragicomedy that teetered on the brink of greatness, but finally fell off the cliff face of good taste to drown in a pool of schlock. It was the defining moment in David Bowie's career, and had a bigger impact on him as an artist than the riches of Serious Moonlight, the greatness of his late 1970s works, or even Ziggy Stardust himself. Bowie would never be the same again. Weighed down by a decade and a half of theatricalisation and, for the first time, with money literally to burn (at the end of the tour the 60-foot-high fibreglass spider designed for the show was set alight in an act of symbolic catharsis), Bowie was like a star at the end of its life span. Glass Spider was a supernova of a concert which saw the old version of Bowie finally explode under the weight of self-parody, only to shrink to the red dwarf of Tin Machine.

For Glass Spider, Bowie thought big but ended up appearing small. When he took the stage at the Feyenoord Stadium in Rotterdam for the very first gig on this six-month world tour, he was decked out in a gaudy red suit, mainly because he had to wear such retina-challenging garb in order to be seen at all. With eleven other players and dancers on stage at the same time as Bowie himself, it's no wonder that the audience, many of whom needed something akin to a radio telescope to see the real-life action, felt rather short-changed. Having lost confidence in himself as a performer after three years of relatively poor records, Bowie decided to blur and camouflage himself on stage, obscured by a superfluity of people and props.

The theory behind Glass Spider was commendable enough. Bowie wanted to inject some much-needed danger into his live performances and had been inspired by the avant-garde dance work of Germany's Pina Bausch and Canada's La La La Human Steps (who Bowie approached initially for the Glass Spider tour). He envisaged a sort of rock'n'roll circus, a pop panto, but the execution was third rate. The stage was enveloped womblike by the fibreglass carapace of the spider itself. This was Bowie at his most literal and least inspired. There was a 'Glass Spider' song, Glass Spider tour, and a bloody great arachnid on stage too. It was incredibly close to Spinal Tap.

Bowie was also never more active during a rock show, sprinting backwards and forwards, abseiling down to the stage for '87 And Cry', belting out 'All The Madmen' on top of scaffolding, and then, at the very top of the spider, singing an actually quite magnificent 'Time' for the show's encore. Never before has a meteorological report actually determined the content of a rock show. If it was too windy sixty feet up, Bowie couldn't perform the song for fear of toppling off his mounting and becoming a rock'n'roll casualty. For the 1987 tour, as if in a fit of menopausal pique, Bowie recast himself as a pop athlete rather than a pop aesthete. In an era in which Madonna jogged on stage, turning the pop spectacle into a reconstruction of a work-out in the gym, and in which the dance routines of Paula Abdul and Michael Jackson passed aerobics off as art, Bowie picked up on the prevailing trend and replaced showmanship with sweat.

At his own suggestion, Carlos Alomar opened the show with a solo. Mildly pissed off at being the tour's *éminence grise* yet again, and with Bowie's old school chum Peter Frampton drafted in for some serious stadium solos, Alomar wanted a piece of the action. As the tour's intro music, a classical updating of Hendrix's 'Purple Haze' by The Kronos Quartet, faded out, Alomar stormed on centre stage looking like he had been connected to the mains backstage, his hair frozen in electrocuted spikes: 'On that tour, I was tired of being the sideman. I wanted my place. Give me a bone, Jesus! That's why he let me do the introduction. Peter Frampton is not Carlos Alomar and I wanted to show I could do all that stuff. That I was more than just a rhythm-guitar player.' Thereafter, a motley collection of curiously attired dancers shinned down from the top of the spider on ropes, including a raven-haired transvestite and a man with sticky-out Alomar hair and a crutch (but why?).

For the most part, the audience didn't know what was going on. A dialogue, part recorded, part spoken live, was conducted between the dancers and Bowie and, at outdoor gigs such as Wembley Stadium, with a huge, rebounding echo on the PA on a swirling, blustery summer's day, all the fans could hear was, 'it's in the cluster (whoosh, crackle, distortion), you ain't been educated (more whooshing, more crackling, more distortion), wrong stuff! wrong stuff!' all spoken in a kind of horribly fake New York drawl. The audience then watched Bowie drag dancer Melissa Hurley out of the crowd for the musically somnambulant 'Bang Bang'. In theory, this was a neat trick. Bowie was parodying that awful moment of true rock'n'roll connection in Bruce Springsteen's 'Dancing In The Dark' video when The Boss, in an immaculately contrived normality of jeans and T-shirt, drags an equally bland 'lady' out of the audience to groove along with. (This was, with bizarre and rather horrible results, actually re-enacted by Bono during U2's Live Aid performance.) Bowie's piece of artifice must have been quite amusing on the opening night of the tour, but since by the third gig everyone sentient had heard about the stunt through press reports, it was wholly contrived and unfunny by the time the show hit week two. The only entertaining aspect for those in the crowd was trying to spot the suckers who genuinely didn't know what was about to happen and tut-tutting disapprovingly at them in a superior and wholly unpleasant way.

Alomar detested the theatricality. 'That was the first time I had ever had an experience like that, with all those dancers. They would constantly push the musicians into the back line because they had so much activity going on in front stage. That was extremely difficult because a lot of the dialogue was on tape and the rest was actually spoken. It's hard running around at a million miles an hour and then catching your breath and saying the line. I thought it was way too much dancing.'

Another major problem arose from putting on the show during a summer that was both rainy and windy, at least in the UK. By the time Bowie took the stage at Sunderland's Roker Park, the crowd were half-drowned, and spent most of the first half-hour throwing empty beer cans at the idiots who still had their umbrellas up, thereby completely blocking a view of the 'activities', which were hard enough to fathom in any case. Not only was it rainy but, on most of the European gigs, it was also light until 10 p.m. Consequently, the flashing neon spider did not become luminous until three-quarters of the way into the set, and the back projections were virtually invisible. And because a curfew operated in many of the places Bowie played (outdoor venues – no noise pollution, please), the shows had to start early and finish by 10.30 p.m. It was not unusual to see Bowie storm off stage a minute past the curfew having just raced through the encore.

There were some good moments. For example, the opener did not lack spectacle. Although an idea borrowed from the *Diamond Dogs* tour, Bowie appearing out of the jaws of the spider, perched like a *Thunderbirds* puppet in an office chair, was an impressive piece of stadium-rock silliness. Bowie was slowly lowered to the ground as he intoned the opening section of 'Glass Spider', but he cocked the lines up so frequently during the first few gigs that he was forced to mime to a backing track for most of the tour. The show's set list originally showed Bowie in confident, non-hit mode. 'Because You're Young' and 'Scream Like A Baby' were rehearsed, but sadly not played. The recent 'Loving The Alien' was tremendous. 'All The Madmen', 'Sons Of The Silent Age' and 'Big Brother' were reworked. As the tour progressed, however, with notices being poor and audience response often muted, some crowd-pleasers like 'Young Americans' and 'The Jean Genie' were installed. During the closing section of 'The Jean Genie', Bowie would leave the stage to change, and Alomar and Frampton would play trade-off guitar solos in a battle to the end.

But the *Never Let Me Down* material sounded rather lame and they played almost the whole album live – at least initially. Not only was the album commercially rather a disappointment (reaching only Number 6 in the UK, the lowest chart position for a new Bowie album for fifteen years, and Number 34 in the States), but artistically it was largely bankrupt. The whole package was wrong, from the new Bowie logo through to the album cover and the terrible mullet hair. For the first time in his career, even the videos were unmemorable. The video for the first single, 'Day In Day Out', was a collage of posing and street violence, including an attempted rape. The video had to be cut in order to be aired on prime-time television, rendering it a nonsense. Even the matey, jokey pitch at the press conferences came over as false. At the start of the tour, just as tickets for the European shows went on sale, someone from among Bowie's PR people must have released a 'Bowie's last tour' story to the press to frighten the fans into buying tickets, since both the *Mirror* and Radio 1 ran 'bye bye Bowie' stories. They needn't have bothered. Ticket sales were healthy throughout Europe, although not quite on the landslide scale of Serious Moonlight.

Bowie's crucial Wembley Stadium gig, on 19 June 1987, was a completely sterile affair with little rapport between audience and performer. The acoustics were terrible, Bowie looked miserable and the windy weather meant no encore. The second gig on the following night was better, with Bowie rescuing a potentially disastrous blow to his reputation in front of his home crowd, but it was obvious he was in some sort of trouble. The new single, 'Time Will Crawl', stalled outside the Top 30 and a *Top of the Pops* appearance was axed from the schedule when the single dropped down the chart.

The tour was corporate rock played to extremes. (Bowie even sought a sponsorship deal with Pepsi and appeared in an ad with Tina Turner.) It was lavish and expensive, but the idea of Bowie now kowtowing to big business was undignified. 'It's a better product than some others I could mention,' was Bowie's lame excuse. While he bemoaned the opening of a McDonald's in Bali and criticised the American government through a pop video and in interviews (he dubbed Reagan 'ole hop-a-long' in a *Tube* interview with 'crazy fucker' Jools Holland that spring), he was allowing his tour to be sponsored by one of the avatars of American imperialism.

Erdal Kizilcay loved the tour. Having received co-writing credits on three songs, 'Girls' (later covered by Tina Turner), 'Too Dizzy' and the excellent 'When The Wind Blows', he was finally playing to the sort of audiences he had hitherto only dreamed of. 'We met Lady Di at Wembley. I'll never forget that. She was such a beautiful woman and such a nice person – she was shining. We met so many great musicians too on that tour, like Bono and Mick

Jagger. But Bowie himself was under stress. He was tired with all the press he had to do, and on top of that, he hated flying. I'm a pilot and David always used to have me sit next to him during a flight so that I could explain what was going on.' During the tour, Erdal, keyboard-wiz Richard Cottle, Peter Frampton and tour photographer Denis O'Regan would form one socialising party, whilst Alomar, Carmine Rojas and Alan Childs formed another. Erdal very much appreciated Carlos' contribution to the overall sound, but, as he recalls, 'There was always a problem with his personality. Even when we were rehearsing in New York, he gave some kind of weird television interviews saying something like David wouldn't be anything without him. David was very angry with him as a result.'

For his part, Carlos Alomar detected that Bowie was not happy and under considerable strain. Bowie was carrying this tour like he had never had to before. With a mammoth performing retinue and support staff, the pressure was incredible. Sometime during the tour, Bowie fell for the beautiful dark-haired dancer Melissa Hurley, his on-stage love in the Glass Spider 'narrative'. Again, fiction was following Bowie into real life. At forty, he appeared to be entering a classic midlife crisis, falling for a woman only a few years older than his own son. 'He kind of went up and down a lot on that tour. He had his friend Peter Frampton, and at the beginning they went out a lot and talked a lot. He did have Melissa at that point, and she was very nice. But he's a very complex individual and it's not always those things that happen on the road that bother him. Company and corporate problems weigh hard on him. He's always had to handle some of his own affairs.'

As ever, there were tensions between band leader Alomar and Bowie's personal assistant. 'Coco and I were going through all sorts of fights and arguments. Carmine and I were the party animals and we always used to party hard. David would always want to come out with us. It really was a bone of contention for Coco. "David mustn't hang out with Carlos or Carmine, because if David were ever going to get into trouble, he would get into trouble with them." We weren't even like that. We weren't into heavy drugs or anything – we'd just take some wine back from the gig. This way we wouldn't have to worry about the musicians being all over the place. As band leader I like keeping all the musicians together, so it's all one big happy family. The happier the family is, the more David is not part of that family, because

David's family is being up there with Coco and the business of the tour. So he had to escape with us once in a while; it's no way to live. They weren't lovers. That was way back in the past; a long-finished thing. But Coco was always in love with Bowie, no doubt about it.'

The year was to get even worse for Bowie when a thirty-year-old Dallas woman, Wanda Nichols, an acquaintance of tour drummer Alan Childs, accused Bowie of raping her at a Dallas hotel on 9 October and was photographed covered in bite marks. News of the alleged rape made the front covers of the British tabloids in a wave of damaging publicity. Six weeks later a grand jury in Dallas threw out her allegations after hearing just two hours of evidence. Bowie admitted having sex with her and agreed to take an AIDS test after Nichols reported that he had told her that he was infected. Just a few months earlier, Bowie had felt moved to caution against unprotected sex at a press conference in London to promote the tour. This happened at the height of the AIDS scare in the UK and the resulting tabloid demonisation was credibility sapping.

In addition to the artistically unfulfilling and personally unhappy tour, Bowie also had to face public disembowelling by the rock critics, particularly in the UK: 'unmemorable tedium' (*NME*), 'the paucity of ideas is quite incredible' (*Melody Maker*), 'desperate hamminess, frenzied schlock and half-baked goofing' (*Sounds*). 'It was time for him to be unfashionable in the media,' Chris Roberts, then a staff writer for *Melody Maker*, recollects. 'His credibility had lasted way beyond any previous character in pop (with the possible exception of Dylan). By rights he should have been out of fashion years before that. Sooner or later everyone becomes unhip. He ran through four careers and it was time for a backlash. Glass Spider was overambitious. He's always ambitious and that's highly creditable, but it was overelaborate and ornate when people were lapsing into a laissez-faire attitude. I don't have any problem with people descending from a huge neon-lit spider, that's fine by me. I think the version of "Time" he did for that tour was absolutely stunning. I was ridiculed for liking it and he was ridiculed for doing it. There was overwhelming peer-group pressure not to like it. It was ambitious, challenging, weird, strange, mental and barmy, and that's got to be good.'

Bowie's voice was on top form throughout the tour, but as a performer he looked extremely uncomfortable, affecting an uneasy mixture of smiles and play-acting. Whereas in the 1970s it was almost as if all he had to do was walk on stage to make an impact, now he cluttered the stage with props and helpers and surface froth. Consequently, he lost his sense of cool.

Bowie ended 1987 moonlighting, rather successfully, in the unlikely role of Pontius Pilate in Martin Scorsese's *The Last Temptation of Christ*. Bowie's part, like that in John Landis' 1985 movie *Into the Night*, was no more than a cameo, but there was something very convincing about his Pilate. Bowie made his screen entrance riding imperially on a horse, and gave Willem Defoe, in the guise of Christ, a brief introduction into Roman politics, before sentencing him to Golgotha.

By 1988, it was obvious that a part of Bowie had been destroyed by the Glass Spider tour. The figure of the lavish stadium rocker was one Bowie found hard to impersonate, and the music he was making was boring him. The problem was maintaining the huge momentum of a superstar rock career. In typically ambivalent style, Bowie decided to follow two seemingly diametrically opposed plans of action. First, early in 1988, he was persuaded, in principle, to go back on the road in 1990 to play a lucrative greatest hits tour. Second, he decided to regain control of his music. In a way, the barrier to this was one man – Carlos Alomar.

Although never verbalised as such, it was obvious to Alomar that Bowie was keen to take over control of his music from his band leader. Alomar explains: 'First of all, there was never any question as to the ownership of the music. It wasn't quite that. I knew that he wanted to have more control over the different directions that his music could take. So I saw the latter part of our relationship as a power struggle. I knew David wanted to do a different kind of music but he just didn't know how. I always thought that if I gave the music back to David, it would end up going back to The Spiders From Mars, and that's exactly what happened.'

The farewell to Alomar signalled the end of Bowie's hit-making, commercial phase. David Bowie, pop star, was dead: 1988 was the first year since 1971 in which there were no David Bowie songs in the UK Top 40. It was at this point that Bowie left 'pop' behind and became a 'rock' star. Bowie had paid far more heed to the journos claiming he was in terminal artistic freefall than he should have. In the previous five years, he had still been able to come up with 'Shades', 'Loving The Alien' and 'Absolute Beginners' – hardly piffling items. But now Bowie began tearing huge chunks of musical flesh out of the body of his music, paring his sound down to a minimalist, guitar-driven unit. Crucial to this development was a man whose analysis of Bowie's predicament was clear. Here was a man who offered a solution – an unknown guitarist by the name of Reeves Gabrels.

In 1988, there was a sort of road-to-Damascus conversion for Bowie and it took place in the unlikely setting of a Turkish restaurant in Switzerland. The new material being demoed by Bowie and Gabrels was vastly at odds with the music on his three previous EMI records. It was time for a decision. 'We were sitting outdoors at this little Turkish restaurant in May 1988 when I said to him, "You have a creative control over your records, right?" ' remembers Gabrels. 'And he said, "Yes. They basically have to accept what I give them." So I said, "The only thing that you have to deal with is criticism and possible lack of sales. If you do exactly what you want, if you think it's going to alienate the people who aren't the true fans, that's up to you. I like what we're doing, but I've got nothing to lose. I've never had the drug of commercial success. The only barrier between you doing what you want and you doing what you think you should do, is you." It was a gentle conversation. I was naive enough to point out the obvious. I had no idea that the conversation had the impact it did have at the time.'

It was this conversation that fundamentally rerouted Bowie's career. From this point on, although there would be world tours, greatest hits records and media pranks and mischief, Bowie was to deliberately scale down his own expectations and that of his audience in terms of his career in music. From 1988 onwards he would write, record and perform largely on his terms. 'He was at a crossroads,' Gabrels points out. 'Either he became Rod Stewart and played Las Vegas, or he followed his heart. I was 31 years old. Prior to that I had been playing four sets a night in country bars, then playing weddings and giving lessons. I had nothing to lose. Anyone with more sense would have quit and got a proper job. The only thing I had to sustain me was a sort of musical integrity. I was also a fan of his music and I wanted to get it back on course for what I thought it should be personally. It was me trying to make a David Bowie record that I wanted to listen to from beginning to end.'

Gabrels saw Bowie very much as a serious rock act, and the *Let's Dance* era as an aberration. He also saw himself very much as an authentic musician, driven by enthusiasm and the creative urge, not by money. 'I had a strong mistrust of professional musicians – what I used to and still do think of as "cheque-book musicians".' Bowie's problem in the 1980s, according to Gabrels, was that too many of these cheque-book musicians had been allowed to shape his music. It was time to get the music back.

Reeves Gabrels was born on Staten Island on 4 June 1956. Unlike Bowie, he had attended both art school and music school. He is unique in the roster of Bowie sidekicks and collaborators in that he is the only one to have been a friend first, collaborator second. 'That's the key to the longevity of our relationship,' says Gabrels. 'I'm the only person David has played with who he has known as a person or a friend prior to making music with them.'

Gabrels used to hang out backstage with Bowie during the American leg of the Glass Spider tour. Gabrels' wife, Sarah, was doing the press for the tour, on a break from her job as a hard-news journalist. 'David and I used to sit and talk about stuff other than music,' says Gabrels. 'I had the same type of art interests, and never said anything to David about being a guitar player. I had two heroes, and they were David and Miles Davis. I have a tape of this band I was in at high school playing this stuff from *Diamond Dogs* and *Ziggy Stardust* and *Aladdin Sane*. I was aware of how people were always trying to get something out of David because of Sarah's job as press person. So I was just enjoying hanging out. I remember saying to Sarah in a pipe dream, "I'd love to work with David and get him back to the rock format." The thing I loved about *Aladdin Sane* and *Scary Monsters* was that they rock harder and they're also more twisted.'

At the end of the tour, Bowie asked Sarah Gabrels if there was anything he could do for her. Sarah gave David a tape of her husband's current work.

The phone call from Bowie resulted in a near-farce. Gabrels: 'I was having a real lousy day, walking round London putting up ads to give guitar lessons. I'd spent more of my money than I had thought on making copies for the posters and I had to walk back to South Kensington from Oxford Circus.

'I got home and, as we didn't have an answerphone at that stage, every time the phone went I had to answer it as Sarah was working. It was like the fourth phone call and I was trying to write some music. I finally picked up the phone and I was really cranky, and this voice says, "Hi, it's David." I said, "Yeah, David who?" "David Bowie." I had told one friend in the US about David Bowie calling me, and he could do a mediocre English accent, so I thought it was him. The voice on the end of the line said, "I listened to that tape Sarah gave me. Why didn't you tell me? You sound like the guitar player I've been looking for." I remember thinking, Wow! If only this was really David Bowie, this would be cool that he said that. His voice didn't seem English enough for it to be David Bowie's. I said, "All right, who the fuck is this?" And he just cracked up. He said to me, "Remember, we used to hang around backstage and watch television with the sound off and make up dialogue for the characters?" I said, "Oh, man, I'm sorry!" He said, "I'll call you in a while and maybe we can get together." I thought, in a couple of weeks, but a couple of hours later he called me back and said, "What are you doing this weekend?" '

Gabrels flew out to Bowie's house in Switzerland in May 1988. 'I went over for a weekend and stayed for almost a month.' Their first collaboration was on an old song from *Lodger*, 'Look Back In Anger', which Bowie was in the process of updating for a performance at the Institute of Contemporary Arts that July. The new, brutal version of the song worked great. They spoke the same language of sound: 'When it came to the guitar parts, we thought about them in terms of architecture – Gothic spirals of sound. This is where the art-school background really helps, because we rarely speak in musical terms. He and I were writing part of the songs that would go on to become Tin Machine songs – "Heaven's In Here", "Baby Universal" (we had a rough version of that without vocals), "Baby Can Dance", "Bus Stop".'

The concert at London's Institute of Contemporary Arts (ICA) in the summer of 1988 was a cool comeback for Bowie after Glass Spider only months before. Bootleg videos of the performance were being sold for extortionate sums at Café Munchen, the rendezvous for enthralled Bowie fans, post-gig. Although his set comprised just one song – a radical, thrash-metal reworking of 'Look Back In Anger' – Bowie had reclaimed the experimental high ground. The music itself was brutal and minimal and driven by a thunderous programmed drum figure and a wall of guitar noise. Visually, he was dangerously theatrical and arty, perform-ing a dance routine with the Canadian dance troupe La La La

Human Steps while a video screen showed prerecorded images of Bowie and dancer Louise Le Cavalier intercut with the live performance. This was his first venture into the world of 'interactivity'. *Melody Maker*'s Chris Roberts gushed: 'It wasn't a relative of pop. It was purely fantastical . . . They slap one another across the face, tickle the chin, hurl, whirl and assault. The flickering video shows Bowie and Le Cavalier, monochrome icons freezing with fear and lust . . .'

Suitably energised, Bowie began work in earnest on his next solo album, and decided to bring in a new producer in the shape of Tim Palmer, who had been recommended to him by Billy Duffy from The Cult. Palmer had made a name for himself as the producer of alternative guitar bands such as The Mission, The Mighty Lemon Drops and Gene Loves Jezebel. 'I was a big fan of Bowie, of course, and to be honest a little nervous about our first meeting,' remembers Palmer. 'I was a big fan of the classic albums, but not so much of the later material. The last album that David made that I had really enjoyed was *Lodger*. My first impression when working with him was that he is so completely open to letting the people who surround him (musicians and producers, engineers, etc.) have their opinions and express themselves freely. He is not too precious about his work. When I became involved in the project, I was under the impression that it was to be a David Bowie record, not a Tin Machine record.'

The whole character of the recording session was to change with the arrival of a rhythm section that epitomised the bigheaded bona fide rock'n'roll ego. Enter the Sales brothers.

Drummer Hunt Sales and bassist Tony Sales were the gale-force winds howling through Iggy Pop's *Lust For Life* album in 1977. They grew up on the periphery of the famous Sinatra 'Rat Pack', and their friends were the children of these people. 'The reason why the Sales brothers came in was to avoid the cheque-book musicians,' says Gabrels. 'We wanted people who were band guys. I think David ran into Tony in LA. I got a message on my answer-machine where I was living in London: "I just thought of it! Check out *Lust For Life*. I've found the rhythm section!" Prior to that the only rhythm section we had discussed involved Percy Jones (fretless bassist with Brian Eno and Brand X) and Terry Bozzio (drummer with Frank Zappa and Missing Persons).' But the Sales brothers were in and everyone knew about it.

'There was a week of like freshman hazing,' recalls Gabrels. 'All they wanted to do was to push me because David was placing a certain amount of trust in me, and I had never done a record that had been released internationally. The Sales brothers' attitude was like, "Well, we all know who we are. Who's this guy?" '

'I worked with David and Reeves on my own,' producer Tim Palmer explains, 'and it wasn't until about six days later that the Sales brothers arrived. Then all hell broke loose. The sessions took on a completely different feel; it was much more chaotic. Hunt and Tony had very crazy, fun personalities and they had very strong ideas of what they wanted to do. On the one hand, this was fun, but at times I found it a little frustrating. Hunt is an exceptional drummer in my opinion, but he can be very undisciplined in his approach, and it can be hard to get ideas across. After it was seen how the music was being created, David decided that it should be called "Tin Machine" as a project, and it is true to say that all the individuals involved were working to their own agenda. Bowie was not directing them.

'At first, I was a little disappointed. When we first started the project I had all these huge ambitions and intentions of how I was going to make the greatest-sounding Bowie album ever. Once I realised the direction we were going, all these dreams went right out the window. I had to get my head round a completely different scenario. It wasn't that I didn't like it, it was just not what I was expecting. I originally wanted a much more controlled environment.'

Gabrels, too, had serious misgivings about Bowie's decision to turn the solo album into a band project: 'I actually tried to talk him out of the band thing because I thought the Sales brothers were nuts! I didn't want to be in a band any more. Bands are a nightmare, and democracy doesn't work as well as benevolent dictatorships in rock'n'roll in my opinion.'

Having been installed only weeks earlier as Bowie's co-collaborator, Gabrels was almost immediately relegated to being one-quarter of a totally unstable whole. 'The Sales brothers gave us the balls,' says Gabrels. 'I learned a lot from those guys about what communicates and what doesn't and what's primal and what's intellectual. We would have thought too much, left to our own devices. Ultimately, it was a magnanimous and kind gesture on David's part because it also meant that we all came out better financially.'

Gabrels forced Bowie into making ad hoc creative decisions – to trust his inspiration, record and be damned. 'David, I feel, was at a point in his career where he just wasn't enjoying making music or liking his own records any more,' is Tim Palmer's succinct appraisal of the situation. 'It had become all too stagnated and thought-out. He seemed to just want the thrill of a group of personalities making music without compromise. This was not about fine details, more about performance. They would work very spontaneously and fast. Sometimes I would still be trying to get a sound but they were done. No chance to go back. The sound of the band playing together in the Casino in Switzerland was electric. Most of the tracks were all played together live. We recorded the album digitally, which is interesting, because many people at that time felt that you could not record grungy, noisy rock on digital. I think this album showed that it can be done.'

'The thing with Tin Machine was that I would have gone for a somewhat more technically proficient and aggressive and slightly experimental rock thing,' says Gabrels, 'rather than a garage thing, which is what we got with the Sales brothers. We were very aggressively going for an audio vérité thing, where you record a song in a day, so we were a handful in the studio, but Tim rose to the occasion wonderfully.

'There was a list of potential names for the band,' says Gabrels. 'The brothers liked "Tin Machine" because it was like The Monkees, having your own theme song! My suggestion for the album name was The Emperor's New Clothes. It was a little too much like setting yourself up; giving your critics ammunition.'

So far the sessions had been frenetic and almost wholly improvisational. The next stage of recording involved a change of locale. 'We finished the first batch of sessions in Switzerland and decided to reconvene in Compass Point Studios in the Bahamas a few months later,' recalls Tim Palmer. 'We also decided to mix the record in New York. In the sessions at the Compass Point Studios in Nassau, the environment was completely different. We were all living in beach huts right by the water's edge, and it was very hot. In the studio, it turned out that we were short of microphone stands because Status Quo had them all next door!'

When *Tin Machine* was released in May 1989, it was the first Bowie album in six years to actually sound of its time. Groups such as Guns N'Roses and Bon Jovi had turned hard rock into a stadium draw, and were reaping huge commercial rewards. And more left-field acts such as Sonic Youth and The Pixies were looking to the properties of sheer noise, to the potentiality of guitar music to form the same sort of musical black hole that was allowing house, rave and techno music to provide the perfect soundtrack to late-1980s hedonism within dance culture. 'I think the first album was important as it was sort of a proto-grunge album,' is Tim Palmer's assessment. 'David was listening to bands like Sonic Youth, Dinosaur Jnr and the Pixies, but none of those bands had broken into the Top 20 US albums. Tin Machine I think opened the door to some of the more chaotic-sounding guitar bands. This, to me, was at least the most vital Bowie album for some time. People seemed to either love it or hate it. At least we got a strong reaction.'

The problem with *Tin Machine* was that, despite its aggression, sonic attack and daring (and all these things are undeniable), it seldom left the era of Led Zeppelin and Cream, and sounded rooted to the blues tradition. Bowie now began to promulgate the joys of 'authentic' emotion within rock, citing the 1960s triumvirate of Cream, Hendrix and Zeppelin as influences, and prizing The Neville Brothers for their 'in yer face' real live sound. In short, he appeared to be championing those very qualities his early career had been aimed at destroying.

The first Tin Machine album did have a number of strong tracks, despite the rather traditional garage bludgeoning inflicted on them by the band. 'Heaven's In Here' was essentially a blues number, with Hunt Sales' drums mixed way up competing for space with Gabrels' lead guitar. Bowie is reduced to a shouting match with the band just to be heard. As for Tony Sales, we can hardly hear him. The lyric of the title track is a sonic admission of Bowie's deadened musical sensibilities. He bawls: 'Raging, raging, raging/Burning in my room/Come on and get a good idea/Come on and get it soon' before the song ends without warning, as if beheaded mid-verse. 'I Can't Read' was cut under a full moon in the Bahamas and mixed in 45 minutes. Bowie again searches for his deserted muse. When he sings, 'I can't read shit any more', it actually sounds like he's singing 'I can't reach it any more' – desperation and despair writ large. On the other hand, Bowie had regained his sense of humour with 'Bus Stop', a punky 1-minute-45 mini-drama about a man finding God while waiting for the bus home. 'Amazing' is lyrical and euphonic, with one of those graceful, melodic lines, ascending effortlessly step by step, which can be heard so often in his work from 'Life On Mars?' through to 'Outside'. The obvious choice for a single, it remains a forgotten gem. Elsewhere, however, Tin Machine either wreak havoc on perfectly good songs like 'Prisoner Of Love' and 'Baby Can Dance', or simply sound oafish and dull.

Bowie had simultaneously released himself from the state of suspended animation which had characterised the somnambulant *Never Let Me Down* and robbed his music of much of its subtlety. As an album, it was not overloaded with great Bowie melodies or hooky choruses either. Sometime Bowie collaborator Adrian Belew echoed many people's sentiments in his assessment of the album: 'My own critique of the record is that it needed some melody. I thought the idea was an interesting one – a sort of noise-based band. I liked the idea, and I liked the people involved. If only David could have fitted in some of the melodic content he's so good at then the songs would have been songs. They were less like songs and more like interesting pieces of music. It's just unfortunate that it didn't contain something a little easier for the rest of us to grab on to.'

The main problem for Bowie was to convince EMI of the validity of both the album and the band. 'I think David realised that the "suits" at the label would have a problem with the new direction he was taking,' recalls Tim Palmer. 'They were always hoping for the new *Let's Dance*, and he enjoyed that. We rented a huge PA to play back the album to the label and it was fun to watch them squirm under the intense volume and chaos.'

Tin Machine was released in May 1989. Although it is traditionally regarded as a ghastly blunder and commercial black hole, this is not necessarily how it was viewed at the time. It sold no worse than *Never Let Me Down*, and in fact improved on the latter's chart position, reaching Number 3 in the UK and Number 28 in the States, thus making it a pretty successful Bowie project, at least in commercial terms. When Bowie announced a small-venue tour to promote the album in the summer, hundreds of fans queued up all night for tickets in the UK. Tin Machine's first gig took place at The Armory, in New York City, followed by another small-scale gig at The World, also in NYC, prior to two dates at the Los Angeles Roxy Club. Next up was a short European tour. When the band played the Paradiso Club in

Amsterdam that May, there were 1,500 inside the club, and 25,000 outside the venue watching a telecast of the gig.

The album was infinitesimally more enjoyable than the ensuing Tin Machine tour, which saw Bowie in the new role of chain-smoking, guitar-tuning journeyman rocker. Tin Machine live was that thing that Bowie had never been, and had no right to be – boring. On stage, a now-bearded Bowie acted out a parody of the rock star he never was, puffing his way through a seemingly endless stash of cigarettes in what was a most unhealthy stage act, coming as it did less than two years after he had sprinted and leap-frogged around on the Glass Spider. On the Tin Machine tour he was the 'diamond geezer', with plenty of band introductions and chats with the audience. For his fans, it was a pleasure to encounter their idol in such small auditoria, although for many he had done away with the very thing that made them want to be Bowie fans in the first place – that sense of daring, of spectacle, of being other. Bowie seemed to want to destroy the idea of being 'David Bowie' altogether. Musically the sound was sloppy, with too many guitar solos, and too little focus. 'Thirty per cent of every night was improvisation and the Sales brothers were rooted in that,' says Gabrels. But unless you were really into massively prolonged rock extemporisation, it was all so much music for musos.

What also alienated fans and critics alike was the insistence that Bowie was merely a quarter of a whole. This, as Reeves Gabrels knew from the very outset, could never be. The result was a false, laddish 'democracy': no amount of media manipulation could ever get Bowie to be interviewed without at least one of his confrères. Bowie, ever the mimic, took this macho bonhomie to great lengths, affecting a blokish, chatty demeanour. For some journalists it was all too much. Jon Savage: 'The forced camaraderie of the Tin Machine project – all those dreadful "boys together in a band" interviews are emetic: they actively make me not want to explore the records further.'

The Sales brothers were all wisecracks and boyish humour, although Gabrels did his best to distance himself from living the ultimate rock'n'roll cliché. 'Yeah, we were sort of revelling in it to a degree, but if you look at my appearance I always wore suits. I was very much anti the image. We don't need limos to meet us at the airport – let's get a van.' The sexual politics of the project, though, were disturbing. It was all big noisy guitars, declamatory lyrics, menopausal angst and four-boys-in-a-band photo oppor-tunities. Gabrels reveals that when he and Bowie compared musical obsessions, their current hobbyhorses were surprisingly similar: 'We realised when we first talked that we were both listening to the same thing – John Coltrane, Miles Davis, Cream, The Pixies, Hendrix, Glen Branca, Sonic Youth, Strauss, Stravinsky. These were all things we wanted this band to be.'

Live, the gang mentality merely added to the homosocial aspect of the project. Lines like 'Tie you down, pretend you're Madonna' on 'Pretty Thing', 'Baby can walk around the town, attract a man, and cut him down' on 'Baby Can Dance', and the moralising tone of 'Prisoner Of Love', a song about entrapment in the female clutches which ends with the command to Bowie's love to 'just stay square', bespeak male insecurity and a sort of clichéd machismo. A later Tin Machine song actually contained the line, 'One shot put her away, hey hey!' Given Bowie's poly-sexuality and gender confusion of the 1970s, the gang warfare of Tin Machine represented a recalcitrant and unpleasant stumble back towards unreconstitution.

Bowie's interviews for this period make for revealing reading. In the early 1980s, he seemed on the surface to be approaching middle age confidently. Now he was full of loathing, and self-doubt, keen to turn his personal dysfunctionalism into tirades against society's ills. Bowie was having a very public midlife crisis. 'What is the purpose of daily life?' he asked *Rapido* rhetorically in May 1989. 'It doesn't seem any more to have any values that mean a thing.' Playing the part of concerned parent, he said of his son, Joe, 'It's very hard for him to understand the structure because, in fact, I think the structure is decaying rapidly.'

For *Tin Machine*, Bowie covered John Lennon's 'Working Class Hero'. Two of his own lyrics also dealt with overtly political themes. 'Under The God' was a shouting match with a neo-Nazi, and 'Crack City' an act of self-sterilisation, a tirade ostensibly directed at 'the master dealer', but symbolically also against his own 'irresponsible' 70s self. Both songs are extremely simplistic lyrically, and deliberately so. Bowie commented: 'I don't wanna go on preaching but I've only heard a couple of anti-drug songs. Frankly, I don't think people are writing them, but I've not heard one that's effective because they're all intellectual, they're all literate, and they're written for other writers.' Of 'Under The God' he said: 'I wanted something that had the same simplistic, naive, radical, laying it down about the emergence of a new Nazi so that people could not mistake what the song was about.' Of the two, 'Crack City', with its brazen use of the 'Wild Thing' riff, works much better, bringing to mind the cautionary tale of the life and tragic drug-related demise of Hendrix. The motivations for these songs were largely personal, but Bowie hid behind the mask of collective responsibility in Tin Machine to publicly atone for his own private sense of shame for some of his past coke-driven predictions. Bowie was not altogether a convincing advocate. His music had never before carried a party-political agenda, and he had always tried to distance himself from the role of white, middle-class, middle-aged pop star with a social conscience. It is a very, very tricky role to play convincingly, as everyone from Bob Dylan to Sting has found out.

Some commentators proclaimed Tin Machine a scam: unconvincing and noisy, it was simply David Bowie's latest shock tactic, and an act of artificial authenticity. Tim Palmer: 'People's ideas of a David Bowie album with the emphasis on constant metamorphosis and direction changes just fuelled the idea that it was just another Bowie concept like Ziggy Stardust. The simple fact that David was at such a different level in the success scale and financial scale, with all his busy schedules, made the idea of him just being a band member seem a little unbelievable.'

So, Tin Machine seemed like the musical manifestation of a midlife crisis. Now well into his forties, Bowie externalised his feelings of insecurity and depression in a shroud of noisy, 'youthful' rock. Despite its shortcomings, and presumably to spite EMI, Bowie continued the project. In the autumn of 1989, Bowie took the band to Australia to record a second album. Cast away in an alien environment, the band became less manic and more self-absorbed. The new material was melancholic and rootless. 'With the second Tin Machine record, my desire was to bring the songwriting a little more to the fore,' says Gabrels. 'I wanted the songs to stand more clearly as songs, and for the ragged edge of the playing on the first record to be preserved but for us to try and bring the songs more to the front.'

With the best part of the follow-up album in the can, Bowie switched back to solo mode again. With Tin Machine Bowie had tried to kill himself off, at least in commercial terms as a 'brand' name. His record company, EMI, bamboozled by the loss of the signifier 'Bowie', were left with a major marketing headache, which they subsequently got rid of by almost apologetically attaching stickers to the album's cover telling potential buyers that David Bowie was in fact alive and well and just part of a new band they didn't know how to promote. With Tin Machine, he had murdered David Bowie, pop star. With his next venture, he would attempt to put his musical history to the sword, to inflict execution by arena rock.

In January 1990, Bowie did what many fans thought he would never, ever do. He agreed to a multimillion-pound greatest hits tour. On the surface, the idea was so Las Vegas that it was indeed something of a shock: songs such as 'Rock And Roll Suicide' had signalled his hatred of schmaltzy, Sinatra-style goodbyes. Surely even a career that had been based on a media profile of constant change and innovation could not accommodate a retroactive measure of this magnitude? But behind the suspicion that Bowie was simply cashing in on his back catalogue in a lull between projects there was a genuine excitement at the opportunity of hearing the old songs again, songs which had helped define popular culture in the post-Beatles age. It was a momentous decision by Bowie to revisit past glories. With the exception of the Serious Moonlight tour, Bowie had never given his fans a show based primarily on hits. He was to indulge himself (financially) and his audience (musically) in equal measure.

Again, Bowie was tuning into the *Zeitgeist*. Popular music around the late 1980s and early 1990s became defined, in part, by retroactivity. By 1990 sales of CDs in the UK amounted to 45.6 per cent of total units sold, a little way ahead of prerecorded cassettes at 41 per cent, with vinyl amounting to just 13.4 per cent of total sales. In the period 1985–90, CDs tended to be bought by affluent sections of society, and the format was originally sold on the basis of its alleged superior ability to reproduce sounds (hence its initial popularity with classical music aficionados). Often CDs were merely a means to update, rather than add to, a personal library of sounds, resulting in old favourites being bought and listened to all over again. In 1990 the launch in the UK of the glossy monthly magazines *Vox* and *Select*, both reactive measures to the success of *Q*, was an attempt to tap into this spirit of retroactivity. *Q* magazine in particular had a refreshingly open idea of what needed to be covered. We might not care much for Phil Collins or Fleetwood Mac, but they were undeniably important in commercial terms and they had stories to tell (stories which other rock weeklies and monthlies weren't telling).

Rock entered the 1990s as an antique cultural form. David Bowie entered the 1990s as a discredited old-school superstar. In the eyes of much of the media and many of his fans, there had been three self-inflicted hammer blows to his career – *Tonight*, *Never Let Me Down*/'Glass Spider' and the entire Tin Machine project – and one which he could do nothing about: his age. The dilemma for Bowie, as for countless other rockers of 'maturing' vintage, was how to deal as a middle-aged rock star with a predominantly thirty-something and middle-aged audience using a cultural form (pop and rock) which was in danger of playing itself out.

Bowie obviously didn't want to become a jukebox, forever recycling his hits for the pop-goes-cabaret circuit. So he became one temporarily, using the *Sound + Vision* greatest hits tour to retire his most popular songs before killing off his past for good. Now 43 years old, with a legacy of 25 years' worth of recorded music, he felt weighed down by his past and by public expectations of what constituted that past. Bowie later claimed, in a radio interview with Capital London's Nicky Horne, that since he regarded himself as an artist, as someone whose art was dependent on its contemporaneity for its lifeblood, the thought of being simply another rocker with a repertoire to repeat tour after tour was deeply depressing. In some ways, Bowie has an almost high-cultural estimation of what the relationship between himself and his art ought to be. There is a sneaking suspicion that, like a classical composer, Bowie would love to debut each new work rather than having to mix and match it with crowd-pleasing oldies. Bowie rather ambiguously said that the tour would 'probably be the last time I will be doing these songs' (i.e. implying that all those oldies not played on the tour were still ripe for further exploitation), before adding a trademark piece of subterfuge, 'And I generally stick by what I say.' He arranged for fans to vote for their favourite tracks, which, he promised, would form the set list for the shows. After that, they would never be performed again. However, most commentators knew that it was a self-denying ordinance that would prove virtually impossible to stick to, and they would be proved right.

The immediate motivation behind *Sound + Vision* was a promotional one. The small American record label, Rykodisc, had been entrusted with the difficult task of tidying up Bowie's back catalogue. In late 1989 they had released the exquisite boxed set, *Sound + Vision*, which later justifiably won an award for package design. Never-before-heard songs included 'Lightning Frightening' from 1971, 'After Today', an out-take from the Sigma sessions in 1974, and Bowie's own reading of Bruce Springsteen's 'It's Hard To Be A Saint In The City'. Enthused by Rykodisc's overall commitment and standards, and with a reissued back catalogue to promote, Bowie's decision to tour his old hits was of mutual financial benefit.

The idea of a greatest hits revue was first mooted back in early 1988, and Bowie had agreed to the concept of a 1990s hits tour even before starting work with Tin Machine. Bowie asked Reeves Gabrels to be the guitarist on the tour, but Gabrels graciously declined and suggested Adrian Belew. 'From my point of view, I didn't want to play old songs; I had too much fondness for the original versions. Adrian was more part of David's history. It seemed more like Adrian's place; he had been on two records in the 1970s. It left me free to chase David around with the tapes of the second album while he was on the *Sound + Vision* tour. We were trying to make the band point, and if I'd have done the tour, the Sales brothers would have been pissed off and it would have confused the issue a whole lot more.'

'I was by the pool in San Diego with the rock band America when I got a call from David asking me to do the gig,' says Belew. 'I thought it was a pretty huge undertaking.' We talked about material, and the list of songs grew longer and longer, and they required quite a lot of different styles and different sounds. The way we decided that we could cover so much material was to put some of the orchestrations into a sequencer. So you could actually have an orchestra play. I remember we kept adding more and more sampling and we kept buying more and more samplers! What I wanted to do was to reach the essence of the songs, yet do them in a fresh manner. Any signatures, a particular guitar line or any particular parts that you really needed, stayed, and everything else was just interpreted by the band.'

Rehearsals, which lasted a month, began in January 1990 in New York City. At the end of January, Bowie appeared in a crisp black suit and white shirt, mercifully beardless, and with an acoustic guitar in hand, to announce the *Sound + Vision* tour at a press conference at the Rainbow Theatre, London. He good-naturedly strummed along to a few lines of the 'Laughing Gnome' before launching into 'Space Oddity'. This, he told the press, was merely a temporary interruption to all things Tin Machine; a chance to wipe the slate clean and carve a greatest-hits-free era for himself in the 1990s. The demand for tickets in the UK was colossal. Two shows at the 12,000-seat London Arena sold out immediately. A third went in eight and a half minutes. A new compilation, *ChangesBowie*, featuring a predictable selection of hits from 1969 to 1984 and terrible cover artwork (a sixth-form cut'n'paste collage of thousand-times-seen photos slapped across the 1976 *ChangesoneBowie* black-and-white shot), was readied for release. A 'new' old single was also planned. Although never a favourite in the UK, 'Fame', as Bowie's older US Number 1 ('Let's Dance' was considered too recent to rerelease), was remixed in a myriad of largely superfluous formats and reissued as 'Fame 90'. Bowie was back as 'living nostalgia'. Through its excesses, Glass Spider had killed off pop star Bowie, and Tin Machine had seen him shrink to a quarter of his original size to become part of a band. Would *Sound + Vision* finish the job?

12. 'IMANCIPATION', 1990–1993

Do you realise we have accumulated 74 years of touring experience in this band? ... Well, that's something to think about, isn't it? ... That means that collectively we're like Muddy Waters. A very poor man's Muddy Waters.

DAVID BOWIE ON TIN MACHINE, 1991

David said to me that he didn't want to compete with Let's Dance. *I said, 'You're crazy. We have to compete with* Let's Dance. *That's our job!'*

NILE RODGERS ON BLACK TIE WHITE NOISE, 1999

'I Believe In Magic/Angel For Life'

BOWIE'S 'WEDDING SONG', FOR IMAN, 1993

With the Tin Machine project put to bed, at least temporarily, Bowie was Bowie once more and his fans turned out in their millions to hear his greatest hits for what they thought would be the very last time. Bowie's audience had aged. His last big hit album was seven years ago. The last album that had spoken directly to the cult of Bowie was a decade ago. His hard-core following were now twenty- and thirty-somethings and they were dwindling fast. In their place was the rump of the *Let's Dance* era, the general rock fan who wanted Bowie to be a singing jukebox. Although he played hit after hit, many of the gigs were strangely muted affairs, as if the audience was over-bloated by the well known. Bowie could hardly have been more crowd-pleasing. His audience pigged out on a diet of hits, from 'Space Oddity' and

'Jean Genie', to 'Fame', 'Golden Years', 'Queen Bitch', 'China Girl', 'Let's Dance', 'Fashion', 'Blue Jean', 'Modern Love', 'Rebel Rebel', 'Changes', 'John, I'm Only Dancing', 'Young Americans' (during which Bowie crumpled to the floor and feigned incapacity after emoting the lines, 'ain't there one damn song/that can make me break down and cry'), and, of course, 'Sound And Vision', but now a Bowie gig was a pleasurable evening out, not a hormonally charged theatrical behemoth of a gig. Bowie himself set the tone, in sombre suit, sensible hair and strumming an acoustic guitar, diffidently conservative and businesslike. The days of him as a teen idol were gone. Even with so many hits in the set, one 'fan' at Birmingham NEC was overheard asking her partner during the intro to 'Station To Station', 'Is this from his Tin Man album or something?' 'There was a certain portion of the audience that knew less about David Bowie than the true David Bowie fans,' says Adrian Belew. 'For them, it's a scene, it's an event; maybe they've heard one or two songs but they know David Bowie's a superstar and they want to be involved – it's almost like a football event. You know, I'm sure that true awareness was only a part of it.'

Did Belew believe Bowie was bowing out his old songs? 'I did, actually, because I knew his commitment to trying to make adventurous new music,' he said in 2003. 'He'd already started Tin Machine, and that's what that was all about, an attempt to strike out into new territory and to stop making popular music per se. And I had had enough conversations with him to know that he wasn't happy with the way things had gone. He especially wasn't proud of the last couple of things he'd done. The Glass Spider tour he'd hated. He told me that from the very beginning he knew that it was just not right. In my mind I envisaged that David would now go to places that he'd never been before. I believed him, and that's kind of what he's done. He's not been back to that level of exposure since then, but it's not just because his music has changed and his attitudes have changed, it's because the world has changed.'

It was always Bowie's intention to go for a small musical unit – the legacy of his Tin Machine experience. Belew had downscaled and contemporised Bowie's back catalogue and his sequenced arrangements gave it coherence. 'Space Oddity', with a big, booming fretless bass, worked well, as did a rocky 'Changes' and a stately 'Ziggy Stardust'. Belew pulled out all the stops on the tour, giving virtuoso performances every night, attempting to cover the ground of two, sometimes three, guitarists. He wrote an eerie backward guitar solo to introduce 'Ashes To Ashes', although Bowie often got nowhere near the falsetto live, his voice cracked and weak. However, on some tracks, such as 'Stay' and 'Young Americans', it was time for Belew and the band to struggle. The sound was starved of essential nutrients, and in dire need of the emergency services of a rhythm guitarist and a saxophonist. 'I played guitar synths, which I could make to sound like violins and trumpets,' says Belew. 'However, a saxophone is vital on "Young Americans", and I always felt that you couldn't fill that role with the guitar. Occasionally, of course, it would have been nice to augment a few things here and there.' What *SoundAVision* conclusively proved was that Bowie needs a big band to really cut it live, but it's a lesson that he has not always heeded.

Visually, the tour was Bowie's best since the 70s and it left even the most die-hard critic with a sense of wonderment. Bowie was killing off old songs and ghoulishness marked the stage presentation on the tour. When the first few bars of 'Space Oddity' started it was just Bowie and an acoustic guitar. Then suddenly a gigantic, computer-generated image of the man appeared out of the ether, hovering magically in front of him and, in an optical trick, seemingly above the first few rows of the audience too.

At preprogrammed times a diaphanous screen was lowered at the front of the stage and films were projected onto it. These films, a brilliant series of images, were constructed to add complementary visual information: a 60-foot pair of legs somersaulted across the stage for 'Space Oddity'; a swirling, gyrating Bowie danced for 'Be My Wife'. In a visual technique mimicking his strategy of ego assembly, Bowie was chopped up and reassembled for 'Let's Dance', and for 'Ashes To Ashes' a quite stunning film depicted him dressed as the Thin White Duke of old – coked out, icy and blank. With the addition of two screens on either side of the stage, acting independently of one another and randomly showing first close-up pictures of the live Bowie, then a variety of computer-generated images, the result was befuddling: Which Bowie should I be looking at? The live, 'real' one, the one on film, or the 'real version' being slowed down, chopped up and turned different colours on the screens as he sang? The process was confused even further by the fact that the film Bowie often lip-synched in time with the real Bowie's live vocal. The most curious moment came when a computer-generated image of dancer Louise Le Cavalier chased the real-life Bowie off the stage. Bowie was able to slice off aspects of his personality and have them dance simultaneously before his audience. There was no need for breathless costume changes. Technology had given Bowie the ultimate self-regarding strategy. During 'Rebel Rebel', he made the song's lyric (an anthem for his glam-era 'children') come to life. The fans became the stars, as Bowie filmed the audience with a video camera, the images instantaneously relayed to the screen.

The stage was lit like a theatre – a vast expanse of blackness with Bowie and Belew illuminated by white light. Just as the monochromatic look of this tour was a direct descendant of the chiaroscuro of the 1976 tour, so Bowie took the stage in a frilly white shirt with crumpled, rakish Georgian sleeves and either black waistcoat and trousers or dark suit. With a deliberate nod to glories past, and in an inspired gesture, Bowie began using an excerpt from Walter Carlos' soundtrack for *A Clockwork Orange* as his opening music, just as he had done for those *Aladdin Sane* shows so many years before. It was a moment of genuine poignancy and not a little sadness for days of glory past.

Only Belew was allowed in front of the scrim to trade off guitar lines and play with Bowie. 'David wanted me to be out on the stage with him because I think he needs some sort of sparring partner. He would occasionally say, "You can be Keith to my Mick!" But he didn't want the rest of the band in the picture.' This, according to Belew, led to a great deal of resentment. 'It was decided that the band would be shunted off to the corner; in fact, behind one of the opera scrims that would come down. I know they were gravely disappointed by it. I think everyone in the band then felt very insignificant. I think Rick Fox, our keyboard player, nearly quit the tour several times.'

As on the *Diamond Dogs* tour, Bowie wanted to fill the stage space with his solo act. This was not a rock show in any accepted definition of the term. 'One night was particularly nasty,' recalls Belew. 'There was a song in which David wore a guitar and somehow he miscommunicated to Erdal Kizilcay, our bassist. He made a motion to Erdal and Erdal ran up to him on stage and started dancing along with David, which infuriated him. He was very upset about it, threw his guitar across the stage, and cut out of there as quickly as he could. At that point, we had a rented jet which we flew in, and it was a very quiet and tense flight that evening. In the event David and Erdal had words and it was all smoothed over, but obviously the idea was that no one was supposed to come out on stage with David and me.'

After the gig Bowie threw his shirt at him, saying, 'Take it, and sing in my place, Erdal.' And, after further words during the flight to the next gig, Kizilcay decided to leave the tour. Prior to the gig, Bowie had given the whole band a pep talk. Reviews of the tour had been decidedly mixed, and Bowie had called for more action on stage. According to Kizilcay, the flashpoint occurred when Bowie begun trading licks with him during 'The Jean Genie' and Bowie missed his vocal cue for when the chorus came back in, thus infuriating him. The argument was soon smoothed over by Bowie, but, in general, the small touring party was not a happy bunch of people.

Sometimes Belew would sneak back behind the opera screen to check that his band was still there. 'Every now and then, I'd duck back just to interact with them a bit. There were occasions when I would see Rick Fox, the keyboard player, eating a sandwich, while an enormous amount of sound would be pouring out from all the keyboard samplers – he wouldn't actually have anything to do! There were also times when he would wear headphones and he would turn off his live keyboard and the guys in the crew could hear what he was playing and he'd be playing some Beatles song or something right on stage whilst we were playing "Space Oddity"! Naturally, some of the songs he did play in real time, but there were stretches where he could have a sandwich too!'

The sheer scale of some of these gigs staggered Belew. It was awe-inspiring and exciting, yet somehow unreal. 'I remember walking on stage every night and the lights would come on and we'd start "Space Oddity" and it was absolutely chilling. There'd be this immense sea of heads and lighters. But, overall, as a musical experience, playing in those kinds of stadia is not the greatest because you're not really sure what the audience thinks. It's a large smattering of indifference. When you play in a club you can see the faces of the audience and you can see when they're responding. David said to me once, "I stretch my arm out and look over here to the right and I see there's my friend Jim over here and I wave and 2,000 people wave back at me." We played the Egg Dome in Japan and the Sky Dome in Canada with anything from perhaps 60,000 to 90,000 people. With that many people, it's almost surreal.'

According to Belew, Bowie himself was a much-changed man, and the two became friends. 'I remember he gave me a guided tour of the Prado Museum in Spain. It was like going round with a professional guide! He just seemed friendly, happier, more at ease with himself. I realised that his life was still complicated and he was still having problems. He was in a problematic relationship with Melissa and I could see he was very distressed about that. I myself was going through a divorce, so we did have "buddy, buddy"-type conversations. More than anything else, he was once again unsure of where to move his career to. He mentioned to me what a disaster he thought the previous tour had been. I think he was embarrassed by that tour.'

Bowie was on a more even keel. He was enjoying life without drugs as a prop, although he did allow himself a beer or two, with often comic results. 'He gets inebriated very quickly,' recalls Belew with a chuckle. 'If he drinks one or two beers then he's drunk. He's very funny when he's drunk; he gets kind of loud, but in a nice way. He reminded me of a modern-day Cary Grant. He had a very good sense of humour about himself. He was still very stylish and fashionable, although he wasn't outrageous any more. He'd moved out of that period into being a grown-up.'

Belew also found that almost the entire management, promotional and touring team of the class of 1978 had been removed. 'The buffer of people had changed completely,' remembers Belew, with, of course, the exception of the 'aide to Mr Bowie', Coco Schwab.

Coco's attitude towards her relationship with David is a protective one; overly protective, I would say. She's very controlling of his image and of everything that happens around him, and either he's telling her what he wants done, and she's doing it, or she's controlling what's happening and he's going along with it. I was never quite sure which was the truth: probably both. If there was someone who had to be fired, or something that needed to be changed, she'd be the one with the bad news.

Sometimes it would just irritate you because it would be so useless. I'll give you a little story about Coco. One time we were in England and I met a fan who was in need of a ride (I think they were hitchhiking), so I gave them a ride back to the hotel. Then I went and had some lunch and I saw Coco, who asked me what I'd been doing. I said I'd been into town and had given a ride to a fan who was really bubbling over about David Bowie. Coco flipped out and said, 'You should never do that. You should never talk to these fans. You don't know what they're capable of.' Her famous quote to me then was, 'You need to be more paranoid!' That's a perfect quote. I wrote it down. That's quite an odd thing to think. I'd rather not be more paranoid. I realise that there is some truth in what she's saying and that there are people out there who might be dangerous, but it struck me as being inappropriate for the occasion, and frankly, I'm not interested in being more paranoid.

There's no denying that Coco has antagonised well-meaning work associates, but there is an important gender-related point to be made about her. To make her voice heard in a male-dominated climate, it's no wonder, in one respect, that a figure such as Coco (and there are many others like her in the music business) had to adopt ruthless, sometimes rude, strategies. Likewise, because of their relative scarcity value within the music business, women arguably tend to be targeted and demonised by men, who feel threatened by the dominance of these women within the power-relationship. If Coco had been a man, comments about her would in all probability be nowhere near as negative, as he (she) would have just been doing his (her) job. The potential threats to Bowie were very real: on tour it was a security nightmare if fans gained access to private suites, hotel lobbies, musicians' rooms, and Coco had the events of 8 December 1980 firmly imprinted on her mind.

Belew and Bowie recorded two songs together, and the rocker, 'Pretty Pink Rose', became a tour staple. Bowie had demoed the song with Bryan Adams' backing band back in 1988. In its original state it sounds incredibly pop-orientated, having as it does some annoyingly MOR keyboard riffs, but it is nevertheless a very strong song and has an insistent synth riff which was removed by Belew when he arranged it in 1990. Belew gave it balls, added a lovely musical introduction which stated its main musical theme, put some avant-garde pop guitar on it and transformed it from pop into rock. 'He sent me a demo and I thought on first hearing, Well, my God, now I've got this offer from David to do one of his songs, but I'm not sure whether I like it!' remembers Belew. 'But I did like it, especially the chorus, so I took it into the studio and doctored it up with lots of guitar playing, and it turned out a lot better. To be in the studio on the same microphone as David Bowie, that's pretty amazing. There's a chill factor. It's kind of unimaginable in some ways. You don't picture yourself standing at the microphone singing with one of the most famous singers in the world.'

Tim Pope, one of the most innovative video producers of the time and The Cure's in-house video-maker, shot the song's video, which had Bowie and Belew hamming it up with actress Julie T. Wallace, who had, in the mid-80s, earned a certain notoriety as the lead in the BBC's adaptation of *The Lives and Loves of a She-Devil*. Inexplicably, the single was a flop. 'Even to have a big-name figure does not guarantee success,' Belew ruefully comments. 'Atlantic promoted it as much as they could until they ran out of budget.'

The tour, however, was big business and the greatest hits package, *ChangesBowie*, became Bowie's first UK Number 1 since *Tonight* in 1984. Even *The Rise And Fall Of Ziggy Stardust And The Spiders From Mars* made a brief reappearance in both the British and American album charts. As the tour played through Europe that spring, it picked up consistently good reviews. For *The Times*' David Sinclair, Bowie's 'presence was little short of majestic'. Giles Smith in the *Independent* located the artifice behind Bowie's surface ordinariness: 'Hoping perhaps to suggest a chummy informality, he occasionally lugged his own microphone stand out of the way, or noisily plugged a guitar in, moments which, in fact, merely confirmed your suspicions of contrivance ... And when a roadie was on hand apparently for the sole purpose of removing the man's cigarette, you realised the extent to which the steps were mapped in advance.' Adam Sweeting was typically less impressed, calling the show 'David Bowie's Antiques Roadshow'. To some critics, revisiting past glories merely indicated his parlous creative state of the moment.

The *Sound + Vision* tour sped on through North America before reaching one of Bowie's heartlands, Japan, in May. Unfortunately, 'The Laughing Gnome' was not on the set list anywhere, despite all the efforts of the *NME* and its 'Just Say Gnome' spoof campaign. With Bowie still adamant in interviews that he was giving up his past repertoire, the final resting place for Ziggy was the Rock In Chile Festival in Santiago on 27 September 1990. The *Sound + Vision* tour had visited 27 countries, played 108 shows and lasted 7 months. In the UK alone he had played to a quarter of a million people, five times more than anticipated when the initial dates were announced. Bowie allegedly made £4.5 million from just ten UK gigs.

Bowie and Belew bade one another farewell. 'We agreed that sometime in the future we'd do something again,' recalled Belew in 1999, 'but time passes quickly. It's already been eight years!' Bowie went immediately into filming for a romantic comedy, *The Linguini Incident*, with Rosanna Arquette. Belew resumed his successful avant-garde pop career as a solo artist and in various other collaborative formations centring around King Crimson and its scions.

During the course of the *Sound + Vision* tour Bowie split up with Melissa Hurley, who was, by this time, his fiancée. The sizeable gap in age between the two had finally taken its toll. On 14 October, Bowie met Iman Abdulmajid (born 25 July 1955, in Mogadishu, Somalia), a long-time Bowie fan. Iman, she of the Tia Maria television ads in the 1980s, had been one of the top models in the world in the 1980s, but by the time she met Bowie she had already given up this career to move into film and to set up her own cosmetics company. 'I saw his relationship with Melissa dissolve,' says Belew. 'We were sitting on the plane and he was leafing through a fashion magazine when he stopped at a picture of Iman and said: "I want to get to know her, I want to have a date with her!" I think lightning struck; just looking at her picture, he got interested in her. That was at the very end of the tour; at the beginning of the tour, I saw that he was going through a lot of personal grief over the relationship he had at that point.'

The two began a quaintly old-fashioned romance that would lead to marriage in 1992. Meeting Iman shook Bowie out of the depression of his early forties. 'We lived together for twenty months and during that time I had to learn how to evaluate what sharing one's life meant,' wrote Bowie in 1998. 'Strange new things like learning to listen, knowing when a reply was not necessary but just being a receptive human being ... Most importantly, though, turning one's asocial possessive and inevitably destructive characteristics around.' In a move sure to keep Interflora on their toes, Bowie apparently sends Iman flowers on the 14th of every month, the anniversary of their first dinner date.

Carlos Alomar was relieved and happy for his friend. 'From the Serious Moonlight tour through Tin Machine and back to David Bowie again, he was going through all sorts of upheavals. A major, major concern was his love life. Here's a guy in the prime of his life. We saw him with Melissa and we thought, "What is he doing with this kid?" I have had a wonderful relationship with my wife Robin for thirty years so he knows what a wonderful family life I had. You've got to be envious of a situation like that. When he met Iman, he must have been crying out to have a different part of his life addressed. Once he met Iman, I knew he would be just fine because the depressions that he was going through during the Glass Spider tour were directly associated with his inability to find love. A lover is not a wife. When he married Iman, I was like, "Wow!" ' Mike Garson had this to say about Iman: 'She is great. She's very dynamic and intelligent. When I see David and Iman together I see a beautiful couple who share a mutual respect and love. They are very supportive of each other's busy lives and careers.

Bowie proposed in Paris in October on the Seine. 'We rented a boat and it was a total surprise,' remembers Iman. 'We had a chef, a piano player, and every time we went under one of the bridges, the lights would come up and he got on his knees and proposed to me.'

If his love life was flowering, his music career was 'hitting an all-time low'. In the space of twelve months Bowie had to endure the double blow of being dropped by his record label, EMI, and of seeing his new album, *Tin Machine II*, become the first for nearly twenty years to miss the UK Top 20. In America it reached only Number 126.

At some point in 1990, EMI heard the tapes for the second Tin Machine album and decided that they weren't going to release it. When Bowie had told Gabrels back in 1988 that his record company had to release his new product, he was perhaps underestimating corporate desire for hummable tunes and rock-star appurtenances. Eventually, Bowie found a new deal with Victory Records. One of the first suggestions from the new label was to turn 'One Shot', one of the catchier tracks on the album, into a radio-friendly hit. Hugh Padgham, who by now had become one of the biggest producers in the world with his work with Sting and Phil Collins, was brought in. 'We recorded it in A&M Studios in LA, and mixed it in New York,' says Padgham. 'I was sent the demo and I thought, Yes, this is a bloody great song.'

Padgham, however, was not a great admirer of what had gone on previously with the band: 'I thought it was terrible, to be honest. I just couldn't believe it. It just sounded like this mad bunch of people. It was only when I started working with them that I realised that Reeves was a master of his instrument in an Adrian Belew kind of way. To the uninitiated it could sound just like a load of noise, but actually when you concentrated on listening, it made more sense. I remember being amazed by Hunt Sales. The Sales brothers were basically mad.'

With Bowie on the road throughout most of 1990, the task of pulling the second Tin Machine album together had gone to Gabrels. His intention was to bring out the songs; to bring a melodic sensibility to bear on the band's grooves. Tim Palmer, the producer of the first Tin Machine record, was called in to mix the new album. 'Bowie could always put on a great performance. On one song, "Amlapura", I remember David resinging the lead vocal slightly flat, very intentionally, to get a sad-sounding performance. That control of pitch really impressed me.'

Tin Machine II was finally released on 3 September. It was an inconsistent, compromised set, varying from the excellent, lilting pop/rock of 'Goodbye Mr Ed' and the chill psycho-drama of 'Shopping For Girls' to the abomination of the tub-thumping slice of authentic Americana that is 'Stateside' and the genuinely excruciating balladry of the schmaltzy epic 'Sorry' (both these tracks, as if in a bid to secure the band as a 'democracy', were sung by drummer Hunt Sales). Most of the other tracks fell somewhere between these two extremes: 'Baby Universal', with its 'hallo humans, can you hear me thinking', might have worked had the backing track been more inventive (as it was when played live by Bowie in 1996). The breezy ballad, 'Amlapura', a paean to Bowie's beloved Indonesia, was also affecting enough. The first single, 'You Belong In Rock'n'Roll', complete with Bowie in hammy Elvis mode, was booming, mechanistic and Bowie barely broke out of a semi-spoken drawl.

Bowie certainly seemed enthused, and embarked on an autumn media blitz which included two *Top of the Pops* appearances, a Radio 1 session and a short world tour. The later VH1 legend, 'Music that means something', could have equally applied to Tin Machine too and their self-conscious attempts to make weighty and 'profound' musical statements. 'We're trying to create a new adult thing,' Bowie told *Rolling Stone* in autumn 1991.

As a man with his own inimitable sense of style, on tour that autumn Bowie paraded a version of himself which showed an almost *Tonight*-era proclivity for loud, clashing suits, bland designer shirts and luminous striped trousers. This was sartorial and musical meltdown combined. The embarrassingly 'kick-ass'-entitled It's My Life tour hit North America, Europe and Japan, playing small- to medium-sized venues through to February 1992. But this time the reception, at least in the UK, was half-hearted. Just two years before fans had camped all night for tickets to see their man in cosy venues. Now ticket sales even for 2–3,000-capacity venues were brisk but hardly overwhelming. The band played the last gig of the tour on 17 February 1992, in Tokyo. It was the last time they ever played together. A second single from the album, 'Baby Universal', missed the Top 40, and 'One Shot', the intended radio-friendly single, wasn't even released in the UK or US.

Tin Machine as a band finally came to a rather demeaning end with the release of *Oy Vey Baby – Tin Machine Live* in the summer of 1992. If Tin Machine on record had been a rather hit-and-miss affair (in some instances certainly much better than most critics have made out), then live they often sounded wearisome and blustering. *Oy Vey Baby*, its title intended as a pun on U2's recently unleashed *Achtung Baby*, remains Bowie's least essential moment to date. The record failed to make the charts in either America or the UK. The British music press savaged it. *Melody Maker*'s Paul Mathur turned a review of the album into Bowie's obituary: 'This is the moment where finally, categorically and, let's face it, lumpily, he ceases to exist as an artist of any worth whatsoever. It's not the glamorous plane crash, not even any sort of paid-his-dues dying candle . . . It's not just dying, it's ensuring that posterity will never know he existed.'

Undeterred, Reeves Gabrels rates this as the best Tin Machine album. For him, it's what the band were supposed to be all about: playing live, improvisation, fleshing out the blueprints of the original songs: 'That band was really about being a live band,' concludes Gabrels. 'It was a garage band on steroids with a big budget!'

In reality, by 1992, the band had run its course, 'People want to see David Bowie,' says Gabrels. 'There are people who would pay £35 to go and watch him grocery shop. People wanted their David Bowie unadulterated; they didn't want to see him playing with these three Americans. They didn't want to see him with a band. They didn't want to hear Hunt and Tony or myself sing. We made the point and we also fell on the grenade of *Let's Dance* and created the situation whereby anything that happened next could be anything. People didn't know what to expect, which is the way it had been previously in his career.'

Tin Machine should have been a one-off project, or simply a Bowie album, rather than a career strategy. Journalist Paul Du Noyer says, 'I still take the courageous minority viewpoint that Tin Machine was (a) an essential step for him and (b) quite a successful experiment. I suppose my only feeling is that the experiment was successfully completed with the release of the first album and he should have gracefully left the laboratory at that point. There was no need for a second one – least of all was there the need for that appallingly entitled *Oy Vey Baby*. It's all so sad because it's such a reactive title. It doesn't seem to be Bowie's job to be blandly responding to someone else's existing success.'

The Tin Machine period, taken as a whole, left us with only a handful of genuinely good Bowie songs. For Bowie, it was a crucial career move: 'Once I had done Tin Machine, nobody could see me any more. They didn't know who the hell I was, which was the best thing that ever happened, because I was back using all the artistic pieces that I needed to survive and I was imbuing myself with the passion that I had in the late 70s.' Tin Machine, then, was a rite of passage. According to Bowie, it salvaged his career. However, the band has not been judged kindly by posterity. In 2004 *Blender* magazine placed Tin Machine 12th in their Top 50 Worst Artists in Music.

No official explanation has ever been given for the demise of Tin Machine. There was no statement to the press, no big bust-up to report, no artistic differences, no nothing, and Bowie remained, out of a sense of loyalty, tight-lipped about the whole affair. So, what were the real reasons behind the split? Most importantly, Tin Machine weren't selling enough records to attract major label support, although it should be pointed out that the band was a genuine democracy. Bowie did not have to bankroll the group, nor did he shoulder the losses. Reeves Gabrels in particular was keen to distance himself from rock-star extravagances. Second, Bowie decided, creative batteries recharged, that he could do it without them, thank you very much. Third, there was a general feeling of things 'having run their course'.

'We just got tired of debating every issue,' confirms Reeves Gabrels. 'We did a very long tour together and I think we realised at that point that he didn't need the burden of a democratic band, to some degree. I always wondered how long it would take him to realise that; the fact that personality-wise, there was a lot of air in one balloon. I could be very wilful and convinced I was right about things. I was probably the one who had the least right to be aggressive in that environment and I'm sure that I was no day at the beach either.'

According to some sources, what disenchanted Bowie in particular was the lifestyle of Hunt Sales. One lighter and rigger at the Zirkus Krone gig in Munich 1991 recalls doing coke with 'the one with all the tattoos'. Reeves Gabrels, though, vehemently denies that hard drugs were a part of Tin Machine's touring lifestyle. 'I have to say that in the whole time – two tours, two albums – I never saw anything. Tony to this day, from the time of his automobile accident, was strictly teetotal. Hunt was a hobbyist. He would smoke pot or do whatever he wanted in his own time, which everyone is entitled to do. I'm sure there were times when I was aware of things that were going on but it certainly would not have included Tony. Tony's sobriety is a very precious thing to him.'

Carlos Alomar, however, is far less circumspect: 'I did find out that David was very unhappy during the Tin Machine stuff. He was very unhappy because of the drug problem they had with one of the band members, Hunt Sales. It's a terrible blow when you find that one of the band members is lying to you and, more importantly, lying to himself. David was depressed because of his inability to deal with that drug problem. You know, if you get ready to do a show and one of the members is totally out of it, it's gonna affect you considerably. Particularly when the die is cast and you've thrown yourself in with the lot of them. What are you gonna do?'

For Gabrels, had it all ended there and then as far as his work with Bowie was concerned, he would have quite happily returned to playing in other bands, and in other musical genres. 'As far as I was concerned, after the first Tin Machine album it could have been over and I would have been satisfied. I had participated in something that brought it back to a position where I thought David's heart was. I didn't really worry about what would happen after the demise of Tin Machine because I knew I'd still be playing in any case. At the end of Tin Machine, the idea that David and

I might work together was there, and we parted amicably and with humour.'

Bowie's next public performance came in April 1992 at the Freddie Mercury Tribute Concert For Aids Awareness. That night Bowie came over as a jokey, good-natured bloke (his references to his promiscuity in the 1970s were, shall we say, inappropriate, given the event). Bowie, in a loud lime-green suit, duetted with Annie Lennox on 'Under Pressure' (the rehearsal was, apparently, miles better). He then accompanied a sprightly and scarcely aged (at least from a distance) Ian Hunter (then already a venerable 52 years of age) for 'All The Young Dudes', and played with the sadly ailing Mick Ronson for a half-fluffed "Heroes".

All this was genuinely moving, particularly the sight of Ronson, then terminally ill with cancer, on stage for what most knew would be the last time. Bowie fell to his knees and recited the Lord's Prayer, in an apparently spontaneous gesture of support to a dying friend of his and Coco's, an Australian playwright called Craig. The effect was startling. It was the most theatrical and controversial thing he could have done. His critics thought it a crass, hypocritical attempt to hijack the show for his own theatrical ends, a publicity stunt in the worst possible taste. His supporters thought Bowie should be commended for his commitment to the overall message of the concert. However, his attempt at 'seriousness' did come across as gauche and overly dramatic, even if the intention behind it was altogether genuine. It was a mix of artifice and heartfeltness, and thus trademark Bowie.

Bowie was entering a reflective, contemplative phase. He was now also very much in love, and on 24 April 1992 Bowie and Iman married in secret in Lausanne. Their honeymoon/house-hunting vacation in LA saw them caught up in the LA riots after the infamous beating of a young black man, Rodney King, by a white policeman, an event which directly influenced a new song, 'Black Tie White Noise'. A church ceremony took place two months later at St James' Episcopal Church in Florence: Eno, Yoko Ono, Eric Idle and Bono were just some of the big-name celebrities on the list. His son Joe, now 21 and calling himself by his first name, Duncan, and studying philosophy at university, also attended, with his girlfriend Jenny Ichida, and was photographed with his smiling dad.

For his marriage to Angie in 1970, Bowie had appeared with hair permed and clothes impeccably post-flower-power. Now he looked healthy and tanned, his smile seemingly reconstructed, his old fangy canines seemingly replaced. Iman, tall and impressive, stood statuesque, a couple of inches above Bowie without heels. Even Bowie's mum Peggy, then 78, made it to the event, as did *Hello!* magazine.

The marriage jump-started Bowie's muse. For the wedding ceremony, Bowie had composed a couple of instrumental pieces using sax and keyboard. For his next project, Bowie made his first concept album since *Diamond Dogs*. Back then the themes were alienation and emotional collapse; now the concept was love. His new album was his 'wedding album', a gift to his wife Iman. Selling a record on the back of one's marriage was either touchingly heartfelt or shamefully naff, depending on one's point of departure. Recording began in New York that autumn on the first solo Bowie album for nearly six years.

Apart from his wedding photos splashed all over *Hello!*, 1992 also brought Bowie back into the public eye somewhat by default. That summer, American composer Philip Glass debuted his new work, *The Low Symphony*. The symphony itself was a surprisingly conventional work for Glass, and the neo-romantic, positive sweep of the music sat uneasily against the bleakness of the original. But the middle movement, 'Some Are', based on a song Bowie had originally left off the album and included only on the 1991 reissue, was a quite spectacular reinterpretation.

As Bowie returned to solo action, he may have been heartened to discover his influence over planet pop was becoming stronger after a decade of minimal credibility. The second half of 1992 also saw the rise and rise of Suede, whose debut single, 'The Drowners', with its arch vocal posturing, disturbing and cavernous drum figures, and teetering, ether-slicing guitar, was an obvious homage to Ziggy-era Bowie. Brett Anderson's vocal, intensely intrusive like Morrissey's, affected an unstable sonic register somewhere between Bowie, Bolan and Steve Harley.

Suede had something truly great. Anderson himself emerged as a classic Bowie casualty, not in any way a sad case, but an archetypal disaffected arty suburbanite (like so many great English rockers), and a genuine fan of Bowie. Suede's toweringly decorous second album, *Dog Man Star*, was the closest thing in ambition to Bowie's *Diamond Dogs* produced by any artist in the

1990s, and paid homage to Bowie by referencing no less than three of his albums in its title.

Journalists commented on the Bowie posters on Anderson's wall, his use of 'A Letter To Hermione' on his answerphone, and his whiplash, aggressively homoerotic stage persona. In late 1992, Brett, in what surely must have been a deliberate echo of Bowie's own initial gender standpoint, told the media that he was 'a bisexual man who had never had a homosexual experience'.

Steve Sutherland, who had almost single-handedly provided sensible comment on Bowie's Tin Machine phase through some excellent interviews in *Melody Maker*, and who was now at the *NME*, brought Brett Anderson and Bowie together in early 1993, just before the release of the debut Suede album and Bowie's own solo offering. According to Anderson, Bowie was approachable and paternalistic ('He's like someone's dad or something', he later commented to Tony Parsons). Bowie greeted the ingénue dressed in a sombre pinstriped suit, black gloves and fedora, almost exactly the same uniform William Burroughs had worn nearly twenty years earlier when Bowie, complete with Ziggy crop, had met him for the first time. Bowie was gently teasing Anderson while simultaneously setting himself up as the godfather of glam, the progenitor of Britpop. One exchange between them was especially revealing:

Brett: It's so necessary for us to play live because, when everyone's so critical and you're under such a microscope, it's necessary to actually go out there and be quite honest about it. I'd never want to appear like a media fabrication which I'm sure a lot of people think we are. Premeditated is one thing we're completely not. We do what we do quite naturally.
Bowie: Ah, therein lies the difference. That's where we vary. I may not have any real understanding of why or how but what I was doing was a fabrication.

Bowie's 'fabricated' pop of the 1970s had, in the hands of Suede, become legitimised. Suede put forward the rhetoric of honesty, Bowie the rhetoric of deceit. It was a microcosm of the clash between 70s culture (about the surface, artifice and a sense of play) and 90s culture (with a new earnest authenticity in place).

It must have given Bowie some satisfaction to see his first solo album for six years, *Black Tie White Noise*, depose the debut

Suede album from the Number 1 spot in the UK album charts in its first week of release in April 1993. Bowie was riding the crest of a mini-wave, and his fans were returning, as if urging him through their wallets to abandon Tin Machine for good.

Advance reports of the album had Bowie in chipper mood, confident enough even to comment to *Rolling Stone* magazine late in 1992: 'I don't think I've hit this peak before as a writer and performer.' The title, *Black Tie White Noise*, was meant as a comment both on the racial mix of his own marriage and on Bowie's working practices – fusing American soul and rhythm-and-blues and overlaying a European melodic sensibility. It was also, rather aptly, a cut-up of a concept he had first come across through talking to William Burroughs in the 1970s. 'I got to know William Burroughs, and he told me that one day he went into the French patent office, and for approximately $5, he bought himself a copy of all the plans for making a black noise bomb . . . It works on the principle of the opera singer and the glass – that there's always a note that will destroy physical substances. And this guy had devised a method that reduces flesh to mush and leaves the building standing. It was not far removed from the frequencies that Pink Floyd were playing around with. When you hear things like that, you wonder why the human race hasn't been wiped out.'

For his first solo offering of the 90s, Bowie reinstalled Nile Rodgers, the producer of his last great album, *Let's Dance*, a decade earlier. For Rodgers, however, the recording of the album was a hugely frustrating experience:

The difference between *Black Tie White Noise* and *Let's Dance* is night and day. When we did *Black Tie White Noise*, I felt my hands were tied to a large extent. It was like, 'Hey, David, let's try this.' 'No, I don't wanna do this.' 'Hey, David, let's try this, then.' 'No, I don't want to do that either. This record is really about my wedding.' I'd say, 'But David, no one cares about your wedding. Let's make a hit!' 'No, I don't want to compete with *Let's Dance*,' would be the reply. 'But David, we've got to compete with *Let's Dance*. Everyone in the world will be asking why are we doing this, and the reason has got to be that we're trying to top *Let's Dance*. Hey, David, we've got to do Let's Dance 2. It's got to be like *Star Wars*. You don't put *Star Wars* 2 out and it's less. It's gotta be better!' I said this to him over and over again. I'd even call Iman, who was my friend, and I'd say, 'Please tell him!' and she'd say, 'No, I like those other songs,' and I'm going, 'Aaaaaaarggghhh!!! No, you don't like those songs. Please, Iman – tell him.' But she would say, 'No, I agree with David.'

I was playing great commercial licks to Bowie, and he was rejecting them almost across the board. I didn't know what to do. I felt that the world was against me. But let's not be too one-sided. Maybe the licks I thought of stank – who knows? But all I knew was that they couldn't all suck! I can't even tell what sort of sound we were going for with *Black Tie White Noise*. Maybe I was drinking and drugging more than I should have done. Well, in fact, I know I was for *Black Tie White Noise* and *Let's Dance*. I'm not sure if I lost the ability to do great records, so it's not all David's fault. When we finished that record, I knew it wasn't cool. I knew it wasn't nearly as cool as *Let's Dance*. Don't get me wrong. I think there's really clever, interesting stuff on it. But the point is, it ain't as good as *Let's Dance*.

I loved that song 'Miracle Goodnight', though. I thought it was incredible. If he'd released that as the first single, he would have had a smash. He had another song, 'Lucy Can't Dance', which was a guaranteed Number 1 record, and everyone around him was totally perplexed when it only appeared as a bonus track on the CD. He was running from success and running from the word 'dance'. Imagine David Bowie and Nile Rodgers together, and we come out with a song 'Lucy Can't Dance'. Smokin'!! I was already accepting my Grammy. But he was not budging. It was an exercise in futility – no matter who I tried to call, it fell on deaf ears.

But the album does have its own distinctive charm. There's a melismatic quality to tracks such as the lead-off single, 'Jump They Say', and the opener, 'The Wedding', a reworking of Bowie's own wedding-day music, a meld of Western chordal progressions (representing the Church Of England side of the Bowie/Jones/Burns family) and microtonal music (for Iman's Muslim relations). But it is Lester Bowie's trumpet-playing which steals the show, adding a debonair jazzy touch throughout the album. When the trumpet line cuts in and solos on 'You've Been Around' and 'Jump They Say', it's as odd a moment as on any Bowie album, and a breath of fresh air after the constant guitar soloing of the

Tin Machine phase. The really striking aspect of the record is how well Bowie is singing. His deep vibrato is allowed full rein, hitting aural distress level 'rock bottom' on his rendition of 'I Feel Free'.

The Cream song is the most touching moment on the album. It was recorded as a kind of tribute to two friends, one long dead, the other sadly about to die. Cream were one of Terry Burns' favourite groups, and long ago Terry had taken the teenage David to see them in London. Bowie also played the song live with The Spiders, and Ronson appears on this new dance version of the song. The two were photographed together for the final time, Bowie looking more Sinatraesque than ever in his trilby and long cashmere coat, Ronson, already stricken with cancer and suffering seizures and blackouts, gaunt but still smiling and joking in his self-deprecating Yorkshire accent.

Three songs midway through the set reveal that Bowie's touch was as sure as it had been for a decade. 'Jump They Say', an eerie psychodrama, beautifully phrased and paced with a backward sax part, is one of his most dramatic numbers. The first single off the album, it was a sizeable European hit and his first to reach the UK Top 10 for seven years. The video, directed by Mark Romanek, was a potpourri of allusion. Bowie is dressed in a dark suit and striped tie, referencing the schoolboy persona of the 'Boys Keep Swinging' video. Indeed, the lipstick-smearing gesture, which had remained in Bowie's video iconography since 'Boys Keep Swinging', resurfaced in 'Jump They Say'. The ending of the video is another visual reconstruction of a past artistic life. The cover of *Lodger* depicted Bowie crushed on the mortuary slab, his vulpine grin pinned back at right angles. On 'Jump They Say', wearing virtually the same clothes and in almost exactly the same distorted and crushed position, Bowie mouths the word 'jump' before his death.

The subject matter of both song and video was Terry's suicide, and his schizophrenic episodes, during which he would hear voices calling out to him, are awesomely realised in the song. Bowie urges his brother not to listen to the demons daring him to plunge to his death: 'Don't listen to the crowd, they say jump!' This very public atonement was a brave thing for Bowie to do. Predictably, cynics in the media merely said that Bowie was cashing in, once more, on personal tragedy for commercial gain.

The video, like the song, fictionalises Terry's death (Terry did attempt suicide by jumping out of his hospital window in 1982, but was unsuccessful) as the focal point for a number of disturbing visual set pieces. Shots of Bowie teetering on the edge of a high building, lip-synching to the song, alternate with a number of other sequences. Bowie is shown as some sort of executive apparatchik, captured with his colleagues for the corporate photograph before being frog-marched out of an anteroom, gagged, connected to an electrical 'torture chamber' and administered violent electric shocks while his torturers take photographs of his contortions and agony. Three women fix Bowie with their telescopes, in an echo of Hitchcock's voyeuristic masterpiece *Rear Window* (1954). Other Hitchcockian devices are used too. The theme – the fear of heights – is a clear attempt to utilise the same psychological currency as in *Vertigo* (1958), while the incorporation of pigeons flapping around Bowie's heels is a reference to *The Birds* (1963). Shot partly in Cinemascope, it's Bowie's best video since 'Let's Dance'.

According to *Melody Maker*'s Chris Roberts, the video was proof, if any were needed, of Bowie's continued relevance. 'If anyone needs to know why Bowie is still relevant and interesting, show them this video and ask them if they could honestly name any other artist who could do a video this fascinating at this stage of his career. In the 1970s, there was kudos to be gained by being intelligent, literate, articulate and having reference points outside of rock. If you try to bring in theatre, literature or film now, you'd expect to be giggled at. I think that's a terrible shame. We'll end up with Nirvana – a bunch of roadies in sweatshirts.'

Two other songs carry the same unnerving, slightly psychotic, allure. On 'Pallas Athena', utterly chilling and basically an instrumental, Bowie is at his most experimental for a decade. The line 'God is on top of it all' is intoned by Bowie in a voice so heavily disguised that he sounds more like a black soul singer than any other vocal style Bowie might himself be expected to provide. The hard-hitting dance track, 'Nite Flights', a brilliant cover of the 1978 Walker Brothers' song, is just as disquieting with its 'On night flights/Only one way to fall' hook and stunning synth swoop from speaker to speaker – the best musical moment on any Bowie record for a decade.

However, elsewhere Bowie is in soppy mood. Lyrically, with its penchant for blandishments and clichés, this is not a great Bowie album. 'Miracle Goodnight' is an elegant pop song, with highlife guitars and one of Bowie's catchiest melodies, but somehow he is far less convincing and attractive when blissful than when blighted. Likewise, the cover 'Don't Let Me Down And Down' (with lines such as 'Still I keep my love for you'), and 'Wedding Song', in which Bowie, without a trace of irony, croons 'I believe in magic', are pretty and homely, but trite.

The wheels of the Bowie comeback bandwagon came off almost immediately. Savage, a small independent label Bowie had signed to in the USA, went bust shortly after the album was released in the States, seriously affecting its promotion. In Britain, without a tour behind it, the album slipped out of the Top 100 after just a couple of months. Savage Records filed a $65 million lawsuit against Bowie, contending that it had lost more than $1 million on *Black Tie White Noise* and had a contract to pay Bowie $3.4 million for his next three albums. Bowie's lawyers allegedly negotiated a termination of the contract after the album didn't sell well. Savage subsequently filed for bankruptcy and sued Bowie and BMG, alleging conspiracy and fraud. However, the lawsuit against Bowie was dismissed without comment by the New York State Court of Appeals.

With *Black Tie White Noise* in the UK Top 40 that April, there was a mini-revival in Bowie's commercial and artistic stock, but this was overshadowed by the death of Mick Ronson of liver cancer in April 1993. Although Bowie donated a cover of Dylan's 'Like A Rolling Stone' to the posthumously released *Heaven and Hull* album, he did not perform at the Mick Ronson Memorial Concert at Labatt's Apollo, Hammersmith (formerly the Hammersmith Odeon), staged the following April and organised by Ronson's sister Maggi and writer and friend Kevin Cann. 'It wasn't big enough, was it?' was Ian Hunter's later assessment. 'Freddie's was big – David knew he'd be seen by a lot of people there.' Trevor Bolder agreed: 'We all were hoping he would come, but he said . . . he was too upset that Mick had died to turn up for a memorial concert. But when Freddie Mercury died, Bowie was straight on stage because it was in front of millions of people. He got there for Freddie Mercury's concert, but he wouldn't get there for Mick Ronson's because it wasn't a big enough audience for him . . . It was a shame because it was a great evening.'

The event featured a reunited Spiders with Trevor and Woody, fronted by Joe Elliott of Def Leppard and with Phil Collen on lead. Also on the bill was Ronson's original band, The Rats (featuring a surprise guest: Tony Visconti on bass), Dana Gillespie, Roger Daltrey, the aforementioned Ian Hunter, Steve Harley and Queen's Roger Taylor.

'I don't understand why he didn't turn up to Mick Ronson's funeral or to the memorial service,' says producer Gus Dudgeon. 'I thought it was a shame. He might have a very good reason and I'm sure he feels he does, but . . . he should have been there. I was there and I was upset that he wasn't there.'

Bowie obviously did not feel able to 'go public' with his thoughts on Ronson at the time. And there would have been a whole phalanx of past friends and collaborators from The Spiders days, some he had not seen or spoken to for twenty years, to cope with in the full glare of the media. The early 1990s were a time when the communication lines to people from his past (such as Tony Visconti) had not yet been reopened. His silence could only be understood as human frailty, but Dudgeon was right: he should have been there. Again Bowie was using his massive stardom as a protective shield to hide behind when a public demonstration of his affection for, and indebtedness to, one of rock's genuine nice guys would have been a very humane act on Bowie's part, media circus or no.

That year, 1993, was to become Bowie's most artistically productive year since 1977, and by the summer he was back recording yet again. This time, the catalyst was the BBC's adaptation of *The Buddha of Suburbia* by Hanif Kureishi, a book which fictionalised aspects of Kureishi's upbringing in Bromley, a Kentish suburb of London. Bowie, of course, was also a Bromleyite.

In the early 1970s Kureishi had envied the local coterie of suburban proto-punks who later transformed themselves into the Bromley Contingent. Hanif Kureishi: 'But they didn't just admit anyone who'd frayed their jeans and dumped their grandfather's tied-up vest in the sink, along with a tin of orange dye. Their sartorial and tonsorial snobbery, along with a freezing coolness, could only have been a version of their parents' resistance to the vulgar. In the suburbs the working class were never far away, on the heels of the lower middle class. I was finally deemed fit to join after I ran away to the Isle of Wight pop festival.'

The Buddha of Suburbia tells the picaresque tale of Karim, a young Asian boy, and his move from marginality (crushing suburban tedium) to centrality (bohemian, big-city opportunity). The book has a lot to say about 1970s youth culture and the allure of stardom and self-re-creation as a viable path out of the rootless ennui of town life. The story also centres on the relationship between the young would-be actor, Karim, and Charlie Hero, the avatar of progressive chic, a Bowie-like figure who progresses from hippy to space-suited glamster to punk before regressing to become a mediocre but commercially successful Billy Idol-style rocker at the end of the novel.

Kureishi was commissioned by an American magazine to interview Bowie in February 1993, and he took this opportunity to ask Bowie to write some original music for the BBC television adaptation of his novel. Bowie took some of the central themes and developed them, with multi-instrumentalist Erdal Kizilcay, in a seven-day recording blitz in the summer of 1993. The resulting album, *The Buddha of Suburbia*, was released in the November of that year.

Since 1983, Bowie fans had got used to the depressing sight of their idol tanned, in a suit, hobnobbing with aristocrats of the rock and royal variety. But the music on *The Buddha Of Suburbia* indicated that he had had a rather drastic rethink. When Bowie sings on the title track, in his best cockney: 'Sometimes I fear/That the whole world is queer' he is recalling a long-forgotten plot.

What underlies the whole set is a feeling of relief and release: relief that *Black Tie White Noise* had at least in part re-established Bowie as a relevant artist after the critical mauling of Tin Machine, and release because here was an album with which Bowie could indulge himself to the full, with no collaborators to mollify, and no audience to appease. Developing songs out of the incidental music from the programme, Bowie turned the project even more clearly into an exercise in auto-cannibalism.

This is most obvious on the title track, one of those slow, anthemic numbers he hadn't written for a while ('Absolute Beginners' in midair collision with 'The Bewlay Brothers'), with a wash of acoustic guitar à la *Hunky Dory*. In it, Bowie also musically plagiarises his own 'Space Oddity' and lyrically steals the 'Zane zane zane, ouvre le chien' section from 'All The Madmen'.

Elsewhere, 'Dead Against It', effulgent with a gorgeously retro melody Blondie would be proud of, has echoes of the late 1970s New York new wave scene (and redeploys Eno's 'cricket menace'). 'Strangers When We Meet' is pure *Flesh And Blood*, disco-era Roxy Music mixed with The Spencer Davis Group's riff for 'Gimme Some Lovin''. And on the sublimely hypnotic mantra, 'Untitled Number 1', Bowie pastiches the sort of hippyesque Indian-influenced music he himself never actually recorded at the time. There's also a cheeky 'Bowie as Bolan' bleat in the coda, an echo of Bowie's original take-off of his friend on 'Black Country Rock' over two decades earlier. This is all clever, inventive stuff: not Bowie at his absolute best, but not far off it.

The rest of the album has very little to do with rock music at all. 'Sex And The Church' has a groove Prince would have killed for. 'Bleed Like A Craze Dad' has the album's best riff, a cross between 'The Harlem Shuffle' and a James Bond movie soundtrack. It builds like a "Heroes"-period epic and has a cinematic compass, a grandiose glare. Bowie's half-spoken vocal is polite white rap and intentionally echoes his remarkable delivery on *Lodger*'s 'African Night Flight'. 'South Horizon', the Dame's personal favourite, is an avant-garde jazz instrumental that folds itself in two and changes gear midway in a quite bizarre fashion.

Mike Garson, who had played on 'Looking For Lester' on the previous album, was back, and at his best: 'David did the whole thing, then he came out to LA and he brought the tapes and in three hours I did the piano work and I just listened to the music on ear phones. Again he directed where to play but I just played on top of it. Right after the *Young Americans* tour he said, "You're going to be working with me for the next twenty years." Then I didn't see him for twenty years! Then he called me and he said, "Let's go." It was as if ten minutes had passed, it was that bizarre. I thought some of the music on *Buddha* was fantastic.'

There are two more instrumentals: 'The Mysteries' is the closest thing to a minimalistic Eno-esque piece of writing Bowie has yet attempted, while 'Ian Fish, UK Heir', a funereally slow retread of the title track's main themes with dollops of surface static plastered over the top for good measure, is so quiet it's hardly there at all. It is intriguingly unlistenable, and surely designed to send those *Let's Dance*-era fans into a blind panic.

Unlike *Black Tie White Noise*, the album was well received by the UK music press. However, the album wasn't so much released as let out on parole: there was no real publicity, no supporting interviews, no pre-album single, no nothing. Moreover, it was incorrectly labelled a soundtrack album, arousing the expectation of fifty minutes' worth of incidental music rather than a bona fide Bowie album. It wasn't even given worldwide release.

Buddha remains Bowie's great lost album. It was released on exactly the same day as yet another greatest hits compilation, *David Bowie: The Singles Collection*, a predictable batch of old chestnuts (some of which, like 'Ziggy Stardust', weren't even singles) which was destined for a moderately good chart run in the pre-Christmas retro-rush. What *The Buddha Of Suburbia* project ultimately afforded Bowie was a ready-made opportunity to reclaim his London, and more specifically his suburban, roots. He had spent the first ten years of his career trying to deny those roots, and to find an alternative, more exciting world. In the 1980s he lived according to the pop-star, jet-set standards of the day, with a base in Switzerland and other residences scattered across the world. However, refocusing in the 1990s on the exciting elements of his 1970s music led Bowie to attempt to reclaim some heritage, some origins for himself.

Bowie began spending more time in Britain. Around the time he befriended Kureishi, he also struck up a rapport with the *enfant terrible* of conceptual art, Damien Hirst. Hirst, of course, became national property following the media rumpus over the show in which he exhibited a dead sheep in a tank of formaldehyde. Bowie was becoming more and more visible in his support for the art world. He had been a collector for over a quarter of a century – his private collection contains work by the masters Rubens and Tintoretto, as well as by modern artists such as Bomberg, Auerbach, and Gilbert and George. In 1994 he stepped in with £18,000 to buy the controversial and graphic *Croatian And Muslim* by Peter Howson, Britain's official war artist in Bosnia, when the Imperial War Museum wouldn't take it because it depicted a rape. He was also finally plucking up the courage to plan an exhibition of his own work.

Hirst was just the sort of new, happening and anti-Establishment cultish figure Bowie was naturally drawn to. He was the nearest thing the British Art world had to a proper 'star'. Bowie bought Hirst's *Beautifully Shattering Splashing Violent Pinky Hacking Sphincter Painting* in 1995 and the same year collaborated on a spin painting with Hirst himself, *Beautiful Hello Space-boy Painting*. In interviews Hirst revealed his love of using body parts as artistic hardware, of seeing beauty in death as a way of turning society's attention to its reality: 'What I really like,' he told the *Observer*'s Robert Chalmers, 'is the contradiction: a really gorgeous photograph of something horrific.' These two main themes, what Hirst called 'the paranoiac denial of death that permeates our culture', and a view of the body as a mere assemblage of tissue, skin and bone which, once dead, could make great art, were to have a direct influence on Bowie's next project.

It is not surprising that the subject fascinated Bowie: in 1974, his own body of skin and bone itself looked perversely plastinated. In his web journal on BowieNet, he wrote (in January 1999) about a visit to the Musée Fragonard in Paris. The anatomist Fragonard II had been given a suite of rooms by the École Nationale Veterinaire and had produced 'ghastly hyper-Gothic' plastinated bodies with preservative lotion pumped into them after death.

The immediate post-Iman phase also saw Bowie get into a little piercing and body art himself. He now sported a fetching earring and a tattoo of a dolphin on his calf. This neo-paganism and fascination with the body captivated Bowie and provided him with the subject matter for his new project. It was this cultural cocktail of end-of-the-millennium neo-paganism, ritual body art and artful anatomisation which, together with an abiding recognition of his own mortality, was to preoccupy Bowie. For David Bowie, the end of the millennium was to occur not in 1999 but in 1995. And it happened Outside.

13. THE MUSIC IS OUTSIDE, 1994–1997

An ageing rock star doesn't have to opt out of life. When I'm fifty, I'll prove it.

BOWIE TALKING TO JEAN ROOK IN 1979

Happy birthday, ma'am!

PAUL DU NOYER, MOJO MAGAZINE

Nineteen ninety-three had been a curious year for Bowie. Relaunching his solo career, he could have capitalised on the manifest enthusiasm with a world tour and an even more commercial album. He might have accepted MTV's offer of an *Unplugged* slot (they had wanted his old hits – Bowie refused). But no. *Black Tie White Noise* would be an aberration. For his next project, Bowie determined to build on the sonic experimentalism of *The Buddha Of Suburbia* and refashion his 70s sonic experimentalism for the 1990s. Rather than seek out new life and boldly go where no man had gone before, however, Bowie raided his old address book for 'new' collaborators in the 1990s. First he revisited his most recent history and brought back Nile Rodgers. Then it was Mike Garson and Mick Ronson. Now it was Brian Eno. Later it would be Carlos Alomar and at the end of the 1990s, even Tony Visconti was back. History was collapsing in on Bowie.

By the early 1990s, Eno had become one of the most respected and innovative rock producers in the business. His work on U2's 1991 album, *Achtung Baby* was a recent case in point: a brilliantly inspired collision of industrial noise, circular beats and great tunes. Recorded at Hansa, the scene of "*Heroes*", it sounded more like a David Bowie album than any which had gone under the real brand name for almost a decade (save Iggy's *Blah Blah Blah*). Eno's own low-profile career as ambient experimenter was, after years of seeming curio interest only, finally making an impact on the mainstream, particularly on dance genres such as ambient house, rave and trance. By the 1990s, Eno had become an arbiter of good taste, with his own record label, his own occasional journal (edited by Bowie writer Kevin Cann), a major publisher hanging on his every word (Faber & Faber) and a sporadic series of lecture tours (always good fun). 'He's one of those people, rather enviable in a way,' said John Peel, 'who has drifted into a kind of elder statesman media role where people take everything he says terribly seriously.'

Philip Glass' symphonic treatment of *Low*, together with Bowie's own newly regained passion for experimental music, made Eno an obvious, though predictable, choice for collaborator on the new Bowie album. After his wedding in the summer of 1992, Bowie gave Eno a tape of work in progress. The new textural, atmospheric music, which would later find its way on to *Black Tie White Noise*, piqued Eno's interest. The first hint of a team-up came in October 1992. In a question-and-answer session after a talk at Munich's Gasteig, Eno said that Bowie had asked him to collaborate on a piece of music to commemorate the 1,200th anniversary of the Institution of Kyoto in 1994. Nothing came of this project, but the ball was definitely rolling.

Bowie and Eno envisaged a series of musical and visual possibilities, a smorgasbord of releases counting down the last five years of the millennium; not just one, but several albums, interactive material, even an operatic performance at the Salzburg Festival in December 1999. Only one of the projects (an album release, *1. Outside*) ever came off.

In that first session in March 1994, several albums' worth of material was recorded. Mike Garson: 'I recorded at least thirty-five hours of music with David that was improvised with Reeves and Eno in Montreux. There's a load of stuff that was never edited, so they have ten albums there if they want. From my viewpoint, it was better than the stuff that made *1. Outside*. Every bit of it was videoed; there were cameras fixed on each of us. David had his charcoals and he had his art set up. It was one of the most creative environments I-have ever been in. We would just start playing. There was no key given, no tonal centre, no form, no nothing.' During this stage an operatic piece (called *Inside*) was recorded, but never edited down to a releasable length.

Bowie has said in subsequent interviews that he had a very hard time trying to convince any record label to release the set of songs which would make up *1. Outside*, and only did so when he added some more conventional songs. 'It was never said to me that it had been rejected for want of commercial material,' says Gabrels. 'I just thought the decision was made that the double CD *1. Outside* operatic set would have been insane to put out from a commercial point of view, which for me is always a questionable criterion, and that we needed to rerecord some more songs.'

Work had continued off and on throughout 1994, culminating in that final session in early 1995. Some of the songs were totally improvised. 'Hearts Filthy Lesson' (for some reason minus the apostrophe), a haunting song with an insistent and harrowing rhythm, started off as a total improvisation, with Garson providing one of the hooks on his jazzy piano. It would later be used to brilliant effect in the film *Seven*. 'When I heard it in the movie, I almost got scared to death,' says Garson.

'I went out to Switzerland every other month for a month at a time till November 1994, the last session was in January/February 1995,' confirms Gabrels. That was when 'Outside' the track came. The other versions of 'Strangers When We Meet' and 'Thru These Architect's Eyes' came from these sessions in New York too, as did 'I Have Not Been To Oxford Town' (original title: 'Toll The Bell'). The slam-dance of 'Hallo Spaceboy' grew out of an ambient instrumental of Gabrels' called 'Moondust'. During this final New York session, Bowie brought back Carlos Alomar on rhythm guitar.

The title of the album obviously expressed a wish to be thought of, again, as being outside of the pop mainstream, but Eno and Bowie's fascination with outsider art also inspired the record. In early 1994 Eno and Bowie went to Guggin mental hospital just outside of Vienna, where some of the famous outsider artists lived and worked. Bowie explains: 'Some of them have been in the painters' wing for, like, thirty years, as an Austrian experiment to see what happens when you allow people with mental disabilities to give free rein to their artistic impetuses. Before you go to the outsiders' wing, there's the other wing you pass through where all the psychos and murderers live, and the only thing written on the wall is 'THIS IS HELL'. But the painters' wing is coloured with graffiti everywhere . . . To see the starkness of the other wing next door is really hard-hitting . . . It's quite obvious that these outsider artists don't have the parameters that are placed on most artists . . . Their motivation for painting and sculpting comes from a different place than that of the average artist who's sane on society's terms.' The lesson to learn from outsider art was that the artist should be primal. Technique or virtuosity didn't matter; that which was unformed and was screaming inside of you, waiting to be released, was the real essence of creativity.

Bowie's new material also possibly reflected an interest in contemporary philosophy. It may be pure coincidence, but some of the phrases and themes on the album are uncannily similar to those developed in a book by Gilles Deleuze and Felix Guattari, *A Thousand Plateaus: Capitalism and Schizophrenia*. For Deleuze and Guattari, contemporary society is increasingly dominated by rhizomic forms; that is, by people, ideas, and/or collectives that form an interconnected mini-community of dependent ideas. Reading through *A Thousand Plateaus*, it is impossible to miss the connections between Bowie's songs and some of Deleuze and Guattari's concepts, if only on the most superficial of levels: 'A book exists only through the outside and on the outside . . . In short, we think that one cannot write sufficiently in the name of an outside . . . try out continuums of intensities segment by segment, have a small plot of new land at all times.' I wonder if Duncan, then reading for a PhD in philosophy in the States, had been sharing some of his academic obsessions with his dad?

It was also obvious that Bowie was tuning in to the pre-millennarian vibe, represented by concern for the future expressed in terms of a negation of the past and a recognition that history was collapsing, folding in on itself, even dying. This idea, the 'perpetual now', 'the depthless present', had long been the currency of certain strands of post-modernism, and a song such as 'Outside' caught this mood: 'But it's happening now/Not tomorrow/Or yesterday'.

This concern for the moment, the feeling that popular culture and pop music exist in a cyclical parallel universe somehow outside of lived 'clock-time', has been picked up most visibly by gay pop performers and writers, and Bowie appears to be distancing himself from his re-heterosexualised self of the 1980s. A decade earlier, in the Pet Shop Boys' 'West End Girls', Neil

Tennant had sung: 'We've got no future, we've got no past/Here today, built to last', while an edited collection of pop writing for Faber & Faber by Jon Savage and Hanif Kureishi, stressed the circularity of pop time. One of Savage's favourite quotes is a passage from gay writer Rodney Garland's 1953 novel, *The Heart of Exile*:

> The Young were living mostly in exile, but exile gave them possibilities of which they had seldom dreamed before ... Nearly all of them, willingly or unwillingly, became creatures of the moment, living in an everlasting present; the past had vanished, the future was uncertain.

Many gay critics deride the heterosexual fascination with history, connections and antecedents which give the illusion that history matters and that a future exists. Writer Bertha Harris argues that the privilege of the homosexual sensibility is 'to make things stop happening. Reality is interesting only when it is distorted, and second ... reality lacks interest because it is controlled by usefulness which is pertinent only to the heterosexual continuum. The positive decision our hypothetical artist makes is to attach himself to the inexpedient and the impertinent.'

For this new exercise in the 'impertinent', Bowie had mustered what he called a team of fellow musical renegades, people who were not only technically proficient but who would respond to surprise tactics. During one of the earliest recording sessions, Eno, updating his Oblique Strategies techniques, handed out some 'flash cards' to the performers. Bowie recalls: 'He said to our drummer [Sterling Campbell], "You are the disgruntled ex-member of a South African rock band. Play the notes you were not allowed to play." And then the pianist [Mike Garson] was told, "You are the morale-booster of a small ragtag terrorist operation. You must keep spirits up at all costs." My card said, "You are a soothsayer and town crier in a society where all media networks have tumbled down," so I knew it was my job to pass on all the events of the day.'

Creative contradiction was thus the name of the game. Bowie himself had returned to an updated Burroughsian cut-up technique for his lyrics. A friend had designed a programme for his AppleMac which randomised the lyrics at the press of a key, completing instantaneously what might have taken hours using the original paper-and-scissors technique (Bowie later co-designed the Verbasizer, a computer which takes apart sentences fed into it, then creates new sentences with the words). The result was a lyrical style more radically fractured than even his late-1970s work, with computer-assembled lyrics rewritten and then fed back into the program. These were living lyrics, evolving, as Eno would later comment, through a process of natural selection.

On 1. *Outside*, words are chosen not so much for their meaning but for how well their actual sounds, when sung, fit the music. The words are used as sound signifiers, as isolated blasts of noise, every bit as much as signifying visual concepts.

There were tensions between Eno (at heart a minimalist) and Bowie (with his much more painterly 'let's layer it on and see what happens' approach). Eno was to comment in his diary: 'In the studio here we're doing just about the exact opposite. My brows wrinkle frequently, and I become the sculptor to David's tendency to paint. I keep trying to cut things back, strip them to something tense and taut, while he keeps throwing new colours on the canvas. It's a good duet.'

'The only thing missing,' Eno was to comment on hearing the final mix, was 'the nerve to be very simple'. In an interview with *NME*'s Steven Wells, Bowie put it like this: 'I mean, Brian's a lot more fearful of testosterone than I am. I LOVE it when it rocks. I love it when it has balls! I love it when it has big hairy massive balls on it! But Brian is a lot more informed by minimalism and I am definitely not a minimalist. Layer it on! The thicker the better! Baroque and roll!'

The sound developed on 1. *Outside* was, however, dense and textural, underpinned by a booming rhythm section. Garson was promoted to lead instrumentalist and his piano frills dominate the album. Haunting and perfect on 'The Motel', demented on 'A Small Plot Of Land', they inhabit musical space somewhere between avant-garde jazz and classical styles. ' "The Motel", that's my favourite track,' says Garson. 'I didn't co-compose it with him, but I mixed in a few harmonies that made it stronger. It's probably in his top-ten songs ever.'

'The songs have a slow, careful build into the pay-off line,' says musician, writer and critic Alan Franks, 'but they're absolutely not written as pop songs and they're not particularly written as rock songs. It's almost like what Jacques Brel would be doing now if he'd gone heavy.'

The rousingly anthemic 'Outside', the insistent, slap-based, almost atonal groove of 'Hearts Filthy Lesson', the disfigured rock of 'The Voyeur Of Utter Destruction (As Beauty)', 'A Small Plot Of Land' and 'No Control' all have this slow build, but it's paced to perfection on 'The Motel'. The song evolves almost impercep-tibly, with Garson's languorous piano refrain and the wearied beat of the rhythm track set against an epically realised piece of singing from Bowie, alluding to the 'This Is Hell' legend he had seen in Guggin: 'There is no hell like an old hell/There is no hell/And it's lights out boys'.

'The Motel' is a very clever song, musically both a homage and a piece of self-appropriation. Musically and lyrically it cribs from The Walker Brothers' glorious 1978 psychodrama, 'The Electri-cian' (the line 'there's no hell, no' is lifted almost wholesale). However, 'The Electrician' itself, with its slow, pulsing synth, was a direct echo of Bowie's own 'Warszawa' on *Low*, so 'The Motel' is part of a friendly dialogue between the two singers, both influenced and influencing. These songs show a new grandeur emerging in Bowie's repertoire. They're beautifully paced and confidently sung in an open-throated vibrato. Despite the lack of literal meaning in many of the lyrics, Bowie's diction remains clear throughout. Alan Franks: 'Bowie has set out to do something else than write a competent, well-crafted and sense-making rock song. To me it's an abnegation of meaning on one level, on a verbal and literal level. It means that if you get something from *Outside*, which I certainly do, some charge, some meaning from it, it is of the kind that is equally difficult to define. My difficulty is in proportion to the meaninglessness of the words.'

Elsewhere, the music nods more approvingly towards pop. 'Hallo Spaceboy' is quite daring, with a hard, industrial menace and great use of dynamics. On it Bowie revisits the old chestnut of pop star/pop fan in a sexual spin à la 'Rebel Rebel' ('Do you like girls or boys?/It's confusing these days'). 'Thru These Architect's Eyes' has a suitably soaring melody and a stunning chorus (and who else would be daft enough to write a pop lyric about famous architects?), while 'I Have Not Been To Oxford Town' is classic Bowie pop and the obvious choice for the lead-off single (naturally, it remains an album track only). Carlos Alomar's clipped rhythm guitar gives a light funky touch, while the chorus is positively sing-along. 'I'm Deranged' is almost as good, carrying echoes of jungle music and throwing some 1980s Kraftwerk into the brew.

The main problem with the record was, however, that it needed much tighter editing, something Bowie himself now recognises: 'It's a good album. It was too long. Much too long.' *1. Outside* did take rather a lot of excess theoretical cargo on board, for it was not simply an album, it was a 'non-linear Gothic drama hyper-cycle'. Calling himself (with tongue hopefully firmly in cheek) 'a mid-art populist and post-modernist Buddhist who is casually surfing his way through the chaos of the twentieth century', Bowie had written a completely unfathomable piece for Q magazine in late 1994 called 'The Diary Of Nathan Adler', and developed this idea for a story included instead of sleeve notes on *1. Outside*. Included on the album was a succession of extraneous narrative sections which simply acted as distractions. Journalist Paul Du Noyer had this to say: 'I think he's overconceptualised it. I know he describes the story as "non-linear". I know when I see the word "non-linear" I reach for my gun. I run for cover anyway. I always remember "non-linear" being one of those shifty buzzwords people used in the 1980s to describe their videos. So I realised that in pop, non-linear means "plotless nonsense".'

1. Outside revealed a new persona for David Bowie – the arty, faintly left-wing, mildly elitist artiste – and this directly reflected his extra-musical interests. In the spring of 1995, he held his first ever art exhibition. Bowie had accepted a place on the editorial board of the journal *Modern Painters* and had shown himself to have far more than a dilettante appreciation of art history. In particular, he appeared fascinated by the figure of the Minotaur, who in Greek legend dwelt in a labyrinth on the island of Knossos. In fact, Bowie, together with body-part fetishist Damien Hirst, actually contemplated recreating the Minotaur. An anonymous man had offered them his body (after his death, of course), and Hirst planned to remove the head and stitch on a bull's head in its place. Bowie schemed to house this new Minotaur in a labyrinth on one of the Greek islands.

It was the figure of the Minotaur, in its computer-generated form, complete with massive balls and penis, which dominated the interesting, if inconsistent, Cork Street exhibition that April. Some of the pieces were excellent. 'Ancestor' was an expressionistic tribalistic painting inspired by a trip to South Africa with Iman. Bowie said, 'One of the stories prevalent in Africa is that the ghost of one's ancestors are white and often when white man was first seen he was thought of as being one of the ancestors of the tribe, and so I just took that and did a series of ancestor figures with kind of Ziggy Stardust haircuts.' But perhaps the most striking piece was an update of that mask made in 1974 for the 'Aladdin Sane' performance on the *Diamond Dogs* tour. Now, in middle age, Bowie's chrome mask looked almost as spooky as the '74 original, a companion-piece study of the ages of man.

As expected, some of the press reaction was hostile ('post-A-level, pre-art school', remarked one critic). In the media, much attention had focused on the idea of the artist as 'hyphenate', with the increasing visibility of rock stars moonlighting as authors (Ray Davies), 'actors' with a yen for the paint pot and artist's smock (Sly Stallone), artists directing movies (Julian Schnaebel) or pop videos (Damien Hirst), and pop stars designing wallpaper (Bowie). It was all supposed to be a desperately new thing, the birth of a 'super-art-form' or 'non-specific creativity'. At best, this new cross-disciplinarity enabled creative people to be more creative. At worst, it gave rich and famous people with little talent the chance to be extremely aggravating in other areas of culture.

In Bowie's defence, it should be pointed out that he had always been a hyphenate. Bowie as singer-songwriter-performer-mime-actor-painter-sculptor-writer has been a hyphenated figure for decades, and the media attention on cultural polyglots was actually only a mirror of developments in contemporary Western society, a society in which many individuals found themselves forced into changing careers and lifestyles. The idea of a job for life was largely a thing of the past, and more and more people had to adapt and be flexible. As the *NME*'s Stephen Dalton put it in 1997, 'Let's face it, everyone's a bit David Bowie nowadays.'

Musically, the mid-1990s in the UK were, of course, dominated by the Britpop wars. Although much was made at the time of both Blur and Oasis' indebtedness to the Kinks and the Beatles, as the scene's chronicler John Harris points out after the fact in his book *The Last Party*, 'David Bowie was a far greater influence on Britpop than any artist of the 60s.' The Britpop groups drew inspiration liberally from Bowie's earlier work, although Pulp and Blur would go on to make music in the image of Bowie's more experimental late-70s work, with *Lodger* being a surprise influence on their more fractured and distant music. *Hunky Dory*'s 'Life On Mars?', 'Quicksand' and 'The Bewlay Brothers' were a huge influence on early Suede and Parklife-era Blur, whilst Oasis were also often close to Bowie's riff-rocking blueprint. The Gallaghers went on to design a pretty effective live version of Heroes (although, as Harris points out, they dropped or forgot the distancing inverted commas). The Britpop groups produced some of the best songs of the decade. But Bowie himself had largely abandoned conventional song structures altogether. *1. Outside*, with all its arty conceptualising and 'anti-songs', was finally released in September 1995. The only thing like it at the time was Scott Walker's *Tilt*, by turns intriguing and unlistenable, and close in style to some of the more operatic flourishes from *1. Outside*.

1. Outside did not, however, make much of a mark commercially. 'Hearts Filthy Lesson', one of the most uncompromising tracks, preceded its release. The video, directed by Samuel Bayer, who had worked on Nirvana's 'Smells Like Teen Spirit', was the most disturbing of Bowie's career, and was obviously not designed for heavy rotation (MTV in fact rejected the original edit). On the video, Bowie is surrounded by Holocaust-like images of deprivation: hangings, decapitations and bodies pierced with giant needles in the name of art. His own body is covered in powder paint, as if bodily fluids, skin and paint have somehow been mixed to form one primeval medium. The stench of death hangs over the scene, in the same way that it infuses the album itself. Bowie had lived more than two-thirds of his three-score years and ten, and the inevitability and potency of death was the album's subtext. It was a great video, but it signalled that Bowie's target audience was a very small section of the mainstream. This was light years away from the work of the 'populist entertainer', who had bored his hard-core fans a decade before.

The single fared disappointingly, reaching Number 35 in the UK charts. It was hardly played by Radio 1, an amazing situation given the aura of the Bowie name and the 'backing' of a major record label. One former Bowie fan was brought temporarily back into the fold by the single: 'I thought it was brilliant,' says Gary Numan. 'There's so much crap, then there's something like that which comes along, which is an absolute masterpiece and only gets to Number 35. On "Hearts Filthy Lesson" every sound is a gem. The arrangement was brilliant and he sang it well. My own feelings are, much as I think his voice is phenomenal, he oversings a lot of the time. He sings harder than he needs to; that's why I prefer his earlier stuff. "Hearts Filthy Lesson" was right back into that not-so-full-on singing. That's the thing I hate about Whitney

Houston. I know she can sing very well but, fuck me, you don't have to sing flat out on every song you do. Too much singing going on here! "Hearts Filthy Lesson" was right to the point. It was right where it needed to be, a very focused track, right up my street, right in the middle of the sort of music I love.'

Before the album's release in late September, Bowie did a spot of moonlighting. Complete with platinum fright-wig and original leather jacket, he played Andy Warhol in painter Julian Schnaebel's film about the black American artist, Jean Michel Basquiat, who died of a drug overdose in 1988. The film, *Basquiat, Build a Fort, Set It On Fire*, opened in the US a year later. It was modish and disappointing, and Basquiat came across as a mumbling jerk, even if the intention was to portray him as a tortured post-modernist. Bowie's performance was striking, though even more camp than Warhol was in real life (an amazing achievement), but the film was dull and had absolutely zero dramatic structure.

Bowie then began an American tour, but it was a tour with something of a difference: he would co-headline with Trent Reznor's Nine Inch Nails, then one of the biggest acts in the States. Reznor's brand of gender-confusion, cloaked in blasts of industrial noise, was a rearticulation of late 1970s Bowie for a hard-core 90s audience. Bowie's profile had very recently been raised in the States, not least due to the popularity of Nirvana's MTV *Unplugged* version of 'The Man Who Sold The World'. Other US acts such as The Smashing Pumpkins and Marilyn Manson were also playing music with Bowie's influence not too far from the surface. The time was ripe for Bowie to restate his case before a new generation of American pop fans.

The sudden appearance of Bowie in the list of influential rock icons in the States was further consolidated (perhaps even engineered) by the Bowie camp itself, keen to make their man relevant again. Bowie's management company, Isolar, based in New York, was very keen to attach Bowie's name to more 'youthful' acts. Indeed, one article on the workings of Isolar posted on one of the unofficial Bowie websites stated that Isolar commissioned a focus-group study comprised of mostly fourteen-year-olds. 'What the survey revealed was that the current record-buying target audience, born in the years 1976–1980, had a brutal disregard for history and legacies. When asked what they considered to be classic rock artists, after a moment of hesitation they volunteered Prince and Michael Jackson and Madonna. When asked what words came to mind regarding David Bowie, they retorted with such telling codes as "Let's Dance" and "gay".'

Subsequent to these findings, the marketing division began to scheme fervently. How could they reconnect with this disrespectful new generation? Proposals: A collaboration with Devante Swing, a Bowie covers album, a new-blood hip-hop and rave album of reworkings of old songs.'

In the light of this, Bowie's move to work with Nine Inch Nails might be seen, in part, to be a premeditated commercial move. However, more accurately, it was Bowie's admiration for Reznor and also his willingness to try and win over a new, and at times relatively hostile audience which was the real motivation. Bowie was in a no-win situation: die-hard fans disliked the fact that he was sharing centre stage with a man who, they claimed, was a poor imitation of one aspect of Bowie's 70s iconography. Others regarded the move as further evidence of Bowie's desperate trendiness and his desire to be seen to be cutting-edge by attaching himself to a 'happening' act. Gabrels: 'It was definitely a risk. We were out playing live almost three weeks before the *Outside* record came out, which was a bit suicidal perhaps. The biggest problem was that we constructed this sort of meld between two bands. We were crossing between the two bands at a time when the band that was on first, Nine Inch Nails, was at the peak of their set, which is a very intense peak, and we would have to come out and do a changeover kind of thing with "Subterraneans". But we didn't have enough of that high-intensity material so that made it difficult. It was interesting to see that at any given point maybe a third of the audience was in the lobby, because they were either David fans who couldn't stand listening to Nails, or Nails fans that couldn't stand David. It was an experiment on the part of both bands; but it was educational for them both. It was a brave move for both bands, probably braver for David.' The two acts did indeed perform a musical bridge together, comprising 'Subterraneans', 'Scary Monsters', 'Reptile', 'Hallo Spaceboy', 'Hurt' (later, of course, brilliantly covered by Johnny Cash), and 'The Voyeur Of Utter Destruction (As Beauty)'. Then came Bowie's main set, which was still devoid of any of the greatest hits performed on the *Sound + Vision* tour five years earlier.

'I like a lot of what happened to us on that tour,' Bowie said in 2004. 'It became progressively better as we continued. And both

Trent Reznor (Nine Inch Nails' lead singer) and I felt we had really accomplished something by the end of the tour. We got off to a very shaky start. But it did help me understand a certain aesthetic that was needed to do live performance in front of younger crowds. Especially ones who expect harder music. On the other hand, I wouldn't want to lose the people who have stayed with me for years. Because they're pretty bright people as well. You've gotta find a balance between not seeming to harness a young crowd and not trying to appease the older crowd.' 'We had to go through the torture of the tour and all the bad reviews to get to where we are now,' is how Mike Garson put it in 2003. Bowie was once again pushing the boundaries of what was possible, striving to break and then remake his art in order to survive.

During the US leg of the *Outside* tour, Bowie renewed his acquaintance with some of the Sigma Kids for a 21st-anniversary meet-and-greet. Both star and fans were now middle-aged. Patti Brett: 'There was a complaint on the *Outside* tour that David never talked to us any more, so Carlos got us twenty backstage passes and they had this little reception for us after the show. David met everyone personally, shook everyone's hand and then talked with us for about an hour and a half whilst we took pictures. He was amazed that everyone had gotten so much older and that some people now had kids. He has this little greyish goatee and he's talking about how old we'd gotten! So I grabbed his goatee and I said, "You're looking a little grey here yourself!" He put his hand through his hair and said, "Yeah, but I still look good up here." I said, "Yeah, and for as long as you and I have both been dying our hair, I'm surprised we have any," and he just roared at that.'

The *Outside* tour hit the UK in November and December 1995. Morrissey, who had just released the mildly disappointing album, *Southpaw Grammar*, was suggested by Bowie's PR consultant, Alan Edwards, as the ideal support act. Sadly, Morrissey left the UK tour midway through the UK leg due to illness. The fact that Morrissey was well enough to play dates in Japan only a week or two later indicates that the reason for his departure was more to do with him being pissed off with the tour than anything else, and it was rumoured that he took off after a bust-up with Bowie backstage.

Bowie himself has remained tight-lipped about the reasons for Morrissey's departure, but Mozza has gone on record as saying that Bowie 'was very odd to me', which, however much we might love one of Manchester's finest sons, is a bit like the proverbial pot calling the kettle black. 'He asked me to sing a few of his songs in my set, which I thought was wrong. And then after a few nights he asked to join in during my set, which I thought was wrong and I said, "I can't do this." And then he would ask me if he could come on at the end and he would appear and I would disappear, so there would be no end and no encore for me . . .' Bowie obviously had in mind a short duet between the two (they had famously sung 'Cosmic Dancer' together at a Morrissey gig in 1991, so there was a precedent). Also, on the recent Nine Inch Nails/Bowie tour, the two acts had indeed segued together.

The muted reception given to Mozza at the few gigs he did play was deeply depressing for him and for some Bowie fans. At one, Morrissey vented his disappointment by taking the mic and announcing, 'Good evening; we are the support band,' making his frustration perfectly clear. In many ways, Morrissey was Bowie's 1980s heir: a charismatic anti-star and a classic commentator on (northern) suburban boredom and angst. And with *Your Arsenal* (produced by the ailing Mick Ronson in 1992) and *Vauxhall And I*, Morrissey had hit a rich vein of songwriting. In many respects, one would have thought that an hors d'oeuvre of psychosexual mini-dramas courtesy of one of Britain's finest lyricists would have pleased Bowie fans a lot more than it apparently did. However, the fact that Morrissey went unappreciated said less about the standard of his performance and more about the traditionalism of Bowie's audience.

For, if reports are true, some of Bowie's British shows saw support visibly haemorrhaging away, as fans voted with their feet and left the shows early. One Bowie fan, Liz Racz, reports: 'I think there were a lot of unhappy people at Wembley. I could see straight away that they had come to hear all the old songs – "Let's Dance", "Rebel Rebel", etc. Boy, were they disappointed. Some left halfway through. Clearly these people were not "real" fans; just people who had one or two albums and thought it would be fun to come along and hear all the old hits again. You may be able to do that with your Rod Stewarts, Billy Joels, etc. Not with Bowie.'

The mid-concert desertions were quite remarkable: it's not often, if ever, that a proportion of your audience, having paid £20 and travelled from afar, actually leave halfway through. These gigs were arty, dour and difficult, certainly, but the pleasure came in wallowing in Bowie's steadfastly uncommunicative pose. For some, though, Bowie was now just plain boring. His decision to revisit hardly any of his former hits was one that perhaps largely backfired.

However, Bowie, if not his audience, was eerie and impressive, and so were his band. Bowie, mercifully without smile or suit for the first time since the 1978 tour, looked cool and menacing, hair cut short and spiky, a little make-up (blue eyeliner) and a cool selection of outfits from the long leather coat to what can only be described as a toga made out of cobwebs. The band played brilliantly, with Garson's quirky jazzy piano runs set against Alomar's pristine, understated guitar work and Gabrels' sonic adventures, which often sounded to be in a different key to that of the song itself. Mojo's Cliff Jones, later to find fame as lead singer of Gay Dad, summed it up perfectly in his review of Bowie's performance at Meadowlands in New Jersey, at which he was pelted with bottles and pretzels by a bemused audience: 'The music itself is a bewildering excursion into a looking-glass world where everything sounds unusual and not quite as it should anyway . . . Bewilderingly random solos and strange sinewy scales battle against a pounding techno backing while inhuman piano runs tumble from the speakers. Extremely unsettling but strangely thrilling, as though someone has randomly rewired the Rock Machine . . . Rock may have become too cool for its own good; afraid to step outside the circle and make a jerk of itself. Bowie, to his credit, is not. Jerk or genius, tonight that circle was broken. This strange show proved that, in some indefinable way, Bowie remains a curious pioneer – and pioneers, as they say, get all the arrows.'

Although not on the scale of some of his previous tours, it was a theatrical show and a welcome return to pop drama after the visual boredom of Tin Machine. After Philip Glass' version of 'Some Are', Bowie and band came on stage in a simulated electrical storm which dazzled the audience for the show's brave opener, 'The Motel'. By the time of 'Hallo Spaceboy', the sound was deafening and pounding and the light show trippy and hypnotic. Not Bowie at his visual best, but daring once more.

At the same time, Bowie and the band did a string of television appearances to promote the album. 'Strangers When We Meet' was also released, a double-A-sided single with a new live version of 'The Man Who Sold The World' mixed by Eno. It fared disappointingly, only just breaking into the UK Top 40, but it gave Bowie the opportunity to put in a cool performance at the European MTV Awards in Berlin that November. Taking the stage in an ankle-length coat, backlit and stately, Bowie sang wonderfully well. It was originally planned for Polly Harvey to duet with him on the song, but the West Country waif backed out after a 'disagreement over the arrangement'.

Finally, Bowie was to see some much-needed chart action – in the UK, at least. The third single off *1. Outside*, a rerecorded disco version of 'Hallo Spaceboy' with the Pet Shop Boys, just missed the UK Top 10 during its brief run in the charts in February 1996. Bowie had performed the track live during that month's Brit Awards and had picked up the Lifetime Achievement Award from prime-minister-in-waiting Tony Blair, a Bowie fan and ex-pop musician himself (photos of a youthfully long-haired Blair getting down have appeared in the press). Bowie, complete with long silver earring and stilettos, managed to look quite normal in the face of the Labour leader's bouffant hair and bug-eyed stare. The two had met backstage during the *Outside* tour, and Mr Blair went on record as 'fancying' Mrs Bowie. As John Harris records, however, the moment when Blair presented Bowie with his award was not without a certain perverse humour. Blair had not taken advice on whether to say Bowie (to rhyme with 'showy' – which would have been correct) or Bowie (to rhyme with 'wowie'). 'There was the merest of stumbles, before Blairite logic kicked in. Somehow he managed to masterfully incorporate both pronunciations and thereby alienate no one: "David Bowie – oh – ie!" said Blair, just as the walk-up music boomed from the speakers and the man himself ran to the stage.'

The award was emblematic of the turning of the tide for Bowie. By repositioning himself outside of the mainstream, by rewiring the rock machine to bizarre effect with his *1. Outside* album, Bowie was beginning to regain some of the danger and sense of outreach of his 70s career.

Bowie turned fifty on 8 January 1997. Like British television's famous Time Lord, Dr Who, he had regenerated again. He was in good shape in artistic terms. He had spent his fortieth birthday skiing, with the flaccidity of *Never Let Me Down* about to be 'unleashed' on his mainstream audience. Now he had *Earthling*, which established him as a member of humankind after decades orbiting planet pop, while at the same time hinting at his continued fictional alien status. He was the only British pop icon of his generation to have survived with most of his massive artistic credibility intact. He had a new sound too.

Earthling was a direct result of the blasted energy of his current band. Bowie had been on the road almost constantly throughout 1996 and the highlight for many was his show-stealing headlining performance at the Phoenix Festival that summer. As Bowie took the stage on the first night, hundreds of fans who were stuck in the lanes leading up to the festival deserted their cars and walked the extra miles in order not to miss a bona fide-pop sensation. Bowie was brilliant that night, his hair spiked up in a carroty explosion, his body bedecked in stained and torn Union Jack dandy frock coat, and he tore through a set of new and old, ending with an emotional version of 'All The Young Dudes'.

Sadly, this gig, and the summer *Outside* tour dates, were without guitarist Carlos Alomar. Bowie and Gabrels had pared down the large *Outside* arena band to a small unit, and in doing so they lost finesse and gained rock attack. For Alomar, the tour had been an unhappy experience both musically and personally: 'When I go on the road I value my fans, and I call them friends. It really is upsetting to come into town and your friends have died of Aids, or they're no longer there, or it's so long since the last time that they still think it's Tin Machine, so they don't even show up. So, from town to town, I found myself extremely lonely. I wasn't able to access David on this tour, because he was married and there were a lot of things that were taking up his time. It just became a question of, when will I have a chance to leave?'

Taking his touring band of Gabrels, Garson, Dorsey and Alford into the studio during breaks between gigs in the autumn of 1996, Bowie had fashioned a state-of-the-art, high-octane blast of ideas and inspirational musical sequences. Central to Bowie's new direction was the New York-based Mark Plati, a producer, engineer and musician. Plati had worked with famed dance producer Arthur Baker at his Shakedown Sound Studio in New York in the late 1980s.

Bowie chose the Looking Glass Studio, owned by Philip Glass, to record *Earthling*. It had a big control room and a window with a view of Manhattan Bridge. Plati was hired as someone who already knew the studio and its workings (he had produced Deee-Lite there). The vibe during the making of this, Bowie's 21st solo album, was cordial and relaxed. The studio was dubbed 'The Clubhouse' by Gabrels and Gail Ann Dorsey. Bowie would interlace studio time with trips to art galleries. Friends would pop in: film-maker David Lynch (who would use 'I'm Deranged' for his *Lost Highway* movie), Tony Oursler (who provided those wonderfully quirky and surreal 'heads' for the 'Little Wonder' video and *Earthling* tour) and Bowie's old sparring partner (literally so in 1979, when a dinner date ended in fisticuffs), Lou Reed. 'David would go from explaining his views on modern art to enjoying watching us throw muffins out the studio window on to the tops of taxi-cabs!' recalls Plati. 'He would make fun of my biker shorts; I'd tell him and Reeves to go piss off and find an art opening when they were bothering me.'

The blueprint for the album was a piece called 'Telling Lies' written by Bowie in Switzerland, a continuation of tracks such as 'I'm Deranged' on *1. Outside*, and part of an ongoing dialogue between Bowie's style and jungle. Plati had come up with the 'Feelgood mix' which was released by Bowie on the Internet (to great success: 250,000 downloads of the track were reported).

Work started on the album with just Plati, Gabrels and Bowie. 'We began putting song ideas and arrangements into the computer, not to tape,' says Plati. 'I had begun getting into hard-disk recording, and at that time I was getting reasonably good at it. It proved to be an ideal way of getting audio information into a format where you could easily move it around. David would say, "Let's hear a verse, a chorus, a verse, a double chorus, a break, etc.," and I would be able to do all that in about thirty seconds.'

Unsurprisingly, Plati was knocked out by Bowie's technique and studio craft as a vocalist and made sure to keep the tape rolling all the time: 'I just wanted to capture everything I could, which meant recording and saving everything from the very beginning. Lucky for me, because the run-through guide vocal for "Little Wonder" ended up being the only one he ever sang on that track! Most of the vocals were first take, which I had never seen before in my career.'

Bowie would concentrate on the lyrics, jotting things down on Post-it notes or on his computer, while Gabrels and Plati busied themselves with the music. Bowie would chip in with certain lines or sounds he wanted to try.

As the session progressed, the rationale behind the album became clear, particularly during the making of 'Battle For Britain (The Letter)'. 'This was a track which sprang from an idea that I'd come up with over the summer; my attempt to do a jazz-tinged jungle track,' says Plati. 'David scrapped the original chords and came up with new ones. I found the chord progression to be real catchy and unique, and I felt like this could be our first real "Bowie" song. I think at this point I felt like the focus of the record had come together; it was the first time that I heard mention of David's intent to make a melody-driven record. There would be actual songs over intense atmospheres, but the atmospheres wouldn't dominate. I got excited.'

In a moment of inspiration, Bowie turned to Garson and suggested that he play a piano solo, like a Stravinsky octet. After a trip to Tower Records and a quick listen, Garson got what Bowie wanted, delivering a signature barking-mad piano run for the middle section. 'Also, I'd been experimenting with chopping things up in the computer and throwing them about,' adds Plati. 'I'd read about The Beatles chopping up bits of tape for "Being For The Benefit Of Mr Kite", and reassembling them in random fashion. My attempt to do this became the break after the piano.'

The amazing percussive figures on the track came about by mixing Zachary Alford's live drums played in half-time with programmed double-timed jungle figures. 'To get the match seamless took days,' reports Plati. 'But the results speak for themselves.'

'Battle For Britain (The Letter)' is filled with loops, clippings of sound and masses of distortion, a great riff from Gabrels and a well-crafted melody from an almost 'Day In The Life' Beatle-esque Bowie. Bowie told Jon Savage that he was hoping to build on the work of Mick Jones' undervalued post-Clash group, Big Audio Dynamite, and it is the sound on tracks such as 'The Bottom Line', 'Medicine Show' and the sublime 'EMC2' from the debut album *This Is Big Audio Dynamite* (1985), and the title track of Iggy Pop's *Blah Blah Blah*, that much of *Earthling* draws on.

'Little Wonder' was originally intended as a nine-minute jungle electronic epic, much longer than on the album. 'At that point I would never have thought we could cut it down to a four-minute single,' remarks Plati. 'The middle was to be filled with all sorts of effects, atmospheres and breaks. Some ideas (the train after the second verse, for instance) made it into the body of the song.' For the lyric Bowie updated *Snow White and the Seven Dwarves*, inventing a few dwarves for himself and generally having fun (self-deprecatory, too, with the 'Dame Meditation, take me away!' line). Bowie premiered the song at the *VH1 Fashion Awards*. He was unforgivably cheeky, daring the audience into a standing ovation.

This new, jungle-inspired music was not finding favour with band member Mike Garson, however. ' "Little Wonder" did nothing for me; neither did "Telling Lies",' is his candid admission. 'He took me and Reeves to a club in London to listen to Goldie and I was thinking, "Where's the melody?" I enjoyed watching people dance, and that was it. *Earthling* didn't have enough melody for me. Although I'm a crazy improviser, I like a good melody – that's what inspires me. I remember telling Reeves I didn't think *Earthling* would have the future power *Outside* would have. I felt that *Outside* wouldn't be recognised for another ten or fifteen years.'

Garson loved 'Looking For Satellites', though. 'I thought that was the best tune on the album. I got so turned off when they didn't follow through with that and release it as a single that I lost my desire, because I thought that was the one. I thought that was a mistake. When I heard those vocals at the beginning I almost died, it was so good.'

'This was the second track we worked on,' says Plati. 'It sprung from an idea I had created over the summer. I hadn't heard much electronic stuff in three-time, so I set out to make one. This was one of the first attempts to consciously make something out of "junk", a theme throughout the record; take any sound and make something musical out of it. I used samples from lots of records I'd done before and reshaped them, twisted them, made them into new sounds. David and Reeves scrapped my chords and built a new progression.'

Although Gabrels didn't even think the song needed a guitar solo, Bowie wanted one in towards the end. Only this would be a guitar solo with a difference. Gabrels was banned from using certain notes and asked to solo on just one string. The result: a typically bizarre and sonically dysfunctional solo, scuppering a pop song and making it dissonant. Bowie was 'throwing in wrenches', as Alomar called it.

'Looking For Satellites' is a gorgeous pop song, though, and the interpolation of Lou Reed's 'Satellite Of Love' for the hook is fabulous. Of the song, Bowie said: 'I used words randomly: "Shampoo", "TV", "Boy's Own". Whatever I said first, stayed in. It's as near to a spiritual song as I've ever written: it's measuring the distance between the crucifixion and flying saucers,' said Bowie cryptically.

'Seven Years In Tibet', one of Bowie's favourite songs, was – like 'Fashion' all those years before – almost dropped before it reached fruition. Gabrels had composed a track called 'Brussels' and the song developed out of this blueprint. Plati says that through a combination of Gabrels' perseverance and the dynamic of the band, the song finally came to life. Garson's farisfa organ solo, inspired by Gabrels, was an incongruous touch. Suitably reinspired, Bowie came up with the lyric and the idea of running his voice through a ring-modulator to create a haunting, disembodied vocal effect. Mid-paced verses are hammered into submission by howls of guitar, and Bowie's alto-sax riff momentarily brings 'Let's Dance' to mind. Gabrels also added a haunting guitar part based, so he reveals, on Fleetwood Mac's 'Albatross'.

For 'Dead Man Walking', Bowie wanted a techno sound close to Underworld, who were currently in the UK charts with their lager-lout anthem, 'Born Slippy'. He reused a chord progression 'given' to him by Jimmy Page and used earlier on his own 'The Supermen'. 'I really took it upon myself to work this track to some conclusion,' says Plati. 'It took five days to sort it out during the mix, but it became a real epic. It begins completely programmed and by the time it's finished it's completely live.' The song simply soars out of the speakers and, with its killer chorus, rattles along at a fine pace.

'Law (Earthlings On Fire)' is the most unnerving piece on the album. Bowie indulges in the sort of sci-fi speculation that marked albums such as *The Man Who Sold The World*.

The closing shot, a quote from Bertrand Russell, 'I don't want knowledge, I want certainty,' delivered in Bowie's best cyborg (Bowie sang into an empty water-cooler bottle, among other things, to get the strange sound), is a chill conclusion to the album. Bowie snobs get the *Low*-era Harmonizer snare-drum sound on this track too.

On 'Telling Lies', the lyric 'I'm the future, I am tomorrow, I am the end' echoes the Book of Revelation: " 'I am Alpha and Omega, the beginning and the ending," said the Lord.'

On 'The Last Thing You Should Do', Bowie and his cohorts spew out ditties and riffs in all directions. Bowie's on top form vocally, with his sanguine tale of post-Aids conservatism/redemption: 'Save the last dance for me/Catch the last bus with me/Give the last kiss to me/It's the safest thing to do.' The semi-comedic 'I'm Afraid Of Americans' strikes a blow for all those of us cowed by the omnipresence of Michael Jackson, Walt Disney and McDonald's.

Other songs were rehearsed and reviewed for inclusion on the album. 'Baby Universal', a track from *Tin Machine II*, had been revamped and massively improved upon during the 1996 *Outside* tour, and a version of it was recorded for the album. Likewise, an acoustic version of the Tin Machine song, 'I Can't Read', was recorded (and was later released on the soundtrack to *The Ice Storm*, becoming a minor hit in 1997). But these Tin Machine songs were left off to accommodate 'The Last Thing You Should Do', originally recorded late in the sessions as B-side material. 'I have to admit I miss "I Can't Read" not being on the record,' Plati says, 'and I disagreed strongly with David at the time. But his argument was that "Last Thing" fitted in better conceptually. I think time has shown him to be correct.'

The artwork and conceptualisation of the album took shape during recording, Plati recalls. 'Every new idea or concept would be put up on the wall. By the end of recording, the walls of the studio were filled with the artwork that would become the album.' The album's title was the first to be chosen by fans themselves. On tour that September, Bowie asked the audience at Roseland, New York, if the album should be called 'Earthling' or 'Earthlings'.

The cover showed Bowie like some Napoleonic-era military dandy, hands behind his back, surveying England's green and pleasant land, made harsh and unrealistic through vivid greens. It's a depopulated mock-up of the real thing, just as *Ziggy Stardust*'s cover looked like alien London. The tattered Union Jack featured on the tour and on the album was co-designed by Alexander McQueen. Bowie had the idea of resurrecting the Union Jack after seeing sculptor and artist Gavin Turk's exhibit *Indoor Flag* back in 1995. The Union Jack, as a symbol in British pop culture, had gone from being a motif of British export confidence in the 1960s to being defaced by the punks in the 1970s and seen as a rightist symbol when paraded by Morrissey at Finsbury Park in the early 1990s. After wearing the frock coat triumphantly at the 1996 Phoenix Festival, Bowie set off a mini-trend of Union Jackers, culminating in the sale of Ginger Spice's Union Jack dress at auction for $50,000.

Earthling was released on 3 February 1997. The first single off the album, the catchy 'Little Wonder', was the most heavily influenced by the 'drum'n'bass' sound. Bowie sings in his best adenoidal 'sarf London' accent, reciting a litany of cheeky cockneyisms. The video, directed by Floria Sigismondi, was actually better than the song. It showed three different ages of the Dame – bemused mid-sixties ingénue, spaced-out space-age androgyne, and the ever more spooky real version, who transforms into a mannequin at the end of the song. This is the first Bowie video to actually look more like a dance video than a rock video: the use of quirky slowed-down shots of the various Bowies set against a speeded-up environment of London's inner-city existence (on the tube, and in busy traffic) is reminiscent of dance videos such as Orbital's 'The Box'.

But according to Mat Snow, editor of *Mojo*, the air of calculation about the project made *Earthling* only a qualified success: 'I think the drum and bass was bolted on purely so that he could get a hit of *Zeitgeist* energy. I think he did it as a fairly cold decision. I don't think that his style and the drum'n'bass style converged on an organic basis, if you will. He was clearly intrigued by this "happening music" and thought that this is the sort of thing that he ought to be acknowledging within his own music. That said, I wasn't actually affronted by it, and enjoyed quite a lot of it. But I suppose there's something less full-blooded about it than, say, *Young Americans*, where he took another contemporary black style and entered into it with such panache and commitment, whilst maintaining his own fundamental melodic shapes. Whereas *Earthling* felt slightly more like an arranged marriage. I felt he wasn't quite as interested in drum'n'bass as a form and he didn't inhabit it as a form quite as well. Also, this is exactly the sort of critical move you would have expected from David Bowie. In fact, it was a pretty good album, but I don't think it was given a fair shake, because people thought, It's grandad down the disco, isn't it? That is a function of people not allowing a fifty-year-old artist just to be an artist. It's ageism, pure and simple, and I think I had a semi-ageist response.'

In fact *Earthling* only has three or four tracks that contain a drum'n'bass element. Before its release, advance reports misleadingly called it Bowie's jungle magnum opus, a fact that put fans off since much drum'n'bass was marked by a paucity of decent melodies. The complete collapse in the market for drum'n'bass (never significant in commercial terms in any case) in the late 1990s gives ample proof that outside a coterie of club-goers and media gurus, the genre was virtually support-free. For Mat Snow, however, *Earthling* was a sign of nervousness, as if Bowie didn't really know who his audience was any more. 'The sleeve didn't help. It looked like a fifteen-year-old Hipgnosis design for a 10 cc album circa 1978. It was disappointing for Bowie. If you looked at the album as a package, *Earthling* felt just too marketed. He calls the thing *Earthling*, which is tremendously self-referential. When people start to get self-referential like that, you worry that they're trying to press the trigger of their core market, saying, "Hey, remember me? I'm Ziggy Stardust, the weird one!" So there was a slight anxiety that he'd lost touch with his market, or that his market had kind of moved on to other things. So it's almost, "Hey, I'm Gary Glitter and I'm back and we're still the same old gang, right?" Yes, I thought it smacked of an insecurity unbecoming of David Bowie, and the sleeve had this curious out-of-touchness and insecurity about it.'

For Snow, *Earthling*, like *Let's Dance*, was a calculated attempt to win mainstream approval. This time, however, it backfired: 'I liked that record, but nonetheless, people did think it was a purely commercial move. He wasn't playing with it in the same way he played with riff rock in the early 1970s and soul in the mid-1970s. This was a way of connecting with a mainstream audience and I felt that the same motivation was at work again with *Earthling*. But it worked much better with *Let's Dance* because he was only 35 then. He had not been through a kind of figure-of-fun phase; he had not made any bad records.'

Eight years after the release of the album, some have argued that the drum and bass elements of the record have dated it. Mark Plati, for one, disagrees: 'Personally, I still love *Earthling*, and not just because I worked on it,' he says. 'When I played it recently, it still sounded fresh, probably because it was done so fast. It was a very "first instinct" kind of record. It felt like it just came about on its own. It really captures a moment.'

At fifty Bowie was, on the surface at least, a saner, more relaxed individual than he was at forty. And a wealthier one. He had a mansion in Switzerland, Hauts de Lausanne, and one in New

York as well as a holiday home in Bermuda. He went public with his intention of starting a family with Iman. He was active as a musician, actor and artist. He had also regained his spirit of adventure, his interest in the new.

That said, the ten years since Glass Spider had seen Bowie removed from the top division of rock superstars, largely of his own making. The general rock fan had heard nothing from him for over a decade. Bowie had not had a major hit album for fourteen years. Apart from his hard-core fans and the serious rock fan, to most Bowie had, to all intents and purposes, retired in the 1980s.

The media hoo-ha surrounding Bowie's half-century had an air of predictability about it. Two new biographies also appeared: George Tremlett's *Living on the Brink* and Christopher Sandford's *Loving the Alien*. The media was full of retrospectives (almost all of them, with a beguiling lack of ingenuity, featuring the words 'chameleon' or 'changes' somewhere in the title). Alan Yentob produced a disappointing Bowie tribute for the BBC, cunningly entitled *Changes*. A question-and-answer session on Radio 1 proved more entertaining. Brian Molko from Placebo took the opportunity to ask Bowie when he was going to work with them. Neil Tennant, The Cure's Robert Smith, Mick Hucknall and long-time Bowie nuts Brett Anderson and Ian McCulloch also quizzed their idol. A moving tribute by Scott Walker appeared to bring Bowie to tears. The show was cheekily compered by Mary Anne Hobbs, who chatted to Bowie about his sagging bottom and sexually transmitted diseases.

Bowie himself topped the celebrations off with a birthday bash at Madison Square Garden on 9 January, at which he performed a selection of oldies with the likes of Robert Smith (who gave him a fossilised chameleon as a birthday present!) and Lou Reed, along with tracks from *Earthling*. The show itself was a disappointment. Visually, Bowie was using the same filmed sequences he had shot seven years earlier for the *Sound + Vision* tour. But even more disappointing was the choice of participants.

Bowie's wish to remain relevant and not to turn into some nostalgia show is understandable. But, just once, it would have been both a poignant and magnanimous gesture to have filled the bill not with contemporary acts who had very little to do with the Bowie story, but with musicians who were actually part and parcel of his history. It would have sent Bowie's hard-core following into raptures to see the old rhythm section of Alomar, Davis and Murray reunited. It would have been a treat to have Eno and Fripp perform on stage with Bowie for the first time, or for Belew, Slick, Ricky Gardiner or Stacey Haydon to make another appearance. Luther Vandross, whom Bowie had discovered and who by the 1990s was one of the biggest soul acts in the world, might also have been asked to tread the boards with Bowie again. Bowie could have swallowed his pride, puckered his lips and reconvened The Spiders. As an act of genuine pop archaeology he might have sought out The Lower Third. He could have grooved with Nile Rodgers. And, although Lou Reed was there, where was Iggy Pop?

The birthday bash was far less a celebration of Bowie's career than a showcase for his current musical obsessions. Even the choice of contemporary artists was strange. The Bowie influence may be visible in the theatricality of The Cure (if not in their music), but The Foo Fighters and Sonic Youth hardly spring to mind as first-degree Bowie casualties. Suede, Nine Inch Nails or even Blur would have been more faithful choices. But, importantly, they were not big US draws and there was Madison Square Garden to fill and television rights to secure.

Carlos Alomar was not terribly impressed: 'I wasn't asked to play. If I had been asked, I would have played. I was just there for moral support. There were a lot of people he could have asked. He could have asked Luther Vandross, who's now a superstar. But that whole thing was a political thing for him, to get together with the people who he thought would project him into the future. But I don't even like some of those groups. Sonic Youth? Come on, give me a break! They're brain-dead! If you're looking at it as a retrospective of his life, who are these people? Everyone that had worked with him could have come on, like Dennis Davis, and if you were a Bowie fan, you would have known who they were but to put the old band back together again, that wouldn't have been political.'

The reason for the virtually all-contemporary line-up was, according to Reeves Gabrels, a very simple one: 'David is generally more about the present than the past.' He remembers the gig as 'a stressful but fun occasion in terms of having only one night to get it right while the cameras were rolling. As far as the people involved . . . I already knew Frank Black and suggested him for the line-up, and had hung out with Billy Corgan and

Robert Smith and I had a number of friends in common such as Tim Pope who worked on the show and lighting designer Gary Wescott. I was concerned that the list of participants would end up being too mainstream. For the longest, Madonna was expected to perform so, as the roster stabilised, I was greatly relieved.'

The spin-off from the pursuit of his current enthusiasms was that the new work was geared to a very different audience than the 'Phil Collins-style' fans who had sat flummoxed at Wembley Arena on the *Outside* tour. It was thus a commercial decision to tour small clubs in the US in the autumn and to play festivals such as Phoenix, Roskilde and Balingen the previous summer. For the first time in over a decade, Bowie began finding a younger audience. Those who attended his shows throughout 1997 were an intriguing mix of forty- and fifty-something Ziggy-lovers, twenty- and thirty-something *Let's Dance* and *Scary Monsters* freaks, and teenagers who thought *Earthling* cool and who were discovering his back catalogue.

Bowie toured *Earthling* almost continuously throughout 1997. He played two sets, a more conventional set of 'songs' (which included such oldies as 'Quicksand', 'Stay', 'Panic In Detroit' and 'Fashion') together with material from *Earthling* and *Outside*, and a second, and at times frankly dull, drum'n'bass set, including extensively reworked versions of some Bowie classics, such as an excellent but almost unrecognisable 'V-2 Schneider', 'Pallas Athena' and a version of Laurie Anderson's 1981 hit 'O Superman' with Gail Ann Dorsey on lead vocals.

Bowie's own live vocal was weakening as the *Earthling* tour progressed. Almost two years of nonstop gigging were taking their toll. Another factor was Bowie's nicotine intake. He had beaten booze, forsworn drugs and even conquered what was possibly an anorexic condition in the mid-1970s, but he couldn't overcome his addiction to the evil weed. In one of his most bizarre interviews, Bowie said to Jarvis Cocker in the *Big Issue* in 1997: 'In my past Gitanes were the ones that I really thought had it all. [They] took me all through the 70s. But they were so strong . . . they get to become really addictive. But then I went from those to Marlboro Reds. I went through the 80s on those and around the time I started Tin Machine, around 1988, I realised I wasn't getting the high notes at all, so I dropped down to Marlboro Lights. I should go even lighter, I suppose, because I know I'm going to have to give up sooner or later when the kid comes. In a general day I get through about forty Marlboro Lights – which is a cut down from what I used to smoke, believe me. When I'm on the road I tend to drop down to about twenty. I think probably that I'd sing much better if I didn't smoke.'

On stage Gabrels had taken to dyeing his close-cropped receding hair, wearing make-up, and coming on like a transvestite Uncle Fester from the *Addams Family*. 'What could be more terrifying than a six-foot-one, 190 lb, kilt-wearing guitar player with bleached hair, heavy eye make-up and light purple lipstick?' says Gabrels. 'Do you know how people press to the front of the stage? If I went to the front of the stage to take a guitar solo, I could feel people draw back, even though they were pressed to the barriers. Maybe it was like a psychic withdrawal. The kilt is very liberating. My father was part Scottish, part Cherokee Indian, part French and part English. I was walking through Glasgow and I saw a place called The Kilt Store. You have to have them custom made, but they had one in which someone had decided not to buy, and it was the same clan as McCloud and it fitted me. Never had a bad show whilst wearing a kilt!'

Bowie undoubtedly reached a new audience with *Earthling*. Playing to crowds who had come as much to see The Prodigy (Bowie's co-headliners) as the Dame, Bowie converted even the most cynical of observers. His new music was muscular and contemporary, his back catalogue peerless. There were some fun moments too, such as an appearance on *The Jack Docherty Show* when Reeves Gabrels played the song with a huge furry mouse head, and Bowie with a pair of mouse's hands. Bowie's appearance on the German TV show *Wetten Dass* was as bizarre as asking Ziggy onto *Bruce Forsyth's Generation Game*. His role as interviewee included having to predict whether a guy in a pair of trunks about to submerge himself in a tank of water could play the trumpet underwater for an entire minute (he failed), and Bowie's face was a study of 'What the hell am I doing on this programme?' faux pleasure.

The biggest success off the album was a Trent Reznor remix of 'I'm Afraid Of Americans'. Reznor stripped the song back to its minimalist beats and produced an eerie, psychotic track which helped it into the lower reaches of the US charts. It reached only Number 66, but it hung around the US Billboard Top 100 for an impressive sixteen weeks and was his first hit since 'Day In Day Out' over a decade earlier. In Canada, a country in which the sentiment of the song obviously struck a chord, the single was in the Top 50 for six months. However, it was not issued in the UK, where the most recent crop of Bowie singles had fared badly. 'Little Wonder' had reached Number 14, a moderate success. 'Dead Man Walking' astonishingly missed the Top 30 and 'Seven Years In Tibet' missed the Top 50 altogether. A version of 'Seven Years In Tibet', sung in Mandarin, did become a Number 1 in Hong Kong, its anti-Chinese sensibility obviously popular in the former colony.

Bowie told Radio 1's Jo Whiley: 'Over the last couple of years, I've felt really guilty about the continuing situation. I wrote a couple of things in 1968 about this situation. One was called "Silly Boy Blue" and another was called "Karma Man". I thought, what a perfect time to release an anti-Chinese song in Hong Kong, just as the Chinese take over. It got super-popular, but I'm not sure we'll be able to tour there now, of course. I'll probably try and play there next year – but we'll see. I've probably fallen out with the Chinese now.'

Earthling was only a moderate-selling album, reaching Number 6 in the UK and Number 35 in the US, despite some justifiably good reviews. Particularly insightful was an end-of-year review in the *Financial Times* by Peter Aspden: '*Earthling* was inspired by the drum'n'bass sound which has become a staple of the British dance scene; but what joy to see it manipulated with such expertise by an old master. If I were in Prodigy or The Chemical Brothers, I would be listening very closely. Both *The Fat Of The Land* and *Dig Your Own Hole* were strong on aggression and aural attack, but lacked the variety and subtlety to last beyond twenty-odd interesting minutes.'

Bowie was nominated in the 40th Grammy Awards in 1998 for Best Male Rock Vocal Performance ('Dead Man Walking') and Best Alternative Music Performance (*Earthling*), awards eventually won by Radiohead and Dylan respectively. The rumoured duet between Radiohead and Bowie never took place: Radiohead had been told that they could not perform on their own at the Grammys because it would 'not be good for ratings'. Bowie was also nominated for Best Male Video in the US MTV Awards for 'I'm Afraid Of Americans'. He went prizeless, but the mere fact that he was nominated after fifteen years of critical pillorying by sections of the media was a massively encouraging experience for him – and for such a hard-hitting, single-minded album.

Bowie still had a few surprises in store too. Take, for example, 1998's Nat Tate hoax. In 1997, Bowie had decided to invest in a publishing venture, 21, to accommodate his passion for art and literary matters. *Blimey! From Bohemia to Britpop: The London Artworld from Francis Bacon to Damien Hirst* by artist and writer Matthew Collings set the tone for the press: chatty, informal, yet dealing with big ideas (high-cultural contexts, low-cultural speak). It was slightly pretentious too, and so signature Bowie. But the Nat Tate book by William Boyd told a very tall tale of the flawed genius of an artist, riven by depression, who committed suicide by jumping off the back of the Staten Island ferry in 1960. Nat Tate, of course, never existed.

It was the classic Bowie-esque scam of the 1990s, the sort of thing he did to pop in the 70s. It was an indication of the power and usefulness of myth and deceit in everyday 'real' life. Once again, Bowie had completely outfoxed his peers. The writer and journalist Bill Buford even imagined Bowie filling the slot vacated when Warhol died in 1987. The art world, leaderless and lacking in glamour, needed a high-profile leader: 'Everywhere [Bowie] went, he was followed by a crowd of forty, fifty people. Some were friends, eager to have a word: some were fans. But many – in this self-consciously hip and groovy crowd – just wanted to be near him. They followed him, mouths open, shuffling behind, going wherever he went.'

Nevertheless, what did any of this matter to those people who put Bowie where he was, the fans of his music? Was Bowie's endless diversification alienating his public for good?

14. THE REVOLUTION WILL BE DOWNLOADED, 1998–2000

And the Internet is, no doubt, the most subversive, rebellious, revolutionary form of communication since, oh, television then, if you must.

DAVID BOWIE, 2000

It is a rather sad fact that in the 1990s, the three events that marked Bowie's highest media visibility were not associated with his music at all. His marriage to Iman was one. His fiftieth birthday was another. And the Bowie Bond scheme was the third.

Cynics have said that the media package surrounding *Earthling* and Bowie's fiftieth birthday was merely a way to draw attention to the Bowie Bond scheme, and that *Earthling* itself was a failed attempt to break Bowie into a youth market and raise his commercial stock amongst the under-thirties. In the eighteen months following his birthday, a number of polls revealed Bowie to be one of the richest rock stars in the world. One survey actually claimed he was the world's richest musician, with an estate of $900 million.

In 1997, Bowie re-signed his back catalogue to EMI, and received an advance of $28.5 million. However, it was the Bowie Bond scheme which provided the copy for the tabloids and broadsheets. It was a scheme designed with one specific aim in mind: to finally buy out ex-manager Tony Defries.

The banker who organised the deal was David Pullman of The Pullman Group, a division of Fahnstock & Co. It was the first time a rock star had undertaken such a deal, which involved royalties on his back catalogue being used as 'asset backing' on an issued bond. In the event, one institution, Prudential Securities, bought all $55 million worth of the securities on the day they were issued. In effect, Bowie received $55 million upfront, in return for agreeing to pay back the full amount (plus interest each year) at a specified time. The value of Bowie's back catalogue was used as 'collateral' in the sense that future royalties would go towards paying the interest. When the bonds expire (repaid in full), the royalty rights will revert to Bowie, and he'll be able to sell them over again. 'There is tremendous value in intellectual property: film libraries, record masters, literary estates – the value of it grows over time,' said Pullman in May 1998. However, investment in rock acts other than those with a long and proven track record is regarded as very risky.

'Almost every singer with a hit record today is the bankruptcy of tomorrow,' said William Krsilovsky, a lawyer specialising in music and entertainment copyright law. Bill Zysblat, who helps manage David Bowie and other rock stars through his company RZO, said Bowie wanted the $55 million upfront rather than having to wait to the end of his multi-year royalty deal. He used part of the money to purchase a share of the publishing rights to his own songs held by a former manager. He also invested a large part of it in the expectation of getting a greater-than-10-per-cent deal.

In the eyes of some, the Bowie Bond scheme merely inflated Bowie's status and made him look greedy. It was a typically innovative move guaranteed to grab the headlines as Bowie turned fifty. Bowie's name and reputation, and everything that signified, was used as a guarantor of a certain sort of cultural kudos, and this was translated directly into dollars for the Bowie estate. It was a move which has since been copied by other recording artists. However, the feeling was that, for the first time since Tin Machine, Bowie was allowing himself and his name to be 'branded', using stardom as a commodity.

Between 1988 and 1996, Bowie and Reeves Gabrels fought to re-establish Bowie's musical credibility. The period from 1997 to 2000 saw just one new album recorded, but a whole range of headline-grabbing business coups undertaken. Bowie the entrepreneur was becoming more and more visible, despite the fact that he always refuses to discuss his business affairs in public. The

Bowie Bond scheme set in train a whole train of money-related Bowie activities, none of which was connected with the one area in which Bowie excelled and was admired for: his music.

During this period, Bowie's main interest became the Internet. Given his interest in knowledge and his eclectic tastes, it was not really surprising that he would be bewitched by the possibilities of the Net. He was already something of an Internet star, becoming the first major rock act to release an Internet-only single with 'Telling Lies' in 1996. By September 1996, in terms of the number of sites relating to him, he was the third most popular solo male artist on the World Wide Web. The Internet was seemingly all he was ever asked to talk about. He viewed the medium as full of creative potential. It could create a space in an unregulated form for genuinely oppositional art. It could create a vibrant community of fans. It was an enabling development which demystified the icon. It was an important educational tool. And it was fun.

On 1 September 1998, at 12.01 a.m., BowieNet was launched. Bowie had been interested in communications technology since the early 1980s, when communications on his Serious Moonlight tour were conducted by the then almost unknown process of email, so he was no arriviste in this field. As ever, he had his finger firmly on the pulse. He appeared to be genuinely motivated by his vision of using the Internet as a proactive device, to create an online community not just of Bowie fans, but of rock fans in particular, and Internet users in general. BowieNet is undoubtedly an attractive place to visit: beautifully and stylishly designed, with plenty of information, it replenishes and develops itself almost by the day. There is downloadable rare material (live and otherwise), a chance to 'chat' with other fans, and celebrity web chats. Users have the opportunity to get closer to Bowie's obsessions, as part of BowieNet is taken up with his current fascinations in the world of literature, art and film. There is also the chance to get inside Bowie's mind, by eavesdropping on his increasingly occasional Web Diary/Log. Not everyone agrees with this approach, though: 'I have no interest in writing a daily journal about my private life,' Reeves Gabrels said. 'I believe it demystifies the artist and gets in the way of the music.'

In a number of interviews following the launch, Bowie said that, had he been a young artist starting out now, he probably would never have become a musician, so alluring and so full of potential was the Internet. 'If I was nineteen again, I'd bypass music and go straight to the Internet,' he told Andrew Davies of the *Big Issue*. 'When I was nineteen, music was still the dangerous communicative future force, and that was what drew me into it, but it doesn't have that cachet any more. It's been replaced by the Internet, which has the same sound of revolution to it.' In another interview he added, 'Music is merely becoming a conveyance of information and is not the revolutionary cycle it once was.' Again, in February 2000, he was singing the same tune: 'When the vocabulary of any art form gets too well known it dissipates its dynamic. Once everybody can play the e chord on a guitar, once everyone can sample what they want at home on a cheap computer, the medium suddenly becomes the message and the message seems to be: "This is lifestyle music not attitude music". I think we probably buy our music in the same way as we buy our clothes now, it's no longer the replacement to church.'

'At the moment I'm looking at the Net decidedly as an art form because it seems to have no parameters whatsoever,' said Bowie. 'It's chaos out there, which I thrive on, actually. But I do see opportunities and I'm quite good at maybe putting my fingers on those opportunities and running with them and I'm quite prepared to jump into just about everything in life in the deep end.' Bill Zysblatt, Bowie's finance man, stated that Bowie, 'spends a fair bit of time in the chat room'. Apparently, Bowie will sometimes post anonymously to chat-room discussions and then later send participants an email letting them know he was there. While most of the emails Bowie receives are handled by someone else, Zysblatt said the singer will personally answer fifty or so a month. This aspect may have two knock-on effects. The pop star becomes dangerously knowable and demystified; a certain aura of mystique and allure is stripped away and, consequently, the star becomes ordinary, which is exactly what our rock heroes should not be. Secondly, even the chimera of a one-on-one relationship between multimillionaire star and fan can result in the sort of twisted identification that leads to pathology.

At the time, it was apparent to many that Bowie was getting overly enthusiastic about the medium. As well as being a source of social and cultural change, the Internet is also an anarchy of deregulation, a world of imaginary friends and enemies. It can serve to make people more alienated, not more connected. You can make a friend or enemy of someone you never have to see in the flesh ('Who to dis, who to truss', Bowie sings in one of his first post-BowieNet songs, 'The Pretty Things Are Going To Hell').

By 1999, BowieNet was valued at £300 million. Computer-world, America's leading computer magazine, listed Bowie as one of its top 25 innovators for 1999, the only entertainment figure on the list. And there were more initiatives to come, as, in the words of the *Financial Times*, Bowie branched out into areas 'unrelated to what business strategists might call his core compet-encies'. In the space of just over a year, 'Bowie' became an Internet Service Provider, a radio station and a bank. In 1999, he started his own David Bowie Radio Network on the Rolling Stone Radio website. But far more significant were the expansion of his Internet company, Ultrastar, and the launch in late 1999 of Bowie.banc.com. Bowie and Ultrastar began running American baseball team websites such as New York Yankees (Yankees-Xtreme) and the Baltimore Orioles (OriolesWorld). 'We [Ultra-star] create little generic ISPs for different companies and universities and colleges and all that, so it's actually quite a major company now,' Bowie said. With BowieBanc, Bowie wasn't risking any of his own money in the venture, though. Depositors get ATM cards, cheques and other banking paraphernalia em-blazoned with Bowie's name and image as well as a year of BowieNet service. All of the actual banking operations are handled by the online banking firm USABancShares.com. Bill Zysblatt explained: 'What we are doing is taking his fan base, which twenty years ago had an affinity for wearing a T-shirt of his, and maybe ten years ago graduated to wearing a golf shirt of his, and in the last three or four years has developed to being part of his online service, and trying to create the same affinity with what he is doing with online banking.'

This is a good financial wheeze, but depressing for those of his fans who value Bowie for his oppositional stance. It's also a tad embarrassing. You might choose to wear a Bowie T-shirt once or twice a year in public during clement weather, but giving out an email address with Bowie's name on it, or having Bowie's face on your flexible friend when you hand it over to buy a six-pack is a different matter. Bowie fans want their man on the road and on the CD player, visible and entertaining, not further embroiled in the machinations of the capitalist establishment. Zysblatt, perhaps aware that there might indeed be cries of 'sell out' from some quarters of the media, had this to say about Bowie's business savvy: 'From the earliest days of David's career, regardless of how avant-garde he may have appeared to the public, it was never really an anti-Establishment message. Maybe we felt it was anti-Establishment because our parents didn't like the fact that he was wearing a dress. But quite frankly, if you look at his savvy, going back to his very first signings with RCA where he retained ownership of his master, the business side of his mind was always working.' So according to the new orthodoxy, Bowie was always as Establishment as they come, his violation of the rock gene pool with the likes of Aladdin Sane and the Thin White Duke just so much brouhaha. It is a depressing message to all those who had championed Bowie as a challenging rock icon who hit back at the Establishment.

This is not to criticise the architect of many of these brilliant business initiatives, as Reeves Gabrels attests, 'Bill [Zysblatt] is a really nice guy and a rarity in the music business side of things. He is a man you can trust. We have often disagreed where music and commerce meet, but he has my complete respect.'

Bowie is not alone in branding his name in this way. An article in the *Financial Times* drew attention to the fact that it wasn't just Bowie the rocker who was getting in on the act: 'In the days when a brand meant the name of a laundry detergent or something in a can, the idea that people could be brands might have been regarded as absurd. It seems less so today,' said Richard Tomkins. 'This week, another old rocker, Mick Jagger, registered his name as a trademark for more than twenty products and services, from toiletries to bars. His agents said this was just to prevent other people profiting from the use of his name, but nobody seemed particularly surprised at the idea of Mick Jagger as a brand of deodorant.'

David Bowie has a curious and, to some, illogical relationship with money. As a pop-art saboteur à la Warhol, we should not be surprised that he wanted to make commercial art. We thanked him and revelled in his 1970s attack on the phoniness of the hippy pose, which held that music was some authentic expression of consciousness, man, and that the musicians were too far-out to be interested in making money.

For a lower-middle-class child such as Bowie, born into the austerity of post-war London, money has a huge importance. Bowie himself is not an ostentatious man. Whilst a lover (and connoisseur) of fine art, and a voracious collector, he is not at all bothered about the flotillas of yachts, the car park full of vintage cars, or the private pleasure parks full of young children that other rock superstars appear to find damn-near essential to getting through a day off between vocal overdubs. This wholly admirable sense of thrift and moral responsibility has stayed with him. But whereas in the past, Bowie kept business away from our pleasure, in the late 1990s it appeared, with Bowie Bonds, BowieNet, and BowieBanc, that his financial managers were very visibly out to make us part with our money in ways totally unrelated to the reasons why we became David Bowie fans in the first place, which were our love of his music and our deep admiration for the man.

One knock-on effect has been the sad trashing of his pristine musical legacy by the business operators themselves. Fans have had to endure "Heroes" being used in TV adverts for the likes of Kodak, Microsoft, CGU (pensions/investments and insurance) and, in 2004, in an actually rather good instrumental version by Nathan Larson, Wanadoo. This fan, for one, has never felt at all heroic when Microsoft Windows flashes up for the umpteenth time: 'This program has performed an illegal operation and will be shut down – invalid page fault in module KERNEL32.DLL'. Nor does the idea of investing in a pension come across as even mildly evocative of the Dunkirk spirit.

Bowie's willingness to allow his music to sell commercial products also bothered his right-hand man. Gabrels has a deep respect and friendship for Bowie, but he became disillusioned with the dilution of the man's musical legacy:

David was one of three of my non-guitar-playing musical heroes, right up there with Miles Davis and George Jones. I always felt like he had a real history and legacy that I was proud to be participating in and also furthering. Your legacy and history is what gets remembered. My attitude has always been, 'Let's make some great music'. In the early Tin Machine days I used to get chided as being the 'art snob' in the band. I never felt that was accurate, but it did point out an aspect of my respect for what I do. I personally don't believe that using your music to sell products is cool. It devalues the art ... it devalues its meaning and emotional content. Unfortunately, sometimes artists have no control over such things due to who owns the master tapes or controls the publishing. But when you can protect it, then, out of love for your fans and your art, I think you should.

Charitably, former *Mojo* editor, Paul Trynka, said in Bowie's defence, 'Good rock stars devour new experiences. He's not exploiting his name, he's too switched on for that. I think it's all part of a wish to keep surprising people.' But fans want to be surprised musically, not by how successful their idol is at developing a media empire. Writer Sean O'Hagan summed up things accurately for a piece in the *Observer* in early 2000: 'Of all the guises adopted by rock's reigning chameleon, this [Bowiebanc.com] is certainly the most astute and most failsafe. One can't help thinking that Ziggy must be turning in his glittery grave.'

By the late 1990s, it had been a dozen years since his last big UK hit single and fifteen years since his last convincing film role. The giant creative strides taken by Bowie on *1. Outside* and *Earthling* had hinted at more daring endeavours, but it seemed that the momentum had been lost. Rather than follow up *Earthling* with another high-energy techno-rock album, Bowie appeared rather to lose the courage of his convictions.

1998 was a busy but bitty year in the career of David Bowie. He made two films scheduled for 1999 release, *Exhuming Mr Rice* (later retitled *Mr Rice's Secret*) and *Everybody Loves Sunshine*, a gangster movie shot in Liverpool and the Isle of Man and co-starring Goldie (and released on video as *Busted*), but there was no new album. The frenzied activity between autumn 1992 and autumn 1996, a period which had yielded four fine albums, was over. For Reeves Gabrels, it was a frustrating time:

I believe that there should have been a follow-up *Earthling*-type album, much in the same way that *Aladdin Sane* followed *Ziggy* . . . an extrapolation of the previous album. The music had evolved, the band was playing great and the window of opportunity (time-wise) was there. David's desire was to put together a live album (produced by him and me) of *Earthling/Outside*-only material, plus two new tracks – a song called 'Funhouse' (an amazing drum'n'bass/rock extravaganza) and a cover of Dylan's 'Trying To Get To Heaven'. Unfortunately, Virgin refused to put it out after it was completed and submitted in late winter 1998. Aside from the obvious, the bad news was that, in the amount of time David, Mark Plati and myself spent compiling and editing, we could have written and recorded the *Earthling* follow-up album that I'd hoped we'd do. The good news is you can get these very same album-quality live tracks online at liveandwell.com.

At this stage it must be said that Bowie himself is adamant that the record was never intended for commercial release. It was, in fact, devised by Bowie to be the first album to be made strictly as a downloadable work from an internet site only, although in the end Virgin got cold feet and cancelled the release, perhaps concerned over the possible repercussions for the industry.

Bowie did make a few forays into the recording studio, though. He was developing a highly mannered, slightly quivery, deep vibrato. His voice was now almost jazzy and fluid, dealing in a somewhat microtonal, unstable register. On Goldie's *Saturnzreturn*, released in early 1998, Bowie sang 'Truth', but, if the truth be told, the music, and Bowie's performance, were boring. Later in the year, he recorded a version of George Gershwin's 'A Foggy Day In London Town' for the latest in a series of AIDS charity albums, this one entitled *Red, Hot And Rhapsody*. He performed the song with Angelo Badalamenti, a composer who had scored the original *Twin Peaks* TV series and worked on the first Julee Cruise album. Again, the song itself, and Bowie's performance, lacked colour. Another song, 'Planet Of Dreams', performed with bassist Gail Ann Dorsey for the benefit CD *Long Live Tibet*, is reminiscent of *Avalon*-era Roxy Music. It was only moderately artistically successful.

There were also two new Bowie compilations, the first fruit of Bowie's new reissue campaign. The *Best Of Bowie: 1969/74* was a reasonably predictable package of undoubtedly brilliant moments which reached Number 13 in the UK Charts. A second compilation, *1974/1979*, fared less well, only just reaching the UK Top 40. A third release, covering the years 1980 to 1987, was planned, but not released.

Then came the Bowie reissues on EMI. Perhaps the most notable feature of these reissues was the compulsory addition of lyrics to the CD booklets. Never again on *Diamond Dogs* would we be able to sing 'Her face her saddest feature but she wears a dolly brooch' as we now know that it's 'Her face is sans feature but she wears a Dali brooch'. Ah, the mystery all gone! Generally, the sound quality was more faithful to the vinyl originals than the Ryko versions of 1989–91. *Young Americans* appeared the most improved, a dominant and lush sound now picking up all of Visconti's brilliant production, whilst *Station To Station* remained largely unimproved and slightly sterile. *Let's Dance*, always a fabulous production, simply soared out of the speakers. None of the newly repackaged albums broke the UK Top 100 however and these reissues came without the extra tracks that for some made the Ryko issues essential.

Seventeen Bowie titles were reissued in all. Originally a second disc was to be included with bonus tracks and an ECD (enhanced CD) section, with videos and other features including an interactive day-by-day chronology. A prototype of *Space Oddity* was actually created by Abbey Road Interactive, but because the whole reissue schedule was delayed, all such plans had to be shelved.

By the late 1990s, Bowie could be satisfied with having built up an impressive post-Tin Machine body of work. However, his musical career was not yet completely back on course. Mojo's Mat Snow had this to say:

Bowie is a legend and he always will be a legend. Yet, at the same time, as a brand, to use a corporate marketing term, he's tainted. What a brand is, is an indicator of a certain reliable quality. For example, if Bowie was Jaguar Cars, and Jaguar put out a couple of really crummy cars, they'd have to come out with a bloody good third one to persuade people to even take an interest. And that's what's happened to Bowie. He made a string of disappointing records. How do you then get people interested? The Rolling Stones theoretically had the same problem, but they've got over it because they've simply turned the record into a souvenir of the tour. The records aren't very good but they come out just as the tour kicks off. What you really want is to go to the tour, but some of the people will also buy the album, because it's all part of the same excitement. They probably don't play the album much, if at all, but, none the less it's still part of a sense of being there. Because Bowie's tours are comparatively low-key, he can't sell an album on the back of a big-event tour. It's the finance of the whole thing. You can only really do big-event tours if you can make lots of profit in North America. And Bowie was just never quite big enough over there.

Before the release of his next album, Bowie indulged us with a few trademark generalisms. In February 1999, he took the stage at the Brit Awards in London's Docklands' Arena with Placebo to duet on Marc Bolan's 'Twentieth Century Boy'. Bowie appeared once again to have put the ageing process into reverse gear. He paraded a new, longer hairstyle. Goatee-less, he looked like a cross between the Thin White Duke and a bisexual Bryan Adams. English soccer fans remarked that he looked like midfielder David Beckham, ironically looked after by the same PR team as Bowie himself. Whatever, his performance was a study of controlled aggression, and the double act stole the show. Bowie also found time to have a go at designing his own mini car, designing Francis Ford Coppola's short story magazine *Zoetrope* and donating a piece to the New York Academy of Art's ninth annual 'Take Home A Nude' auction (Bowie's piece was a black canvas with the word 'nipples' spelled out in Braille!). But, for almost the whole of the first half of 1999, Bowie was readying himself for one last crack at the pop scene the right side of the millennium.

The album that was released in October 1999 under the title *hours* . . . had provisionally been called The Dreamers until Reeves Gabrels pointed out that the title made him think of a Mariah Carey or Celine Dion album. It had a confused genesis. In part, it was a song sequence revolving around the midlife crisis of a regretful man who may, or may not, be based on Bowie himself. In part it was the soundtrack to a computer game, *The Nomad Soul*, released in November 1999 by Eidos (Bowie, who appeared in the game as Boz, made it a 'condition' that he was morphed back to the age of 24, so as to appear as a young androgene). The album also included one track that would be included on a soundtrack album, *Stigmata*, and another that would be used for a BowieNet writers' competition.

Gabrels was a natural choice for the game soundtrack, having already worked extensively in that genre: 'I was asked by David to write a couple of songs with him for *Omikron*. After we met with the Eidos team, I suggested that we should do all the music. It seemed only natural to me, as I had already done many television and film soundtracks (for example, *David Lynch's American Chronicles*, and various documentaries and independent films). As it turned out, we wrote eight songs for the game (all on *hours* . . .) and then I wrote about two to three hours of instrumental themes for it.'

It had been a long time since Bowie had demoed songs, and honed and crafted them before going into the studio. It was a method which had worked brilliantly on albums such as *Let's Dance* and, before that, *Ziggy Stardust*, but one which Bowie had largely abandoned in the late 1980s. So, for Bowie to become a craftsman again was an unexpected, though potentially exciting, volte-face. Reeves explains: 'The music on *hours* . . . was influenced by a couple of things. The fact that, firstly, we sat down and wrote songs with just guitar and keyboard before going into a studio. Secondly, the characters we appear as in the game performing the songs are street/protest singers and so needed a more singer/songwriter approach. And, lastly, it was the opposite approach from the usual cheesy industrial metal music one would normally get.'

The album also showcased a new style of guitar playing for the many fans who associated Reeves Gabrels with avant-garde, microtonal blasts of noise: 'Because the album was taking a decidedly more introspective turn, it meant that I needed to approach the guitar-playing in a different way in order to wrap around the vocals and support the mood of the song in the solos. As co-writer and co-producer I had to be extra careful that the guitar player in me was responding to the lyric content of the songs. The music for 'We All Go Through' (Japanese album track), 'Survive' and 'The Pretty Things Are Going To Hell' came from songs that I had started for my solo record. On the other hand, 'Thursday's Child' and 'The Dreamers' were from keyboard/vocal ideas that David had had.'

Although Gabrels wanted Mark Plati, who had worked so effectively on *Earthling,* in on the sessions earlier, he was not called in by Bowie until halfway through recording. 'My involvement in *hours* . . . began one evening in April 1999 when I received a page with a phone number followed by a few sixes' – the number of the Gabrels. He goes on:

I rang back and David and Reeves were at Chung King Studios, wondering if I'd like to put fretless bass on some of the new songs they'd written. Within two hours I had biked to the studio with a couple of bass guitars, and unknowingly settled in for the next few months. David and Reeves had been writing and working on the songs which would become *hours* ... for a few months by that point, working in fits and starts in Bermuda and other places. David and Reeves had convened in New York, looking to wrap up the project. A lot of it was already recorded – basic guitars and keyboards, drum loops and programs, some vocal ideas. My involvement grew from being a bassist to doing some additional production and recording and, eventually, mixing the album.

I hadn't even counted on being involved in this album. Rumours abounded – David and Reeves were doing it on their own in an underproduced 'home-grown' fashion, in direct contrast to the last few albums, which were of course full-on studio affairs. Also, it was strongly rumoured to be Tony Visconti's return to the fold, and since Tony and I are both producers/engineers/bassists, I figured that I'd be about the last person they'd need to call! But call they did, and a treat it was.

Plati was involved as a musician and as a mixer and producer. He later became part of Bowie's touring band, as well as the musical director, fulfilling the role that the likes of Garson, Alomar, Belew and Gabrels had held before him.

According to Plati, the vibe in the studio was one of relaxed creativity, Bowie himself being much calmer than during the frantic, pre-fifty adrenaline rush of *Earthling*:

I hadn't seen him since early 1998, and his hair was a lot longer and no longer dyed. He seemed a bit calmer, no doubt due to the conclusion of the *Earthling* tour and surrounding activities. It occurred to me then that I'd only worked with him while he was doing either a lot of press or live shows – both very draining, especially while trying to record at the same time. As a result, we spent more time discussing the news events of the day and life in general, a lot more so than on *Earthling*, when the pace was a lot more hectic, and we didn't know each other as well. David would tell stories, talk about books he was reading, films he'd seen, and art he was interested in. He loves kids, so I'd fill him in on my six-year-old daughter's shenanigans (when she would visit the studio she would lecture Reeves and David about smoking – they were polite, but it didn't stop them smoking). He'd go on about the Internet ... He was very into eBay at that time, just amazed at the things people would put up for auction (Reeves would ask him daily if he'd bid on an island yet). And the humour between David, Reeves, myself and Jay Nicholas (our assistant) – we'd often go off at a tangent and be howling for hours.

As far as Reeves Gabrels was concerned, however, Bowie had embarked on a new musical journey, away from the sort of experimentation he had fostered: 'Sharing the writing and production chores with David always makes for an interesting ride and for some very healthy and amusing debates. At the end of the day, it is his name on the album cover and so he is the one who needs to be most happy. Having said that, if it had been up to me I would have brought Mark Plati in sooner at the very start of the finishing touches, tightening up the tracks and mixing. Sonically, left to my own devices it would have been edgier or creepier (like the "B" side "We Go To Town").' Indeed, a semi-instrumental track, '1917', a sort of psychotic update of the riff from Led Zeppelin's 'Kashmir', was one of the best things under the Bowie name from the 1990s, but its lack of conventionality saw it released as a 'B' side only.

hours . . . initially makes for alarming listening. One American fan posting his comments on the Net just after its release summed up the disappointment when he said that it sounded like Boz Scaggs! Consistent in pace, it has a world-weary quality, as if Bowie was drained after the mania of *Earthling*. However, there are richer textures and innovative moments. Melodies, links, hooks and guitar lines have obviously all been well crafted, in contrast to the spontaneous blasts of energy found on *Earthling* and *Outside. hours* . . . showed that Bowie could still write a perfect pop melody. Take 'Survive', for instance, a pop song with a mellifluous and sensationally poetic guitar line from Gabrels, and one of Bowie's most awesomely realised melodies of the decade.

However, Gabrels pinpointed the real weakness of the album. Some of the tracks appear sonically staid, or underdeveloped. 'Thursday's Child', for example, is crying out for strings, or some sort of lush adornment. As it stands, it appears underproduced, almost like a demo. The same can be said for 'The Dreamers', which was tweaked and pulled in the mixing stage, with overdubs added, but still fails to deliver. Two of the songs, however, are Bowie classics. The aforementioned 'Survive' was eventually the second European single. 'It's probably my favourite track on the record,' enthused Plati. 'To me it's very epic in a late-1960s kind of way, both in its composition and in how the production builds and peaks.' 'Something In The Air' is one of Bowie's best-ever moments. It is an emotionally cracked tale of a love gone bitter: 'Lived with the best times/Left with the worst/Danced with you too long/Nothing left to save'.

Bowie's voice catapults upward towards the end of the song, making it his best vocal moment for an age. According to Mark Plati, 'David pulled out the ring modulator once again for this one, making his vocal nearly unrecognisable in the outro. It's a wonderful vocal in general, very tortured. Great guitar work from Reeves, not what you'd expect from a man the press calls 'Mr Noisemeister'. Sometimes he'd remind me of the Eagles' 'Hotel California' with some of his lines!'

The first European single was, however, the melancholic ballad 'Thursday's Child', a great Bowie single, but flawed by its staid arrangement. Bowie claims that the song is not autobiographical, but biographical. Dealing with regret for a life of missed opportunity, it is sung by a middle-aged man who finally finds a new love (surely a theme not wholly lacking in autobiographical features?). Bowie is, in fact, a Wednesday's child, and the title of the song is a clever and typically obscure lift from a biography of Eartha Kitt Bowie remembered from the 1960s.

What completed the package was, as ever, the video for the single, which was a departure not only for Bowie, but also perhaps for ageing rock stars in general. Directed by Walter Stern, who made the classic foetus video for Massive Attack's 'Teardrop', Bowie is pictured staring into a bathroom mirror, preparing for bed, his wife beside him removing her make-up. It's an exercise in the mundane, until the Bowie character suddenly starts hallucinating, seeing in the glass a younger version of himself, with whom he performs a 1990s version of the famous scene from the Marx Brothers' *Duck Soup* in which Harpo and Groucho mimic each other's actions through an imaginary mirror. The young Bowie looks painfully unnatural, almost like a Tussaud's waxwork. It's an everyday scene given a disquieting, almost paranormal twist (the video for 'Survive', also directed by Stern, continues this theme with Bowie levitating in his kitchen). The middle-aged Bowie also sees a past love, who cheekily laughs at her wrinkly ex-lover before the two kiss and the hallucination ends. Self-regarding and narcissistic the video may intentionally be, but it's a haunting and most unusual piece of work. Seldom, if ever, has a rock star of Bowie's vintage attempted to confront the ageing process full-on like this, and the song and video are genuinely moving and very sad.

The song was in fact originally intended to be a major-league collaboration between the former Glam-meister and some 1990s swing-beat divas. Gabrels: 'David originally wanted TLC to sing on "Thursday's Child", which I wasn't really into at all. Through a stroke of good fortune I managed to get Holly Palmer, who is a friend I used to write songs with in Boston.' Before Palmer was called in, however, Bowie hit upon an inspired, though sadly unrealised idea: 'As far as the backing vocals are concerned, David had the idea of a child singing the "Monday, Tuesday" part,' says Plati, 'so we asked my six-year-old daughter Alice to come in and do it. However, Alice wanted no part of it. She said she'd rather sing with her friends than with grown-ups (her class from school had come to the studio on a field trip recently, and I had recorded them singing various kids' songs and burned them all CDs. She assumed it would be in the shops). So we called Holly and she auditioned for David over the speakerphone, with him giving her some direction, like 'more vibrato, less vibrato'. In a couple of hours she joined us on Varick Street and cut the backing vocals. Alice later had misgivings about turning down the session once she saw Holly performing with us on *Storytellers* and *Saturday Night Live*. After all, she could have been on tour with Dad!'

'The Pretty Things Are Going To Hell' features the finest riff Gabrels ever played for a Bowie album, one which can inspire even the most guitar-weary of listeners to strike a few air-guitar stances. ' "Pretty Things" is actually one of the first songs we recorded, but one of the last to get completed vocals,' remembers Gabrels. 'The main guitars took me about twenty minutes to do in London in February 1999, and the vocals are largely from a rough vocal done in May 1999. I thought that one was going to remain unfinished, but it lived through David's period of dislike long enough for it to become a fan favourite (much like "Seven Years In Tibet").' Mark Plati: 'On this track we went for something Reeves and I called "bonehead", playing the simplest Neanderthal part possible (I'll bet you never thought Reeves would advocate such a thing). It's harder to do than you think – it's always easier to play loads of things. The bass in that song is low and ugly and simple – and perfect. The guitars just chug along nastily, little flourishes poke out now and then but for the most part it is kept under tight, gnarly, control. The solo is boneheaded perfection! The drums, however, were anything but simple. Mike Levesque had been reading a biography of Keith Moon around this time [presumably *Dear Boy* by Tony Fletcher], so I think he saw an opening to rise to the occasion. I think he's the instrumental star of that track.'

'The Pretty Things Are Going To Hell' is a 1990s take on glam rock, referring as it does to Bowie's own 'Oh! You Pretty Things' and also Iggy's 'Your Pretty Face Is Going To Hell'. Bowie's chosen children may be on the road to eternal damnation, but they have attained everlasting heroism through style.

The rest of the album varies from good-ish to weak. The filmic 'New Angels Of Promise', in the doomy-romantic style of 'Sons Of The Silent Age', is energised by the recalled Sterling Campbell's blistering drum patterns and reminiscent of the 1980s work of Peter Gabriel (on 'San Jacinto', for instance), whilst the instrumental 'Brilliant Adventure' has Bowie plucking his koto and resurrecting his Buddhist muse. 'Seven' is pure pop and fitted in to the five-song sequence of tracks dealing with worn-out regret. It is hard not to interpret the lines: 'I forgot what my brother said/I forgot what he said' as autobiographical. 'What's Really Happening' is the first song ever to be co-written by a rock star and a fan, via the Internet. Bowie posted a lyricless melody on his website and was deluged with lyrics from 80,000 would-be collaborators. Even members of The Cure decided to have a bash (and failed). The eventual winner, Alex Grant, recorded the song live on BowieNet with Gabrels and Mark Plati. It was another first for Bowie. Sadly, it's not a great song to begin with, whatever lyric happens to be bolted on to it, and should not have been more than a 'B' side at best. Alex Grant himself was apparently in a state of almost clinical shock throughout, and what fan wouldn't be? Mark Plati: 'That was a fun session. Alex was great. He was there with a friend, and they seemed a bit numb just being in New York and in a recording studio, especially that particular session. There were lights, cameras, journalists, and catering (I actually wore pants as opposed to bike shorts, which left David and Reeves a bit numb). But Alex was fine with David, and a good sport. He and his friend ended up singing background vocals on the track. Still, he seemed to be in a state of disbelief the entire session.'

Throughout the set, Bowie under-sings. Although high in the mix and skilful, his voice is neither stretched nor affected. Like everything else on *hours . . .* the setting in which the songs emerge is unobtrusive and helps to serve the meaning of the lyrics, while the lyrics themselves are plain and unadorned. Bowie describes it thus: 'Because the words, the lyrics generally on the album are very simplistic, the simple things, I think, are expressed quite strongly. The music that we wrote for them is more of a supportive kind of music – it doesn't create two or three different focuses.'

hours . . . is a sad, often bitter album. The cover is a pietas: a fictive, floppy-fringed young Bowie, like an angel at Heaven's gate, cradling a middle-aged version of himself (a man reduced to a babylike, helpless state, or perhaps even in his death throes?). Indeed, on 'If I'm Dreaming My Life' Bowie is in an almost dreamlike state of disorientation at the altar steps, while Gabrels' neo-psychedelic guitar line picks out the melody in the cloisters. 'I hate albums that are really happy,' Bowie told the press. 'When I'm really happy, I don't want to hear happy albums, and when I'm really sad, I don't want to hear happy albums. So for me personally, there's not much place in my life for them. And I tend to gravitate towards the lonely and the isolated in my writing.'

Bowie said that the title of the album was meant to be a play on the word 'ours', an album of songs for his own generation. 'The impression I wished to give with this album was that there was a certain amount of autobiographical material in there,' Bowie said. 'Maybe biographical is a more accurate word, because for so much of it I drew upon peers and contemporaries and people that I grew up with and other guys that I know who are of my age group who maybe have not ended up in a situation where they feel quite so buoyant as I do. I'm incredibly fortunate. I'm a very, very lucky man. I've got a wonderful life.'

Bowie had yet another surprise prepared to coincide with the release of *hours . . .* When the chance came to release the new album on the Internet before the scheduled retail release, Bowie jumped at it. Beginning the musical 'striptease' on his official site on 6 August 1999, he ran a review of the album track-by-track, as each 45-second snippet was released to the fans. The album's cover was likewise revealed plate by plate. Bowie fans were being given a flirty taster of the new work.

Then, on Tuesday 21 September, the following was posted on BowieNet: 'For the first time in the history of the music business, a major recording artist and a leading record company are joining with retailers to bring a complete album to music fans via download from the Internet.' 'I am hopeful that this small step will lead to greater steps by myself and others, ultimately giving consumers greater choices and easier access to the music they enjoy,' Bowie said. HMV harrumphed: 'If artists release albums on the Net before other people can buy them in the shops, it's not a level playing field. Records should be available to everyone at the same time, and not everyone has access to the Internet.' While prepared to give Bowie a second chance, the company issued this warning to other would-be web pioneers: 'It's unlikely that we would stock the artist in question. Retailers are not going to stand for it.' A big chain in Holland, Free Records, announced that it was boycotting *hours* ... With hindsight, one can now say that Bowie was streets ahead of the game. 'Bowie was early in building his Internet presence,' says Michael Plen, Virgin Records' Vice-President (Promotion). 'There was a great foresight on his part in knowing where the Internet strength was; even though it hadn't reached any critical mass for quantity, he certainly knew its qualitative reach and its power.' Bowie had accurately foreseen the revolution in the music industry that would be brought about by the download generation.

Reeves Gabrels explains the attraction of the format to artists: 'I can now create and make music available within a week of completion. I also do not have to run what I see as my art through the screening and filtering process that is the function of the A&R department at record labels. For better or worse, what you hear is what I wanted you to get. There are no compromises.'

For Bowie and Gabrels, the Internet had opened up a whole range of new ways of getting music across to their target audience. Gabrels again:

Well, I view it like this (and this is not a particularly singular or original idea, as it is shared by many others): in the late 1960s and early 1970s there was the open radio format revolution that opened the airwaves up to a lot of music that we now view as seminal, vital and classic. After that came video music television and that, while largely visual in impact, set the stage for another music surge and movement. Since then, many of us have been either waiting or looking for some new frontier. I think music online, being made available by the artists (through conduits like CD Data Base, Inc) represents precisely the opportunity we've all been waiting for, and that is a very big deal. The revolution will not be televised, the revolution will not be broadcast, the revolution will be downloaded. When I got involved in releasing my music exclusively online, I knew that we were ahead of the learning curve for the general populace. In just the few months since the original beta-testing phase the public's ability to deal with mpeg downloads has changed dramatically. My dentist has bought personal mpeg players for his two pre-teenage daughters. That tells me something good about the acceptance of the technology. Every new idea takes time to seep into popular culture. I'm willing to wait for people to catch up if it means I can have greater control over what I do. Plus, it's fun. As far as using the Net to build a community, I am not online to make friends. I am simply there to make my art available. By doing so I hope that I reach people with music in a more meaningful way with music than I ever could with words. I intersect with the public at large at the sounds I make. Hopefully, it provides the same catharsis for them as it does for me.

Bowie's single, 'Thursday's Child', was a hit in the UK, reaching a respectable Number 16 (remarkably his 56th Top 40 UK hit), on the back of minimal radio exposure. Perhaps as a sign of things to come, the single was a Radio 2 record of the week, as was the less successful follow-up, 'Survive'. The album itself dropped out of the charts very soon after reaching Number 5, thus only marginally improving on the performance of *Earthling*. In America, it was a resounding flop, not even cracking the Top 40. Elsewhere though, *hours* . . . was a success. It made the Top 10 in France, Germany and Italy, and the Top 20 in Japan.

Bowie supported the album, not with the full-scale promotional tour it perhaps needed, but with a succession of one-off gigs and television dates. Of his appearance on VH1's *Storytellers*, executive producer Bill Flanagan said: 'This is going to be the best thing that VH1 has ever shown. Scratch that, this is probably the best thing you're going to see on TV this year.' Bowie appeared with long hair and in a hooded sweatshirt, and revealed that he was almost as good a stand-up comedian as he was a singer. The set list was full of surprises too. 'Word On A Wing' had made a comeback, as had 'Drive-In Saturday'. When the band rampaged through the mod-stomper 'Can't Help Thinking About Me', unperformed for a third of a century, it was so old it sounded like a new track.

Mike Garson was back on keyboards. For Garson, it was a magical performance: 'I have to tell you, opening with him on 'Life On Mars?' meant a lot to me. It's not like I played on the original, because that was Rick Wakeman, but I played it live with The Spiders and just to do it with piano and voice meant that it had a lot of beauty for me.' *Storytellers* would be Bowie's last performance with the man who, all those years ago, had helped to lead him away from the mainstream, towards experimental music.

It was reported in the press that the split was amicable and that Gabrels had simply taken time off to complete his solo work before rejoining the Bowie Roadshow. In fact, this is not entirely true. Gabrels did have his own solo work to finish but, in truth, he and Bowie had drifted apart artistically. He was, in fact, the first major Bowie collaborator/guitarist to leave of his own volition, as opposed to being overlooked for the next project:

As I have said in the past, I never really wanted to play any of the 'old' songs as they mean too much to me in their original form. They are too much a part of my musical roots (my mother bought me *Ziggy Stardust*) and I would hate to do a disservice to those memories. Maybe I'm too precious about it. I always tried to be aware of David's legacy. But a big part of that legacy is the pursuit of the new. When I became more aware of the desire to do more old songs and to eliminate the sequential information and loops from our new music, I realised that what David wanted from the music was quickly diverging from what I needed. I needed to finish my album, and seek out new scenarios where I don't know what will happen next. I was ready to move on, take control of my life and pursue my own course. Hence the title of my new album, *Ulysses (della notte* [of the night]). It is about the journey through the night of the last few years, creatively and spiritually. And about finding your way home. I had a really good eleven years with David. He is my friend and he changed my life, personally and creatively, in ways he may not even know. I hope that I did the same for him. During the recording of *hours* ... I had a sense of the circle being completed. I had my solo record to finish and other projects to begin. I needed the shock of the new and the rush of the unexpected. It was obvious to me that it was time for me to tell David that I was leaving. On August 27th I told him that I needed to go. My statement was met with a combination of concern, as I was obviously tired from the work of the previous six months, and disappointment, because I was bowing out of the promo tour that was due to start the beginning of October. He understood. Out of respect for him and the music we made in our time together, I had to go.

Gabrels had certainly brought the elements of invention and the unexpected back to Bowie's music. And what is undeniable is that he shook Bowie out of the corporate torpor he had slipped into in the late 1980s.

After the shock of losing Gabrels, Bowie quickly regrouped, drafting in Page Hamilton to take over as lead guitarist. Bowie was now playing a mix of oldies and new songs, including album tracks such as *Lodger*'s 'Repetition' and hits such as 'Rebel Rebel'. For Mike Garson, the songs from *hours* . . . came alive the more they were honed on the road. Garson was happy with Bowie's new, more melodic approach, for it presaged a brighter future: 'There are potential signs for the future that the melodies will be coming back and that they'll be getting better. I just wish six more months had been spent on the album and that maybe Tony Visconti had come in and that it had been produced a little further. I played those songs for four months, they improved as the days and weeks went on. We took the songs where they really should have gone because they were underdeveloped in the studio.'

Bowie worked extremely hard on the road, fitting in myriad television appearances too, despite a bout of gastric 'flu. He appeared on Chris Evans' high-rating *TFI Friday* show in the UK and, on entry, was mobbed by a delirious audience. The biggest show was the Net Aid concert at Wembley Stadium in October 1999. Billed as a 1990s re-enactment of Live Aid, and reportedly receiving a massive number of hits on the Net, by the end of November it had raised £8 million, whilst Sir Bob brought in £120 million. 'We walked out on stage in front of 80,000 people and we opened up with "Life On Mars?",' said Garson. 'I mean, I was frightened to death because I had no band to hide behind and we're connected, musically, me and David. If I'm a little uptight, or he's a little uptight, we kind of feel it in each other. We were able to grow above it and bigger than it, but it was scary!'

But there were other, smaller gigs too, in the likes of Dublin, Paris and Copenhagen, all of which were, in the estimation of Mike Garson, 'phenomenal'. However, there was a particularly nerve-wracking affair at London's Astoria: 'We were all so nervous because there were all these famous people in the audience. Mike Jagger was there, and Pete Townshend, and they all went backstage. David was great in that show, although the band, I thought, didn't play its best.'

The scale of the tour disappointed some fans, particularly when it turned out that audiences at some of the shows were at least partially filled with invitees. As one fan bluntly put it: 'I find it hard to swallow that David Bowie is playing such a small gig when he knows that he has such a large hard-core following. I heard about the gig weeks ago and was really excited about it. I was told by the Astoria and Virgin not to ring for ticket bookings until 10 a.m. on the Monday. So like a good boy I started ringing them at 10.00. The Astoria was engaged, so I tried the Virgin line, and to my delight I got through at exactly 10.04, only to be told all the tickets had gone. I couldn't believe it. I have been a fan for about fifteen years, and to me this is another example of him mistreating his fans. I understand that he doesn't want to tour fully, but why do such a small venue, especially when his showbiz friends have first choice of tickets!'

This short tour had a whiff of preaching to the converted about it. Bowie was chatty, telling jokes, but there was little real drama. The old edginess, present as recently as the *Outside* tour, was gone. Moreover, a small number of fans were seriously inconvenienced by the cancellation of Bowie's scheduled performance at the Gisborne 2000 'First Light' Festival in New Zealand, on the eve of the new millennium. Poor ticket sales had created major financial problems. The promoters had overpriced tickets at $400, and had perhaps overestimated the pulling power of the line-up, which was headed by Bowie, a specially re-formed Split Enz, and Dame Kiri Te Kanawa and the New Zealand Symphony Orchestra. It was rumoured that fewer than 2,000 of the 35,000 tickets had been sold. Bowie had no choice but to pull out, to the sound of understandable howls of protest from those fans who had already booked their flights and accommodation for the celebrations at a venue which had been touted as the most easterly point on the globe to welcome in the new age. The event fell foul of the millennium hype, in that punters decided to forgo the sky-high pricing and to stay at home with their families and loved ones instead. Which is exactly what Bowie did too.

Bowie actually ended the 1990s in the pop charts. In fact, he was enjoying one of his biggest hits of the decade with an oldie, 'Under Pressure'. It was, so the press release went, 'a three-way collaboration between Queen, David Bowie and Microsoft to mark World AIDS Day, December 1 1999, with a global Internet-based AIDS fund-raising event. WindowsMedia.com, from Microsoft, will host a free video download featuring Queen and David Bowie and will provide people with an opportunity to donate money to fight AIDS. The free download will feature the recent groundbreaking video of Queen and David Bowie – breakthrough technology has brought these two great performers together for the first time using unique footage.' The single was put on commercial release too, reaching Number 14 in the lucrative and high-selling pre-Christmas market. The video, though, was woeful. For those who remembered with embarrassment the video for 'Unforgettable', in which Natalie Cole duetted with her dead dad, the 'Under Pressure' video, which segued live footage of Freddie from 1986 with Bowie's live performance of the song in 1992, made for uncomfortable viewing. Even if it was for a supremely worthy cause, Bowie was once again allowing his back catalogue to be exploited without due regard for the quality of the product. More depressingly still, its success showed that Bowie was actually more saleable as a nostalgia act.

In 2000, news spread that Bowie had plans to reactivate Ziggy Stardust. It was now almost thirty years since, in a dazzling display of theatricality, Ziggy stole the authentic heart of rock'n'roll from the hippies and the singer/songwriters. As recently as 1997, Bowie had stated that there wasn't a 'snowball's chance in hell' of him doing another Ziggy project. So why the about-turn?

There has always been something of a 'cult of Ziggy'. In July 1998, Bowie's Ziggy swan song was re-created over two nights at the ICA in London. 'A Rock'n'Roll Suicide', devised by Iain Forsyth and Jane Pollard, featured Steve Harvey in the lead role, wearing costumes by original Bowie designer, Natasha Korniloff.

A more direct challenge to Bowie came, of course, in 1998, with the fun but flawed film, *Velvet Goldmine*. Bowie was asked to act as a consultant on the film and to contribute seven songs for the soundtrack, five of which were to be sung by the characters and two – 'Let's Spend The Night Together' and 'Lady Grinning Soul' – to feature in the original, but, after reading the script, he declined to be involved. According to Mike Harvey's Ziggy Companion Website, 'It has been reported that Haynes sent the script to Bowie to elicit his co-operation and songs for the movie, but Bowie was said to be appalled by the project, telling friends that all his character did was spend his time administering blow jobs.' Just months earlier, Bowie had instructed his legal·team to research into the viability of producing his own glam-era film and, having received favourable reports, he had begun assembling material and ideas.

The *Velvet Goldmine* film portrays David Bowie in a very unsympathetic light. The main character, Brian Slade, is based overwhelmingly on Bowie. But was Bowie really as crass and manipulative as the Slade figure in the film? And was the Iggy Pop/Kurt Cobain/Kurt Wild figure really the wellspring of all things glam? That said, it is an entertaining and, at times, beautifully shot film, with a great soundtrack (the Bowie pastiches are surprisingly effective). But, as a whole, it remains unconvincing. Actors Ewan McGregor et al are all far too well nourished to play authentic glam-rock figures. Eno was apparently spied at one cinema, laughing all the way through the film. Visconti dubbed it a 'gay porn movie'. There are indeed some semi-explicit gay snogging scenes, which is somewhat ironic, as 'Velvet Goldmine' is a heterosexual love/lust song, and the title a metaphor for the vagina.

Together with his friend and original Ziggy photographer and promo-maker Mick Rock, Bowie planned a series of linked releases to mark the thirtieth anniversary of the *Ziggy Stardust* album: 'On film, I want to translate the audience's perception of Ziggy. The theatre piece will be about Ziggy's interior life. And the Internet [project] will be about things like "who's his mom?" – a huge exploration of his background.' Bowie appeared to be set to demystify the magic of Ziggy by tampering with the legend and adorning it. Reeves Gabrels for one was unconvinced: 'David mentioned to me the possibility of recording additional songs to expand the original *Ziggy* album into a double CD/album set for

2002. Personally, I think it is a dangerous idea in so far as how the fans will view it. It may be akin to going back and adding songs to *The Dark Side Of The Moon* or *Never Mind The Bollocks, Here's The Sex Pistols*. My idea was that, in order for this to work you would need to record it in a 16-track studio, with a Trident console, using no recording equipment or instruments made since 1972, and get Ken Scott [who did *Ziggy*] or Tony Visconti to record and mix it. It would be important to examine the original track sheets [one electric guitar, 12-string acoustic, vocal, drums on four tracks only, mellotron/real strings, saxes, pennywhistles etc.] and stay within those limitations. It will be interesting to see if this path is pursued.'

Eventually, all such plans were dropped. Perhaps Bowie simply ran out of time? Or maybe a wiser counsel prevailed, and Bowie was persuaded that the whole Ziggy 2002 concept was a bad idea. Updating and improving a record which palpably did not need either updating or improving was never going to lead to anything other than disappointment. That said, there is a cache of songs and demos from the period that will one day hopefully be released.

In 1998, the friendship and working relationship between Tony Visconti and David Bowie was restored. The first fruits of the new collaboration were a cover version of John Lennon's 'Mother', intended for a tribute CD to commemorate what would have been the great man's sixtieth birthday (the project was ultimately scrapped), and one new song.

In the spring of 1999, Bowie and Visconti talked about starting work on their first album together since 1980. In March 1999, Bowie recorded his vocal for the Placebo track, 'Without You I'm Nothing', with Tony producing. How did Visconti feel about being back in the hot seat? 'To tell the truth, I wasn't really bothered by being "sent to Coventry" during those years,' Visconti said in 1999. 'I never said any of those things maliciously and I felt, if that's all it takes to be on the outs with him, then so be it. I've always had a life full of family, friends and career. It was only in very recent years, around the time he made contact again, that I realised how much I had missed him. We had both grown and changed, so the time was right to open the channels again. However, I've discovered how sensitive he is about his privacy and I've learned to respect that.'

Visconti was justifiably displeased, however, about having his contribution to Bowie's late-1970s work downplayed. 'When

David and Brian [Eno] got together for their 1990s ventures it was often reported erroneously that Brian produced *Low*, "*Heroes*" and *Lodger*. I can't blame David or Brian for this, it was just irresponsible journalism. I don't even have to defend myself, one only has to read the credits on those album sleeves. It's a shame the mistake was made, and that it's been repeated so often in print, and also on the Web. I would just like to remind people that by the time Brian Eno was involved with David Bowie, I had already produced, or co-produced, six of his albums. I played bass, guitar and keyboards, sang, arranged instruments and conducted string sections. I mixed every Bowie album I've worked on except *David Live*. After the 'Triptych' and Brian Eno's involvement I went on to produce the *Scary Monsters* album, which Bowie's later albums are judged by.'

Visconti was pleased to be recording with his friend again. He reported that, although Bowie had lost some of his top range, he was singing with more confidence than ever before and was even more professional. 'I can listen to his voice all day,' he said.

In the pollfest that was such a feature of the millennium, Bowie was heaped with plaudits. The readers of the *Sun* newspaper voted him the biggest music star of the last hundred years. In *Q* he was rated the sixth biggest music star of the century. America's *Entertainment Weekly* made him No. 1 Classic Solo Artist of all time with 35 per cent of the votes, more than double his nearest rivals, Barbra Streisand and Elvis. Bowie was also awarded one of France's highest honours, Commander of Arts and Letters, for his lifetime achievements in music.

In May 1999, Mr Bowie became Dr Bowie. The conferment of an honorary music doctorate by Berkeley (the seat of the University of California) was a touching and wholly deserved tribute to Bowie's huge contribution to music past, present, and future. In his acceptance speech to the crowd of 4,000 at the Hynes Convention Center he described music as 'my doorway of perception and the house that I live in'.

When the nominees for the best solo act for the 2000 Brit Awards were announced early in the New Year, Bowie, at 53, was not the oldest candidate (that honour went to the 59-year-old Tom Jones, the eventual winner). He took his place in a superannuated line-up of veterans: Ian Brown (a spring chicken at 36), Van Morrison (54) and Sting (48). Did their selection merely reflect the interests of the selection panel? Or did it indicate real star quality? Or was it simply a sign that the link between 'pop' and 'youth' was no longer important? Perhaps most tellingly, whilst there may be plenty of interesting music produced by indie and dance acts, the absence of young solo male artists revealed that the status of the male rock and pop singer was moribund. To those of us who remember pre-1990 pop, it was final confirmation that, after almost two decades of dance triumphalism, the era of the great rock icon was dead. The music business had finally redesigned itself around anonymity, in a scene almost wholly devoid of traditional 'star quality'. Tom Jones with his thunderous voice and terrifying leather trousers and Bowie with his angsty midlife-crisis album were totems of a dying rock configuration. Did we actually need rock gods any more?

Bowie for one didn't appear to think so. For many of his fans he had succeeded in hitting his very best form in the 1990s, albeit intermittently, something which would have been thought impossible back in 1987. However, for those who found him an irrelevance, or only sporadically listenable, his myriad extracurricular activities were reason enough for his inconsistency. In the 1970s, Bowie lived his music and his stage shows. Everything was ultimately devoted to that end. In the 1980s and, undoubtedly, in the 1990s, Bowie's music-making competed with other interests, interests which don't necessarily feed back into his music. There was clearly some sort of organic link between the *Station To Station* album, the Thomas Newton character of *The Man Who Fell To Earth*, and the Thin White Duke character. Bowie was working in different media, but the whole package fitted together. But how did a speak-over for an art exhibition (for the controversial 1999 installation, 'Sensation'), the institution of a website, and the compering of a fantasy/horror television series (Bowie was the guest presenter for a TV version of *The Hunger*) all fit together? Bowie appeared to be tiring of the rock world. On playing live he said: 'It's not my life. I could give it up tomorrow.' For the first year of the new century, he had other things of more consequence than his career to attend to.

Bowie fans around the world reacted to the announcement on Sunday, 13 February 2000 of Iman Bowie's pregnancy with a deluge of congratulatory emails. The couple had always wanted to have children. Mike Garson recalls that Bowie had mentioned starting a family as long ago as the *Outside* tour. Both had children from previous marriages. Bowie's son Joe (now known as Duncan) is involved in film and video production, whilst Iman has a daughter, Zulekha.

Of course, there were some in the media who couldn't resist a little tease. Here's Iain Lee from *The Eleven O'Clock Show* (Channel 4): 'It was announced this week that David Bowie and wife Iman are expecting a baby. The last time David Bowie took delivery of anything weighing 6 lb 11 oz he immediately stuck it up his nose.' Or this, from the same show's Daisy Donovan: 'When asked if he preferred a boy or a girl, David replied that he is married now and those days are behind him.'

Away from the rigours of the antenatal class, Bowie the pop singer made a comeback with aplomb. His date with destiny came on 25 June 2000 when, on a piece of farmland in Pilton, Somerset, he appeared at Britain's best-loved outdoor pop event, the Glastonbury Festival.

It was in the knowledge that the Glastonbury crowd was not primarily a Bowie audience that he elected to perform his first greatest-hits set for a decade. Bedecked in what looked like a frock coat made out of Granny's leftover curtain material, and with a barking-mad mane of mousy locks, Bowie was fully aware that, with a two-hour set containing more bona-fide culture-defining hits than anyone else who had ever played Glastonbury, he could not fail. And he didn't. In a scene which must have echoed the video to R.E.M.'s 'Everybody Hurts', when they heard that Bowie had started his set, late-comers stuck in a traffic jam outside the festival grounds simply abandoned their cars in the middle of the road and walked.

Bowie had last played Glastonbury when Edward Heath was prime minister and the UK was struggling to come to terms with the new-fangled decimal currency. Now, on the eve of the Euro, Bowie stood eerily reminiscent of his pre-Ziggy frock-attack self of all those years ago. This look was to lead to Britain's influential style bible, *GQ*, awarding him their 'Most Stylish Man Of The Year' award in autumn 2000.

As a live performer, Bowie now recognised that a certain amount of crowd-pleasing material had to be included on his set list. Like Banquo's ghost, Bowie's back catalogue was coming back to haunt him. By the start of the new millennium, it appeared that Bowie had given up denying his past. The nagging question remained though – could he build a future?

On a personal level, the answer appeared to be a resounding yes. On 15 August 2000, Bowie became a father for the second time, when Alexandria Zahra Jones was born at 5.06 a.m., weighing in at 3.3 kg (7 lb 4.6 oz). Dad assisted in the delivery and cut the umbilical cord. On a commercial level, Bowie had, like Dylan and The Rolling Stones, long since stopped worrying the upper echelons of the singles charts. But with albums, it was an altogether different story. An utterly mind-boggling run of hit albums was extended for a further year when *Bowie At The Beeb*, a double CD of live recordings from a series of radio sessions dating from 1968 to 1972, made Number 7 in the UK charts. On a creative level, Bowie again elected to look back rather than to stride confidently into the new. After years of neglect, his pre-'Space Oddity' cache of songs had come under his scrutiny, and he had concluded that they weren't quite as bad as most of us had thought. So he recorded a set of minor oddities, including three new songs to complement the reshaped old material. The album, entitled *Toy*, went into production in 2000. By the end of that year, Bowie's standing amongst pop practitioners, if not the pop public, was unassailable. A poll conducted by the *NME* among top musicians themselves hailed Bowie as the 'most inspiring musician', the biggest influence on the current generation of musicians. He beat the Beatles into third place. It was fifteen years since his last global hit record, and twenty since the last unanimous critical success. But the next five years would see a wonderful Indian summer in the career of Britain's most import-ant living musician.

15. '... LIKE STRAUSS, AT 84', 2001–2005

'I desperately want to live forever ... I want to still be around in another forty or fifty years'

DAVID BOWIE SPEAKING IN 2003

Munich, 2002: Bowie is beaming, a rudely healthy, light-brown floppy centre-parted fringe tumbling sexily over his eyes. For a man in his mid-fifties, Bowie cuts an astonishingly alluring figure, preserved, pert and radiant, and seemingly several pounds lighter than the long-haired incarnation that had appeared at the Glastonbury Festival two years earlier. Dressed in a cool, gleaming, blue silk suit replete with waistcoat and fob chain, he walks to the centre of the stage, pauses and examines his audience as Mike Garson's piano intro to 'Life On Mars?', jazzier but no less powerful than Rick Wakeman's original played all those years ago on *Hunky Dory*, weaves its way to the moment when the music gives way to his vocal entry. And he nails it. Singing as if his vocal emanates from parts of the body other singers can't reach, he soars above the naked accompaniment, his voice booming out across the arena, the audience captivated. David Bowie is on tour again, but this time it feels different, this time it's as if he is genuinely connecting with his audience. No longer playing a character, or hiding behind props and poses, this, so it seems, is simply David Bowie. After so long, is he finally allowing us to come to know him?

Bowie's new album, *Heathen*, the 25th of his career (that's if we count the Tin Machine twosome), had been garnering not just the sort of reviews that pumps the confidence and gladdens the heart, but possibly the most positive press of any David Bowie album in many a year. One would have to be pushing forty to remember when *Record Mirror*'s Simon Ludgate bagged an advance copy of *Scary Monsters* and awarded it seven out of five stars, and perhaps closer to a personal half-century to remember when it all started, when 'Space Oddity' crept into the Top 50, steadily ascended the charts, and gave David Bowie his first ever hit. *Heathen* was the first David Bowie album for twenty years to be spoken of in the sort of hushed tones usually reserved for out-and-out pop classics.

Heathen's success, although unsurprising and well deserved, was, in a perverse way, almost galling. It was by now a given of rock journalism that every new Bowie album would be subjected to death by cliché: 'Bowie's best since *Scary Monsters*' would be the sage assessment, as it had been, off and on, ever since 1987. Even the best journalists were, it seemed, unable to write a review without mentioning the 's' and 'm' words. Yet Bowie himself had stated many times in interview that he had been happy with his songwriting for well over a decade. Few Bowie fans were disappointed with *Heathen*: many saw no real difference in quality between the newie and any number of other Bowie releases since 1993. What Bowie had suffered from throughout that period, though, was the lack of a suitable musical climate into which he could fit. In 2002, he found it. With dance music dying a death, a new wave of UK acts – polite, confessional and melodic – took over. In the 1990s, Bowie had sought a fusion between beats and rock rhythms, but critics had harangued him for genre-hopping, and mocked him for being too old to be down the disco. So, it was with an unrestrained sense of relief that, on putting *Heathen* into the CD changer, what they heard was an epic and very adult re-statement of the classic Bowie theatrical themes, with hardly an unwelcome electronic bleep in earshot. The print and broadcast media began to take a genuine interest in his music for the first time in a generation.

However, in a number of crucial ways, his new album was little different from any of his others. Bowie himself has been at pains to stress the threads of continuity running through his vast body of work. His fans and the critics have, so Bowie hints, simply on occasion been fooled by the musical and visual shape-changing. 'There's a very strong continuity to the work I do,' Bowie opined.

'The sensibility of the lyric from 'Space Oddity' [1969] is really no different from something from *Heathen* [2002]. The sense of disorientation and solitude, the feelings are really not that different.' Look beneath the musical form (whether it be pop, rock, soul or drum'n'bass) and the subject matter is largely constant: an often harrowing journey of self-realisation, a spiritual quest, a thirst for knowledge, a snapshot of the year he had lived through. And that year was 2001.

Bowie entered the year smarting from his record company's indifference to the planned follow up to *hours* . . . Not for the first time had a new Bowie record been treated with a certain disdain by his label. *Toy*, a collection of reinterpreted Bowie songs (some officially released such as 'Conversation Piece', others hitherto officially unreleased, such as 'Shadow Man') plus two new compositions, 'Afraid' and 'Uncle Floyd', was apparently rejected by Virgin Records, leaving Bowie 'terribly hurt'. It does seem astonishing that a new CD by an artist of David Bowie's stature might fall foul of 'scheduling conflicts' (the music business shorthand for rejected product), as *Toy* would have been guaranteed at least a Top 20 UK placing, even if bought only by Bowie's hard-core fans. That said, *hours* . . . had sold modestly, and a new record whose appeal was likely to be restricted to a hard-core fan base was obviously not the stuff that business executives were dreaming of.

Toy had always been conceived as an interim album. Recorded with Bowie's touring band of Sterling Campbell, Gail Ann Dorsey, Mike Garson, Earl Slick and Mark Plati (who, as on *Earthling*, played a leading role in helping to define the sound of the sessions), the idea was to rehearse the songs during the day at Studio C in Sear Sound in Manhattan, and then record them almost as live tracks, giving the sessions a less studied quality. Later, multi-instrumentalist Lisa Germano and ambient-guitar specialist Gerry Leonard were brought in for the overdubbing sessions.

Toy was on the schedule for many months. As 2001 progressed and the album still hadn't hit the shops, puzzled fans began to fear that it had encountered difficulties. In a posting on a Bowie message board, one fan remarked, not without humour, that *Toy* reminded him of Area 51/Hangar 18: 'We hear a lot about it, and know that it exists, but nobody ever gets to see it.'

Several of the songs have been made available subsequently on official releases as bonus tracks or on maxi CDs. They include an outrageously fun stomp through 'Can't Help Thinking About Me', a reflective and poignant 'Shadowman', and a pretty 'Conversation Piece'. However, along with the so-far unedited instrumental suite of music recorded in 1994 which currently goes by the name of *Inside* (and which Mike Garson considers to be generally superior to the official *1. Outside* CD) it still awaits official release.

One of the reasons why *Toy* never saw the light of day was of course the speed of Bowie's songwriting. The mid-80s ennui, during which Bowie must have encountered something akin to writer's block, long behind him, he was now writing at a furious pace. During what must have been months of protracted behind-the-scenes negotiation with his record company, he had already started to move on to his next project. Towards the end of the making of *Toy*, Tony Visconti had been brought in to write an orchestral arrangement for one of the songs, and to mix the record. Now Bowie turned to him once more to produce his next studio album proper.

To cut the new album, Bowie and Visconti decamped to Allaire Studios in Shokan, situated two hours north of Manhattan in the grounds of a 1920s estate. Bowie was so taken with the beauty of this mountainous region that he bought a tract of land in the vicinity. 'It's hard to imagine a recording environment more physically beautiful and more conducive to meditation and creativity than Allaire,' is how Paul Verna put it in *Mix* magazine in 2003. 'David was very jovial. But he would go somewhere in the mornings when he was writing these songs,' Tony Visconti told the Guardian. You could see he was really struggling with questions. After a few weeks I said: "It seems like you're addressing God himself." The concept of *Heathen* is a godless century. He was addressing the bleakness of our soul ... and maybe his own soul.'

One bright morning in early September was to bring a tragedy of biblical proportions. Bowie and Visconti looked down on their home town in disbelief. 'All night we could see the flames,' says Visconti, recalling 11 September 2001. 'For that whole day we lost contact with our loved ones. Iman was very close to it. He [Bowie] got hold of her for ten minutes and the phones went down. My son lived very close. His business partner lived across the street and managed to get out five minutes before the building collapsed. All of us have stories like that.'

'When I first went back to have a look at the World Trade Center area I thought, Oh my God, it looks like London's East End when I was a kid,' said Bowie. 'That's what it looked like when I was about seven. Then it brought it all back, what London was like in that particular time.' The first lines of Bowie's next album would be 'Nothing remains . . .'; the opening lines of the final song, 'Steel on the skyline/Sky made of glass/Made for a real world/All things must pass'.

Critics speculated that the tone of the album had been directed, at least in part, by the dread events of 9/11. Mark Plati, however, doubts this as a prime motivation:

As far as 9/11 is concerned . . . it had an impact on everyone I know, especially those of us that live here. I think of David as a New Yorker and I don't think you can help but be affected on many levels by such a thing happening in your town. After all, even when you switched off CNN you'd still see the diverted traffic, hear the sirens of the emergency vehicles and the rumble of huge trucks carting away debris, the fighter jets patrolling overhead . . . and, you could smell the fires burning for months afterward, day and night, wondering what exactly you were taking in with each breath. There were constant reminders of death just walking down the street. I don't think David would set out to write a '9/11 album' or anything like that, but I think in *Heathen* you can feel the overall mood of where we all were during those times.

Yet some of the imagery on the album is so incredibly evocative of the devastation (both psychic and physical) wreaked on the day itself, and of the long period of reconstruction, that Bowie must surely have written at least part of the album after the event? Bowie is adamant that this is not the case. 'It was quite spine-tingling to realise how close those lyrics came. There are some key words in there that really just freak me out. It was written before 9/11 both lyrically and melodically. It wasn't written about that and I just felt that as long as I could make it absolutely clear that I'm not trying to exploit the situation, then I should just let it be. Because that's my work last year. That's what I did.' Asked whether 9/11 influenced the record, Tony Visconti replied: 'Undoubtedly, but a lot of those lyrics are very prophetic. I swear to you only a few lines were amended after September 11th.'

At the *Concert For New York City*, a charity concert held on 20 October 2001 at Madison Square Garden in aid of the Robin Hood Relief Fund, Bowie opened the proceedings with a moving version of Simon and Garfunkel's 'America', sitting cross-legged on the stage and accompanying himself on an 80s Omnichord keyboard, before going on to sing the obligatory, although on this occasion genuinely rousing, "Heroes". 'I didn't want to open with a celebratory mood. We were all devastated,' said Bowie. 'I felt there was a lot more apprehension. People were feeling displaced and nervous and had caution about the future. It just felt, symbolically, that "America" had that resonance to it – it had a certain sensibility of "Where are we going?" that for me personally felt right for the occasion.'

Bowie felt the loss of so many brave people very deeply. 'We have a fire station not one and a half blocks from where we live, and ever since Lexi was born, she has gone past that with me on Sundays. And all the guys know her. They lost quite a few guys, you know, and it really had an effect on me,' Bowie told Rachel Sklar in 2002. 'It was really heartbreaking, it really was, to then go past that fire station and it was covered in bouquets and flowers and gifts and it was just, it was really tough. I was only too happy to do something in recognition of the service that they gave the city.'

Bowie and Visconti, for so long estranged, resumed their work together with all the fluidity of old. Although never ones for resting on their laurels or relying on tried and tested formulas, Visconti and Bowie did revive certain old techniques for the recording of the new album. 'On some tracks, like "Sunday" and "I Would Be Your Slave", we decided to resurrect the "Heroes" vocal sound,' Visconti told Blair Jackson of *Mix* magazine. 'You need a big studio, and Allaire's room is huge and not treated – other than a few carpets and tapestries judiciously placed on the floors and walls. The pitched ceiling is about 35 feet high, and the floor is something like 25 by 40 feet. The way we did it, the main mic was augmented by two more, placed about 12 feet and 30 feet from David . . . I carefully adjusted the thresholds of the gates to open when David sang above a certain volume. The mic at 12 feet would open when he sang mezzo forte, and the mic at 30 feet would only open when he sang fortissimo. Of course, the mic at 12 feet would be open then, too. I put the distant mics in omni mode to catch more of the reflections off of the walls and ceiling rather than David's direct voice.'

There are genuinely great tracks on *Heathen*. 'Slip Away' is one. Originally recorded as 'Uncle Floyd' the previous year for the unreleased *Toy* project, and reshaped by Bowie for the new album, its wonderful melody and haunting chorus, stylophonic ending and weirdly anachronistic fretless bass work perfectly together. Another slam-dunk was '5.15 The Angels Have Gone', a quasi-reggae ballad, again with that ghostly quality that is *Heathen*'s sombre leitmotif. The incantatory opener, 'Sunday', detonates into life after 3 minutes 45 seconds, as Bowie's octave-scaling scream reaches sublime heights, while the closing track, 'Heathen (The Rays)', with it's ominous militaristic drum figure and 'Warszawa'-like ending leaves us seemingly without hope or consolation.

Heathen may have a conceptual unity, but musically it's one of Bowie's most playful records. 'Cactus', a wonderful cover of a minor Pixies classic, comes closest to the edgy rock of *Scary Monsters*. The second cover, 'I Took A Trip On A Gemini Spacecraft', is techno, whilst a third, Neil Young's 'I've Been Waiting For You', is squarely American punk. 'I Would Be Your Slave' is a drum'n'bass ballad, a new genre if ever there was one. 'Afraid' is riff rock, whilst the UK Top 20 hit, 'Everyone Says Hi', is, despite its almost heartbreaking lyric, a slab of near 'Kooks'-era pop. Peel away the smiley surface, and this is the album's saddest song. It deals with bereavement, and how one copes. Here, the song's protagonist can't accept the death of someone close, and so deludes himself into thinking that they're simply away on an extended vacation. But despite the style-hopping, the experiments never jar or sound premeditated, and, like all the best Bowie records, it repays repeated listening, as new surfaces and textures reveal themselves with each play.

Sombre, moody, spiritually questing and reflective, *Heathen* is Bowie's post-millennium hangover record. It lacks the optimism of the likes of *Earthling*, which was written and conceived in the run-up to 2000. 'I had rosy expectations for the twenty-first century, I really did . . . The whole idea was lifting my spirits quite a lot during 1998 and 1999,' Bowie told the press in 2002. *Heathen* reflects the more troubled times and scenarios of the early part of the Noughties. And it also encodes Bowie's own anxieties for his daughter. 'Since my daughter's been born, I am changing as a writer. There has been a shift in the weight of my responsibilities, relinquishing my own concerns about myself and

Iman as a couple, and instead thinking about Lexi and what her world is going to be like.'

Heathen was released in June 2002. At the end of 2001, Bowie left Virgin Records and formed his own label, Iso, which then cut a licensing deal with Columbia, who were owned by Sony Music Entertainment Inc. Bowie was happy with the new arrangement. 'I gotta say, going with a new label, Columbia Records, they certainly made my presence far more known with *Heathen*,' Bowie told Gene Stout. 'I think that pricked everyone's ears and showed that I hadn't slid off the radar.' Although not quite the commercial success it for a time threatened to be, *Heathen* reached Number 5 in the UK, staying in the charts for 18 weeks. In the US it reached Number 14. Estimated global sales for the record are around two million units, a substantial improvement on Bowie's albums in the 90s.

Heathen met with almost blanket critical approval. A four-star *Q* review by 'grumpy old man' David Quantick set the tone for the album's positive, though rarely gushing, reception. Alexis Petridis in the *Guardian* pointed out that the album was 'packed with fantastic songs, liberally sprinkled with intriguing touches ... the sound of a man who has finally worked out how to grow old with a fitting degree of style. When you consider the state of his peers, that is a unique achievement in itself.' He then added the caveat: 'It would be wrong to herald *Heathen* as a complete return to 1970s form. It lacks the thrilling sense of artistic tumult that marks *Station To Station*, *Low*, or 1980's *Scary Monsters (And Supercreeps)* albums, on which ideas appear to burst forth, barely marshalled. But those records were made by a decadent gay saxophone-playing cokehead alien Pierrot with an interest in fascism and the occult. *Heathen* is the work of a multimillionaire 55-year-old father of two.' Petridis' assessment of the record was just about on the mark: whilst failing to match the astonishing creativity of much of his work in the 1970s, it was nevertheless a valid and at times excellent piece of work. But then so were *1. Outside* and *The Buddha Of Suburbia*, and neither of these records were given the praise they deserved. It was simply time again for Bowie to be liked, and to be found cool. In the 1990s it was fashionable to be critical of Bowie. By 2002, it was no longer folly to admit one's appreciation.

The covers of Bowie albums are often an indicator of the quality of the records inside them. The slightly contrived pietas of *hours* . . . for example, or the Gilbert-And-George-gone-wrong image used for *Tonight*, were a reflection of the lack of confidence of some of the music within. *Heathen*, however, had one of his best ever covers. In semi-profile, staring like a grown-up Midwich Cuckoo, Bowie looks possessed. The accompanying booklet contains a series of defaced works of art and literature, featuring words crossed out. Here Bowie was alluding to one of *Heathen*'s central themes – the lack of understanding between the Christian West and the Muslim Middle East, the reduction of what the other doesn't understand to the status of 'un-art'.

In 2002, Bowie took to the road to promote the album. Again, the critics were on his side. In the summer, he joined Moby's Area Two tour, along with acts such as experimental performance artists The Blueman Group, and Busta Rhymes. During one gig, perhaps either misremembering, or revealing a new nugget of information, he announced: 'I lied when I said there's not going to be anything from the 60s. I recorded this in the 70s, but I wrote it in the 60s.' The song? 'Changes'.

Back in the UK early that summer, Bowie curated the Meltdown Festival. His choice of artistes reflected his avant-garde leanings (The Legendary Stardust Cowboy), populist tastes (Coldplay and Suede), and his more high-brow inclinations (Philip Glass performing Bowie's *Low* and "*Heroes*" symphonies). Writing in *The Times*, critic Stuart Maconie slated what he regarded as the conservatism of Bowie's choices, which led Bowie to pen a rejoinder and Maconie to make an unreserved apology on BBC Radio 2 for 'a joky piece I wrote about him [Bowie] recently'. The highlight of the Festival was, of course, an appearance by Bowie himself. Bravely, Bowie decided to play two albums in their entirety, *Low* and his latest work *Heathen*, before ending the show with a short blast of hits. 'Looking, at 55, like David Beckham's (slightly) older and better-groomed brother, he strode on in a black waistcoat and white shirt, a resplendent vision of lithe, ageless cool,' wrote Dave Sinclair in *The Times*. 'Only Bowie, of all the pop icons in their fifties, could still convince as a Beautiful Boy, with his shaggy hairstyle, trim physique and skinny tie (worn undone, hanging loose and flapping in the wind of several outbursts of applause from a sycophantic audience who doesn't seem to realise that you're supposed to clap only when something good happened, and not all the time like mentally deficient seals),' is how Barbara Ellen viewed the revitalised Boy

David. Bowie dedicated '5.15' to John Entwistle, whose death had been announced the day before.

On 2 October 2002, Bowie returned, triumphantly, to the Hammersmith Odeon (now known as the Carling Apollo), a venue whose place in Bowie lore had been guaranteed when Bowie played his last live gig with The Spiders there almost thirty years earlier. Three decades later, fans were paying up to £250 on the black market for tickets to the gig. Inside was a cross-section of high-profile media supporters who presumably didn't have to fork out that sort of cash. They included Liberal Democrat leader Charles Kennedy, Travis, Glen Matlock, Queen's Roger Taylor, Brian Eno, Placebo, the Pet Shop Boys, Boy George, Jonathan Ross, Ricky Gervais, Frank Skinner, David Baddiel and Ben Elton. Somehow, one couldn't have imagined this sort of turn-out for the second Tin Machine tour a decade earlier. In fact, comedian and presenter Jonathan Ross had, through his high-profile TV and radio shows, been almost single-handedly responsible for bringing Bowie back into the public spotlight. Ross was so transparently awestruck that it was impossible not to miss the reverential nature of the admiration shown by Ross and the forty-something media who had grown up listening to Bowie and were now in a position to indulge their obsessions.

The concert was introduced by Radio 1's Mark and Lard, two massive fans who were just about the only people on the network still playing Bowie records. 'Not only is this the last show of the tour, but it is the last show we'll ever do when there's a fucking tube strike!' Bowie laughed, the very model of blokey charm. John Aizlewood reviewed the gig thus: 'For one previously so determined to shed his past, Bowie now embraces nostalgia. Seemingly tension-free, Bowie 2002 is a willing entertainer, full of bonhomie ("This place! Blimey!"), willingly churning out a battalion of hits and the occasional elderly album track – *Lodger*'s 'Look Back In Anger' was especially lambent – alongside most of the current album, *Heathen*.'

For the 2002 shows Bowie performed a winning mixture of songs from *Heathen*, album tracks (the *Low*-era material shone in particular) and an ample dose of big hits and Bowie standards. The shows would end with a heart-stopping rendition of the song which, back in 1990, he had vowed to never play again: 'Ziggy Stardust'. What was apparent was just how well Bowie was now singing. It sounded as if he had rediscovered his late-1970s' singing range. One possible explanation was that, sometime towards the end of 2001, Bowie had finally given up smoking. Whatever the case, his powerful, full-throated voice indicated that his lungs seemed to be in a much healthier condition.

During October 2002, Bowie returned home and played a series of intimate gigs in New York. In fact, Bowie ran with the idea of following the route of the New York marathon, which crosses all five boroughs. With shows in Staten Island, Brooklyn, Queens, the Bronx and Manhatten, the NYC Bowie-thon thrilled fans. Myriam Santos-Kayda's collection of moody black-and-white studies in her book, *David Bowie: Live In New York*, provided a touching keepsake of the event for the rest of us.

Emboldened by the success of the record and the tour, Bowie came off the road to spend time with his family in New York. However, work began almost immediately on the follow-up to *Heathen*. Having been cut free from the tired old scheduling conflicts, he was now able to write, record and release just about when he liked. 'Well the deal I've got with my label ISO for Columbia is a lot looser than the ones I've had before,' confirmed Bowie. 'It means that I can put out stuff whenever I want to. I really get frustrated because I write an awful lot and it's very hard when you are sort of stockpiling songs not to be able to just put them out, but most of the majors really want a long sell-off period, you know, before they put out anything else, but it's pretty cool with Columbia, so it looks like I will be able to do what I used to, which is like one a year ... I'm really kind of autonomous ... I'm an *autonomous entity* ... so I can virtually do what I want, which is great.'

For his next album, Bowie drew inspiration from his immediate locale. To all intents and purposes, he is now a New Yorker. Contrary to some reports in the media, Bowie, as he is at pains to point out, owns just one residence there, an apartment in the SoHo area of Manhattan purchased in the early 1990s. New York affords relative anonymity. In recent years, the singer Björk has set up home there for much the same reason. In New York Bowie is able to walk the streets without the constant media intrusion he might encounter in LA, Paris or London. 'I have a great time here: we can go where we want, eat where we want, walk out with our child, go to the park, ride the subway, do the things that any other family does. I'm very happy with that situation ... I'd never dream of employing a minder unless I'm working. I have always found that that type of behaviour attracts more attention than anything else.' With just one tabloid newspaper, New York is relatively sleaze-free. Bowie claims that he finds the whole media fixation on celebrity 'crap'. 'I cannot understand anybody who wants to be on the front of a newspaper all the bloody time if they don't have something to sell.'

At a time when many Europeans take a very dim view of Bush-era foreign policy, and have demonstrated their disapproval in the form of various anti-American stances, including actively campaigning against foreign policy, or simply refusing to visit the country, Bowie appears increasingly Americanised. He may sing on stage, 'I'm afraid of Americans/I'm afraid of the world', but behind the irony and the mildly critical position of that song, Bowie appears more at home in New York than anywhere else in his life. 'What he was saying to me was that what attracted him about New York has changed over the years,' says writer Paul Du Noyer, who has interviewed Bowie over three decades. 'In his younger days, it would be the city that never sleeps, endless opportunities for recreation of one sort or another. Whereas now, he probably values New York for its generally cultural ambience, the opportunities it affords for privacy and comfort.'

One of the first songs Bowie tracked for the new record ended up providing the title for the new CD: 'Reality'. In fact, even more so than with "Heroes" Bowie ought to have put some distancing inverted commas around the whole concept. The title was meant, in part, to comment ironically at the media obsession with reality-television shows. 'On the concept of "reality": it's a broken, fractured word now. It feels at times that there really is no sense any more, in a major way, and that everything is being broken down for us, and the absolutes have gone, and you end up with bits and pieces of what our culture was,' Bowie explained. In essence, Bowie wasn't saying anything much new here, at least nothing that a post-modernist thinker might not have said fifteen years ago about the fracturing down of our society, the existence of temporary mini-realities, the end of the grand narratives of class, religion, and race. Post-9/11, however, there was indeed a collective collapse of confidence in America's march towards economic and political global hegemony. 'There's kind of an implosion there because of the tragedy of 9/11 and, after that, the gradual picking up of the pieces,' is how Bowie described it in 2004. 'I think now you're finding a New York that's coming out of that, physically as well as intellectually. Physically, there's a whole restructuring of lower Manhattan, and there's also a new pattern. The artists are starting to move out to Jersey or Brooklyn, so the vibe is becoming very different.'

The title also encapsulated the prosaic nature of the project itself. 'I just wanted it to be songs that were written at home where I live,' Bowie said in 2004. 'That was the only line I gave myself: "Here I am, at home. What songs come to me, just living around town, doing what I do, going out with the family and being on the streets?" It was that kind of feel, and it was really no more complicated than that.'

'*Heathen*'s aesthetic is far more serene [than *Reality*], although there's something somewhat disturbed about it,' he added. 'A lot of *Heathen* is questioning one's spiritual connection, and it has the unease you get from being in the mountains. There's something disturbing about being up there! Down here there's a different kind of disturbance. There's an aggression to the urban situation. So *Reality* is less about the spiritual life and more about the – I have to use the word – reality of living in a town left with such a tragic residue.'

Tony Visconti was once again co-producer, and the personnel on the record was basically the *Heathen* touring band. The whole ambience of *Reality* was less taut than on its predecessor; there was a looseness to the playing, a rockier sound. Ahead of the album's release, he dubbed the sound 'a bit thrusty' and told the press that it was written in order to be played live. The problem with *Reality*, however, is its very laxity. Possessed of neither a really coherent musical identity nor any thematic trajectory, it sounds underwritten. This was the flip side of Bowie's new, looser arrangement with Columbia records: he may now have the freedom to make records more quickly, but he could also record and release what he wanted, unfettered, one suspects, by the wise counsel of intermediaries and gatekeepers. It is probably true to say that Bowie lacks a critical presence within his entourage, someone who can tell him when a song isn't up to scratch, when an idea needs more work, when a project lacks coherence. The result is that, whilst around a third of the songs on *Reality* are Bowie near top form, the remainder vary from good to merely pleasant.

The opener, 'New Killer Star', with its punning title, was probably the strongest track on the album. With an unmistakably

Bowiesque riff, the song depicts the emotional and physical scarring of his home town – 'See a great white scar/Over Battery Park' – but, filtered through Bowie's surrealistic lyrics, the result could never be called a 9/11 song per se. For many, the first taste of the new album was a snippet from a second great track, 'Never Get Old', which was posted on BowieNet to accompany a promotional campaign for Vittel mineral water. Bowie featured in the ad along with David Brighton, an LA-based Bowie lookalike whose live tribute to Bowie has been endorsed by no less than *Station To Station* producer Harry Maslin himself. In the ad the real Bowie wanders through a house populated by various alter egos ('Ashes To Ashes' Pierrot, *Diamond Dog*, *Ziggy/Aladdin Sane* clone, The Thin White Duke), all convincingly played by Brighton. It's a shame that a real video for the song along those lines was not made. The song itself mined the same ore of outré funk riffing and rousing melodies that had turned 'Modern Love', 'Fame' and 'Fashion' into such brilliant singles. The third classic cut on the album was 'Fall Dog Bombs The Moon', a wonderful song. Bowie sings: 'These blackest of years, that have no sound/No shape, no depth, no underground, what a dog', in what is a better record of early-Noughties uncertainty and disquiet than any other song of the time.

With its flamenco-guitar opening and vibrant alternative-rock-styled twists and turns, the cover of Jonathan Richman's 'Pablo Picasso', positioned second on the album (like the cover of the Pixies' 'Cactus' on *Heathen*), was also an effective treatment. At one stage Bowie had tentatively planned a Pin-Ups Two, and on the shortlist for this particular project was George Harrison's 'Try Some, Buy Some'. Bowie had chosen the track, as covered by Ronnie Spector, as part of his famous radio performance on *Star Special* in May 1979, so it's obviously a song dear to his heart. Yet Bowie's interpretation, although densely packed, is just too grand for its own good. And there are other miscalculations on the record too. 'The Loneliest Guy' might possess the sort of sombre piano refrain which gave *1. Outside* its psychotic menace, but Bowie's vocal, quivering and unstable, is just too much. As music writer Alex Petridis correctly put it, the song was sadly 'overcooked'. Another song Bowie had written for *Black Tie White Noise* and had attempted again for *Earthling*, 'Bring Me The Disco King', was finally released here as a jazz number, with trademark

Garsonic piano fills and an understated accompaniment. But after spending a decade trying to get it right, the *Reality* version still ended up inferior to the second recorded treatment of the song from 2003, the edgy electronica version which was included on the soundtrack to the film *Underworld*.

The rest of *Reality* is, nevertheless, never less than listenable. The Motownesque stomp of 'Looking For Water', the Tin Machine-styled squawl of the riff-rocking blitz that is 'Reality', the prettiness of 'Days', and the harmonica-fired reportage of 'She'll Drive The Big Car' are all well crafted and enjoyable, though they don't quite move you like *Heathen* did.

And yet, the critics went mad for the record. For the first time ever in his career, the reviews were better than the album deserved. 'Touching, intelligent and – a bonus – listenable,' was Caroline Sullivan's assessment in the *Guardian*, while *Q* magazine, in what one hopes is an in-joke within the journalistic community (but probably isn't), dubbed it, 'Bowie's best music since *Scary Monsters*.' 'Comically callous in a way Bowie hasn't been since *Scary Monsters*', was the verdict of the *Sunday Independent* (on his cover of 'Pablo Picasso'), while *Dotmusic* opined: 'Bowie's best since *Scary Monsters*, yet again.' There were many, many more reviews saying almost *exactly* the same thing. Bowie should pre-emptively sticker up his next album 'Best Since *Scary Monsters*' and have done with it.

The public, however, were largely unimpressed by the hype and by the record itself. Although debuting at a lofty Number 3 in the UK album charts, it dropped out again after just four weeks. In Europe *Reality* sold solidly enough for a time, but in America it was a flop. However, the relative lack of success was neither wholly unanticipated nor in any way career-threatening. That said, *Heathen* had raised expectations of a genuine big-selling album as a follow-up. Bowie was already committed to a long world tour, his first major trek since the *Sound + Vision* tour in 1990, and, for a man in his mid-fifties, a gruelling schedule.

But Bowie seemed to be in good shape. He had quit smoking in December 2001, and was living a healthy lifestyle. He rose around 5 a.m., sometimes before Lexi, organised his day, dealt with emails and phone calls to Europe, and then began his own work. The days of self-abuse were history. Lithe and, for many, still stylishly sexy, he could pass for a man approaching fifty rather than someone facing the reality of his on-coming sixtieth birthday.

He meditated regularly and also worked with a boxing trainer three times a week. 'I'm fast and agile, so technically I think I'm pretty good,' Bowie told Tim Cooper. 'But whether I have any power in my punches or any ability to stay away from the other guy I don't know, because I've never been in a fight. My trainer is a huge man who wouldn't dream of even tapping me on the forehead 'cos it would lay me out.' When not working he would take it in turns with Iman to play with Lexi. Less the nappy-changing new dad, Bowie saw his role as more 'educational'. 'I do a lot of reading aloud.' A nanny would come in daily to take care of Lexi when Iman and David were working.

For the tour, Bowie assembled a band of all the talents. This was not the riff-rocking aggro of The Spiders, the art-rock collision of the musicians of the 1978 tour, or the cold if beguiling musical pioneering of the mid-1990s, Gabrels-era Bowie. No, this was a band which was professional and flexible, able to recreate the textures and nuances of Bowie's long and musically varied career relatively faithfully without, perhaps, striking out in any massively unexpected direction. Mark Plati, who had been band leader on the *Heathen* tour, left to work with Robbie Williams, and Gerry Leonard took over. In his early forties, this friendly Dubliner had developed a career, under the moniker Spooky Ghost, as an outré guitarist specialising in ambient sonics. It would be his guitar playing, on the likes of 'Sunday' and, most dramatically, 'Heathen (The Rays)', which would provide two of the musical highlights of the show. Mike Garson (keyboards), Earl Slick (guitar), Gail Ann Dorsey (bass and vocals), Catherine Russell (guitar, keyboards, percussion and mandolin) and Sterling Campbell (drums) were all retained from the *Heathen* tour, Garson (1972–75, 1992–2004) becoming Bowie's longest-serving musical compadre.

The *Reality* album was launched by a brilliant piece of Bowie shock tactics. Way back in early 1981, Bowie had spoken to Radio 1 about an idea he had had of supporting his *Scary Monsters* album not by a tour but by relaying a select bunch of concerts via video link into cinemas around the world. Twenty-two years later and the will (and the technology) were there. On 8 September 2003, Bowie performed the entirety of *Reality* at London's Hammersmith Riverside Studios, and, although fans reported glitches with the sound mix in some cinemas, 68 cinemas in 22 countries took the broadcast, making it a very special event for Bowie's hard-core fans. Bowie himself couldn't remember the logistics of how many cinemas and how many countries, joking with the audience, 'I can never remember facts – that's what made my life so much fun!' And he wasn't a hundred per cent sure of his own lyrics either, as we watched on, amused, by the sight of the Rock God of all Rock Gods occasionally sneaking a furtive glance at a ledger containing the words to his new album. Played live, the songs from the album sprang to life, just as Bowie said they would. During the concert, fans' text messages scrolled along the bottom of the screen, and after the performance, there was a Q&A for the fans which, as Alexis Petridis described it in the *Guardian*, 'simultaneously recalls the Eurovision Song Contest and a particularly chaotic phone-in on 1980s kids show *Saturday Superstore*'. 'The questions are staggering. Josephine in Berlin wants to know what happened to a dog Bowie owned in the 1970s. Unsurprisingly, Bowie replies that the dog died. He wears a regretful expression. Whether he is regretting the passing of the hound or his decision to take part in the Q&A is unclear. His answers reveal less than his skin-tight trousers do.'

The band learned around fifty songs for the gigs, and kept rehearsing and adding more as the months rolled by. Bowie could never be accused of short-changing his fans. Concerts would regularly run way past two-and-a-half hours. Some songs, such as 'The Jean Genie', were played only a handful of times before being dropped, whilst others, such as 1975's classic 'Win', were rehearsed but not performed. Although Bowie was at pains to say in interviews that this was not a crowd-pleasing set, how could an evening's entertainment which regularly included 'Ziggy Stardust', 'Rebel Rebel', 'Changes', All The Young Dudes', "Heroes", 'Fame', 'Fashion', 'Under Pressure', 'Ashes To Ashes' and 'China Girl' really be anything other than just that? True, Bowie did retain several songs from *Heathen*, but as the tour progressed the percentage of the show made up by songs from the new album dwindled. Bowie did resurrect the odd brilliant album track such as 'Fantastic Voyage' or 'Be My Wife', whilst *Earthling*'s 'I'm Afraid Of Americans' became something of a standard, but overall, there were enough hits to keep casual Bowie fans happy, including the sort who, on hearing the first bars of 'The Man Who Sold The World' exclaim, 'Ooh, he's covering a Nirvana song!'

The 'A Reality' tour kicked off on 7 October 2003 in Copenhagen. 'You've got your mother in whirl, she's not sure if you're a boy or a squirrel', sang Bowie during 'Rebel Rebel'. 'I tell you it's a T-shirt-and-jeans-type show, believe me, that's what it is,' Bowie said. 'If you like the idea of me just singing my songs, you're going to be thrilled.' Bowie's very presence was, of course, enough. Dressed like a slightly older member of The Strokes, he commanded the stage, his voice once again brilliant. But this was in no way a theatrical or dramatic event. There were some concessions to the arena rock spectacle: a massive LED screen flickered into life depicting the band in crude animated form, before the real-life players took their positions. Mark Adams on BowieNet pointed out that 'the screens high above the stage gave it the feel of a boxing match'. There was a raised catwalk, two platforms either side of the stage, and two snow-white trees, but it was hard to see how the design was in any way related to the musical contents of the evening. Those fans hoping for rock theatre would be disappointed; this was not art, it was Bowie and his band playing brilliant songs. It is a shame that, for the last decade, Bowie appears to have lost interested in the possibilities of rock as theatre. Hopefully it's an area he will return to on future tours.

'C'mon kids, wake up, your granddad's here,' harangued Bowie at the MEN in Manchester. This was Bowie clearly at ease and enjoying himself. In Dublin he reportedly said to the 16,000 audience, '*Tiocfaidh Ar Lia*', 'our day will come'. 'He said it near the start, so the pretext was, our day will come, we'll have a great concert tonight,' said long-time Bowie fan and writer Dara O'Kearney. 'However, judging by the sly grin on his face, there's not a shadow of doubt that he knew exactly what he was saying, and that it's an IRA slogan.' During an emotional 'All The Young Dudes', musician Ricky Warwick used his mobile phone to relay the performance live to Def Leppard 5,000 miles away in Moscow! The show was edited and released on DVD in 2004.

The reviews were ecstatic. However, the tour was not running as smoothly as Bowie had hoped for. In November, one date was lost because of laryngitis. In December he had to postpone five shows due to a bout of flu. Given the fact that, historically, Bowie has hardly ever had to miss dates, this was a surprise. In May 2004 a lighting technician fell to his death just before Bowie took to the stage at a concert in Miami. Then, on Friday, 18 June, at the Norwegian Wood Festival in Oslo, Bowie was three songs into his set when an overzealous female fan, swinging her arms around, let go of a lollipop which, by some astonishing fluke, managed to hit him in the eye. The show was stopped. Bowie, not surprisingly none too pleased, asked for the person to identify him or herself, although no one came forward at the time. Regaining his composure, he joked, 'Lucky you hit the bad one' and, not seriously injured, after a two-minute break managed to continue the gig and play a full show.

However, just five days later, on 23 June, he was taken seriously ill nine songs into the set in the T-Mobile arena in Prague. After singing 'Reality', Bowie left the stage. The band continued with the instrumental, 'A New Career In A New Town', followed by 'Be My Wife', with Catherine Russell on vocals. Bowie then restarted the show, only to leave the stage again a few songs later. Starting the concert for a third time, it was clear that he was in agony. The press, however, were told that his condition was down to nothing more serious than a pinched nerve in his shoulder.

Astonishingly, Bowie appeared two days later at the Hurricane Festival in the North German town of Scheessel, astonishing because, as it turned out, he was actually suffering from a heart problem. Although no official statement was ever made linking the pinched nerve in his shoulder with heart trouble, it's a medical fact that such conditions are sometimes 'warnings' of more serious heart problems. After the concert Bowie's condition worsened and he was reported to be doubled up in agony backstage. He was rushed to the St Georg Hospital in Hamburg, where he was diagnosed as having an acutely blocked artery and underwent a procedure known as an angioplasty, used to promote the normal flow of blood around the heart. A catheter is threaded along the artery to the site of the narrowing and then inflated, thereby crushing the atherosclerotic plaque into the wall of the artery. According to the British Heart Foundation, at least nine out of ten such procedures are successful, with most patients able to go home the next day. This was not major heart surgery, therefore, but neither was it a minor illness.

The remaining fourteen European dates were cancelled, but the seriousness of Bowie's true condition was kept from the media until he was well enough to fly back home two weeks later. Newspaper reports claimed that 'Staff said he was "very poorly".' Sources close to the singer said he was 'run down' on the tour and had 'missed his family and was tired'. Julian Stockton, from Bowie's London-based PR company, The Outside Organisation, quoted Bowie as saying: 'I'm so p'd off because the last ten months of this tour have been so fuckin' fantastic. Can't wait to be fully recovered and get back to work again. I tell you what, though, I won't be writing a song about this one.'

Even with the cancellation of the final dates, the 'A Reality' tour had been a huge success, playing across Europe, the USA, Canada, New Zealand, Australia and Japan to an estimated total audience of 722,000. It netted Bowie $45.4 m (£22.3 m), the highest grossing tour of 2004. Whether Bowie would ever attempt such a tour again is, however, debatable. For health reasons alone, shorter tours may well be the order of the day from now on.

A month into his convalescence, Bowie was spied shopping in the Chinatown district of New York. Sporting a cowboy hat and a pale green T-shirt, he happily chatted to well-wishers whilst stocking up on herbal tea and ancient remedies from a local Chinese grocery. Reports commented on how well he looked, but published photographs showed him looking understandably somewhat drawn. Later in the year, Bowie was rocking with a moustache and looking much healthier, although by 2005, the 'tache had (possibly wisely) been removed!

What then for the future? Well, one can be certain that part of the future for David Bowie will revolve around his illustrious back catalogue. Under the auspices of EMI, a reissue campaign is in process which will be an ongoing concern for many years to come. Three of Bowie's classic studio albums, *The Rise And Fall Of Ziggy Stardust And The Spiders From Mars*, *Aladdin Sane* and *Diamond Dogs*, have been reissued with new artwork, a bonus CD of collectable material, a chronology (by Bowie expert Kevin Cann) and sleeve notes by someone whose name I can't quite remember. Just to have them back out there, being played, discussed and reviewed all over again, is marvellous. And for those of you new to the Bowie scene, it all makes for a joyous act of discovery. At the time of writing, there are on-going discussions regarding a reissue of *Young Americans* and for a refurbished *Hunky Dory*. There has also been talk of a new version of Bowie's forgotten classic *The Buddha Of Suburbia*, and a DVD release of *Serious Moonlight*. There will doubtless be more to come, leading, one hopes, to the first ever multi-disc David Bowie anthology.

It is with some frustration that those connected with the EMI reissues read postings on Bowie-related message boards from disgruntled fans annoyed about the lack of bonus material on these commemorative records. Although such material may, indeed, exist, it doesn't exist in the quantity some fans think it does, nor is it often of a quality David Bowie deems worthy of release. Yes, 'Rupert The Riley' does exist, so does the instrumental demo 'A Lad In Vain'. But whether they are artistically up to the strict quality-control standards Bowie has set himself for all his product is another matter. In some cases songs have been tracked but remain unmixed. Others are crude demos of questionable audio quality. And then, of course, there are the documentaries and live footage. Very often negotiations with television companies break down because of the exorbitant fees charged for the rights. And, whilst film footage does exist from Bowie's classic tours of the 1970s and 1980s, the task of editing them and bringing them up to a releasable quality takes time, effort and money. At nearly sixty, Bowie is still much more interested in making new music than in reliving past triumphs. And most of us would not want or expect anything else.

Bowie, of course, still has other business interests away from music. Bowieart, although not so much in the news these days, is still a going concern, still championing new talent. It is possible to buy signed prints of Bowie's artwork and look at Bowie's new second career (art having long overtaken film as his major side project). He is a distinctive though underrated painter, his *Self Portrait*, produced whilst on the island of Mustique in 1988, as iconic an image of the man as any album sleeve.

Bowie freely admitted to being something of a 'Webaholic' in the mid-1990s, but today he tries to limit the amount of time he spends on-line. His major Internet experiment, BowieNet, continues apace. Under the stewardship of the redoubtable Blammo (aka Mark Adams), it manages to keep Bowie fans supplied with rolling news content, competitions and the occasional word from the Master himself. Bowie (who goes by the name of 'Sailor') has been known to post relatively frequently. Why 'Sailor'? Well, he is, as we know, 'adrift on the sea' and, of course, he 'can't dance like you', but above and beyond the references to the songs themselves, the name is an anagram of Bowie's company, Isolar. 'I think it's something to do with solitude, freedom, and travelling the unchartered waters ... or something,' says Bowie. Other Bowie fan sites continue to have their following, of course. Paul Kinder's *Bowiewonderworld*, though unofficial, provides up-to-the-minute news and contains an important archive of Bowie-related writing and ephemera. Stefan Westman's *Bassmanbowie* is also an important site with some excellent features. And Evan Torrie's *Teenage Wildlife*, whilst at the time of writing not updating its news pages, has a message board which is very much alive and well. In print, the *Voyeur*, the longest running David Bowie fanclub in the world, offers a quarterly magazine. Finally, Bonster's, 'David Bowie Newsletter For The Lazy and Web-Impaired' is a handy round-up of news.

In the age of downloads, i-Pods and the constant availability of music, the way in which we consume music has changed dramatically since Bowie's heyday in the 70s and 80s, and this may, in part, explain why someone like David Bowie belongs, in essence, to a different era in pop's development. Back then, the first listening of a new album was an event. Not only that, the iconography of the cover was also an essential ingredient in the overall experience. The magic of *Diamond Dogs* can only really be appreciated by listening to it from start to finish. Bowie made music which worked on several connected layers. It said little or nothing about the concerns of the everyday, but it still managed to articulate a profound meaning. 'Bowie operated outside the field of conventional discourse,' is how Paul Du Noyer puts it. '*Ziggy Stardust* had nothing in particular to say about the miners' strike or the three-day week, but it didn't need to; it was operating on an entirely different level. Most great art tends to work on the level of the collective subconscious rather than the conversation of the day.'

Now, music fans are almost completely unused to experiencing music in this way. Individual songs are prioritised over any attachment to a particular artist. The possibility, therefore, of making a powerful statement in a collection of songs intended to be consumed as a whole is becoming less and less likely. 'I think the context of the music has changed immeasurably since I started making it,' Bowie told writer and journalist Jim Derogatis in 2004. 'Like it or not, it has become merely an adjustment to lifestyle rather than the kind of manna from heaven it was when I was a kid. It just seems to have a different context altogether – it's like water from the tap or electricity from the plug. Kids just presume it's there for the taking, and you can't dispel that idea.' Perhaps surprisingly, Bowie is coming round to the idea that he too may have to rethink the way in which he works as a musician within the business. 'I'm coming very quickly to the stage where

I'm tempted to just start writing songs and putting them out. I really like [Apple's] iTunes – I think it's a pretty cool idea to just assemble the album of your choice, and it makes absolute sense to me. These days, I find it very hard to find more than a couple of tracks on anybody's album that are something I want to play again and again.'

As evidence of Bowie's enthusiasm for the changing pattern of music consumption, in 2004 he actively encouraged his fans to bootleg his songs. BowieNetters were allowed to download a vocal line from an old Bowie song and use it over the instrumental backing track of one of the *Reality* songs to create a 'mash-up', two songs blended together using computer music software. The winner was to receive an Audi car. Critics argued that Bowie was merely cynically exploiting a technique to kindle interest in his new album. And, of course, the technique wasn't altogether new. In 2002, the Sugarbabes' 'Freak Like Me', a mash-up by producer Richard X of two songs, 'Are Friends Electric?' by Tubeway Army and Adina Howards' 'Freak Like Me', had been a UK Number 1. But many mash-ups were illegal and record companies had threatened action. Bowie was the first rock star to actively encourage his music to be used in this way. The winning contribution was 'Big Shaken Car', a mash-up of *Let's Dance*'s 'Shake It' and *Reality*'s 'She'll Drive The Big Car'.

Bowie remains a huge music fan. His talent for spotting a great band a mile off was revealed in the autumn of 2004 when he let it be known to the world that a hitherto-unknown band, Arcade Fire from Canada, were poised to be the next big thing, six months before the critics raved about their debut album and astonishingly intense stage show. However, Bowie takes a dim view of a lot of pop music, arguing that it's disconnected from the needs and desires of the listening public, and that it's music made by the industry for the industry. 'I listen to really odd stuff and a lot of it is out on the edge,' he told the BBC in 2002. 'I know about Kylie and Robbie and *Pop Idol* and stuff like that. You can't get away from that when you hit the shore, so I know all about the cruise-ship entertainment aspect of British pop.'

Today, music no longer carries with it the sense of danger it once had; it no longer plays such a crucial role in shaping the thoughts and personalities of young people. In fact, as Bowie observes, the sense of moral indignation felt by his parents in response to the sounds of rock music is largely a thing of the past.

'A lot of guys in my generation grew up with rock music. Not Sinatra. Not big band. They grew up with the Stones and The Beatles and all that. So there's not quite such a divergence between the generations as when I was a kid. It was called the generations [sic] war. He likes Sinatra and he likes Jagger and never the twain shall meet. In a way it was true. As much as I love my father and all that, we didn't share anything like the same musical tastes. But my son and I, we pretty much have the same tastes. We can look at each other's albums. He'll pick out a Lennon album and a Hendrix album and say they're cool. I can go for a Grandaddy or Mercury Rev album and say, "I understand this. I know all about this, what they're doing." '

Bowie admits that there's often a deep vein of melancholy in his own music: 'gloom is my default attitude, I suppose', is how he described his art to Tim Cooper in 2003. But after all the years of shape-changing, are we now seeing the real man? For the first time in his life there's certainly a consistency there, both personally and professionally. Personally Bowie is married, with a family, and happily domiciled in New York. The frantic days of the torrid yet inspiring quick-fire Beckenham–London–New York–LA–Berlin changes of locale which fed a fervently creative mind during the first half of the 1970s have been replaced by sane stability. Professionally, Bowie has kept roughly the same team of people together for many years. His PR company, his management, his financial advisors and most of the musicians he works with have been part of the David Bowie Story now for a very long time. With age comes experience, and acceptance of the 'if it ain't broken, why fix it' dictum. 'It's stretching it as an analogy, but you think of the musicians as characters,' says Bowie. 'Their musical sound is a character for the song. You think, here's a little play – who would you people it with? How does the character of this song sound?' And the older he gets, the happier Bowie appears with those people he knows and can trust. Like a cast of characters in a long-running soap, it's sometimes tough to write a particular favourite one out. The days of short-lived appearances in Bowie's musical career seem over, replaced by a trend towards more stability within his entourage.

In concert, Bowie is consistently good, and frequently outstanding. With a brilliantly drilled band and four decades of stagecraft, he can give some of the best shows to be seen in rock. Having the best repertoire in the business and an astonishingly committed fan base also helps. What Bowie concerts now lack, though, is a sense of real tension and drama. He is now a brilliant singer and entertainer. He connects with his audience, he jokes, he introduces, he smiles, he *entertains*. There is, of course, absolutely nothing wrong with this. However, it obviously wasn't always like that. There was a time when his very physical presence, the freakiness of his performance and the spellbindingly intense music came together to create an aura of shamanistic power around a Bowie performance. It was less concert, more magical initiation ceremony, as Bowie's followers were inducted into the growing cult of the emotionally wonky, the sexually not-sure and the blessed cool. Bowie would hardly ever smile, would hardly ever even *speak* to his audience. He wouldn't mobilise the audience to clap along with 'Rebel Rebel', he wouldn't give them the visual cues, the standard fare of the pop gig. In the 70s Bowie just had to *be*.

'The trouble is that it's almost impossible to make a valid comparison between what he does in late middle age and what he did as a young man, as it's impossible to sustain that type of creativity,' is how Paul Du Noyer puts it:

> This is not a criticism of Bowie specifically; it's something you find in artists in pop music almost universally. It's hard to find anyone who can recapture the kind of potency they had in their twenties. And that might be as much a failing on their part as a failing in the audience, really. When they're in their twenties they are catering to an audience that is typically the same age or a bit younger than they are. And that is an audience that is looking for meaning in the music it consumes. Later on, however, they are catering to an audience that is no longer looking for meaning, because they've found it elsewhere in life. They are catering for an audience that simply wants entertainment and nostalgia, and I think this cannot help but have an influence on them as performers. In a way it implies a lowering of the game. Maybe they're acquiring expertise as they go along. Maybe they're acquiring stagecraft. Maybe, in Bowie's case, as he says, he's simply relaxing a lot more. A certain tension goes out of the whole proposition, and that might be what you intuitively are missing.

Bowie has sold somewhere in the region of 140 million albums in the course of his career. Estimates of his personal fortune vary wildly, from £100 million to £500 million. Yet despite this, Bowie himself is not a particularly extravagant man. Unlike some other rock stars of his vintage, he's not a shopaholic; indeed, he positively dislikes shopping. His 'uniform' when about town is a baseball cap and a T-shirt. 'I've found that, if I hide the hair under a cap, I somehow become almost invisible. I blend so much with the rest of humanity it makes me feel almost normal!' His only addiction these days appears to be to tea-tree-flavoured toothpicks. Today, by rock-star standards, Bowie lives an unpretentious life in New York. Iman's career flourishes; she runs her own cosmetics company, and, in 2003, she landed a $1 million contract as the face of De Beers. 'David is like me and Lou Reed,' says Mick Rock. 'We're city people. I need the fumes, and I think David and Lou are of that ilk.' Bowie and Iman have a fried breakfast every Sunday morning – 'a little bit of England', says Bowie. About once a month, the Bowies throw a dinner party, followed by the screening of a documentary or of one of David's current comedy favourites such as *The Office* (written, of course, by Bowie-nut Ricky Gervais, the only comedian with David Bowie teeth). Moby and Lou Reed live nearby and are friends, but, mainly, Bowie's friends and acquaintances are unconnected with the business. However, despite for the most part leading the normal life of a rich New Yorker, he is *still* David Bowie. 'I've recently got friendly with a father and his little boy I met in the park with my daughter,' said Bowie in 2003. He's there every single weekend and we really buddied up to each other. But we've only talked about music twice in all that time. The first time we started talking, he said: "I would never have thought I'd find you in a park." And it kind of upset me: why wouldn't you believe I would take my own daughter out? ... I suppose that's the impression one has of celebrity.'

Bowie is also completely indifferent to honours, titles and plaudits. Although he takes quite seriously, and to heart, what others say about his work, he himself, as he always says, is in the business for himself, not to please others. And this selfishness, if that is what it is, may lead him up blind alleys on occasion, but more often than not results in brilliant music. He has joined the select band of celebrities, including Albert Finney, Vanessa Redgrave, Alan Bennett, John Cleese, Helen Mirren, Honor Blackman and George Melly, who have turned down an honour. According to reports, Bowie was offered a CBE in 2000, but declined it. 'I would suggest that they give it to somebody who would give a damn,' Bowie once said when asked whether he would ever accept such an honour. 'I'm not sure what I'd do with it. I'd lose it or break it, or put it in the drawer and lose the key.'

However, there are, of course, a number of past colleagues and loved ones who Bowie never discusses and with whom he no longer has a relationship. Ex-wife Angie and ex-manager Tony Defries are just two of the people for whom the lines of communication are all but closed. Defries still has a high regard for David, but the feeling is not reciprocated. Yet Bowie has remained friendly with many others from his long career. The artist George Underwood has been a close friend since school days. Geoff McCormack is another very old friend. But Bowie's main priorities are, quite rightly, his family, and his daughter, Lexi. 'I don't want to start doing what I unfortunately did with my son, inasmuch as I spent an awful lot of time on tour when he was a young child. I really missed those years, and I know he did too. Fortunately we were together by the time he was six and I brought him up from that point on. It was a one-parent family. I don't want to repeat the same mistakes with Lexi.' 'I just wanna be there for Alexandria,' Bowie told the *Scottish Sunday Mail*. 'I desperately want to live forever. You know what I want [is] to still be around in another forty or fifty years.' He goes on, 'She's so exciting and lovely so I want to be around when she grows up.' Now in his mid-thirties, Bowie's son Duncan works in the film business. 'He's doing it all on his own. He doesn't expect anything from me. He's a very nice man, he's lovely. I love him very much indeed, I really do.'

Bowie remains fascinating and, when he makes himself visible, a quite brilliant media figure. Sir Elton John might win hands down in terms of self-deprecation and the ability to show a human side which mainstream Britain can identify with, but Bowie still retains an aura of indefatigability. Up to date with cultural references, he always gives journalists good copy, and this keeps him interesting and afloat, when other rock stars of his vintage have simply run out of anything even remotely interesting to say. He's well read and, has up-to-the-minute opinions on everything from *The Office* to the new Blur album. He thinks very quickly under pressure. He's completely spontaneous. And, he can be very funny. At his best, there's almost a sort of surreal stand-up quality to him. Very few, if any, pop stars have this mixture of fierce intelligence and what seems like utter self-belief. Friend and photographer Mick Rock put it like this: 'David wants to get into people's heads a bit, and he's a talker. David would talk the hind legs off a donkey. You don't have to feed him too much to get him excited and buzzing. I had dinner with Kate Moss a couple of nights ago – she's a friend of mine and of David's. She had met David only recently and she said, "Oh blimey, oh boy, can't he talk, love? He wore me out!" And I thought, That's David! Of course David says the same thing about me: "That Mick Rock. You can't turn her off when she's started," he said to a mutual friend recently. And David will talk and talk, and he'll get stronger and stronger, and he'll build on it. He has that slightly renegade thing, but charmingly renegade. David is also extremely articulate, as you know. There are reams and reams of interviews and yet he always says something interesting. Most of these guys, with all due respect, are like photographers; they should get on with their fucking business and shut up,' said Mick with an ironic laugh.

Understandably, after his illness Bowie took an extended period of downtime, staying at home and taking time out from being 'David Bowie', allowing David Jones to begin to feel better. By the spring of 2005, when Bowie was photographed out and about in New York with Iman, he looked fully recovered. His hair seemingly dyed a darkish brown, he smiled to the camera with a look that belied both his years and his period of illness. In December 2004, Bowie reported that he was currently writing material for his next album. 'I'm heading for another period of experimentation. [I'm at] a time when I'm collecting myself before I break all my own rules.'

'He certainly gives the appearance of being a contented cove,' says Paul Du Noyer. 'He's on a plateau now of success. He's no longer at the stage where he lives or dies on the success of his latest album. If the album does badly then it'll be a disappointment for him, but it won't be career-threatening to any degree.' At long last, it appears that even David Bowie is at ease with himself. 'I'm not a temper person. Am I passive–aggressive? I don't think so. Earlier in my life, there was more of the bipolar in me – I would vacillate quite aggressively between depressed and euphoric. I think I'm very even.'

And with this contentment has come a complete switch in terms of what Bowie wants out of music. 'There are no yearning ambitions any more,' he told Tim Cooper. 'There are things I'd like to do but none are crucial. I sense that I've become the person I always should have been. It's been a kind of cyclical, almost elliptical journey at times, but I feel like I've finally arrived at being instead of becoming, which is kind of how I feel about being young – there's always a sense that you are becoming something, that you're going to be shocked by something new or discover something or be surprised by what life has in store. I'm still surprised at some things, but I do understand them, I know them. There's a sense that I know where I am now. I recognise life and most of its experiences, and I'm quite comfortable with the idea of the finality of it. But it doesn't stop me trying to continually resolve it: resolve the questions about it. And I probably will. I think I'll still be doing it – hopefully – like Strauss, at 84.'

In the next twenty years we will see a completely new phenomenon in pop music history, something that would have been altogether unimaginable forty years ago, but which now seems inevitable: the pop musician in old age. For David Bowie, the story goes on.

UNFURL THE FLAG

*I can't think of any other musician in the twentieth century who has
impacted on popular culture and music more than David Bowie. It's safe
to say none of the records we like would sound the way they do
without David Bowie. I've met princes, I've met nobility and aristocracy,
but I've never met anyone who is as regal as Iman and David Bowie. I do
see them as titular monarchs of the world in which we live.*

MOBY, 2005

*David Bowie's contribution to rock and roll has been wit and
sophistication. He's smart, he's a true musician, and he can really sing.*

LOU REED, *ROLLING STONE,* 2004

*The most important thing for an artist is to pick through the debris of a
culture, to look at what's been forgotten or not really taken seriously.
Once something is categorised and accepted, it becomes part of the
tyranny of the mainstream, and it loses its potency. It's always been
that way for me: the most imprisoning thing is to feel oneself
pigeonholed.*

DAVID BOWIE, 1998

*There doesn't ever seem to be any self-doubt with Bowie and this is to
be commended. He seems to be very good at getting the best out of
himself. I'm always riddled with doubts and self-criticism.*

BRYAN FERRY, 1999

I t is seldom that pop figures become pop icons; it is both a
blessing and a curse when it happens. For the pop legend is
traditionally the stuff of a certain type of fantasy, a myth of the
romance of the tortured (male) pop romantic. The pop icons of

the 60s (Dylan, Lennon, Morrison) were of this number, their power was their poetry. They spoke to culture in a new language, enriched our understanding of what it is like to live through our times.

Bowie is not of their number. Like his 60s forebears he appealed, in his artiness, to the pop intelligentsia, and, in his sexiness, to teenage men and women. But he subverted the whole notion of what it was to be a rock star; he spoke in tongues. Bowie parodied pop stardom, he played the part of the rock star but never really became one himself (certainly not the sort of pop star people could believe was real). In his sly, sexual ambiguity, he unlocked the great forbidden forces of rock. Before him, the gay subculture influenced pop culture covertly, with its ambiguity, its sense of play, its nowness and its style obsession. Bowie unleashed all this into the mainstream and destroyed the myth of 60s pop iconography for ever. Together with punk rock, Bowie blew the rock era apart to leave it where it is now: a stylistic free-for-all, a mix-and-match culture.

Bloated, self-important, leather-clad, self-satisfied, the pop world needed to be parodied and plagiarised, ripped open and remodelled. Bowie challenged the very core belief of the rock music of its day. He was a pansexual, pangeneric pop behemoth. He floated in and out of identities, sexualities and musical styles in a way that seemed to some calculating or pseudo. In fact, it was a prediction of how popular culture would be in the last two decades of the century: far more playful, the divisions between the arts far less stable, music far less static, combinations of ideas and styles a commonplace, our own lives less rooted to one direction or orientation. Bowie's work predicted all this, over thirty years ago.

If punk made life tough (even only momentarily) for existing pop stars, then Bowie too engendered this sense of harrowing partisanship. Bowie defined cool for a dozen years. To be a Bowie fan was almost a calling. It made life for other pop stars bothersome as Bowie redefined cool to mean a change of image and style for each album. It was a fabulous challenge to others after years of stasis. By destroying the macho myth and the romance of rock, he spoiled the party for everyone else. The old rock formation of the 60s died.

After Bowie there has been no other pop icon of his stature, because the pop world that produces these rock gods doesn't exist any more. It's impossible now for pop musicians to work at the rate Bowie, Dylan, the Stones and The Beatles did; artistically and commercially, two albums a year would be suicide. Recording techniques and the pace of promotion have meant that the velocity of change has slowed. After Bowie, it became almost impossible to frighten or challenge a mainstream pop audience. Theatricality became increasingly played out, and even when great visual artists appeared, they were pastiches of what were often parodies themselves.

Pop music is still great and there is more great music now than there ever was, but its central defining role for youth culture has passed to other art forms. Since 1980, the pop world has disintegrated into niche markets. It means that no one figure has been able to dominate that world again. The 1990s and the 1980s did not throw up a comparable figure. There was Michael Jackson, Prince, Madonna, Springsteen, Morrissey and Cobain, but they could never define the pop world again because it no longer really existed.

The fierce partisanship of the cult of Bowie was also unique – its influence lasted longer and has been more creative than perhaps almost any other force within pop fandom. Talented, wealthy, good-looking – Bowie is the mythic embodiment of what his fans would wish for themselves. Fred and Judy Vermorel's book, *Starlust* (1985), revealed the secret fantasies of fans and is dominated by contributions from Bowie followers. Today, those fans remain as partisan and as precious as ever. For some, being a Bowie fan is still a way of life; a way of looking at the world; a way of being special. Many Bowie fans remain resolutely idiosyncratic and separatist, buying not only into a musical credo but a lifestyle as well. Bowie's message preaches individuality, not collectivity. In 1990, *Punch*'s Richard Cook put it like this: 'You had to be a fan, maybe even a fan's fan, if David Bowie was going to mean anything to you at all. Liking this or that record never came into it. Bowie stood for fanaticism.' A female fan simply says: 'Basically, I tell strangers I'm a Bowie fan and then clam up if they don't reply, "I'm a Bowie fan too!" I feel I've told them my station in life and everything about me in those four words.'

Bowie is both star and icon. The vast body of work he has produced, from *Ziggy* through to the comparatively mainstream films such as *Labyrinth*, has created perhaps the biggest cult in popular culture. The theoretician Umberto Eco defines a cult text as follows: 'the work must be loved, obviously, but this is not enough. It must provide a completely furnished world so that its fans can quote characters and episodes as if they were aspects of the fan's private sectarian world, a world about which one can make up quizzes and play trivia games so that the adepts of the sect recognise through each other a shared experience.' This is perhaps why Bowie is such a strong presence on the Internet, why there are still numerous fan meetings around the world, why the fan quoted above feels that saying she is a Bowie fan defines her more accurately than any statement about her gender, ethnicity or class.

The fierceness of their identification with Bowie as icon led commentators to dub his fans 'Bowie casualties' or 'Bowie freaks'. Inspired by Bowie's sense of style and cool and won over by the logic of his own career in self-re-creation, these fans have had an even greater influence on popular culture than Bowie himself. A particularly interesting feature of this identification is the way in which fans allow aspects of Bowie's personality to spread into their own, either consciously or unconsciously. Not only do they copy him stylistically, but they also copy mannerisms from videos, memorise parts of interviews and repeat them as if they were their own thoughts, and model their own likes and dislikes on his. Since Bowie took to wearing one in the mid-70s, a number of fans now also wear a cross. Asked when they became Bowie fans, many reply with a specific time and date, as if recollecting a conversion of almost religious proportions. The following extracts from letters written in 1993 by a nineteen-year-old female fan give an indication of the psychological pull the singer can have.

Ever since I've been a fan (6 years, 1 month, 28 days, 7 hours and 23 minutes exactly!), I've put all my energy into buying all kinds of Bowie-related stuff. Apart from the obvious, like records, videos, books, posters and every scrap of paper merely mentioning Bowie, I've also bought a garden gnome (as in 'The Laughing Gnome'), a little model of a Buddha (a link to Bowie's interest in Buddhism), waistcoats à la Bowie '76 and '90, plenty of wash-in, wash-out red hair dye and so on – everything to try and connect every part of my life to his basically. I've just surrounded myself in everything Bowie-esque so I can live in my own dream world . . .

I'm forever quoting things Bowie has said in interviews, copying his mannerisms and trying to develop my taste in music to identically match his ... I really can't tell whether I would have liked all those different albums had I not known Bowie liked them. I suppose I'll never know. I have, however, stopped short of drugging myself up to the eyeballs with cocaine! ...

I think the crux of the matter is that I love David Bowie and it's such a strong emotion that I can't explain anything terribly well. All my thoughts and ideas on Bowie must be the usual ones you get through loving someone ...

I would really like to be inside his head so I could piece together his whole life – the private Bowie and the public Bowie. I'd like to follow him around everywhere without me actually being there if you see what I mean – like an invisible person to just observe the proceedings without actually being part of them.

The extreme emotions felt by this fan are not at all out of the ordinary. A number of other fans recounted their fandom as if it were a calling. David Gough wrote: 'The first time I became aware of Bowie ... well, everybody remembers the first time. It's like, "Where were you when JFK got shot?" Or "The first time you touched a girl's breast?" Like some bizarre contrived initiation, or a celestial vision of the Magi, its imprint has a resonance on a subterranean level. It's personal and yet it unites us.'

Other fans have commented on how their own personalities have become strangely infected by Bowie's. One man wrote about his 'possession' in the 1980s: 'my love for Bowie grew and grew to the point not just of obsession but of actually thinking I was Bowie. I would spend whole evenings with friends conducting Bowie interviews, laughing in cockney tones and walking in what I thought was an exact replica of the great man. I drove people mad and for at least two years had absolutely no interest in anything but Bowie. People would say: "Oh, one day you'll realise how stupid you are." I'm now 28, married, with three wonderful children, but when it comes down to it I'm as obsessed as ever.'

A teenage girl recounts a similar tale: 'When I say that I copy his movements and mimic him, I mean just that. For instance, when I watch one of his movies or concert videos I copy all the moves he has made and I know a lot of the dialogue by heart. When I see him cross-legged on a couch, I copy him. Or any facial expressions he does, I try and mimic. I frown, walk, talk, sleep, eat and drink in mimic of him. I bought a guitar similar to his, I try and read all the same books he does, and I even have his top-ten list of books. I read Nietzsche and Burroughs because he reads them, and I also like any other personality he does. Tina Turner, Chuck Berry, John Lee Hooker, Tricky and Goldie are all in my record collection. I tell myself that I will listen to these until I like them.'

However, if Bowie consciously promulgated an idea in the 1970s, it was that fans could interact with the star and, by using him as a model, change themselves and find new aspects of their own personalities for themselves. Not only could they find in Bowie a way to identify and possibly come to terms with their own sexual or emotional difference, but they could also find out more about themselves. Most Bowie fans are able to exercise discernment; to use Bowie as a positive influence on their lives. 'I am perfectly comfortable with the amount of influence Bowie has had on my life,' wrote one female fan:

He may be my 'hero' (although I'm not sure it is a word I would personally subscribe to to describe my feelings), but I'm still able to sift out the good from the bad in his views and opinions. What David Bowie has encouraged me to do is to be more receptive to new ideas and experiences. I have listened to music, been places and seen things I probably never would have done if it had not been for him. For me Bowie represents more than just music, however great that is. He represents a whole different way of thinking. He does not align himself to any one group of people, religion or school of thought. I know he pinches ideas from other people, but then who doesn't? His talent is to take an idea and mix it up to make it into something new.

For this fan, Bowie is the template for a new way of being a person. In a culture which often discourages difference and encourages deference, Bowie as an icon challenges the notion that fundamental ideas are in any way valid or any more true than the mix-and-match pluralism and ambivalence he himself feels so keenly.

In the eyes of some Bowie fans, his influence was and is a totally liberating one. One male Canadian fan contends that Bowie's restlessness and low boredom threshold became a guiding principle in his life: 'Watching David's interviews, reading and quoting some of his lines at times and adapting some of the general ideas and changes made in his life made me analyse what was going on with my life. For example, the idea of when things get boring and you feel "like you've painted yourself into a corner", then that's when you should throw yourself into unfamiliar territory. I've done this socially many times. When I get bored with the same social group and find it getting monotonous I'll branch out into a group where I may know one person then expand friendships just because I enjoy learning about "new ways of thinking".'

For a good many of these fans Bowie's main influence was that he brought a sense of cool to their lives; showed them how to carry themselves in social situations and how to present a 'public' self: 'Watching Bowie physically move, as far as the way he enters a room and carries himself is concerned, helped me overcome a lack of self-confidence and basic shyness at one time. Even now, when I feel uncomfortable walking into a large group of people, I remember how David would approach the situation. Don't get me wrong – I have never had any intention of wanting to become David Bowie. He's simply the biggest influence on my life and continues to be.'

Finally, in the lives of many fans, Bowie's music has been a constant source of both solace and release. Many write that Bowie's music has helped them overcome personal tragedy. Of course, there is nothing particularly unique in this. In her article on Elvis Presley, 'Sexing Elvis', Sue Wise wrote about how Presley became for her an unmacho, feminised icon and a source of comfort and inspiration as she came to terms with her sexuality. So Bowie has often fulfilled the same healing function. In the words of one male fan: '*Low* was the soundtrack of my life. *Low* got me through college, through the death of a close friend and the loss of countless loves. I found my voice when I walked through the rain-sodden streets of derelict Liverpool terraces. I could see the post-apocalyptic vestiges of Berlin, and the Brucke Museum and the expressionist-rendered corpses of Kirchner and Dix.'

Bowie aficionados are another matter entirely. These fans are obsessed with listing and collecting, and some are commodity fetishists par excellence. Apparently, many of the old Bowie collectors from the 1970s and 1980s have sold their collections, but have been replaced by a new, younger cohort of Bowie nuts.

For these people, a rare acetate of even the most execrable song is gold dust. For in collecting circles, vinyl equals prestige, its value confirmed by its scarcity in the age of the CD. There are, of course, gradations of aficionadohood, from those who would willingly spend hundreds on one item to others who simply 'content' themselves with buying every new Bowie product – an expensive task in itself, considering the variety of formats in which each single comes.

For some fan-club organisers and traders in unofficial DVDs, tapes and memorabilia, Bowie is not simply a source of enjoyment but also of profit, and the field is highly competitive and jealous, sometimes even cut-throat. To be fair, this mini Bowie industry has grown up because of Bowie and his management's own failings. For a long period his back catalogue was in a messy state: before Ryko/EMI's rerelease programme in the early 1990s it was extremely difficult to find Bowie's work on CD (save for his 1980s EMI-America work). Up until 1993, there was no official collection of his videos either.

And much of his finest work remains undocumented. With the exception of DA Pennebaker's slightly disappointing film of the Ziggy Hammersmith show, it remains impossible to see Bowie in his glam pomp. There are official videos of his 1983 and 1987 tours only. The result is an enormous demand for both unofficial Bowie DVDs (often of shows filmed privately by fans) and bootleg CDs.

Bowie has never had an official fan club. Indeed, in 1987 he remarked: 'I'm not really a fan-club type person.' But the hard-core Bowie fans who travel the globe to see their man scour the press for information or subscribe to the many unofficial fan clubs and magazines which have been set up by Bowie fans over the years. These have varied from friendly, homespun fan-driven magazines like *The Bowie Connection* and *Zi Duang Provence* to the 'semi-official' glossies such as *Crankin' Out!* and the late, lamented *Starzone*. This gap in the market was exploited by a myriad of unofficial Bowie sites in the second half of the 1990s, in response to the demand for information which had arisen since the music press had stopped covering Bowie's activities on a regular basis. These unofficial websites were often helped along by Bowie's PR people and management, Bowie realising the importance of maintaining links with his hard-core following. In the end, BowieNet was official recognition that this fan base deserved a bona fide source of information.

Some fans go to the most extraordinary lengths to see or gain information about their idol. Some overstep the mark. Bowie fans have a reputation for being some of the most (over)zealous in the world. For some, obsessing is their very *raison d'être*. And they will seek out the strangest of memorabilia. For example, in 2005, you could bid on eBay for 'David Bowie Used Cigarettes from 1995 Son's Graduation'. That's right, three genuine Bowie fag-ends ('all tobacco removed').

Some are rewarded for their perseverance with sneak previews of unreleased material (always a Bowie fan's dream), backstage passes and exhibition and party invites. Neville Judd's story of the graciousness shown by Bowie, Coco and his publicist Alan Edwards back in 1993 eventually ended up reported in the *Sun*: 'Bowie came out and helped us with the coffee before taking us through to the studio. He cleared away some clutter from the settee in the studio and said, "Park yourselves down here, then." He put on the DAT of *Black Tie White Noise*, chatting to us all of the time, and spent the whole time saying about how they chose the songs and bits he liked in particular songs. He played the whole album and spent some time listening to what we all had to say, and for more pictures. Then it was time to go, with lots of "thank you so much" and hugs, I remember. I think he's a genius and a very nice man too. The Angelman, definitely.'

It would appear that Bowie is very caring towards his fans, despite his in-built wariness of fandom itself. For Bowie is primarily a pop star fan himself. He has always been very upfront about his influences. Ziggy Stardust, the album and the character, was so convincing because it was conceived by someone deeply knowledgeable and enthusiastic about the currency of superstardom. His career is full of homages, pastiches and appropriations and, as it has developed, Bowie has become a big fan of himself. In the 1990s every release has been marked by a sort of musical auto-cannibalisation – a slither of *Diamond Dogs* here, a dash of *Scary Monsters* there. It is this construct of pop star as pop fan which gives his music much of its sense of play and purpose, and does, of course, prefigure the rise of the DJ as performer or pop curator, each new record a collage of past favourites, a rearticulation of past obsession.

Bowie is undoubtedly the most criticised rock star of his generation. He seems to be judged by a different standard than other rock stars of his vintage. His recorded legacy is so impressive that even when a new product only falls slightly short of past glories, the assessment is normally harsh and unforgiving. It is very hard to be indifferent towards him. He elicits a very clear-cut response from people. To some he is a saviour, a mentor. To others he's a preening dilettante and a charlatan. Bowie-bashing has been a favourite sport of journalism since the Serious Moonlight tour, and up until 1993, his defenders had very little with which to fight back. But the tide began to turn in the late 1990s and, as we have seen, by the time of the release of *Reality*, Bowie records were garnering uniformly positive and almost reverential reviews.

But despite his media presence, few people would actually be able to name so much as one song from his post-*Let's Dance* catalogue. One female fan wrote: 'In many ways, I think he has become a "cult" artist, with a small but dedicated following of fans. The average person in the street will still know him as the bloke with the earrings and make-up and bright red hair. They forget that he's given all that up now. (Well, at least he had, until very recently.) I don't suppose for one moment any of them could tell you what sort of music he now plays. So while his name is constantly in the public eye (for example, on one day recently he appeared in such diverse publications as the *London Evening Standard*, *Empire* magazine and the British Rail magazine for first-class travellers), and he is acknowledged as an innovator and an artist who has influenced others, his own music seems accessible to only a tiny minority.'

'I see him as an interesting kind of fringe figure,' said John Peel in 1990. 'I know most people would disagree with that, but he's always struck me as being rather on the outskirts of things. I think that's probably to do with hearing those very Anthony Newley-influenced things that he started off with, and thinking of him more as a kind of stage singer than as a pop singer.' Bowie represented musical progress at a particular moment of rock stagnation, before punk really shook things up: 'I liked the idea of him reinventing himself because it was at a time when audiences wanted a kind of predictability, perhaps even more so than now. The one distinguishing feature about early-70s progressive rock was that it didn't progress. Before Bowie came along, people didn't want too much change.'

Now, almost all the best bands have bits of Bowie somewhere in their creative gene pool. By theatricalising rock, 'debasing' it musically, and opening it up to all sorts of musical and extra-musical influences and ideas, Bowie struck a blow for all those people who were sick to death of rockers going out on stage in denim, pretending that they were really just one of the boys and patronising their audience with songs about what they should be feeling. For a rock superstar can never be just one of the boys, as Tin Machine showed. Rock stars are meant to be weird, disquieting and discomforting. In the 1990s, groups such as Nine Inch Nails, Smashing Pumpkins, Marilyn Manson, Suede and even Blur were in the spirit of Bowie. In the Noughties, Bowie's musical DNA is to be found in the arty and intricate music of Arcade Fire and in the genre-hopping brilliance of Bowie-nut Moby.

Critics and fans, on numerous occasions, have bought Bowie's rhetoric about posing, and have concluded that he actually thinks and behaves in this way. The result, of course, is to see all of Bowie's art as mere sham; as facile and having no depth. This book has argued that this is simply not the case. Bowie is an extremely skilled singer, musician and writer. The sheer weight and enormity of his back catalogue is startling. He has at least six albums which could be regarded, even by the most mean-spirited of critics, as classics. And despite what Bowie and others have said subsequently, these albums were both critical and commercial successes. *Aladdin Sane* was the top-selling album in the UK in 1973, *Diamond Dogs* was Number 1 for a month, *Ziggy Stardust* spent nearly 200 weeks in the UK album charts, and *Hunky Dory* over 100. *Station To Station* was a huge seller in America. Even *Young Americans* and *Low* reached Number 2 in the UK.

Rather than being a poseur in reality, Bowie posed at being a poseur. Peeling away the layers of artifice reveals a body of work of considerable depth and maturity. Writer Alan Franks:

I don't think he's a pseudo-intellectual at all. I think he's interested in a wide range of subjects. He always was. I don't think he has a butterfly mind. When he wanted to learn mime he did it the proper way, through Lindsay Kemp. When it came to singing, he studied the older generation of crooners like Anthony Newley. He's a great shape-changer. I don't think the desire to change should be mistaken for flippancy or for surfing through styles. I don't think the two things should be mistaken for each other. The world is full of people who reinvent themselves, Picasso being the obvious example. Underneath there's still the same well of creativeness. I think that anyone writing Bowie off as a pseud or a poseur is in trouble. The burden of proof is always going to be on that individual, because Bowie's work is very, very substantial and at best is extremely impressive.

The rhetoric from the post-Thin White Duke Bowie has been that he's now 'normalised', more in touch with his 'real' self, more in tune with the world. But some doubt whether Bowie is actually as normalised as is made out, including journalist Paul Du Noyer: 'It often occurs to me that people in rock music are essentially quite normal individuals attempting to project themselves as something other than normal. Whereas with Bowie, the reverse seems to be the case, in that he's a genuinely weird individual who affects normality – at least, he does nowadays. Certainly since the 1980s he's come across as a regular guy. Of course, in the 1970s he made no attempt at it!'

Bowie remains a brilliant parodist and mimic, a truly protean character, and this is what makes him special. One need only look at Bowie being interviewed to realise that his speech, his phrasing, his entire personality, are subject to wild redefinitions. One male Bowie fan said: 'He will always tell you what you want to hear. He has five or six stock answers and will pluck out whichever one he feels you want to hear. You're never going to get the real deal. I've seen so many people in his face before. Like at the end of the "Be My Wife" video, he looks exactly like some guy I knew five years ago, and there's a part in the 'Cracked Actor' documentary where he says, "I've been really messed up, man," and he chuckles and he looks exactly like Kylie Minogue! It's this Greek gift he has, like a mythological gift, where you can see flashes of people appear. It's very odd. He's not a schizophrenic. Real schizos are in pain – he's not in any pain. But he can draw on different aspects of his own personality and he will present them to anyone who feels that is the part they want to see. Who will know what he's really like?'

The essence of Bowie's contribution to popular music can be found in his outstanding ability to analyse and select ideas from outside the mainstream – from art, literature, theatre and film – and to bring them inside, so that the currency of pop is constantly being changed. There had, of course, been theatrical moments in popular music before Ziggy Stardust, but no one had ever conceived of an entire rock show as a theatre production. Likewise, before Bowie's admission of bisexuality, few pop stars felt free to flout gender codes. The gay activism of a figure such as Tom Robinson in the late 1970s would have been impossible without Bowie's stand back in 1972. Bowie gave gays courage. The fact that he has seemingly reneged on the gay side of his sexuality should not mean that we should regard his 70s career as a cynical media charade. Alan Franks again: 'I think he gets an enormous pleasure out of ambiguity in almost everything he does ... Bowie's intrigued by the opposites within things, the contradictions any proposition might contain or anticipate, and sexuality is just one of those things.'

For his fans, this artificiality, this ambiguity, this impersonation, is the very stuff of what he's about. Bowie is the very antithesis of figures such as Bruce Springsteen. In 1976 he said, 'You can't go on stage and live – it's false all the way ... I can't stand the premise of going out in jeans and a guitar and looking as real as you can in front of 18,000 people. I mean, it's not normal!'

For journalist Mat Snow, Bowie's music will always be timeless because it articulates that special state of in-betweenness-adolescence. The key is in his theatricality and self-dramatisation:

Those were the records [between 1970 and 1974] which seemed to make being an adolescent so terribly exciting. This was music of and for my generation. I loved The Beatles and the Stones and Hendrix and Dylan, but essentially I felt that that had happened when I was a child. Whereas Bowie was making wonderful, exciting records right there and then. You had an artist of real stature who you could put in the same pantheon with all those 1960s people because he had a talent of that scale. He just kept doing interesting things. He was like The Beatles; every year he would change. People keep going back to those records in the 1970s. They're peculiar because they don't fade for me. They're so tied up with my adolescence, and the themes they address are in some ways so adolescent, yet I never feel embarrassed about listening to them – they still get me. There's something very rich about the way in which he addressed adolescence which resonates still with older people.

What Bowie's records have about them is this tremendous self-theatricalising, which is, of course, a tremendously adolescent thing. You know, when you're an adolescent you're always trying to find out where you stand within your peer group. You always want to make a bit of sense to yourself because you're clearly no longer a child, but you're very worried about what the adult world is about to throw at you. And, at the same time, curiously enough, as confused and depressed as you often feel in that period, this is often also the time when convention says that you should be having the most fun you've ever had in your life. I think he articulated this without putting it into so many words. There's something about the big emotional gestures he made, the combination of extreme artifice and heartfeltness – the heartfelt artifice, if you like – which resonated particularly with adolescents and those people still connected with their adolescent past: the search for identity, but the real pain behind that search.

What does the future hold for Bowie? He's now in his late fifties, so will we see Bowie the crinkly seventy-year-old up on stage singing 'The Jean Genie' to an audience of pensioners? The thought is too frightful to contemplate but, with The Rolling Stones in their sixties and still cutting something of a dash on their stadium tours, the idea is not perhaps as fanciful as it might seem.

The lives of so many people have been empowered by Bowie's enthusiasms. In 1998, he told interviewer Charlie Rose, 'I would have loved to have been like Sting and been a teacher. I really would've liked to have done that. What really gets me off is to be able to introduce people to new things. I love the feeling of introducing a new subject or something, especially to younger people, that maybe excites them, and gets them going on something, and it influences them to do something – you know, opening up some kind of world. I love taking people to art galleries and really corny things like that. I love taking them to museums as well . . . I always felt it was a gift when anybody ever took me anywhere, or showed me a new way of doing things. I always felt that that was the greatest gift that they could give me. And I love doing that back; I love showing people things like that.' But Bowie needn't worry. His artistic legacy has educated people in ways more profound than he could ever imagine.

From perfect pop ('Space Oddity'), cool Americana ('Golden Years') and soaring electronica ('Sound & Vision') to dance-floor perfection ('Let's Dance'), bittersweet irony ('The Buddha Of

Suburbia') and pulsating abjection ('Hearts Filthy Lesson'), Bowie defines human emotion (and the lack of it). At his best, he actually achieves the near impossible: he puts into sound the inexpressible and the unexplainable; he comes closer to emotions there are no words for, and makes them real. His influence has been unique within popular culture – he has permeated and altered more lives than any comparable figure.

His words of prophecy, self-realisation and self-mythologisation from way back in 1971 have guided him (and us) through the last third of the twentieth century. They will guide him into the next and will be his eternal legacy: 'So I turned myself to face me/But I've never caught a glimpse/Of how the others must see the faker/I'm much too fast to take that test'.

NOTES

Below is a brief summary of the main sources used in the writing of each chapter. Readers wishing to track down individual books, authors, records, DVDs, videos, films and other cultural bric-a-brac mentioned in the text should refer to the Documents section.

INTRO: UNCAGE THE COLOURS

The opening quote comes from an interview with Fred Hauptfuhrer in the September 1976 edition of *People* magazine.

CHAPTER 1: ELVIS IS ENGLISH 1947–1967

In this chapter, I drew on my interviews with Mike Vernon and the late Gus Dudgeon. Other ideas and quotations were drawn from a wide variety of sources, such as the excellent Radio 1 fiftieth birthday tribute to David Bowie, 'ChangesnowBowie', the academic anthology, *Visions Of Suburbia*, the work of sociologists Simon Frith and Howard Horne on the British art-school tradition in their 1987 book *Art Into Pop*, and the work of Terrence McKenna and Rogan Taylor on the relationship between pop culture, intoxicants and shamanism. I also gleaned very useful information about Bowie's unreleased work from the 1960s from Bowie fan David Priest. The unofficial Bowie website, Teenage Wildlife, was an invaluable source of information, as was the excellent Bowie website Bowiewonderworld. Bowie's quotes about family life as a youngster are from his own BowieNet web journal. Visual sources included Bowie's first ever television interview, conducted by Cliff Michelmore on the *Tonight* programme, where he appeared as the chairman of the Society For The Prevention Of Cruelty To Long-Haired Men, and the 1969 promotional film, *Love You Till Tuesday*, released on video in 1984 and on DVD in 2004. Thanks to Kevin Cann and Nicholas Pegg for their eagle-eyed detection of factual inaccuracies present in the earlier editions of the book. Kevin Cann also offered invaluable beyond-the-call-of-duty assistance and sage advice on reshaping some of the material, not only in this chapter but throughout the first third of the book.

CHAPTER 2: BECKENHAM ODDITY, 1967–1970

For this chapter I was fortunate to be able to speak to Ken Scott and Paul Buckmaster, both of whom worked with Bowie in the 1960s. An extensive email correspondence with Tony

Visconti also yielded some excellent material. I spent a lovely afternoon discussing Bowie and Bolan with John Peel at 'Peel Acres' in September 1996. A letter written by Bowie to Peel in 1969 was also made available to me. The quotes by journalist and biographer Mark Paytress on Bolan and Bowie are from private correspondence with the author. The most important secondary source for this period is ex-manager Ken Pitt's memoir, *The Pitt Report*. I also drew upon the work of Bowie biographies by Peter and Leni Gillman and Christopher Sandford. Kerry Juby's excellent edited account of Bowie through the eyes of his friends and colleagues, *In Other Words ... David Bowie*, was invaluable. The Bowie quotes are sourced from a variety of printed and Internet sources. The section on the 'Estate of Gus Dudgeon versus David Bowie' legal battle was sourced from BBC News online. Again, the help of Kevin Cann was invaluable in updating this section.

CHAPTER 3: LOOK OUT ALL YOU ROCK'N'ROLLERS, 1970–1972

Tony Visconti and Ken Scott, producers of Bowie's classic albums *The Man Who Sold The World* and *Hunky Dory*, provided invaluable information for this chapter. I also drew on interviews with Bowie's ex-producer Gus Dudgeon, and David Stopps, the manager of Friar's Aylesbury, a venue which played its part in breaking Bowie in 1971/72. Among the most useful secondary sources was Legs McNeil and Gillian McCain's *Please Kill Me: An Oral History of Punk*, providing witty anecdotal evidence for Bowie's initial reception by the Warhol crowd in 1971. My reading of Bowie's 'coming out' in 1972 was contextualised through consulting Marjorie Garber's *Vice Versa* and John Gill's *Queer Noises*. Angie Bowie's autobiography, *Backstage Passes*, was also consulted. I drew upon a wide range of contemporary press reports from the Anglo-American music press (see the documents section for references). I am once again indebted to Bowie archivist David Priest for information on Bowie's multifarious recording projects in 1970 and 1971, many of which await official release. However, the biggest debt of gratitude is owed to Kevin Cann, who made a number of invaluable suggestions on how to improve the text.

CHAPTER 4: COSMIC SURGERY, 1971–1972

The Legendary Stardust Cowboy's official website www.stardustcowboy.com is the least essential though most amusing place to start here, giving as it does a shot of the ridiculous and an idea of the sort of fringe culture Bowie was hip to. Ken Scott, John Peel and David Stopps again weighed in with some meaty exclusive contributions to this chapter. Bryan Ferry's first-hand testimony was also invaluable. Bowie fan and journalist Chris Roberts added colour to the seismic impact Ziggy had on his children (and on their terrified mums and dads), while David Priest provided some exclusive information on Bowie's cache of unreleased songs from the Trident era. Rogan Taylor imaginatively discussed Bowie's indebtedness to shamanism with me during my time at Liverpool University. For background reading on the link between Bowie and the 'black glam' of the likes of Sun Ra and George Clinton, start with John Corbett's *Extended Play*. Chris Charlesworth's 2003 essay for *Mojo* on Bowie and the media yielded some excellent material for this chapter too. However, the biggest source of new material comes from those interviewees I contacted whilst writing the booklet to be included in EMI's Thirtieth Anniversary Edition of *Ziggy Stardust*. Ken Scott, Mick Rock, Ian McCulloch, Gary Kemp and Marc Riley all provided excellent anecdotal material. My thanks go to Nigel Reeve for permission to reuse this work, which is under the copyright of EMI Records Ltd./Jones Tintoretto Entertainment Co. LLC. Finally, thanks to Kevin Cann, who prompted me to rethink many sections in this chapter.

CHAPTER 5: KILLING THE KABUKI MONSTER, 1972–1974

Ex-MainMan Dai Davies, together with Ken Scott, provided exclusive information on this period. Scott also spoke to me in detail about the making of the ground-breaking *Aladdin*

Sane, and *Pin Ups*, and on the split with Bowie. Mike Garson was a treasure-trove of info too. Bryan Ferry discussed his solo covers project, *These Foolish Things*, released the same day as Bowie's own *Pin Ups*. Chris Charlesworth, then a journalist with *Melody Maker*, provided a useful insight into the 'hostility' of Bowie's US MainMan operation. The *Nationwide* feature on Bowiemania, originally broadcast in June 1973, is an essential piece of televisual rock history and shows how Bowie, in 1973 at least, had a teen audience à la The Osmonds and David Cassidy. Those wishing to explore the cult of Bowie should look at Simon Frith's article 'The Art Of Posing'. Little factoids and trivia snippets came courtesy of Paul Kinder's excellent Bowie website, Little Wonderworld, on which you can also read a selection of the fraudulent Mirabelle diaries. Equally useful was Mike Harvey's incredibly detailed website on the early David Bowie, The Ziggy Stardust Companion. Lou Reed's quote on the making of 'A Walk On The Wild Side' comes from a BBC Radio 2 documentary, whilst Bowie's voice was recreated from a wide range of recent and not so recent interviews. Extensive correspondence with Tony Visconti provided me with exclusive material about Bowie and the *Diamond Dogs* project. However, the bulk of new material for this chapter came from my own work on the EMI reissues of *Aladdin Sane* and *Diamond Dogs* (copyright of EMI Records Ltd./Jones Tintoretto Entertainment Co. LLC).

CHAPTER 6: SHILLING THE RUBES, 1974–75

This was when Bowie finally broke America. The poetic decadence of the period was captured perfectly by Alan Yentob, whose *Cracked Actor* documentary, shot in 1974, remains one of rock music history's most important texts. Footage of Bowie's spooky appearance on *The Dick Cavett Show*, with Bowie tapping the floor with a cane, sniffing and disconnected, is available on a DVD *The Dick Cavett Show – Rock Icons*. For this chapter, I drew heavily on my exclusive interviews with Carlos Alomar, Earl Slick and Mike Garson, who played extensively with Bowie during this period, as well as on correspondence with producer Tony Visconti. My interview with Sigma Kid Patti Brett was also invaluable. Coco's interview material is sourced from a BowieNet Q&A, whilst Bowie's voice is recreated from a wide variety of sources, including 1976's excellent *David Bowie Story* from Radio 1, the 1993 update with interviews by John Tobler, and the three-part *David Bowie Story* produced in 2000 by Wise Buddha for Radio 2. Angie Bowie's *Backstage Passes* and Kerry Juby's *In Other Words . . . David Bowie* helped sketch in some contextual material. Among the many articles consulted were Lester Bang's review of Bowie's soul tour to be found in *Psychotic Reactions and Carburetor Dung*, and Robert Elm's 1985 *Face* article on the influence of Bowie's soul period entitled 'All You've Got To Do Is Win' (see Documents for details on these and other articles consulted).

CHAPTER 7: MAKING SURE WHITE STAINS, 1975–76

Interviews contained in *Creem*, *Rolling Stone*, the *NME* and *Melody Maker* give ample evidence that Bowie was somewhat confused during this period, but the real gem is Bowie's satellite interview with the late Russell Harty, recorded in November 1975 (available on the Bowie-fan trading network), which shows our man looking forward to returning home the following spring but eerily paranoid. Bowie's scary performance as song-and-dance man on *The Cher Show* is also worth tracking down (Bowie claims not to remember recording the session at all!), as is his bleary-eyed stroll through 'Golden Years' on *Soul Train*. Bowie's comment on his performance that day is taken from *The David Bowie Story*, Radio 2, 2000. The tour rehearsals for the 1976 tour, including Bowie's superior version of a song later recorded by Iggy Pop, 'Calling Sister Midnight', is now available in quite good quality from traders. Bowie's unfortunate interest in the forces of the Far Right was pieced together from articles in *Spearhead* and *Bulldog* pamphlets (and many thanks to Liz Thomson for sharing this source with me). Bowie's occultism was contextualised through a reading of, among others, Brennan's *Occult Reich*, Peter R Koenig's short essay, 'The Laughing Gnostic', and

Symond's biography of Crowley. Earl Slick, Carlos Alomar and Paul Buckmaster again provided first-hand testimony. Writers Chris Charlesworth, Paul Du Noyer and Alan Franks also made useful contributions. Gary Numan spoke freely to me about his Bowie fandom, while other eyewitness accounts of the 1976 tour, possibly Bowie's finest, come from Kevin Cann and Paul Du Noyer. Quotes from Bowie himself are drawn from a wide variety of documentary sources, including both versions of Radio 1's *The David Bowie Story* (1976, 1993), as well as television and print media interviews.

CHAPTER 8: THE NEW SCHOOL OF PRETENSION, 1976–1977

Bowie's most radical work came during a rush of creativity which produced four albums, two Bowie, two Iggy Pop. Thanks to Tony Visconti for his detailed reconstruction of the *Low* and *'Heroes'* sessions. Thanks to Carlos Alomar for his thoughts too. Eno and Schmidt's *Oblique Strategies* cards, which were being sold by Eno's Opal company in the early 1990s, provide an invaluable insight into Eno's contrary modus operandi. The best piece of investigative journalism on Bowie's Berlin phase can be found in a 1991 *Independent* article by Steve Turner, 'The Great Escape Of The Thin White Duke'. The interviews by Charles Shaar Murray ('Who Was That (Un) Masked Man?') and Michael Watts are essential pieces of reportage. For Iggy, dip into the *Mojo* article listed in the Documents section. Thanks again to David Stopps for his recollections of Iggy's gig at Friars Aylesbury. Footage of the *Marc* television show exists among Bowie fans, as do interviews given to the European media to promote *'Heroes'*. The quote by Michael Rother of Neu! is taken from his own website. Jon Savage's recollections of *Sounds'* 'New Musick' articles is sourced from my article on electronic music for a *Mojo* Special Edition. The promo for 'Be My Wife' is a study in surreal strangeness as is, in a rather different way, the duet with Bing (which is a staple of yuletide TV programmes in the UK). For Bowie's impact on youth culture style see Steve Redhead's *Football With Attitude* and Peter Yorke's *Style Wars*. For his impact on punk, see Dave Laing's *One Chord Wonders* and Jon Savage's *England's Dreaming*. *The David Bowie Story*, presented by Paul Gambaccini and first transmitted in 1993, has some excellent material on the era.

CHAPTER 9: AN AXE TO BREAK THE ICE, 1978–1982

An exclusive interview with Adrian Belew provided a wealth of information for the first half of this chapter on the 1978 world tour and Bowie's *Lodger* album. The Numanoid versus Bowie-freak face-off was a feature of the pop-culture politics of 1979. Bowie's recent comment on this 'feud' is sourced from *Q*'s 'Cash for Questions' feature in July 2000. Carlos Alomar spoke to me about *Lodger* and *Scary Monsters*, whilst Tony Visconti also contributed via email. The videos for *Lodger* and *Scary Monsters* are all essential viewing and have been collected on the anthology *David Bowie: The Best Of Bowie* (EMI, 2002). For the 1978 tour the *Musikladen* performance is often shown on music channels, but is inessential. Much better is the official footage of Bowie live in Dallas in spring 1978, available from Bowie traders. An hour-long live special from the Budokan, Tokyo, on the final leg of the tour, was also broadcast. The two performances on *The Kenny Everett Video Show* in 1979, featuring a rum 'Boys Keep Swinging' and a great acoustic version of 'Space Oddity', are worth tracking down too. The stunning live performance on *Saturday Night Live*, with Bowie ending the set in a dress, sees our man at his most telegenic. 'The David Bowie Star Special', a two-hour slot on Radio 1 from May 1979, which saw Bowie guesting as DJ, is a great snapshot of his musical obsessions of the time. The Allan Jones 'Lou Bops Bowie' story originally ran in *Melody Maker* in the spring of 1979, was relived in an *Uncut* 'Stop Me If You've Heard This One Before' section, and is still remarkably good fun. The quote from the Human League's Adrian Wright was sourced from an interview with the author for a *Mojo* special on electronic music. Finally, the cult of Bowie in the new romantic era was explored through numerous interviews and correspondence with Bowie fans themselves. Thanks to two Bowie fanzines, *Zi Duang Provence* and *Crankin' Out!*, for their help in putting me in touch with fellow fans. The Sean Mayes quotes are taken from another fanzine, *Starzone*. Sean Mayes' diary of 1978, *We Can Be Heroes*, was published in 1999.

CHAPTER 10: DAVID BOWIE: SUPERSTAR, 1982–1987

A fascinating and under-researched period of relative artistic failure actually started with a huge artistic triumph, *Let's Dance*. Nile Rodgers spoke exclusively about the making of what was Bowie's biggest album, while Tony Visconti shared his thoughts on the break-up of his friendship with Bowie, and Carlos Alomar provided information on the 'power struggle' of the mid-1980s. Producers Alan Winstanley and Hugh Padgham and guitarist Earl Slick provided much useful material for this section, as did Erdal Kizilcay. One can trace Bowie's slide into a rigid conformity throughout the mid-1980s, particularly in Chris Bohn's 1983 piece on the Serious Moonlight-era Bowie, Charles Shaar Murray's 1984 piece for the *NME*, and David Thomas's article from 1986 (see Documents for details). The official video for *Serious Moonlight* makes a slick show even slicker, but is entertaining nonetheless. The videos from the period are included in *David Bowie: The Best Of Bowie* (EMI, 2002). Footage of Bowie's Claridges press conference is available from traders and was covered at the time by *Newsnight* and *The Tube*. A curious TV programme, *North of Watford*, is also worth tracking down; part history of Milton Keynes, part assessment of Bowie and his sellout concerts at the Bowl that summer. All Bowie's films from the period have, at some stage and in various forms and formats, been officially released – *Merry Christmas, Mr Lawrence* is the only essential purchase, however. Bowie's comments come from a variety of printed and Internet sources, whilst Alomar's tribute to Tony Thompson is taken from the former's website.

CHAPTER 11: 'THE EMPEROR'S NEW CLOTHES', 1987–1990

Bowie's own 'rock'n'roll suicide' baffled critics and fans. In this section, Carlos Alomar and Erdal Kizilcay described the *Glass Spider* tour, Reeves Gabrels the Tin Machine project and Adrian Belew the preparation for *Sound + Vision*. Thanks, too, to the producer of the first Tin Machine album, Tim Palmer, for his recollections. A song suite covering many of the tracks from the first album was made with Julien Temple and is well worth seeking out. The articles by Steve Sutherland on Tin Machine, together with Adrian Deevoy's *Q* profile, provide us with the most sensible journalistic comment on Bowie's middle-age artistic collapse.

CHAPTER 12: 'IMANCIPATION', 1990–1993

Far from being fazed by Tin Machine's false start in 1989, Bowie emerged as a compact and confident hit-reproducing machine for the *Sound + Vision* tour the following year. An interview with the show's musical director, Adrian Belew, sets the scene for this section. I also spoke to Adrian for a *Mojo* Bowie Special in 2003, and some of the information in this chapter is sourced from this piece. The tour effectively killed off the Tin Machine project, which lurched slightly messily to an inconclusive end in 1992, a period discussed by Reeves Gabrels and Hugh Padgham. Carlos Alomar shed some light on the reasons behind the split. 1992 saw Bowie married and happy (his thoughts on this come from his own Internet journal). In 1993, he was back in the charts with *Black Tie White Noise*. Producer Nile Rodgers provided exclusive material about what he saw as a missed opportunity to re-establish Bowie as a mainstream superstar. The meeting of glam godfather Bowie and pretender to the crown Brett Anderson was arranged and reported on by Steve Sutherland at the *NME*. The story of the swift and unseemly demise of Bowie's US record label, Savage, was reconstructed by the author from subsequent press reports featuring on the Teenage Wildlife and Bassman Bowie websites. Producer Gus Dudgeon discussed Bowie's decision not to attend Mick Ronson's funeral. Thanks to Hanif Kureishi for his quote about his Bromley days, taken from his article on the making of *The Buddha Of Suburbia*. Mike Garson's quote about the project was drawn from a three-hour interview with the author. The official video *Tin Machine Live: Oy Vey Baby* is not essential. The *Black Tie White Noise* video, originally released in 1993, is now available on DVD. The *Sound + Vision* tour has sadly never been given an official release, although any number of privately filmed shows are available from traders, as are copies of official television broadcasts from South America and Japan. Bowie's August 1990 Milton Keynes show was broadcast in its entirety by Radio 1, together with an interview, and the following year Bowie was back at the Beeb for the first time in almost twenty years to record a session with Tin Machine. Radio 1's 1993 programme, *The David Bowie Story*, a six-part biography of Bowie presented by Paul Gambaccini with John Tobler as the interviewer, contains contributions from the likes of Ken Pitt, Carlos Alomar and Tony Visconti, and is essential listening.

CHAPTER 13: THE MUSIC IS OUTSIDE, 1994–1997

For the *Outside* project, Bowie again enriched the mainstream with some unusual cultural bric-a-brac. The history of this period was pieced together through interviews with Gabrels and Alomar, supported by critiques by Alan Franks and Paul Du Noyer. The Bertha Harris quote is taken from *The Art of Today* by Brandon Taylor. Eno's splenetic 1995 diary, entitled *A Year With Swollen Appendices* and published by Faber, provided useful information too. I also consulted a variety of art histories, philosophical ruminations and journalistic accounts of both album and tour; most of these are listed in the Documents section. Bowie's significant contribution to the art world can best be explored by visiting his official art website, www.bowieart.com. The video for 'Hearts Filthy Lesson' is essential viewing and can be found on the EMI release *David Bowie: The Best Of Bowie*. Thanks to Gary Numan for his comments on the single. *Basquiat* is now available on DVD but is inessential. No official DVDs for the *Outside* or *Earthling* tours exist, although Bowie's fiftieth birthday bash at Madison Square Gardens was filmed and broadcast. Numerous unofficial films of both tours exist in the Bowie trading network as do many good-quality audio bootleg tapes and CDs. Thanks to Reeves Gabrels, Mark Plati and Mike Garson for their thoughts on the *Earthling* album and to writer Mat Snow for his comments. A transcript of the full interview with Mark Plati about the making of *Earthling* is available on Mark's own website (see Document section for details). The Isolar market-research report was taken from Bassman's Bowie website. For Bowie at fifty, try Radio 1's tribute *ChangesnowBowie*. The Bill Buford article on Bowie's Nat Tate scam is from the *Guardian* – details in the Documents section. Bowie's quotes are from a variety of printed and Internet sources, whilst Morrissey's assessment of Bowie's appearance on the *Outside* tour is from an interview with Dave Fanning. Some of the quotes from Mark Plati and Mike Garson originally appeared in an article written by the author for a *Q/Mojo* Bowie Special in 2003. John Harris' excellent *The Last Party* also provides good material on Bowie's influence on Britpop, and includes the marvellous quote about Tony Blair at the Brit Awards.

CHAPTER 14: THE REVOLUTION WILL BE DOWNLOADED, 1998–2000

For the Bowie Bond scheme section I am indebted to Dara O'Kearney and Evan Torrie, who wrote about Bowie's finances for the Teenage Wildlife website. For Bowie's interactive activities, it's best to simply check out BowieNet itself (www.david-bowie.com), a feast for any Bowie fan. The *Nomad Soul* computer game with music composed by Bowie and Gabrels was released by Eidos in the autumn of 1999. For the *hours . . .* era, I was fortunate to have three wonderful first-hand testimonies. Mark Plati produced a detailed and fascinating account of the *hours . . .* album and its promotion. Sadly, space dictated that I could only use samples from it in this chapter. Mike Garson was again a wonderfully sympathetic interviewee (thanks to Matt Gilbert for arranging the interview). Reeves Gabrels, Bowie's cohort for a dozen years, signed off his involvement with David Bowie with his candid, and touching, contribution to this edition of the book. As readers will notice, the titles of both Chapter 14 and Chapter 11 are, in fact, Reeves' own words. This entire chapter is also indebted to the work of Bowie fan Bonnie Powell (aka Bonster), whose internet newsletter, the 'David Bowie Newsletter for the Lazy and Web-Impaired', gathers together articles, hot news and gossip in a compact and fun format. Details of how to subscribe to this newsletter can be found in the Documents section. Philip Norman's insightful article on the *hours* . . . -era Bowie, Richard Tomkin's article from the *Financial Times*, and Sean O'Hagan's critical overview from the *Observer* were all helpful (see the Documents section for details). *Velvet Goldmine* is now officially available on DVD and is worth a watch.

CHAPTER 15: '. . . LIKE STRAUSS, AT 84', 2001–2005

An interview with writer and Bowie fan Paul Du Noyer provided some very useful material for this section. The contributions by Mick Rock come from an interview with the author for a *Mojo* Bowie special in 2003. The opening description of the Bowie concert at the Olympiahalle in Munich is the author's own eyewitness account. A review of the concert by the author was posted on BowieNet in 2002. Several sections of this chapter also appeared in the aforementioned *Mojo/Q* Bowie special – a big thank you once again to Mark Blake for permission to reuse this material. Bowie's voice has been reconstructed from numerous articles in the likes of the *Guardian*, Dotmusic, *Sunday Independent*, and BBC News online. For a full list of all articles consulted, please see the Documents section.

OUTRO: UNFURL THE FLAG

The Moby quote on Bowie comes from Mute Records' official press release for the *Hotel* album in 2005. The Lou Reed tribute comes from *Rolling Stone* magazine. Many thanks in particular to writers Paul Du Noyer, Alan Franks and Mat Snow for their contributions here. The real stars of this chapter, though, are the fans who have provided me with exclusive material over the years.

DOCUMENTS

This section is not meant to be an exhaustive or definitive guide to Bowie's work or to work on Bowie. Rather, it is a guide to what readers who have had their curiosity piqued can do if they want to explore Bowie further.

SECTION 1: READING

Books on Bowie

One of the best books on David Bowie was written long ago and is now sadly out of print. Charles Shaar Murray and Roy Carr's *David Bowie: An Illustrated Record* (Proteus, 1981) marries sharp, investigative journalism with insight and wit. Kevin Cann's *David Bowie: A Chronology* is full of useful anecdotes and incredibly detailed. Nicholas Pegg's *The Complete David Bowie* is an astonishingly detailed reference book and justifiably highly regarded by Bowie fans. Sean Mayes' memoir, *We Can Be Heroes: Life On Tour With David Bowie*, provides a fascinating insight into the *Stage* tour from the much-missed keyboard player. Lavishly illustrated and perceptive, *Bowiestyle*, written by Mark Paytress and co-written by Steve Pafford, is an essential purchase for the hard-core Bowie fan. *Blood And Glitter*, a brilliant collection of photos of the glam era by Mick Rock, defines the period through images as well as anyone has ever done in print. Philippe Auliac's *David Bowie – Passenger* is a fascinating photo-documentary of the period.

Of the major biographies, the Gillmans' *Alias David Bowie* has much to say about Bowie's ancestry, though markedly less about his work and its meaning; it remains, however, a well-crafted and important book. *Stardust*, by MainMan-insider Tony Zanetta and journalist Henry Edwards, contains one man's often fascinating view of the media circus, whilst the more recent *Loving the Alien*, by renowned rock journalist Christopher Sandford, is typically well written, though somewhat humourless, and paints Bowie in a rather unsympathetic light. *The Bowie Companion*, edited by Elizabeth Thomson and David Gutman, is an anthology of important articles up to 1992. Kerry Juby's *In Other Words . . . David Bowie* and the *Starzone Interviews*, edited by David Currie, collect together interviews on Bowie from the mid-1980s.

At the time of writing, at least five other David Bowie books are about to hit the shelves. Nicholas Stevenson's as yet untitled book promises to be an in-depth cultural analysis and is due to be published by Polity in January 2006. Before then comes *Beaming David Bowie*, a memoir about the digital age by Marc John, *David Bowie: The Shirt He Wears*, a 'psychological study of Bowie's life and art' by Jonathan Richards, and the trade version of

David Bowie and Mick Rock's book, *Moonage Daydream: The Life And Times of Ziggy Stardust*. Finally, in what looks like being a real treat for Bowie fans, Kevin Cann has written a book on Bowie's early career up to 1974 (publication date to be announced).

All places of publication London, except where stated.

Auliac, Philippe, *David Bowie – Passenger*, Sound And Vision Editions, 2004.

Bowie, Angie, and Carr, Patrick, *Backstage Passes: Life On The Wild Side With David Bowie*, Orion, 1993.

Bowie, David and Rock, Mick, *Moonage Daydream: the Life And Times of Ziggy Stardust*, Genesis Publications, 2002.

Buckley, David, *The Complete Guide To the Music of David Bowie*, Omnibus, 1996.

Buckley, David, *David Bowie: The Complete Guide To the Music*, Revised Edition Omnibus, 2004.

Cann, Kevin, *David Bowie: A Chronology*, Vermilion, 1983.

Carr, Roy, and Murray, Charles Shaar, *David Bowie: An Illustrated Record*, Eel Pie, 1981.

Charlesworth, Chris, *David Bowie Profile*, Proteus, 1981.

Currie, David, *The Starzone Interviews*, Omnibus, 1985.

Currie, David, *David Bowie: Glass Idol*, Omnibus, 1987.

Flippo, Chet, David Bowie's *Serious Moonlight*, Sidgwick & Jackson, 1984.

Gillman, Peter and Leni, *Alias David Bowie*, New English Library, 1987.

Hopkins, Jerry, *Bowie*, Corgi, 1986.

John, Marc, *Beaming David Bowie*, Marc John, 2005.

Juby, Kerry, ed., *In Other Words . . . David Bowie*, Omnibus, 1986.

Matthew-Walker, Robert, *David Bowie: Theatre of Music*, Kensal Press, Buckinghamshire, 1985.

Mayes, Sean, *We Can Be Heroes: Life on Tour with David Bowie*, Music Sales Ltd, 1999.

Miles, Barry, *Bowie In His Own Words*, Omnibus, 1980.

Miles, Barry and Charlesworth, Chris, *David Bowie: Black Book*, Omnibus, 1988.

Paytress, Mark, *Ziggy Stardust*, Schirmer Books, 1998.

Paytress, Mark and Pafford, Steve, *Bowiestyle*, Omnibus, 2000.

Pegg, Nicholas, *The Complete David Bowie*, Revised and Expanded Third Edition, Reynolds and Hearn, 2004.

Pitt, Kenneth, *Bowie: The Pitt Report*, Omnibus, 1985.

Richards, Jonathan, *David Bowie: The Shirt He Wears*, Helter Skelter, 2005.

Rock, Mick, *Blood And Glitter: Glam – An Eyewitness Account*, Visionon Publishing, 2001.

Sandford, Christopher, *Loving The Alien*, Little, Brown, 1996.

Santos-Kayda, Myriam, *David Bowie: Live In New York City*, foreword by David Bowie, Power House Books, 2003.

Thompson, Dave, *Moonage Daydream*, Plexus, 1987.

Thomson, Elizabeth, and Gutman, David, eds., *The Bowie Companion*, Macmillan, 1993.

Tremlett, George, *The David Bowie Story*, Futura, 1974.

Tremlett, George, *David Bowie: Living On The Brink*, Century, 1996.

Weird And Gilly, *Mick Ronson: The Spider With The Platinum Hair*, Independent Music Press, 2003.

Welch, Chris, *Changes: The Stories Behind Every David Bowie Song 1970–1980*, Carlton, 1999.

Welch, Chris, *David Bowie: We Can Be Heroes: The Stories Behind Every David Bowie Song 1970–1980*, Thundermouth Press, 1999 (US version of previous book).

Zanetta, Tony, and Edwards, Henry, *Stardust: the Life and Times of David Bowie*, Michael Joseph, 1986.

Articles on Bowie

The Bowie Companion (see above) is a rich source. Below is a list of the most important articles consulted in the writing of the text. Since the arrival of the Internet, some of these reports have been sourced from transcriptions on websites of radio interviews and online news stories.

Anon, 'A Message From Dave', *Melody Maker*, 26 February 1966.

Anon, 'Don't Condemn Pop', *Spearhead*, 150, April 1981.

Anon, 'Isolar', on Bassman Bowie website, 1996.

Anon, An Interview with Michael Rother of Neu!, */www.junkmedia.org*

Anon, Interview with Trevor Bolder, *Let It Rock*,http://dmme.net/interviews/bolder.html, October 2003.

Anon, 'Bowie Dismisses Kylie And Robbie', BBC News Online, 5 July 2002.

Anon, 'Bowie Asks Fans To Bootleg Songs', BBC News Online, 26 April 2004.

Anon, 'Bowie Leads Year's Tour Earnings', BBC News Online, 16 July 2004.

Aizlewood, John, 'Look Back In Pleasure', *Evening Standard*, 3 October 2002.

Aspden, Peter, 'Angst Back In Fashion', *Financial Times*, 27–28 December 1997.

Bailey, Doug, 'Jarvis and Bowie Light Up', *Big Issue*, 8 December 1997.

Bebbington, David, 'David Bowie And The Beckenham Free Festival At Croydon Road', West Beckenham Residents Association, www.wbecra.com.

Bohn, Chris, 'Merry Christmas, Mr Bowie', *NME*, 16 April 1983.

BowieNet, Q&A with Coco Schwab, www.davidbowie.com/bowie/specialFeatures/coco, 27 June–13 July 2001.

Bowie, David and Gervais, Q&A, the *Observer*, 21 September 2003.

Brazier, Chris, 'Bowie: Beauty Before Outrage', *Melody Maker*, 4 September 1976.

Bream, Jon, 'Post-Flu, David Bowie's Back In Action And Ready For His First-Ever Solo Date In Minneapolis', *Minneapolis Star Tribune*, 9 January 2004.

Brown, Gary, 'Monster Maestro', *Record Mirror*, 9 August 1980.

Buckley, David, 'Sleeve Notes for the Thirtieth Anniversary Edition of *The Rise And Fall Of Ziggy Stardust And The Spiders From Mars*, EMI Records Jones/Tintoretto Entertainment Co., LLC, 2002.

Buckley, David, 'Sleeve Notes for the Thirtieth Anniversary Edition of *Aladdin Sane*, EMI Records Jones/Tintoretto Entertainment Co., LLC, 2003.

Buckley, David, 'Renaissance Man', *Loving The Alien, Bowie Mojo Special Limited Edition*, Emap, 2003.

Buckley, David, 'Reborn Again', *Loving The Alien, Bowie Mojo Special Limited Edition*, Emap, 2003.

Buckley, David, 'Sleeve Notes for the Thirtieth Anniversary Edition of *Diamond Dogs*, EMI Records Jones/Tintoretto Entertainment Co., LLC, 2004.

Buckley, David, 'New Music Night And Day', *Q/Mojo Special Edition, Depeche Mode + The Story of Electro-Pop – When Machines Ruled The World*, Emap, 2005.

Buckley, David, 'Empire State Human', *Q/Mojo Special Edition, Depeche Mode + The Story of Electro-Pop – When Machines Ruled The World*, Emap, 2005.

Buford, Bill, 'That Nat Tate Hoax', the *Guardian*, 10 April 1998.

Charlesworth, Chris, 'Watch That Man', *Loving The Alien, Bowie Mojo Special Limited Edition*, Emap, 2003.

Cocks, Jay, 'David Bowie Rockets Onwards', *Time*, 18 July 1983.

Cohen, D.R., 'David Bowie Eats His Young', *Rolling Stone*, 25 December 1980.

Cohen, Howard, 'Hunky Dory: David Bowie Content With His 'Reality'', *The Miami Herald*, 8 September 2003.

Coleman, Ray, 'A Star Is Born', *Melody Maker*, 15 July 1972.

Collis, Clark, 'Dear Superstar', *Blender*, Issue 8, www.blender.com, 2002.

Cook, Richard, 'Ziggy Popped', *Punch*, 23 March 1990.

Cooper, Tim, 'Star Man', the *Observer*, 9 June 2002.

Cooper, Tim, 'Thirty Years On, Bowie Brings Back The Stardust', *Evening Standard*, 3 October 2002.

Cooper, Tim, 'I've Beaten Vices Thanks To My Daughter', *Evening Standard*, 20 November 2003.

Copetas, Craig, 'Beat Godfather Meets Glitter MainMan', *Rolling Stone*, 28 February 1974.

Costa, Maddy, 'David Bowie: Live Review, Royal Festival Hall', the *Guardian*, 1 July 2002.

Crowe, Cameron, 'Ground Control To Davy Jones', *Rolling Stone*, 12 February 1976.

Currie, David, 'Tony Visconti: a Producer's Tale', *Starzone* 11, 1984.

Davies, Andrew, 'Starman Lost in Cyberspace', *Big Issue*, 11–17 January 1999.

Davies, Stephen, 'Performance: David Bowie, Radio City Music Hall', *Rolling Stone*, 29 March 1973.

Deevoy, Adrian, 'Boys Keep Swinging', *Q*, June 1989.

Derogatis, Jim, 'David Bowie's New Scary Monsters', *Chicago Sun-Times*, 9 January 2004.

Du Noyer, Paul, 'Please God Let It Be Me', *Q*, April 1990.

Du Noyer, Paul, 'Contact', *Mojo*, 104, July 2002.

Du Noyer, Paul, 'Do You Remember *Your* First Time?', *Word*, 9 November 2003.

Ellen, Barbara, 'David Is A Goliath', 7 July 2002.

Elms, Robert, 'All You Have To Do Is Win', *The Face*, May 1985.

Fanning, Dave, Interview with Morrissey on *2FM*, 4 November 2002.

Ferris, Tim, 'David Bowie In America – The Iceman, Having Calculated, Cometh', *Rolling Stone*, 9 November 1972.

Finn, D.E., 'Moon and Gloom: David Bowie's Frustrated Messianism', *Commonweal*, 1, 1983.

Flynn, Paul, 'David Sticks The Boot In', the *Guardian*, 27 April 2004.

Franks, Alan, 'Keeping Up With The Jones', *The Times magazine*, 9 September 1995.

Fricke, David, 'The Dark Soul of a New Machine', *Rolling Stone*, 15 June 1989.

Frith, Simon, 'Only Dancing: David Bowie Flirts with the Issues' (1983), in McRobbie, A., ed., *Zoot-Suits and Second-Hand Dresses: an Anthology of Fashion and Music*, Basingstoke: MacMillan Education, 1989.

Gabrels, Reeves, 'Letter to the editor', *Sydney Morning Herald* reprinted in Bonster's *David Bowie Newsletter for the Lazy and Web-Impaired,* June 2002.

Gallagher, William, 'Bowie Thrills The Crowd With Cinema Gig', BBC News Online, 9 September 2003.

Gillman, Peter, 'Going Straight, A New Role For The Rebel', *You*, (*Mail On Sunday magazine*), 6 April 1986.

Glaister, Dan, the *Guardian*, 19 February 1996.

Hauptfuhrer, Fred, 'Rock's Space Oddity, David Bowie Falls To Earth And Finds His Feet In Film' *People Magazine*, September 1976.

Hilburn, Robert, 'Bowie: Now I'm A Businessman', *Melody Maker*, 28 February 1976.

Holden, Stephen, 'Rock Kings, Drag Queens: a Common Strut', *New York Times*, 1 June 1998.

Horkins, Tony, 'Golden Years', *Rock On CD*, 1992.

Hughs, Tim, 'Bowie For A Song' (1970), reprinted in Elizabeth Thomson, and David Gutman, eds., *The Bowie Companion*, 1993.

Ives, Brian and Bottomley, C., 'David Bowie: Reality Bites', VH1.com, 2003.

Jackson, Blair, 'Recording Vocals', *Mix*, 1 November 2002.

Jerome, J., 'A Session with David Bowie', *Life*, December 1992.

Jones, Allan, 'The Great White Hope Versus The Thin White Duke', *Melody Maker*, 21 April 1979.

Jones, Allan, 'Stop Me If You've Heard This One Before', the above *Melody Maker* story relived, *Uncut*, May 1999.

Jones, Cliff, David Bowie/Nine Inch Nails, Meadowlands Arena live review, *Mojo*, 25 December 1995.

Jones, Dylan, *The Times*, 9 October 1994.

Kane, Peter, 'Bowie: Cash For Questions', *Q*, 166, July 2000.

Kirkup, Martin, Review of *Diamond Dogs*, *Sounds*, 4 May 1974.

Koenig, Peter R., 'The Laughing Gnostic', Internet essay.

Kureishi, Hanif, 'The Boy in the Bedroom' (unpublished article), 1993.

Laing, Dave, and Frith, Simon, 'Bowie Zowie', *Let It Rock*, June 1973.

Loeffler, Mark, 'Designer Remedies For Bowie's Theatre Bug', *Theatre Crafts*, 21 November 1987.

Maidment, Kevin, *Heathen* Review, Amazon.co.uk, June 2002.

Malins, Steve, 'Duke Of Hazard', *Vox*, October 1995.

MacKay, Patricia, 'Serious – and Stunning – Moonlight', *Theatre Crafts*, 18 January 1984.

MacKay, Patricia, 'Surrealism and Di Chirico: Mark Ravitz Designs', *Theatre Crafts*, 18 January 1984.

Mackinnon, Angus, 'The Elephant Man Cometh and Other Monstrous Tales', *NME*, 13 September 1980.

McNeill, Phil, 'The Axeman Cometh . . .', *Wire*, 92, October 1991.

Membery, York, 'Bowie Sued for '1m by Major Tom producer', the *Guardian*, 9 June 2002.

Mendelsohn, John, 'David Bowie? Pantomime Rock?' *Rolling Stone*, 79, 1 April 1971.

Moeller, Sean, 'Ziggy Stardust Grows Up: A Q&A with David Bowie', *Quad-City Times Newspaper Online*, 12 May 2004.

Mohan, Dominic, David Bowie Interview on *Virgin Radio*, 15 June 2003.

Morgan, J., Review of *Stage*, *Creem*, January 1979.

Mulvey, John, *Heathen* review, *Dotmusic*, 7 June 2002.

Mulvey, John, *Reality* review, *Dotmusic*, 15 September 2003.

Murray, Charles Shaar, 'Sermon From The Savoy', *NME*, 29 September 1984.

Murray, Charles Shaar, 'David Bowie: Who Was That (Un) Masked Man?', *NME*, 12 November 1977, reprinted in *Shots From The Hip*, Penguin, 1991.

Murray, Charles Shaar, 'And The Singer's Called Dave . . .', *Q*, 61, 1991.

Murray, Charles Shaar, 'The Man Who Fell To Earth', *Arena*, May/June, 1993.

Norman, Philip, 'No Hiding Face', *Sunday Times*, 19 September 1999.

Odell, Michael, 'Clash Of The Titans', *Q*, 207, October 2003.

O'Grady, Anthony, 'Dictatorship: the Next Step?', *NME*, 23 August 1975.

O'Hagan, Sean, 'Major Tom.com', *Observer*, 16 January 2000.

Orshoski, Wes, 'Bowie Gets Back To 'Reality'', *Billboard*, 6 October 2003.

Paphides, Peter, 'Cyberspace Oddity', *Time Out*, December 1998.

Parsons, Tony, Bowie interview, *Arena*, May/June, 1993.

Paulson, Diana (transcriber), 'Chat@Eden Online' (a David Bowie webchat), 2 February 2000.

Penman, Ian, 'What Was That All About?', *Guardian*, 7 November 1996.

Petridis, Alexis, 'A Star Is Reborn', the *Guardian*, 31 May 2002.

Petridis, Alexis, 'David Bowie: Odeon Cinema, Brighton', the *Guardian*, 10 September 2003.

Pond, Steve, 'Beyond Bowie', *Live!*, March 1997.

Quantick, David, 'Mr Universe' [*Heathen* album review], *Q*, 191, June 2002.

Reed, Lou, 'Walk On The Wild Side', Sold On Song – Song Library, BBC Radio 2.

Reed, Lou, 'David Bowie', *Rolling Stone*, 946, 15 April 2004.

Rice, Anne, 'David Bowie and the End of Gender', *Vogue*, 173, November 1983.

Roberts, Chris, 'David Bowie with La La La Human Steps', *Melody Maker*, 9 July 1988.

Robinson, Lisa, 'Clockwork Orange In Black & White', *Creem*, May 1976.

Rock, Mick, 'David Bowie Is Just Not Serious', *Rolling Stone*, 8 June 1972.

Rook, Jean, 'Bowie Reborn', *Daily Express*, 14 February 1979.

Sandall, Robert, 'Demolition Man', *The Times*, 1995.

Sanneh, Kelefa, 'A Regular Guy And Friends, Just Touring', *New York Times*, 2 August 2002.

Savage, Jon, 'The Gender Bender', *the Face*, 7 November 1980.

Shrorer, Steve, and John Lifflander, 'David Bowie: Spaced Out in the Desert', Creem, December 1975.

Simpson, Dave, 'Ground Control', the *Guardian*, 5 June 2002.

Simpson, Dave, 'David Bowie Live Review, Manchester Arena', the *Guardian*, 18 November 2003.

Simpson, Kate, Interview, *Music Now!*, 1969.

Simpson, Richard, 'Bowie Feeling Hunky Dory', *Evening Standard*, 28 July 2004.

Sinclair, David, 'A Star Who Will Never Fall To Earth', *The Times*, 1 July 2002.

Sinclair, David, 'All The Old Dude Had, He's Still Got', *The Times*, 18 November 2003.

Sischy, Ingrid, Bowie interview, *Interview*, September 1995.

Sklar, Rachel, 'Bowie Motivated By Fatherly Fear', *Canadian Press*, 5 June 2002.

Sloan, Billy, 'I Missed My Son Growing Up . . . I'm Not Going To Make The Same Mistake With My Daughter', *Scottish Sunday Mail*, 23 November 2003.

Snow, Mat, 'Mr Bowie Changing Trains', *Mojo*, October 1994.

Spencer, Neil, 'Space Invader', *Uncut*, August 1998.

Stout, Alan K., 'Bowie Knifes Into NEPA', *The Times* leader, 26 May 2004.

Stout, Gene, 'Gettin' Ziggy wit it? No, Bowie Builds His New Set Lists Around The Here And Now', *Seattle Post-Intelligencer*, 12 April 2004.

Sullivan, Caroline, 'Kitsch 'n' Synch Adds Up To Art', the *Guardian*, 16 November 1995.

Sullivan, Caroline, 'David Bowie, Reality', the *Guardian*, 12 September 2003.

Sutherland, Steve, 'Metallic KO', *Melody Maker*, 27 May 1989.

Sutherland, Steve, 'Tin Machine: Metal Gurus', *Melody Maker*, 1 July 1989.

Sutherland, Steve, 'Tin Machine: The Industrial Blues', *Melody Maker*, 8 July 1989.

Sutherland, Steve, 'Bowie: Boys Keep Swinging', *Melody Maker*, 24 March 1990.

Sutherland, Steve, 'Bowie, Ch-Ch-Ch-Ch-Changes?', *Melody Maker*, 31 March 1990.

Sutherland, Steve, 'One Day, Son, All This Could Be Yours . . .', *NME*, 20 March 1993.

Sutherland, Steve, 'Alias Smiths and Jones', *NME*, 27 March 1993.

Sweeting, Adam, 'The Star Who Fell To Earth', the *Guardian*, 3 and 4 March 1990.

Sweeting, Adam, 'Tin Machine Live Review', the *Guardian*, 12 November 1991.

Thomas, D., 'Bowie's Profile', *Extra*, 9 March 1986.

Thompson, Ben, *Independent*, 28 March 1996.

Tomkins, Richard, 'Bowie – The Man Who Sold the Web', *Financial Times* (on-line edition), 28 January 2000.

Trainer, Adam, 'Well, I Wouldn't Buy The Merchandise: David Bowie As Postmodern Auteur', *Sense Of Cinema*, August 2003.

Turner, Steve, 'The Great Escape Of The Thin White Duke', *Independent*, 4 May 1991.

Tyler, A., 'David Bowie', *Superpop – A Disc Special*, 1973.

Verna, Paul, 'New York Metro', *Mix*, 1 September 2003.

Walker, Andrew, 'David Bowie: Banking on Success', BBC News Online, January 2000.

Watts, Michael, 'Oh You Pretty Thing', *Melody Maker*, 22 January 1972.

Watts, Michael, 'Confessions of an Elitist', *Melody Maker*, 18 February 1978.

Welch, Chris, 'Beckenham Arts Lab', *Melody Maker*, September 1969.

Wells, Steven, 'The Artful Codger', *NME*, 25 November 1995.

White, Timothy, 'David Bowie: a Fifteen Year Odyssey of Image and Imagination', *Musician*, 55, May 1983. Reprinted in *Rock Lives*, Omnibus, 1991.

Wild, David, 'Bowie's Wedding Album', *Rolling Stone*, 21 January: 14, 1993.

Wooley, Charles, 'Bowie And Me', Transcript of an Interview with David Bowie on Channel 9's *Sixty Minutes*, 28 July 2002. (http://sixtyminutes.ninemsn.com.au/sixtyminutes/stories/2002 . . . 07 . . . 28/stor y . . . 650.asp)

542

Yates, Paula, 'Bob, Blitz & Bowie', *Record Mirror*, 18 September 1979.
Yates, Robert, 'Back On The Outside Looking In', the *Guardian*, 29 September 1995.

Bowie Fanzines/Tributes

There have been any number of Bowie fanzines since the 1970s, and their usefulness in promoting the work of Bowie and in helping fans to access information has been vital. With the institution of BowieNet and the existence of dozens of Bowie fan websites, most of the fan-based activity is no longer taking place in the print media. However, three UK Bowie fanzines are worth further investigation: *Starzone*, edited by David Currie (glossy and competent, featuring numerous insightful interviews with Bowiecentric people. Ran from 1981 to 1987); *Zi Duang Provence*, edited by Dean Baalam (idiosyncratic, homespun, but intensely enthusiastic fanzine. Ran from 1987 to 1993); and *Crankin'Out!*, edited by Steve Pafford (glossy, professional fanzine).

In the US one of the longest-lived fanzines running in the late 1980s and early 1990s was *Rumours and Lies and Stories They Made Up*, edited by Mike Alford (again homespun but full of information).

Fan groupings exist throughout the world and celebrate Bowie at concerts, exhibitions, conventions and meetings. Currently the biggest is probably The Voyeur (http://go.to/bowiefanclub). Dating back to 1982, it claims to be the longest-running Bowie fan club in the world. Based in the Netherlands, it provides a newsletter three times a year.

The Cult of Bowie and Pop Fandom

One new book is definitely worth investigating. Dave Thompson's *To Major Tom: The Bowie Letters* tells, in epistolary form, the fictional story of one David Bowie fan, and comes highly recommended. Also well worth reading is broadcaster Mark Radcliffe's mildly Bowie-obsessed and very funny memoir, *Showbusiness*.

Frith, Simon, 'The Art Of Posing', in *Music For Pleasure*, Frith, S., ed., Oxford: Blackwell, 1988.

Hebdidge, Dick, *Subculture: The Meaning Of Style*, Methuen, 1979.

Jenson, J., 'Fandom As Pathology: The Consequences of Characterization', in Lewis, L.A., ed., *The Adoring Audience: Fan Culture and Popular Media*, Routledge, 1992.

Kureishi, Hanif, *The Buddha of Suburbia*, Faber, 1990.

Miller, Harland, *Slow Down Arthur, Stick To Thirty*, Fourth Estate, 2000.

Radcliffe, Mark, *Showbusiness: Diary Of A Rock 'N' Roll Nobody*, Hodder & Stoughton, 1998.

Redhead, Steve, *Football With Attitude*, Manchester: Wordsmith, 1991.

Sampson, Kevin, *Awaydays*, Jonathan Cape, 1998.

Taylor, I, and Wall, D., 'Beyond Skinheads: Comments on the Emergence and Significance of the Glamrock Cult', in Mungham, G. and Pearson, G., eds, *Working Class Youth Culture*, Routledge: 105–123, 1976.

Thompson, Dave, *To Major Tom: The Bowie Letters*, Sanctuary, 2002.

Thorne, T, *Fads, Fashions and Cults*, Bloomsbury, 1993.

Vermorel, Fred, and Judy, *Starlust: The Secret Fantasies of Fans*, Comedia, 1985.

Vermorel, Fred, and Judy, *Fandemonium!: the Book of Fan Cults and Dance Crazes*, Omnibus, 1989.

Willis, Paul, *Profane Culture*, Routledge, 1978.

Willis, Paul, *Common Culture*, Buckingham: Open University Press, 1990.

York, Peter, *Style Wars*, Sidgwick & Jackson, 1980.

Bangs, Lester, *Psychotic Reactions & Carburetor Dung: Literature as Rock'n'Roll, Rock'n'Roll as Literature*, Greil Marcus, ed., Mandarin, 1991.

Bracewell, Michael, *England Is Mine: Pop Life in Albion from Wilde to Goldie*, Harper Collins, 1997.

Chambers, Iain, *Urban Rhythms*, MacMillan, 1985.

Corbett, John, *Extended Play: Sounding Off From John Cage To Dr. Funkenstein*, Durham, North Carolina: Duke University Press, 1994.

Easlea, Daryl, *Everybody Dance: Chic and The Politics of Disco*, Helter Skelter, 2004.

Eno, Brian, and Schmidt, Peter, *Oblique Strategies* (boxed set of over 500 cards), Leigh-on-Sea: Opal Information, 1975.

Eno, Brian, *A Year With Swollen Appendices: Brian Eno's Diary*, Faber & Faber, 1996.

Frith, Simon, *Sound Effects: Youth, Leisure, and the Politics of Rock'n'Roll*, New York: Pantheon, 1981.

Frith, Simon, 'Essay review: Rock Biography', *Popular Music 3: Producers and Markets*, in Middleton, R., and Horn, D. eds. Cambridge: Cambridge University Press, 1983.

Frith, Simon, *Art Into Pop* (with Howard Horne), Methuen, 1987.

Frith, Simon, 'After Word. Making Sense of Video: Pop into the Nineties' in *Music For Pleasure*, Oxford, 1988.

Frith, Simon, 'The Suburban Sensibility in British Rock and Pop', in *Visions Of Suburbia*, ed., Roger Silverstone, 1997.

Frith, Simon, and McRobbie, Angela, 'Rock and Sexuality' (1978), in *On Record: Rock, Pop and the Written Word*, Frith, S., and Goodwin, A., eds., Routledge, 1990.

Gill, John, *Queer Noises, Male and Female Homosexuality in Twentieth-Century Music*, Cassell, 1995.

Grant, Linda, 'Cut And Thrust', *Guardian*, 5 February 1996.

Harris, John, *The Last Party: Britpop, Blair And The Demise of English Rock*, Fourth Estate, 2003.

Herman, Gary, *Rock'n'Roll Babylon*, Plexus, 1994.

Hill, Dave, *Designer Boys and Material Girls*, Poole: Blandford Press, 1986.

Hipgnosis, and Dean, R., *The Album Cover Album*, Dragon's World, 1977.

Holdstein, Deborah, 'Music Video: Messages and Structure', *Jump/Cut*, 1, 1984.

Hoskyns, Barney, *Glam! Bowie, Bolan and the Glitter Rock Revolution*, Faber & Faber, 1998.

Hunter, Ian, *Diary of a Rock-and-Roll Star*, Independent Music Press, 1996 (1974).

Jones, Cliff, and Paul Trynka, 'Whatever Turns You On' (Iggy Pop special), *Mojo*, 29, April 1996.

Keil, Charles, *Urban Blues*, Chicago: University of Chicago Press, 1966.

Laing, Dave, *One Chord Wonders: Power and Meaning in Punk Rock*, Milton Keynes: Open University Press, 1985.

Longhurst, Brian, *Popular Music and Society*, Cambridge: Polity, 1995.

McDonald, Ian, *Revolution In The Head: the Beatles' Records and the Sixties*, Fourth Estate, 1994.

McNeil, Legs, and Gillian McCain, *Please Kill Me: The Uncensored Oral History Of Punk*, Abacus, 1997.

Marcus, Greil, *Lipstick Traces*, Secker & Warburg, 1989.

Melly, George, *Revolt Into Style: The Pop Arts in the 50s and 60s*, Oxford: Oxford University Press, 1970 (1989).

Miller, James, *Flowers In The Dustbin: the Rise of Rock and Roll, 1947–1977*, Fireside, 1999.

Moore, Alan F., *Rock: The Primary Text*, Buckingham: Open University Press, 1993.

Murray, Charles Shaar, *Crosstown Traffic: Jimi Hendrix and Post-War Pop*, Faber & Faber, 1989.

Needs, Kris, *Needs Must: A Very Rock'n'Roll Life Story*, Virgin, 1999.

O'Brien, Lucy, *She Bop: The Definitive History of Women in Pop*, Penguin, 1995.

Paytress, Mark, *Twentieth Century Boy: The Marc Bolan Story*, Sidgwick and Jackson, 1992.

Paytress, Mark, *Bolan: The Rise And Fall Of A Twentieth Century Superstar*, Omnibus Press, 2002.

Peebles, Andy, *The Lennon Tapes*, BBC Publications, 1981.

Redhead, Steve, *Football With Attitude*, 1991.

Reynolds, Simon, *Blissed Out: The Raptures of Rock*, Serpent's Tail, 1990.

Reynolds, Simon, and Press, Joy, *The Sex Revolts: Gender, Rebellion and Rock'n'Roll*, Serpent's Tail, 1995.

Rimmer, Dave, *Like Punk Never Happened: Culture Club and the New Pop*, Faber & Faber, 1985.

Rimmer, Dave, *New Romantics – The Look*, Omnibus Press, 2003.

Savage, Jon, 'Androgyny', *The Face*, June, 38, 1983.

Savage, Jon, 'Humpty Dumpty and the New Authenticity', *The Face*, July 1985.

Savage, Jon, 'The Enemy Within: Sex, Rock and Identity', in Frith, Simon, ed., *Facing The Music*, New York: Pantheon, 1988.

Savage, Jon, 'The Age of Plunder' (1983), in McRobbie, A., ed., *Zoot-Suits and Second-Hand Dresses: an Anthology of Fashion and Music*, Basingstoke: MacMillan Education, 1989.

Savage, Jon, 'Tainted Love', in Tomlinson, A., ed., *Consumption, Identity and Style*, Routledge, 1990.

Savage, Jon, *England's Dreaming, Sex Pistols and Punk Rock*, Faber & Faber, 1991.

Savage, Jon, and Kureishi, Hanif, eds., *The Faber Book Of Pop*, 1995.

Savage, Jon, *Time Travel: From The Sex Pistols To Nirvana: Pop, Media And Sexuality, 1977–96*, Chatto & Windus, 1996.

Shore, Martin, *The Rolling Stone Book of Rock Video*, Sidgwick & Jackson, 1984.

Sinclair, Dave, *Rock On CD: The Essential Guide*, Kyle Cathie, 1992.

Street, John, *Rebel Rock: the Politics of Popular Music*, Oxford: Blackwell, 1986.

Sutherland, Steve, *NME Originals – Glam*, IPC Ignite! 2004.

Tamm, Eric, *Brian Eno: His Music and the Vertical Color of Sound*, Faber & Faber, 1990.

Media, Society, Ideas

The following is a list of predominantly non-music books and articles which helped provide the cultural context for the book.

Ansell Pearson, Keith, ed., *Deleuze and Philosophy: the Difference Engineer*, Routledge, 1997.

Ansell Pearson, Keith, *Viroid Life: Perspectives on Nietzsche and the Transhuman Condition*, Routledge, 1997.

Bockris, Victor, *Warhol*, Harmondsworth: Penguin, 1989.

Booker, Christopher, *The Seventies: Portrait of a Decade*, Allan Lane, 1980.

Boyd, William, *Nat Tate: An American Artist*, 1928–1960, 21.

Brennan, J.H., *Occult Reich*, Futura, 1974.

Bulldog (paper of the Young National Front), 'White European Dance Music', November/December, No. 25, 1981.

Burroughs, William S., *Naked Lunch*, Palladin, 1992.

Collings, Matthew, *Blimey! From Bohemia to Britpop: The London Artworld from Francis Bacon to Damien Hirst*, 21, 1998.

Deleuze, G., and Guattari, F., *A Thousand Plateaus*, Trans. B. Massumi, Athlone Press, 1998.

Edwards, Frank, *Strange People*, Secaucus: Citadel Press, 1961.

Garber, Marjorie, *Vice Versa: Bisexuality and the Eroticism of Everyday Life*, Hamish Hamilton, 1995.

Harrer, Heinrich, *Seven Years In Tibet*, Flamingo, 1994 (1953).

Hoggart, Richard, *The Uses Of Literacy*, Penguin, 1992 (1957).

Hunt, Leon, *British Low Culture: From Safari Suits To Sexploitation*, Routledge, 1998.

Lydenberg, R., *Word Cultures: Radical Theory and Practice in William S. Burroughs' Fiction*, Urbana: University of Illinois Press, 1987.

McKenna, Terrence, *Food Of The Gods: a Radical History of Plants, Drugs and Human Evolution*, Rider, 1992.

Medhurst, Andy, 'Negotiating The Gnome Zone: Visions of Suburbia in British Popular Culture' in Silverstone, R., ed., *Visions Of Suburbia*, Routledge, 1997.

Metzner, Richard, *Maps Of Consciousness*, Collier-MacMillan, 1971.

Morgan, Ted, *Literary Outlaw: The Life and Times of William S. Burroughs*, New York: Henry Holt, 1988.

Morley, Paul, *Words And Music: a History of Pop in the Shape of a City*, Bloomsbury, 2003.

Silverstone, Roger, ed., *Visions Of Suburbia*, Routledge, 1997.

Singer, June, *Androgyny: Towards a New Theory of Sexuality*, Routledge, 1977.

Sontag, Susan, 'Notes On Camp' in *Against Interpretation and Other Essays*, Eyre & Spottiswoode, 1967.

Sulloway, Frank, *Born To Rebel, Birth Order, Family Dynamics and Creative Lives*, Little, Brown, 1996.

Symond, J., *The Great Beast: The Life and Magick of Aleister Crowley*, MacDonald, 1971.

Taylor, Brandon, *The Art Of Today*, Weidenfeld and Nicolson, 1995.

Taylor, Rogan, *The Death And Resurrection Show: From Shaman to Superstar*, Anthony Blond, 1985.

The Legendary Stardust Cowboy (real name: Norman Odam), 1969, 'My Life', short biography taken from his official website, Paralysed, 1998.

Waldrep, Shelton, *The Aesthetics Of Self-Invention: Oscar Wilde To David Bowie*, University of Minnesota Press, 2004.

Willet, J., ed. and trans., *Brecht On Theatre: the Development of an Aesthetic*, Methuen, 1964.

SECTION 2: WATCHING

The following section includes the most important television performances and Bowie specials consulted during the writing of this book. Of these, *Cracked Actor*, by Alan Yentob, originally broadcast by the BBC in January 1975, is nothing less than a piece of rock history and the best thing on Bowie yet produced for television. VH1's *Legends* special, narrated by surrealist and comedian Eddie Izzard, is the best recent summary of Bowie's career.

Bowie on TV

The Tonight Show, BBC, 1964: Bowie's first-ever TV performance, as the President of the Society for Prevention of Cruelty to Long-Haired Men. Interviewed by a bemused Cliff Michelmore.

Top of the Pops, BBC, 1972: singing 'Starman'.

Nationwide 73, BBC: feature on Bowiemania from 1973, with interview and live footage of Bowie, and interviews with fans.

The 1980 Floor Show, NBC, 1973.

Cracked Actor, BBC, 1975: the classic rockumentary.

Bing Crosby's Merrie Olde Christmas, 1977: performs a duet with Bing – 'Peace On Earth'/'Little Drummer Boy' – and sings his own 'Heroes'.

Marc television show, Granada, 1977: sings 'Heroes' then unfinished duet with Bolan.

Kenney Everett Video Show, LWT, 1979: performs 'Boys Keep Swinging' and slapstick with Everett.

Kenny Everett New Year Special, LWT, 1979: chill, acoustic 'Space Oddity'.

Saturday Night Live, NBC, 1979: classic performance with Klaus Nomi and Joey Arias.
Johnny Carson Show, NBC, 1980: sings 'Ashes To Ashes' and 'Life On Mars?'.
The Snowman, Channel 4, 1983: introduces the classic animated film in tight-fitting jumper
   and with peroxide-blond, sculptured hair.
Top of the Pops, BBC, 1987: performs 'Time Will Crawl' (not shown until the 1990s).
VH1, 1998: *Legends: David Bowie*.
VH1, *Storytellers*, 1999: a short live set interspersed with Bowie stand-up and anecdotes.
David Bowie Live By Request, 2002: a short concert performed for television networks.

Bowie on Video and DVD

Below is a list of the most important official pop promos featuring David Bowie:

'John, I'm Only Dancing' (1972). Directed by Mick Rock.
'The Jean Genie' (1972). Directed by Mick Rock.
'Space Oddity' (1973). Directed by Mick Rock.
'Life On Mars?' (1973). Directed by Mick Rock.
'Be My Wife' (1977). Directed by Stanley Dorfman.
'Heroes' (1977). Directed by Nick Ferguson.
'Boys Keep Swinging' (1979). Directed by David Mallet.
'DJ' (1979). Directed by David Mallet.
'Look Back In Anger' (1979). Directed by David Mallet.
'Ashes To Ashes' (1980). Directed by David Mallet.
'Fashion' (1980). Directed by David Mallet.
'Wild Is The Wind' (1981). Directed by David Mallet.
'Under Pressure' with Queen (1981).
'Little Drummer Boy/Peace On Earth' (1982, shot in 1977).
'Let's Dance' (1983). Directed by Bowie and David Mallet.
'China Girl' (1983). Directed by Bowie and David Mallet.
'Modern Love' (1983). Directed by Jim Yukich.
'Jazzin' For Blue Jean' (1984). Directed by Julien Temple.
'Blue Jean' (1984). Different promo to above, filmed at the Wag Club, for US promotion.
'Loving The Alien' (1985). Directed by David Mallet.
'Dancing In The Street' (1985). Directed by David Mallet.
'Absolute Beginners' (1986). Directed by Julien Temple.
'Underground' (1986). Directed by Steve Barron.
'As The World Falls Down' (1986). Directed by Steve Barron.
'When The Wind Blows' (1986). Directed by Steve Barron.
'Day In Day Out' (1987). Directed by Julien Temple.
'Never Let Me Down' (1987). Directed by Jean-Baptiste Mondino.
'Fame 90' (1990). Directed by Gus Van Sant.
'Real Cool World' (1992). Animated promo, not featuring Bowie.
'Jump They Say' (1993). Directed by Mick Romanek.
'Black Tie White Noise' (1993). Directed by Mark Romanek.
'Miracle Goodnight' (1993). Directed by Matthew Rolston.
'The Buddha Of Suburbia' (1993).
'Hearts Filthy Lesson' (1995). Directed by Sam Bayer.
'Strangers When We Meet' (1995). Directed by Sam Bayer.
'Hallo Spaceboy' (1996). Directed by David Mallet.
'Little Wonder' (1996). Directed by Floria Sigismondi.
'Dead Man Walking' (1997). Directed by Floria Sigismondi.
'Seven Years In Tibet' (1997). Directed by Doro Productions.
'I'm Afraid Of Americans' with Trent Reznor (1997). Directed by Dom and Nick.

'Thursday's Child' (1999). Directed by Walter Stern.
'Under Pressure' (1999). Queen and David Bowie (RAH Mix).
'The Pretty Things Are Going To Hell' (1999, though unreleased). Directed by Dom and Nick.
'Survive' (1999). Directed by Walter Stern.

Bowie does not actually appear in person on either 'Under Pressure' (original version) or 'Real Cool World'. He does, however, appear in a cameo role in the videos 'Mercy Mercy Me' (The Ecology) by Marvin Gaye and the 1998 'Various Artists' version of Lou Reed's 'Perfect Day'. A photo of Bowie with Iggy Pop on the day they met Kraftwerk in Spring 1976 is included in the latter's promo for their 1977 single, 'Trans Europa Express'. Several TV programmes have sporadically been used for promotional purposes too, such as Bowie's performance of 'Rebel Rebel' on *Top Pop* (1974), his appearance on *The Dick Cavett Show* singing 'Young Americans' (1974), his guest slot on *The Cher Show* in 1975 singing 'Fame' and his *Soul Train* performance of 'Golden Years' the same year. In the absence of video footage, these were used on television shows such as the BBC's *Top of the Pops*. *Top of the Pops* would often also construct unofficial promo films for Bowie's singles, such as for his 1974 hit, 'Knock On Wood'. His live performance of 'Starman' on *Top of the Pops* in 1972 is also much shown. Bowie also performed 'The Jean Genie' in the *Top of the Pops* studio in December 1972, though the tape has apparently been wiped.

There are two essential DVD purchases. The first is *Best Of Bowie* (DVD EMI: 490 1039, 11 November 2002), the best place to start for new and not so new Bowie fans. An excellent collection featuring hidden material called 'Easter eggs'.

DISC 1: 'Oh! You Pretty Thing', 'Queen Bitch', 'Five Years', 'Starman', 'John, I'm Only Dancing', 'The Jean Genie', 'Space Oddity', 'Drive-In Saturday', Ziggy Stardust', 'Life On Mars?', 'Rebel Rebel', 'Young Americans', 'Be My Wife', 'Boys Keep Swinging', 'DJ', 'Look Back In Anger', 'Ashes To Ashes', 'Fashion', 'Wild Is The Wind', 'Let's Dance', 'China Girl', 'Modern Love', 'Cat People (Putting Out Fire)', 'Blue Jean', 'Loving The Alien', 'Dancing In The Street'.

DISC 2: 'Absolute Beginners', 'Underground', 'As The World Falls Down', 'Day-In Day-Out', 'Time Will Crawl', 'Never Let Me Down', 'Fame '90', 'Jump They Say', 'Black Tie White Noise', 'Miracle Goodnight', 'Buddha Of Suburbia', 'Hearts Filthy Lesson', 'Strangers When We Meet', 'Hallo Spaceboy', 'Little Wonder', 'Dead Man Walking', 'Seven Years In Tibet', 'I'm Afraid Of Americans', 'Thursday's Child', 'Survive'.

The second is *Ziggy Stardust and the Spiders From Mars: the Motion Picture* (DVD: EMI 492 9879, 24 March 2003). Although of great historical import, the film unfortunately doesn't really do justice to the wonderful Aladdin Sane costumes. The parent CD soundtrack won *Music Week*'s Best Catalogue Release award in 2004.

For a taste of contemporary Bowie, fans need look no further than *David Bowie – A Reality Tour* (Sony Music Video 2004). At the time of writing, the DVD has been a commercial success, selling over 100,000 copies in the US alone. In 2003, a special tour edition of his then current album, *Reality*, contained a bonus DVD of Bowie's live performance of the entire album, recorded at London's Hammersmith Riverside Studios. Bowie's excellent performance at Live Aid is to be found in its entirety on the official release, *Live Aid* (Warner Vision 2004). Anyone interested in the post-Tin Machine Bowie should check out *Black Tie White Noise* (EMI Records 2005). Hard-core fans will also want Universal Music's 2004 release *David Bowie – Love You Till Tuesday*, which includes 'The Looking Glass Murders' from 1970.

Several unofficial Bowie rockumentaries are also to be found, including *David Bowie: Sound & Vision* (Stax Entertainment Ltd, 2003), *David Bowie: Origins Of A Starman* (Chrome Dreams, 2004), and *Inside David Bowie 1969 To 1974* (Classic Rock Legends, 2004).

A poignant performance of 'America' and a rebel-rousing version of "Heroes" can be found on *The Concert For New York City* (Sony Music Entertainment 2002), while the Freddie Mercury Tribute Concert (EMI, 2002) also contains a performance by Bowie. The Serious Moonlight tour awaits full reactivation on DVD. The Glass Spider tour was issued on DVD (Panorama Music Video, 2001).

Bowie's film career has been uneven, although two of his starring roles are essential: *The Man Who Fell To Earth* is now available on DVD (Warner Home Video, 2002), as is *Merry Christmas Mr Lawrence* (Optimum Home Entertainment, 2005). Other film appearances include *Christiane F* (Second Sight Films Ltd, 2000), *Everybody Loves Sunshine* (Cinema Club, 2002) *Basquiat* (Pathe Distribution Ltd, 2003), *Mr Rice's Secret* (Odyssey Video, 2003), *The Hunger* (Warner Home Video, 2004) and *Labyrinth* (Columbia Tri-Star Home Video 2004). Bowie's introduction to the children's classic *The Snowman*, is also featured on the latest DVD release (Universal Pictures Video, 2004).

Bowie on Film

Below is a list of Bowie's major screen roles.

Absolute Beginners (1986). Directed by Julien Temple.
Basquiat (1995). Directed by Julian Schnaebel.
Christian F. – Wir Kinder vom Bahnhof Zoo (1981). Directed by Ulrich Edel.
Everybody Loves Sunshine (1999). Directed by Andrew Goth.
Exhuming Mr Rice (1999). Directed by Nick Kendall.
The Hunger (1983). Directed by Tony Scott.
Ill Mio West (1998). Directed by Giovanni Veronesi.
Into The Night (1985). Directed by John Landis.
Just A Gigolo (1978). Directed by David Hemmings.
Labyrinth (1986). Directed by Jim Henson.
The Last Temptation Of Christ (1988). Directed by Martin Scorsese.
The Linguini Incident (1991). Directed by Richard Shepard.
The Man Who Fell To Earth (1976). Directed by Nicolas Roeg.
Merry Christmas Mr Lawrence (1983). Directed by Nagisa Oshima.
Twin Peaks: Fire Walk With Me (1992). Directed by David Lynch.

Bowie in the Theatre

Bowie's only major acting role to date came in 1980 when he starred, to great acclaim, as the lead in Jack Hofsiss' production of *The Elephant Man*, which played Broadway in the autumn and winter of 1980–81.

Interactive Bowie

Jump: The David Bowie Interactive CD-ROM, BMG/ION, 1994.
The Nomad Soul, Eidos Interactive.

SECTION 3: LISTENING

Bowie Singing (official releases)

ALBUMS:
All of David Bowie's studio albums from 1969 to 1989, including the first Tin Machine album, were re-released by EMI in September 1999. EMI have continued this reissue programme with thirtieth anniversary editions of *Ziggy Stardust*, *Aladdin Sane* and *Diamond Dogs*, a refurbished and expanded *Black Tie White Noise*, a new, award-winning edition of *Ziggy Stardust The Motion Picture*, and various other releases. Below is a list of Bowie's studio albums and a selection of currently available compilations, their original release date and UK

catalogue number, and their chart performance in both the UK and the US since the time of their original release. Inferior or deleted anthologies or compilations, of which there are legion, have been omitted. Those interested in Bowie's very earliest recordings from the mid-1960s should try *David Bowie: Early On* (1964–1966) (US CD Rhino R2 70526), *David Bowie: Rock Reflections* (Australian CD: Deram/Polydor 820 549 2) and *David Bowie: the Deram Anthology 1966–1968* (Deram 844 784-2). Below is a manageable and listenable selection of some of the best pop music ever recorded.

David Bowie, Deram DML.1007 (June 1967)

David Bowie, Philips SBL 7912 (November 1969).†* (UK highest chart position 17, weeks in chart 38, US highest chart position 16, weeks in chart 36)

The Man Who Sold The World, Mercury 6338041 (US November 1970, UK April 1971).‡* (UK 26/31, US 105/23)

Hunky Dory, RCA SF8244 (December 1971).* (UK 3/122, US 93/16)

The Rise And Fall Of Ziggy Stardust And The Spiders From Mars, RCA SF8287 (June 1972).* (UK 5/174, US 75/81)

Aladdin Sane, RCA RS 1001 (April 1973).* (UK 1/72, US 17/22)

PinUps, RCA RS 1003 (October 1973).* (UK 1/39, US 23/21)

Diamond Dogs, RCA APL I. 0576 (April 1974).* (UK 1/39, US 5/25)

David Live, RCA APL2.0771 (October 1974).* (UK 2/12, US 8/21)

Young Americans, RCA RS. 1006 (March 1975).* (UK 2/16, US 9/51)

Station To Station, RCA APLI-1327 (January 1976).* (UK 5/17, US 3/32)

ChangesoneBowie, RCA RS 1055. (May 1976). (UK 2/28, US 10/39)

Low, RCA PL. 12030 (January 1977).* (UK 2/24, US 11/19)

'Heroes', RCA PL. 12522 (October 1977).* (UK 3/26, US 35/19)

Peter And The Wolf, RCA RL 12743 (May 1978) (US 135/7)

Stage, RCA PL 02913 (September 1978).* (UK 5/10, US 44/13)

Lodger, RCA BOW LP I (May 1979).* (UK 4/17, US 20/15)

Scary Monsters (And Super Creeps), RCA BOW LP 2 (September 1980).* (UK 1/32, US 12/27)

Christiane F – Wir Kinder Vom Bahnhof Zoo, RCA 4239 (soundtrack) (April 1981) (US 135/7) Re-released in 2002 on EMI 5330932

ChangestwoBowie, RCA BOW LP 3. (November 1981) (UK 27/17, US 68/18)

Let's Dance, EMI America AML 3029 (April 1983). (UK 1/58, US 4/68)

Ziggy Stardust – The Motion Picture, RCA PL 84862 (October 1983).* (UK 17/6, US 89/15)

Tonight, EMI America DB1 (September 1984). (UK 1/19, US 11/24)

Absolute Beginners, Virgin V 2386 (March 1986) (features three tracks by Bowie) (UK 19/9)

Labyrinth, EMI America AML 3104 (July 1986) (features tracks by Bowie and 6 instrumentals by Trevor Jones) (UK 38/2, US 68/8)

Never Let Me Down, EMI America AMLS 3117 (April 1987). (UK 6/16, US 34/26)

Tin Machine, EMI-USA MTLS 1044 (May 1989).** (UK 3/9, US 28/17)

Sound + Vision (4-CD boxed set) Rykodisc, RCD 90120/21/22. (November 1989) (US 97/16) EMI reissue

ChangesBowie, EMI DBTV 1 (March, 1990). (UK 1/29, US 39/27)

Tin Machine II, 8282721 (September 1991).** (UK 23/3, US 126/3)

Tin Machine Live – Oy Vey Baby, Victory/ 828 328 (August 1992).**

Black Tie White Noise, Arista 74321 13697 (April 1993). (UK 1/11, US 39/8)

The Buddha Of Suburbia, Arista (November 1993). (UK 87/1)

David Bowie: The Singles Collection (November 1993). (UK 9/15)

Santa Monica, '72, Trident International, GY 002 (May 1994) (UK 74/1)

RarestoneBowie, Trident Music International, Golden Years GY014 (UK 101/1)

1.Outside, RCA 74321 31066 2 (September 1995) (UK 8/4, US 21/6)

Earthling, RCA 74321 44944 2 (February 1997) (UK 6/4, US 39/6)

The Best Of Bowie: 1969-73, EMI 7243 8 21849 2 8. (October 1998) (UK 13/19)

The Best Of Bowie: 1974–79, EMI 7243 4 94300 2 0. (April 1998) (UK 39/2)
hours . . . VIRGIN CDV2900 (October 1999) (UK 5/6, US 47/4)
Bowie At The Beeb, EMI 72443 528629 2 40 (September 2000) (UK 7/4, US 181/1)
Heathen, Columbia 5082222 (June 2002) (UK 5/18, US 14?)
The Rise And Fall Of Ziggy Stardust And The Spiders From Mars (Thirtieth Anniversary
    Edition), EMI 5398262 (July 2002) (UK 36/2)
Best Of Bowie, EMI 5398212 (November 2002) (UK 11/36)
Reality, Columbia 5125552 (September 2003) (UK 3/4 US 29/4)

†This album was re-released as *Space Oddity* in November 1972 and is referred to under this
name in the text.
‡This album was re-released by RCA in November 1972.
*Reissued with extra tracks (with the exception of Aladdin Sane) by EMI between 1990 and
1992.
**Recorded as part of Tin Machine.

SINGLES:
Below is the formidable list of Bowie's hit singles in the UK and US, and proof that he is one
of the most durable rock stars in the business.

UK CHARTS

The following is a list of Bowie's Top-75 chart hits (compiled with the help of the excellent
British Hit Singles And Albums). The information given runs: week entered the chart, title,
original record label and catalogue number, highest chart position and total weeks in chart.
Bowie has debuted at Number 1 only once, with his duet with Mick Jagger, 'Dancing In The
Street'. Bowie's fastest selling solo single was 'Ashes To Ashes', which entered the Top 75 at
Number 4 and reached Number 1 the week after. Although no official figures have ever been
given, it seems that Bowie's biggest seller in the UK is 'Space Oddity', with sales close to a
million, followed by 'Let's Dance', with sales of around 750,000.

Date	Title	Label	Pos	Wks
6 Sep 69	'Space Oddity'	Philips BF 1801	5	14
24 Jun 72	'Starman'	RCA 2199	10	11
16 Sep 72	'John, I'm Only Dancing'	RCA 2263	12	10
9 Dec 72	'The Jean Genie'	RCA 2302	2	13
14 Apr 73	'Drive-In Saturday'	RCA 2352	3	10
30 Jun 73	'Life On Mars?'	RCA 2316	3	13
15 Sep 73	'The Laughing Gnome'	Deram DM 123	6	12
20 Oct 73	'Sorrow'	RCA 2424	3	15
23 Feb 74	'Rebel Rebel'	RCA LPBO 5009	5	7
20 Apr 74	'Rock'n'Roll Suicide'	RCA LPBO 5021	22	7
22 Jun 74	'Diamond Dogs'	RCA APBO 0293	21	6
28 Sep 74	'Knock On Wood'	RCA APBO 2466	10	6
1 Mar 75	'Young Americans'	RCA 2523	18	7
2 Aug 75	'Fame'	RCA 2579	17	8
11 Oct 75	'Space Oddity' (re-issue)	RCA 2593	1	10
29 Nov 75	'Golden Years'	RCA 2640	8	10
22 May 76	'TVC15'	RCA 2682	33	4
19 Feb 77	'Sound And Vision'	RCA PB 0905	3	11
15 Oct 77	'Heroes'	RCA PB 1121	24	8
21 Jan 78	'Beauty And The Beast'	RCA PB 1190	39	3
2 Dec 78	'Breaking Glass'	EPRCA BOW 1	54	7
5 May 79	'Boys Keep Swinging'	RCA BOW 2	7	10
21 Jul 79	'DJ'	RCA BOW 3	29	5

Date	Title	Label	Pos	Wks
15 Dec 79	'John, I'm Only Dancing' (Again) (1975)/'John, I'm Only Dancing' (1972)	RCA BOW 4	12	8
1 Mar 80	'Alabama Song'	RCA BOW 5	23	5
16 Aug 80	'Ashes To Ashes'	RCA BOW 6	1	10
1 Nov 80	'Fashion'	RCA BOW 7	5	12
10 Jan 81	'Scary Monsters (And Super Creeps)'	RCA BOW 8	20	6
28 Mar 81	'Up The Hill Backwards'	RCA BOW 9	32	6
14 Nov 81	'Under Pressure'	EMI 5250	11	1
28 Nov 81	'Wild Is The Wind'	RCA BOW 10	24	10
6 Mar 82	'Baal's Hymn' (EP)	RCA BOW 11	29	5
10 Apr 82	'Cat People (Putting Out Fire)'	MCA 770	26	6
27 Nov 82	'Peace On Earth – Little Drummer Boy'	RCA BOW 12	3	8
26 Mar 83	'Let's Dance'	EMI America EA 152	1	14
11 Jun 83	'China Girl'	EMI America EA 157	2	8
24 Sep 83	'Modern Love'	EMI America EA 158	2	8
5 Nov 83	'White Light, White Heat'	RCA 372	46	3
22 Sep 84	'Blue Jean'	EMI America 181	6	8
8 Dec 84	'Tonight'	EMI America EA 181	53	4
9 Feb 85	'This Is Not America'	EMI America EA 190	14	7
8 Jun 85	'Loving The Alien'	EMI America EA 195	19	7
7 Sep 85	'Dancing In The Street'	EMI America EA 204	1	12
15 Mar 86	'Absolute Beginners'	Virgin VS 838	2	9
21 Jun 86	'Underground'	EMI America EA 216	21	6
8 Nov 86	'When The Wind Blows'	Virgin VS 906	44	4
4 Apr 87	'Day-In Day-Out'	EMI America EA 230	17	6
27 Jun 87	'Time Will Crawl'	EMI America EA 237	33	4
29 Aug 87	'Never Let Me Down'	EMI America EA 239	34	6
7 Apr 90	'Fame 90' (re-mix)	EMI-USA FAME 90	28	4
22 Aug 92	'Real Cool World'	Warner Bros. W 0127	53	1
27 Mar 93	'Jump They Say'	Arista 74321139422	9	6
12 Jun 93	'Black Tie White Noise'	Arista 74321148682	36	2
23 Oct 93	'Miracle Goodnight'	Arista 74321162262	40	2
4 Dec 93	'Buddha Of Suburbia'	Arista 74321177052	35	3
23 Sep 95	'Hearts Filthy Lesson'	RCA 7432137032	35	2
2 Dec 95	'Strangers When We Meet/The Man Who Sold The World (Live)'	RCA 74321329402	39	2
2 Mar 96	'Hallo Spaceboy'	RCA 74321353842	12	5
4 Nov 96	'Telling Lies'	RCA 74321 397392	81	1
4 Feb 97	'Little Wonder'	RCA 74321 452072	14	4
16 Apr 97	'Dead Man Walking'	RCA 74321475842	32	2
18 Aug 97	'Seven Years In Tibet'	RCA 74321512542	61	1
21 Feb 98	'I Can't Read'	Velvet ZYX 8757 8	73	1
26 Sep 99	'Thursday's Child'	Virgin VSCDF 1753	16	3
12 Dec 99	'Under Pressure (RAH mix)'	EMI 72438 88033	14	7
30 Jan 00	'Survive'	Virgin VSCDT 1767	28	2
23 Jul 00	'Seven'	Virgin VSCDT 1761	32	2
11 May 02	'Loving The Alien (re-mix)'	Positiva CDTIV 172	41	1
28 Sep 02	'Everyone Says "Hi" '	Columbia 6731342	20	3
12 Jul 03	'Just For One Day (Heroes)'	Virgin DINST 263	73	1
26 Jun 04	'Rebel Never Get Old'	Columbia 6750406	47	2

Tin Machine

1 Jul 89	'Under The God'	EMI-USA MT 68	51	2
9 Sep 89	'Tin Machine/Maggie's Farm (Live)'	EMI-USA MT 73	48	2
24 Aug 91	'You Belong In Rock'n'Roll'	London LON 305	33	3
2 Nov 91	'Baby Universal'	London LON 310	48	3

US CHARTS

Bowie's chart success in the States has been uneven, with two big Number 1s overshadowing many minor hits. The data provided goes as follows: week (or month) single released, title, original record label and catalogue number, highest chart position and total weeks in chart (where information is available).

Jan 72	'Changes'	RCA 740605	41	
May 72	'Starman'	RCA 740719	65	
Nov 72	'The Jean Genie'	RCA 0838	71	
Feb 73	'Space Oddity'	RCA 0876	15	10
Feb 74	'Rebel Rebel'	RCA AP BO 0287	64	
Jan 75	'Young Americans'	RCA 10152	28	4
Aug 75	'Fame'	RCA 10320	1	14
Nov 75	'Golden Years'	RCA 10441	10	16
Apr 76	'TVC15'	RCA PB106664	64	
Feb 77	'Sound And Vision'	RCA PB 10903	69	
1 Nov 80	'Fashion'	RCA PB 12134	70	
14 Nov 81	'Under Pressure'	Elektra 47235	29	8
10 Apr 82	'Cat People (Puttin' Out Fire)'	Backstreet Records	67	
26 Mar 83	'Let's Dance'	EMI America 8158	1	14
11 Jun 83	'China Girl'	EMI America 8165	10	11
24 Sep 83	'Modern Love'	EMI America 8177	14	9
Feb 84	'Without You'	EMI America B8190	73	
22 Sep 84	'Blue Jean'	EMI America 8231	8	10
8 Dec 84	'Tonight'	EMI America	53	
9 Mar 85	'This Is Not America'	EMI America 8251	32	4
7 Sep 85	'Dancing In The Street'	EMI America 8288	7	9
15 Mar 86	'Absolute Beginners'			
1 Apr 87	'Day-In Day-Out'	EMI America 8380	21	7
29 Aug 87	'Never Let me Down'	EMI America 43031	27	5
Nov 1995	'Heart's Filthy Lesson'		92	
14 Oct 97	'I'm Afraid Of Americans'	EMD/Virgin 72438 3861828	66	16

Bowie Singing (unofficial releases)

Planet Bowie is awash with unofficial recordings. Bootlegs are, as we all know, illegal. Many are of piss-poor quality. Some are on offer at fan-fleecing prices. However, Bowie himself has been known to turn a blind eye to websites with downloadable bootleg material, and once even asked fans to send in their illegally taped and photographed performances of his *Earthling* tour to his own official website! While some have grown richer than they should on the back of bootlegging Bowie, turning the Bowie black market into one of the most cut-throat in the business, there is one Bowie bootleg, superbly recorded and packaged and repackaged over two decades by a variety of illegal sources, which should be in every Bowie fan's collection, and that is *The Thin White Duke*, a ferocious live performance recorded in early 1976 at the Uniondale Coliseum, Nassau.

For more info on bootlegs, surf the Net, but be warned: you'll frequently be disappointed and almost certainly emerge with a black hole in your pocket!

Bowie talking

A brief list of some of Bowie's most important radio appearances and radio documentaries.

Grundy, S., *The David Bowie Story*, Radio 1, four parts, May 1976.
Bowie, D., *Star Special*, Radio 1, Bowie spins the discs, May 1979.
Gambaccini, P. (presenter), Tobler, John (interviewer), *The David Bowie Story*, Radio 1, six parts, 3 April – 8 May 1993. Update of 1976 broadcast featuring interviews with Bowie and his workmates.
ChangesnowBowie, 1997. A Bowie tribute presented by Mary-Anne Hobbes and aired in January 1997. Guest questioners included Sean Ryder, Scott Walker, Damon Albarn and Brett Anderson. Bowie also played acoustic versions of half-a-dozen oldies.
Golden Years – The Story of David Bowie, BBC Radio 2, three parts, March 2000. Presented by Mark Goodier.

SECTION 4: SURFING

Official sites

Bowie has two excellent official websites, BowieNet (www.davidbowie.com) and www.bowieart.com.

Unofficial sites

There are dozens and dozens of Bowie-related fan websites. Here are my personal favourites:

Bassman Bowie – www.algonet.se/bassman
Teenage Wildlife – http://teenagewildlife.com
Bowiewonderworld – http://www.bowiewonderworld.com
The Ziggy Stardust Companion – www.5years.com

Bowie-related sites

Philippe Auliac – www.netgalerie.net/auliac/philippeAuliacfr.html
Adrian Belew – www.murple.com/adrianbelew/
Angie Bowie – www.bettyjack.com/angie
Reeves Gabrels – www.reevesgabrels.com
Mike Garson – www.nowmusic.net/
Iman – www.i-iman.com
Outside Organisation (Bowie's UK publicists) – www.outside-org.co.uk
Mark Plati – www.markplati.com
Mick Rock – www.mickrock.com/
Earl Slick's website and cyber record label – www.slickmusic.com/
Tony Visconti – www.tonyvisconti.com

For regular updates of Bowie news you can also subscribe to Bonster's 'David Bowie Newsletter for the Lazy and Web-Impaired' at http://dbfan-list-requestietete.com/.

INDEX